An American History

An American History

MERLE CURTI
UNIVERSITY OF WISCONSIN

RICHARD H. SHRYOCK
JOHNS HOPKINS UNIVERSITY

THOMAS C. COCHRAN
UNIVERSITY OF PENNSYLVANIA

FRED HARVEY HARRINGTON
UNIVERSITY OF WISCONSIN

VOLUME TWO

HARPER & BROTHERS, PUBLISHERS, NEW YORK

Contents

Maps

Preface

Through most of the nineteenth century, the United States was an agrarian republic, and was of secondary importance in the world's diplomatic and military patterns. But by the middle of the twentieth century, this same republic had become a great industrial nation, and was in every sense a major world power.

Our first volume covered American history in the agricultural age, including a treatment of the sectional conflict down to 1877. The present volume deals with the United States in the industrial age—the transition to a manufacturing economy; the problems connected with industrialization and urbanization; the emergence and development of the United States as a world power.

Following the design of our first volume, we have combined the chronological and topical approaches. This book is divided into three parts, each representing one time period. Part I, which deals with the transition from a farm to a factory civilization, centers chiefly on the years from 1877 to 1896. But, to make clear the nature and significance of the transformation of the American economy, we have treated the rise of industry in broad terms, covering the entire second half of the nineteenth century. This section stresses the impact of the industrial revolution on American institutions, and concludes with an account of the unsuccessful effort of farmers to gain political control of a changing America.

Part II concerns the quarter-century from 1896 to 1919, a period in which the new factory economy reached maturity. We have here stressed the concentration of economic power, the progressive movement (a political effort to meet the problems of industrialization and urbanization), and the recognition of the world-power position of the United States. Part III deals with the difficult years since 1919, years in which the United States has faced the domestic and foreign problems of a mature industrial nation. In this section we have given particular attention to the increasingly important role of the government in American economic life, and the significance of the United States as an economic, military and cultural force in every part of the globe.

This volume is a history of the United States as an industrial power. In consequence, each of the three sections begins with a treatment of the economic patterns of the period. Next comes an analysis of social and intellectual developments for the same years, with stress on the interaction of economic and cultural forces. The conclusion of each section is devoted to political and diplomatic trends, and the relationship of these trends to economic and cultural history.

Because of the increase in government activity in the twentieth century, we have given a substantial amount of space to political history. At the same time, we have endeavored, as in our first volume, to include a good deal of material bearing on the history of American business, on scientific progress, on changing values and ideas, and on the relationship of the United States to the outside world.

In planning *An American History*, we have attempted to keep the reader constantly in mind. Thus, we have aimed at clarity and readability. We have tried to provide the details essential for an understanding of industrial America, without including so many names as to confuse the reader. And we have held the volume to its present length so as to leave time for additional reading in the rich materials available in recent American history. The bibliography is intended as a preliminary guide to such reading.

The maps were drawn especially for this volume by James J. Flannery of the University of Wisconsin. Arthur H. Robinson of the same institution acted as general adviser on map problems.

M. C.

R. H. S.

T. C. C.

October, 1950   F. H. H.

Part I

The Triumph of Industry
(1850-1896)

 In the middle of the nineteenth century, the economy of the United States was still predominantly agrarian. By the end of the century, the American economy was basically industrial. Given world trends, and the natural resources of the United States, the transformation was inevitable. Just as logically, the change profoundly affected social and economic institutions in the republic and led American farmers to protest—rather ineffectively—against the dominant trends.

1

Industrial Expansion

A New America

In the whole of world history, there are few movements or events that compare in importance with the industrial expansion of the United States during the second half of the nineteenth century. Even now we cannot assess the results with complete accuracy. It is clear, however, that the rise of manufacturing from 1850 to 1900 transformed American agrarian society into the urban and industrial civilization of today. The shift profoundly affected the political, economic, and cultural interests of the American people. It also changed once and for all the role of the United States among the nations of the globe.

The Industrial Age

The *rate* of growth in manufacturing— the annual percentage increase—was not so very high. It was lower in the five decades after 1850 than it had been in the two decades before 1850. It was lower than the rate of growth in certain other countries during the early stages of industrialization. But the whole process was on a grander scale. Save for the 1860's (when the Civil War upset normal patterns), the half-century saw a continuous upward movement in the production of raw materials for the factory. The output of finished products nearly kept pace. Given the size and resources of the United States, this meant that the American republic would presently be able to produce greater quantities of goods than any other nation on earth.

During these two generations of industrial growth the physical surroundings of citizens changed more rapidly than in any comparable

period before or since. In 1850 the life of Americans much resembled
that of their ancestors. Fifty years later many of the old landmarks
were gone, and the people of the United States lived in a new world

Let us specify. In 1850 most farmers were far from the railroads and
the telegraph lines, knew nothing of plumbing, and had, of course,
never heard a telephone or seen an electric light. City dwellers also
lived much as they had a half-century before. There were no skyscrapers; "rapid transit" was by horsecar; light was supplied by flaring
gas jets, whale-oil lamps, and old-fashioned candles. Bathtubs were
few, and most urban areas relied on outhouses and cesspools rather
than on sewers. Stores, business offices, and homes looked much as
they had in 1800, lines of telegraph poles providing the one striking
new feature of downtown streets.

By 1900 the farmers were served by a tight network of railroads and
by long-distance (interurban) electric trolleys. Most rural centers had
telegraph connections; many also had telephones. Spurred by stories
and advertisements in national magazines, farmers were beginning to
install plumbing, and even electric lights. Automobile owners had
already joined the bicyclists in lobbying for hard-surfaced roads, both
in the country and in the cities. In this and other matters, urban
changes were spectacular. Even in small cities electric lights and signs
made the main streets sparkle. In New York and Chicago office buildings rose above twenty stories and massive apartment houses were
being constructed to supply living quarters for the urban middle
classes. Downtown areas were crowded with streetcars, and for more
rapid transportation there were elevated lines and a few subways.
Beneath the streets, water, gas, and sewer pipes and telephone, electric light, and telegraph wires wove complex patterns.

What did all this mean to the average citizen? It is hard to say.
Certainly these years were marked by economic progress. That is, production increased more rapidly than did population, and there was a
sharp rise in the average citizen's purchasing power. This, however,
tells very little about human happiness and the general welfare.
Although people who commute to work in crowded cities normally
consume more goods than do farmers, the city dwellers are not

necessarily more fortunate than their country brethren. Things made at home may give pleasure in the making and the using. But home-made articles (unlike poor imitations sold in stores) are not recorded in the national income. Nor is there any sure way of comparing the quality of goods sold in the market from one generation to another. Statistics showing average income are also deceptive. A large increase for the richest tenth of the people and a slight decrease for the remaining nine-tenths might cause a rise in the total national income. Yet in this situation most citizens would be in worse circumstances than before.

When one has considered all these points, it still appears that the American people were better off in 1900 than in 1850. This statement would not hold true for slum dwellers and sharecroppers. It seems clear, however, that most Americans obtained some benefit from the 70 percent per capita rise in purchasing power from 1850 to 1900; and that, on the economic side at least, the United States had gained in the transition from the agrarian to the industrial age.

Why the United States Became Industrialized When It Did

The industrialization of the United States was in line with world trends. Before 1800, the industrial revolution had been confined largely to Great Britain and a few small regions on the European mainland. Then others came into the field. By 1850 the political and economic leaders of the Western world were convinced that prosperity and power were associated with a manufacturing economy. Wherefore many nations set out to build factories. Germany became industrialized between 1850 and 1900. France, Austria, Italy, and other European countries began to build up manufacturing; and, outside Europe, Japan and the United States entered the industrial competition.

Desire alone could not create a factory economy. Industrialization was impossible without access to raw materials. (In particular, there was need for coal as the basic source of power, and for iron ore as the key to heavy industry.) Capital was also necessary, as was a satisfactory labor supply. Well-developed transportation was absolutely essential, for raw materials had to be taken to the factories, and finished products to the market. There was need, too, for technological and managerial skill and a government favorable to industrialization.

Before 1850 the United States did not come close to satisfying these requirements. Technological difficulties and deficiencies of transportation had prevented the exploitation of many natural resources (for example, the mineral wealth of Minnesota and the Rocky Mountains). Despite an inflow of investment capital from London and immigrants from Germany and Ireland, the United States in 1850 was painfully short of capital and labor. Though rapidly growing, the American population at mid-century was still too small to provide an altogether satisfactory market for a large industrial structure. What was more, the scattered character of the population made it doubly difficult to solve the transportation problem. The country had all too few trained engineers and factory managers. Finally, the agrarian-dominated government of that day did little to encourage manufacturing.

From 1850 on, the picture changed with great rapidity. A high birth rate, a declining death rate, plus heavy immigration from Europe more than trebled the population of the United States in fifty years. It stood at 75,000,000 in 1900, exceeding that of any state in western Europe. The population increase yielded the labor needed for industrialization and presented a great potential market for factory products. The supply of capital was also greater than before. British money continued to pour in for investment purposes and was supplemented by domestic funds, accumulated through the piling up of profits in the United States.

With capital and labor more readily available, enterprising businessmen were able to improve the transportation network and to exploit the nation's high-grade natural resources. Improvements in science and technology (notably the rise of the engineering profession) helped speed the process, as did the development of managerial efficiency. To top things off, the federal government, and most state governments as well, favored industrial development after 1860. The industrialization of the United States thus became possible.

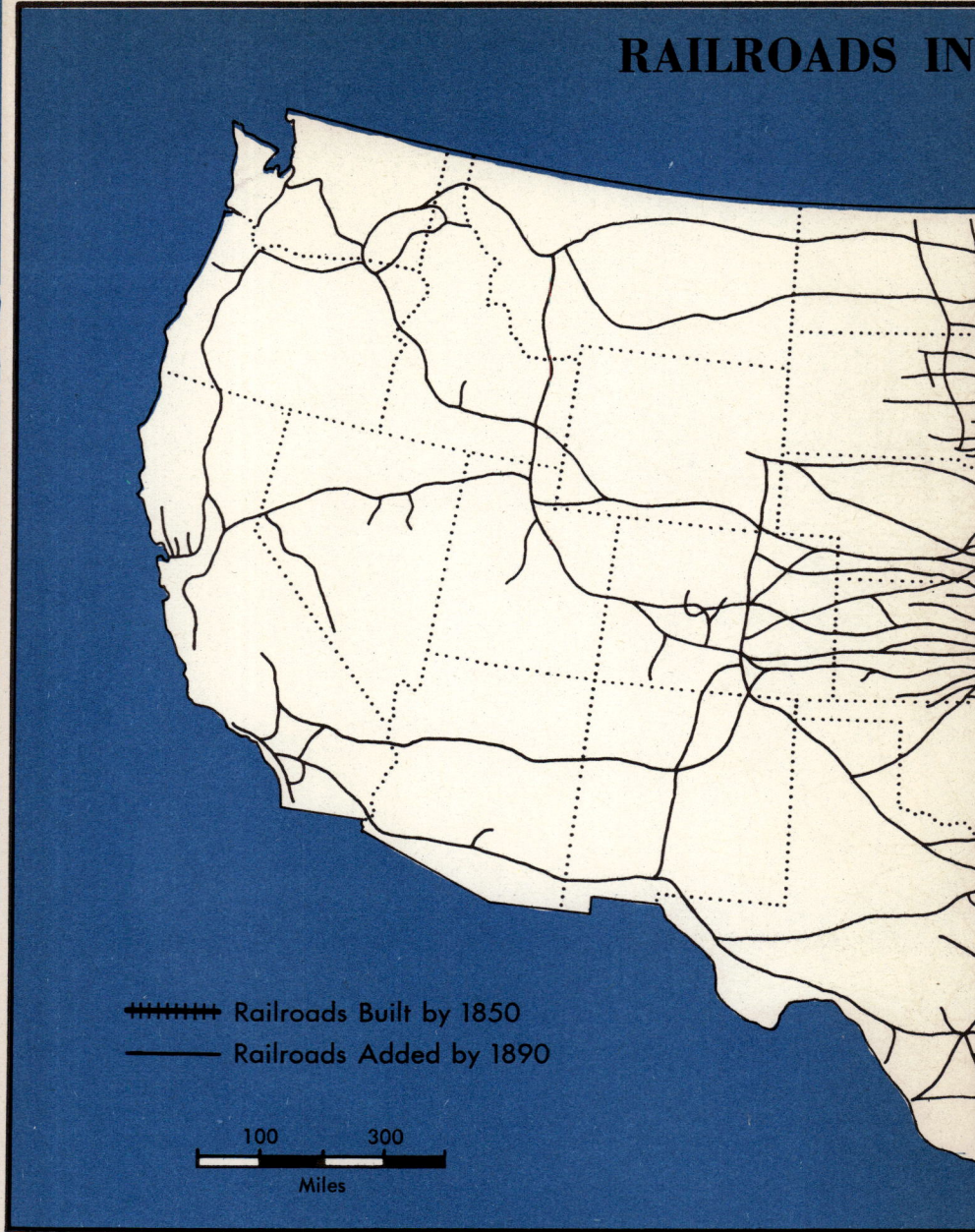

┼┼┼┼┼┼┼ Railroads Built by 1850

───── Railroads Added by 1890

100   300

Miles

When railroad building began, most Americans felt the new lines would be useful chiefly as a means of hauling agricultural products to market. They did prove important in that field. At the same time, the railroads were able to carry coal and other raw materials to industrial areas, and to transport manufactured goods to consumers. Railroad construction thus played a key role in the transition from an agrarian to an industrial economy. It was no accident that the great era of railroad building (1850-90) coincided with the industrialization of the American republic.

There were few miles of railroad in the United States of 1850, and

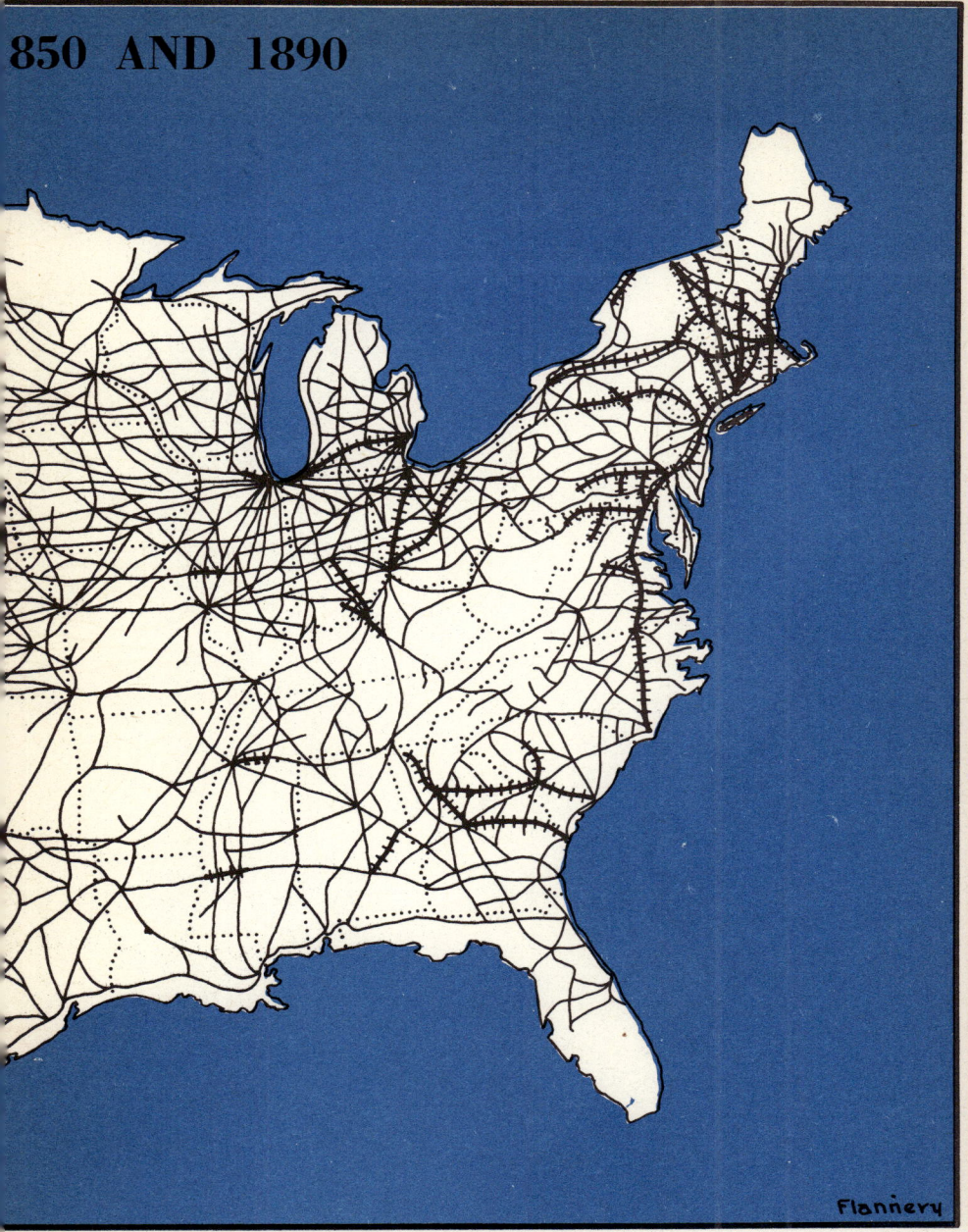

Flannery

most of the existing mileage was in the Northeast. In the next four decades, track was laid down in all parts of the country. The areas of heaviest concentration, however, were the Northeast and the Middle West. The South, held back by the Civil War and Reconstruction, continued to lag behind the northern sections of the country. And most major lines ran east-west rather than north-south.

Relatively few new lines were laid down after 1890. Existing roads were improved, and (in the West especially), companies built branch lines. But the major part of the work was done by 1890.

Railroads Change the Nation

In the transition from an agricultural to a manufacturing economy, the steam railroad was of key importance. Indeed, railroad building affected every side of American life. Railroads hauled raw materials to the factories, carried factory products to the consumer. Railroad securities attracted capital from abroad; railroad promoters drew immigrants to the United States by advertising cheap land. Money made in railroad ventures provided capital for manufacturing plants. The railroads were the best customers of the all-important iron and steel industry. Besides that, the rise of the engineering profession was closely associated with railway building, as was much technological advance. And railroad promoters were among the first to persuade government officials to support the new economic trends.

These were the great years for American railway builders. In 1850 the whole country boasted less than 10,000 miles of first-line track (that is, total mileage omitting yards, sidings, and double track). Fifty years later the figure was just short of 200,000 miles. Only during the Civil War had the annual addition to railroad track fallen below a thousand miles; and in boom years it had risen to eight or ten thousand miles. Altogether, American building roughly equaled the mileage constructed in all the European nations combined.

Much capital was required for the construction of thousands of miles of track at a cost of from $10,000 to $50,000 per mile. The railroads therefore dominated the security exchanges, and their profits provided a continuing incentive for investment. Looking back over this period, Henry Adams said that his generation had mortgaged itself to the railroads. Certainly it looked that way. By 1900 the American people had as large an investment in railroads as in all types of manufacturing put together. The financial sections of the newspapers listed railroad securities by themselves and put "all other" securities on another page. Everyone seemed to regard railroad investments as sound. Bankers would lend money on railroad bonds but not on industrials. Foreign investors, though reluctant to risk money in American manufacturing schemes, bought enormous quantities of American railroad securities.

As they were completed, the railroads changed city and country, commerce and agriculture, manufacturing and finance. They made business truly national. Freight and express service broadened marketing opportunities. Manufacturers all over the country were put into competition with each other; and their traveling salesmen filled the new Pullman cars.

The railroads decided the fate of many cities. Such western centers as Omaha, Denver, and Billings were products of the railroad. In the East, manufacturing cities at junction points profited from their good rail connections and their low competitive railroad rates. They were able, therefore, to wage a war of extermination against competitors on less accessible, high-rate branch lines. Thus the railroad system, as a whole, tended to locate industry in the larger towns, reinforcing trends established in the days of water transportation. But uniformity was lacking. Some individual railroads promoted manufacturing in the smaller cities along their rights of way by offering special freight rates and other concessions to businessmen.

Some railroads relied heavily on direct connections with the new factories. Others fared well without such ties. The coal railroads made profits by hauling that vital raw material. And any number of lines served purely agricultural communities. In such states as Illinois, Wisconsin, and Iowa, it was not necessary for a railroad to connect large cities to return a profit. A promoter could do very well by extending a cheaply built line into a rural area and hauling farm produce.

Railroad building speeded the development of sparsely settled agricultural areas, especially in the West. This was natural, for the new link with the market meant a real chance for farmers to make profits. Also important was the fact that the railroad construction jobs took native and immigrant workingmen westward. A substantial number of these construction workers stayed on after the job was done, settling down as farmers.

The railroads themselves were often involved in the settling process, for the national and state governments gave railroad entrepreneurs great gifts of land. By selling the land, the entrepreneurs obtained funds to build their lines; and the purchasers then provided freight for the railroad. In consequence, the railroads paid much attention to land operations. Advertising for settlers at home and abroad, selling on credit, and directing settlement, the railroads became, in a sense, regional development organizations, not unlike the chartered companies of early colonial days.

Railroad influence was many-sided. When the railroads came, farmers who had previously been unable to market their products shifted from subsistence to commercial agriculture. This often meant an expansion of operations, with new credit relations and new mortgages. Many rural communities went into debt to buy railroad bonds, this being one way of attracting a branch line.

As soon as the railroads opened a new region, grain elevators were constructed, and new banks and new stores. Local businessmen expanded their horizons, and grew rich or went broke speculating on what the railroad would do for real estate, crops, or trade. Life lost its easygoing seasonal timing and became geared to the schedule of daily trains and the speed of telegraph communication. By the middle 1870's the local sundial was obsolete: time had been standardized in zones, and the station clock was the local authority.

The Railroad Industry

Federal land grants made possible the first transcontinental railroad, the Union-Central Pacific, completed in 1869. This, however, was only the beginning. Promoters asked for and obtained land grants for other transcontinental lines. The states joined the central government in aiding the prospective builders, so that all parts of the West would have an equal chance for development. Even that did not suffice. Each crossroads demanded a rail connection. Local communities all over the nation bid against each other in subscribing to railroad bonds, for to be passed up meant permanent inferiority to rail-connected neighbors.

In a competitive, free-enterprise society, such frantic bidding was bound to attract the corrupt along with the honest, the parasite as well as the genuine builder. Nor was it easy to tell one from the other. Sometimes a turn in the stock market transformed a good man into a villain or converted a small-time manipulator into a solid citizen.

In general, lines were started as small ventures to connect inland communities with existing railroad centers or with lake or river ports. The local businessmen soon discovered that they could not swing the deal themselves. They therefore went hat in hand to the New York, Boston, or Philadelphia financiers. The eastern money men surveyed the project and decided whether or not to invest their own or their clients' capital. Since money was hard to raise, the terms were usually harsh. Big-city financiers were likely to insist on retaining the controlling stock as a bonus; and they insisted that the inland communities take a good share of the bonds.

Although they found the terms burdensome, the inland promoters were forced to accept. But there were ways of getting even. Construction had to take place far from Wall Street; and local men provided much of the supervision, labor, and materials. Building costs were difficult to estimate, and those on the ground tried to make sure that they would not lose money on construction contracts. So while the local people complained that they were being exploited by eastern capitalists, the capitalists moaned that they were being fleeced by their small-town associates. "Landowners and road contractors," said one Boston investor, "are the ones who too often get the whole benefit of the money that capitalists put into the West."

Railroad financing was often very involved. Many lines were never built at all, villainy, incompetence, or depression having dissipated the original investment before a single tie was laid. Few railroads fulfilled the grandiose plans of the promoters; usually the initial capital was exhausted long before these plans were realized. The railroad might then function as a short line, and finance extensions out of profits, if any. Or the officers might seek additional capital.

Where to get the extra money? It might be obtained from the eastern capitalists who had helped out at the start. But, since the venture was shakier than before, the financiers might now insist on terms even harsher than those exacted earlier. ("I shall increase my . . . interest if necessary . . . ," wrote one eastern capitalist, "but . . . we will make them pay for our doing their work.") Another possibility was to raise money by selling stock in the construction company, as distinguished from the railroad itself. With this new support, the construction company might be able to finish its job, taking in payment large quantities of the stocks and bonds of the railroad. The result was over-capitalization, large profits for the holders of the construction company securities, large losses for the original investors in the securities of the railroads. And more often than not the original investors included many ordinary citizens who had put up their cash and pledged their credit in hopes of attracting a railroad to their region.

It is difficult to generalize about the railroad financiers. Certainly a good number behaved very badly. Many breathed the public-be-damned spirit wrongly associated with the name of William H. Vanderbilt of the New York Central system. Some raised money without any intention of building railroads. Others made a practice of laying track parallel to existing lines, the aim being to profit from construction contracts, then to force the older railroad to buy them out. A large percentage of the most unsavory figures were associated with minor lines. But the trunk lines had scoundrels, too—"Jubilee Jim" Fisk, for instance, who with his partner Jay Gould manipulated stock and politicians and milked the Erie Railroad dry.

This was one side of the picture. The only side, said some reformers. In fact, however, many railroad financiers were well intentioned. Good intentions did not always mean efficiency, for many honest promoters were overoptimistic or extravagant. (Henry Villard, for instance, the man who built the Northern Pacific.) But there were those who combined integrity with good judgment and a high level of ability. One example was John Murray Forbes, a Boston capitalist whose group financed the Michigan Central, the Chicago, Burlington and Quincy and other lines. Though very profit-conscious, Forbes dealt fairly with stockholders and tried to build efficient railroads at minimum cost. In the process he enriched himself; but he also added to his nation's wealth and prosperity.

A chief incentive in railway building was the value added to nearby lands. Virtually every group of railroad promoters organized land companies to buy up property along the proposed right of way. Much of the net profit in the early years came from these operations.

The tie was even closer in the case of the western roads that received federal or state land grants; these companies were directly in the real-estate business. The ultimate value of most of the principal roads from Illinois west depended on the successful sale of their land grants.

The main problem was that of price. Selling the land quickly to settlers meant traffic for the road; but this meant bottom prices. Holding out for high prices was tempting; but delay in sales meant delay in settlement, and little freight for the railroad. High prices also caused the public to attack the railroad as a grasping monopoly that retarded land development. Most roads, therefore, finally decided to sell at low rates.

Various types of abuse entered into the handling of government land grants. One involved holding land off the market. The original land-grant acts set broad limits. Within these limits the railroads could claim a certain amount of land. Until they made their choice all land between the designated limits was withheld from homesteading by the public. Some companies which ran into construction difficulties failed to indicate the land they wanted for more than a decade. Some never made a choice, and the land eventually reverted to the government. But meantime citizens were deprived of the opportunity to acquire much valuable western land. Congress and the state legislatures could have handled this problem by terminating grants where there was no construction. The railroads, however, had friends at court; and little was done until the middle 1880's.

Another type of abuse concerned special privileges for favored individuals. Insiders were able to find out where stations and yards would be located. Then, with the connivance of company officials, they bought large tracts of land from the railroads at minimum prices and made huge profits on the deals. This practice deprived stockholders of their legitimate profits from land sales; and it helped make the public suspicious of the railroads.

Rates and Regulations

Many citizens disapproved of the financial and land policies of the new railroad companies. But when demand for government regulation of the railroads appeared in the 1870's and 1880's, it was the rate question which was considered basic.

One side of the rate problem was the short haul–long haul differential. A large part of the cost of hauling freight by rail or water is for loading at the beginning and unloading at the end of the journey. This was as expensive for a ten-mile trip as for one of a thousand miles. Consequently, the railroads always charged a higher rate per mile for short hauls than for long ones.

This was understandable; but it did not tell all the story. Rates for long runs were also affected by competition. Long-haul freight (say from Chicago to New York) could go by a variety of different routes. With several railroads bidding for the business, rates went down—far, far down during rate wars like that of 1874. There was no such competition and there were no such rate reductions on short hauls. Normally a farmer had access to only one railroad. The line did not need to cut rates to keep the farmer's business. On the contrary; it could use its monopolistic position to boost the rate, thus making up for losses on long hauls. It cost more, therefore, to ship wheat a few miles from Nora, Illinois, to Chicago than to send the same product the much longer distance from St. Paul, Minnesota, to Chicago.

Naturally enough, the farmers and merchants who had to pay the high rates complained bitterly. They and others also raised objections to the special favors given to big shippers. To get the business of such giant concerns as the Standard Oil Company, railroads offered bargain rates or gave rebates. So general did these deals become that railroad presidents could not keep up with all the secret arrangements entered into by their traffic managers. When the railroads themselves began to suffer under the pressure of shippers and cutthroat competition, the stronger roads formed pools. These involved agreements to maintain rates and share the business on a percentage basis. By the middle 1880's much competitive traffic was pooled. But, since pooling agreements were unenforceable at law, secret rate cutting continued. What was more, many Americans regarded pooling as additional evidence that railroad officials thought in terms of monopoly rather than the public interest.

As criticism of rate policies mounted, more and more citizens demanded governmental regulation of the railroads. At first (from the 1860's to the 1890's) the focus was on state action. As early as 1869 Massachusetts set up a commission to investigate railroad abuses. In that same year an Illinois constitutional convention empowered the state legislature to set maximum rates. Thereafter Illinois and other states tried to fix rates by legislative act or through state railway commissions. The movement centered in the Middle West and reached its peak in the depression years of the mid-1870's, when the Grangers were at the height of their political influence.

In the end, however, this state rate-fixing drive proved unsuccessful. Some commissions were so anti-railroad that a reaction set in—for, after all, the Middle West was still trying to attract new lines. The Grangers, chief sponsors of regulation, lost ground rapidly after 1875 and finally faded out of politics. Meantime, the railroads fought regulation tooth and nail, using money and working through journalists and politicians friendly to their cause. And by 1880 many of the regulatory laws were repealed, amended, or ignored.

Then the federal courts stepped in. During the 1870's the United States Supreme Court upheld the right of state legislatures to regulate rates (the so-called Granger cases, notably in Peik *vs.* Chicago and North Western Railway, 1876). But in the next decade the judges took different ground. In the Wabash case of 1886, the Supreme Court held that states had no power to fix rates on routes that involved interstate commerce. Since most rail routes fell in this category, the decision was a paralyzing blow for the friends of regulation.

With state regulation a failure, there was increasing demand for action by the United States government. Small shippers in every part of the country threw their weight behind the movement, and in 1887 Congress passed an Interstate Commerce Act. Theoretically, the law gave an Interstate Commerce Commission the right to declare rates unjust, to prevent long haul–short haul discrimination, and to outlaw pooling. Actually, the statute was not very effective at the start. The Interstate Commerce Commission could enforce its duties only through the courts; and the federal judges found various loopholes in the 1887 law. Even so, the establishment of the Interstate Commerce Commission was a landmark in the advance of national power and in the movement toward greater government regulation of economic life.

Meanwhile, technological improvements, expansion of routes, and a general price decline produced a nearly steady downward trend in rates from 1873 to 1896. By the end of the century there were half a dozen transcontinentals, plus a dozen other long lines from the Mississippi Valley to the Rocky Mountains. There had been much railroad building in the South; and the East and Middle West were crisscrossed by rails seldom more than twenty miles apart. This meant that by 1900 farmers and other small shippers were likely to be near competitive points.

Although the essentials of railroad technology remained unchanged throughout this period, heavier rails, more powerful engines, and the Westinghouse air brake speeded freight and passenger service. So did the combination of short lines into large railroad empires (Cornelius Vanderbilt's New York Central system, for example). In the 1850's it had taken three days over many separate railroads to make the trip from Chicago to New York. By 1900 express trains were covering this distance in less than a day. Crossing the continent by train and stage had required a month on the eve of the Civil War. By 1900 the transcontinental railroads had cut this time to less than a week.

Production of Raw Materials

Over half the tonnage hauled by the new railroads consisted of a single item, coal. From the beginning of the industrial revolution in eighteenth-century England, coal was the most important raw material; and it remains so to this day. The emergence of the United States as the greatest industrial power on earth is closely related to the fact that this country possesses half the known coal reserves of the world.

Coal not only supplied freight for the railroads; it also provided fuel for the locomotives. As the years went by, coal warmed more and more American homes, stores, and offices. In manufacturing, coal became and remained the major source of power, running far ahead of water power and petroleum. The manufacture of iron and steel required more coal than iron ore. Coal heated the blast furnaces. It drove the steam engines that made the factories function. It made possible the new electrical industry.

The first commercial coal in America was the anthracite, or hard coal, of eastern Pennsylvania. The annual production of that region doubled each decade from 1850 to 1900. But geologists, combing the United States for minerals, found no important new deposits of anthracite. Consequently bituminous, or soft coal, ultimately became the chief source for heat and power. In the last half of the nineteenth century, anthracite production rose from 4,000,000 to 60,000,000 tons per year. During that same period, the annual production of bituminous jumped from 3,000,000 to 200,000,000 tons.

Unlike anthracite, bituminous coal was found in every major region of the United States. The largest and best-quality veins are in the Appalachian Mountains, extending from western Pennsylvania through Virginia, West Virginia, Tennessee, and Kentucky. But many other areas contain commercially valuable deposits. The location of coal in Illinois, Missouri, and Alabama promoted a westward and southward movement of heavy industry in the 1880's and 1890's.

Coal was basic in the power picture; but water was not to be ignored. From earliest colonial days, millers had located by waterfalls and had used water power for their manufacturing enterprises. As the United States became industrialized, manufacturers continued to exploit this source of energy. With the development of the electrical industry after the Civil War it became possible to transform water power into electrical energy, supplementing the supply of electricity obtained from coal. By the mid-1890's, the hydroelectric industry was firmly established, and power was being transmitted distances of twenty miles. The future appeared promising. There were, however, certain complications. Most troublesome of these was the fact that the major untapped sources of water power were in the Rocky Mountains, far from the major industrial centers.

In the twentieth century, petroleum products have become important sources of power. But that was for the future. From the 1850's to the 1890's the petroleum industry centered its attention on kerosene, used chiefly for illumination. Inventors, however, were working on internal-combustion engines. Their work would transform transportation after 1900, though coal and the steam engine would continue to dominate the factories.

There are, of course, other sources of power—wind power, animal power, man power. But as the United States became industrialized, the accent would be increasingly on mechanical power. Between the late 1850's and the late 1890's the population of the United States increased by 150 percent. The number of animals used for draft purposes increased roughly in proportion. In these same years the nation's total installed mechanical power went up from less than 5,000,000 to more than 40,000,000 horsepower, an increase of more than 700 percent. Later increases would be still more spectacular.

Besides coal and other sources of power, an industrial nation needs iron ore. Here again the United States was fortunate, having more and richer ores than competitor nations. The eastern seaboard ores, scattered from the Canadian border of New York to Alabama, had been worked on a small scale since the colonial period. As the nation moved into large-scale iron production, around 1850, Pennsylvania took the lead. Her supremacy came from a strategic combination of resources, for she had both iron ore and coking coal. Virginia had the same combination, but made less headway because she was not so close to the chief markets for iron.

The discovery of iron ore around Lake Superior (in upper Michigan, Wisconsin, and especially Minnesota) ultimately added to the advantages of Pennsylvania. Since there was no coal available in the Lake Superior region, and since the manufacture of iron required twice as much weight in coal as in iron ore, the logical move was to send the ore to the coal. This meant shipping iron ore down the Great Lakes by steamer to the Pittsburgh coal area. The opening of the great Mesabi Range in Minnesota about 1890 provided whole mountains of iron ore; and by 1900 the Lake Superior mines were supplying the ore for most of the iron and steel production of the United States. Much of the ore still went to western Pennsylvania. Some, however, went to new furnaces and mills along the Great Lakes in Ohio, Indiana, and Illinois. Meantime, ore deposits of lesser importance had been opened in a score of other states, from Alabama and Tennessee to California and Oregon. Manufacturing establishments sprang up near each of these local fields.

In 1850 the American iron and steel industry specialized in iron production. Blast furnaces produced 600,000 tons a year, whereas steel output was negligible. Fifty years later, the concentration was on steel. Nearly 70 percent of the 15,000,000 tons of pig iron produced by the furnaces in 1900 was turned into steel. The change-over came in the 1870's, and was associated with the introduction of technological processes from European steel centers.

The years from 1850 to 1900 saw great increases in the production of other minerals—lead, zinc, copper, silver, gold. All were important, gold and silver being particularly significant in the field of politics. From the industrial point of view, copper counted most. It was the basic metal of the electrical industry, which played a vital role in American industrialization after the 1870's. Copper had been mined in colonial New Jersey, and in Michigan during the 1850's; but there had been no incentive for large production until the need arose for copper wire. By then copper ore had been located in the West, from Montana to Arizona. This became the great producing area as copper production increased tenfold from 1880 to 1900, and the United States took the world lead in copper mining.

Aside from cement, stone, sand, and other materials generally available locally, lumber was the remaining raw material essential for physical progress. The cutting of hardwoods moved across the northern part of the country from Maine and New York to Michigan and Wisconsin, then on to Minnesota and by the 1890's to the Pacific Northwest. From 1850 to 1890 boards cut in sawmills near the Great Lakes made Chicago the center of the industry. But production continued in the older areas also, and a new soft-pine industry developed in the South. Coal was replacing wood as fuel, but the new industrial system needed lumber in a thousand ways. Hence in 1900 lumber products had approximately the same value as pig iron.

In raw materials as in railroads, these were days when one could "get rich quick." Cornelius Vanderbilt, Jay Gould, Leland Stanford, C. P. Huntington, and others made fortunes promoting railroads. At the same time, Marcus Daly and William A. Clark went from rags to riches in copper and fought each other for control of Montana politics. The Weyerhaeusers made a lumber fortune in the Great Lakes region and later increased it by operations on the Pacific coast. John

D. Rockefeller's wealth came from another raw material, petroleum, though his control was at the refining rather than the producing level. Similarly, Henry Clay Frick's first successes were in coke, a coal product of great importance to the steel industry. (Frick, incidentally, was financed by the Mellons of Pittsburgh. In the twentieth century, these same Mellons would again figure in the history of natural resources, by securing control of a newly important raw material, aluminum.)

Many were lost along the way. In iron ore one of the great names was that of Leonidas Merritt. With his brothers and other relatives, Merritt opened the Mesabi iron range. For a time the "seven iron men" seemed to be on the way to enormous wealth. Then they were caught short in the depression that followed the panic of 1893. The wealth of the Mesabi went to other men—to John D. Rockefeller, Andrew Carnegie, Henry Clay Frick, James J. Hill.

These four names suggest the ways in which the raw materials were interrelated, and how all were linked to transportation. Carnegie and Frick were iron and steel magnates. Frick had started out in coal, Carnegie in railroads. Coal and railroads, Mesabi ore and the manufacture of iron and steel thus formed a single pattern. Hill was another railroad man, the builder of the Great Northern. Rockefeller was in oil. But that meant transportation, too, including control of pipelines. Nor was Rockefeller unwilling to enter other fields; he moved into the iron ore business, lending money to the Merritts and acquiring lake steamers which transported the ore to the steel centers.

Land grants greatly speeded the building of the western railroads. In like fashion land policy influenced the exploitation of raw materials. In 1850 a great many of the nation's mineral and timber resources were located on United States government land. By 1900 most of these resources had been transferred to private hands, often for prices that were absurdly low.

The transfers were in line with land policies established in the early days of the republic. From the beginning Congress had been anxious to shift public lands to private hands as rapidly as possible. The tendency from the 1790's on was to reduce the price. After the passage of the Homestead Act in 1862, some lands were given away to settlers;

and, of course, enormous tracts were handed to railroad promoters. The plain intention was to promote settlement and aid private enterprise by getting rid of the public domain as soon as possible.

This trend was not reversed until the twentieth century. A series of laws of the 1870's did set lands of special value outside the provisions of the Homestead Act; but these lands were sold far below their true value. Under the Mining Act of 1872 mineral lands were to be sold at from $2.50 to $5.00 an acre. The following year Congress set a price of $10 to $15 an acre for coal lands. A Timber and Stone Act of 1878 set a $2.50 to $5.00 price per acre. Although these were minimum figures, government officials made virtually no effort to get more than the lowest permissible price. Nor did the government try hard to enforce all the provisions of the statutes. The Timber and Stone Act called for development of the property by the purchaser; but much of the land acquired under this legislation was transferred to big lumber companies.

In the nineteenth century many Americans assumed that individual self-seeking would produce public gain. The exploitation of natural resources did not point to that conclusion. Big or small, most exploiting companies sought profit without regard for the future. Lumber companies were unbelievably wasteful, and took no interest in reforestation. Poverty-stricken, unproductive "cut-over" lands were their gift to later generations. Petroleum producers were even more prodigal with that irreplaceable raw material. Owners of coal mines skimmed the cream, seeking quick profits and leaving properties in bad shape for their successors. Yet few Americans objected. The conservation movement would not take hold until the United States had wasted much of its rich heritage.

Growth in Consumer's Goods

The years from 1850 to 1890 saw a spectacular increase in consumers' goods. Of the many fields affected, two stood out. These were the petroleum industry and the business of preparing processed foods.

As has been noted, oil would eventually enter industry as a major source of fuel and heat; but before 1900 its chief use was in kerosene for the ubiquitous oil lamp. Gas obtained from coal had started the rapid advance in lighting in the 1830's, and electricity topped this off in the 1880's. But both of these developments were confined at first to the cities. For small-town and rural Americans (still a majority of the population in 1890) the great change was the replacement of light from expensive whale oil or unsatisfactory candles by the cheap and reliable kerosene lamp.

Residents of northwest Pennsylvania had long been familiar with oil as a seepage from certain lands. Then, in 1859, E. L. Drake, a geologist representing New York and New England interests drilled the first commercial oil well. The crude oil was refined by simple distillation and put on the market as a lighting fluid. When it proved successful, drillers and refiners rushed in to exploit the new product, buying farms, leasing oil rights, and creating fortunes for Pennsylvania farmers, if not always for themselves. The boom went on during the Civil War, even when General Robert E. Lee was threatening the state with invasion. Aside from buying substitutes for the draft, the boomers seem to have been little concerned about the war.

Shrewd young John D. Rockefeller went into the oil-refining business in Cleveland at a time when hundreds of small producers were glutting the market (1862). Rockefeller had a good location; and he was a resourceful, hard-driving businessman. Within two decades he and his Standard Oil group had a virtual monopoly of refining and a dominant position in the field of oil transportation. Opponents of Standard Oil claimed that Rockefeller used his monopolistic position to raise the price of kerosene. Rockefeller partisans replied that Standard Oil created a uniform product readily available in all parts of the United States and most of the civilized world.

Americans had long used food preprocessed in mills or factories. In value of product, flour milling was in 1850, and had long been, the chief industry of the United States. Meat packing also ranked high. In addition, factory-packed food in cans and jars, first appearing in the 1820's, had won a small market among those not afraid to experiment.

As urban needs increased, and as transportation improved, processing at strategically located shipping points became big business. Flour milling centered at Minneapolis, and to a lesser extent at Kansas City,

Richmond, and Buffalo; meat packing shifted from Cincinnati to Chicago. Minneapolis won ascendancy in flour through new milling processes introduced there in the 1870's. Chicago came to dominate the packing business because of rail connections, efficient stockyards, and large-scale operations. The introduction of the refrigerator car in the 1870's increased Chicago's importance by enabling her packers to ship fresh beef to eastern and foreign markets.

As flour milling and meat packing moved ahead, other processed foods increased in popularity. City dwellers tried canned salmon and canned soup, prepared cereals and bottled pickles. Advertising was used to break down public resistance to each new product; and the manufacturers felt that they had made real progress by 1900. Undoubtedly they had. Even so, home cooking and preserving remained the rule in most American homes.

Food did not tell all the story. Bit by bit factory goods were replacing handmade products in the home. The commercial adaptation of the sewing machine, first to cloth, then to leather, lowered the price of factory shoes and ready-made clothes. Furniture from plants in Grand Rapids, Michigan, and elsewhere began to displace the products of the local cabinetmaker. Homemade rugs slowly gave way to factory-produced floor coverings. Meantime, mass production reduced the price of stoves, brooms, matches, and scores of other household articles.

New Locations for Industry

The emerging pattern of mass production, mechanical power, and railway transportation produced an interconnected, national market. In this situation it seemed best to manufacture at the points where costs were lowest. This caused many industries to migrate, generally in a westerly direction. Others remained in physically uneconomic locations because of inertia, business traditions, existing capital investments, or proximity to buyers, bankers, or exporters.

For heavy industry the controlling force in location was the cost of transportation. In locating a steel plant, Andrew Carnegie had to balance cost of transporting coke, iron ore, and finished steel in such a way as to produce the lowest total. This kept the center of this industry in western Pennsylvania.

In industries where the value added by manufacture was large and the weight of product small, the supply of skilled labor might be the most significant factor. New England illustrates this point. The New England states are located far from the geographical center of the United States—far, too, from the center of population. Nor are they near the most important raw materials. Yet, in defiance of the pressure of transportation costs, New England remained a manufacturing center from 1850 to 1900, specializing in hardware, clocks, firearms, silverware, and other products which required skilled labor.

As in earlier decades, New England led the nation in textile production. That industry, however, required few skilled workers. The call was rather for a large supply of cheap, unskilled labor. Hence the textile industry began to migrate from New England to the southern states. There the manufacturers could employ back-country farm families at low wages. New England had no comparable labor supply; many of her back-country districts had been depopulated by the westward movement. Attempting to hold their lead in textiles, New England businessmen brought in French-Canadian and European immigrants. But the southward trend continued.

Since textile manufacturing required bulky machinery and large buildings, reasonably priced land was a factor of importance in locating textile establishments. Other industries needed cheap labor but very little land. In this category is the manufacture of furs, clothing, jewelry, novelties, and notions. Those who produced these items also wanted to be near the markets so as to predict trends and fashions. Hence these industries stayed in the heart of the big cities, particularly New York, and employed immigrant labor. By 1900 such enterprises plus those that used cheaper land on the outskirts of New York had concentrated 15 percent of the value of the nation's manufactured products in this one big city.

Despite this concentration of manufacturing activity, the nation's industry was spreading out. By 1900 all five of the states of the Old Northwest (Ohio, Indiana, Illinois, Michigan, Wisconsin) ranked among the first ten states in number of people engaged in manufacturing. Only New York, Pennsylvania, and Massachusetts ranked ahead of Illinois and Ohio in this particular. Factories were also springing up in other traditionally agricultural regions. Georgia, California, and North Carolina, for example, stood fourteenth, fifteenth, and sixteenth in number of industrial wage earners.

This spread of manufacturing had not been caused by economic forces alone. Impressed by the wealth that came from industrial operations, states all over the nation had made special efforts to attract factories. So had cities in every section. State and local governments had offered cash to those who would build factories, or tax exemption over a period of years. Communities had advertised their advantages: good transportation, power possibilities, a supply of cheap labor. Chambers of commerce had joined in the bidding, speaking for merchants and lawyers, realtors and bankers. Plainly, the industrial age had arrived, and was making its impact felt in every corner of the land.

Technological Advance

The phenomenal growth of American industry during the second half of the nineteenth century would have been impossible without a major advance in technology. Without improved technology—that is, without new inventions and improvements in engineering—the railroads would not have been nearly as efficient as they had become by 1890. Without improved technology much of the coal and iron ore would have remained indefinitely within the hills. Without improved technology the United States would not have been in a position to bid for world influence by 1900.

Technical progress after 1850 was based in part on what had gone before. That is, the desire to save labor and secure profits led inventors to add by trial and error to what they had inherited. But there was something more, something which speeded up the process of invention. This was a changing relationship between theoretical (basic) and applied science.

Down to 1850, industries had increased efficiency, if at all, on the basis of empirical, trial-and-error methods, without benefit of scientific principles. Agriculture and textile manufacturing, ironmaking and medicine were all largely unrelated to theoretical science. But such basic sciences as physics, chemistry, and pathology were moving ahead rapidly. Prior to 1850 these sciences had influenced technology here and there (as when astronomy had aided navigation). From 1850 on, the influence was extended all along the line. The result was an extraordinarily rapid advance of technology. For a single scientific principle—for example, that of electromagnetism—suggested many applications.

Invention, moreover, encouraged further invention. This had been true even in the days of trial-and-error methods. Better spinning machines, for instance, had produced a need for and stimulated the development of improved weaving equipment. But when basic science came into play, everything moved faster. Research not only answered social needs, as in providing chemical fertilizers. It also suggested new needs which the public could not have anticipated. Thus science, in providing the steam engine, created a hitherto-unfelt need for locomotives; and the availability of the latter led to demands for a whole series of inventions from steel-making processes to air brakes and automatic couplers.

The result was a transformation of Western civilization. To put it in another way, technology had long operated at a low temperature produced by trial-and-error advances. Then, when the heat of science was turned on, the whole process burst into flame.

No country was more transformed by technology after 1850 than the United States; and in certain respects the American republic was peculiarly successful in developing and exploiting inventions of every kind. Americans had worked out superior techniques even before 1850, as in the making of farm machinery. This was natural. As an underpopulated country, the United States had a special need for labor-saving equipment. At the same time, American wealth in natural resources provided unusual means for meeting this need. Americans also shared the general European enthusiasm for "progress." But citizens of the United States gave a special twist to this enthusiasm by their zeal for "practical" achievements. Hence after 1850, as before, they showed little concern for theoretical or basic science.

American indifference to basic science reflected the attitudes of farmers and businessmen alike. Both took pride in being "practical." Also significant was the lack in the United States of the aristocratic traditions which in Europe upheld the prestige of pure scholarship and science. In consequence, most nineteenth-century discoveries in basic science were European rather than American. Generally, too, the initial applications of these discoveries to technology were first worked out in the Old World rather than the New. After 1850, as before, the typical American invention was of the trial-and-error sort. Beyond that, Americans excelled in getting inventions into mass production, for the benefit of the people as well as the producer. This trend had been earlier foreshadowed in Eli Whitney's development of standardized (interchangeable) parts in the firearms industry.

The neglect of theoretical science by nineteenth-century Americans was very striking. Neither business nor the masses nor the government displayed much interest in research. Few corporations set up research laboratories before 1900, and government aid to science was largely limited to useful projects in agriculture, mining, and the like. The colleges viewed their professors primarily as teachers rather than as research men. The few who were interested in research received scant encouragement. Thus Willard Gibbs did basic work on mathematical physics for years at Yale but did not even receive a salary until Europeans called attention to his genius. In 1876 the Johns Hopkins University was established in Baltimore along German lines, to devote itself basically to research and research training; but faculties in most colleges and universities continued to give nearly all their time to undergraduate instruction.

Some Americans deplored this situation. Those who complained included scientists who wanted aid or recognition for their research work, and others whose national pride was hurt by the fact that American science was still colonial in dependence on Europe. A few far-seeing individuals said that the United States would pay heavily for neglecting pure research. Work done in chemistry and physics laboratories built great German industries after 1870 and pushed Germany far ahead in the production of drugs and dyes and lenses.

But few Americans were worried. Trial-and-error methods had enabled the United States to build an efficient transportation and manufacturing system. Why not continue to pursue that line? If basic theory worked out by Europeans brought technologic change, Americans could eventually import the new process and fit it to the mass production system of the United States.

Trial-and-Error Inventions

The sewing machine which Elias Howe "invented" in 1846 is a good example of technologic advance achieved in the United States. A stitching machine had been patented in England as early as 1780, a workable sewing machine in France in 1830. Howe then added the eye-pointed needle and the double-lock stitch and turned out a highly efficient machine. Howe's work required no research in basic science. But it was ingenious, and solved the problem of finding an automatic equivalent for the complicated finger motions of sewing. And when marketed, the sewing machine had great social significance. It became one of the first modern improvements lightening labor in the home. At the same time, its employment in factories made possible the rapid and therefore cheaper production of woolen, cotton, and leather products.

Or take the linotype. This was made by a German-trained American mechanic, Ottmar Mergenthaler, in response to a definite social need. The earlier invention of the rotary press enabled newspapers to turn out rapidly great numbers of sheets; but the hand-setting of type slowed down the total process of producing the papers. Working on the problem, Mergenthaler finally produced the linotype in 1884. This machine operated through a keyboard, a device earlier employed in the piano. Molten lead poured into a mold so as to cast an entire line of type at a time. Printing of newspapers, books, and magazines promptly became cheaper as well as more rapid. This happened just when the expansion of advertising brought increasing income to periodicals. Advertising and the linotype together made for mass circulation, which in turn brought important changes in American society.

The years that saw the introduction of the linotype also saw the development of the typewriter. Various "writing machines" had been made by European and American inventors between 1820 and 1870, but none operated quite so rapidly as did handwriting. There was, moreover, no great demand for very rapid machines; handwriting served well enough in those early days. But as the tempo of business increased after 1870, the advantages of rapid writing became apparent. Then, in 1873, Christopher Sholes produced a typewriter which was more rapid than the hand and which was simple enough for commercial production. The machine was marketed by Remington, and by 1890 typewriters were selling briskly.

Useful though the typewriter was, it took fifteen years to become a definite success. People were so accustomed to handwriting that they disliked typewriting—it was too impersonal. (To this day, very personal messages are often written in longhand.) Moreover, typewriters were expensive and at first seemed hard to use. But business offices soon found that the machine was worth the cost. As for the skill, it soon became the custom to hire trained typists. Men were hired at first, but were soon replaced by women for the simple reason that the latter's services were cheaper. Thus by 1900 women were moving into offices as they had earlier invaded the factories.

In time, other office machines were invented—mimeographs, addressographs, calculators, and many more. Some of these were outgrowths of the typewriter. With them came improved office procedures such as systematic filing and indexing, and the correlation of typing with the old process of shorthand. Later, the phonograph (Dictaphone) was used in business. The cumulative impact of these devices produced a revolution in office management, this revolution being related as both cause and effect to the evolution of large-scale business. The old-fashioned merchant's office, with a few clerks on high stools handling written accounts and correspondence, could no more carry on a modern business than could stagecoaches handle present-day transportation.

Other inventions rested on knowledge of basic science. Here the American contribution was less impressive; American developments came generally after Europeans had laid the foundations.

Lighting illustrates the point. There was little improvement in this field from classical times to 1800. Although people would certainly have enjoyed better light, there had been no strong demand for it.

Trial-and-error experiments offered few possibilities, save in such minor advantages as the use of whale oil as a new source of fuel for lamps. But in the late eighteenth century, growing knowledge of the chemistry of gases suggested to European scientists the possibility of gas lighting. This was tried in London, and introduced into American cities after 1800. New York's Broadway stores were so illuminated by the time of the Civil War. By then research scientists were turning to other materials. A Canadian geologist obtained kerosene from petroleum in the 1850's; and the kerosene lamp was soon used all over the world.

Meantime the chemists had opened an even more promising field. At the beginning of the nineteenth century Sir Humphry Davy, an Englishman, found that an electric current generated by chemical decomposition in a battery would in turn decompose other chemicals. Observing this process of electrolysis (later vital in the chemical industry), Davy tested the effect of current on chemicals and metals. This led to his invention of the arc light (1809), used to light American cities as late as the early 1900's. Davy also found that some metals burned very slowly when a current was passed through them, and in so doing gave out light. Following this line, English and French scientists developed incandescent lights in the middle of the century, and lighted rooms on an experimental basis. During the twenty-five years before 1870, various inventors used carbon filaments and partial vacuums in the bulbs. That is to say, the basic theory had been established, and some technologic paths explored.

At this point the American Thomas Alva Edison entered the field. Edison was a self-trained man who lacked, at least in his earlier career, basic scientific knowledge. He was, however, exceedingly ingenious and persevering. Given the elements of a problem, he came up with effective solutions that baffled more original thinkers. This was the case with incandescent lights. They had "worked" abroad but were neither cheap nor durable. Just what metals were best for wires, just what degrees of vacuum? What substances made the toughest and best filaments? The problem, in other words, was in the trial-and-error stage. Taking it up there, Edison produced in 1879 an effective light that used carbon filaments, platinum wires, and a high-vacuum bulb. Simultaneously, others were developing and marketing incandescent bulbs in Great Britain.

In his great work, Edison cared little for abstract problems. If such questions arose, he said he could "hire a mathematician." What excited Edison was not the "pure" curiosity of the scientist. Rather his was a zeal for turning out products that could be made available to the public. He thus reflected the view that democracy had a distinctive mission: to put technology to work for the welfare of all the people.

This outlook helps explain Edison's interest in the telephone and phonograph. It also helps explain his active interest in producing and distributing his products. He was, of course, interested in personal gain; but he was even more interested in having his countrymen benefit from his work. Unlike many inventors, he had the ability to put his inventions into commercial production. He showed this when he opened the famous Pearl Street power plant in New York City in 1882 to supply current for electric lights.

Edison's success was linked to the general situation of the American public. Relatively low living standards cut down the market for new inventions in Europe. The majority of Europeans simply could not afford to buy the gadgets. Conditions were different in the United States. The desire to provide better products for the masses was supplemented by their ability to buy them. Although many Americans were far from prosperous, average income levels had long been higher here than in the European countries. They so remained in the second half of the nineteenth century, providing a large market for new inventions.

Not that new inventions were accepted right away. The older generation liked the "good, old-fashioned way" and resisted Edison's lights and Alexander Graham Bell's telephone. Younger citizens were more receptive, but it took time and salesmanship to convince potential customers. Sometimes the delay was associated with price and quality, for it took a decade or more to make many new devices cheap and efficient. Prejudice and apathy were also in the picture. Antiseptic methods in surgery, introduced in Britain around 1860, were not generally used by American surgeons until after 1885.

There is a popular belief that inventors starved in garrets while predatory corporations made millions from their inventions. Sometimes it did work out that way. On the other hand, a number of inventors made fortunes on their patents; and many businessmen lost heavily in backing particular inventions. Successful inventors won great popular acclaim from 1850 to 1900, at a time when Americans ignored theoretical scientists. Thus Edison became the "Wizard of Menlo Park" while the mathematical physicist Willard Gibbs remained unknown.

Technology in Iron and Steel

Of the technologic changes made between 1850 and 1900, none were more important than those achieved in iron and steel. Here was a key industry, and one in which the United States had great advantages, owing to abundance of natural resources. Technologic gains here meant economic gains for the whole United States.

Europeans had used iron since remote times and had gradually acquired knowledge of different grades and alloys. Ore was smelted in charcoal furnaces, and rule-of-thumb methods produced cast iron and pig iron (hard and brittle), wrought iron (soft and malleable), and steel (hard and tough). The differences in these depended largely on the amount of carbon present.

Relatively brittle grades of iron were at first the only ones that could be produced in large quantities at a reasonable price. Hence the rails used on early railroads had an annoying habit of breaking and tearing through the floor of the cars above. Iron boilers were also unreliable; boiler explosions accounted for most of the "Great Steamboat Disaster" headlines of the 1830's and 1840's. Plainly needed was a cheap and reliable steel.

Part of the answer was found by the trial-and-error method, by William Kelley in the United States (1846) and William Bessemer in England (1856). These men found that when one melted pig iron (high in carbon) the carbon in it would burn under an air blast and thus provide its own fuel. The burning could then be stopped when enough carbon remained to provide the qualities of steel. It was no longer necessary, as before, to remove nearly all the carbon to make wrought iron, then go through a second process of adding carbon to make steel. Bessemer also invented a converter to control air blasts; and with the introduction of this device began the manufacture of relatively cheap steel.

Difficulties remained. The percentage of carbon which gave a good steel with one ore proved unsatisfactory with other ores. Here science entered the picture. Analytical chemists found that the quality of steel depended in part on the amount of phosphorus and manganese in the original iron ore. With this knowledge, manufacturers could tell just when to turn off the blast with each ore. Chemists also learned how to improve steel by adding silicon and manganese; and their research made it possible for producers to grade the product.

Patent difficulties delayed American steel production until the Bessemer and Kelley groups merged. Then, from the late 1860's on, the industry moved ahead. There were further technologic improvements, many of them brought from Europe. Notable was the German-developed open-hearth process, in which gases escaping from the furnace were combined with air to form a super-hot flame which was played over the surface of the molten metal. In this process it was possible to determine even more exactly what the quality of the steel product would be. Andrew Carnegie used this technique to advantage, and after 1900 it became more widely used than the Bessemer process.

For improvements based on scientific research the steel manufacturers of the United States depended heavily on Europe. American supremacy was in the field of mass production. By the 1880's the steel production of the United States had surpassed that of Great Britain. By 1900 the American republic was making a third of the world's steel. Production on this scale was made possible by expanding uses— locomotives and battleships, railroad rails and business machines, wire and cans, bicycles, rivets and girders for the new skyscrapers.

The Power Engine

In 1850 the steam engine had largely replaced horses in long-distance land transportation and was beginning to replace wind power in ocean transport. Steam power was also being substituted for water power in textile mills and for man power in the printing industry. Many saw the whole future wrapped up in the steam engine. "It rows, it pumps, it excavates, it lifts, it hammers, it carries, it spins, it weaves . . . ," cried Daniel Webster. "No visible limit yet appears beyond which its progress is seen to be impossible."

In line with Webster's glowing prophecy, the steam engine did become more useful after 1850. During the preceding decade an English physicist had defined the mechanical equivalent of heat. It now became known that energy as well as matter was indestructible and that all forms of energy (heat, electricity, mechanical energy, and so on) were mutually convertible. In the case of the steam engine, this knowledge made it possible to compare the amount of heat generated in the firebox with the amount of mechanical power actually delivered at the wheels. One could thus measure the relative efficiency of boilers, valves, governors, and the like. With such yardsticks and by continuous experiment, engineers were able by the 1890's to produce locomotives and stationary engines far superior to those of a half-century before.

The future of technology, however, did not lie entirely with the steam engine. By 1890 scientists and inventors were tapping other sources of energy. They were harnessing electrical power. They were using the energy that bound together the atoms of chemical combinations. (Later, with the development of atomic physics, the much vaster energy which held together the interior systems of atoms would also be liberated for man's use or misuse.)

The energy locked in chemical combinations had been employed since medieval times in the form of exploding gunpowder. Thus the cannon may be called an early form of internal-combustion engine, doing work by instantaneous combustion or explosion. In terms of physics or chemistry, the cannon was a sort of heat engine, for it required a spark or flame to raise the gunpowder to a temperature at which it would combine with air (sudden oxidation or explosion). The resulting gases expanded rapidly, forcing the cannonball out with great speed. In a steam engine, by contrast, heat raised water to a temperature producing steam, and the expansion of steam forced out a piston. A chief difference between these two heat engines is that in a steam engine the fuel is burned in a separate furnace. In cannon and other gas engines the fuel is burned within the tube or motor cylinder. In other words, the combustion is internal.

The development of the internal-combustion engine was closely tied up with basic scientific research. When the chemists discovered hydrogen, they found that this gas, when ignited, united explosively with air. Why not utilize the force of these explosions to drive pistons? Experimenters in England, France, Germany, and elsewhere worked along this line and finally produced commercially practicable internal-combustion engines by the 1870's. The use of gasoline as a fuel made these new engines very efficient.

It was in transportation that the internal-combustion engine became most useful. During the 1880's Gottlieb Daimler and other German engineers adapted the engine for use in land vehicles, while the French built the engine into a practical automobile. The English followed suit; and in the United States the Duryea brothers, Elwood Haynes, and Henry Ford all produced gasoline-powered internal-combustion-engine automobiles between 1892 and 1895. These vehicles looked like buggies (some even had whip sockets), just as the first railroad cars resembled stagecoaches. In many of the early automobiles the engine was under the seat, and was connected with bicycle-type tires by chains. There were only one or two cylinders, but the cars embodied the basic features of the modern automobile.

Despite its ultimate triumph, the internal-combustion car did not at first seem as promising as the steam automobile and the electric. These dominated the market until after 1900. To be sure, it was a nuisance to handle the fire in a steamer; and the batteries of electric cars needed recharging after a few miles. But the first gasoline cars had problems, too, connected with cranking and gear-shifting. Hand cranking was necessary to turn the flywheel over and compress the "mixture" for the initial explosion. It was not eliminated until the invention of the self-starter just before World War I.

In time, the gasoline engine won. It was the same with small vessels—the early steam and electric launches were superseded by gasoline-driven motorboats. So, too, in a new field, aviation. Early experimenters had tried to use man power (wings) and steam power. But

man power was too feeble, and steam engines were too heavy for flying machines. The internal-combustion engine was the answer. It was
used by the Wright brothers in 1903. Hence the internal-combustion
engine had brought forth the modern automobile and the airplane in
the same generation.

Basic research, so important in the history of the internal-combustion engine, was no less vital in the harnessing of electrical energy.
The discovery that electricity produces electromagnetic fields led early
in the nineteenth century to the invention in England of the electro-
magnet. This helped bring about the invention of the telegraph. It
also pointed toward the invention of the electric motor. Could not
magnets be arranged so as to pull a bar or turn a wheel (that is, to do
work)? Following this line, the American Joseph Henry built a primitive electromagnetic motor in 1831; but, being a "pure" scientist, he
took no further interest in making the machine practical.

Both Joseph Henry and Michael Faraday of England also found
that, just as current would produce magnetism, so magnetism would
produce current. If a coil of wire were revolved between the two poles
of a magnet, a current was induced in it. Here was a way of producing
electricity without recourse to chemical decomposition (batteries). In
other words, the discovery that current would create magnetism led to
the invention of the electromagnetic motor; and the discovery that
magnets would produce current contained in germ the idea of the
electromagnetic generator or dynamo.

As these principles of electromagnetic induction became known,
practical inventors tried to use them. After seeing Henry's electro-
magnet operate, a Vermont blacksmith named Thomas Davenport
actually built electric motors in the 1830's. He connected magnets
with a battery, arranged these in a wheel, then caused the wheel to
turn by reversing the current and causing the magnets alternately to
attract and repel each other. The wheel could now do work; it was an
electromagnetic motor. Davenport applied his motor to the running
of an electric car and even a player piano by 1850. But, lacking capital,
he failed to achieve commercial success.

Most inventors of Davenport's generation were hampered by the
fact that their electric motors depended on batteries, which were soon

exhausted. Not until the development of the dynamo did electric power come into its own. Faraday constructed a primitive dynamo, which produced alternating current (AC). This type of current proved very useful later on; but nineteenth-century experimenters were accustomed to the continuous or direct current (DC) produced by batteries. By 1870 European technologists (an Italian and a Belgian) had made the necessary adjustments, and there were dynamos capable of producing direct current. Edison used such a machine in setting up his New York City power station in 1881–82.

Other inventors were quick to develop the possibilities of operating motors by wire connection with distant dynamos. In 1882 Frank J. Sprague, an American, worked out the trolley device for supplying electric current from wires to streetcars. Five years later he gave Richmond, Virginia, the first electric street railway system. The trolley car was so obviously superior to the horsecar that a hundred other cities sought Sprague's service in the next two years. Sprague later supervised the electrification of terminals and railroads. Meantime, an alternate method of supplying current to cars appeared in the invention of the third rail, to be used extensively in subways and elevated railways.

In time internal-combustion engines and electric motors competed with steam power in the stationary-engine field (for such jobs as pumping) and in railroad transportation (Diesel and electric locomotives challenging the supremacy of steam locomotives). On the whole, however, steam continued to do the bulk of the heavy work on steamships, for railroads, and in industry. Electric and internal-combustion engines performed work for which steam engines were too complicated or too heavy.

There was, in any case, no sharp division among the different sources of power. Electrical devices (for instance, the self-starter) would eventually make internal-combustion engines operate efficiently. And electrical energy was produced by both steam and water power. From the 1840's on, engineers developed turbines, these being elaborations of the vanes long employed in water wheels and windmills. Water or steam could be forced into these turbines in such a way as to utilize far more of the original energy than had been possible with clumsy wheels. The turbines could in turn be used to revolve the coils of dynamos and create electric current. The most spectacular application of this was in the hydroelectric field—the harnessing of Niagara Falls in 1895 to develop 15,000 horsepower for adjacent cities. The steam generation of electricity, though less dramatic, was even more important.

The new power engines developed between the 1850's and 1890's made possible inventions which have had enormous influence on American life. Part of the impact was evident even before 1900. The electrification of street railways, as an example, had helped build up urban areas. The telegraph, the telephone, and the electric light were already important. In the twentieth century the automobile, the radio, the washing machine, the vacuum cleaner, and a hundred other items would affect social patterns in the city and the country. Some of the new devices had bad effects as well as good (thus the automobile would raise living standards and at the same time would become a major cause of death). But in the 1890's much the greater part of technologic advance pointed toward human betterment. American faith in progress therefore reached its highest level in that era.

Science and Invention

The second half of the nineteenth century was an age of great advancement in many different fields. In photography as with power machines, Europeans had done basic investigational work before 1850. The years from 1850 to 1900 saw improvement in existing processes, and the commercial development of the photographic industry. The key American figure was George Eastman, who at the end of the 1880's marketed the first roll-film camera (Kodak). Like other American producers, Eastman used mass production methods and made his product available to a large public. At the same time, others were applying electrical devices to photography to produce the moving picture and other marvels.

Photography illustrates the impact of physics on technology. So does the discovery of X-rays in 1895 by the German physicist Roentgen. In like fashion analytic chemistry was becoming increasingly valuable in metallurgy, pharmacology, and other fields. By isolating the key ingredients in plant drugs, chemists made an enduring contribution to medicine. Geologists became more and more important, for they could help locate and assess the importance of newly significant mineral deposits. Meteorologists, using many observation points and bringing together data by the telegraph, evolved methods of weather prediction that began to have a fair degree of accuracy. The development of medical bacteriology led to the use of antiseptic techniques in surgery; and knowledge of genetics, the science of heredity, began in the 1890's to have some meaning for plant and animal breeders.

Noting all this activity, Americans gradually came to appreciate the need for trained scientists and engineers. The educational system slowly responded to the new needs. A few technical schools had been founded before the Civil War. The rising state universities established engineering courses from the 1860's on, and private schools began to give attention to the field. As it developed, distinctions were made in training, students being specially prepared for civil, mechanical, or electrical engineering. The training given was primarily of a practical sort, including such basic science as was essential in ordinary engineering practice. At the beginning, there was some resistance to the college-trained engineer. Gradually, however, engineering graduates found employment with the railroads, and, in time, with mining and industrial concerns.

Meanwhile, colleges and corporations were giving greater attention to basic research. In 1850, most American inventors were self-trained mechanics who worked in homemade laboratories. Five decades later, the pattern was changing. Science and invention were becoming increasingly complex. Would-be inventors found that they needed educational background and money for staff, equipment, and materials. Universities and business concerns began to assign funds for research. When Elihu Thompson, a physics professor, began inventing electrical devices, he was hired by a company that wished to exploit his patents. Given a steady income and assistants, Thompson was able to work out his ideas as he pleased. Edison developed his own research laboratory at Menlo Park, New Jersey, where he and a corps of assistants made invention a systematic business.

Despite the success of Edison, Thompson, and others, most American business leaders remained "100 per cent hard-boiled and sceptical about . . . organized research" in basic science. But times were changing. German corporations were finding that laboratory work in theoretical science paid off in the long run. American businessmen would eventually reach that same conclusion; and in 1900 the new General Electric Company would establish a research laboratory in Schenectady, New York.

The new trend would mean that future inventors would have basic science training and would exchange the fame (and uncertainties) of private invention for the secure anonymity of the scientific employee. The inventive process, like the production and distribution of goods, would become less an individual matter than before.

2

Business and Labor

A National Economy

Americans were talking about big business in the 1890's, about trusts and monopolies and $100,000,000 corporations. Actually, however, the United States was still a land of medium and small business. There were nearly twice as many men in business for themselves as there were professional and managerial employees of companies.

But into this older type of business world had come new elements. The changing transportation system had affected every local dealer or storekeeper. Until the arrival of the railroad the local businessman might largely control the trade of the community. After it came, dissatisfied customers could order by mail from distant suppliers, or could board a train and shop in a larger center. So the country town became part of a national economy.

In this new national economy, citizens of creative imagination had exceptional opportunities for profit. One could seek wealth by making direct investments in natural resources, transportation, manufacturing, or merchandising. Or it was possible to put money into stocks and bonds. With the expansion of American business, the public sale of securities increased. Fortunes were made and lost by speculation in stocks and bonds. Investment bankers became as important as industrial magnates; and by 1900 many industrial establishments were controlled by financial leaders. Control of industry by the manufacturers (industrial capitalism) was beginning to give way to control by bankers (finance capitalism).

While affecting markets and securities, the nationalization of American business also influenced the labor situation. The need for workers

40

led to heavier immigration than ever before. Meantime, there were drives to organize the workers in booming enterprises—mining, railroading, construction, iron and steel. Although these organizing efforts were generally unsuccessful, the period did see the launching of one permanent labor combination, the American Federation of Labor.

The Business Cycle

The shift from an agrarian to an industrial economy did not eliminate the business cycle. Business activity continued to be characterized by violent upswings and declines. It was prosperity, then depression, then prosperity again. The boom-and-bust cycle had been bad enough in a farming nation. Industrialization made things worse, for the economy was more complex, and the urban unemployed faced actual hunger in hard times.

In the years from 1850 to 1900 there were four major Wall Street panics, each followed by an economic depression affecting most of the United States. These panics came in 1857, 1873, 1883, and 1893. All appear to have been the reaction to overinvestment, particularly in railroads. Each was preceded by a period of rising prices, wages, and interest rates, and by speculative booms in land and securities. Then the boom was broken, accompanied by spectacular business failures.

When the break came, confidence evaporated. Stocks and bonds declined, prices and production slumped, and the country entered a period of economic depression. There were such periods from 1857 to 1862, 1873 to 1879, 1883 to 1885, and 1893 to 1896. The depression eras saw widespread unemployment in the industrialized areas, gloomy forecasts as to the future of the economic system, and a temporary slowing down of physical progress. A depression normally spelled a change at the next presidential election, a national defeat for the party in power. But political reactions were only one sign of the deep discouragement felt by citizens in an age when federal and state governments took no steps to prevent bankruptcies and provided no unemployment relief.

After a time the depression lifted, and good times returned. Factories went back into full production, freight car loadings increased, laborers were called back to work. Prices of agricultural and industrial products moved upward, as did stocks and bonds; and soon the United States was again experiencing an inflationary boom (1850–54, 1863–65, 1869–72, 1880–83, 1890–92). Such booms brought Americans to greater heights of optimism than were scaled by their European neighbors. Enthusiasts projected new railroads and sold lots in townsites that would surround future depots. (Prices ran $100 to $200 a half-acre for western townsites in the early 1880's, whereas the surrounding prairie, in no way distinguishable save on paper, went for $5 to $10 an acre.) With equal optimism men bought stock in mines and cattle companies and factories, with an underlying faith that the nation's growth would eventually give value to all investments.

Rise of the Corporation

Although factories grew steadily in size between 1850 and 1900, the average plant remained small all through this period. A factory typical of the 200,000 functioning at the end of the century yielded only about $25,000 in gross annual income. This had to be divided among the proprietor, one or two salaried assistants, and a score of workers. These "average" factories made such things as tools, stoves, textiles, clothing, house furnishings, jewelry, silverware, musical instruments, books, luggage, beer, whiskey, drugs, and most of the other products that sustained the American standard of living. Larger plants were required for the manufacture of railway locomotives, sheet steel, heavy machinery, and refined oil.

Within the industries still dominated by small business there were great variations in size. Although the average textile mill employed only a few dozen workers, some mills hired more than a thousand. Retail establishments ranged from the small shop staffed by the proprietor's family to giant department stores like those of Marshall Field in Chicago and John Wanamaker in Philadelphia and New York. Sometimes the small unit grew into a big one. In the early 1870's Lydia Pinkham and her children bottled a vegetable compound in their own kitchen. Two decades later production of the same thing required a substantial factory with many employees.

Excluding farms and household manufacture, there were 500,000 individual business enterprises in the United States in 1850, and more

than twice that number in 1900. Most of these were individual pro-
prietorships or partnerships; but for large undertakings the corporation was becoming increasingly popular. It was easier than before to
form a corporation. By the 1870's most states had general incorporation laws. These enabled businessmen to launch a corporation with a
minimum of trouble, after registering and paying a moderate fee.

There were several advantages in corporate organization. A corporation could sell stocks and bonds; and the company and its officers
gained prestige from corporate names and titles. Most important of
all, however, was the liability question. Proprietors and partners
normally had unlimited liability, were personally responsible for the
debts of their firms. The liability of stockholders in corporations, on
the other hand, was limited to the amount of stock held; the debts of
the company could not be assessed against stockholders personally.
This limited liability feature made it possible for the new corporations
to secure the capital needed for large-scale ventures.

The stock of most corporations, even the large ones, was closely
held by the founders and their families. These persons not only owned
the corporation; they also took an active part in management. So it
was with the Rockefeller-dominated Standard Oil Company and with
Andrew Carnegie's steel combine. So it is today with such twentieth-
century concerns as the Ford Motor Company.

But there was another trend, discernible by 1880 and highly significant by 1900. Persons with stock in several corporations found that
they could not spare the time to govern the affairs of each company.
Nor, as minority shareholders, could they wield the influence necessary to make their ideas effective. They ceased, therefore, to try to be
"owners" in the old sense of the word, and became passive investors.
As this process spread, more and more of the property of the nation
came to be held in this new tenure. The nominal owners had less control over their property than did managers, bankers, customers, and
even workers. The owners' (stockholders') claim was just one of many
claims against the gross income of the company; and management
decided what the owners should receive.

Popular journalists and academic economists were noting the new
phenomenon as early as the 1880's and the 1890's. Observing that the

individual investor was losing control of his capital, these commentators talked of "industrial feudalism" and warned of the perils of an
economic order dominated by managers. But nothing was done to
alter the trend, which gathered force each decade after 1880.

The first general incorporation laws did not give corporations the
right to own the stock of other corporations. The legislatures of Pennsylvania, Kentucky, and other states did grant this right in special holding company charters; but the privilege was not generally extended
until the late 1880's. Then, in 1888, New Jersey passed its famous
holding company law. This statute was of great importance in the history of American corporations. It made it easy for businessmen to form
holding companies in New Jersey. That done, they could secure control of any industry anywhere by buying a controlling share of the
voting stock of the leading producers. Holding companies were to be
empire-building agencies in the business world.

Business and the Market

While the nation's corporate structure
was changing, the railroad was revolutionizing marketing. In the early
nineteenth century, merchants from the interior had made semi-
annual trips east and had hauled goods home by wagon, barge, or
steamer. The railroads brought traveling salesmen with illustrated
catalogues. These salesmen came frequently, took the orders of western merchants, and saw to it that goods were supplied relatively
quickly by freight or express. In consequence, the merchant could buy
less at a time and could make payment more rapidly. Credit terms of
six months to a year shrank to sixty or ninety days. Improved credit
information and the credit ratings worked out by Dun and Bradstreet
enabled manufacturers and wholesalers to grant the short-term credits
with greater liberality. For the inland consumer this meant a better
selection of goods, fresher wares, and all-around improved service.

Before the day of the railroads there had been many local and regional agreements for the control of competition. The railroads shattered these agreements by introducing nation-wide buying and selling.
Shoemakers of Lynn, Massachusetts, were put into competition with
those of Chicago; and a New England trade association could not

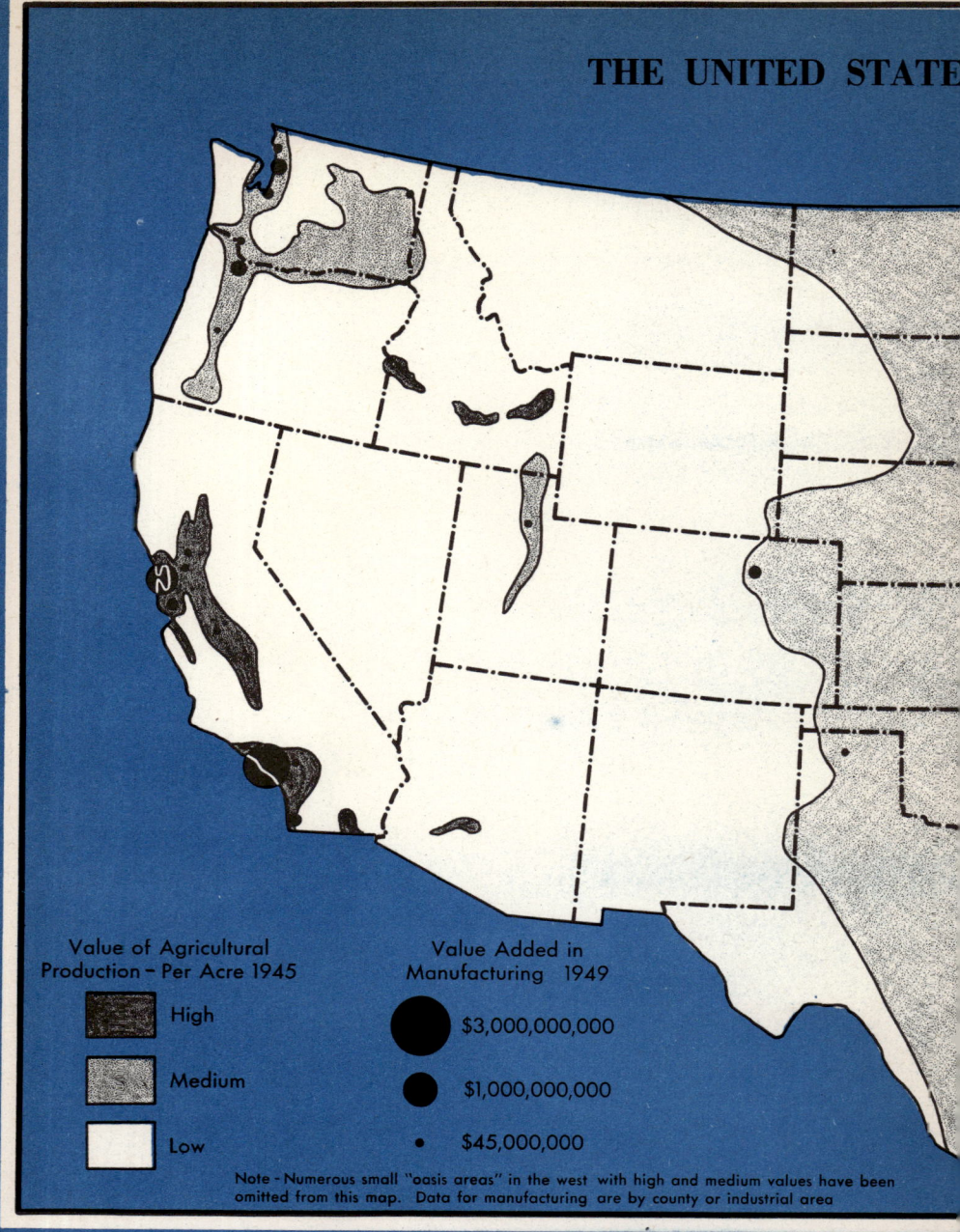

**Value of Agricultural
Production – Per Acre 1945**

High

Medium

Low

**Value Added in
Manufacturing 1949**

$3,000,000,000

$1,000,000,000

$45,000,000

Note - Numerous small "oasis areas" in the west with high and medium values have been
omitted from this map. Data for manufacturing are by county or industrial area

Much of the history of the United States during the past century is reflected in the development, character, and location of economic enterprises. This map clearly shows the concentration of manufacturing
between Boston and Chicago-St. Louis, with the heaviest concentration
in the Northeast (Boston to Baltimore). Note the great industrial activity
in New York's Mohawk Valley and around Pittsburgh, and the rise of a
factory area on the Pacific Coast. Manufacturing in the "new South,"
notable Piedmont textile development, is indicated; but, as can be seen,
southern industry does not yet approach northern factory areas in value-

Flannery

added-by-manufacture.

In the industrial age, the United States remains one of the great farming nations. This map shows the location and relative importance of the various farming regions: the tobacco area of Virginia, the Carolinas, and westward; the cotton belt, with the high production of the Mississippi River and Texas cotton regions emphasized; the citrus fruit areas of California and Florida; the dairy and truck gardening of the Northeast; the corn-and-hog and dairy production of the Great Lakes area, with the wheat region to the west, and the cattle kingdom beyond.

regulate an industry that had spread into Ohio or Indiana. Many manufacturers complained of the result—fierce competition all over the United States. Others were pleased to be able to move outside the local market and sell their brands in many regions.

Building a nation-wide market for soap, patent medicines, or sewing machines called for national advertising. In covering local areas businessmen had dealt directly with the business managers of local periodicals, often buying space on an annual basis. To attempt this on a national scale would require knowledge and experience not available in the ordinary company. As a result, advertising agencies took over. There were a few of these in the days before the Civil War; but their great period of growth was from 1865 on. The agencies dealt in space in dailies and weeklies. They also came to advise their clients as to types of campaign displays and the probable circulation and audience of various journals. It was no accident that a leading advertising agent, George P. Rowell, prepared a pioneer newspaper directory.

Technological advance also aided advertising. The sulfite process for making cheap wood-pulp paper was developed during the Civil War decade. This process, combined with the earlier development of the rotary press, virtually ended the limitations on newspaper space. Previously editors had frowned on elaborate pictorial displays as a waste of precious paper. Now a new world opened for the commercial artist; and the advertising agencies added art departments.

In improving advertising techniques, Americans studied methods worked out in Europe, where the art was highly developed. Partly as a result of that study, "reason why" copy began to replace extravagant overstatements and meaningless jingles in the 1870's and 1880's. Products like Sapolio soap and Eastman Kodak cameras were pushed by campaigns costing hundreds of thousands of dollars a year. Advertising, previously associated largely with patent medicines and local stores, began to gain the dignity of bigness.

It was in the 1890's that Americans really became converted to faith in advertising. Department stores filled urban dailies with pictures of their wares. Sedate magazines like *Harper's* were enlivened by full-page histories of great moments in beer consumption; new slick-paper monthlies including the *Ladies' Home Journal* were read for their

advertisements as well as for their copy. Billboards lined railroad
tracks, posters appeared on roads used by bicyclists. Railroads and
circuses, soapmakers and buggy manufacturers, producers of shoes and
cereals, books and linaments launched elaborate campaigns. Bible societies and aspirants for political office joined the procession. Everything seemed to be advertised.

Big money brought a new maturity to the advertising agencies.
They hired nationally known artists for displays. They called on
campus psychologists for advice. They bore down on the false circulation claims of irresponsible journals, began to talk of the science and
the ethics of advertising. More and more was said of "educating" the
public. Not that this was new. Railroad and land promoters had used
"educational" pamphlets, articles, and speeches in the 1850's, and
producers of consumers' goods had begun to follow suit in the 1880's.
But now the agencies pressed harder than before. Out of their efforts
would come the modern science of public relations.

Limiting Competition

Producers who did not sell directly to
the public were slow to see the value of advertising. The more efficient,
who could force the pace, considered price warfare a profitable device
for securing the lion's share of the market. Price cutting, they said,
would force the most feeble and inefficient out of competition, and
leave the field to the strong.

In such price warfare the rank and file of manufacturers suffered;
plants with new machinery and the largest output had the distinct
advantage. But even the efficient producers suffered. In a competitive
situation prices quickly dropped to a point that barely covered operating expenses and paid little if any return on invested capital. Yet
no one would leave the field willingly, for closing down meant even
greater losses. Aggravating the situation was a long-run, world-wide
decline in prices from the 1860's to the mid-1890's, accentuated in
the United States by a rapid fall from the price peaks of the Civil
War.

Efficient national trade associations might have checked this jungle
warfare. But national trade associations were difficult to organize and

harder still to keep in operation. Most industries had so many producers that "gentlemen's agreements" were always being broken; and the American courts (in contrast to those of Europe) were hostile to contracts controlling prices or production.

Pools were also tried. The whiskey distillers, for example, found that they could produce double what the market could absorb. They therefore formed a selling pool in 1881. Under this arrangement each distiller paid an assessment to the pool based on production. The pool used the money to finance the sale of surpluses in foreign markets.

But pools, like gentlemen's agreements, tended to break down. There was no legal basis for prosecuting a member who cheated on his assessments and sold secretly outside the pool. Federal and state courts in the United States interpreted selling agreements as conspiracies in restraint of trade. This made it difficult for individual producers to band together in a pool to control production.

What next? Competition was still troublesome, and the manufacturers, said Andrew Carnegie, were "willing to try anything." Specifically, more and more industrialists were becoming convinced that they should keep prices up by getting together. "We saw . . . the need to save ourselves from wasteful conditions . . . ," explained John D. Rockefeller, adding that coöperation among corporation leaders was inevitable, that "the day of the combination is here to stay. Individualism has gone, never to return."

Rockefeller's preference was for merger of many individual companies into one concern. In 1879 his Standard Oil Company showed one way of doing this. Let each individual producer incorporate, then turn his stock over to a group of trustees. The trustees (or "trust") would hold the stock of all the competitors and could run an industry just as though it were one big company. "This movement was the origin of the whole system of modern economic administration . . . ," said John D. Rockefeller of the trustee device. "The time was ripe for it. It had to come."

The "trust" was just one method of merging companies. It was equally possible to charter a giant corporation and buy up the various competitors. But in the popular language of the 1880's and 1890's all big companies were called trusts. As the number of companies increased, the term came to be used in a derogatory sense as a synonym for monopoly and lack of consideration for the public welfare.

The consolidated company or group could make profits by holding prices artificially high. It could also increase efficiency by closing high-cost plants and operating those with the lowest costs at full capacity. Over eighty distillers entered the Whiskey Trust, but the trust kept only a dozen plants in operation. Partly offsetting the gains of such operations was overcapitalization. It cost a lot to buy the stock of individual properties and to market additional securities to pay high legal and financial fees and obtain more working capital. Many of the early trusts failed to earn satisfactory dividends on their inflated capital structures.

Mergers were sometimes arranged openly. Control could also be secured by a secret stock-purchasing campaign. Jay Gould was expert at buying control of companies without their managers' becoming aware of his operations. He bought carefully through many brokers, thus building a business empire that included railroads from New York to Texas, and the nation-wide Western Union Telegraph Company. By using the device of the corporate lease he made his money go a long way. That is, he bought control of a corporation, then used his control to lease the company's property for twenty to ninety-nine years to one of his other companies. After that he could unload the stock of the leased corporation and invest his money elsewhere.

With stock purchases and leases, the railroads came under the control of fewer and fewer individuals. A thousand different corporations were bought or leased by a few great systems, such as the Pennsylvania and the Southern Pacific. This gave great power to the promoters and managers who dominated these systems; and it added to the influence of the investment bankers who worked with these key persons.

Economics of Monopoly

The emergence of a few strong leaders depended on a variety of factors. Effective promotion and operation, up-to-date technology, tariff protection, political influence, and control of key patents were all important. It was also necessary to have a cost per unit that decreased as volume increased, so that one could take advantage of mass production economies. Important, too, were willingness and ability to take advantage of every opportunity to crush one's competitors. Here depressions were useful, for they aided the strong in eliminating the weak. Almost anyone could survive in a boom, but only those with efficient production methods and strong credit could keep going in a shrinking market.

The history of the Standard Oil Company illustrates most of these points. John D. Rockefeller, the man behind this company, was determined to secure complete control of oil refining. Like many other leading figures, Rockefeller was interested in having power. But that was not the entire story. The continuance of competition, Rockefeller felt, meant instability and financial uncertainty in the petroleum industry. Eliminating competition, on the other hand, would mean stability and assured profits.

As he moved toward his goal, this Cleveland businessman left nothing to chance. He made his company as efficient as possible. He surrounded himself with able associates. He introduced cost accounting. He employed experts who improved the technique of oil refining. He secured political connections. He built good credit ties by borrowing capital from many banks. He obtained control of such subsidiary operations as cooperage and carting. But he stayed out of well drilling. That was a risky, uncertain, and tremendously competitive business. Better to let the small operators do the drilling, then buy from them. Producing was so highly competitive and the producers were so weak and divided that it was easy to keep the price of crude oil down.

Rockefeller's location in Cleveland was one of his great advantages. He was as near the oil fields as were the Pittsburgh refiners. Pittsburgh, moreover, was a "captive town" of the Pennsylvania Railroad; those who shipped oil out of Pittsburgh had to use that one railroad and pay the rates the Pennsylvania chose to charge. Cleveland, by contrast, was served by more than one line. Rockefeller could play one railroad against another, or could play the water routes against all the railroads. In that way he was able to force rates down and down.

Nor was that all. Once in the lead among Cleveland refiners, Rockefeller pressed home the advantages of mass production. This cut his manufacturing costs. It also meant that Standard Oil had reliably large freight shipments. This increased its bargaining power with the railroads. As one railroad official put it, the "magnitude and regularity" of Rockefeller's business made it worth while to cut rates to the bone to get him as a customer. Rockefeller efficiently used this advantage. Later, he reduced transportation costs still more by laying pipe lines.

Standard Oil had a commanding position in the Cleveland area by 1870. The depression that followed the panic of 1873 enabled the company to bid for national monopoly. The plan was simple: Take in efficient producers through mergers arranged on generous terms and force the less efficient to sell out at bargain rates. Naturally enough, the weaker competitors resisted such tactics. But Standard Oil was strong. It could use its control of transportation against competitors. It could persuade producers not to sell to some refiners. It could afford to hire away the best officers of rival firms. It could drive competitors to the wall in price wars. So Standard won. By the end of the 1870's the Rockefeller interests had secured control of all the firms in the major refining centers.

It was the same in many other fields. When John D. Rockefeller was using the panic of 1873 to win control of oil refining, Henry Clay Frick was taking advantage of the hard times to dominate the coke industry. Simultaneously, Andrew Carnegie was doing much the same in iron and steel. Frick presently joined Carnegie; and, as manager of the Carnegie enterprises, he squeezed out many competitors after the panic of 1893. Such victories were made possible by the fact that the Carnegie-Frick enterprises were efficient, employed the best machinery and the best minds, and reduced unit costs. This meant that they could undersell rivals, and get the business in hard times, when there were not enough orders to go around. In addition, Carnegie and Frick, like Rockefeller, plowed profits back into the business. This made for financial strength, all-important in a period of crisis.

So in sugar refining, where the Havemeyer brothers secured a stranglehold on the industry; in meat packing, with such men as Philip Armour forging to the top; in the sleeping car business, dominated by George Pullman; in Frederick Weyerhaeuser's lumber kingdom. Many failed. Those who succeeded built great economic empires, monuments to their efficiency and their ability to exploit to the utmost every opportunity that came their way.

Rise of Finance Capitalism

Many of the great industrial monopolies of the late nineteenth century were owned by small groups of individuals actively interested in the management of their companies. In consequence, the last quarter of the century was the period of the highly independent captains of industry in the United States. But these very same years also witnessed the rise of the investment bankers, who dealt, not in factories, but in stocks and bonds. These finance capitalists grew more important each decade, and by the 1890's had come to control a sizable proportion of the economic wealth of the American republic.

In time, the investment bankers came to have great influence in manufacturing. At the start, however, they were less active in industrial ventures than in other fields. In the 1850's and 1860's, trading in securities largely centered around government issues and the stocks and bonds of railroads, banks, and public utilities. Railroad issues led the rest; in the late 1850's they made up about 40 percent of the hundred-odd securities listed on the New York Stock Exchange.

By then the investment markets were well established. Stocks and bonds were regarded as a normal investment for the upper middle classes—those who lived in the new brownstone houses, went away for the summer, and sent their sons to college. In addition, prosperous southern planters and western real-estate operators were beginning to invest some of their savings in issues recommended by their brokers. Activity was further increased by the purchases made by American agents of European investors. New York was the center of the trading, and telegraphic quotations from the New York Stock Exchange set prices on local exchanges in other cities.

Investment in securities increased enormously during the Civil War era, mainly because of the large issues of the United States government. Under the direction of Jay Cooke, salesmen hawked these bonds from door to door, tapping sources of capital hitherto unexploited by investment bankers. Merchants and professional men who

had previously kept their savings in real estate were cajoled into showing their patriotism by investing in the Union cause. Small businessmen who were enjoying wartime prosperity were persuaded to use
their surplus in this fashion.

As a result, prosperous citizens fell into the habit of trading in securities. When the war was over, numerous investors sold their government bonds to banks and insurance companies, then sank the proceeds
in the securities of private companies, which promised a better return
on investment. This meant a more active market, and easier financing
for the railroads, utilities, and mining companies in most of the years
from 1865 to 1873.

Unfortunately, many of the new investments did not turn out well.
These were the years when Daniel Drew, Jim Fisk, Jay Gould, and
Cornelius Vanderbilt were demonstrating all the advanced techniques
of stock manipulation. Unwary investors were fleeced, and even experts found the going rough. Since the most reprehensible practices
concerned common stocks, this type of security obtained a bad reputation. Conservatives preferred to deal only in bonds, where the return
was relatively small but also relatively certain. One might make more
on common stock, but it was very likely that one might make nothing
whatsoever. (When asked about the intrinsic value of Erie Railroad
stock, Jay Gould replied, "There is no intrinsic value to it, probably;
it has speculative value.")

The degradation of common stock continued until about 1907.
This was unfortunate, for stock represented ownership, and the sale
of stock should have been a fundamental part of business finance. The
unwillingness of investors to buy this kind of security forced railroads
and public utilities to finance largely through bonds. This meant a
heavy load for interest payments, for bondholders were creditors, not
owners, and had to be paid regularly, whether times were good or bad.
Companies that had raised large sums of money through bond issues
found it difficult to meet their fixed charges in periods of depression;
and many of them went into bankruptcy.

As the sale of securities increased, the investment banker took on
new importance. He was the wholesaler necessary for the marketing
of securities. There had been a few investment houses in the United

States before the Civil War. The number greatly increased during and after that conflict, as trading increased in government and railroad securities. Then came the panic of 1873. The severe depression that followed eliminated the smaller and weaker houses, particularly those without close foreign connections. Even the larger houses were affected. The great firm of Jay Cooke and Company, which had borne the brunt of Civil War financing, failed dramatically in its attempt to carry the burden of constructing the Northern Pacific Railroad.

The houses that survived were stronger than ever. Among these were such famous firms as Lee, Higginson and Company and Kidder, Peabody and Company, both Boston houses; August Belmont and Company, a New York concern connected with the Rothschilds of Europe; and, most important of all, Drexel, Morgan and Company of New York and Philadelphia. This last firm was the American side of an Anglo-American combination. Renamed J. P. Morgan and Company in 1895, it became one of the major influences in American economic life.

Before the depression of the 1870's, many banking houses had followed reckless policies. Those who survived the dark days were inclined to be somewhat more cautious than before. The result was that the major houses stayed out of financial difficulties for a long time thereafter. And as they grew stronger, the investment bankers began to influence the policies of the companies that they financed.

It gradually became a custom for each company to do all its financing through one banking house. This did not always exclude other bankers from a share in the profits. To speed the sale of securities and to spread the risk, the leading houses formed syndicates for the marketing of large issues of securities. Friendly bankers and brokers were invited to take some of the stocks and bonds for sale and to participate in some degree in the anticipated profits. Consequently, the financial community became more of a unit than other types of business. All members of the community shared a common interest in maintaining the group practices, which were called "sound finance."

What was "sound finance"? The banker saw his role as that of physician to patient. The banker helped bring a company into being by selling its securities. He gave advice for its continuing health, injected new capital to speed its growth, operated when serious trouble developed. The latter emergency usually resulted from inability of the company to pay interest on its bonds; and the operation consisted of reorganizing the company's capital structure. Here the law courts came into the picture. Creditors—in most cases the bondholders— could take their case before a judge in the state where the corporation had its home office. The judge could appoint a receiver temporarily to take over the management of the defaulting company in order to conserve the value of the property. While the receiver ran things the various creditors met, usually under the leadership of the investment bankers, to find a formula that would satisfy everybody.

Now the ordinary relations in a company were reversed. The common stockholders, who normally controlled the company, had little to say. The first mortgage bondholders, ordinarily passive creditors, had the power of life and death. If no compromise suited them, they might try to recover their investments by selling the property at auction. But few railroads and utilities were actually put on the auction block; and when they were it was usually to get rid of some junior creditors who had refused to follow the lead of the investment bankers. Normally, the ceremony of receivership led rather to reorganization than to foreclosure and sale in bankruptcy.

In the reorganization, security holders might have to make some sacrifice in income. The investment houses would market a new bond issue to pay off the floating or unfunded debt due to suppliers, banks, and employees. Fixed charges were reduced by the slash in interest rates; but the new issues tended to increase total indebtedness. About 30 percent of the railway mileage of the country was in receivership after the panic of 1893, but only in 1896–97 was there a net decrease in funded debt.

The investment bankers, then, were in command in good times and in bad, during prosperity and during depression. In company after company the board of directors came to be swayed by the great investment houses; and the tendency was to ask Wall Street advice at every step. By the 1890's, J. Pierpont Morgan (the most important investment banker) was one of the most influential persons in the United States. Having mastered the transportation field, he and his financial colleagues were beginning to move into manufacturing. And the nation was entering an era of finance capitalism that would continue until the depression of 1929.

Banking and Insurance

The house of Morgan and other investment banking firms held deposits for their clients and performed most of the other services of commercial banks. It was their practice, however, to restrict these operations to a few large accounts. The ordinary citizen made his deposits in, drew his checks on, and borrowed from a commercial bank. There was nothing in nineteenth-century laws to keep these commercial institutions from forming syndicates to market new stock and bond issues. But commercial banks generally did no more than take a few new securities to sell to their own depositors.

The commercial banking problems of the first half of the nineteenth century persisted after 1850. Small, weak local banks and conflicting state banking laws continued to be the rule. Bank failures after the panic of 1837 had led nine southern and western states to pass laws prohibiting banks. The boom times of the 1850's caused the repeal of most such laws, and a new crop of state-chartered banks entered the field. Regulatory legislation held up standards in some parts of the Union. But in most states there was adequate supervision neither at the incorporation nor at the operating level. As far as banking was concerned, the United States was still in the wildcat age.

When the National Banking Act was passed in 1863, conservatives hoped that a new day had dawned. There was now to be a system of national banks, privately owned but subject to inspection and regulation by the United States government. In 1865, when Congress imposed a prohibitory tax on paper money issued by state-chartered banks, the national institutions obtained a monopoly of bank-note issue. This, it was felt, would force all state banks to take national charters, so that they could issue paper currency; and in the process they would become subject to regulation by the national government.

For a time, this was the trend. By 1868 there were over 1600 national banks, as against less than 250 banks of all other types. Even then there was no truly national banking system; the national banks were mainly small, and independent of each other. But it was a start, and, had the trend continued, the next generation might have brought greater strength, uniformity, and interdependence.

That, however, was not to be. National banks had the privilege of issuing bank notes based on bank holdings of United States government bonds. The rising market value of government bonds after the Civil War led many banks to sell these securities. This made it necessary for them to contract their bank-note circulation. As a substitute for bank notes, they urged their depositors to make use of checks. This worked so well that many banks decided they could get along without issuing any bank notes at all; that is, they could use coin and checks, and the paper currency of other institutions. If a bank no longer issued bank notes, it no longer needed a federal charter, no longer needed to submit to the inspections and regulations of the United States government.

Statistics told the story. By 1887 state and non-chartered banks were more numerous than were national banks. The confusion and uncertainty of the 1850's had returned to the banking field. States seeking to encourage business expansion permitted individuals or groups to organize banks with as little as $5000 in capital; and these institutions, feeble from the start, were not adequately inspected or supervised. In the single year of 1893, 228 of these banks failed.

Thus the American desire for easy credit and local autonomy continued to dominate commercial banking. No central national institution, no nation-wide chain of banks could dictate local credit conditions. To be sure, the big banks of New York could exert influence on the small-city banks that kept deposits in the metropolis. The larger cities of each section could likewise use pressure on the country banks nearby. Nevertheless, no one could tell the small-town or village banker what he could or could not do. If his local pride caused him to lend too much to overoptimistic businessmen, his bank might fail. But none could say that a dead hand on credit had checked the home-town boom.

In the urban communities a new type of bank was rapidly gaining ground. This was the trust company. Trust companies originated as organizations for managing estates, and did the banking business for heirs to those fortunes. Although one was chartered as early as 1822 in

New York, the general spread of these institutions dates from the boom of the 1850's. Gradually the trust company came to do a commercial banking business. Its great advantage was the fact that its form of incorporation permitted it to invest its assets in common and preferred stocks as well as in bonds. State-chartered banks, on the other hand, were usually restricted by law to certain types of bonds. With their broader base, trust companies became valuable customers of the investment bankers. They tended, therefore, to form close ties with the investment banking houses and to share in the rapid growth of finance capitalism.

An important newcomer to the financial world was life insurance. Marine insurance had long been important in the United States and in Europe. Fire insurance became significant in the first half of the nineteenth century, particularly after the great New York fire of 1835. Meantime, a few adventurous businessmen were entering the life insurance field. They encountered difficulties at the start, for many citizens thought it immoral to "gamble" on human life. The census of 1860 indicated that the life insurance policies in force came to less than $200,000,000, the figure for marine and fire insurance being fifteen times that large. Marine and fire insurance kept on growing after that, as property values increased; but the real rise was in life insurance. By 1890 there was general appreciation of the benefits involved; and $13,000,000,000 in life insurance policies were in force in the United States.

Life insurance companies found it necessary to build large reserves against claims. They therefore became important investors in bonds; and, like the trust companies, they drew close to the investment bankers. By 1900 the "pooled savings" in trust companies, banks, and insurance companies provided the principal market for American transportation and industrial bonds.

New Employees

The growth of banking and insurance helped swell the growing ranks of white-collar workers. Trade and transportation also contributed to the increase of this new middle class. So did manufacturing.

This phenomenon was not limited to the United States. The nineteenth century saw office employment increasing throughout the Western world. But in the United States the white-collar group was larger than in any other nation and possessed far more capital and purchasing power than it did elsewhere. This directly reflected the triumph of mass production in the United States. The American industrial machine required proportionately fewer workers and proportionately more administrators than did the hand-labor processes still used in many European nations.

It would be difficult to overstate the importance of these new employees. By 1900 clerical, sales, professional, and managerial employees were half again as numerous in the United States as were the men in business for themselves. They were outnumbered, of course, by the farmers and urban laborers; but there were nearly a third as many office workers as there were nonagricultural manual workers.

These white-collar employees were scorned by such industrial capitalists as Andrew Carnegie, who defined businessmen as individuals who were their own bosses. But this was underrating the new middle class. This group represented the men of the future, Americans who were to grow more numerous and more prosperous with the passing years. Even in the 1890's the white-collar workers came closer than any other group to representing "public opinion" and establishing the standards of American life.

It would be a grave mistake to look on all white-collar workers as a single class. Still, there was no sharp break in the social and economic hierarchy between the $12-a-week clerk and the $200-a-week vice-president. Both were office workers; both were administrative employees. Furthermore, business was expanding so fast in the 1890's that able clerical employees had many chances for rapid advancement.

The middle range of employees—those having actual administrative responsibilities—had salaries that were good in relation both to labor and to top management. Workers earned $400 to $600 a year toward the end of the nineteenth century, and presidents of large companies were rarely paid more than $10,000 to $12,000. At this time members of the intermediate group could command from $1500 to $7500 annually.

This new world of salaried business management was a man's world.

Few women could expect to rise above the level of stenographers or clerks. A few rich women had influence as large stockholders; but the top executive positions were reserved for men. Women did, however, have a place in the new pattern. Wives of white-collar employees gave tone to the new suburbs. They built and furnished (or overfurnished) comfortable homes, had immigrant girls as servants, showed some interest in culture and a great deal in "respectability."

Conditions of Manual Labor

The opportunities in the white-collar field weakened the labor movement at the top, while competition from low-paid immigrants weakened it at the bottom. Nevertheless, workers did make progress in the second half of the nineteenth century, gaining shorter hours and somewhat higher wages. In addition, these years saw the first faltering steps toward national labor organization.

Neither businessmen nor economists understood the causes of wage movements. The ordinary employer expected to get labor at the same rate as his competitors did. When in doubt he asked his competitors what they paid. But what started it all? Some said that the productivity of the worker was the basic regulator. In the sense that laborers were certain not to be paid as much as the total market value of what they made, this was correct. But this extreme limitation had relatively little to do with day-by-day wage scales. These showed wide difference between neighboring cities like New York and Albany. Among the factors involved were price changes, local shortages or surpluses, strikes, unions, the sex, race, and color of the workers.

Regional variations in wages were greatest in businesses that produced for local markets: breweries and bakeries, the construction industry, the service trades. In such activities there was no national labor market, but a host of separate local markets. Theoretically, workers would move to the area of highest pay until the resulting surplus of labor at that point reduced rates to the common level. In practice, this happened slowly, if at all. Home, family, friends, security, and inertia kept workers tied to their communities; and the newcomers from Europe went to cities where their relatives were already located.

Migration, therefore, did not wipe out local wage differences. For at least a generation, coopers earned 15 percent more an hour in Chicago than in Milwaukee. Yet there was no great trek of coopers across the eighty miles that separated the cities.

Nor were wage scales uniform within a local area. The Polish and German Jews who poured into New York at the end of the nineteenth century were employed in the garment industry at near-starvation wages. At the same time, in the same city, electrical and some construction workers obtained wages far above the national average. Similarly, Negroes received less than whites for the same jobs, women less than men. Many of the better-paying jobs (especially those involving supervisory functions) were closed to all except native-born white males. Unionized skilled workers usually claimed better pay than unorganized workers with similar skills; but through most of this period union members were too few to have much influence on the general wage structure.

In 1850 there was a clear distinction between skilled and unskilled workers. The unskilled were common laborers; the skilled were journeymen who had served an apprenticeship and learned some special trade. During the next half-century these classifications began to lose their meaning in a substantial part of the American economy. As factories became mechanized, the call was for workers with some education and intelligence but no special skill. Minute subdivision of operations made it possible to assign a man to two or three operations at which he might become proficient in a few days. One could use the term "semiskilled" for this type of labor; but the expression had no precise meaning. The truly skilled crafts were gradually disappearing save in such strongholds as the building and railroad industries.

Census figures show the trend. By 1900 about 20 percent of all working Americans owned or operated farms. The professional and business group, with their clerks, accounted for about 25 percent. Subtracting 5 percent for servants, the remaining 50 percent represented labor, divided fairly evenly between skilled, semiskilled, unskilled, and agricultural. For all types of manual workers, except some of the skilled crafts, real wages increased from 1865 to 1896, after a decline in the previous decade and a half. The major element

in the rise was the long decline in prices. In many industries $1.50
remained the standard daily wage for common labor from the mid-
1860's to the mid-1890's. But, with prices on the decline, that dollar
and a half would buy more in 1896 than in 1865. In some industries
the situation was made still better by a slight upward trend in actual
daily wages. Meanwhile, the average number of hours in the working
day dropped from nearly eleven to about ten.

Higher wages and shorter hours were somewhat offset by less convenient working and living conditions. Machines went faster; hence
the worker of 1900 might be as tired after ten hours of labor as the
worker of 1865 had been after eleven. Residence was another problem.
The percentage of workers residing in large cities more than doubled
during the second half of the nineteenth century; and by 1900 half the
industrial workers lived in cities large enough to have slum and transportation problems. If it took a man half an hour longer to get to
work each day, an equivalent reduction in the working day would give
him no added leisure. If trolley fares, higher rent, and more expensive
amusements raised his living costs, he lost his increase in real wages.
In addition, his children were likely to be brought up in undesirable
locations, surrounded by disease, crime, and vice. Taking all these
factors into account, it is difficult to conclude that the big-city worker
of 1900 was as well off as the small-town laborer of fifty years before.

The Labor Movement

The trade-union movement had its ups
and downs from the 1850's to the 1890's. For a brief period in the
1880's an industrial union movement flourished (the Knights of Labor); and the 1890's saw the rise of the American Federation of
Labor, a league of unions organizing skilled workers. On the whole,
however, these were disappointing years for American labor leaders.
In Europe, the labor movement grew by leaps and bounds, becoming
important in political and economic fields alike. In the United States,
the movement lagged. Organizers were hampered by conflicts among
workers (native Americans versus immigrants, whites versus Negroes),
by antiunion policies of employers, and by the indifference or opposi-

tion of the public and the government. In 1896 the members of trade unions numbered only 3 percent of the nonagricultural labor force of the United States.

This, however, does not indicate the total influence of the unions. Strikes led by unions often involved thousands of nonunion workers. If the strikes won, the latter benefited. The mere threat of unionization sometimes caused employers to improve the pay and working conditions of unorganized skilled workers.

Sometimes, too, the leaders of the unions spoke for labor as a whole. Sometimes, not always. Most labor leaders of the late nineteenth century were associated with skilled craft unions, organizations formed by the "aristocrats of labor." As was natural, these craft unions were basically interested in getting something for their own members, and only incidentally concerned about labor as a whole. They could give little attention, therefore, to the political, economic, and social needs of the great mass of underprivileged semiskilled and unskilled workers.

There was no nation-wide labor association in the United States in 1850; and few crafts had tried to organize on a national basis. The strength of organized labor was in the local craft unions that had survived the depression which had followed the panic of 1837. During the prosperous 1850's, these craft unions built up their membership and renewed their efforts to secure better pay and improved working conditions. Some of the strongest—the typographers, the iron molders, the locomotive engineers—took advantage of the boom years to create national organizations. The generally prosperous 1860's saw a continuation of this trend, and by the time of the panic of 1873 there were some two dozen national labor organizations, boasting a total membership of around a quarter of a million. The ensuing depression, however, reduced this number sharply.

From the late 1850's until his death in 1869, William Sylvis of the Moulders Union was the chief American labor leader. Sylvis had no such power as do twentieth-century labor leaders—most Americans did not even know his name. But the Moulders were a strong bloc of well-organized skilled workers in a key industry. As their spokesman, Sylvis could win the attention of other workers, and of businessmen and politicians, too. During the secession crisis Sylvis used his influence against coercion of the South; but when war came, he and his men vigorously backed the Union cause. After the war, Sylvis and others formed the short-lived National Labor Union (1866).

Although the National Labor Union failed, it has importance in the history of American labor. The organization represented an attempt to form a national association of workingmen, and claimed more than 500,000 workers at the start. Its national congresses attracted active union men like Sylvis; such able leaders of the shorter-hour movement as Ira Steward; Wendell Phillips and other intellectuals interested in labor reform; and even the woman-suffrage advocates, including Elizabeth Cady Stanton and Susan B. Anthony.

The rising labor leaders were in part responsible for the Congressional legislation establishing an eight-hour day for United States government workers (1868), and for agitation for state laws extending this principle further. The movement also led to some Labor Reform victories in local elections in the Northeast, and an unsuccessful attempt to name a National Labor Reform presidential ticket in 1872.

In the end, however, the National Labor Union failed. The death of Sylvis removed one able leader. More important, the union had paid too much attention to political reform and the organization of producers' coöperatives, too little to the practical job of strengthening union organization and raising workers' standards. The workingmen had lost interest in the experiment even before the panic of 1873 cut into labor strength; and the union in its final stages was run by kind-hearted but ineffectual intellectuals.

After the collapse of the National Labor Union, there was no immediate effort to form another national labor association. It was hard enough to keep the local craft unions going, for the unions lost a majority of their members during the depression of the mid-1870's. Organized labor suffered further as a result of the railway strikes of 1877—strikes caused by wage cuts and by the black-listing of union members. Federal and state officials took the side of the employers, and the strikers were defeated.

After this setback, labor organizers had reason to give up in despair. Some did; others kept on working. Their efforts built the

Knights of Labor, an organization that reached its peak in the mid-1880's. For a while it looked as though the Knights would be a permanently strong nation-wide industrial union.

Founded in 1869 as a secret society of Philadelphia tailors, the Order of the Knights of Labor grew rapidly. In 1878 it became a national organization for all workers, skilled and unskilled, male and female, native and immigrant, white and Negro. Shortly thereafter, the Knights obtained a new leader, Terence V. Powderly, who was also Greenback-Labor mayor of Scranton, Pennsylvania.

Under Powderly's direction, the Order grew in membership, going from 10,000 in 1878 to 50,000 five years later. This increase was caused by several things: the improving economic situation, which enabled all labor organizations to gain members; the willingness of the Knights to welcome anyone interested in labor; the low initiation fee (one dollar); the abolition of the oath of secrecy (1881); and Powderly's strong personal appeal. But the organization had its weaknesses. Most local chapters were composed of men from many occupations, and the Knights of Labor were not very strong in any single industry.

So far, the growth of the Knights had been been impressive rather than amazing. Then came the great days. From mid-1885 to mid-1886 membership soared from 100,000 to 700,000. The spurt was related to the fact that the Knights had wrung some concessions from Jay Gould's railroad and telegraph empire. Then, too, many laborers were stirred by a kind of mass excitement and hope for a better future.

In the end, the great increase proved unfortunate. Members poured in too fast to be assimilated, too fast to be disciplined in union practices. "The position I hold is too big for any ten men," groaned Powderly. "It is certainly too big for me." To make things worse, this leader of the Knights gave too much time to such side issues as temperance and coöperatives. He presently found himself unable to control his men. The rank and file undertook unwise strikes. Skilled workers in the Order quarreled with the common laborers in the mixed locals. By 1887 the membership had melted away. The great day of the Knights ended as suddenly as it began.

Some had predicted catastrophe even when the Knights were riding high. Experienced union leaders had found it difficult to keep craft unions going in nineteenth-century America. Yet the craft unions had as members men of more than average intelligence, training, and experience, men with common interests and a common skill (carpenters, for instance, or printers). It was bound to be more difficult to keep all types of workers together in a common organization, in an age when Americans did not think of labor as a unit.

Industrial unionism might have worked if the Knights of Labor had organized slowly, industry by industry, putting all the textile workers into one union, all the iron and steel workers in another, and so on. Each industrial group could then have worked on its own problems, under the general direction of the national officers. But Powderly and his associates moved too fast; and they aimed at one big union. The one-big-union plan did not succeed; when it failed, the whole idea of industrial unionism was discredited.

With the collapse of the Knights, the craft unions again took hold. To strengthen themselves, these unions of skilled workers formed an American Federation of Labor (1886), under able young Samuel Gompers of the Cigarmakers. Beginning with 100,000 members, the A.F. of L. grew slowly to about a quarter of a million members ten years later.

In the A.F. of L., each member union had autonomy and could handle its own affairs. As a consequence, there were substantial differences among the unions. The United Brewery Workers and United Mine Workers had an industrial union basis and took in all the workers in their fields. More typical were the craft unions like the United Brotherhood of Carpenters and Joiners, the International Brotherhood of Teamsters, and the Cigarmakers International Union. Most of these unions excluded, not only unskilled workers, but also women and Negroes.

It is possible to criticize the A.F. of L. for its policies of exclusion. The Federation failed to help those who needed help the most, and concentrated on skills at a time when improved machines were eliminating skills in industry. At the same time, it must be remembered that the Knights of Labor, by trying to do too much, had ended by accomplishing nothing at all. The American Federation of Labor, attempting less, achieved a limited success.

The victories of the A.F. of L. were in large part the work of its president, Samuel Gompers. Although Gompers did not try to dominate the member unions, he did set the standards in the organization. In particular, he kept the A.F. of L. unions out of politics, would not let the national organization endorse any party program. The A.F. of L. concentrated rather on a "business" approach, whereby skilled workers would emphasize negotiations with employers, aiming at contracts for higher wages and shorter hours.

Although the A.F. of L. attracted most of the craft unions, it did not get them all. The strongest of those that stayed outside the fold were the railroad brotherhoods. Formed between 1863 and 1883, these unions embraced the men who rode the trains: engineers, firemen, conductors, trainmen. Skilled and relatively well paid, the members of the brotherhoods preferred to handle their problems in their own way, and not to affiliate with the American Federation of Labor or any other national organization.

Employers and Unions

The opportunities for advancement, the competition from immigrants, the narrow interest of skilled crafts all helped explain the failure of American labor organizers from the 1850's to the 1890's. In addition to these deterrents, anyone interested in building union membership faced well-organized opposition from employers. It is doubtful if any considerable number of employers have ever believed in the value of trade unions. But in the nineteenth century most employers were so violently opposed to unions, in principle and practice, that they were ready to fight labor organizers to the death, with every available weapon.

Until the rise of large corporations at the end of the nineteenth century, most industrial establishments were managed by their owners. Industrialists therefore thought of their factories much as they thought of their homes. If workers came to the factory, they did so at the pleasure of the owner of the property; and union organizers were not invited. Some owners regarded complete freedom of control so essential that they would have preferred selling out to negotiating with representatives of a union.

In the early days there was no distinction between associations for fixing prices and those for regulating conditions of labor. As late as the 1850's associations of railway managers combined several functions. Presently, however, the labor problem became paramount. This was the case in the 1860's, when the emergence of strong craft unions led to the formation of local employers' associations. As an illustration, the successful unionization of printers around New York City led to the establishment of an employers' organization in this field, the New York Typothetae (1862). Twenty-five years later this employers' group joined with other regional associations to form the United Typothetae, a national employers' association.

As the unions grew in strength, the employers strengthened their associations. To defeat able union organizers and able union lawyers, the employers needed equally skillful agents. An association offered the cheapest means of retaining competent full-time specialists. How, in a given situation, should an employer handle a labor dispute? Should he compromise with the workers, offering a wage boost or recognition of the union? Should he use the lockout, shutting the plant until the workers came around? Should he discharge members of the union and have them black-listed throughout the industry? Should he go to court to get an injunction against the workers? The employer might not know just what to do. The association, with a view of the whole industry, could give useful advice.

The method used depended somewhat on the times. If business was good and orders had piled up it might be best to compromise, or to hire strikebreakers to maintain the flow of goods. If business was poor there was little to be lost by a shutdown. One could appeal to a court for an injunction against strike activity as a threat to property. But the courts were slow, and lawyers were expensive, and any ensuing litigation involved unknown costs. Most employers and employer associations therefore preferred lockouts or the hiring of strikebreakers.

Violence was always a possibility in labor disputes. This violence might hurt the employer (by destroying his property) or it might help him (by bringing him public support and government troops). Employer associations maintained contact with the Pinkerton Detective Agency and other concerns that would supply armed guards. These men would guard property and would protect strikebreakers from attacks by pickets. Sometimes the guards would deliberately create disturbances, causing the government authorities to send in troops to help defend the plant.

Labor and the Public

Middle-class public opinion usually reflected the economic views of the employers. Most middle-income citizens believed that wages were set by competition and could not be permanently influenced by collective bargaining. When strikes attracted national attention (as in the strike at Carnegie's Homestead, Pennsylvania, plant in 1892), news reports and editorials condemned the workers for combining to achieve the economically impossible. But in the meantime, thousands of smaller, less publicized strikes resulted in wage increases and shorter hours.

In many cases employer associations and the newspapers misled the public on some labor question. This happened in the late 1880's, after the Haymarket riot. At that time the anarchists were making a bid for public support, with a program of direct individual warfare against the tyranny of the bosses and the government. This program had a certain appeal in the mountain states and the Far West, in recently settled areas accustomed to weak law and strong personal action. Elsewhere the movement made little headway. But the anarchists preached violence; and in 1886 a Chicago court connected them with a Haymarket Square bomb outrage. Four anarchists were hanged and others imprisoned after a trial featured by disregard for the legal rights of the accused. Having no sympathy for anarchists, and being forced to rely on distorted press accounts, the American public generally approved of the verdict.

The Haymarket affair hurt the anarchist movement. But then, the anarchists would not have been important in any case. The more important point was the influence which this episode had on the union movement as a whole. Few labor leaders were anarchists; and anarchist doctrines made no impression whatsoever on the union rank and file.

Nevertheless, employer associations and many editors blamed the labor movement for the Haymarket outrage. For years thereafter, foes of labor called union organizers "anarchists."

Or "socialists." Here the antilabor forces were on sounder ground. Many European and some American labor leaders were influenced by socialist doctrine. Early in the 1890's Daniel DeLeon and other members of the Socialist Labor party tried to get control of the American Federation of Labor. Working with various other groups, they did manage for just one year to have the bitterly antisocialist Samuel Gompers dropped as president of the A.F. of L. But Gompers came back stronger than ever, and socialist influence declined. Although antiunion agents continued to denounce labor as "socialistic," the overwhelming majority of union members voted Democratic or Republican.

In general, the United States government stayed out of labor disputes; but when it did intervene, it was on the side of the employers. The most celebrated case was that of the Pullman strike of 1894. This strike involved Eugene V. Debs, who had been an officeholder in a railroad brotherhood and had dabbled in politics as a Democrat. Feeling that the brotherhoods did not reach enough railroad workers, Debs organized a new, industrial-type American Railway Union. The new union quickly gained many members on the midwestern railroads and in the Pullman Company. A defensive strike against paycuts by this sleeping car company forced Debs to test his strength in 1894, during a deep depression.

In order to help the Pullman strikers, members of the American Railway Union refused to handle Pullman cars in the Chicago yards. The railway managers maintained that Debs was interfering with the United States mails. Taking this line, a federal district judge issued a sweeping injunction against all types of activity needed to maintain the strike. President Grover Cleveland then rushed in federal troops to guard the trains. This was done over the protests of the governor of Illinois, John P. Altgeld. Like Cleveland, Altgeld was a Democrat; but he did not share the President's antilabor views. Cleveland, however, persisted. The strike and the American Railway Union were broken, and Debs was sent to jail.

The Pullman strike is interesting for several reasons: the crushing of an industrial union; the use of a court injunction and federal troops against organized labor; the conflict between state and federal governments, resulting in another defeat for states' rights. Most interesting of all, however, was the public reaction. A few Altgeld partisans, some labor leaders, and a few others denounced Cleveland's actions. But the people as a whole thought that the President had acted wisely. Organized labor had not yet come into its own.

3

Urban Growth and
Problems

Industry Creates Large Cities

Industrial expansion was an urban development. To the trade which had built the earlier towns was now added a manufacturing system that concentrated factories and workers in the cities. As large centers developed, their possession of banks and transportation and a labor supply attracted still more industrial establishments. Immigrant and native workers came in to claim the new jobs; and the cities became ever bigger.

The process was under way in the decades before 1850. New York City, which had been a town of 20,000 in Revolutionary days, had gone beyond 500,000 by 1850. In the next half-century it jumped to nearly 3,500,000. Similar expansion took place on a smaller scale in commercial and industrial centers throughout the Northeast and the Middle West. Cleveland, a small town of 17,000 in 1850, could boast of almost 400,000 inhabitants by the end of the century. More striking still was the transformation of Chicago, which soared from 30,000 to no less than 1,700,000.

Urban growth lagged in the agricultural South. Even so, new textile factories did bring workers to Georgia, Carolina, and Alabama mill towns. New Orleans, the southern export center, grew moderately from a little over 100,000 to a little less than 400,000. Like the South, the Rocky Mountain and Pacific coast areas had few large cities. An exception was San Francisco, a major west coast port which mushroomed from 34,000 to ten times that figure.

Growth was not confined to metropolitan districts. Improvements in transportation and the establishment of small factories turned villages into towns, towns into small cities. Connecticut and a few other states developed many small industrial centers ranging from 10,000 to 100,000 in population.

The combined growth of small and large cities brought an ever increasing proportion of the country's population into urban areas. In 1850 the nation was still overwhelmingly rural, the urban population amounting to only 15 percent of the total. By 1900 this figure had grown to nearly 40 percent.

New Problems

However farmers might view this situation, most Americans of the 1890's were proud of the record of urban growth. Unlike Europeans, Americans of this period took a great pride in numbers. Conscious rivalries developed between cities, not on quality but on quantity of inhabitants. In a way, this was understandable. The growth of a city was highly visible, was focused in a small area which all residents could see. And rise in numbers was in many cases closely related to an increase in wealth and resources.

But the picture had another side. What of Thomas Jefferson's fear of cities as breeding grounds for disease, poverty, and crime? Rural people continued to suspect the worst; and their suspicions provided overtones to the agrarian political crusades of these years. To farmers, the city was a dangerous place, which would lure farm children away from their healthy heritage of the soil.

Although it was easy to ridicule the rural fear of cities, the description had some point. The sprawling growth of urban areas was entirely unplanned. In colonial days, leaders like William Penn and James Oglethorpe had carefully laid out their green country towns with a view to light, air, and civic dignity. But now, in the mad rush of industrial expansion, cities poured out into adjacent territory without much thought of the complex problems of housing, traffic, recreation, and public safety. Local authorities were caught unawares by the rapidity and scale of growth; and in any case they would have hesitated to try to control the process. Businessmen, increasingly influential in public life, would have resented government interference.

City governments did wrestle with a few problems. They provided in one way or another for street paving and maintenance, for police and fire protection, for water supplies, and in some cases for health services and sewage disposal. The necessary expansion of these services was paid for by increased tax income, based chiefly on mounting real-estate values. In the process, city officials handled ever greater funds—at just the time when the number of citizens became so large that the average individual lost touch with City Hall. Treasuries were now worth looting, and corrupt officials made the most of their opportunities. Sometimes theft was direct. More commonly contracts were awarded to friends, from whom the politicians obtained their cut. Political morality was at a low level.

One consequence of corruption was that little money was left for badly needed municipal services. Certain of these services were rendered inefficient by graft even when funds were adequate. Building inspectors and the police might look the other way if they were provided with gratuities. The unorganized public was not easily aroused to these evils. The poor, who suffered most, lacked influence; the upper classes were prosperous anyway, so why worry? Hence American cities of 1890 compared unfavorably with their European counterparts. The latter were usually cleaner, more orderly, and more impressive than those in this country.

Most American cities were laid out in squares and rectangles, following such early models as Philadelphia. Only a few seaports, notably Baltimore and Boston, retained in their older districts the medieval pattern of winding lanes and thoroughfares. City streets were cleaner than in colonial times, and rough cobblestones were being replaced by asphalt pavements; but dirt and trash still testified to the inefficiency of municipal collecting services. Water-front areas were notoriously crowded and filthy, in contrast to the neat quays which lined some western European harbors. American business streets were usually narrow and noisy, overhead networks of telegraph and telephone wires adding to their ugliness.

Residential neighborhoods had a monotonous appearance, with their rows of buildings all looking much alike. Once a pattern of domestic architecture was established, such as that associated with the red-brick-and-white-steps of Philadelphia and Baltimore, it was cheap and easy for builders to follow it through the whole town. Separate houses predominated in small cities, but solid blocks became the rule in metropolitan centers. Population pressure forced the less prosperous New Yorkers into large tenements, "flats," and apartment houses. Skyscrapers were yet to come. The low urban skylines were relieved by church spires, but the general appearance of American cities was otherwise nondescript and unimpressive.

Rich Men, Poor Men

As cities grew, the poor, and especially the immigrant poor, crowded into the older parts of town. Congestion was worst in New York, which was swamped by waves of eastern and southern European immigrants after 1880. By 1900 some 1,500,000 persons lived in New York City's slums. Here and in other large cities national groups crowded into adjacent blocks, creating a "little Greece" or a "little Italy," which so segregated special elements as to delay their Americanization. Meantime, business sections moved back from the water fronts, and the middle- and upper-income residents (largely of native stock) escaped uptown. By the 1890's many were also moving out into nearby villages or into newly established suburbs. Already more people were living close outside Boston than within the corporate limits.

The wealthy provided themselves with elaborate suburban homes (as along Chicago's North Shore) or built expensive residences on aristocratic avenues and squares in town. In most established cities these mansions were dignified rather than ostentatious, and followed the prevailing architectural pattern. In New York and the newer cities, the millionaires of the gilded age reared elaborate palaces in imitation of those of the European nobility. These paraded the wealth of their owners and thus accentuated the social contrasts with the slums, which in some cases were located near by. By walking two or three blocks, the poor could compare their own misery with the luxury of the rich. This experience was especially bitter during hard times, when families dependent on bread lines and soup kitchens saw the conspicuous waste associated with elaborate entertainments in the mansions of the plutocrats. How could such a situation be reconciled with American traditions of equal opportunities and the rights of the common man?

Middle-income families, a relatively large class in American society, occupied uptown neighborhoods. Many of these people lived in relatively comfortable houses on side streets. Since they could not afford carriages, these middle-class citizens rode bicycles or streetcars to work. They mingled in the business section with the poor, returning to their quiet neighborhoods at nightfall.

The Urban Family

Urban living conditions gradually became more comfortable for the middle as well as for the upper classes. City dwellers found it easier to secure modern conveniences than did isolated farm families. By the 1890's, prosperous urban citizens were lighting their homes by electricity or by improved Welsbach gas mantles; and a few were introducing telephones. Immigrant maids relieved the housewife of much drudgery, enabling her to give some time to interests outside the home. Summer vacations for mother and the children were becoming more common, although father could not tear himself away from the desk except on week ends.

Boys enjoyed these vacations well into their teens, for schooling was being extended. Formerly, many destined for business had left school at the end of the elementary grades. Now a high school education seemed desirable. Prosperous families were also coming to feel that a boy should go to college, regardless of his vocational objectives. Perhaps this would give him time to decide what he wanted to do. A few liberal parents were even sending their girls to the new women's colleges or to coeducational state universities.

College education for girls reflected a continued improvement in the position of women, both in the family and in society at large. It is true that the husband still insisted on being head of the household, and might not tell his wife much about his business or even the family income. But women by 1900 had almost complete control of their own property, and a half-century of agitation for women's rights had begun to change family patterns. Middle-class urban women were the chief beneficiaries of these trends. Poor women, without property or advanced education, were less able to assert themselves.

Women of both the poor and middle classes were increasingly

employed outside the home. Girls had invaded factories long before 1850. Industrial expansion increased such employment after mid-century, especially in the textile mills. Middle-class girls had gone into teaching early, too. During the Civil War era they came to dominate that field; and by 1890 a man teacher was a curiosity in the elementary public schools. The business world resisted feminine invasion longer than did industry and education, but technologic innovations turned the tide by the 1890's. The first telephone exchanges were operated by boys, but their tendency to swear at unseen customers resulted in replacement by girls. Simultaneously, the introduction of typewriters into offices and the growing volume of business correspondence called for additional stenographers and clerks. Although male typists were used first, they were rapidly replaced by young women. A few diehards objected to the complication of having the other sex around; but most employers found girls cheaper and more decorative than male stenographers.

Upper-class parents still expected their daughters to remain at home until marriage. But there was less to occupy them than formerly. Their mothers had maids, and as the upper-class birth rate declined, there were fewer young brothers and sisters to supervise. To some well-educated girls a purely social life under these circumstances began to seem frustrating, and a few sought voluntary or even paid employment outside.

Working-class women of necessity contributed to the support of their families. Some took jobs in factories and stores. Others worked out as domestic servants. The new compulsory attendance laws kept children at school a good part of the day. Nevertheless, the absence of the mother from the home was unfortunate; it left the children on the streets outside of school hours in the very neighborhoods where this environment was most demoralizing.

The Slums Breed Crime

The evils of urban life were of course most obvious in the slums. Parks were few. Neither the public nor the parochial schools considered the provision of recreational facilities a part of their function. The churches could do little, for Catholic parishes in the slums were poor; and the Protestant churches had fled the slums along with their parishioners. Children could play only on the streets or in the back yards; and adults were driven to the saloons.

There were plenty of these in all poor neighborhoods. New York City had 7500 in 1890, one for every 200 citizens. The saloon served as a sort of poor man's club, where one could relax, talk to friends, and if desired purchase forgetfulness. Where else could one find bright lights, talk, and music after ten hours on the day or night shift?

Unfortunately, the easy access to saloons and the hard-drinking habits of Americans promoted widespread drunkenness in slum districts. "Drunks" were a common sight on the streets. Drunkenness also led to street brawls, and was responsible for the beating and neglect of wives and children.

In middle-class neighborhoods, on the other hand, drinking had been discouraged by the temperance movement. The "better people" viewed the swinging doors of the saloon with distaste, and gave support to the antiliquor crusade. By the 1890's, the foes of alcohol were beginning to demand the complete prohibition of intoxicating beverages; and the Anti-Saloon League was organized in 1895 to carry forward this aggressive campaign.

Crime as well as drunkenness was commonly associated with the poorer districts. Children growing up in slum dwellings lacked normal outlets and restraints, and life on the street led easily to delinquency. It was a short step from petty thievery to robbery, then on to murder. While homicides were decreasing in European cities, they were increasing in American urban areas. In 1881 there were 25 murders per million population in the United States; by 1898 the number had jumped to 107. Such single cities as New York and Chicago listed more crimes of violence per year than did all England and Wales.

Why so? There were slums in Britain as well as in the United States; yet murder was rare in England. Some blamed the American frontier traditions and the American passion for individualism. Others talked of culture conflicts growing out of immigration, or mentioned the inefficiency and corruption in American police and court systems.

The increase in crime impressed new burdens on a long-inadequate prison structure. Earlier experiments with solitary confinement were abandoned as too severe and also too expensive. But even with two or more inmates per cell, additional buildings were badly needed. Attempts to secure them led to reconsideration of the whole penal system.

At this point social reformers as well as prison officials came into the picture. Private charities were multiplying, settlement houses were being established in the slums, societies were seeking to protect the interests of poor children. Supplementing these voluntary efforts, state boards of charity were striving to coördinate the activities of such tax-supported welfare agencies as poor houses, orphanages, and hospitals. Prison reform was a closely related activity. New state and local societies studied crime and punishment. A National Prison Association, organized in the 1870's, carried on in the tradition of earlier reforms and employed the more scientific approaches then being developed by European penologists.

This National Prison Association urged, first, that custodial care be improved in terms of better buildings and less brutal discipline. Second, emphasis was to be on reformation rather than punishment. If successful, this program would help human beings and at the same time save the taxpayers money. In the 1870's Massachusetts began placing minor offenders on probation rather than in prison. During the next two decades, many states liberated prisoners on parole, continued freedom being based on good behavior. In 1877 New York pioneered in the establishment of special reformatories for youthful first offenders. Reformation was more likely if the young delinquent was kept separate from habitual criminals.

These experiments brought encouraging results, and similar procedures have been employed down to the present time. The greatest improvements were made in the large state institutions. It was more difficult to modernize city and county jails. Since prisoners were committed to these institutions for short terms, there was less concern about their treatment. Besides, jailers and other local officials were almost always untrained and frequently corrupt. Average citizens were indifferent, and generally unwilling to have their taxes increased to improve the situation.

Street fighting by organized gangs seems to have declined in this period, perhaps because of the introduction of uniformed police. Individual crime, however, flourished, especially in and near degraded sections known as "tenderloins." Distinct from ordinary slums, these districts developed in older parts of town on the fringe of business sections. The tenderloins attracted chronic misfits—down-and-outers, tramps, alcoholics, dope addicts, sex perverts, petty criminals of every kind. Such persons lived in cheap hotels, lounged around the streets without visible means of support, and preyed on adjacent neighborhoods.

In or near the tenderloins were the "red-light districts" of commercialized prostitution. Always an urban phenomenon, these districts flourished in cities which contained large numbers of unmarried men. Experience seemed to indicate that, given this situation, prostitution was virtually impossible to suppress. But because of the moral issue, prostitution was not legalized in this country as it was in Latin Europe. Hence it expanded as an illegal business. Management of the houses was often tied to saloons and gambling interests. Since the houses had to pay for protection, the police and local politicians were drawn into the complex underworld picture. Patrons were mostly poor or of moderate means; wealthy men could maintain mistresses.

The Slums Breed Disease

Apart from moral implications, the most serious consequence of prostitution was the spread of venereal diseases. Since infection was considered a social disgrace, and since Victorian prudishness placed a taboo on discussions of sex, a conspiracy of silence prevailed. This made it impossible to enlighten the public on the medical aspects of the situation and prevented health authorities from dealing with venereal diseases by notification and isolation. Such circumstances facilitated the spread of these plagues throughout a society which would not even admit their existence.

The slums were natural breeding places for all infectious diseases. To begin with, the poor were overworked and undernourished, consequently ill-equipped to resist illness. Crowded and unsanitary surroundings also involved ever present dangers. Lack of fresh air increased the risk of tuberculosis, and filth brought vermin and the threat of typhus fever. Morbidity and mortality were high in poor neighborhoods, keeping urban death rates above those for rural areas. In 1900, when the gross death rate for the whole United States was seventeen per thousand, it was about twenty for New York City, and as high as sixty-two for that city's tenement districts.

Disturbed by epidemics especially, physicians, engineers, and statisticians organized national sanitary conventions in the late 1850's. These groups urged cities to clean their streets, supply pure water, and provide proper disposal of garbage and sewage. The same appeal was taken up by the new American Public Health Association after 1872. Though less dramatic than the feminist or abolitionist crusades, this sanitary movement was one of the major social reforms of the century. Unfortunately, the chief sanitarians are now forgotten—such men as Lemuel Shattuck, who worked out in Massachusetts the plan for the first state board of health (1850), and Dr. Wilson Jewell, a Philadelphian who inspired the first national health association seven years later.

Divided authority plagued health officials at the start. Power needed to be concentrated in city boards of health instead of being split among quarantine officers, sewer commissioners, and sanitary inspectors. Public health administration was so reorganized in New York in 1866, elsewhere later. In 1870 Massachusetts launched a movement to create state boards of health.

Meantime, large towns were outgrowing existing water supply and sewage disposal systems. As late as 1877, such large places as Providence and Milwaukee had no public water supplies, and Philadelphia still possessed over 80,000 private vaults and cesspools. During the 1880's, sanitary arrangements began to catch up with urban expansion. Only 600 cities had public waterworks in 1878; nearly six times that many possessed them two decades later. Sewage systems also extended into long underground networks whose mileage equaled that of the streets above them. This process was greatly facilitated by engineering improvements, as in the better construction of pipes and closer estimates of the volume of flow. Unfortunately, cities continued to dump sewage in rivers and harbors, thus contaminating their own and their neighbors' water supplies.

By promoting cleanliness, the new water systems reduced such diseases as typhus. Water also protected lives and property by making better fire protection possible. Fire risks mounted with the growing urban congestion and the installation of electric wiring. In the early 1870's great conflagrations nearly destroyed Chicago and Boston; and by 1883 the country's annual property loss from fire exceeded $100,-000,000. To combat this menace, the larger cities introduced uniformed, professional firemen in place of excitable volunteer companies. Horse-drawn fire engines were improved, and fireboats were used in the harbors. Inventors produced automatic sprinklers and fire towers and began to experiment with fireproof building construction. These measures cut fire losses in proportion to the wealth exposed in buildings after 1900.

Technology had its limitations, however, when it came to the protection of public health. When a water supply was contaminated, improved engineering systematically pumped typhoid germs into homes. What was needed here was medical as well as mechanical knowledge. This came after 1885, when European discoveries in bacteriology called attention to the need for safe as well as sufficient water supplies.

Boards of health took notice, and the gross mortality of cities began to decline. The annual death rate of Boston, New York, Philadelphia, and New Orleans had remained constant between 1870 and 1890. It fell from twenty-five per thousand in 1893 to twenty, seven years later. This improvement resulted from a drop in the death rates for the chief infectious diseases—typhoid, typhus, scarlet fever, smallpox, tuberculosis. Typhoid mortality in New York City fell from thirty-seven per 100,000 in 1893 to twenty-one in 1900 (by 1920 it was only two). Once again, faith in progress seemed to be confirmed. The most-feared enemies of man were at last coming under his control.

Sanitary reform lagged in rural areas; hence mortality rates fell more slowly. The remarkable 20 percent decline in the death rates of large cities during the 1890's was about double that recorded for the country as a whole. Urban death rates remained a little higher than the rural, but the margin was closing. No longer could the cities be condemned as the graveyards of mankind. Science and technology, in conjunction with economic forces, had brought masses of people together in urban centers at a very considerable social cost. As if in recognition of this responsibility, science was now finding means for preserving these people in their crowded and complicated urban environment.

Religion and Urban Life

The urbanization of American life did not at once change American Protestantism. When times were good, middle- and upper-class urban congregations built more costly edifices, installed pipe organs, employed paid choirs, and encouraged a dignity in services in conformity with sophisticated taste. But in social outlook Protestantism continued, as in the rural age, to emphasize individual morality and salvation. Few ministers or congregations paid much attention to the vice and poverty of the immigrant-crowded slums. Even the revival of 1857–58 was a middle-class affair, hardly felt at all in the poorer districts of the growing cities.

Not that the churches were inactive. During the Civil War they poured much energy into providing for the spiritual and physical well-being of the armed forces. After that struggle ended, many denominations turned their attention to planting churches in the rapidly developing West. Significant, too, was the growing interest in foreign missions. Each of these trends was in line with the traditional, evangelical aims of rural Protestantism; none struck at the most acute problems of the new urban society.

The hold of the older evangelism was again shown in the most spectacular religious phenomenon of the 1870's and 1880's, the revival led by Dwight L. Moody and Ira D. Sankey. Moody was a lay preacher of great sincerity and eloquence; Sankey was his singing assistant. Addressing huge urban audiences, Moody urged all to cast aside sin and to find peace and salvation in Jesus. The concentration, however, was on reclaiming erring souls among the middle classes rather than on making converts in the slums.

Exponents of the old-time religion looked with alarm on the growing secularization of the Sabbath in American cities. Concern increased with the coming of European immigrants who regarded the Sabbath as a day of recreation. Many native American city workers also turned their thoughts to pleasure on their one free day. It therefore became necessary to operate streetcars and places of amusement (including beer gardens) on Sunday.

Interpreting such Sabbath activities as evidence of a decline in faith, orthodox Protestants tried to enforce Sunday-closing ordinances, and even to secure national legislation to prevent trains from running on the Sabbath. In 1888 an American Sabbath Union organized local branches to arouse public opinion. To fit the changing times, this organization shifted the argument from a purely religious basis to a humanitarian one. That is, Sabbath-breaking was condemned less as a sin against God than as an offense against man's need for a weekly day of rest. But, save in strictly rural areas, it was a losing struggle. Such urban states as New York and Massachusetts relaxed their Sunday-closing laws, and the old-time Sabbath retreated as American life was urbanized.

Protestants did not rely exclusively on traditional approaches in their effort to keep a hold on the urban middle classes. The Young Men's Christian Association, which migrated from England to the United States in 1851, experienced a remarkable growth immediately after the Civil War. Its early emphasis was on temperance and on providing a religious atmosphere for country boys who were seeking their fortunes in the cities. Without abandoning this interest, the Y.M.C.A. gave increasing attention to providing recreational and educational facilities for young men in the larger urban centers. Interdenominational in its support and outlook, the organization performed services which the churches were unable or unwilling to provide. The Young Women's Christian Association, founded in 1866, did similar work for young women, concerning itself from the start with the welfare of working girls.

Another development of this period was the rise of Christian Science. The founder, Mrs. Mary Baker Eddy, gathered around her in Lynn, Massachusetts, a group largely composed of artisans and factory workers, and expounded a system which she set forth in *Science and Health* (1875). This book taught that disease and poverty were illusions that could be dispelled by working in harmony with Eternal Mind as Jesus Christ had revealed it. Since it rejected poverty as an illusion of mortal mind, Christian Science had little appeal for working people. It did, however, attract a middle-class following in the cities. These adherents found comfort in its therapeutics and solace in a doctrine which, without rejecting the advantages of material well-being, disparaged the urban middle-class emphasis on materialism.

The rural heritage of American Protestantism and the financial support it derived from the comfortable urban classes caused many Protestant leaders to ignore the problems of the industrial workers. When church leaders discussed labor questions, they often displayed lack of sympathy and understanding. In 1877, a year of widespread labor disturbances, one religious editor favored applying to riots "with unsparing severity the law of force. If the club of the policeman knocking out the brains of the rioter will answer, well and good; but if not, bullets and bayonets, canister and grape, constitute the one remedy and the one duty of the hour." During these sad days of unemployment and suffering, Henry Ward Beecher, a well-paid clergyman, said that "God has intended the great to be great and the little to be little. . . . A dollar a day is . . . not enough to support a man and five children if a man insists on smoking and drinking beer. . . . But the man who cannot live on bread and water is not fit to live."

The lack of sympathy for workingmen was shown in many ways. When the bakers' union petitioned 500 New York clergymen to preach sermons against compulsory labor on the Sabbath, all but six ignored the appeal. As late as 1894 a church at Oshkosh, Wisconsin, excluded trade unionists on the ground that the law of God forbade membership in a labor organization. Small wonder that Samuel Gompers of the A.F. of L. denounced churchmen as allies of the capitalists in the exploitation of the working people.

The Social Gospel

Yet this was only one side of the picture. The 1880's and 1890's also witnessed a growing concern for the problems of the poor. Some Protestants were led to the new position by way of the temperance movement. Foes of liquor had long noted the connection between poverty and heavy drinking. After 1850 a growing number of temperance crusaders conceded that the saloon was an escape from, rather than the cause of, slum conditions. Observers then recalled the doctrine of the Reverend Horace Bushnell, a mid-century Connecticut Congregationalist. Bushnell taught that organized religion could not confine attention to converting sinners; it must also eliminate from the community factors that warped personality and led individuals astray.

English example was even more important. At this very time a group of Anglican clergymen was maintaining that the church must fight the evils of industrialism and extend a helping hand to working people. A few promoted the idea that the teachings of Jesus should lead to socialism. More preferred a direct approach, and entered social settlement work.

Following the British example, a handful of American Protestants began in the later 1880's to preach and work for the poorest industrial workers. The Reverend W. D. P. Bliss, an Episcopalian, founded a Church Organization for the Advancement of the Interests of Labor in 1887. Two years later he launched a more radical Society of Christian Socialists. Bliss also associated directly with workingmen, joining a union and establishing a Church of the Carpenter in a working-class neighborhood. Early in the 1890's, the Baptists and Congregationalists formed committees to study social and economic problems; and at least one Protestant clergyman, Washington Gladden, mediated in disputes between employers and employees. Gladden (who was a Congregationalist) also investigated industrial conditions in Ohio as a step toward working out a program of profit sharing for workers.

Many books helped to popularize the new movement, which was called social Christianity or the social gospel. Two in particular caught on with the general public: *Our Country* (1885), by the Reverend Josiah Strong, a Congregationalist home missionary; and *In His Steps* (1896), by the Reverend Charles M. Sheldon, of Topeka, Kansas. Sheldon's book sells to this day. Seven million copies have been disposed of, making *In His Steps* one of the best sellers of all time. Catching on quickly, the book became the *Uncle Tom's Cabin* of the social gospel. It told the story of a congregation that resolved to live for one year in full accord with the teachings of Jesus. "If the church members were all doing as Jesus would do," asked Sheldon, "could it remain true that armies of men would walk the streets for jobs, and hundreds of them curse the church, and thousands of them find in the saloon their best friend?"

Aware that words were not enough, advocates of the social gospel went into action. The new social settlement houses sprang from lay efforts, but social Christianity inspired the founders. The institutional church was another example of the awakening social conscience. As early as the 1880's, Episcopalian, Baptist, and Congregationalist churches in New York, Philadelphia, and Denver were setting up day nurseries, social clubs, recreation centers, and vocational courses for those who lacked all the "advantages." The institutional church caught on, membership increasing rapidly.

The growing desire to put Christian principles into practice led to many experiments in interdenominational coöperation. The Y.M.C.A. and Y.W.C.A. were pioneer experiments, as was the United States Christian Commission, which ministered to the needs of soldiers during the Civil War. The Woman's Christian Temperance Union, founded in 1874 and led by Frances Willard, drew support from all evangelical bodies in its fight against the saloon. An Evangelical Alliance also won interdenominational backing. This organization, founded in Great Britain, combated skepticism, rationalism, and Catholicism both in the Old World and the New. In addition, many social settlement projects were backed by more than one sect.

Interdenominational coöperation extended into other fields as well. The growing secularization of urban society made a united religious front almost a necessity. At the same time, coöperation was made easier by a decline of the traditionally bitter rivalry among the Protestant sects. Minor theological points seemed less important than before when clergymen faced the immense challenge of the new industrialism.

Critical Bible scholarship was also changing points of view. Study of existing Christian texts in the light of archaeological discoveries and an improved philology compelled learned and open-minded religious leaders to reverse long-accepted authorities, including the King James Version of the Bible. In some instances the labor of revision was an enterprise coöperatively sponsored by several denominations. In any case, it became difficult to hold many of the long-cherished theological dogmas which had promoted sectarian strife.

Involved, too, was the Darwinian theory of evolution, which cast doubt on the Biblical account of creation. At the time, this theory seemed to increase conflict within church ranks, by pitting the Protestant leaders who advocated the theory against those who rejected it. In the long run, however, the widespread acceptance of Darwinism would lead to a further breaking down of denominational lines.

These trends were far more noticeable in the cities than in rural areas. In the country, the traditional, individualistic type of Protestantism continued to be the rule. There was a slow decline in sectarian rivalries in the country, and a trace of interest in the social gospel. Otherwise, the situation was much as it had been before.

Catholic Advance and the A.P.A.

While the Protestants slowly and painfully adjusted themselves to urban life, Roman Catholicism flourished in the immigrant-packed districts of the major cities. In fact, one of the most striking facts of American religious history since the Civil War has been the growth of Catholicism in numbers, wealth, and influence. In 1865 the Catholics accounted for about 9 percent of the population—in round numbers, 3,000,000. By 1900 the census reported 15,000,000, a fivefold increase in absolute numbers with Catholics making up nearly 16 percent of the total population. No less striking was the fact that the Catholic Church, which owed its rise in membership to the influx of immigrants, was augmenting its property holdings even more rapidly than its membership.

The church did not maintain its hold on all Catholic immigrants; some Italians, for example, drifted away. But the great majority stayed in the fold. One factor in the situation was the failure of Protestant groups to establish churches in the lower-class neighborhoods. More important was the Catholic policy of having immigrant priests take care of immigrant groups. This meant that religion was closely associated with Old World experience, learning, and culture.

No less significant was the establishment of parochial schools for elementary education. The Catholic hierarchy in the United States was well aware of the importance of keeping the young faithful. Hence the Third Plenary Council, meeting in Baltimore in 1884, commanded Catholic parents to send their children to parochial rather than to the public schools. The Council further ordered that a parochial school be built beside each parish church within two years. There followed a successful campaign to raise funds for carrying out this directive.

In this period most American Catholics belonged to the working classes. Members of the Catholic hierarchy in the United States were therefore disturbed when the Canadian Catholic bishops had the Knights of Labor condemned (as a secret society). With the backing of a number of American bishops, Cardinal Gibbons of Baltimore came to the defense of the Knights. Pointing out that the head of the Order, Terence Powderly, was a practicing Catholic, Cardinal Gibbons maintained that the Knights were not a secret society in the canonical sense. In the end, the Vatican accepted the Cardinal's view (1886).

Five years later, Pope Leo XIII issued his famous "labor encyclical," *De Rerum Novarum*. While rejecting socialism, this document pleaded for justice to the workingman, and for moral considerations in industry. Thanks to this stand, the more progressive members of the Catholic hierarchy in the United States developed a policy comparable to that of the social gospel within Protestantism. Archbishop Ireland of St. Paul mediated two great railway strikes, and other prelates took part in movements for social justice. From 1882 on, the Catholic Church also sponsored the Knights of Columbus, which, like the Y.M.C.A., provided recreational and educational opportunities for urban youth.

It was inevitable that the growth of Catholicism should revive the traditional religious fears of old-stock Protestants. The reaction was economic as well as religious, for Catholic immigrants competed with American-born Protestants for jobs. There was also a political side, for many rural Protestants feared and distrusted the city machines run by Irish Catholics. Nor was culture conflict absent. In language and in customs, the Catholic newcomers were different from most native

Americans. And Protestant unwillingness to associate with immigrants, as well as the Catholic parochial school policy, may have tended to delay the elimination of those differences.

One result of the friction was the appearance of the American Protective Association. Formed in Clinton, Iowa, in 1887, this organization picked up about 70,000 members within five years and made further gains during the depression of the mid-1890's. Members pledged themselves not to vote for or employ Catholics if Protestants were available. The A.P.A. won a few city elections and for a time held the balance of power in several rural areas. But it faded fast, and was of little consequence after 1896.

From the beginning, many Protestants had criticized the A.P.A. as intolerant and had pleaded for fair play to men and women of all faiths. Catholic leaders, too, worked for good will. Tension did not disappear; but as the century ended many writers and speakers were emphasizing common spiritual traditions rather than ancient sources of conflict.

Education and the City

By 1850 the principle of publicly supported elementary schools had triumphed in the Northeast and Middle West. That is, the states required all urban and rural areas to provide tax-supported elementary schools. Some states also set a minimum school term—generally twelve weeks a year—and a few required the larger towns to maintain public high schools.

This loosely organized state system of locally run public schools spread westward as new states entered the Union from the 1850's to the 1890's. There was progress in the South as well. In that section the Civil War cut short a promising public school movement, and plans laid in the Reconstruction era failed to materialize. Later there came improvement, and the development of public education in the South was comparable in many ways to that of the North and West.

Although teacher training was becoming more important, most elementary school teachers had no special preparation when they began "keeping school." The teacher training courses offered by the new normal schools and the high schools took care of only a part of the need. County training institutes, held for a few days each summer, helped fill the gap. Meanwhile, a number of states were pointing toward a better future by setting educational standards for teachers, requiring graduation from high school for certification.

Even so, the country schools remained inferior. In rural America the school had always been a minor factor in preparing the rising generation for the responsibilities of adulthood. More important were the experiences on the farm, the round of chores, helping in the workaday business of making a living. A minority of brighter or more ambitious lads did find in nearby academies the opportunity to go beyond the reading, writing, and arithmetic ("three R's") of the one-room district school; and from these academies some got the start necessary to go on into a profession or into trade. But for most rural youth, book learning began and ended with a little figuring and reading picked up in a few short terms of school.

The second half of the nineteenth century saw a slow change for the better. Teachers were improving. So were schoolbooks, maps, and globes; and the traditional three R's no longer provided the total subject matter. In the 1880's, Massachusetts pioneered in developing consolidated schools in towns and villages to replace the rural district schools. This movement spread, but very slowly. In many states the dispersed character of the population made consolidated schools expensive. Equally important was the fact that many farmers were not interested in education or did not want their children to go into town to school. Not until after 1900 did rural leaders begin to see that the city would continue to lure an undue proportion of farm youth until the country school became more attractive, and more effectively prepared boys and girls for rural living.

Education changed more rapidly in the city. There the basic economic processes took place, not in and around the home (as in the country), but in the factory, shop, and office. Thus the city home did not equip boys and girls with the skills they would need in later life. Increasingly, the task of providing these skills was assigned to education.

Frequently the impetus came from the employer group. Massachusetts textile manufacturers attending the Crystal Palace exhibition in

London in 1851 were impressed at the way in which the British were applying art and science to industry. Returning home, these industrialists demanded that drawing and design be taught in the public schools. As a result, the Massachusetts legislature of 1860 permitted schools to introduce these subjects. Ten years later the legislature required their introduction into all schools in the larger towns. An Englishman was employed as public school supervisor of drawing and art, and the state created a Normal Art School to train teachers in that field.

Or take another example. In 1876 the president of the new Massachusetts Institute of Technology attended the Philadelphia Centennial Exposition. While there he was deeply impressed by the exhibits of iron and wood work done at the Russian Imperial Technical School in Moscow. Speaking out on the subject, he influenced St. Louis businessmen, who in 1880 founded the first manual training school in the United States. Other cities followed suit; and manual training became important both in elementary and in secondary education.

Commercial training had long been available in private schools (generally called "business colleges"). Then, in 1871, John Eaton, head of the recently established United States Bureau of Education, urged the public schools to add commercial subjects. A decade later he was able to report substantial progress, notably in the new high schools. The victory was not achieved without a struggle. Taxpayers objected on the ground that the addition of manual training and commercial subjects meant extra costs. Conservative educators said the trend involved debasing standards. But the movement won support from those who knew the needs of industry and the needs of young people who would enter business without benefit of college. So in cities where existing schools refused to introduce vocational subjects, separate commercial and technical schools were started.

Simultaneously, other trends were discernible. In the country, youngsters became productive workers at a tender age. In the early stage of the industrial revolution the same situation obtained in town; children of the poor provided cheap labor for mines and factories. But the need for child labor declined as hordes of immigrants arrived in the United States. Humanitarian considerations also reduced the employment of children. All of which meant that the period of economic dependence became longer for city children than for rural youth. This in turn led to demands for statutes to require school attendance, to lengthen the school year, and to provide better opportunities for children to continue studies into high school.

The first compulsory-attendance law was enacted in Massachusetts in 1852. This required all children from eight to fourteen to attend school twelve weeks a year. By 1895 most northern and western states had some such statute. The industrial states also led the way in increasing the length of the school year. As late as 1880 the average American received less than four years of schooling; by 1896 the amount was almost five. Compulsory attendance helped; so did the development of the kindergarten at one end of the public school system and the addition of the high school at the other. In 1870 there were only 500 high schools in the country. Twenty years later there were five times that many.

In asking for better schools, educational reformers pointed to the special problems of urban areas. Community restraints on the individual counted for less in the city than in the country and in small towns. Could not the school provide the needed restraint, thus checking juvenile delinquency and adult crime? Church and family had less hold on many city people than on the rural population. Might not the schools instill the moral values which religion and the home could not adequately provide? Immigrants, many felt, did not understand American institutions, hence fell prey to unscrupulous politicians and radical agitators. Could not educators combat these influences, turning the children of immigrants into useful and loyal Americans?

Many of those who sought larger school budgets tried to sell their program to conservative businessmen. "The high school education detects and exposes the fallacies of socialism," said a leading educator in 1885; "the poor learn that they have an interest in respecting the property of the rich." United States Senator Justin Morrill urged Congress to support vocational education so that the laborer might, by earning higher wages, steer clear of "the imported barbarous despotism reigning over trade unions." Others urged the study of economics to give the young an understanding of the industrial environment and instill in them "sound" ideas about capital and labor.

The traditional classroom, wedded to rote learning and "mental discipline," was ill suited to the newer educational programs. Fortunately, new theories came forward to justify broadening the educational base. Charles Darwin's evolutionary theory, by stressing individual differences, challenged the lock-step routine of the classroom and the assumption that rigid uniformity was necessary in the educational process. In the last two decades of the nineteenth century American educators returning from study in Germany introduced the Herbartian psychology, which stressed the importance of arousing a child's interest by making schoolwork meaningful in terms of past and potential experiences. Refusing to be bound by the traditional curriculum, the Herbartians helped introduce such subjects as literature, history, economics, typewriting, and cooking.

Others worked in the same direction. Americans influenced by the English philosopher Herbert Spencer echoed Spencer's view that education must be useful, must prepare young people for an urban, industrial society. Finally, the rise of modern experimental psychology took much wind from the sails of those who argued that mathematics and the classics provided the only sound mental discipline. Thus there was sound theoretical justification for the extension of education into other fields, particularly those that would help young Americans adjust themselves to the actualities of the new urban and industrial civilization.

Colleges and Universities

More than 260 new colleges and universities opened their doors between 1860 and 1890. Meantime, older institutions grew in strength. All this was definitely related to the urbanization and industrialization of the United States. To be sure, most American colleges were in rural areas. But, save for a few state universities, the largest, most progressive, and most prosperous institutions of higher learning were tied to urban centers. Plainly, upper-middle-class parents were finding it possible and desirable to send their sons and—a striking innovation—their daughters to college.

The expansion of this period depended in considerable part on the contributions of state and federal governments to public-supported universities. At the same time munificent gifts of business leaders invigorated older institutions and established new ones. A flour magnate and a real-estate speculator provided Wisconsin and California with astronomical observatories. A Pennsylvania coal operator founded Lehigh, a New England industrialist planned Clark. Cornelius Vanderbilt endowed the Tennessee institution that took his name. Leland Stanford, another railroad promoter, put some of his wealth into the California institution he and his wife established in memory of their son. Ezra Cornell (telegraph and lands) put part of his fortune into a university in New York, and Johns Hopkins (trade and finance) endowed a university in Baltimore. John D. Rockefeller gave liberally to the new University of Chicago. Vassar, Wellesley, Smith, and other rising colleges for women owed their foundation to well-to-do citizens who wanted to give women an opportunity to achieve the highest standards in collegiate instruction.

Even before 1850, college presidents and professors had debated the issue of classical versus practical education. Although science and technology had won a few victories, the classicists had held their ground. The impact of the industrial age changed the story in the next half-century. The classical curriculum with its prescribed course of study for all students gave way with the introduction of the natural sciences, the social studies, and the elective system.

The Civil War decade saw the establishment of a score of new scientific institutions. Much of the impetus came from the Morrill Land-Grant Act of 1862, which was designed to encourage mechanical and agricultural education. Lack of experience, personnel, or funds held the land-grant colleges back for a while; but they soon made up for lost time. The state-supported University of Illinois pioneered in introducing shop courses. From the time of its opening in 1868, Cornell University (which combined land-grant support with private benefactions) gave scientific and practical education an equal status with liberal arts. Nor were the land-grant colleges alone. The older private institutions added science and engineering courses, or improved existing offerings. New technical colleges were established to meet the needs of the urban age: the Massachusetts Institute of Technology, the Case Institute of Technology, the Drexel Institute, the Armour Institute, among others. Most of these were designed to train the engineers required in transportation and in industry.

The business community also wanted personnel trained in the social sciences. In 1881 the banker Joseph Wharton gave the University of Pennsylvania a liberal gift for establishing a school of finance and commerce—the first modern institution of its kind. Other colleges and universities introduced courses in economics and allied social disciplines. As early as 1872 Yale appointed William Graham Sumner to the first chair in political economy and sociology. Johns Hopkins took the lead in these fields, but other private and public universities were only a little way behind. Important work was done both at graduate and undergraduate levels.

Some of the new social scientists ran into trouble when their teachings did not square with the ideas generally accepted in business circles. Thus tariff protectionists tried to have William Graham Sumner ousted from Yale. One economist was compelled to leave Cornell when he expressed himself frankly on the Gould strike. Another was virtually dismissed from Chicago when he criticized certain public utility corporations. Nevertheless, the social scientists did manage to increase their influence in this period; and bit by bit they won the right to air their views.

Adult Education

The lyceum reached its height in the decade before the Civil War. This voluntary, informal association of townspeople enabled villagers and some farmers to hear well-known lecturers hold forth on morals, literature, and reform. Since these "people's colleges" were willing to schedule speakers whose unorthodox views made them unwelcome in many universities, they rendered an important service.

After the Civil War James Redpath, an enterprising journalist, opened a central booking office. Lecturers could secure engagements through this agency, and local lyceums could engage speakers. This was convenient on both sides. But quality was sacrificed to organization and efficiency. As the older stars like Ralph Waldo Emerson died or retired, Redpath pushed less serious entertainment—humorous readings, travelogues, musical varieties.

As the lyceum changed its character, Chautauqua took its place. This movement was launched in the 1870's, one of its founders being

John H. Vincent, later a Methodist bishop. Interested in training Sunday School teachers, the sponsors staged summer camp meetings at Lake Chautauqua, New York. Then the founders broadened their approach, in a democratic and Christian effort to supply plain people with a rich cultural fare. Leading scholars addressed the summer assemblages on literary, social, economic, and political topics.

Similar outdoor meetings were organized elsewhere throughout the nation. There were seventy in all by the late 1890's. Meanwhile, the original Chautauqua had taken its offerings on tour, thus coming into contact with townspeople and farmers who were unable to attend the summer assemblies. Study groups were supplied with syllabuses and books. Americans who lived in the small towns and villages were thus exposed to the classics and to new writings as well.

Culture patterns were more complex in the city. There were lectures there, as in the smaller towns. In addition, many cities acquired evening schools. The first of these were private; as the years went by, an increasing number had public backing. The evening schools offered standard elementary subjects and also vocational courses intended to help mechanics move ahead.

The public library movement was also city centered. When the Boston Public Library opened its doors in 1854, it led the way in developing a characteristically American institution. Before the end of the century, private benefactors had made it possible for Chicago, Baltimore, New York, and other leading cities to establish public libraries.

The greatest figure in the public library movement was the iron and steel magnate, Andrew Carnegie. A self-educated immigrant, Carnegie well knew the value of books; and when he obtained wealth, he used some of it to make books available to others. His first gift in the library field was made in Pittsburgh in 1881. By the end of the century he had given almost $6,000,000 to communities for library purposes. The community furnished the site. Carnegie then built the library, which the community agreed to maintain.

Thanks to Carnegie and others, many of the larger towns had free public libraries by 1896. Much remained undone; but the movement had already helped a good number of Americans to develop the reading habit. With continued improvement, the free public library was to be viewed as one of the great bulwarks of American democracy.

Literature for Everybody

The new reading habits and the growth of urban population brought prosperity to American publishers. Improved book circulation also helped. As before, books were sold on a subscription basis, through traveling book agents, and through bookstores. The number of stores increased in this period. Editions became larger; books were advertised more widely than before. As in other businesses, growth brought concentration; and the publishing business became centered in New York and a few other metropolitan areas.

Until 1891 the copyright situation was chaotic. The United States legislation protected American but not foreign authors. Many publishers therefore ignored native writers (to whom royalties had to be paid) and brought out cheap editions of such popular English novelists as Charles Dickens (paying Dickens nothing for the privilege). Both European and American authors were better off when Congress finally extended protection to foreigners, in the international copyright law of 1891.

From the 1850's on, there was an enormous increase in the production of dime novels and other "literature for the masses." Hack writers ground out this material in quantity; Harlan P. Halsey, creator of the *Old Sleuth* detective series, penned 650 dime novels. Publishers sold the product by the tens of thousands. Love and adventure were major themes. Juveniles went for Buffalo Bill Wild West titles and for Horatio Alger's stories about country boys who made good in the city. Adults liked suspense and sugary sentiment, and showed a definite preference for tales that linked love, piety, and moral uplift. Comic pictorials and joke books also sold handsomely.

Critics rightly held that few of these items had enduring literary value. These same critics, however, did not always recognize real talent. Some of them underrated the great Samuel L. Clemens (Mark Twain), mistakenly identifying his racy and Rabelaisian humor with the "low tradition." Keepers of many public libraries even refused to stock *Huckleberry Finn*. More acceptable to the self-styled intellectual elite were the local-color writers: George Washington Cable, who wrote of Louisiana Creoles; Joel Chandler Harris, whose stories concerned southern Negroes; Thomas Nelson Page (a bygone Virginia); Edward Eggleston (backwoods Indiana); Hamlin Garland (prairie frontier); Bret Harte (the Far West); Sarah Orne Jewett (down-east Maine).

Many novelists dealt with the new urban regions. Walt Whitman was the first major poet to find inspiration in the bustling anonymous city crowds. William Dean Howells laid bare the saga of a self-made man (*Rise of Silas Lapham*) and probed various problems of urban life, including divorce. Stephen Crane handled another city type in *Maggie, A Girl of the Streets*. John Hay's *Breadwinners* dealt unsympathetically with trade unions, and Edward Bellamy's utopian *Looking Backward* described the potentialities of an urban society under socialism.

Some of the best American writing appeared in magazines. Periodicals sold better than ever before, especially in the cities. The reasons were various: the rise of mass advertising; improvements in printing and in the reproduction of illustrations; the second-class mailing privilege granted by Congress in 1879.

The quality magazines included *Harper's New Monthly Magazine*, which first appeared in 1850. The *Atlantic*, founded in 1857, specialized in New England authors. What the *Atlantic* did for New England, *Scribner's* and *Century* did for the West and South, the *Overland Monthly* for the Far West.

More spectacular was the rise of the popular, mass-circulation magazine. The *New York Ledger*, launched in 1855, quickly soared to the then-unheard-of circulation of 400,000. The publisher, Richard Bonner, became a millionaire; and the high prices paid for contributions made the writing profession more attractive than before. Henry Wadsworth Longfellow, Harriet Beecher Stowe, and others were glad to write for the *Ledger*. Also popular were the illustrated weeklies, notably *Leslie's* and *Harper's Weekly*, both of which backed reforms. *Leslie's* crusaded against the pollution of milk; and Thomas Nast's brilliant cartoons in *Harper's Weekly* helped expose Boss Tweed's corrupt New York City machine.

In 1865 some 700 magazines were published in the United States. Two decades later the number had reached 3300. Many of the new periodicals appealed to special groups. The *Independent*, a widely circulated weekly, used a religious approach, whereas E. L. Godkin's *Nation* was aimed at the intellectual elite, and *Popular Science* interested those who wanted to know about the new technological discoveries. New magazines for women—*McCall's*, the *Woman's Home Companion*, the *Ladies' Home Journal*—overshadowed the venerable *Godey's Lady's Book*, which gave up the fight in 1898. The new pacemaker was the *Ladies' Home Journal*, especially after the crusading Edward K. Bok became editor in 1889.

Newspapers reached even more readers than did magazines. The number of dailies more than doubled in the last two decades of the nineteenth century, and circulation went up even faster. Technological improvements enabled publishers to get out larger and more frequent editions at lower cost. To reach more customers, journalists tried to stress reader appeal. Editorials were played down. News was presented in a livelier style, headlines became bolder, and special features multiplied. There were pages for homemakers, sports sections, comic strips, cartoons, health hints, columns of advice for gardeners and theatergoers and the lovelorn.

As circulation increased, newspapers bought outside services. In 1884 S. S. McClure set up the first agency to provide syndicated features to subscribing newspapers. At the same time the growth of such news-gathering agencies as the Associated Press added to the speed and efficiency (and uniformity) of the American press. Since advertising helped pay for the new services and features, and since newspapers were themselves big businesses, the editorial pages frequently reflected ideas of the industrial and mercantile leaders.

In the second half of the nineteenth century a new sort of publisher replaced the older, Horace Greeley type of journalist. Greeley had used his New York *Tribune* to air his economic and political views. The new men cared less for this than for sensation. Charles A. Dana of the *Sun* and the James Gordon Bennetts of the *Herald* pointed the way in New York journalism by playing up scandals, gossip, and human interest stories. Out in the Middle West, the Scripps brothers made several contributions to the new journalism. They, too, favored sensationalism. In addition, they demonstrated the possibilities of the evening paper, which made a special appeal to the tired office worker and laboring man. With organs in Detroit, Cleveland, St. Louis, and Cincinnati, the Scripps brothers also blazed a trail in the chain newspaper field.

Still more influential was Joseph Pulitzer, an immigrant who bought the St. Louis *Post-Dispatch* in the 1870's. Dedicating the paper to "people rather than . . . purse-potentates," Pulitzer championed civic causes, exposed bribery and corruption. At the same time, he featured crime, sex, and human interest stories and introduced departments designed to appeal to average readers. A few years later Pulitzer used the same formula to build up the run-down New York *World*.

From 1895 on, Pulitzer had a rival in the New York field—William Randolph Hearst. The newcomer had started out in California, with the San Francisco *Examiner*. Branching out, Hearst acquired the New York *Journal*, the second link in what eventually became a nationwide newspaper-and-magazine chain. The mid-1890's saw Hearst and Pulitzer engaging in a New York circulation war, each trying to outdo the other in news coverage, features, sensations, and reforms. In the process, both influenced American foreign relations by playing up the Cuban insurgent cause (1895–98) and demanding that the United States drive Spain out of the island of Cuba.

The City Transforms Rural Life

The years after 1850 witnessed the slow, uneven impact of urban culture on rural life. The result was that the city and the country came to be less sharply distinguished than before. For bit by bit the whole United States was becoming urbanized.

Not that farmers wanted to live like city dwellers. Most country people continued to regard rural living as more healthy and desirable than city life. The old generation of farmers deplored the tendency of their children to seek their fortunes in the city. Rural clergymen and educators denounced the corruption and worldliness of society leaders, city bosses, urban businessmen, and factory workers. Perhaps this was conscious propaganda to stay the tide of migration cityward. Perhaps it was a defense mechanism associated with the uncomfortable fact that urban prestige and power had replaced the traditional leadership of rural America.

Nonetheless, urban ways exerted increasing influence on rural areas. Farm journals and agricultural colleges urged farmers to imitate city businessmen, to study market conditions, keep careful accounts, and adopt a business outlook. Village editors read and copied metropolitan newspapers, and city magazines like the *Ladies' Home Journal* invaded rural districts. These urban periodicals and mail-order catalogues familiarized farmers with city customs. Better merchandising and faster deliveries made it possible for country people to buy soap, overalls, furniture, carpets, and a thousand other items formerly made at home. Farm boys who had moved to the city talked of metropolitan ways when they went home for visits. Rural free delivery (R.F.D.) of mail and, in the 1890's, telephones and improved roads were further links between town and country. Taken all together, these factors gradually urbanized rural America. Without altogether realizing it, farmers and villagers were absorbing urban culture.

4

A Changing Culture

An Age of Specialists

The industrialization and urbanization of America made the national culture far more complex than before. The new age brought a need for all sorts of specialists. Old disciplines were subdivided. Professional standards were raised, and the passing years brought a new respect for learning.

The trend toward specialization could be seen in every field. The medical arts afford an illustration. Colonial doctors had given medicine, pulled teeth, and treated animals. These several jobs were divided during the nineteenth century. Colleges of dentistry were founded after 1850, veterinary schools after 1875. Specialties also developed within medicine proper, some physicians concentrating on obstetrics, others on surgery, and so on.

As specialization increased, each group of specialists became "guild-conscious" and talked of raising standards. The first step in this process was to effect professional organization. This had been on a broad scale before 1850, in such fields as theology, medicine, and law. After mid-century, the tendency was to found more specialized groups. Those interested in the care of the ear set up the American Otological Society in 1869; and surgeons created the American Surgical Society eleven years later. The same generation saw the organization of national associations for civil engineers (1852), mining and metallurgical engineers (1871), mechanical engineers (1880), and electrical engineers (1884).

While setting up their special societies, the specialists did not neglect the larger view. Members of the American Surgical Society continued to back the American Medical Association, which represented physicians in general. The American Association for the Advancement of Science, launched by the geologists in 1848, won the support of many different disciplines and sub-disciplines. Yet there was a growing conviction that many problems could be discussed most effectively by professionals with a common background and experience.

The new professional associations put heavy stress on formal education. In the old days, young men had "read law" in an attorney's office, or had served an apprenticeship under a country doctor, or (as in teaching) had launched a professional career without any special training. The professional societies endeavored to change this situation, to require training in professional colleges. Motives were varied. Protection from competition was often involved; a college-training requirement reduced the number of persons entering a given field. But there was more to it than that. The professional bodies wanted to eliminate charlatans who fleeced the public and dragged down the reputation of the specialty. Furthermore, the associations recognized the obvious fact that specialized preparation was more necessary in a complex urban culture than it had been in the simpler agrarian society of an earlier age.

Besides stressing training, the professional societies did their best to improve their specialties. This could be done by having conferences or conventions, at which new developments could be discussed. Professional journals were also useful. These were often edited by professors in institutions which trained young people for professional careers.

Growing Interest in Research

In the development of specialties, there was strong emphasis on practical considerations. The specialist (a surgeon, for example) could claim higher fees and acquire more prestige than a general practitioner. Specialization, however, also led to an interest in special problems, and this in turn tended to encourage basic research. The trend was weakened by the fact that Americans had long regarded theoretic approaches with contempt. (In 1850, the American Medical Association found only two medical research projects under way in the whole country, one concerning the "physiology of the alligator".) But by the 1890's quite a lot had been accomplished.

The colleges led the way. Instead of insisting that all professors devote themselves exclusively to teaching, some university presidents began to encourage research. President Charles W. Eliot of Harvard appointed research men to his faculty and provided laboratory equipment. Following a similar policy, Provost William Pepper of the University of Pennsylvania set up research institutes which had no general teaching functions. More striking still, the Johns Hopkins University in Baltimore, established in 1876, devoted itself primarily to research. Modeled on German institutions, this new university had no undergraduate liberal arts college. Its professors, chosen for research reputation, therefore had no heavy load of undergraduate instruction. Instead, they gave their time to original work and to the research training of a few advanced scholars.

The Hopkins experiment had great influence in American university circles. By 1896, therefore, a number of institutions were equipped with men and laboratories capable of basic scientific investigations. Industry, too, had begun to see the value of theoretic research. In the generation to follow, American contributions to scientific knowledge would be accorded world recognition. Here, indeed, was a turning point in American intellectual history.

The Humanities and Social Studies

The new enthusiasm for research affected all branches of knowledge, the humanities and social disciplines as well as the natural sciences. Many of these subjects had been studied since ancient times. But approaches changed rapidly as the "scientific spirit" made its impact felt on language studies and on history, on economics, sociology, and law. Investigators borrowed some of the methods of the natural scientists. They tried to observe phenomena more exactly and systematically. They made some effort to be objective, that is, to exclude prejudices and other subjective elements from the thinking of investigators. The effort produced striking advances in many fields.

Here, as in science, American scholars leaned heavily on Europe. In philosophy, for example, many Americans became interested in the positivism of Auguste Comte, a Frenchman who urged that all speculation about a final explanation of the universe and man was useless, and that philosophers should concern themselves with the nature and interrelations of the sciences. Historians introduced the seminar technique from Germany; and college-trained "scientific historians" who strove for objectivity replaced the earlier, literary historians. Statistical methods developed in both Europe and America enabled economists and sociologists to study institutions and problems more analytically than before.

Despite the new methods, those who worked in the social studies were less objective than those devoted to the natural sciences. It was very difficult to observe human behavior with the same calm detachment that one applied to chemical combinations. Those who studied history, and those who did research in economics, sociology, and government generally elaborated doctrines which justified the systems they preferred. Some, like the Englishman Herbert Spencer, used the available knowledge to defend laissez-faire capitalism. Others, including the German Karl Marx, used much the same information to attack existing institutions.

In choosing sides, American thinkers were likely to be guided by their own attitudes and by their view of national interests. Thus European economists who defended capitalism won approval in the United States, whereas Marxian socialism, with its doctrine of class struggle, made little impression. Herbert Spencer had a great vogue, partly because his Darwinian slant pleased businessmen who felt that they represented the "survival of the fittest" in a free-for-all economic struggle.

The Natural Sciences: Darwinism

These were years of great advance in the natural sciences. Physicists expanded their knowledge of energy, thus making possible all sorts of technological improvements. Chemists learned how to proceed by analysis and synthesis—how to break down substances into their constituent elements and how to build up products by combining elements. These advances in the physical sciences were of direct aid to the biologic sciences. Advances in physics gave biologists and physicians improved microscopes and cameras; advances in chemistry revolutionized physiology and pharmacology. A new specialty, physiologic chemistry, was introduced into the medical schools; and, later, biochemistry and biophysics came into the picture.

Meanwhile, the theory of evolution was transforming the whole field of biology. Back in the eighteenth century, zoologists and botanists had collected and classified thousands of specimens of plants and animals. While doing so, some of these scientists had become intrigued by the close resemblance of some species to others. It was discovered that closely related species of animals and plants could be crossbred, producing hybrids in some cases superior to one or both of the parent species.

This posed a problem: If breeders could produce new types, might this not also have occurred in nature? The traditional religious explanation of the origin of species was that God had created each one separately. Nineteenth-century biologists began to suspect that in plants and animals, as in languages, similarities indicated common origins. Wolves, foxes, dogs must have come from common primitive canine ancestors. But how?

Several scientists worked on this question early in the nineteenth century. The French scientist Lamarck advanced the now generally discredited view that acquired characteristics were inherited. A few others, including American-born Dr. William Charles Wells, suggested that all animals faced disease and competition, and that only the fittest would survive to perpetuate their kind. Animal types ill suited to the struggle for existence would become extinct, whereas the successful competitors would survive and gradually evolve new species. By 1860 Charles Darwin and Alfred Russel Wallace, two Englishmen working independently, presented this same basic theory and supported it with a mass of evidence from comparative anatomy, natural history, animal breeding, and geology. Darwin's book, *The Origin of Species*, profoundly impressed both scientists and the educated public.

Many churchmen condemned Darwin on the ground that his view implied that men as well as animals were descended from lower forms —the most immediate ancestor of man apparently being some sort of prehistoric ape. Just as astronomers had dethroned the earth from a central position in the universe, so biologists were tumbling man from his unique position. Was nothing sacred to these scientists? Did scientists feel that man (like the earth) had been of no particular concern to God? This, some thought, pointed toward a materialistic view of nature and man. Others, including the American writer John Fiske, defended Darwin by saying that evolution was God's design for producing man.

In earlier centuries Darwin's theory might have been suppressed as heresy. This was not possible in the free atmosphere of the nineteenth century; and by 1900 Darwinism had won general acceptance among educated Europeans and Americans. Biological research was greatly stimulated by the theory. Specialists in the new field of genetics gave their full attention to the mechanism of heredity. (Here Americans took the lead after 1890.) The evolutionary doctrine also influenced social thinkers, for the concept of the survival of the fittest could be applied to social classes, business competition, and even conflicts between nations.

The Fight Against Disease

Urban growth brought with it special problems of public health. Sedentary city jobs did not provide as much exercise as did farm work. Nor did diets suited to country living fit all city workers. Most important of all, slum conditions lowered resistance and increased exposure to disease. Typhus fever, for instance, was an often fatal infection spread by body lice in crowded areas. The disease persisted in American cities until after the Civil War.

What to do about such problems? Some health "experts" claimed that they had the answer. If men lived right, said these "physiologic reformers," they would not need doctors. Emphasis was on cleanliness, diet, and the avoidance of bad habits. Exercise was stressed. Gymnastic exercises were imported from Germany and Sweden, and city dwellers began to show an interest in organized sports. Most popular was baseball, evolved from old British games in the 1850's and popularized in army camps during the Civil War.

All this, of course, was an upper- and middle-class affair. The health reformers failed to reach many of the poorest people. And in any case, exercise and diet were not enough to prevent the spread of disease in cities which contained overcrowded and filth-laden slums.

Realizing this, many urban leaders tackled the problem of epidemics. Some thought that these mass disasters were caused by contact with infected animals or humans. Others blamed "noxious airs" and odors arising from filth and refuse. The first group favored quarantine of ships and isolation of diseased individuals. The second stressed the need for sanitary reforms—clean streets, food inspection, pure water. A controversy between these two factions dragged on until the 1890's, with the advocates of sanitary reform gradually gaining ground.

Whichever view one held, it was necessary to work through political channels. Quarantines could be enforced only through a government; and only a government could institute community-wide sanitary reforms. Debates over the prevention of epidemics therefore centered around city boards of health. Larger cities established such bodies early in the nineteenth century; the smaller municipalities followed suit a little later. State boards of health were set up after 1870 to advise city governments. Congress even established a national health board in the 1870's; but when it spent all of $10,000 for research within three years, it was abolished as extravagant.

By the second half of the nineteenth century physicians had begun to identify diseases. No longer did they say simply that a patient was "bilious," that his "system lacked tone." Instead, they tried to diagnose a special disease, as indicated by special symptoms.

To perfect the new technique, medical scientists had to perform many autopsies and observe symptoms very closely. Hence they invented instruments to make bedside observations precise—the stethoscope, for example, and the clinical thermometer. The introduction of exact measurements in medical practice and research indicated that medicine was finally taking advantage of quantitative procedures, as the physical sciences had much earlier.

Knowledge obtained through autopsies was quickly applied to medical practice. This was most apparent in surgery. For centuries, surgery had been largely limited to amputations and the setting of fractures. Physicians had gone no further, for they had blamed illness on impurities of blood rather than on diseases located in particular parts of the body. Hence the doctor of 1840, finding a patient with an acute pain in his right side, talked about the "state of the system" and gave purges that killed the patient. In the same situation, the doctor of 1890 diagnosed a condition in a particular organ (appendix) and advised its immediate removal by a surgeon.

Surgery was first attempted on the abdominal organs, since the abdomen was the safest major cavity to open. Only at the end of the century were chest and brain operations tried. By then surgeons had greatly improved their methods. Effective anesthetics had been discovered in the 1840's, probably because the growing interest in surgery had prompted a search for helpful techniques. The later discovery that infections were caused by microörganisms led surgeons to use antiseptic dressings that eliminated these organisms, and to make sure that their hands, instruments, and operating rooms were absolutely clean (antiseptic and aseptic surgery). Operations therefore became less painful, safer, and more helpful.

Dental surgery deserves special mention, for it was one of the first specialties in which Americans excelled. During the 1840's American dentists gave the world the first effective anesthetics; and by the 1860's even Europeans had come to regard American dentists as the best on earth. Dentistry affected the appearance as well as the health of patients. It therefore appealed to a practical people like the Americans, who at the same time were in a relatively good position for paying dental bills.

By 1850, medical scientists had identified a large number of common diseases. They had consequently reached much the same stage as the biologists when the latter had earlier identified the many animal species with which they had to deal. The biologists had then begun to inquire into the origin of species. In like fashion, medical science began to seek the origin of disease.

One theory was that disease was caused by inhaling "noxious airs"; but a search for particular poisons in the air led to no result. More fruitful was another old theory, that diseases were caused by minute animals or plants ("germs") which upon gaining access to the body attacked it as parasites. Using the improved microscope, French and

German medical scientists demonstrated that particular diseases could be traced to particular microörganisms. In the last three decades of the century Pasteur, Koch, and other bacteriologists found the causative organisms of tuberculosis, typhoid fever, diphtheria, and other dread diseases.

Once the causative organisms were known, the way was open for preventive measures. Investigators found that typhoid and cholera germs were carried through water and food, and that these diseases could be prevented by purifying water and by pasteurizing milk. In other cases (including diphtheria) it was discovered that germs spread by contacts between persons. As a result, public health workers knew after 1900 just what diseases could be handled by isolation, and which required sanitary controls.

Pasteur also discovered that killed or weakened germs, when injected into the body, stimulated defense mechanisms in the blood. The germs could not multiply and cause disease; but they protected the body against later invasion by live and virulent organisms. Only a few protective vaccines were known by 1900, but others (notably that against typhoid) were developed soon thereafter.

Armed with greater knowledge, public health authorities could build better programs. City and state health boards improved their quarantine and sanitary measures. They prepared vaccines for the use of physicians. They began to offer diagnostic services, and looked forward to the day when all major infectious diseases would be eliminated.

In these years of progress, little was done for the mentally ill. Thanks to the efforts of Dorothea Dix, government institutions for the insane had been set up even before the Civil War. Study of patients at these and European institutions enabled doctors to distinguish between mild conditions (neuroses) and more serious ones (psychoses). Investigators, however, were unable to discover any physical basis for mental illness. The tendency, therefore, was to commit to an asylum—and forget—serious psychotic cases, and dismiss neurotic patients with the remark that "it is just your nerves."

Public attitudes operated along the same line. The nineteenth-century notion was that mental illness was a personal disgrace, that it might come from some "hereditary taint" in a family. Those with "insane" relatives tried to have them put away. That was the end of the matter; it was not polite even to refer to the patient after that. This attitude promoted general indifference to conditions in mental institutions.

The problem, however, could not be permanently ignored. While physicians were conquering other diseases, mental illness was increasing. It was related, apparently, to the stress and strain of modern living. But how to treat it? Was the answer in mesmerism (hypnotism), which the French clinicians revived and tried in the treatment of neurotic cases? Was it in the elaborate questioning procedure (psychoanalysis) being developed by Sigmund Freud of Vienna? The answer lay in the future; modern psychiatry is a twentieth-century phenomenon.

During the two generations before 1870, many Americans lost confidence in physicians. In that period, medical research was concentrating on identifying disease; but doctors had few cures. Earlier, they had been sure that bleeding and purging were "good for what ails you"; and patients had been encouraged by this confidence. But in the middle of the nineteenth century, physicians were beginning to distrust the traditional cures. Patients consequently felt that they were receiving little aid. This caused many to turn to medical sects whose practitioners promised cures (for example, homeopathy, imported from Germany after 1830). By the 1850's it looked as though the American medical profession might be broken into a number of warring sects, of which the "regulars" would be only one.

Medical progress at the end of the century cleared up the confusion. American physicians who studied in Germany brought back news of discoveries that held out real hope for suffering mankind. Public confidence in medicine was quickly revived. Following the trend, many states limited practice largely to regular physicians, and required these to pass a state examination before starting practice.

Down to the 1890's the United States benefited from, but played little part in, medical research. This was partly because of the general American indifference to basic science, partly because Americans had a peculiar aversion to permitting the autopsies essential for pathological studies. But from the 1890's on, the United States would do its full share. For at long last Americans had become convinced of the utility of basic science and were ready to support it with enthusiasm.

The Fine Arts: Painting

In the fine arts as in science, nineteenth-century Americans leaned heavily on Europe. Many American painters, sculptors, and musicians chose native themes and used their talent for patriotic purposes. But it was not enough to know what thought one wanted to express. It was also necessary to know how to express it. Trained in Europe and by European-trained masters, American artists tended to rely on techniques worked out in Europe. Only toward the end of the century did a few figures, including the painter Albert Ryder, strike out on their own.

The rise of American nationalism, then, did not immediately transform the fine arts in the United States. Thomas Eakins was almost alone among painters who responded creatively to the new scientific, urban culture; Louis Sullivan was one of the few architects who tried to meet the challenge of the city. But urbanization did affect the arts in another way. The accumulation of wealth in urban areas enabled private individuals and city governments to pay substantial fees to architects, sculptors, and artists, and to establish art museums and patronize good music. This gave support to many persons and greatly stimulated all of the fine arts.

In the generation before 1850 the most significant development in painting had been the rise of the Hudson River school of landscape painters. The members of this school employed European techniques. They were, however, American nationalists who combined a romantic interest in the countryside with the conviction that the American scene offered the artist both inspiration and subject matter. Several painters continued this tradition down into the 1870's. Chief among these was Frederic E. Church, probably the outstanding representative of the Hudson River school. Traveling all over the world, Church picked awe-inspiring subjects and greatly pleased his countrymen with his paintings of icebergs, waterfalls, and mountain ranges.

Church and others of the Hudson River school saw landscapes as collections of forms and colors to be imitated exactly. In this emphasis on detail they frequently failed to catch the overall impression. A vital defect, said William Morris Hunt, who in the 1850's brought to the United States the technique and points of view of the French Barbizon school. Like his European masters, Hunt looked for "the big things first," tried to capture mood as well as detail. "When you paint what you see, you paint an object," Hunt told his pupils. "When you paint what you feel, you paint a poem."

The same trend away from literal presentation can be seen in the work of George Inness, whom many regard as the greatest of American landscape painters. A self-taught artist, Inness did his first work under the influence of the Hudson River school. His early canvases, therefore, were literal and detailed representations of what he saw. Later association with members of the French Barbizon school led Inness to subordinate detail to feeling, and his romantic landscapes of the 1880's caught the harsh and pleasant moods of nature.

Meanwhile, other painters were rejecting romanticism and demanding realism. This group included James McNeill Whistler, Winslow Homer, and Thomas Eakins. All three were influenced by the French realists and tried to paint what they saw. But they did not return to the literal representation of detail of the Hudson River school. Rather they suppressed irrelevant details and gave their paintings unity and force as well as accuracy.

Though an American, Whistler preferred to live abroad. Homer and Eakins, however, lived in the United States and gave their work what may be called an American character. Homer was most successful with marine paintings, pictures of fishermen and the foaming surf. His was a talent for making the usual seem fresh and unexpected. Few have matched him in an ability to treat the great forces of nature and the plain people who contended against it. Most of Eakins' themes were peculiarly American, and many represented aspects of the new urban society: a medical clinic, prize fighters, a cello player, a dancing Negro boy, business leaders. The pictures show the scientist's knowledge of anatomy and the poet's feeling for color and rhythm. "Get the character of the thing," Eakins told his students; and with searching objectivity he painted his clients as they looked to him, not as they wished to look.

Thomas Eakins' individualistic realism kept him from becoming a popular painter. Others among the better artists had a wide public following. Winslow Homer, for example, could please both the discriminating critic and the people. During the Civil War he drew sketches of military life for the widely circulated *Harper's Weekly*; and his oil paintings, too, attracted wide attention.

In general, though, there was a distinction between the work of the great artists (the high tradition) and art by and for the people (the low tradition, or genre art). The great artists painted for themselves, for the critics, and for posterity. Genre art was for the average citizen. "Paint pictures that will take with the public," said William Sidney Mount. "Never paint for the few, but the many." Mount did just that, and had no trouble selling his cheerful pictures of Negro life.

Mount and other genre artists were influenced by European models. They managed, however, to give their work a distinctively American character—were, in this one particular, more successful than those who painted in the high tradition. And some of the popular artists did surprisingly good work. An example is George Caleb Bingham, whose illustrations caught the spirit of life on the western rivers and along the frontier. Though primarily a genre artist, Bingham had sound training, including three years in Germany. He could paint portraits in the high tradition; and he also served as professor of art at the University of Missouri.

Much of the work of the popular artists reached the public in lithograph form. This type of art came into its own in 1857 when Nathaniel Currier (a businessman) and J. Merritt Ives (an artist) combined their talents to become "print-makers to the American people." Employing a crew of artists, this firm put out thousands of lithographs illustrating public disasters, sporting events, tender moments in the life of the family, national progress, and regional peculiarities. Especially appealing to urban Americans were the nostalgic images of New England farms in deep snow, with the ox team fetching wood for the fireplace, and with an outward semblance of peace and security. Many rivals challenged Currier & Ives, but the firm held its own until the end of the century.

The magazine and book publishers also distributed popular art. They, like Currier & Ives, took advantage of the improved techniques of reproduction, which ranged from wood engravings to process blocks, and finally to half-tones. There were so many able artists then active that the last four decades of the nineteenth century have been called the golden age of American illustration. Among the leaders in the field were Joseph Pennell, one of the great figures in the history of American graphic arts, and Frederic Remington, sculptor, illustrator, and chronicler of the old West.

To the art of the people also belonged the panoramic canvases that depicted American progress in semi-documentary fashion. Artists accompanied western explorers and recorded their impressions of buffalo and Indian, prairie and plain, desert and mountain. Some of the records (one of the Mississippi River, for example) reached the people through rotating canvases three miles in length. Others found their way into the popular mind through illustrated books about the Indians and the West.

As in earlier times, some of the plain people created artistic objects for themselves. The Pennsylvania Dutch and the Shakers maintained their folk art traditions. Even after 1850 New England whittlers carved handsome figureheads for clipper ships. Limners (though in diminishing numbers) continued to roam the countryside making portraits. Sign painters remained active; and housewives kept on making bedspreads and decorating wallpaper.

Despite this activity, the folk arts were definitely on the decline. New recreational opportunities absorbed time formerly spent on folk arts. Machines replaced the whittlers; and the new lithographing processes made good prints available at a low cost. So the old traditions faded in a changing age.

The Fine Arts: Sculpture

The equivalent of genre painting in the field of sculpture was the popular work of John Rogers. This machinist-draftsman executed a whole series of group statuettes dealing with scenes from American life. Some of the Rogers groups concerned everyday living ("Going for the Cows"); others represented military action ("One More Shot") or great political events ("The Emancipation Proclamation"). Turned out in quantity at a low price, these composition statuettes sold very widely.

Sculpture in the high tradition fitted in with the upsurge of nationalism and the increase of urban wealth. Cities provided commissions for fountains in public parks and for Civil War memorials. New libraries and capitol buildings often called for sculpture; and the new-rich began patronizing sculptors. The result was a large increase of activity in the field, signalized by the formation of the National Sculpture Society.

At mid-century, American sculpture was under Italian influence, and was dominated by academic and uninspired neoclassicists. The next two generations saw a revolt, with the neoclassicist influence replaced by that of the French modernists. A key figure in the transition was Henry Kirke Brown. Italian-trained, Brown at first worked in the neoclassical tradition; but as he turned to American western themes, his work took on a new boldness and vitality (as in his "Indian and Panther"). His greatest achievement was his equestrian statue of George Washington in Union Square, New York (1856). In this project, Brown was assisted by his pupil John Quincy Adams Ward, who went on to do many patriotic bronzes of his own. Ward is also remembered for his "Indian Hunter," his "Freedman," and his "Pilgrim." Daniel Chester French, who studied very briefly with Ward, prepared "The Minute Man" for the centennial of Lexington and Concord in 1875; and he later created the great statue in the Lincoln Memorial in Washington.

It was Augustus Saint-Gaudens, however, who dominated American sculpture at the end of the nineteenth century. Like Brown, Ward, and French, Saint-Gaudens helped liberate his art from the arid conventions of the neoclassicists; and, like them, he interpreted heroic events and figures of American history. Irish-born and European-trained, Saint-Gaudens was nevertheless able to capture and communicate American ideals. His statues of Farragut in New York and Lincoln in Chicago set new standards for public monuments. Out-

standing, too, was his memorial for Mrs. Henry Adams in the Rock
Creek Cemetery, Washington. This bronze figure, seated and shaded
in heavy drapery, suggested the brooding mystery of death. Saint-
Gaudens also directed the sculptural harmonies at the Chicago
World's Fair in 1893.

The Fine Arts: Architecture

The Greek revival in architecture was on
the way out in 1850. It was succeeded by a romantic confusion of
styles. During the 1850's the design books of American builders included Swiss chalets, Oriental houses, Old English cottages, Norman
and Tudor mansions, with broken towers, peaked roofs, and orna-
mental gewgaws which showed what the new jigsaw could do.

Those who could afford pretentious houses increasingly preferred
the fanciful hodgepodges which architects called Gothic. So-called
Gothic detail, added everywhere, increased the artificiality of the
mode. The interiors, darkened by stained-glass windows and dark
woodwork, presented a bewildering array of inlaid tiles, fancy mantles,
fretted carvings, and bracketed shelves groaning under the weight of
bric-a-brac. Furniture was heavy, cumbersome, and highly ornate.
"Italian Gothic" public buildings, featuring varicolored stone and
terra-cotta decorations, also reflected the new enthusiasm.

To add to the confusion, a new style came in from the France of
Napoleon III. This was a fussy neoclassical style, used in scores of
public buildings, notably the State Department building in Washington. An elaborate Queen Anne's style also appeared, and there seemed
to be no end to the ransacking of Europe's past. The Philadelphia
Centennial Exposition of 1876 also introduced some Oriental styles.

In the next two decades, American builders continued to put emphasis on ugliness and discomfort. The poor in the growing cities
lived in miserable tenements; the lower middle classes inhabited
dreary rows of gloomy houses. The homes of those in better circumstances were more pretentious but far from beautiful. Nor were the
small towns and rural areas better. Prosperous farmers ruined fine old
simple-lined houses by adding turrets and gingerwork.

Yet many signs pointed to progress. The Philadelphia Centennial made Americans aware of the superiority of European designs in the decorative arts; and a movement set in to improve the quality of American consumers' goods. At the same time structural technique and standards of taste for public architecture and the residences of the rich were improved by two architects in the romantic tradition, Henry H. Richardson and Richard Morris Hunt.

Richard Morris Hunt (brother of William Morris Hunt, the artist) built a series of French Renaissance chateaux on Fifth Avenue and at the country seats of the well-to-do. Though showy and ill suited to the American environment, these chateaux were at least good imitations of the originals. Hunt also advanced the interests of his profession by founding the first American training center for architects and by helping to organize a professional association, the American Institute of Architects.

Hunt's prestige was rivaled by that of the European-trained Henry H. Richardson. Richardson revived the Romanesque form of southern France and Spain. His massive solid masonry structures with rounded arches had a certain dignity and beauty; and he dealt a blow to the Gothic revival. In his later years, Richardson put up office buildings in Boston, Chicago, and elsewhere, and moved toward the modern idea of adapting the form of a structure to its function.

Ultimately, the urban and industrial needs of the United States would necessitate the creation of a new American architectural style. One can trace the origins back to factory buildings erected before the Civil War. More important were the post-Civil War suspension bridges which made use of steel. The Roeblings, in building the Brooklyn Bridge, and James B. Eads, who bridged the Mississippi at St. Louis, made notable use of new materials. Another American innovation was the elevator, which made it possible to build tall structures in downtown districts where real-estate values were high.

Although American contributions were substantial, industrial architecture also owed much to Europe. The Crystal Palace Exhibition in London in 1851 showed how large areas of glass could be used in building. A decade later, a Frenchman devised a system of reinforcing steel with concrete.

Combining European and American discoveries, Americans produced the skyscraper. William LeBaron Jenney of Chicago led the way; and his ten-story Home Insurance Building (constructed in the 1880's) is generally regarded as the first skyscraper. Until this time builders had been unable to achieve height without using heavy walls. Jenney solved the problem by supporting walls and floor on a metal framework. Heavy walls were no longer necessary; all one needed to do was to cover the steel skeleton with a veneer of bricks or glass.

The possibilities of the new construction were best expressed by Louis Sullivan, a Chicago architect who worked for Jenney for a time. Since the new steel construction was truly revolutionary, Sullivan felt that it called for a revolutionary style of architecture. Form, said Sullivan, should follow and be determined by use. That is, the use of a building should be shown in its appearance. Sullivan developed his theory partly from Walt Whitman's democratic ideology, partly from Darwin's principle of adaptation to environment. And it was more than theory. Sullivan showed what he meant when he built the Wainwright Building in St. Louis and the Transportation Building at the Chicago World's Fair of 1893.

In the years to follow, the views of Sullivan would prevail. At the time, his was a minority voice. The governing committee for the Chicago World's Fair turned down his proposed scheme of functional architecture. It accepted rather a design submitted by McKim, Mead and White, three French-educated partners who were promoting a classical revival. As a result, classical influence would be strong on into the twentieth century; but in time Sullivan would be heard.

The Fine Arts: Music

The second half of the nineteenth century was marked by a rising level of musical competence in the United States and a growing appreciation of good music. This change would not have been possible without the help of music-loving immigrants, especially Germans. These newcomers taught piano. They organized singing societies, string quartets, and orchestras. They founded conservatories and manufactured instruments (making famous such names as Knabe and Steinway). The results were marked, especially in cities with large German communities—New York, for instance, Chicago, Cincinnati, Louisville, St. Louis, and Milwaukee.

Most important of the German immigrants was Theodore Thomas. Arriving in New York with his family in 1845, Thomas made his way against great odds. He gave one-man concerts in the South. He organized a New York orchestra and took it on tour. He directed the Cincinnati School of Music. He conducted the New York Philharmonic Society and the Opera. Finally, in the 1890's, he provided leadership for the Chicago Symphony Orchestra.

Leopold Damrosch was another European-born missionary of musical taste. Coming to the United States in 1871, he organized musical festivals and was conductor for the New York Symphony Society. In 1884 he successfully introduced German opera at the Metropolitan Opera House—the first challenge to the dominant Italian school. Leopold Damrosch's sons, Frank and Walter, carried on their father's work and were notably successful in introducing young Americans to good music.

The development of choral societies, symphony orchestras, and opera owed much to civic pride and to the interest and support of wealthy patrons. Opera furnishes an example. Introduced into New Orleans and New York before the Civil War, opera appealed both to music lovers and to "society." But it required large subsidies. These came in time from the urban rich; and by the 1880's New York's Metropolitan Opera gave promise of permanence. Boston patrons also supported opera, and the New York and Boston companies now and then went on tour, carrying opera to other major centers.

The rise of music education is also associated with the cities. Here the pioneer was Lowell Mason. A composer of hymns who began his musical career in Savannah, Georgia, Mason soon became interested in having music taught in the public schools. He was successful in Boston as early as the 1830's. Later, he advanced the cause of teacher training in the music field. Progress was rapid. By 1896 (a generation after Mason's death) many urban public schools and a fair number in smaller towns offered some sort of instruction in music.

In composition, too, there was some advance after 1850, and a great deal after 1890. A few Americans ventured into opera, and many composed orchestral and choral works. Some of the most successful were immigrants, like Dublin-born Victor Herbert, of light-opera fame. Most of the American-born composers did their chief work after securing training in Europe. Thus Ethelbert Nevin and Edward A. MacDowell, known for their art songs and piano pieces, studied in Germany.

American national characteristics were best revealed in popular music. The minstrel show, firmly established by 1850, continued to enjoy great popularity in succeeding decades. These traveling troubadours familiarized the people with Stephen Foster's sad, sweet songs, which remain popular to this day. And Daniel D. Emmett wrote "Dixie" for the minstrel stage.

The Civil War stimulated the writing of many famous songs. In the South, "Maryland, My Maryland" was a favorite, as was "The Bonnie Blue Flag." Meanwhile, Union composers produced the spirited "Battle Hymn of the Republic," and "Marching Through Georgia." The postwar years brought cowboy and immigrant songs, and songs of urban America.

By the 1890's the new urban tempo produced a sprightly type of song about Negroes oddly in contrast with the slow music of Stephen Foster. Such songs as Barney Fagan's "My Gal Is a High-Born Lady" heralded a new fashion for syncopated scores. Presently labeled "ragtime," this music embraced the whole of city life and pointed the way toward twentieth-century jazz.

As people change, so does their music. Stephen Foster, who died in 1864, had caught the spirit of an earlier, agrarian America with his "Oh, Susannah" and "My Old Kentucky Home." A mood of the changing, urbanized republic was reflected in such new songs as the one that C. B. Lawler brought out in 1894—"The Sidewalks of New York."

The Image of America Overseas

The United States had always interested those who lived in other lands. There had, however, been no single image or mental picture of the New World republic. The ruling classes of the Old World regarded the United States in one way. The liberal intellectuals and the plain people took quite a different view.

To kings and nobles, to great landowners and the higher clergy of the established churches, the United States meant defiance of authority and tradition. It presented a picture of lawlessness, of a crude and culturally mediocre democracy in which the rule of the masses debased standards and jeopardized morality and religion. What was more, emigration to America disturbed landlords and factory owners eager to keep a cheap labor supply, and clergymen who wished to keep their flocks intact. Consequently these groups joined government officials in discouraging emigration. One way of doing this was circulating stories about the misery and disappointments of poor folk who had chased the rainbow across the Atlantic.

Those hostile to America expressed their views in various ways. A German scholar lecturing in Vienna in 1828 blamed the spread of revolutionary ideas on the example of the United States. He warned European authorities that American influence was already endangering the *status quo*, and predicted a grave outcome if this influence were not checked. When visiting central Europe in the 1850's, a European-born American intellectual found men of culture speaking of the United States with contempt, as "a grand bedlam, a rendezvous of European scamps and vagabonds." In 1858 the King of the Two Sicilies imprisoned a University of Naples history professor for declaring in a lecture that George Washington was a great man whose example might be worth imitating. At about the same time a German university professor was arrested for substituting for a lecture on Denmark one on so dangerous a subject as the United States. In like fashion, French intellectuals who openly admired the liberal institutions of the United States met with government disfavor.

On the other hand, champions of liberalism, democracy, and reform regarded the United States with favor. They hailed the American nation as the successful example of a constitutional republic based on the will of the people. They hailed the American separation of church and state as a triumph of religious freedom. They applauded the victory of manhood suffrage in the United States, the abolition of imprisonment for debt, the establishment of free public schools, the rise of an organized labor movement. The Chartists in Great Britain appealed again and again to the American example in their efforts to win a greater measure of political and social democracy.

The revolutions of 1848 saw an upswing of American influence. The revolutionary governments temporarily in power in many European countries frankly adopted American principles of government in the constitutions they framed. The revolutionists also looked to the United States for sympathy and help. Sympathy they received, and even a little help from private persons and voluntary associations. And when the revolutions collapsed the United States opened its arms to refugees from European political reaction.

The American republic also welcomed official and private European missions which came to study United States commercial policies, internal improvements, and public schools. The American jury system influenced Norwegian practices, the American public library movement stimulated the adult education movement in Sweden. American prisons, based on the principle of reforming the criminal rather than merely penalizing him, exerted influence in several European countries.

Latin America was more closely tied to Europe than to the United States. Yet Latin-American liberals were often inspired by the example of the republic north of the Rio Grande. United States success in overthrowing a transatlantic overlord encouraged Latin-American leaders who wanted to win freedom from Spain. Patriotic merchants from the United States scattered copies of the Declaration of Independence and the Constitution in Latin-American ports. Although it would be easy to overemphasize the American influence on the federal system of Mexico, Colombia, and Argentina, these countries all owed something to the example of their northern neighbor. A leading Argentine reformer and statesman, Domingo Sarmiento, modeled his country's public school system on that of the United States.

The plain people of Europe shared the enthusiasm of liberal intellectuals for America. Many talked of the possibility of migrating to the new land. They read and listened eagerly to letters from relatives who had already crossed the Atlantic. These letters told of high standards of living, of good wages, of cheap and fertile land. They told, too, of the relative social equality that prevailed in many parts of the United States.

The letters home did much to influence European views of the United States. "Now for the first time I am able to breathe freely," wrote a Norwegian who had migrated to America in 1837. "No restrictions are set upon freedom of occupation; and every one secures without hindrance the fruits of his own work and by wise and liberal legislation the American citizen is made secure from the assaults of oppressors." An American who visited Europe in 1853 found that the United States was "the ideal world to the peasantry of Europe . . . the Eldorado, the land of golden plenty, where every man can have a home of his own, and leave his children comfortable when he dies."

When the Civil War broke out in 1861, most European liberals took the side of the Union. Conservatives, by contrast, rejoiced at the breakup of the American republic. They called this proof of the "fundamental weakness" of republican and democratic institutions. They made no secret of their sympathy for the Confederacy, based as it was on slavery and a landed aristocracy. And when Union agents appeared to recruit immigrants to replace workers who had gone into military service, the established classes sourly insisted that immigrants would be sucked into the army and come to a bad end.

The final victory of the North confounded conservative Europe as it justified the faith of liberal leaders and of the plain people in the Union. And the triumph of arms, together with the obvious strength of American industry, compelled European conservatives to admit that the New World experiment could no longer be laughed out of court. At the same time, government officials, clergymen, landed aristocrats, and industrialists kept on discouraging emigration by belittling America, pointing to the chaos of Reconstruction, the race problem, the recurrent depressions, and the backwardness of social legislation.

Liberals continued to praise the United States. The abolition of slavery removed an institution that had long troubled European admirers of America. Henry Thoreau, Ralph Waldo Emerson, and Walt Whitman kindled enthusiastic admiration in the democratic poets and writers of the Old World. Such literary figures as Ibsen and

Gorky found inspiration in American democracy. Henry George, the American champion of land reform, and the socialist novelist Edward Bellamy enjoyed an enviable reputation in Europe. Karl Marx and Frederick Engels incorporated into their socialist theories examples taken from the writings of the American ethnologist Henry Lewis Morgan. Later the American device of commissions to fix the rates of public carriers and to control the practices of corporations found favor in Great Britain.

Even so, European liberals and radicals were disappointed in certain American trends. They deplored the American abandonment of the low-tariff policy after 1861. They expressed alarm at the evidences of growing inequalities in the distribution of wealth in the United States, at the rise of the gigantic trusts, at the virtual disappearance of cheap land, at the sluggishness of the movement for social legislation in the interest of industrial workers. American expansion overseas in the 1890's convinced many Europeans that the United States was following Old World paths of empire. And Latin Americans, long suspicious of United States diplomacy, spoke of the "Yankee peril."

These misgivings of liberal intellectuals did not change the image of America cherished by Europe's common people. To millions of emigrants and potential emigrants the United States continued to seem a land of incredible opportunities. Steamship companies and railroad agents, anxious to sell tickets or land, spread this picture throughout Europe. To many America meant economic advancement. Others thought in terms of religious freedom, exemption from compulsory military service, educational opportunities for their children.

Remittances from immigrants to relatives in the Old World gave credence to such views. (In 1907 Italian immigrants sent $85,000,000 to the folks back home.) The same impression was conveyed when immigrants returned to their native villages with good clothes and spending money. American philanthropy further reinforced the image of the United States as a land of milk and honey. For Americans poured money into Europe when there were famines in Ireland in the 1840's and in Russia five decades later.

Meantime other images of America were developing. These were

associated with American economic growth. For one thing, the opening of the last frontiers and the use of new machinery increased agricultural production in the United States. This meant sharp competition for the grain- and cattle-producing countries of Europe. Some
met the competition by shifting from cereals to livestock. This in
turn sent many farm workers to the cities, for cattle required fewer
hands than did grain culture. Other countries, beginning with Germany in 1879, erected tariff barriers and used other devices to keep
out American farm products, especially meat.

As the United States became industrialized, Europe began to feel
competition from American factories as well as American farms. By
the 1880's European manufacturers were clamoring for tariffs to protect their home markets. At the same time these industrialists complained of the difficulty of meeting the competition of mass-
manufactured American goods in the markets of the world.

European industrialists recognized the many advantages of their
American competitors: a great home market in the United States;
rich farmlands; abundant resources of coal, iron, and copper. Old
World observers also noted that Americans had great technical skill
or "know-how." American exhibits at world's fairs made it clear
that the United States had gone far in developing labor-saving devices, in the mass production principle, and in the use of interchangeable parts for machines.

Interested in American methods, London engineers listened atten-
tively to the Connecticut firearms manufacturer Samuel Colt in 1853.
A year later the British Board of Ordnance sent a committee to visit
Colt's factory. This group recommended that Britain order a full set
of American machines for the making of small arms, and import
American workers to set up and demonstrate the use of the machines.
And other Old World governments lost no time in soliciting Colt's
services.

During these same years a British parliamentary commission studied
American manufacturing establishments in an effort to discover the
secrets of American success. The committee reported that the Yankees
put great faith in the adaptation of tools and machines to the specific
purpose at hand. The investigators found that Americans were con-

tinually experimenting in order to improve methods of production. Furthermore, many American employers gave attention to the comfort of workers and to the satisfaction that high wages brought.

American technology excited criticism as well as admiration. Europeans rightly noted that the United States neglected basic research. They claimed that the New World put a premium on quantity rather than on quality. But the more perceptive industrialists, alarmed at the American threat to their markets, saw the necessity of changing their methods to meet the competition. "The American invasion of Europe" and "the Americanization of Europe" were terms heard even before the American demonstration of industrial power in World War I.

Thus by 1900 the United States had begun to export, not only liberal ideas and farm surpluses, but also industrial goods and tech- image of industrial and

Farming in the Industrial Age

Farmers and Factories

How did the farmer fare in the industrial age? There had been difficulties even in the era of agrarian predominance. The farmer had profited from the American Revolution, only to lose in the ensuing peace. His enterprises had boomed again during the wars of the French Revolution and Napoleon, then had languished after 1815. The ups and downs continued as the nation moved into the years of industrial power. Farmers prospered in the 1850's, then ran into depression after the Civil War.

But the difficulties after 1865 were more than routine. The period of depression was unusually long, running from the mid-1860's nearly to the end of the century. At the same time it was becoming apparent that the American economy now centered around the factory rather than the farm. The farmer would have to make his way in a machine age.

It was no easy way. Discouraged about prospects, many young people moved to the city. Others continued the struggle on the farm. To meet the changed conditions, they became more businesslike, mechanized their farms, used scientific methods, and organized economically and politically into special-interest groups.

Many Farmers, Many Problems

The "farm problem" is generally described in terms of the agricultural group that is hardest pressed or most vociferous. Actually, there have been many contrasting farm problems in every period of American history. In the latter half of the nineteenth century the difficulties of the prairie farmers, who were less than a quarter of the nation's agriculturalists, held the center of the stage. But the tenth who lived in New England and the Middle states, and the half who farmed in the old South also had serious problems.

New England farmers could no longer compete commercially with Westerners in producing grain, beef cattle, sheep, and hogs. To make a decent living, the New Englanders had to supply chickens and eggs, milk and fresh vegetables to nearby urban centers. The change from wheat and corn was anything but simple. It took money to buy dairy cows. Truck gardening called for new techniques and hazardous experimentation. Chicken raising was arduous, uncertain, and generally despised as "women's work." Hence many New Englanders abandoned agriculture. From 1850 to 1900 improved acreage in the section fell by more than a third.

Although farmers of the Middle states had similar problems, they had certain advantages. Their better soils, climate, and terrain and their superior agricultural traditions enabled them to compete successfully with the West in some crops. They were also able to develop profitable specialties, such as fattening western beef cattle for market. New York and Pennsylvania remained the leading producers of rye, and New York led in potatoes and wine making. But, save for local use, the production of wheat and corn became unprofitable.

The Pacific coast states had a special problem of distance. They could produce out-of-season fruits and vegetables that might command high prices in Chicago and New York. It took time, however, to overcome the transportation and marketing obstacles. Only in the 1890's did transcontinental freight become cheap and fast enough to enable west coast shippers to invade eastern markets.

Transportation was also the major problem of the cattle and sheep ranchers of the West. They, too, had products much demanded in the East—and in Europe as well. Their fortunes suffered, though, until there was a satisfactory rail network in the area from Texas to Montana. When the railroads came (in the 1870's) the range enjoyed some years of real prosperity. But here too there were problems. Argentine competition and European tariffs and prohibitions cut into foreign sales. Blizzards, droughts, and locusts caused heavy losses. Freight rates were high; the land laws left much to be desired. And by the 1880's wheat farmers were invading the cattle kingdom.

Southern Agriculture

It was the South that presented the major farm problem. Down to 1900 half the nation's tillers of the soil were located south of the Mason-Dixon line. The difficulties of these southern farmers were part of the pattern that produced the Civil War. The war and Reconstruction brought changes without providing satisfactory solutions; and southern agriculture remained in a state of depression. Southern farm regions had a higher percentage of tenants (mostly sharecroppers),[1] a lower standard of living, and less immediate prospect of improvement than agricultural areas elsewhere.

Southern agriculture centered around the production of staples: tobacco, rice, sugar, and (especially) cotton. But subsistence farming held on, too. Hill people kept on trying to scratch a living from their submarginal land. They suffered nearly all the woes of their ancestors, and more besides, for the woodlands no longer contained the game that had helped support the early settlers.

Before and after the Civil War, tobacco planting was concentrated in the border states of Virginia, North Carolina, and Kentucky. Rice and sugar cultivation took a sharp dip downward in the Civil War years. Southern sugar production did not reach the prewar level until the 1890's; and in that decade sugar beets (grown in such northern and western states as Michigan, Colorado, and Utah) became more important than Louisiana cane. Meantime, the center of rice production shifted from the Southeast to the Southwest, from South Carolina and Georgia to Texas and Arkansas. The great southern crop, cotton, also moved westward across the Mississippi, and Texas in time became the leading cotton state. But by using fertilizer, the Southeast also kept in competition.

Cotton production reached the prewar level before the end of the

---

[1] Under the sharecrop system, the owner provided the land, the tenant's cabin, and, perhaps, the farm equipment, livestock, and seed. The sharecropper supplied the labor. At the end of the season, the crop was split into shares. The tenant received a third or more, the amount varying with the area, the time, and the extent of the sharecropper's contribution. (He received more, of course, if he had his own livestock and farm equipment.)

1870's. Thereafter it soared far beyond the slave-day totals. The product found a ready market in England and in the textile factories of New England and the South. This, however, did not spell prosperity for the cotton belt. World prices were low because of high production in the United States and competition from Egypt, India, and other cheap-labor areas. Unlike the wheat farmers, the cotton growers did not cut costs by using new machines. Nor did they diversify crops. That might have helped; but creditors called for a cash crop, and the sharecroppers lacked the education and the incentive to produce a change.

In the days before secession, seven-eighths of the cotton crop was produced by Negro slave labor. Whites accounted for a higher proportion after emancipation, especially in the newly opened lands west of the Mississippi. But whether whites or Negroes were involved, the plantation system persisted. To be sure, there were more individually owned small cotton farms than there had been before the Civil War (and a fair number of these units were owned by Negroes). Even so, the large landowning unit was the rule in many areas. The owner cut his land into small pieces, these being assigned to Negro or white sharecroppers. Borrowing from the owner, and buying at the owner's store, these tenants quickly slipped into debt servitude. And the owner, too, was a debtor, pressed for payment on his mortgage or his bank loans.

Southern agricultural distress had many aspects. The states south of the Mason-Dixon line had suffered heavily in the Civil War. Lack of capital remained critical, as in the days before secession. Also troublesome was the fact that cotton prices continued to be set in the world market. No less important was the South's lack of political influence. And after 1892, the cotton country was invaded by a new enemy, the boll weevil.

On top of all these handicaps, the South has a race problem. Some southern whites contended that the southern states had "settled" the Negro question after Reconstruction, by establishing "white supremacy" and adopting the segregation system. Under this system, Negroes were denied the vote and had separate—and inferior—accommodations in the schools, on the trains, and in theaters and churches. Deprived of equal economic opportunity, the Negro had little incentive to build a better South. And many white men, concentrating on "control" of the Negro, also failed to give adequate attention to the economic improvement of their section.

The Prairie Farmer

Although much of the acreage of the twelve North Central states is not prairie land, most farmers from Ohio to Nebraska shared the problems of the prairie farmer. That is, they raised wheat or corn-and-hogs for sale in distant markets. Generalizations, however, are difficult, for there were many contrasts. While eighty-acre wheat growers were eking out a bare existence in Dakota Territory, their neighbor Oliver Dalrymple was clearing $200,000 a year on his 100,000 acres in the Red River Valley. Well-located Iowa producers of corn and hogs built considerable fortunes while mid-Kansas farmers were ruined by drought.

From the 1840's on, cheap transportation by rail and water opened world markets to American grain producers. Wheat was second only to cotton among American agricultural exports, and pork products (representing corn) ranked third. On the one hand, this export business allowed American cotton, wheat, and corn producers to expand their operations with little fear of permanent overproduction. On the other hand, the situation geared United States agriculture to world price movements and destroyed the possibility of gain from a protective tariff.

Save for the price recession immediately after the Civil War, returns were generally good until about 1883. Thereafter Kansas, Nebraska, and Dakota farmers suffered from severe winters and from summer droughts, and all American agriculturalists encountered increased world competition and declining prices. Fortunately, production costs fell, too. Machinery increased the efficiency of the wheat farmer. So did the increasing size of prairie farms, and in the 1890's a bushel of wheat could be produced for half the dollar cost of 1850. Machinery effected a nearly equivalent saving for corn. But mechanization and the need for large-scale production made grain farming a more complicated business, that tended to squeeze out the small operator.

Free Enterprise in Land

Those desiring to launch new farming ventures faced an initial business problem in buying land. At one time the bulk of the land west of the Appalachians had belonged to the federal government. Much remained unsettled in 1850. Theoretically, a private individual might "squat" on land not open for sale. He might then be able to preëmpt it under the law of 1841—that is, buy it for the standard price of $1.25 or $2.50 an acre. Or, after 1862, the settler might acquire his farm free under the Homestead Act. In reality, however, the government's land-grant policy made squatting dangerous after 1850, and it was difficult to find homestead land that was both fertile and well located.

The difficulties increased each decade. When the United States government granted land to railroad companies, the areas adjacent to the new routes were withdrawn from preëmption and homesteading. Other grants to states, and the sale of Indian, timber, stone, and mineral lands removed enormous tracts from the operation of laws designed to aid the small farmer.

As in earlier days, the chief economic flaw in the government's sale policy was the fact that most commercially usable land was worth more than the government maximum ($2.50 an acre). It therefore paid corporations and wealthy individuals to buy land for investment. These purchasers could operate ahead of the small settler. Thus the settler could neither homestead the better land nor use preëmption to purchase it at the government price. Instead he had to buy from the private owner.

Homesteading, then, was not of major importance in the settlement of the West. In the three decades after 1862 only about 10 percent of the new farms were acquired under the five-year-residence provisions of the Homestead law. Most farms were bought from individual or corporate landlords, many of whom had been connected with the land-grant railroads. These were the men who knew where the railroads were to go, and their consciences would have condemned them had they not profited accordingly.

It is possible, however, to overstate the evils of railroad and corporation sales policies. The western migrant needed more than land.

He needed protection from Indians, from claim jumpers, and from corrupt public land office officials. He needed transportation and credit. Railroads could supply all of these along with land (the land selling at an average price just over $4.00 an acre). Some railroad agencies also gave agricultural advice to newcomers, extended credit at less than the prevailing local rate, and aided farmers when crops failed. The railroad, of course, hoped to take a good share of the farmer's profit through local freight rates. But that very interest in profits made the railroad interested in attracting farmers to their route and having those farmers produce large crops.

As lands were taken up, settlers pushed farther into the interior. By 1850 the westward movement had built up the first tier of states west of the Mississippi; and a few settlers had located along the Pacific coast. In the four decades that followed, the lines of settlement pushed westward from the Mississippi and eastward from the Pacific. By 1890 these two movements had joined, and the census taken in that year showed that there was no longer any continuous frontier line. There was unsettled land, but it was in isolated patches rather than in one big bloc of western territory.

The passing of the frontier would mean a good deal to American farmers. Down to 1890 the ambitious and the dissatisfied could go west. Speculators and railroad companies, Indians, the climate, and the government might make the going rough. But if he persisted, the western migrant could become established and have a farm of his own. After 1890 the old opportunities gradually passed away. No longer could farmers hope to improve their lot by going west. Instead they had to move to the city, or tackle and try to solve their problems where they were.

The Problem of Transportation

Of these problems, none was more serious than that of transportation. As farmers took up land 1500 miles from eastern markets, transportation inevitably became the most important single cost. The government's land-grant policies aggravated the difficulties. By encouraging railroads to build straight west, the government needlessly dispersed population. Grain farmers were

lured by cheap land adjacent to railroads into areas that might better
have been left to sheep and cattle. Once there, they found their profits
eaten up by high freight rates.

Complaints over transportation costs were not confined to the
remote West. From California to Ohio, from Idaho to Florida farmers cried out against high rates. It is hard to tell how much more the
farmer paid than was necessary to maintain rail service. On the short
haul from local shipping points to the nearest primary grain market
most farmers paid high noncompetitive rates. On the long haul from
such primary markets as Minneapolis and Chicago to the East or
Europe the rates barely covered railroad and steamship operating expenses. Farmers could not calculate the exact benefit they derived
from the cheap long haul. They were well aware, however, of the adverse economic effects of the local rates. These were especially burdensome in a period of falling prices; and after 1865 the railroads became
the prime target of those interested in agrarian reform.

Machines, Land, and Credit

In the eastern and southern United
States, farmers used little machinery. In 1850 and for some years
thereafter plows, hoes, rakes, and hand cultivators were the standard
equipment. The threshing was done by portable machines, moved
from farm to farm. It was quite different on the prairies. There large-
scale operations were essential; there the mechanized farm became a
reality.

Mechanization meant that the farmer had to understand machinery
and keep it in repair. He had to select the best types for his farm in
the face of conflicting arguments by competing salesmen. He found,
too, that one cost led to another. In addition to the expensive machines, he needed horses or mules to pull the equipment, and a large
acreage to make efficient use of his mechanized power.

Most farmers embarking on new ventures had to secure credit. This
meant buying land or equipment on time, or securing credit at a store.
To move their crops to market, farmers also had to obtain bank loans.
Some mortgaged their farms. This, however, was less common than
it is today, and in many sections few farms were mortgaged.

Down to 1880 it was fairly hard to borrow money on farm mortgages; and the lender was likely to prefer a short term. Then, in the
early 1880's, financiers found that they could interest eastern investors
in long-term farm mortgages. For half a dozen years prairie farmers
were literally coaxed into borrowing money. Although the rates of 8
to 10 percent seem high at present, they were in accord with those
which established western merchants paid for bank loans.

Drought hit the West just as this boom reached its peak. Thousands
of the mortgages were foreclosed, and both the farmer and the investor suffered heavily. The supply of eastern funds dried up overnight. This cycle, however, left its mark upon the West—built a
suspicion of eastern money men that influenced political as well as
economic trends.

Despite all difficulties, those who owned western and southern
farms remained optimistic about the future. If one could hold on,
there was every reason to believe that his land would appreciate in
value. Hence even if a farmer màde little profit from his operations,
he would be reasonably well off when he reached middle age.

The rise in land values was of course a great incentive to land
speculation. Much of the best land in the Mississippi Valley, therefore, came to be held by absentee landlords who would rent, but not
sell. In fact, the richest soils were the most likely to be farmed by
tenants. In central Illinois and in the highly productive Mississippi
Delta country the percentage of farms operated by tenants was very
high. By contrast, the percentage of tenants was low in the southern
hill country, and in the poorer regions of the Dakotas, where land
values were less certain.

In the country as a whole, tenancy rose rapidly after 1865. After a
few southern landowners had experimented with hired labor, there
was a general shift to sharecrop tenancy. Owners put tenants on the
old plantations and also on the newly opened lands in the Southwest.
In the upper Mississippi Valley, weak and speculative farmers went
down the line to tenancy when they were broken by floods and
droughts and price declines. Farm hands and newly arrived immigrants
also became tenants on farms held by banks and insurance companies
and individuals. Farmers' sons, who in earlier generations would have

gone west, now started out as tenants. Many would remain in that relationship for their whole lives.

Some tenants fared extremely well. A few in the corn and wheat country became wealthy. As a rule, however, tenants did less well than did owners. And as the years went by it was increasingly difficult to move up to ownership. Farms cost more than they had before. The new commercial agriculture also required costly equipment. Many tenants, consequently, never found it possible to move into the owner class.

The Farmer and the Market

The new commercial agriculture presented many marketing problems. Tobacco and cotton, fruits and vegetables, butter and cheese, hogs and cattle, corn and wheat all needed special handling. Wheat will serve for illustration. The basic difficulty was that in each locality the many hundred farmers had to sell through a handful of grain dealers. The dealers could, and sometimes did, combine in setting prices. A farmer could buck the combination by shipping to some central elevator (storage company). But that took cash and required time. Most farmers could not afford to wait, for they had borrowed their working capital for harvesting expenses on short-term notes from local banks.

Besides the dealers, the railroads, elevators and millers made profits from handling the farmer's grain. (The farmer, in fact, received less than 20 percent of the price the consumer paid for grain products.) Where competition was not strong, local dealers made good profits. The railroad's share varied according to locality. Strategically located elevators yielded satisfactory returns, though the abler railroad executives rated storage companies as poor investments. The broker's fees were set by law. But the farmer appeared to be the one man in the chain who had no direct control over price. In consequence, he suffered.

Seeking a Way Out

American farmers had inherited a pattern of exploiting soils, in contrast to the European peasant tradition of intensive cultivation. The American method had originally been encouraged by the cheapness of land, so that even subsistence farming had been wasteful. As western farmers joined Southerners in raising money crops, the tendency was to farm anywhere and in any way that would bring cash profits. Such a motivation led sooner or later to soil exhaustion.

In general, American farmers avoided the laborious tasks associated with intensive farming as inconsistent with high living standards. This explains, for example, why Italian and Polish immigrants replaced Yankees in eastern truck farming. Among older settlers only a few groups were willing to take the pains to farm in a careful and efficient manner. The Pennsylvania Germans were successful in Pennsylvania, Iowa, and Alabama partly because (unlike most Americans) they were devoted to farming as a way of life. In addition, close religious bonds provided morale and solidarity. Religion was also a vital factor in the Mormon communities, where organization brought agricultural success even in the semiarid lands of the Rocky Mountain area.

These groups were highly exceptional in nineteenth-century America. The average farmer was isolated and individualistic. In normal times he was content to go his own way. On occasion, though, crises forced him to modify his attitude.

Such a crisis came in the 1870's and 1880's, a period of acute distress for many American farmers. Seeking a solution, some sold out and moved to town. Others imitated their ancestors by going west. But this took them to the western plains, where they encountered thin soils and an unreliable climate.

There were other possibilities: improving agricultural techniques, coöperating in joint business ventures, entering politics to secure favorable legislation. In adopting these approaches, farmers were simply following the lead of big businessmen. The latter, by the 1870's, were already using improved technology, were coöperating effectively, and were active in politics in their own interest.

Even with farmers these procedures were not altogether new. "Scientific farming" had been tried before 1860; and southern planters had defended their interests by political action. Their defeat in battle during the Civil War was a definite setback for agrarianism. When farmers once more sought favorable legislation after 1870, they had in a sense to start all over again. And this time they found themselves opposed by business interests that had become more powerful than ever before.

Coöperatives

The first post-Civil War attempt of farmers to combine came through the Granges. These were at first secret societies, similar to other bodies which Americans liked to join, and intended to provide more social life for lonely families. The Patrons of Husbandry, launched in 1867 and commonly called the Grange, was a national organization tying together such local groups. Hard times after the panic of 1873 increased membership to more than 2,000,000 and drove the Grangers to consider plans of action. Businessmen were arranging to stop cutthroat competition. Why, then, could farmers not do likewise? The laissez-faire system of production and marketing was clearly operating to the disadvantage of those on the soil.

Moved by such considerations, some Grangers set up coöperative banks and insurance companies to relieve credit shortages and to provide lower premiums and interest charges. To reduce the cost of tariff-protected manufactured goods, the Grangers organized coöperative stores and farm-equipment factories. They also established coöperative marketing agencies that shipped wheat directly to Chicago or Liverpool, in an effort to eliminate middlemen's profits and the charges of monopolistic elevators.

Unfortunately for the farmers, most of these ventures failed. Coöperative stores and factories, usually unable to secure bank loans, shut down for lack of working capital. Discriminatory freight rates made it difficult for coöperative marketing bodies to compete with private grain elevators. Defeated in politics, too, the Grangers went back to their old role of social organizations.

New farm organizations appeared when price decline and drought on the western plains made distress even more acute in the 1880's. Chief among the new groups were the Southern Alliance and the Northwestern Alliance. The latter alone had over a million members. Like the Granges, these bodies cultivated social life among farmers, then tried coöperative enterprises, and finally moved into politics (as the Populists). But their business ventures, like those of the Grangers, usually failed for lack of capital and effective business direction.

The business failures were not surprising. It was difficult for isolated farmers to coöperate. Even when they did combine, inexperience and the lack of capital made defeat almost certain. And such chances as there were for success faded before the opposition of active and experienced business groups.

Mechanization and Irrigation

More successful than the business experiments were the efforts of farmers to improve their techniques. Scientific farming was too complex and mechanization too expensive for many of the farmers who most needed help. Yet improved methods did enable some agriculturalists to hold their own in the competitive process.

The reaper appeared just in time to replace the labor lost to military service during the Civil War. Harvesters, binders, and other machines were introduced during the next generation. These machines worked best in level areas and were most economical on large farms. Mechanization therefore made the greatest progress in the corn and wheat empires of the Middle West. In those regions some tried to push mechanization even further, by using steam tractors to pull the new machines. But since steam engines were clumsy and expensive, most farmers continued to rely on horse power.

Mechanization made less progress in the South and East. Most New England farms were too small or stony for machines to be used with profit; and no devices were invented to revolutionize cotton and tobacco planting. Only recently has a mechanical cotton picker been developed. And even now, most cotton and tobacco is harvested by hand.

Where agricultural machinery was available, it was not always used. The advantages had to be calculated against the cost. If costs were high, a group of farmers might get together to buy one machine. This, however, involved the usual difficulties in securing coöperation.

The same problem existed in connection with irrigation. The need for irrigation projects became apparent when semiarid western regions were opened to settlement. Here the quality of soils was often high, but there was no chance of getting enough water through rainfall.

The Mormons were the first to show the possibilities of large-scale irrigation, in their remarkable cultivation of desert areas in Utah after 1850. Then Congress passed the Desert Land Act of 1877. This provided for the sale of arid lands at bargain prices to persons who would launch irrigation projects. Although 50,000 irrigators filed for land under this statute, the results were far from satisfactory. For one thing, it was difficult for individuals to finance irrigation projects. For another, the act was unpopular because it prevented purchasers from getting title until they had actually brought in water.

In 1894, therefore, Congress offered land to states that would irrigate a portion of any area settled. Colorado, Nevada, Wyoming, and other mountain states accepted the terms, then arranged for private companies to build irrigation works and lease water rights to settlers. During the next two decades, settlers applied for over 7,000,000 acres under this arrangement. Yet less than half a million acres were actually reclaimed. Private companies did not rush into the irrigation field, perhaps because of the uncertainty of returns. Those concerns that did operate had trouble apportioning water and securing payment from land owners.

The farmer, on his part, found it hard to add the high cost of water to the usual expenses of cultivation. Apparently the problems of irrigation were too great to be solved by private initiative. Mormons could succeed because their religious discipline made possible unusual cooperation. But the majority of settlers had little solidarity, and some outside organization was needed to provide them with water at a lower cost than private companies required. Government assistance, however, was not made available until after 1900.

Science and Agriculture

Irrigation and mechanization involved the application of technology to agriculture. Equally important were the contributions of chemistry and biology. In the early nineteenth century, "scientific farming" meant little more than careful trial-and-error experimentation by individual farmers. By the end of the century, however, it became possible to apply certain scientific principles to farm processes. Since these applications were of a technical nature, they were rarely developed by the farmers themselves. Rather they were the discoveries of a new professional group of agricultural scientists.

The rise of these scientists was connected with the establishment of the federal Department of Agriculture in 1862 (elevated to cabinet rank in 1889). The Morrill Act of 1862 provided land grants to states for the support of agricultural and mechanical (A & M) colleges. The faculties of these new agricultural colleges devoted much attention to the use of basic principles in farming. After 1890 Congress provided annual subsidies for the land-grant schools. Three years before, in the Hatch Act, Congress had begun to subsidize state experiment stations devoted to agricultural research. These stations coöperated with the agricultural colleges and with the United States Department of Agriculture; and in time the combined efforts did much to increase the total output of American farms.

Nor was this all. State appropriations advanced the work launched by the federal government; and private agencies coöperated actively. Wisconsin furnishes an excellent example. In the days before the Civil War, this state had specialized in grain production. When states further west began growing wheat, Wisconsin suffered. Looking for a way out, many of the state's farmers shifted to dairy farming. Research at the state land-grant college (the University of Wisconsin) helped make the transformation profitable. Short courses at the university familiarized farmers with improved techniques. *Hoard's Dairyman*, a privately-owned farm journal, also spread the word; and a state dairymen's association located markets, publicized Wisconsin cheese, and otherwise supported this agricultural revolution.

Since agriculture was an applied science, various specialties arose which did not entirely coincide with the usual divisions of basic science. "Soil science" involved not only soil chemistry but also biology and geology. Much was learned about the various types and levels of soils, and their potentialities in relation to different crops and fertilizers. All these variables had to be considered in the apparently simple matter of selecting a particular crop for given land, and of the most effective treatment of this land in cultivation. This was a far more effective way of dealing with actual problems than the old trial-and-error methods of the dirt farmer.

There remained many practical matters which called simply for intelligent observation and common sense. The old difficulties with erosion, for example, could be met by more careful handling of the land —by terracing or by contour plowing. Even here, however, science came into play. Erosion on a large scale through floods or dust storms was traced to wasteful deforestation upstream, or to the wide destruction of binding grasses. The forests and grasses had to be preserved over large areas if the soils of individual farms were to be saved; and this called for the expert knowledge of botanists and foresters.

Botanists and geneticists also began to serve agriculture. When soil or climate made it difficult to raise a common cereal in a certain region, botanists sought varieties more adaptable to the particular circumstances of the area. Geneticists would later produce strains of hybrid corn which resisted adverse conditions and greatly increased yield. Biologists who specialized in insects (entomologists) and those who dealt with vegetable molds and fungi were called in to study the life of pests so as to suggest means of eradicating them. The study of plant diseases assumed increasing importance.

Animal husbandry benefited from science in much the same manner. Geneticists improved livestock by careful breeding. Many of the advances made in human medicine were applicable to veterinary medicine. Training schools in this field were established at A & M colleges and state universities, in close association with animal husbandry departments. Here, too, entomologists were needed, for animal as well as human diseases are spread by insect vectors.

Farm boys who studied at the new agricultural and veterinary colleges encountered all these scientific approaches to farming. But change came slowly. Old-time farmers distrusted "newfangled" methods, calling them impractical. In this they resembled the conservative industrialists who still doubted the advisability of bringing scientific research into their factories.

The older farmers also feared that scientific training would make their sons give up dirt farming to become teachers and experts. This did happen in many cases. What was more, graduates of agricultural colleges sometimes found it difficult to apply general principles to the operation of small farms. But it was plain that by 1900 applied science was moving into agriculture, just as it was moving into industry.

The Farmer Turns to Politics

In the long run, science would provide the answer to many American farm problems. Humans, however, live in the short run. The debt-ridden farmer of the late nineteenth century was not convinced that science would help him out of his predicament. Scientific farming would, in fact, call for a larger cash outlay. Coöperatives also failed to take care of the farmer's needs; and migration west offered less than in earlier periods. The farmer therefore turned to politics, hoped to find in government action some way of improving his situation.

Agriculturalists had done this many times before. The Jefferson and Jackson movements had been made possible by a union of western and southern farmers, coöperating with some city workers. Might not these triumphs be repeated?

Some thought they could. But there were major difficulties. To begin with, the United States was no longer predominantly agrarian. Hence national success depended on efficient organization, which was not easy to obtain. For the sectional conflict had shattered the old Jeffersonian and Jacksonian combination of western and southern farmers. After 1865 most western farmers were Republicans, and most southern rural voters were Democrats. Split between the major parties, and unable to control either, the farmers had a dim outlook.

During the 1860's the Republicans made a determined bid for the farm vote. Lincoln and others attracted western agrarians by talking of the Republican party as the party of the Union and by passing laws popular with rural voters: the Homestead and Morrill Land-Grant laws, legislation to build transcontinental railroads, the act establishing a Department of Agriculture. At the end of the Civil War, Lincoln planned to add southern farmers to his organization, by appealing to Negro agriculturalists and the poorer southern whites. This, though, did not work. Sectional hatred, race conflict, and various political accidents kept the Republican party feeble in the South. And, though the Republicans held the midwest farmers, the party was obviously run by urban leaders.

Meantime, the Democrats were tackling the problem. Assured of the southern rural vote, they sought farm backing elsewhere. Their most effective leader was George H. Pendleton, whose Ohio Idea called for payment of most of the Union debt in unsupported paper currency (greenbacks). This plan was designed to appeal to western farmers. First, it involved an attack on eastern bondholders, long unpopular with rural citizens. Second, the plan called for some inflation of the currency. This would raise farm prices, giving farmers more cash with which to pay debts or buy equipment or additional land. By endorsing this program, the Democratic national convention of 1868 made a definite bid for rural votes.

The Democrats, however, did not follow through. Instead of nominating Pendleton for President, they chose Horatio Seymour, a New York man who definitely disapproved of inflationary schemes. And Democratic leadership, like that of the Republicans, was overwhelmingly urban. In six of the seven presidential campaigns from 1868 to 1892 the Democrats picked a New Yorker to head their ticket.

Grangers and Greenbackers

Unable to control either major national party, the farmers tried other methods. The most effective was operation on a local or sectional basis. Thus the Grangers, active in the Middle West in the 1870's, centered their attention on the states rather than entering the national arena.

For a time the Grangers were quite successful. Focusing their political efforts on the transportation question, they forced seven state legislatures to adopt regulatory legislation. The Granger laws regulated the rates charged by railroads and grain elevators, prohibited pools, rebates, and other monopolistic devices, restricted the granting of passes (which the railroads had used to influence politicians). The farmers behind the movement were encouraged when the United States Supreme Court called Granger legislation constitutional

(Munn *vs.* Illinois, and Peik *vs.* Chicago and Northwestern Railway, 1876).

Then came reverses, ending in the collapse of the Granger movement by 1880. An improvement in economic conditions temporarily took the edge off farmers' grievances. Meantime, lack of experience had caused the Grangers to make serious blunders in their political and business affairs. Regulation proved less effective than had been anticipated, partly because transportation problems went beyond the confines of any single state. The railroads, fighting hard, had secured repeal of many Granger laws even before the United States Supreme Court declared that most Granger legislation was unconstitutional (Wabash case of 1886, on the ground that the states could not regulate rates on interstate carriers).

Some farmers went from the Granger movement to the Greenback party, which ran presidential candidates from 1876 to 1884. The Greenbackers made an interesting but unsuccessful effort to form a farmer-labor party on a national scale. Their appeal to rural voters centered around their demand for inflation, which would increase farm income. In addition, they reflected Granger interest in transportation problems; but instead of concentrating on the states, they asked for Congressional regulation of the railroads.

There were several reasons for the failure of the Greenbackers. They entered national politics before they had enough effective local machines. In any case, it was difficult to buck the major parties. And the Greenbackers made two strange presidential nominations, picking an industrialist, Peter Cooper, in 1876, and an unpredictable professional politician, Benjamin F. Butler, eight years later. General James B. Weaver of Iowa, the 1880 nominee, was a happier choice. Weaver polled a respectable vote in the Middle West. But the General could not achieve a farmer-labor alliance; as an agrarian, he won little backing among workingmen.

That, in fact, was a key to the whole situation. Like the farmers, the city workingmen opposed monopoly. Like the rural voters, the urban laborers stood to gain if a farmer-labor combination secured political power. But such a combination was not forthcoming. As always, city and country people viewed each other with suspicion. Farmers wanted to raise prices; city workers wanted to hold them down. Laborers took little interest in railroad rates, which deeply concerned agrarians; and farmers were indifferent to the labor-sponsored shorter-hour movement.

The Populist Crusade

As one farm movement faded, another rose to take its place. The Grangers gave way to the Greenbackers; and as the Greenback party died, the Alliance movement took the center of the stage. Formed during the 1880's, the Alliances immediately entered politics and in 1892 created a new and powerful political organization—the Populist or People's party.

There were two National Farmers' Alliances. The Northwestern Alliance, in old Granger country, reflected midwest reaction to drought and dwindling prices. The Southern Alliance brought together several groups that represented the growing dissatisfaction of white farmers of the South and Southwest. Since this Southern Alliance drew the color line, there was also a National Colored Farmers' Alliance.

The Alliances were in politics from the beginning. They did extremely well in the state and Congressional elections of 1890. Which, of course, pointed to the need for national organization. This was achieved in 1892, when the first convention of the Populist party assembled in Omaha.

Like the Grangers, the Populists were against the railroads. Like the Greenbackers, they felt that inflation would help agriculture. But, formed in desperate times, the People's party did not stop there. The Populists attacked the tariff and demanded tax reform, including the use of a graduated income tax. They denounced grain speculation and the national banks. They called for government ownership of the railroads, the telegraph, and the telephone. They demanded a postal savings system and direct election of United States Senators. They asked for government aid to agriculture, through extension of credit to farmers.

Here at last was a fighting program for rural voters, something far more promising than the lackluster planks of the major parties. Farmers took to the Populist cause with a fervor bordering on the religious. They flocked to hear the movement's fiery orators: Tom Watson of Georgia, spokesman of the hard-pressed cotton farmer; Mary Ellen Lease, who told her Kansas followers to "raise less corn and more hell"; Jerry Simpson, another Kansan, the "sockless Socrates of the prairies"; Ignatius Donnelly of Minnesota, a veteran champion of the wheat farmer; Davis H. ("Bloody Bridles") Waite of Colorado, who pleaded the cause of the ranchers and the miners of the Rocky Mountain region.

Eastern journalists and other foes of Populism made fun of the People's politicians. They jeered at Mrs. Lease for daring to invade man's realm of politics. They said all Populists were vicious cranks. (Did not Donnelly pose as a Shakespearean expert and write books about the lost continent of Atlantis?) Certainly it was true that many Populists lacked dignity and polish. But they spoke for voters long neglected; and they spoke with force and with conviction.

In 1892 the Populists chose as their presidential candidate General James B. Weaver, who had been the Greenback nominee a dozen years before. Weaver did well at the polls, obtaining a million of the 12,000,000 votes cast and picking up electoral votes in a half-dozen states. This was the strongest showing made by any third party since the Civil War, and many predicted that there would hereafter be not two but three major parties.

But this was not to be. From the beginning, the Populists had certain limitations from the national point of view. The most important of these were a weakness in the Northeast and a general failure to capture the votes of city workers. The People's party was essentially a combination of southern and western farmers. In the national convention of 1892, Texas had more votes than New York, North Dakota more than Pennsylvania. The presidential nomination went to an Iowan, Weaver, the runner-up being from South Dakota. A Virginian was chosen over a Texan for the second place on the ticket; and the platform stressed agrarian demands.

As a sort of afterthought, a Populist committee on resolutions did bid for labor votes by praising the eight-hour movement and criticizing the strikebreaking tactics of employers and the government. But there was scant response. Some small-town members of the Knights of Labor joined the Populists. The Knights, however, had passed their period of strength; and other workingmen showed little interest in the cause. In 1892 the Populists ran behind the feeble Prohibition ticket in most industrial states. In New York, they also trailed an even weaker minor group, the new Socialist Labor party.

Failure to attract the workingmen was not the only problem of the People's party. Also significant was the fact that most Americans were attached to the two-party system. In general, the Populists did best in states where they captured or coöperated with a major party. Thus Weaver polled his biggest vote in 1892 in Kansas, where the Populists had taken over the Democratic machine. In the South, Populists often found it useful to form coalitions with the Republicans. Such a combination carried North Carolina in 1894.

It followed that the Populists might give up the fight if a major party adopted Populist views. In a way, this is what happened in 1896. By then, the nation was in the great depression that followed the panic of 1893. There were cries for reform within both major parties. In the end, the Republicans chose to remain conservative. But the conservative (Grover Cleveland) Democrats lost control of their party to William Jennings Bryan's free-silver agrarians. The Populists thereupon endorsed Bryan for President; and the People's party slid into oblivion. A handful of determined Populists continued the struggle, and named tickets on into the next century. But for all practical purposes the Democrats swallowed the Populists in 1896.

Bryan and the Election of 1896

To put it in another way, the farmers had recaptured the Democratic party. Southern and western farmers had been two of the strongest elements in the Democratic organization back in the days of Andrew Jackson. Coöperation had been maintained down into the 1850's, with Southerners led by Jefferson Davis working with western followers of Stephen A. Douglas. After the Civil War, the Pendleton forces had tried to reëstablish the old southern-

and-western-farmer control, only to meet with defeat. Thereafter, the Democratic party had been run by city bosses and businessmen, working in league with conservative Southerners.

In the 1880's and 1890's agrarian distress brought new Democratic leaders to the fore. Down in South Carolina "Pitchfork Ben" Tillman denounced the party's national leadership and said that the Democratic party must come out for reform. The same call sounded in the West, where "Silver Dick" Bland of Missouri and young William Jennings Bryan of Nebraska demanded Democratic action for the farmer. And at long last, in 1896, these southern and western agrarians secured control of the Democratic party and named the golden-voiced Bryan as candidate for President.

In some ways this new development strengthened the agrarian cause. Unlike the Populists, the Democrats were organized the nation over. They were strong in labor circles, where the People's party had been extremely weak. There were well-oiled Democratic machines in northeastern cities in which the Populists had polled next to no vote at all. The Democrats also controlled the solid South. Although the Populists had done well in the southern states, they had run into the race question. When they had allied themselves with the Republicans (as in North Carolina), the Populists had been denounced as Negrophiles. Elsewhere, as in Alabama, the Democratic politicians had marched Negroes to the polls to vote against the new party. Alarmed at such developments, many white Southerners had concluded that new parties might be dangerous, and that agrarian reform should be sought through the Democratic organization.

Finally, the decision of 1896 gave the embattled farmers a great leader, a much more vigorous and effective candidate than old General Weaver. The late nineteenth century produced many politicians of greater intellect than William Jennings Bryan, and some with better insight. But Bryan had the magic touch. He could excite a rural audience, could turn interest into enthusiasm, enthusiasm into burning zeal. As they looked at Bryan's young and handsome person, as they listened to his rich, persuasive tones, the country people felt that now at last they had their leader. Here was the new Thomas Jefferson;

PATTERN OF REPUBLICAN VICTORY IN 1896

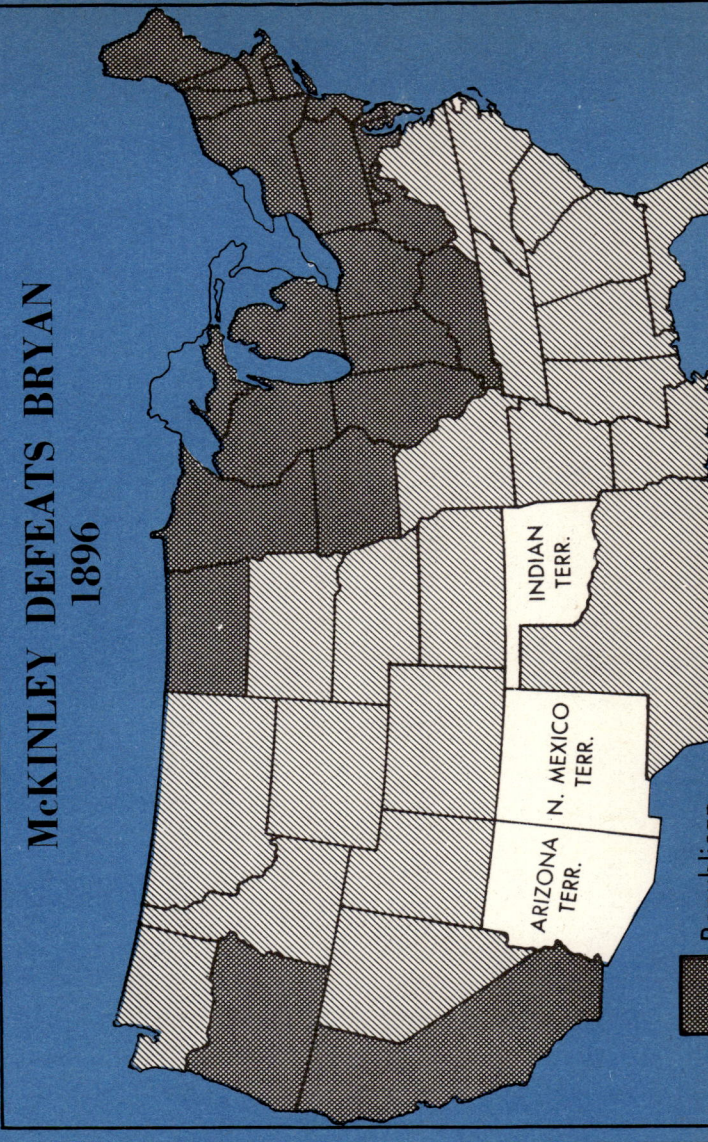

McKINLEY DEFEATS BRYAN
1896

ARIZONA TERR.

N. MEXICO TERR.

INDIAN TERR.

Republican

Presidential contests seldom present clear-cut issues. The election of 1896, however, saw the agrarian forces, under the Democratic presidential candidate, William Jennings Bryan, lined up against the urban and industrial backers of the Republican nominee, William McKinley. The Republicans won by carrying the industrial Northeast and the newly industrialized states of the Middle West. Bryan carried the southern and western farm states, and the mining states of the Rocky Mountains. This, though, was not enough to bring him victory.

CHIEF MANUFACTURING STATES

PER CAPITA VALUE OF MANUFACTURING IN 1900

INDIAN
TERR.

N. MEXICO
TERR.

ARIZONA
TERR.

Miles

100 300 500

Miles

$120 and Over

Under $120

Flannery

The campaign showed plainly that the agrarian economy traditional to America had given way to an industrial one, and that there would be no turning back. It was clear, too, that agrarian politicians could not hope to win national contests without support from the cities — for example, from urban workers. By attracting city laborers, Woodrow Wilson and Franklin D. Roosevelt were to succeed where Bryan had failed.

here was the new Andrew Jackson. Indeed, Bryan was closer to the farm voters than either of those leaders of an earlier day.

That was on the credit side. Yet much was lost when the People's party threw in its lot with the Democrats. For most of the Populist program was sacrificed in the process. The Bryan Democrats put all their weight behind the inflation issue. To them, free silver was the cure-all, the panacea for the farmers' woes. That is, the Bryan people wanted the United States to base its currency system on silver as well as gold. Silver was to be given an artificially high value (sixteen ounces of silver were to be considered worth an ounce of gold, though one could buy twice that much silver with that amount of gold). Since silver was plentiful, the result would be expansion of the paper money in circulation. The downward trend of farm prices would be reversed. Rural people would be able to pay their taxes and debts and buy much-needed equipment. Farm prosperity would help the whole country, and the crippling depression would pass away.

Focusing on free silver, the agrarian Democrats pushed aside the other Populist demands: government ownership of transportation and communication agencies; tax reform; credit for the farmer. Some Populists believed that these things could be obtained later, after the farmers had won control of the government and taken care of the immediate problem of farm prices. Others felt that inflation was a snare and a delusion and did not get at the basic problems of agriculture in an industrial age. Some of the doubters expressed themselves bitterly. "The free silver movement is a fake," mourned Henry Demarest Lloyd, who wanted to keep the People's party as a broadly based reform organization. "Free silver is the cowbird of the reform movement. It waited until the nest had been built by the sacrifices and labors of others, and then it laid its eggs in it, pushing out the others which lie smashed on the ground."

Most farmers, though, were willing to give Bryan a try. Perhaps the Nebraska Democrat did overemphasize free silver. Still, the average farmer was most concerned over prices. And Bryan won rural voters by telling them what he himself believed—that the American economy was based on the farm, not on the factory. He said this with great eloquence in his cross-of-gold address, made at the Democratic convention just before his nomination to the presidency: "The great cities rest upon our broad and fertile prairies. Burn down your cities and leave our farms, and your cities will spring up again as if by magic; but destroy our farms and the grass will grow in the streets of every city in the country."

In the campaign that followed, Bryan carried his message to the people. He traveled up and down the land, covering nearly 20,000 miles and speaking 600 times. On this tour the Democratic candidate won the hearts of farmers everywhere . . . but Bryan lost. William McKinley, the Republican candidate, was elected President of the United States.

Bryan's defeat is easily explained. He had most of the farmers; but the farmers were in a minority in the industrial age. Bryan's foe McKinley swung the urban and industrial Northeast and carried the newly industrialized states of the Middle West. That was enough to turn the contest, and to show that the farmers of the United States were no longer strong enough to carry a national election.

Looking Toward the Future

Where did that leave the country people? Had they fought and lost their last campaign? Had they worked in vain in building up the Granger movement, in organizing the Populist crusade? Had they gone down with William Jennings Bryan?

In 1896, it was hard to tell. Bryan in defeat looked forward to a "second battle" four years later. He would lose that, too. But the agrarian crusade would not altogether fail. The embattled farmers had made an impression. When the progressive movement flowered after 1900, its leaders would try to help the farmers as well as the city workers. And though the rural voters could not carry national campaigns alone, they had learned how to operate politically in an industrial society. After the 1890's farmers would use pressure politics to influence politicians in both major parties. They would insist and would obtain consideration from the government. Farmers would become an ever smaller part of the nation's population; but they would be heard.

6

Politics and Politicians

The Quest for Power

As agricultural history shows, the coming of the factory age had a profound influence on politics. Those who opposed the new industrialism carried their fight into political channels, attacking monopolies and demanding governmental regulation of railroads and other business combinations. At the same time, those who approved of the current economic trends sought influence in politics to speed the transition to a manufacturing economy, and to defeat anti-business groups.

Business Influence

The relationship between the government and industry had been apparent long before the Civil War. Back in the days of Andrew Jackson, agrarian control of politics had caused the defeat of Henry Clay's American system, a plan designed to promote manufacturing. By 1850, the factory age was at hand but the political influence of southern agriculturalists still acted as a restraining force. Southern votes prevented northern businessmen from getting many of the things they wanted: a protective tariff, railroad land grants, subsidies for ocean-going steamships.

This situation changed during the 1860's. The secession of the southern states enabled northern commerical and industrial interests to secure legislation to their liking. In rapid succession they obtained from Congress a protective tariff (Morrill Tariff of 1861), land grants for a transcontinental railroad (the Union-Central Pacific, completed in 1869), contract labor and national banking laws (1864).

In the three decades that followed, business interests sought to retain and extend their political influence on national, state, and local levels. They were willing to grant certain favors to farmers and workingmen—homestead laws, for instance, and pensions for Union veterans. But, as was natural, the captains of industry were much more interested in obtaining government backing for their own projects and in heading off attempts to check, control, and regulate their enterprises.

On the whole, the businessmen succeeded in the period from the 1860's to the 1890's. They gained and held more influence than they had possessed before the Civil War, more than they would have in the twentieth century. As a result, they succeeded in postponing effective government control of American economic life. In the states they obtained favorable corporation laws, such as the holding company legislation of New Jersey. They won state and national land grants for their railroads, tariff protection for their industries, currency and tax legislation that they considered satisfactory. Finally, in disputes between employers and labor, the local, state, and national governments were almost always on the side of the employer.

How did the industrialists, financiers, and other businessmen acquire and hold their political power? They were, after all, a small minority of the American people. The South and West were traditionally opposed to eastern business domination. In all sections, farmers and laborers, white-collar workers and small businessmen regarded the financial and industrial giants with suspicion. Confidence in business leadership was shaken by the panics of 1873 and 1893. Yet business continued strong in politics to the end of the century. Why so?

Part of the answer can be found in the weakness of the opposition. As has been seen, the farmers lacked effective national organization for much of this period; differing party loyalties and the memory of the Civil War made it difficult to bring together western and southern agrarians. It was much the same with labor. Even in the heyday of the Knights of Labor, the unions reached only a small fraction of the American workingmen. Frequently there was dissension in labor ranks; and labor chieftains always found it hard to coöperate with farm leaders.

Other foes of big business were even less effective. These included

white-collar workers, small merchants and manufacturers, and some
professional people. Many of these groups had no organization whatsoever (the white-collar workers, for example). Others organized for
professional but not political purposes. All wished to improve their lot;
but all looked down on workingmen and farmers, all were reluctant to
join hands with labor and agrarian elements.

Business control of politics was also linked to public indifference
toward political affairs. In the first half of the nineteenth century,
politics had been an honored calling, and those in pubilc life had been
the objects of admiration. This changed after the 1850's, and many
persons came to feel that politics was a field to be avoided at all cost.
The new accent was on business success; ambitious young men looked
to industry or the professions rather than the Senate. Politics seemed
to be increasingly corrupt, and run by sordid professionals. Citizens
were disturbed by the scandals associated with the Republican politicians of the Grant administration and the Democratic politicians of
Boss Tweed's New York machine. But instead of rising to correct the
situation, many Americans turned away from politics in disgust. This
enabled political bosses and pressure groups to run the show.

Political Techniques

Those who sought political influence
sometimes resorted to bribery. Political standards were distressingly
low in and after the Reconstruction era. Moreover, government salaries were insufficient to support officeholders who lacked private
means. This, said one bribe-taking Congressman, made many public
officials dependent on "financiers, speculators, monopolists, lobbyists,
robbers and thieves."

It was the same at every level. City trolley franchises and state land
grants frequently went to those who lined the politicians' pockets.
State legislators and judges often sold their influence to such businessmen as Jay Gould and Jim Fisk, Daniel Drew and Cornelius Vanderbilt. (One group of New York legislators, the "Black Horse Cavalry."
was said to have sold its votes as a unit to the highest bidder.) On the
national scene, Congressmen of both parties made personal profit out
of land grants to railroad promoters.

Sometimes the pay-off was indirect, as when legislators were given opportunity to buy valuable securities at bargain rates. Often the operation was more direct. "Enclosing a check which I hoped you would accept . . . ," wrote a manufacturer of watches to his Congressman in 1867. "May I inquire what probability there is that the tax on Manufactures will be lowered?"

When reformers exposed such relationships, the public was apt to turn against both the bribers and the bribed. In the long run, therefore, bribery was less effective than were campaign contributions. Farmers, laborers, and small businessmen were not yet well enough organized to make large contributions to political campaigns. Big business, though, could pour substantial sums into party treasuries. A politician who received such aid took no pledge to obey the contributors. But if he wanted support in future campaigns, he was unlikely to bite the hand that fed him.

Party discipline often operated in the same fashion. Many of the largest contributions went to political parties rather than to individual politicians. Party bosses came to depend on the money to finance state and national campaigns. They therefore set party policy in such a way as to insure a continuing flow of funds. Party officeholders were expected to coöperate. Those who did could count on political favors. Those who did not found it difficult to secure patronage or nomination for better jobs.

Campaign contributions were tied closely to the lobby system. Industrialists, financiers, and others who desired to influence the government maintained paid agents at the seats of government. These lobbyists checked on the activities of lawmakers and executive officials; and campaign contributions often depended on their reports. Lobbyists also testified before Congressional and state legislative committees, as experts on the needs of their employers. They supplied facts and wrote speeches for friendly legislators. They tried to persuade others, combining arguments with pressure from the politician's home district. They provided entertainment; they furthered their cause by supplying newspapers with copy.

In time both labor and the farmers would have effective lobbies. But, save in a few state capitals, neither group was adequately represented in the period before the 1890's. The efficient lobbies were those of the Union veterans, the temperance people, and, above all, the rising business groups.

Typical of the more successful lobbyists was John L. Hayes, Washington representative of the National Association of Wool Manufacturers. Hayes worked chiefly through Republican Congressmen from New England and the Middle Atlantic states. Year after year he saw to it that Congress retained high tariff duties on woolen goods. During the Civil War tariff schedules had been forced upward, partly because domestic producers were carrying an extra burden of manufacturing and income taxes. The taxes on income and manufactures were eliminated after the war, but (partly because of lobbyists like Hayes) the tariff duties were not reduced. Later, when the Ohio growers demanded protection, Hayes called for and obtained still higher duties on manufactured woolens, to offset the expected rise in the price of the raw material.

Along with lobbying went a variety of other activities. Businessmen influenced and controlled newspapers. They and their partisans wrote books and articles promoting their ideas. Industrialists swung votes by advising and even threatening their employees. Sometimes men of capital themselves entered politics, seeking to add to wealth prestige and political power. Two who represented this trend were Abram Hewitt, iron and steel manufacturer who was elected mayor of New York City, and Mark Hanna, an Ohio traction magnate who became a United States Senator and is best remembered as the power behind William McKinley.

Businessmen also tried to identify business leadership with such basic American ideals as democracy and opportunity. As citizens of a rising nation, Americans had long prized their chance to get ahead, the opportunity of every man to improve his economic status. Recognizing this, business spokesmen made much of the fact that Andrew Carnegie and other leading industrialists were self-made men. The industrial community, in other words, was run by democratic-minded leaders who understood the people; and every hard-working laborer had a chance to reach the top. So said Andrew Carnegie, in essays that associated industrialism with democracy. So said Horatio Alger, Jr., whose rags-to-riches yarns sold nearly 20,000,000 copies.

While hammering on this point, business leaders also stressed patriotism and the American tradition of individualism. Americans loved freedom, had worked and fought for freedom. How, then, could they favor governmental regulation of business? Patriotic appeals were equally important. After the Civil War, Union bondholders insisted that the honor of the nation required that they be paid in gold, not in depreciated greenbacks. Likewise, the tariff was defended on patriotic grounds, as a device to protect the United States and American workers from unfair competition with impoverished foreigners.

The Two-Party System

In the Civil War and Reconstruction periods, industrialists, financiers, and merchants tended to line up with the Republicans. This was logical, for the Republican party was tariff-minded and interested in a national banking system and in land grants for railroads. Then, too, the Republicans were stronger than the Democrats, better able to achieve results in Washington and in most of the state capitals.

Once established, the combination between the Republicans and business continued decade after decade. Yet business did not limit its attention to Republicans. That would have been suicidal. To be sure, the country was "normally Republican" in the half-century after Lincoln's election to the presidency. But the Democrats were always strong. The Republicans controlled both houses of Congress only a third of the time in the three decades from 1867 to 1897; and the Democratic popular vote exceeded the Republican in four of the nine presidential contests held in those years. In other words, the Democrats were powerful enough to wreck the political plans of the men of capital. Consequently, business sought the support of Democrats, made contributions to Democratic as well as Republican campaign funds.

On the whole, this program worked. Take the case of iron and steel. Andrew Carnegie, Henry Clay Frick, and most of the other major figures in the industry were Republican. But Abram Hewitt, of the Cooper-Hewitt interests, was an influential Democrat. It followed that the industry had a voice at court whichever party was in power.

If the Republicans controlled the House of Representatives, iron and steel's need for tariff protection could be set forth by Representative William D. ("Pig Iron") Kelley, a Pennsylvania Republican. When the Democrats took over, the same arguments could be presented by Representative Samuel J. Randall, a Pennsylvania Democrat.

Nor did it matter very much which party occupied the White House. There were great railroad strikes in the 1870's, and again in the 1890's. In each case the United States government intervened on the side of the employers, dispatching troops to the scene of conflict. In the 1870's, the troops were ordered in by a Republican President, Rutherford B. Hayes; in the 1890's, by a Democratic Chief Executive, Grover Cleveland.

So, too, on state and local levels. In the North, industrialists and financiers generally obtained franchises, land grants, and the like through the Republican organization. In the South, the leading businessmen worked through the Democratic party. Yet many of these southern Democratic businessmen were agents of northern Republican financiers. Party labels meant less than did the lines of power.

Failure of Third Parties

Those who desired a change could attempt to gain control of a major party; or they could set up a new organization, a minor or third party. The first alternative was generally preferred. Some, though, felt that the old parties were beyond redemption, and that reform-minded citizens must make a new start. "We denounce the Democratic and Republican parties as hopelessly and shamelessly corrupt, and, by reason of their affiliation with monopolies, equally unworthy of the suffrages of those who do not live upon public plunder," said one group of extremists. "We therefore require of those who would act with us that they sever all connection with both."

The most persistent minor party was more interested in moral than in economic issues. This was the Prohibition party, which nominated presidential candidates regularly after 1872. Besides attacking liquor, the Prohibitionists denounced gambling and speculation, prostitution, polygamy, and nonobservance of the Sabbath; and they worked for woman suffrage, cheaper postage, educational and civil service reform. Some Prohibition candidates were able and experienced politicians— for example, Neal Dow of Maine, Prohibition nominee for President in 1880. Still, the Prohibition vote was always very light, and did not begin to reflect the strength of the temperance movement. Most foes of alcohol opposed the third-party approach and preferred to work as a pressure group, influencing major-party politicians through such agencies as the Woman's Christian Temperance Union (W.C.T.U.).

Early efforts to form a third party in the labor field met with almost complete failure. After achieving local successes in Massachusetts and elsewhere, the Labor Reform party held a national convention in 1872. The delegates nominated Lincoln's old friend David Davis for President. They hoped that Davis would also be acceptable to the Liberal Republicans, who had broken with the regular Republicans for this campaign. The Liberal Republicans, however, showed no interest in coöperating with Labor Reform. Instead, the Liberal Republicans lined up with the Democrats. Judge Davis refused to run; and the candidate finally chosen by the Labor Reformers made a poor showing. The whole party, like other worker groups expired in the depression that followed the panic of 1873.

After that, some Labor Reformers tied in with the Greenback party, which tried to build a farmer-labor combination (1876–84). In this effort, the Greenbackers endorsed labor demands: they opposed child and contract labor, asked for Chinese exclusion, shorter hours, government inspection of mines and factories. But the Greenback movement, with its inflation emphasis, appealed to farmers rather than laborers. Only in 1884 did the Greenbackers show any sort of urban strength; and that was because of the personal appeal of Ben Butler, the party's popular but shifty presidential nominee.

When the Greenback party died, some of its sponsors brought forth a Union Labor ticket in 1888. This, like the Greenback organization, did best in Mississippi Valley rural districts; and it gave way naturally to the Populist or People's party. As has been noted, the Populists developed amazing strength in the early 1890's and gave promise of becoming a real political influence. But then they joined the Democrats in the Bryan campaign of 1896, and faded from the picture.

The last presidential campaign of this period—the celebrated Bryan-McKinley contest of 1896—saw many minor tickets in the field. Although the Populists endorsed Bryan, they would not accept Bryan's Democratic running mate, and ran their own vice-presidential candidate, Tom Watson. The anti-inflationist gold Democrats refused to support Bryan, and nominated General John M. Palmer on a separate ticket. The Prohibition party also divided on free silver, and split its tiny vote between two presidential candidates. Rounding out the field was the Socialist Labor party, a feeble left-wing group that had first entered the arena four years before.

There were, then, no less than six presidential candidates in 1896. But just two counted. Plainly, all efforts to form a powerful third party had failed. Nonetheless, the minor parties had influenced politics in the United States. More than once minor parties had spearheaded reform drives, had set forth ideas rejected by the major parties. As public interest mounted, one or both of the major parties took over the issue. The activities of Labor Reform and the Socialist Laborites forced Republican and Democratic leaders to pay more attention to workingmen. Prohibition gains in certain rural districts affected the attitude of major-party workers in those areas. The Greenbackers caused some leading politicians to reconsider their views on public questions; and both Republicans and Democrats were deeply influenced by the Populist crusade.

The Major Parties

Even so, most of American history must be told in terms of the major parties. They controlled the offices; they passed, enforced, and interpreted the laws. Pressure groups and average voters both operated within the framework of the major-party system.

Many Americans backed one party consistently, regardless of the current issues and candidates. Others shifted from time to time, because of hope or disgust, or the personalities of the leading candidates.

The major-party politicians therefore used pressure and persuasion to get all their regular supporters to the polls; and they did all they could to attract the undecided voters. The politicians also gave some attention to those who regularly voted the opposition ticket, searching for useful openings.

The regular strength of the Democrats was largely concentrated in the solid South and in a few major northern cities. This had been true in the decade before secession (1851–61). It remained the case down to the 1890's.

The opposition did its best to break this combination. The Republicans tried to secure power in the northern cities by exploiting Democratic scandals and appealing to special-interest groups (the Irish-Americans, for example). Sometimes they succeeded. In 1888, for instance, they turned enough urban Irish voters against President Grover Cleveland to insure his defeat for reëlection. Again, in the 1890's, a Republican-dominated "good government" group defeated the Tammany Democrats of New York City. (Young Theodore Roosevelt became police commissioner in the reform administration.) These victories, though, were impermanent. Tammany regained control the next time out; and the Irish and other "immigrant groups" in the northern cities generally remained Democratic.

The Republicans had even harder sledding in the solid South. Reconstruction (1865–77) gave them a chance to work in all the southern states, to try to build Republican machines around carpetbaggers, newly emancipated Negroes, and the poorer whites. By the 1870's, however, the latter group had lined up with the Democrats; and the old slave states were lost to the Republicans. Disenfranchisement of the Negro tightened the Democratic hold, and in the 1880's Republican strength in the South was largely confined to such border states as Missouri and Delaware.

The next decade saw the Republicans again attacking the problem. Some backed Henry Cabot Lodge's Force Bill, which would have used federal power to protect the voting rights of southern Negroes. This bill passed the House in 1890, only to die in the Senate. Meantime, some southern Republicans were flirting with the Populists. By the late 1890's, however, the southern Democrats had reëstablished one-party rule. The Populists were gone; and the disenfranchisement of the Negroes was made virtually complete by new laws. A typical statute barred those who could not read and write, and "understand" the Constitution. Since white election officers decided what was meant by "understand," Negroes could be excluded easily. Illiterate whites, however, were allowed to vote under "grandfather clauses," which opened the polls to descendants of those who had voted in slavery days.

Weak in the South, the Republicans were strong elsewhere. Most of the big and little businessmen of the North and West were regular Republicans. So were many professional people. A large percentage of the Union veterans consistently backed the Republican candidates, as did nearly all the northern Negro voters. Some northern cities were run by Republican machines, the party being especially strong in such industrial areas as the Pittsburgh region. The Republicans had some strength among skilled workers, including those who disliked the foreign-born voters controlled by the Democratic machines. Finally, the Republicans were well organized in northern and western farm districts.

When invading Republican territory, the Democrats aimed chiefly at the workers and the farmers. Success was limited until the 1890's, when William Jennings Bryan did take thousands of farm votes away from the Republicans. But, as an agrarian leader, Bryan had limited appeal to workers. That fact, and great activity on the part of business groups, gave the Republicans the crucial election of 1896.

Congress and the White House

The political history of the national government is bound to center around the White House. For one thing, the President has great constitutional powers. For another, he and his running mate are the only American officials chosen on a national basis. And, by virtue of his position, the President is head of one major party and the target of the other. Presidential power, however, has shifted from time to time. Party strength, personal ability, and crisis situations have made some Chief Executives the dominant figures of their day. Others have been almost completely ineffective.

The decade before the Civil War was one of weak Presidents: Millard Fillmore (1850–53), last Whig occupant of the White House, an accidental President who moved up from Vice-President when Zachary Taylor died; Franklin Pierce (1853–57) and James Buchanan (1857–61), Democrats chosen because of their lack of enemies rather than for qualities of leadership. No one of these three was renominated for President, let alone reëlected. A few cabinet officers were important in this prewar decade—Pierce's Secretary of War, Jefferson Davis, for example. But the strongest national figures were members of Congress—such men as Stephen A. Douglas, the Illinois Democrat, and William H. Seward, the New York Whig who turned Republican.

Then, in 1860, the Democratic party split on sectional issues, and Abraham Lincoln became the first Republican master of the White House (1861–65). Though a minority President, Lincoln nonetheless developed into an effective leader. This was owing partly to his own high talents. Secession and war worked in the same direction, for secession decreased Democratic strength within the Union, and the state of war gave Lincoln special military powers. Lincoln was thus able to bring back Andrew Jackson's concept of the strong executive.

When he ran for reëlection in 1864, Lincoln was far from confident of victory. He and his party's managers consequently sought to strengthen their ticket by giving the vice-presidential nomination to a war Democrat, Andrew Johnson of Tennessee. At the time, this looked like good politics; but it made for party confusion when, on Lincoln's death, Johnson became President (1865–69). As President, Johnson won some support from moderate Republicans and from Democrats; but he failed to win the backing of the then-dominant radical Republicans (Thaddeus Stevens of Pennsylvania, Charles Sumner of Massachusetts, among others).

Strong in Congress, these radical Republicans had looked with disfavor on the growth of presidential power during the Civil War. They had also frowned on Lincoln's moderate reconstruction plan. Their preference had been for "thorough" reconstruction, which would punish Confederates and keep southern states out of the Union until the Republicans could organize in the South. When Johnson continued the Lincoln policies, the radical Republicans checked him, overrode his vetoes, and tried to remove him from office. Although they failed to get the two-thirds vote necessary to convict at Johnson's impeachment trial before the Senate (1868), the radical Republicans did sharply reduce presidential power. Not until the twentieth century (and the age of Wilson and the Roosevelts) would there be a return to effective executive leadership.

Four Republican Presidents

Once Johnson had served out his time, the Republicans managed to control the presidency for sixteen years (1869–85). For the first half of this period the occupant of the White House was Ulysses S. Grant, the only Republican ever to serve two full terms as President. The general prosperity of the day helped Grant win election in 1868 and reëlection four years later. Important, too, was Republican control of southern states still under military rule. These factors would have benefited any Republican nominee. Grant, however, had an additional point of strength: his military reputation. This meant votes. It also meant that Grant, as a national hero, was in a position to reëstablish presidential leadership.

But that Grant did not do. New to politics, the General did not know how to use his popularity. Nor did he learn; he remained incredibly naïve in politics. He never discovered how to present issues in a manner likely to impress the public. He accepted the spoils system but did not know how to turn it to his political advantage. He chose some good subordinates, then failed to work in harmony with many of these individuals. Often he relied on incompetent and ineffective or vicious and corrupt advisers.

As a consequence, General Grant could neither control Congress nor handle his own executive subordinates. Though personally honest, Grant was unable to prevent a wholesale looting of the government by his appointees and associates. And the President's efforts to influence the legislative branch of the government were singularly unsuccessful. In 1870, when his party controlled both houses of Congress, Grant was badly beaten in his effort to effect annexation of Santo Domingo.

Despite his status as hero, Grant began to lose support. Carl Schurz, Charles Francis Adams, Charles Sumner, Horace Greeley, and other prominent Republicans left the party in 1872 to fight against Grant's reëlection. As Liberal Republicans, they nominated Horace Greeley for President. Although Greeley was also endorsed by the Democrats, the Republicans managed to pull Grant through to victory. But then came serious reverses. The panic of 1873 ushered in a long depression. Voters who had given the Republicans credit for prosperity now blamed the administration for the downward turn in the business cycle; and the Democrats gained in the Congressional elections of 1874. Scandals such as the Crédit Mobilier affair further damned the Grant administration. In addition, many citizens were saying that Grant's reconstruction policies had failed and that the Republicans had neglected to heed demands for tariff and civil service reform.

Given these developments, it seemed probable that the Democrats would win the presidential election of 1876. Republican defeat seemed the more likely when the Democrats named a reform candidate, Samuel J. Tilden of New York. But the Republicans also had a reform nominee, Rutherford B. Hayes, an Ohioan who had not been connected with the Grant gang. Hayes could count on the regular Republican vote. Having been a Union officer, he was sure to do well among veterans (Tilden had not been in uniform). As a foe of the spoils system, Hayes also won the backing of Carl Schurz and other liberal Republicans who had deserted Grant four years before.

Would that be enough? First returns indicated that Tilden had the edge in popular votes and would have a majority in the electoral college. Some Republican managers, however, refused to concede defeat. The contest ultimately turned on electoral votes in Oregon and in three states still held by federal troops—Louisiana, South Carolina, and Florida. There were double returns from these four states. By counting all against Tilden, a Republican-dominated electoral commission gave the victory to Hayes by a single electoral vote (185–184). The Tilden forces felt that their opponents had stolen the election; but Hayes was inaugurated and served out his term (1877–81).

As President, Rutherford B. Hayes labored under several handicaps. A conscientious, honest man, he was not outstanding in ability. Many of his countrymen considered him illegally elected. The Democrats controlled one house of Congress all through Hayes' administration, and both after the mid-term elections. Finally, the President's own Republican party was torn by dissension. The chief division within the party was between the Stalwarts and the Halfbreeds. Both factions were headed by self-seeking politicians, the Stalwart chieftain being Roscoe Conkling, the Halfbreed leader James G. Blaine.

Hayes, though, did his best, and made a spirited attempt to restore dignity to the presidential office. This involved defying the Senate, which wanted to control presidential appointments and removals. Grant had lacked the will and competence to challenge the Senate on patronage. Hayes, by contrast, specifically refused to follow the wishes of the Stalwart Senator Roscoe Conkling, a vain and dictatorial spoils-man from New York. In the end, Hayes won. He thereby struck a modest blow for presidential leadership and to some slight extent advanced the cause of civil service reform.

In other matters, too, Hayes took decisive action. It was he who ended the reconstruction process by withdrawing the last occupation troops from the South (1877). Disturbed by the labor conflicts of that same year, he used federal troops to help break the railroad strikes. He also employed his veto power to prevent Congress from barring Chinese immigrants, which said Hayes, would violate treaty obligations. Congress proved unable to pass the bill over Hayes' veto, and Chinese exclusion legislation was delayed until 1882.

Hayes, however, did not always have his way. When he asked for civil service reform, Congress pointedly refused to follow the President's lead. And when he vetoed the Bland-Allison Act of 1878, the Senate and House passed the measure over the veto.

This Bland-Allison statute involved the currency. During the Civil War the Union had issued some unsupported paper money (greenbacks). After 1865, some farm politicians urged the continuation of this policy, as a means of raising prices. Business opposition, however, caused Congress to vote against increasing the number of greenbacks. What was more, those outstanding were made redeemable in gold (resumption of specie payments, 1879).

By then, farm inflationists were adopting a new approach. Down to 1873, the United States was on a bimetallic standard. In other words, the monetary system theoretically rested on both gold and silver, an ounce of silver being rated as worth one-sixteenth as much as an ounce of gold. Since silver brought more on the commercial market, and since gold was in good supply after the California gold rush, the United States came to rely almost exclusively on gold. Silver was therefore demonetized by Congress in 1873; and the country was on a single (gold) standard.

Just at that time, vast quantities of silver became available with the opening of new western mines. The result was a sharp drop in the price of silver. Silver miners then desired to sell their product to the government, preferably at the old price (one-sixteenth that of gold). Southern and western farmers also demonstrated interest. If the government bought silver, and issued silver coins or paper money on the basis of these holdings, there would be more currency in circulation, and prices would rise—a development much to be desired in the hard times after 1873. Bimetallism would thus have the same inflationary result as the issuance of greenbacks. Hence demonetization was termed the "crime of '73," and there were cries for "free silver," "16:1," and "the dollar of our daddies." As a result, Congress passed the Bland-Allison Act, which provided for a limited coinage of silver.

It was understood that Hayes would not seek renomination in 1880. Roscoe Conkling brought out Grant again and suggested nominating the General for a third term. James G. Blaine and other foes of Conkling checked this strange movement, and the Republican nomination went to James A. Garfield of Ohio, a party regular who had a distinguished war record and had been a capable Congressman. To placate the Grant forces, the second place on the ticket was awarded to Conkling's political crony, Chester A. Arthur of New York. The Garfield-Arthur team went on to win the election. Returning prosperity worked for the Republicans, for in good times voters favor the party in power. What was more, the Democrats had an unusually weak ticket, headed by General Winfield S. Hancock. The Democrats carried the solid south, New Jersey, and two far western states; but northeastern and middle western votes took the Republicans to victory. It was close. Garfield was only 7000 ahead of Hancock in the popular voting (4,449,000 against 4,442,000), and the shift of New York would have meant a Democratic triumph in the electoral college.

In his few months in office in 1881, Garfield showed energy and political competence. Like his predecessor Hayes, he was interested in increasing presidential influence and in modifying some of the worst features of the spoils system. Like Hayes, Garfield locked horns with Roscoe Conkling; and in the contest Conkling was driven from the Senate and out of politics. But Garfield was killed by a frustrated office seeker; and the presidency went to Conkling's friend Arthur.

Chester A. Arthur was not so bad a president as might have been expected. All his life, Arthur had been a party hack. Elevation to the White House (1881–85) seemed to change his standards. He took on dignity, prosecuted the star-route mail frauds, and declared for civil service reform (helping to effect passage of the Pendleton Act of 1883). His term also saw the beginnings of the modern navy. But on the whole, Arthur was ineffective. An accidental President, without much prestige or ability, he was frequently ignored by Congress and by the leaders of his own party. The public also denied him anything above a middle rating; and the Democrats gained in the mid-term elections of 1882. So when 1884 rolled around, Arthur was dropped, and the Republican presidential nomination went instead to the famous James G. Blaine, from the state of Maine.

Cleveland and Harrison

Now, for the first time since 1856, the Republicans were to lose a presidential contest. Many of their victories had been narrow ones, and they had seldom controlled both houses of Congress at the same time. It therefore took a shift of only a few voters in a few states to turn the election the other way. The shift came in 1884.

James G. Blaine, the Republican candidate that year, was one of the master politicians of his day. Though not a veteran, Blaine was popular with the "boys in blue." Though a foe of reform, he won the support of many humble citizens. Though a political spoilsman exposed in the "Mulligan letters," he was famed as the "Plumed Knight." As Speaker of the House, as Senator from Maine, as Secretary of State under Garfield, he had impressed his magic personality on other politicians and the public. His was a logical nomination, and many guessed that he would coast to victory.

Instead, Blaine was beaten. In a long political career he had accumulated many enemies. Some were spoilsmen who envied Blaine's success (Roscoe Conkling, to mention one). Others were reformers who disliked Blaine as a machine politician and corruptionist. When Blaine was nominated in 1884, some liberal Republicans ("Mugwumps") bolted and threw their support to the Democratic candidate, Grover Cleveland, who had made a reputation as reform governor of New York.

Though sorry to lose the mugwumps, the Blaine leaders did not consider the loss irreparable. They could make it up, they thought, by attracting voters who disapproved of Cleveland's Civil War record (he had hired a substitute) and disliked the Democratic candidate's reputation as one who drank and was the reputed father of an illegitimate child. Since Blaine was anti-British and had Roman Catholic relatives, the Republicans also expected to pick up some votes from the normally Democratic Irish-Americans. But here they met with disappointment. At the very end of the campaign, Blaine antagonized the Irish when he allowed one of his Protestant backers to call the Democrats the party of "rum, Romanism and rebellion."

In a close election, Blaine lost New York by less than 1200 votes; one-tenth of one percent of the total cast in that state. Had he carried New York, he would have been elected President. It could be said, therefore, that the loss of a few Irish voters in New York cost Blaine the election. Or one could say that the shift of a few mugwumps to Cleveland had determined the result. Putting it another way: Cleveland carried the southern states from Maryland and Delaware to Texas. In addition, he won four northern states: Indiana, New Jersey, Connecticut, New York, just enough to give him victory.

In any case, Cleveland became the first Democratic President since the Civil War (1885–89). The new chief executive was a cut above the average occupant of the White House. A stolid, heavy-set and unexciting individual, Cleveland had relatively little popular appeal. He was, however, a determined and intelligent man more attached to principle than to political expediency. A conservative, he felt that the government should limit its activities as much as possible. Within the sphere of governmental action, however, he favored vigorous, decisive action, above the level of party politics. Thus he was a reform mayor of Buffalo, a reform governor of New York, and a reform president in his first term.

Even so, Cleveland did not greatly alter American political patterns. There was a substantial turnover in the government service, with an increase in the number of Southerners holding posts in Washington. Cleveland also showed himself to be a man of courage and conviction in establishing a new veto record. (Most vetoes were of private pension bills. General legislation covered Union veterans disabled in service, and Cleveland rightly felt that many of the private bills involved unworthy cases.) Still, Cleveland lacked the party strength, the public backing, and the political finesse needed to produce presidential domination of Congress.

At the end of 1887 Cleveland dramatized the tariff issue by devoting his entire annual message to a plea for lower rates. This was in preparation for the 1888 campaign. Again, as in 1884, Cleveland polled more popular votes than his Republican opponent. Again, as in 1884, he carried the solid South and picked up a few northern states. But this time Cleveland lost New York; and once more New York turned the tide. As in 1884, the New York vote hinged on less than one percent of the state's total ballots. Among the reasons for Cleveland's defeat was the loss of some Irish-Americans who considered him too favorable to Britain.

The Republican victor in 1888 was Benjamin Harrison, an Indianian whose grandfather had been President a half-century before. Benjamin Harrison had several points of availability. He was a Union veteran, a proved vote getter from a doubtful state, a decent and respected individual. His friends thought him capable and forceful; others found him cold and undistinguished. As President (1889–93), he did try to build a vigorous foreign policy. Otherwise, he made little effort to provide leadership. He let Congress run the show.

Congress was very active in these years, the winter of 1889–90 being especially important. It was then that the Republican Speaker of the House, Thomas B. ("Czar") Reed, streamlined the rules so that business could be handled quickly and in line with the wishes of the dominant party. Another member of the lower house, William McKinley, gave his name to a new high-tariff bill. There had been tariff changes from time to time since the passage of the Morrill Tariff of 1861, notably a slight reduction in 1883. The McKinley bill of 1890, however, was the most significant revision of rates since the Civil War. By moving levels sharply upward, it demonstrated how committed the Republicans were to a high protective policy.

In the same year, Senator John Sherman's name was attached to two important statutes: an antitrust law designed to curb monopoly and a silver-purchase act intended to pacify the western inflationists. With the Interstate Commerce Act of 1887, the Sherman Antitrust Act of 1890 indicated that the national government was beginning to recognize the necessity of regulating certain aspects of economic life. The Sherman Silver Purchase Act represented an effort to conciliate the silver owners and farm inflationists by stepping up the silver-buying program provided for in the Bland-Allison Act of 1878. Like the earlier measure, the 1890 statute helped the silver interests more than it did the farmers.

In addition, this "billion-dollar Congress" spent money with a lavish hand. The government's income from the tariff and from liquor and tobacco taxes had created an embarrassing surplus. The Republicans, however, did not want to cut the tariff. They therefore chose to spend the surplus. The Congress of 1889–90 passed pork-barrel river and harbor bills, voted a bounty for domestic sugar growers, increased silver purchases, appropriated money for a big navy, and increased the number of veterans on the pension rolls. Once formed, the spending habit proved hard to break; and the government was to run into difficulties when the surpluses evaporated after the panic of 1893.

Republican leaders thought that the laws of 1889–90 would increase their party's strength. They hoped, too, that Republican fortunes would be advanced by the admission of new western states. Colorado had been brought in during 1876. North Dakota, South Dakota, Montana, and Washington all followed in 1889, Idaho and Wyoming the next year. But there were unexpected results. Some of the new states developed an interest in Populism; later, all espoused Bryan-style Democracy. Nor did the Republicans fare well elsewhere. In 1890, halfway through the Harrison administration, the President's party suffered a crushing defeat. Many Senate seats were lost by the Republicans; and the Democrats gained control of the House of Representatives.

Two years later, in another Cleveland-Harrison contest, Cleveland increased his popular lead and carried the electoral college. In this 1892 campaign, Cleveland captured New York by a substantial margin. He could have won the election even without the Empire State, for he carried, in addition to the solid South, three states in the Middle West (Indiana, Illinois, Wisconsin). Further west, the Populists showed strength, and the Republicans received their smallest electoral-college total since their first presidential race in 1856.

Back in the White House for a second stay (1893–97), Grover Cleveland had to contend with an economic depression, ushered in by the panic of 1893. Here was a real opportunity for presidential leadership. But Cleveland, basically conservative, felt that he should not step in to lessen the effects of depression. The people should support the government, he said, but the government should not support the people.

Not that Cleveland was inactive. He urged tariff reduction, and obtained it, after a fashion, in the Wilson-Gorman Tariff of 1894. But the President was hostile when Jacob Coxey's army of the unemployed marched on Washington, demanding a public works program to provide jobs for the needy and to get money into circulation. When the marchers reached the nation's capital, some leaders were arrested for walking on the grass. In the same year (1894) Cleveland had federal troops help crush the Pullman strike. The President also opposed agrarian demands for higher farm prices. Instead of espousing free silver, he persuaded Congress to repeal the Sherman Silver Purchase Act, which was draining the Treasury of gold. In addition, Cleveland used his influence inside the Democratic party against such rural leaders as William Jennings Bryan.

Mark Hanna's Victory

For a full generation before the panic of 1893 the two major parties had been very much alike. Depression and the Cleveland policies finally brought a change. Southern and western agrarians captured the Democratic national convention in 1896. Junking the conservative Cleveland crowd, they demanded that something be done for the depression-ridden farmers; and they named for President the Populist-influenced Bryan.

This was more than a normal party change. Bryan's nomination shifted control of the Democratic machinery from the eastern cities to the West and South. It changed the party emphasis from laissez faire to a demand for government participation in social and economic reform. It provided leadership such as the Democrats had not known for decades. Bryan would move from inflation in 1896 to anti-imperialism and an assault on the trusts four years later; and the Democrats would help bring in the progressive era (1901–17).

The Republicans met the challenge of depression in a somewhat different way. Their nominee of 1896 was William McKinley of Ohio, author of the high-tariff bill of 1890. McKinley and his manager, Marcus Alonzo Hanna, lined up with hard money against free silver; with big business against the farmer; with the *status quo* against reform. Using techniques developed in earlier campaigns (1888 in particular), Mark Hanna collected an enormous campaign fund from business leaders. Bryan obtained what he could from the silver interests and from his farm supporters; but he was hopelessly outclassed by Hanna. And Bryan lost the election, his rural strength being offset by Republican influence in the growing cities.

There were many party changes in this campaign of 1896. The Populists endorsed Bryan and were absorbed by the Democrats. Bryan lost many Cleveland Democrats. Some, like President Cleveland himself, sat out the election without endorsing any candidate. Others went to McKinley, or backed John M. Palmer, a gold Democratic presidential candidate who helped the Republicans by drawing votes from Bryan. Meantime, Henry M. Teller of Colorado and other inflation-minded silver Republicans from farm and silver states left Republican ranks and lined up with Bryan.

The campaign of 1896 resulted in a triumph of gold over silver, manufacturing over agriculture. The contest also centered attention on the national character of political and economic questions. Interesting, too, was the fact that Congressional leadership was fading.

Each party emphasized the leadership qualities of its presidential candidate; and after 1896 the White House would have new prestige. And, though the victory went to the conservatives, a revitalized Republican party would presently, like the Democrats, begin to weigh the possibilities of progressive reform.

Role of the Courts

Congressional influence was the major force in the national government from the Civil War to 1896, although there was an occasional show of presidential strength. These years, however, also witnessed some increase in the power of the judiciary.

The federal courts fared badly in the 1850's and 1860's. When the Supreme Court took a stand on slavery (Dred Scott case, 1857), many Northerners refused to respect the verdict. The same antagonism toward the courts ran through the next decade. Suspecting that many judges were pro-Confederate, Lincoln suspended the writ of habeas corpus and sometimes operated through military tribunals. Congress reflected the same attitude when it increased the number of Supreme Court justices, enabling Lincoln to alter the complexion of the Court.

Reconstruction saw these trends continued. Congress by-passed the regular judiciary when it established military courts in the occupied South. Further legislation limited appeals to higher courts, lest reconstruction laws be declared unconstitutional. And judicial prestige suffered another blow in 1870–71, when the Supreme Court reversed itself overnight in the Legal Tender cases. (At first, the judges expressed doubt as to the government's right to issue unsupported paper currency. Then, after Grant had filled two vacancies with jurists of another turn of mind, the Court, in a case involving slightly different circumstances, upheld the constitutionality of the Civil War greenbacks.)

From then on, the federal courts gained in prestige and became a major force in the national government. In general, the judges were exceedingly conservative, disposed to protect property rights against any form of public interference. Although the Supreme Court upheld some state regulatory legislation in the Granger cases of the 1870's, the Wabash decision of 1886 severely limited the right of states to regulate railroad rates. In this decision the judges hammered home the point that Congress had exclusive power to regulate interstate commerce. But when the national government entered this field in 1887, the courts interpreted away the power of the Interstate Commerce Commission to adjust rates. The Maximum Freight Rate decision of 1897 is a case in point.

The Supreme Court also made use of the Fourteenth Amendment to the Constitution. When adopted in the Reconstruction era, this amendment was considered primarily as a device to protect Negroes against discrimination. Nevertheless, southern whites developed the segregation system, with which federal courts were reluctant to interfere (Civil Rights cases, 1883). The amendment therefore became a dead letter so far as the Negro was concerned. But the courts were presently using it to protect corporations (legal "persons") against regulation by state governments. This was the doctrine set forth in the so-called Minnesota Rate case (Chicago, Milwaukee and St. Paul Railroad *vs.* Minnesota, 1889).

Equally interesting were the court decisions in the taxation and trust fields. A tariff cut and a depression slump in federal revenues caused Congress to seek new sources of revenue in 1894. The House and Senate therefore revived the income tax, which had been used during the Civil War. But the Supreme Court stepped in and declared this tax unconstitutional (Pollock *vs.* Farmers' Loan & Trust Company, 1895). The legal problem concerned the direct tax provision of the Constitution. The judges, however, also thought of the tax as an "assault upon property," a threat to the conservative interests which the judges desired to protect; that is, they correctly saw the income tax as the most dangerous weapon the government could wield against those with large incomes.

The Sherman Antitrust Act of 1890 also ran into judicial difficulties. The statute clearly outlawed combinations in restraint of trade. In the E. C. Knight case of 1895, the Supreme Court refused to crack down on the sugar trust, although that combination had a virtual monopoly of sugar refining within the United States. This was a manufacturing combination, said the Court, not a combination in restraint of trade. But simultaneously the learned judges used the Sherman Act against labor, in the Debs case, which grew out of the Pullman strike.

In a way, the McKinley victory of 1896 seemed to ratify decisions such as these. But they would not satisfy twentieth-century Americans.

Part **II**

The New World Power
(1896-1919)

 *By the middle 1890's, the United States had become one of the greatest manufacturing nations on earth. The triumph of industry had, however, aggravated old problems and created new difficulties. Reform was necessary because of humanitarian considerations, and to make sure that discouraged citizens would not turn toward radicalism. As a consequence, the early years of the new century brought a progressive movement, aimed at eliminating corruption from politics and aiding labor, agriculture, and small business. At the same time, an expansion drive increased the world power and influence of the United States.*

7

The Industrial Nation

Economic Trends

By 1896 the United States was in population and production the leading industrial nation of the world. It had passed Germany and Great Britain in the production of iron and steel and had pulled level with the latter as a great producer of coal. The new power sources of the twentieth century, oil and electricity, would give the United States an even more striking supremacy.

For the next two decades, however, the patterns of American economic growth followed lines laid down in the nineteenth century. It is possible to classify the entire period from 1830 to 1920 as one major era of industrialism in America—that devoted to the initial development of coal, iron-and-steel, lumber, textiles, and railroads. Judged by number of workers employed, or by value added by manufacture, or by capitalization, these were the country's largest industries in 1900. Railroads continued until 1914 to be the greatest consumers of new capital. And the early years of the twentieth century resembled the preceding century in still another way: there was a rapid westward movement, particularly into Oklahoma and Texas.

Technological Change

Changes in technology, though, were already pointing industry in new directions. Electricity for light, power, and communication, together with the internal-combustion engine and new alloyed metals, would presently alter patterns of investment, population, and physical growth. Nineteenth-century progress had centered around the coal-burning steam engine and the railroad. Twentieth-century change would be associated closely with electric

181

power and communication, and with lightweight motor vehicles and airplanes.

As has been seen, the inventors had done much of the foundation work before 1896. Europeans had worked out the gasoline-powered internal-combustion engine, creating the automobile and pointing toward the day when the Wright brothers would successfully fly an airplane at Kittyhawk, North Carolina (1903). By 1895 Old World experimenters had done the basic research in wireless telegraphy (radio), and in alternating-current electricity, the type suitable for long-distance transmission. The electric trolley, the incandescent lamp, the telephone, the motion picture, the phonograph had all come into being.

There remained the job of development; and here Americans excelled. A typical American contribution was a new method of treating high-speed tool steel. This was worked out at the turn of the century by Frederick W. Taylor (better known as the "father of scientific management") and Maunsell White. The improvement made it possible to double the speed of cutting machinery, and pointed the way toward experimentation with other alloys.

The key to American industrial success was mass production. Improvements in machine tools helped make this possible. Rods, shafts, and bearings were machined to closer tolerances (less variation in measurement), and continuous, mechanized assembly lines were introduced. Some hundred years after Eli Whitney had demonstrated that he could put muskets together from piles of similar parts, three Cadillac automobiles were dismembered in a test by Royal Automobile Club officials in London. Their parts were shuffled, and three good new cars were assembled from the resulting assortment. In 1917 nearly 800,000 Ford chassis moved through the assembly line, each one interchangeable with every other. Astonishing to many Europeans, such demonstrations were becoming routine to American engineers. The stage was being set for the virtual disappearance of hand grinding and fitting.

Meantime, there opened a whole new world of the reproduction of sight and sound. By improving the vacuum tube, Lee De Forest (an American) opened the way for the commercial success of radio. Phonograph records introduced Americans to classical as well as popular music; and the movies became the chief entertainment medium of the American people.

New Industries

The revolution in technology brought new industries that would ultimately displace the old leaders. The automobile industry went beyond steel in value of product in the 1920's, and the electrical industry came by the 1930's to exceed steam railroads in capital investment. Furthermore, the automobile led to a government outlay for highways that exceeded $300,000,000 a year by 1919.

Urban areas were electrified between 1896 and 1910. Businessmen and prosperous homeowners installed power, lights, and telephones; interurban lines, trolley cars, new elevated and subway systems spread the net of rapid transit. Since there were only a few big hydroelectric stations (as at Niagara Falls), electric current for power and light in most communities was supplied by coal-powered steam-generating plants. By 1912 there were more than 5000 of these local power stations. The telephone spread even more rapidly. In 1895 there were less than 350,000 phones. By 1910 there were nearly 8,000,000, or about one for every ten persons. This ratio changed slowly thereafter, and stood at one telephone for every four persons by 1950.

By the turn of the century the electric trolley had become the standard means of city transportation. Lines extended into suburban areas, and trolley-run trains connected major cities. This brought new areas into the commuting zone and threatened the short-haul passenger service of the steam railroads. Electric subways and elevated lines were also becoming more common in the largest centers.

The automobile industry advanced with equal rapidity. Although mechanics and sportsmen had been building racing cars since the early 1890's, no American automobile was built for general sale until after the middle of that decade. Then, instead of copying the expensive French models, Americans set out to build cheap, light "horseless carriages."

The time and place were admirably suited to the new industry. No

other major Western nation needed the automobile so badly to overcome distances; no other contained so many persons who could afford
a thousand-dollar machine. American manufacturers of bicycles, wag-
ons, and machinery could easily supply the parts required. And the
Dingley Tariff of 1897, with its 45 percent import duty on foreign
cars, helped keep European competitors out of the low- and medium-
price market. Local manufacturers were also at an advantage because
of the need for access to spare parts and to mechanics familiar with
the machines.

Small producers dominated the new industry at first. In 1900 some
4000 American cars were turned out by a host of small firms, each selling in a local area. To become "manufacturers" the energetic pioneers
needed only a barn for assembly purposes, credit with suppliers, a few
nearby dealer outlets, and enough capital to meet the initial pay rolls.

The modern industry had emerged by the time of the First World
War. Henry Ford introduced his standardized Model T in 1909, and
never varied its essential specifications until he abandoned it in 1927.
After 1914 Ford cars were made on a mechanized assembly line by
men receiving the then-phenomenal minimum wage of $5.00 a day.
As Model T sales climbed to over 500,000 a year, Fords became an international symbol of American mass production and a part of the national folklore. Jokes about "flivvers" or "tin lizzies" took the place of
the standard Irish and Jewish dialect stories, and popular songs celebrated the reliability of Fords.

The second largest producer, General Motors, shared in none of
this popular humor, but was ultimately to capitalize the fact that its
cheapest car was not so "common." The two giants, Ford and General
Motors, and some twenty smaller companies accounted for the great
bulk of the 1,600,000 cars and trucks turned out in 1916. Although
the Model T was a somewhat primitive automobile, the expensive
cars with eight- or twelve-cylinder motors were not fundamentally different from the automobiles of the 1950's.

Toward Bigger Business

Large-scale operations benefited indus-
tries using heavy power machinery and assembly line techniques.
Small automobile companies were able to compete with big plants

like those of Ford and Buick only because they bought from large suppliers who had in turn the advantages of mass production. The small plants disappeared in many industries where such arrangements were impossible. In iron, for instance, the capacity of the most efficient blast furnaces increased tenfold from 1885 to 1919, and the big furnaces of the twentieth century were beyond the means of a small producer.

Even so, business consolidation ran far beyond the needs for economy through increased size. Many companies became so enormous that they deliberately decentralized operations to avoid the inefficiencies of an overextensive single plant. For these and other concerns control of the market was the prime consideration leading to bigness.

Oddly, the judicial interpretation of the Sherman Antitrust Act of 1890 also promoted consolidation. In theory at least, American courts and legislatures had always favored free competition and demanded restraints on monopolies. But in 1895, in the E. C. Knight case, the Supreme Court of the United States held that a monopoly of manufacture was not necessarily a restraint of trade under the 1890 statute. Four years later, in the Addyston Pipe decision, the justices held that a voluntary association of producers for the regulation of prices (what Europeans might call a cartel) was a conspiracy in restraint of trade and hence prohibited by the Sherman Act. The lesson seemed clear: it was legally safer for competitors to form one big company than to try to control the market by agreements. In time, therefore, the Sherman Antitrust Act came to be called "the mother of trusts."

Consolidation came so fast at the end of the century that the United States appeared to be headed toward some form of monopoly capitalism. In 1897 there were only a dozen manufacturing companies with as much as $30,000,000 in capital; by 1903 the number had climbed to forty-one. The same pattern prevailed in railroads. Following the panic of 1893 railroad financiers and investment bankers bought control of the weaker properties. They then combined the most important routes into half a dozen major systems, each held together by common ownership of strategic blocs of stock. Meantime, the communications field was coming under the domination of such giants as American Telephone and Telegraph (A.T. & T.), Western Union, and Postal Telegraph.

The aim of many of these companies was complete monopoly of the market for their products. When Presidents Theodore Roosevelt (1901–09) and William Howard Taft (1909–13) set out to enforce the Sherman Antitrust Act, major capitalists decided that it would be best to leave some competition. The Supreme Court suggested as much in 1911. In ordering the dissolution of the Standard Oil combination, the justices used the "rule of reason." That is, they distinguished between "reasonable" and "unreasonable" restraint of trade (the judges to define the terms in every case). Presumably complete domination of the market by one concern would be "unreasonable"; but domination by a handful might be regarded with less disfavor.

As a consequence, the monopolies of 1900 gave way to domination of individual industries by a small number of companies. The almost complete control of John D. Rockefeller's old Standard Oil trust was replaced by leadership of around a dozen companies. A like situation developed in tobacco after the breakup of James B. Duke's American Tobacco Company by Supreme Court order (1910). In steel, the giant United States Steel Company came to be content with about half the market.

The result was neither free competition nor monopoly, but a mixture that economists call monopolistic competition. Competition was maintained in advertising, service, and quality, but not in price. In other words, the decline of single-company control did not restore a free market. The drift was rather toward an era of "stable prices," set by intercompany understanding.

The Bankers Take Hold

Consolidations and mergers always involved exchange of stocks and bonds, and usually the marketing of new securities. This was the business of investment bankers. As financial operations increased in size, the dozen leading investment houses rose steadily in importance, with the house of Morgan in the lead.

Banking influence was not confined to the marketing of securities. Experience with overambitious railroad promoters had convinced J. Pierpont Morgan and other financiers that it would be wise to keep an eye on the management of reorganized or refinanced corporations. In a number of railroad reorganizations of the middle 1890's (that of the Southern system, for example) Morgan had the common stock placed in the hands of trustees. These trustees, appointed by Morgan, then directed the management of the road. As other major investment houses such as Kuhn, Loeb and Company took similar measures, the railroads came to be at least partially controlled by investment bankers.

The generally satisfactory securities market from 1897 to 1902 encouraged the bankers to take an active part in promoting consolidations and mergers. The operations became so profitable to all concerned, except some investors, that James J. Hill of the Great Northern Railroad said that corporations were merged by the bankers "not for the purpose of manufacturing any particular commodity . . . but for the purpose of selling sheaves of printed securities which represent nothing more than good will and prospective profits to promoters."

J. Pierpont Morgan engineered the biggest mergers and added to his stature as a leader in the banking community. In 1901 his firm attracted world attention by combining the Carnegie interests and a number of smaller steel companies into United States Steel. The new corporation had a nominal capital of $1,400,000,000, and was by far the biggest manufacturing company ever organized anywhere on earth. Other Morgan creations included General Electric, International Harvester, and the International Mercantile Marine. The Morgan firm also assumed leadership in transportation, finance, and public utilities (as with the Southern Railway, the Bankers Trust, and A.T. & T.).

Big corporations had large bank accounts, which they placed in the most influential banks. Hence fewer and larger producers meant concentration in financial resources. As telephones and fast trains enabled the trusts to control their business empires from New York, that city became more than ever the center of American finance. Within the city a group of already large banks grew until they completely overshadowed financial interests elsewhere in the nation. The National City Bank, the First National Bank, the National Bank of Commerce, and a few others in downtown Manhattan, together with such private banking houses as J. P. Morgan and Company and Kuhn, Loeb and Company came to dominate American finance.

Among the commercial banks National City took the lead. It handled the accounts of the oil, meat, copper, and other raw material producers, forging far ahead of its competitors. Holding the largest gold reserves outside the United States Treasury, National City ran the principal market in federal government bonds and held the reserve deposits of 200 out-of-town banks. Its aggressive president, James Stillman, was a leader among the New York bankers, who informally set discount rates, eased or restricted credit, granted or withheld large loans.

The power of the New York group was in part a recognition of the need for national coördination in financial matters. The national banking system established during the Civil War had no central bank or steering committee. The New York financiers therefore stepped in and performed many of the functions that in other Western nations belonged to a central bank.

The minor panic of 1907 dramatically illustrated the operation of the New York combination. Backed by Stillman and by George F. Baker (of the First National), J. Pierpont Morgan assumed responsibility for the entire financial community in time of crisis. Morgan and the Committee of the New York Clearing House, representing the chief banks, decided which banks could be permitted to fail and which had to be saved. The United States Treasury Department coöperated by entrusting funds to this group. Morgan did the rest, using his forceful personality and his great economic power. When bankers gathered at the Morgan Library seemed reluctant to advance sufficient funds to save a faltering institution, Morgan persuaded them to coöperate.

The Money Trust

On the one hand the successful support of the financial markets by the New York financiers lessened the impact of the panic of 1907. On the other hand the episode indicated an alarming concentration of financial power. Exposures by reforming journalists (the so-called muckrakers) further alarmed the public, as did the haughty manner of J. Pierpont Morgan. The national House of Representatives under progressive influence therefore had a special subcommittee headed by Arsène Pujo of Louisiana investigate the concentration of financial power. The widely publicized hearings and report of this committee (1912–13) convinced many citizens that a "money trust" dominated the American economy.

In support of this view, the Pujo investigators named as the inner group the house of Morgan, their affiliates, the Bankers Trust and the Guaranty Trust, together with the National City and the First National. The partners, directors, and officers of these institutions held 341 directorships in 112 corporations with resources of $22,000,000,-000. It was implied that through these posts the inner group dominated the major insurance, banking, railroad, and public utility corporations, plus a considerable segment of ocean shipping and heavy industry. Morgan and George F. Baker were each directors in forty-eight companies, and, said one railroad official, where Morgan sat was the head of the board. Besides the inner group, the Pujo subcommittee identified an outer circle of bankers whose aims and influence were generally in harmony with those of the Morgan bloc. Included in the outer circle were Kuhn, Loeb; Kidder, Peabody; Lee, Higginson; August Belmont; J. W. Seligman; and Brown Brothers.

Unquestionably the Pujo investigators ascribed to Morgan more power than he actually possessed. There was much internecine warfare in the financial world, and little of the carefully planned policy that should issue from the head office of an efficient monopoly. Morgan and Baker were so overloaded with duties that they frequently failed to use the power at their disposal. Curiously, too, the leading bankers had no staff of experts to coördinate the activities of partly controlled railroads and public utilities. In many Morgan-connected companies, the financiers came into the picture only when large expenditures were involved. And when the banker did give advice, it was likely to be confined to matters related to the securities market.

At the same time, it was clear that banker influence was increasing, that finance capitalism had replaced industrial capitalism in many fields. When Morgan, Baker, or Stillman actually spoke up at board meetings, their opinions were close to decisive. Though bankers competed for business, nearly all represented the same conservative Wall Street point of view. They knew each other intimately and thought and acted alike on most national problems. Morgan had enormous prestige, particularly between 1907 and his death in 1913. Undoubtedly his opinions strongly influenced the entire banking world.

This was all for the good, said Morgan partisans; it meant economic stability. "With a man like Mr. Morgan at the head of a great industry," said one New York merchant, "production would become more regular, labor would be more steadily employed, and panics caused by over-production would become a thing of the past." In defense of this position, it was pointed out that conservative banker influence kept speculators out of key posts, and that the Morgan group offered strong support to some financial institutions in time of trouble.

It is true, of course, that there were no long or severe depressions between 1896 and 1919. But the bankers could not claim exclusive credit for the industrial expansion, the rising farm prices, the war boom of these years. Nor could it be said that the bankers always operated with discretion. Overoptimism and the ease of floating securities led Morgan and his colleagues to create unnecessarily high capitalization. In the name of "sound finance" they increased bonded indebtedness enormously, and advised the issue of common stock in foolishly large quantities. Morgan and his friends felt that monopoly or community of interest would guarantee profits notwithstanding this watering of securities. But sometimes (as with the New Haven Railroad) the profits did not materialize. Instead, the heavy capital burden led to receivership and bankruptcy.

The Federal Reserve System

The unusual power of the finance capitalists came in large part from rapid economic expansion, relative scarcity in capital, and lack of a central bank. Only the bankers could mobilize the savings of the community in large quantities. Only through their influence could the reserves of bank credit be drawn upon in emergencies.

Could this be changed? Many thought it could if the United States developed a central banking system. Such a system might create a more elastic currency, so that credit would be available when most needed. At the same time, the central system might end the power of the money trust over bank credit.

The problem was frequently discussed after the panic of 1893.

Aside from fractional currency (pocket change), circulating money in the United States consisted of certificates for gold deposited in the Treasury, gold coins, national bank notes, a fixed amount of Civil War greenbacks, and the silver dollars and certificates for silver dollars that had been issued under the Bland-Allison and Sherman Silver Purchase acts. All these mediums were relatively fixed in quantity and could not be expanded or contracted rapidly to stabilize the money market. In panics and depressions fear of bank failures led citizens to close their accounts and hoard cash. This led to a shortage of money and made a bad situation even worse.

Clearing houses—associations to settle accounts between banks—did make an effort to provide the money needed in emergencies. From 1860 on, clearing houses in New York and other cities issued certificates during periods of crisis. This paper, however, did not help the whole country; and it was nonlegal. Those who advocated greenbacks and free silver claimed that their proposals would take care of emergencies. The Greenbackers, however, counted for little after the resumption of specie payments in 1879; and the silver forces went down with Bryan in 1896. The Gold Standard Act of 1900 closed the door to the possibility of unsupported paper currency or an expansion of silver certificates.

For a time it seemed that the situation would be solved by an increase in gold production (associated with an improved cyanide process and the opening of new fields in Alaska, South Africa, and Australia). Prices moved upward, and there seemed to be no scarcity of specie. But then the panic of 1907 produced the usual temporary famine.

With greater determination than before, Congress set out to find a remedy. As a temporary expedient the House and Senate passed the Aldrich-Vreeland Act of 1908, designed to provide extra bank notes in a crisis. The long-range problem was taken up by a National Monetary Commission. After surveying all the banking systems of the world, the Commission framed a conservative central banking act. Since the proposed central bank would be a privately owned and operated monopoly, the progressives in both major parties joined in defeating the measure (1912). The issue, now encased in politics, carried over into the administration of Woodrow Wilson (1913–21).

The Federal Reserve Act of 1913 was essentially a Democratic party bill containing few concessions to the Republicans. In keeping with the American tradition of localism and fear of federal power, it established a decentralized system rather than a national bank. The one central agency was a Federal Reserve Board composed of the Controller of the Currency, the Secretary of the Treasury, and five members appointed by the President. The act divided the country into twelve districts, each with a Federal Reserve Bank. The Federal Reserve Banks were to be bankers' banks, serving the system's member institutions, which would in turn serve the public. The local banks supplied the capital and two-thirds of the directors of each Reserve Bank. All national banks had to join the system, and other banks could do so by subscribing to Federal Reserve Bank stock to the extent of 6 percent of their capital and surplus. Only members of the system could use the twelve Reserve Banks.

The Reserve Banks provided a more elastic currency through their ability to issue paper money in return for certain kinds of agricultural or commercial paper offered as security by the member banks.[1] The Federal Reserve notes had to be backed to the extent of 40 percent by cash. But since all member institutions had to keep their reserves on deposit at the Reserve Banks, cash on hand was sufficient to permit a very large note expansion during emergencies. In practice, an extra supply of notes was made more certain by requiring that members normally be out of debt to the Reserve Bank at least once a year.

The Reserve Banks could encourage or discourage member-bank borrowing by raising or lowering the rediscount rate. If the rediscount rate were only 2 percent, and customers of member banks were anxious to borrow on eligible paper at 5 percent, the local bankers could make a good profit by lending at 5 percent and rediscounting at 2 percent. If the rediscount rate was raised to 5 percent, there would be no gain in such operations. The Reserve Banks could also influence the

---

[1] Local banks lent money to individuals on a short-term basis, taking as security a claim on goods moving to market. The banks obtained their profit by "discounting" the promissory notes. The local bank could then take these promissory notes and borrow on them (have them "rediscounted") at a Federal Reserve Bank. In this transaction the Federal Reserve Bank would lend paper money (Federal Reserve notes) to the member bank. The amount of paper money in circulation would depend, then, on business activity and business needs as well as on the gold supply.

money market by buying or selling government bonds. Buying bonds added to the Federal Reserve notes in circulation, whereas selling bonds reduced the quantity of circulating currency. Normally each Reserve Bank regulated these matters to suit itself, but the central board could and sometimes did override local decisions.

Since membership involved submitting to strict federal regulation of banking practices, most state banks preferred to stay outside the system. At the time of the passage of the Federal Reserve Act, the American Bankers Association warned that "those who do not believe in socialism" would find it very difficult to accept the law. Many financiers continued to feel this way. Only a little more than a quarter of the country's banks were members in 1917, although the members controlled two-thirds of all banking resources.

In solving the problem of an elastic currency, the Federal Reserve Act in no way interfered with the investment banking activities of the money trust. Even the death of J. Pierpont Morgan in 1913 did not reduce the influence of the house of Morgan. One year after that, with the outbreak of World War I, the firm increased its activities by becoming American purchasing agent for France and Great Britain.

The America of Big Business

Big business and increased government activity were rapidly producing a new kind of American life. Earlier assumptions regarding the rights of individuals and the social virtue of selfish enterprise were challenged by many sorts of collective agencies. The classic or Jeffersonian concept of democracy, as a system whereby the individual citizen expressed his will directly, was yielding to a vague recognition of the fact that democracy in practice often meant a balancing of pressure groups. The citizen, therefore, could be effective only through organizations.

Business had pioneered in forming such organizations, and big business meant a steadier pressure in politics and on the press. "As business . . . has learned the secret of combination," boasted the *Banker's Magazine* in 1901, "it is gradually subverting the power of the politician and rendering him subservient to its purposes." The then-rising progressive movement demonstrated that business was far from

political control; but it also showed that reformers had to be well organized to succeed.

Nor did the process end here. As regulatory legislation went on the
statute books, business leaders felt called upon to improve their organization, to pool their resources and fight harder than ever on both
state and national levels. Meanwhile, urban newspapers were becoming big businesses in themselves, sensitively geared to the advertising
revenues that accrued from fighting on the "right side."

Possibly the most basic change of these years came in the life and
expectations of ambitious Americans. The chances for a man to start
a manufacturing or transportation enterprise on a shoestring became
fewer each decade. Andrew Carnegie's advice to go into business for
yourself was increasingly difficult to follow. Aside from the professions, trade, and retailing, the only reasonably safe opportunity for
most men was in taking a job in a company.

If employed by a really large concern, the aspiring youth found himself in a world quite different from that described in the old success
stories. There were few chances to show originality. The road to advancement lay in avoiding errors in a routine job, and pleasing superiors by work and personality. If successful, the employee could rise
step by step through the company hierarchy until in late middle age
he might secure a well-paid officership.

In this type of ascent the man with a business family background,
a good education, and proper connections had a great advantage over
persons coming from the worker or farmer class. Most of the top-rank-
ing big businessmen of the decade 1900–1910 had been born in cities
or large towns and came from middle- or upper-class business and professional families; and nearly half had some college training. Only one
in fifty was the son of a laborer. The standard business pattern was
still to start at the bottom, often at a salary too low for self-support.
But promotion was more rapid for those with good connections.

These social changes were gradual. The expansion of trade and
service industries still offered good openings for the small businessman. From 1890 to 1930 the number of independent business enterprises increased by more than a third. Meantime, however, the number of white-collar, professional, and managerial employees doubled.

This trend was to continue in the next generation. The typical middle-class American had become a company employee rather than a farmer or an independent businessman.

Workers in the Factory Age

For the businessman able to share in the profits of ownership, and for farmers selling at ever higher prices, the early twentieth century was a period of prosperity. For white-collar and industrial workers it was an era of frustration. Although real per capita income increased by a third in the two decades after 1898, these groups failed to share in the rise.

To put it in another way, the rich were becoming richer, the poor were becoming poorer. There was much talk of the new "consumer economy" at a time when most Americans could buy less than before. An upper-middle-class standard of living featured by automobiles, telephones, phonographs, and electric lights grew up alongside the unimproved tenements, flats, and shanties of the "other half." Furthermore, national advertising created acute dissatisfaction among those unable to afford the new luxuries. Schools also improved, widening the horizons and expectations of the multitude just when jobs became increasingly monotonous and promotion less likely than before.

Americans had long been proud of their high standard of living, had boasted of their equality of opportunity and democratic rule. In consequence, they were unwilling to accept the new order without protest. A vigorous progressive movement threatened the old guard of both major parties. Radical movements gained strength—it was in these years that socialism and anarchosyndicalism reached their all-time highs in the United States. Artists and intellectuals spoke out strongly; and labor organizations made new advances.

It was no accident that the radical and reform movements drew heavily on the white-collar workers. Although the cost of living rose 150 percent from 1896 to 1918, the yearly earnings of nonagricultural workers rose 140 percent. But the annual income of white-collar workers went up only 80 percent. Since standards of living are relative, the situation would have been more tolerable had all classes been held back by some failure of productivity or international calamity. But in these same years of hardship for clerical employees, the 40 percent of the population that depended on agriculture, managerial salaries, and profits enjoyed an aggregate income that rose faster than the cost of living, and by 1918 had outstripped prices by 70 percent.

Conditions of life and work for industrial workers continued to deteriorate. In the 1890's less than a third of the population lived in cities of over 8000 inhabitants. By 1919 the number was approaching a half. Partially effective tenement-house legislation prevented sanitation and overcrowding from becoming any worse than before in New York and a few other places. In most cities, however, the slums continued to spread, unchecked and unregulated. Nor was bad housing confined to big centers. Cities of 50,000, like Holyoke, Massachusetts, had immigrant-crowded slums as bad as those of Chicago, Philadelphia, and New York.

The average work week did decline, from fifty-eight to fifty-two hours from 1896 to 1918. Yet conditions tended to become less pleasant for the quarter of the labor force that worked in factories. The minute subdivision of labor in big plants led to tedious, repetitive operations that gave the employee little of the pleasure of good workmanship.

More general than the insistent monotony of the assembly line was the problem of the loss of personal relations with those in ultimate authority. Since most employees worked for firms employing over 100, and since multi-plant operations had become common, the employee lost contact with anyone above his immediate superior. These immediate superiors were foremen and straw bosses, many of whom were petty tyrants. Foremen could discriminate against Negroes and foreigners, and could give the best jobs to their friends and relatives. Unless the results were clearly manifested in reduced productivity, higher officials were not likely to interfere.

Would owners and managers have ordered things differently had they known what was happening? It is hard to say; but it is clear that top management was generally concerned with finance and the market rather than with labor. And the bankers, who controlled some big-company policies, regarded employee relations as quite beyond their sphere of interest.

The A.F. of L.

It is tempting to explain the spread of trade unionism by picturing the poor immigrant or country boy plunged into a big city. Crushed by a feeling of loneliness and rootlessness, his childhood symbols and ceremonies lost, his living quarters bare and ugly, his work made onerous by a tyrannical foreman, he seizes on the union as a refuge, a way of restoring meaning to life. Similarly, the strike can be seen as an emotional release, a participation in a group effort to assert rights, privileges, and human dignity.

Such feelings were certainly present in the city dwellers who labored in big, impersonal factories. But it was not in these plants that unionism spread rapidly. Throughout this period the principal mass production industries were able to prevent the unionization of the rank and file of their workers. The great area of union growth at the turn of the century was in the building trades, in mining, and in transportation. And most of these activities were spread through the small and medium-sized cities.

The areas of unionization were largely dictated by the remaining elements of skilled craftsmanship that fitted into the traditional organization of the American Federation of Labor. Where these elements were weak or lacking, the A.F. of L. organizers generally met defeat and ultimately lost interest. Yet at this very time the trend was away from skills and toward machine production. Thus the main pattern of unionism represented the past rather than the future and was highly vulnerable to the advance of the machine.

Union membership grew rapidly after 1897, and stood at 2,000,000 in 1904. Although this was only 6 percent of the labor force, it represented a fivefold increase in less than eight years. If the trend continued, a majority of the workers would soon be organized.

But the trend did not continue. Employer opposition and the limitations of the craft approach imposed effective checks on growth. Union membership remained almost stationary for the next five years. Then unionization of clothing workers caused a rise, but less than 6 percent of the labor force was unionized in 1914.

Shortage of workers during World War I paved the way for a great gain in trade-union strength between 1916 and 1919. Also important was the passage of the Clayton Antitrust Act of 1914, which specifically exempted unions from prosecution under the antitrust laws. The attitude of President Woodrow Wilson was an additional element in the situation. During the war Samuel Gompers of the A.F. of L. gave Wilson a no-strike pledge. In return the President saw to it that manufacturers who held war contracts allowed Gompers to approach their workers.

The results were spectacular. By 1919 there were over 4,000,000 union members, nearly 10 percent of the labor force. The gain, however, was not to prove permanent. A decline set in soon after the end of the war. Losses were associated with employer activity, with the collapse of war industries, the loss of strikes in 1920, and the Big Red Scare. It was apparent, too, that labor could not register long-term gains in the mass production industries while its leaders clung to the skilled-craft pattern.

Some independent unions rebelled against the strictly defined craft unionism of the A.F. of L. The opposing plan was to organize all workers of one industry, regardless of skills, into one big union (industrial unionism). This might be called a vertical type of unionism, running from top to bottom of a plant, as contrasted with the horizontal type, which attached each kind of skilled worker to a different union and left the unskilled unorganized. The Western Federation of Miners and later the Amalgamated Clothing Workers broke away from the A.F. of L. and maintained industrial organization. But the strength of the conservative Samuel Gompers in union politics, and threats of jurisdictional warfare prevented most of the unions from attempting industrial organization.

The I.W.W.

Disgusted by the "aristocratic" craft unionism and conservative politics of the A.F. of L., a group of radical leaders formed a new national organization in 1905. They used the name Industrial Workers of the World (I.W.W., nicknamed "Wobblies"). The plan, like that of the Knights of Labor, was to include all workers in one big union. The professed radicalism and open espousal of violence of the I.W.W. scared employers and journalists. As a result, lurid publicity made the organization seem large and menacing.

But membership was probably never over 70,000, and the I.W.W. failed to develop a stable organization in any industry.

The Wobblies had their chief influence in fields neglected by the A.F. of L. Big Bill Haywood and other I.W.W. organizers worked in the eastern textile centers, and staged bloody strikes in Lawrence, Massachusetts, and Paterson, New Jersey, just before World War I. They built up a following in western agriculture, especially among migratory workers. They organized northwestern lumber camps, and aided the Western Federation of Miners in the Rocky Mountain region.

I.W.W. activity was everywhere associated with violence. For this the union was partly responsible; it was not unwilling to use sabotage, sit-down strikes, and the slowdown ("poor work for poor pay"). What was more, the I.W.W. operated in company towns and other areas where the employers controlled the law-enforcement agencies and were disposed to use those agencies against labor organizers.

World War I marked the downfall of the I.W.W. Vaguely anarchosyndicalist in political philosophy (believing in internationalism and individual perfectionism), the union's leaders violently opposed American entry into the war in 1917. As a consequence, they were arrested in wholesale lots, tried, convicted, and given long prison sentences. Disorganized by loss of its leaders and seizure of its offices, the organization failed to recover its strength after the armistice. The I.W.W. doctrines of extreme individualism, coöperative production, and a negligible state belonged in any case to an older America and had little place in the increasingly state-dominated large-scale industrialism of the middle twentieth century.

Employer Attitudes

Because of its doctrine of warfare against capitalism, the I.W.W. was beyond the pale of possible recognition by businessmen. But even the conservative A.F. of L. failed greatly to alter the employers' opposition to collective bargaining. "I do not believe that a manufacturer can afford to be dictated to by his labor . . . ," said one employer to a Congressional committee, "and I shall never give in. I would rather go out of business." Shoe manufacturers of Marlboro, Massachusetts, did in fact shut down their plants and ruin their business rather than deal with unions. Some textile manufacturers moved from New England, where unionism was gaining, to nonunion sections of the South.

As unions gained strength after 1900, employers combined to oppose the new trend. The National Association of Manufacturers, the Citizens Industrial Association, and the League for Industrial Rights all fought unionism tooth and nail. The chief issue, then as later, was the closed shop. In many cities the A.F. of L. had succeeded in restricting the building trades and other skilled crafts to union men. Then the Citizens Industrial Association, representing 250 employers' associations, took up the fight. The Bureau of Education of the C.I.A. mobilized local business leaders against the closed shop. Lectures and articles, reinforced by the antiunion attitude of most newspapers, brought the support of the middle class. As a result, the spread of unionism was checked; and business was given fresh assurance that, despite union gains in the British Empire, a united front could keep America open shop.

Meanwhile, the League for Industrial Rights used the Sherman Antitrust Act to check the American Federation of Labor strategy of boycotting unfair employers. From the date of its organization in the 1880's, leaders of the A.F. of L. had circulated "We Don't Patronize" lists of firms unfair to labor. The net effect of these lists was not very great; but employer groups disapproved of the practice. After many years of litigation, the United States Supreme Court finally held in the Danbury Hatters' case (1908) that such nation-wide boycotts violated the Sherman Act. The hatmakers' union was therefore fined over $200,000.

As in earlier times, employers' associations were chiefly useful to medium-sized and small businesses which could not afford their own specialists. The large concerns needed no outside advice as to where to hire armed guards or strikebreakers and how to secure injunctions against labor unions. Until menaced by the New Deal of the 1930's, many of the industrial giants did not even bother to join the National Association of Manufacturers or to support the lobbyists of the League for Industrial Rights. Rather the big companies took care of their own problems through specialized staffs. In a strike of 1901, United States Steel demonstrated its ability to defeat the Amalgamated Association of Iron, Steel and Tin Workers; and in electricity, motors, foods, and chemicals, unionism was confined to a few skilled workers. The bitter labor wars of this era mainly involved smaller employers in construction, mining, textiles, and clothing.

Labor Legislation

As machinery grew more complicated and operated at higher speeds, there was a sharp rise in industrial diseases, injuries, and deaths. In the older owner-managed shops the proprietor had been able to judge each case on its merits and had sometimes granted paternalistic care to injured and sick workers or to their widows and children. But in the big manager-run plants of the twentieth century this personal relationship no longer existed; and nothing came to take its place. Commercial accident insurance was prohibitively expensive, and lodge or union benefit plans usually paid little more than funeral expenses. Great tragedy faced the dependents of the 20,000 workers killed and 1,000,000 injured each year.

Theoretically, an injured worker had the right to sue for damages. In practice, the right meant little. To begin with, a legal action involved lawyers' fees and costs that the poor man could not advance. Even if he went to court the laborer had to prove that he had not contributed to the accident by his own negligence. Further, if another employee was to blame, the common law assigned responsibility to this impecunious fellow worker rather than to the employer. The need, plainly, was for compulsory workmen's compensation legislation.

Child labor, long hours, and bad factory conditions also affected the health of the working people. Nearly 2,000,000 children under sixteen were employed in 1900—twice as many children as trade unionists. Many men and women still worked twelve hours or more at a stretch, in dusty, humid, and ill-ventilated plants.

The nations of western Europe had already brought most of these evils under control. Only the United States, once the great center of reform, had refused to face these problems realistically. Why so?

Partly, no doubt, because aggressively individualistic American industrialists opposed regulation on principle. Partly, also, because conservative labor leaders like Samuel Gompers failed to fight hard for social legislation, preferring to devote their energies to bargaining with employers for higher wages. Little was done until urban upper-class reformers, concerned over public health, brought pressure on state legislatures.

Some intelligent employers tried to ward off state action by improving conditions in their own plants. The majority, however, did nothing to improve conditions. Instead, they prepared to fight the reform lobbies and progressive politicians. In the battles that followed, James A. Emery of the National Association of Manufacturers developed many of the techniques of modern pressure politics. He showed the effectiveness of deluging legislators with telegrams from their constituents, and of pointing out to politicians the power of the interests affected by their acts. "No objectionable bill will pass through the hands of any committee after Mr. Emery has a chance to tell them what it is," gloated the president of the N.A.M. in 1909. "If he gets a chance at them I will promise you the bill is dead from that moment."

Persuasive though Mr. Emery was, the reformers did achieve some measure of success. Between 1901 and 1917 the legislatures of many industrial states passed laws compelling employers to insure against accidents to workers; prohibiting child labor; requiring school attendance; and limiting hours of labor for women.

Labor and the Courts

Many of the apparent gains for labor were undone by the courts. Conservative judges threw out compulsory-insurance laws on the ground that such statutes deprived employers of property without due process of law. Laws regulating hours of labor were scrapped because, it was said, they violated freedom of contract.

Gradually, though, the picture changed. Regulatory laws were rewritten to meet constitutional objections. Liberals were elected or appointed to posts previously held by conservatives. State tribunals reversed previous decisions; and in 1908 the United States Supreme Court approved state legislation limiting hours of work for women (Muller *vs.* Oregon). It took nine years more to bring approval of a state law limiting the working day for men (Bunting *vs.* Oregon). By 1913 state workmen's compensation and child labor laws were generally meeting the judicial test. More advanced social legislation covering pensions and minimum wages continued to be disallowed.

In issues arising from labor disputes the courts adhered to traditional interpretations. The loosely drawn Clayton Antitrust Act of 1914 attempted to limit the use of injunctions in labor cases. Nevertheless, judges kept on issuing court orders against strikers, saying that this was necessary to protect property. In Coppage *vs.* Kansas (1915), the Supreme Court declared unconstitutional a state law prohibiting employers from forcing workers to sign yellow-dog contracts (pledges not to join a union). Two years later, in the Hitchman Coal and Coke decision, the same tribunal denied union delegates the right to organize workers where such contracts were in effect.

Scientific Management

Although hostile to reform legislation, some owners and managers did turn their attention to labor problems. Hoping to increase output, some employers worked out incentive schemes and improved factory conditions. And many took interest in the work of Frederick W. Taylor, the "father of scientific management."

As early as the 1880's Taylor was impressed by the low efficiency of American shops. Lost motion, wasted time, listless work seemed too often the rule. Resigning an executive post, Taylor became in 1893 the first specialist in "systematizing shop management and manufacturing costs." He sold his services to many companies; and others picked up such parts of his system as incentive pay for higher production. By 1912, Taylor had imitators all over the world.

In developing his system, Taylor used time-motion studies to analyze given jobs and to set standards of performance. He also urged the proper placing of machines and careful division of labor under trained foremen. To achieve maximum exertion from each worker he favored paying wages on a piece-rate basis "scientifically" adjusted to be fair to all operatives. Unions had no place in the Taylor system.

Although no company adopted Taylor's ideas in their entirety, workers disliked what they saw of scientific management. If employees responded well to piecework rates and doubled their wages, the company cut the rates. If workers went all out in some competition for bonuses, the employers expected them to maintain the accelerated rate thereafter. The president of a business machine concern, for example, exulted: "The gowns were offered as prizes for excellent work. . . . Output increased 100,000 pieces in two weeks. The girls showed themselves what they could do when they needed to, and since that time the production has never fallen below these records." To workingmen, then, Taylorism seemed merely a rationalized speed-up, and they wanted none of it.

Welfare Capitalism

As social legislation went into effect, employers found that it did not hurt them as much as they had feared. Workmen's compensation laws caused businessmen to install safety devices. These devices reduced accidents and resulted in increased production. Statutory limitation of the work day saved light and fuel; and workers turned out about as much product in nine hours as they had formerly in ten.

Some managers further discovered that better lighting and more comfortable working conditions yielded good results. Cafeterias, clean washrooms, rest periods, and recreational facilities attached workers to a particular plant and cut down the need for training replacements. Shortage of labor in the World War I boom emphasized all these matters and led to personnel studies aimed at picking the right man for the job, and keeping him at it.

A few industrialists counted on profit sharing to increase incentive and promote attachment to the company. Some firms experimented with annual bonuses based on profits. Others tried plans calling for the installment sale of common stock to workers. Neither program was successful. Corporate profits were too variable to have employees' living standards geared to them. Workers preferred to have the company pay good wages rather than to have it dispense unpredictable windfalls. Stock purchase failed because the worker could not save enough to buy any meaningful holding, and the installment plan tied him to the company, often to a nonunion contract.

After 1900 a growing number of business leaders became conscious of the workers' desire for democratic self-expression. As early as 1904 the American Rolling Mills established a work council to represent employees. Edward Filene introduced a similar system in his Boston department store. But it was the system established in the Rockefeller-owned Colorado Fuel and Iron Company, after a bloody strike in 1914, that first attracted general attention to the "company union." The spread of such unions was greatly aided by the attitude of government boards during World War I. These boards took the position that companies receiving war contracts should bargain with representatives of their employees. As a consequence, General Electric and 125 other large companies instituted their own unions.

At first Samuel Gompers regarded the movement with favor. He thought it would accustom workers to union membership, and that they would presently swing over to affiliation with the A.F. of L. The error of this calculation soon became apparent. The leaders of company unions hoped for promotion within the company; hence they could not afford to quarrel with their employers. They might urge better work conditions, they might bring up reasonable grievances. But they could not work for affiliation with the A.F. of L. without forfeiting chances for promotion, and perhaps losing their jobs. Company unions, therefore, were often a bar to true collective bargaining.

The dilemma of the company union was typical of the problem of the relations of labor and management. Even in the factories where welfare plans were tried, the managerial emphasis was on lowering costs. Few plant superintendents would dare to argue the value of a welfare program save on a moneymaking basis. This largely explains the limited results of such efforts. Workers came to suspect that each improvement was either a device to stall off pay increases or a subtle means of increasing production. The same attitude applied when welfare programs extended to improved company housing and model company towns. Almost invariably the worker sensed a loss of independence and a tendency on the part of the company to give him pleasant conditions only in return for harder work.

Like other human beings, workers value prestige as well as pay. It was in this area of personal values that the welfare programs ran into the chief barrier between management and labor. The companies that did the most for their workers were in general strongly antiunion. The heads of these firms were unwilling to admit labor to any real participation in policy or planning. Able management sought rapid change, displacement of labor by machines, a dynamic situation in which no job could be guaranteed. Unions stressed fixed rules and the right of the worker to his job. Most managers could see no way of bringing these views together, no hope of treating organized labor as a partner in the enterprise.

Yet the worker was taught in school to believe in majority rule and the importance of the rights of every individual. How could these doctrines be reconciled with the system of authoritarian leadership in business? In his doubts and resentments the employee was mirroring the twentieth-century struggle between administrative efficiency and social democracy. Great complex business machines had been built under aggressive, autocratic leaders. How could the structure be fitted to the traditions of majority rule?

Better Times for Agriculture

For the farmers, the first two decades of the twentieth century were years of relative prosperity. They were years, however, in which little was done to attack the fundamental problems of agriculture. Hence those who tilled the soil were to be ill prepared for the difficulties which would press down on them after World War I.

Rural problems had gone from bad to worse after the Civil War, reaching a climax of calamity in the drought and depression of the early 1890's. Then, rather suddenly, many farmers found their situation improved. Rain returned to the prairies. Farm prices rose as the gold supply increased and as the growth of urban population swelled the demand for food and textiles. The wholesale prices of manufactured goods went up 30 percent between 1900 and 1914. The increase in farm prices was double that amount, 60 percent.

As their lot improved, many farmers became optimistic. Higher income permitted some owners to pay off mortgages and to buy the equipment which improved technology was making available. The discouragement and bitterness of 1896 therefore yielded to a spirit of hope and confidence. Money was coming in. New roads brought the farmer nearer to his market. The new machines were increasing production. And a whole new world was coming into being, with the phonograph, the telephone, the movies, the automobile, electric lights, and septic tanks. Although these luxuries were beyond the reach of most farmers, rural standards of living were rising all along the social scale.

Urged on by science and by improved market opportunities, farmers turned to new crops: citrus fruits, for instance, in Florida, California, Texas. At the same time, agrarians took up new lands, continuing the westward movement which had been in progress since colonial days. Although 1890 marked the end of the frontier as a continuous line, there remained much unsettled government land. Part of it was in isolated patches here and there; but there were also enormous tracts of land on the western plains, from the Dakotas and Montana to Oklahoma and Texas. Americans took up these lands with enthusiasm, the new land booms resembling those of earlier days. Wheat and cotton both moved westward in this period. There was much land speculation; and there was more homesteading in the ten years after 1900 than in the preceding decade.

While completing the settlement of the United States, farmers were trying to work together. The Grangers had experimented with coöperation, as had the Populists. Success, however, had been very limited. There were less than a thousand farmers' coöperative societies in the nation in 1896. By 1921, the number had grown to more than 11,000. Coöperatives were especially strong in the Middle West, and had proved notably successful in the marketing field. Of the several groups behind the movement, two stood out: the American Society of Equity, started in Indiana in 1902; and the Farmers' Union, organized in Texas that same year.

Agriculture also registered gains through government channels. Though disappointed in the defeat of Bryan in 1896, the farmers stayed in politics. Many stuck with the Democrats; others built influence among the Republicans. And in 1910, at long last, agricultural groups organized an effective farm lobby in the national capital.

The decade that followed saw the emergence of two important farm groups—the Nonpartisan League and the American Farm Bureau Federation. The Nonpartisan League, which was founded in North Dakota in 1915, soon became influential in several wheat states. Not exactly a political party, the Nonpartisan League endorsed major-party candidates who favored the establishment of government warehouses, easier credit, and the like. Under the leadership of Arthur C. Townley, the Nonpartisan League temporarily captured the Republican machinery in North Dakota and strengthened a new Farmer-Labor party in Minnesota. But after 1920, the League lost ground.

Meantime, the more conservative Farm Bureau Federation came into being (1920). Working through county agents, this organization sought to improve agricultural methods and to promote the organization of coöperatives. At the same time, the Farm Bureau Federation entered the political field as a lobbying agency. Through its efforts and those of other interested associations a bipartisan farm bloc was organized in Congress in the early 1920's.

Working at all government levels, the farmers obtained a good deal between the middle 1890's and the early 1920's. They secured better roads, first from the state and local governments, then (in Woodrow Wilson's administration) from the United States as well. Congress and the state legislatures voted increased sums for agricultural research and agricultural education. Landmarks here were two Congressional statutes, the Smith-Lever Act of 1914 (which provided for demonstration work through county agents) and the Smith-Hughes Act of 1917 (which promoted agricultural education through the high schools). With the passage of the Hepburn (1906), Mann-Elkins (1910), and Valuation (1913) acts, federal regulation of the railroads became more effective than before. The credit situation also improved, especially after the creation of the Federal Farm Loan System in 1916.

And United States government support of irrigation became significant with the adoption of the Reclamation Act of 1902.

Unsolved Problems
Despite these measures and the general
agrarian prosperity, the farmers did not solve their basic problems in
this era. First of all, they failed to tackle the question of farm tenancy.
With land and equipment going up in price, it became more and more
difficult to acquire a farm. Tenancy therefore increased; and a young
man starting out as a renter was likely to be one when he died. As in
earlier years, the situation was at its worst in the South, where the
sharecrop system was tied to racial as well as to economic questions.

Nor was tenancy the only labor problem. Large-scale farming became the rule in the wheat empire and in some fruit-growing regions.
This brought a demand for farm labor—mainly migratory workers
who were hired as harvest hands. Mexicans as well as natives were
used for this work, which paid little and made a settled life impossible.
Yet almost no one tried to improve the lot of these unfortunates—
neither the government, nor the employers, nor the major religious
and labor leaders. The I.W.W. did try to organize in this field, but
with only limited and temporary success.

Farmers could have used the good times of 1900–19 to diversify
their crops. Had they done so, they might have decreased their dependence on uncertain foreign markets. Perhaps, too, diversification
would have reduced the severity of the "overproduction" problem of
a later day. But diversification called for skill in planning and in execution. Tenants and hired hands generally lacked the desire or the
ability to experiment. Owners, too, preferred soil-exhausting staples,
because they feared change and wanted a cash crop.

In this picture, the foreign market was a major factor; and one
could see trouble ahead. Cotton and tobacco commanded a good
European market in the decade and a half before the First World
War. Meat and wheat did not do so well. Americans were producing
more pork than ever on Iowa corn-and-hog farms; more beef than
ever on western cattle ranches; more wheat than ever as the western

plains went under the plow. But simultaneously production was soaring in Canada and South America, in Australia and New Zealand. After 1900, foreign markets for American meat and cereal products began to melt away; but neither the government nor the farmers gave much study to the matter.

American agriculturalists were also failing to take care of their nation's land resources. One-crop agriculture exhausted the soil. Erosion went unchecked. Forest fires destroyed much of value. President Theodore Roosevelt and his successors in the White House developed a conservation program, as did many state officials. But at the same time, other government officials seemed to encourage waste of natural resources. Congress, for example, made homesteading easier between 1900 and 1914 by increasing the amount of land one could homestead and by allowing settlers to obtain title in a shorter time. This encouraged some to settle land that should have been left for grazing. For in many areas, plowing the plains led to wind erosion; and the topsoil blew away.

8

The People and
Maturing Capitalism

A New Standard of Living

Rising prices from 1896 to 1919 were a real benefit to the farmer and businessman and added to the appearance of prosperity in the nation as a whole. Gold from Yukon mines increased bank reserves and credit. Export surpluses of farm and factory products brought the currencies of the world to New York and improved the terms of dollar exchange. But more important than these in raising the middle-class standard of living was the increased variety of goods for sale at moderate prices. Here was the beginning of an age of continuous marvels in consumers' goods, a period that would lead many to regard such possessions as the chief aim of life.

The range was wide. Factory-processed goods improved the American diet. Prepared cereals took the place of meat, baked beans, and grits at breakfast. Canned fruits and vegetables added variety to a previously limited winter menu. Improved transportation served the same end. In the 1890's large quantities of citrus fruits began to come east from California, and at the same time new railroads developed orange-growing areas in Florida. During cold weather fast freight trains brought fresh vegetables to the northern cities from the Gulf coast and the Southwest.

By 1900 one could buy at low prices ready-made women's clothing of the latest Paris style (put together by immigrant labor in New York loft buildings). The well-to-do could now afford to buy and discard ready-made hats, shirtwaists, and dresses in response to annual changes in fashion. All members of the family could have the thrill of selecting stereopticons, sports equipment, musical instruments, and hundreds of other new possessions from an increasingly wide and cheap assortment. Installment plans brought more expensive goods like pianos and phonographs within the reach of working-class families. Even the Sears, Roebuck mail-order house, which had denounced such practices in earlier years, advertised pianos at $5.00 a month in 1915.

Equally important in reshaping American society was the increased mobility of the people. Bicycles, trolley cars, and automobiles gradually extended the normal range of individual movement. Down to 1880, farmers seldom traveled more than a dozen miles from home, except when changing residence. The city dweller's world was even more restricted. Then the "safety bicycle" revolutionized travel possibilities. By the 1890's single- to seven-seaters were the standard American vehicle. Urban families with sturdy legs pedaled twenty miles on their multiseated machines for picnics in the country. Despite bad roads, farm families found it easier to go to town now that they did not have to hitch the horse and take him away from the farm work. Bicycle clubs lobbied for better roads, and induced New Jersey and other states to start spending considerable sums on hard surfacing. This rebirth of the turnpike age presently helped the introduction of the automobile.

Electric trolleys with their cheaply laid tracks and low fares also broadened the daily range of travel in and around cities. From 1915 on, buses came to do the same work more economically. The trolley then declined in importance; and eventually much of the 45,000 miles of trolley track was torn up or abandoned.

Of all the new consumer utilities, the automobile was the most important. It gave a thrill of power to the city dweller suffering from a depersonalized world; and in time its use profoundly altered American economic life. By 1910 cars were sufficiently cheap and reliable to encourage long trips and regular use for commuting purposes. Ten years later there were 7,000,000 passenger automobiles in operation, more than one for every four families in the United States. Through highways were already relocating country towns and diverting local business from small-town general stores to the bigger establishments in nearby cities. Farmers were enjoying a new range of markets, schools, and recreation. Suburban areas accessible only by automobile were attracting upper-class families away from Main Street mansions. As standardized apartments took the place of individual houses in many cities, the car came to be one of the most significant marks of social prestige. And whereas an expensive house was a symbol of success that could be noted only in one's home town, the Packard or Pierce Arrow could accompany its owner everywhere.

Population Trends

In 1896 the population of the United States was just over 70,000,000. Twenty-five years later it was half again that large, and stood at 105,000,000. Immigration accounted for roughly half of the increase. The rest represented the excess of the birth rate over the death rate.

Although the increase was substantial, the rate of increase was declining. In the generation before 1896 the population of the country nearly doubled. It would take two full generations after 1896 to have it double again. Part of the explanation for this could be found in the slowing down of immigration after 1914. Fully as important was the relationship of the birth rate to the rise of the cities.

The rise of the cities continued to be a striking feature of American growth. In 1896 less than two-fifths of the American people lived in places of 2500 or more inhabitants. By 1921, the figure was more than half. In 1890 there were fewer than sixty cities with a population above 50,000. The census of 1920 listed more than 150 such places. Many cities grew tremendously. Los Angeles, barely 50,000 in the early 1890's, was well beyond half a million three decades later. Atlanta and Cleveland more than trebled their population in the same years, Detroit increased by 400 percent, and joined New York, Chicago, and Philadelphia in the million-inhabitants class by the 1920's.

This urban growth was a world-wide phenomenon. All over the globe men and women were flocking to the cities, spurred on by waning opportunities in agriculture and by the economic, social, and cultural advantages of urban areas. The children of old-stock American farmers left rural areas to seek their fortunes in the city. In the nineteenth century, many European immigrants to the United States had settled on the land. In the twentieth, nearly all newcomers crowded into the industrial cities. They came in quantity, more than a million a year by 1910. Every northern and western city had its large immigrant community; and in the early 1920's more than 30 percent of the population of New York, Boston, Cleveland, and Chicago was foreign born.

Meantime, Negroes who saw no future in southern agriculture moved to southern and northern cities. This migration was impressive in the first decade of the twentieth century. It became even more so after 1914. Altogether, more than 1,700,000 Negroes moved to urban areas between 1896 and 1919, nearly half of these going to northern cities.

A Declining Birth Rate

The movement cityward definitely contributed to the slump in the rate of population growth. The urban birth rate was less than that of rural areas. City people found it difficult to bring up big families in crowded surroundings. The economic insecurity of urban life was also a factor in the situation, as was the middle-class belief that small families were associated with a higher standard of living.

The decline in the birth rate was marked in the middle and upper classes in the cities. This began to cause public comment as early as the 1840's. Children were becoming more and more of an economic burden, what with mounting bills for medical attention and for prolonged education. Obviously, the fewer the children, the more one could do for those one had. Besides that, the health of mothers was better assured if they did not bear children too frequently. Selfish motives were sometimes involved—the more children, the more trouble and expense. Mixed motives, therefore, led an increasing number of middle-class couples to limit the size of their families. The middle-class tendency to delay marriage until one had a little money saved affected the situation. Also significant were the contraceptive devices made available by commercial concerns.

Reactions to the declining birth rate were varied. Catholic authorities and conservative Protestants condemned as sinful the use of contraceptives even by married couples. Fighting on the other side was Margaret Sanger, a nurse who had witnessed the suffering of poor women burdened by frequent childbearing. After her arrest for circulating a pamphlet on family limitation (1914), this advocate of birth control organized a national association which eventually led to the creation of the Planned Parenthood Federation of America. In 1921 Mrs. Sanger opened a birth control clinic in Brooklyn. Although this was closed by the police, a higher court ruled that in New York physicians could give contraceptive information when childbearing would impair a patient's health. Similar victories followed in many other states.

Critics of the birth control movement often noted that the advocates of family limitation had most influence with the upper- and middle-class parents best able to support large families. The poor, both in the cities and in the country, continued to have many children. There was some point to this argument; but after World War I the birth rate would decline among all social, economic, and religious groups, even among the poorest urban and rural classes.

A Declining Death Rate

The decline in the national birth rate was partly offset by a simultaneous drop in the death rate. This had been decreasing slowly for many years; in Massachusetts, for instance, it fell from twenty-one per thousand inhabitants in 1865 to seventeen in 1899. The national rate went down from seventeen to thirteen during the next two decades. (By 1948 it had dipped below ten.)

The death rate was not uniform. It was higher for males than for females; higher for the colored population than for whites. Down to 1915, rural areas had a somewhat lower death rate than did urban regions. Thereafter, several large cities claimed to have brought their rate down as low as that of country districts in their respective states. Within cities, the lowest death rates (like the lowest birth rates) continued to obtain in the so-called better neighborhoods.

The drop in the death rate, especially in the cities, was related to the more varied diet; to better medical care of small children; and to sanitary improvements and special preventive measures against infectious disease. Since little progress was made against the degenerative diseases of the older age groups (cancer and heart trouble, for example), it was chiefly the children and young adults who benefited. Thus the death rate for infants under one year declined dramatically between 1900 and 1920 from 162 per thousand population of that group to ninety-two. For adults between sixty-five and seventy-four years of age, the rate fell only from fifty-six to fifty-two.

Despite improved life expectancy for children, the drop in the birth rate was such as to decrease the percentage they represented in the total population. The median age of the entire population gradually rose from less than twenty-three at the beginning of the century to more than twenty-five two decades later. Americans, on the average, were slowly becoming an older people.

Combined with the difficulties of caring for old people in urban homes, this trend would eventually lead to conscious efforts to improve the lot of elderly people. Senior citizens displayed some initiative themselves in this connection. Those who could afford it migrated in the winters (or permanently) to Florida and California. There they could enjoy associations with others of their generation. At the same time professional groups and some of the larger corporations organized retirement plans. Those outside began to hope for old-age pensions.

The New Immigration

A notable population trend was the changing character of immigration. Until the late 1880's most of those who crossed the Atlantic to settle in the New World came from northern and western Europe, especially from the British Isles, Germany, and Scandinavia. After 1890, eastern and southern Europe provided the majority of immigrants. The change was dramatic. During the 1880's less than a fifth of the immigrants came from southern and eastern Europe. In the 1890's the proportion jumped to more than half; and it went beyond 70 percent in the first decade of the new century.

Several circumstances explained the shift. In the first place, British, German, and Scandinavian industry enjoyed prosperity during this period. Standards of living improved, and social legislation provided

THE COUNTRIES OF ORIGIN OF THE NEW AND OLD IMMIGRATION

1840-1860

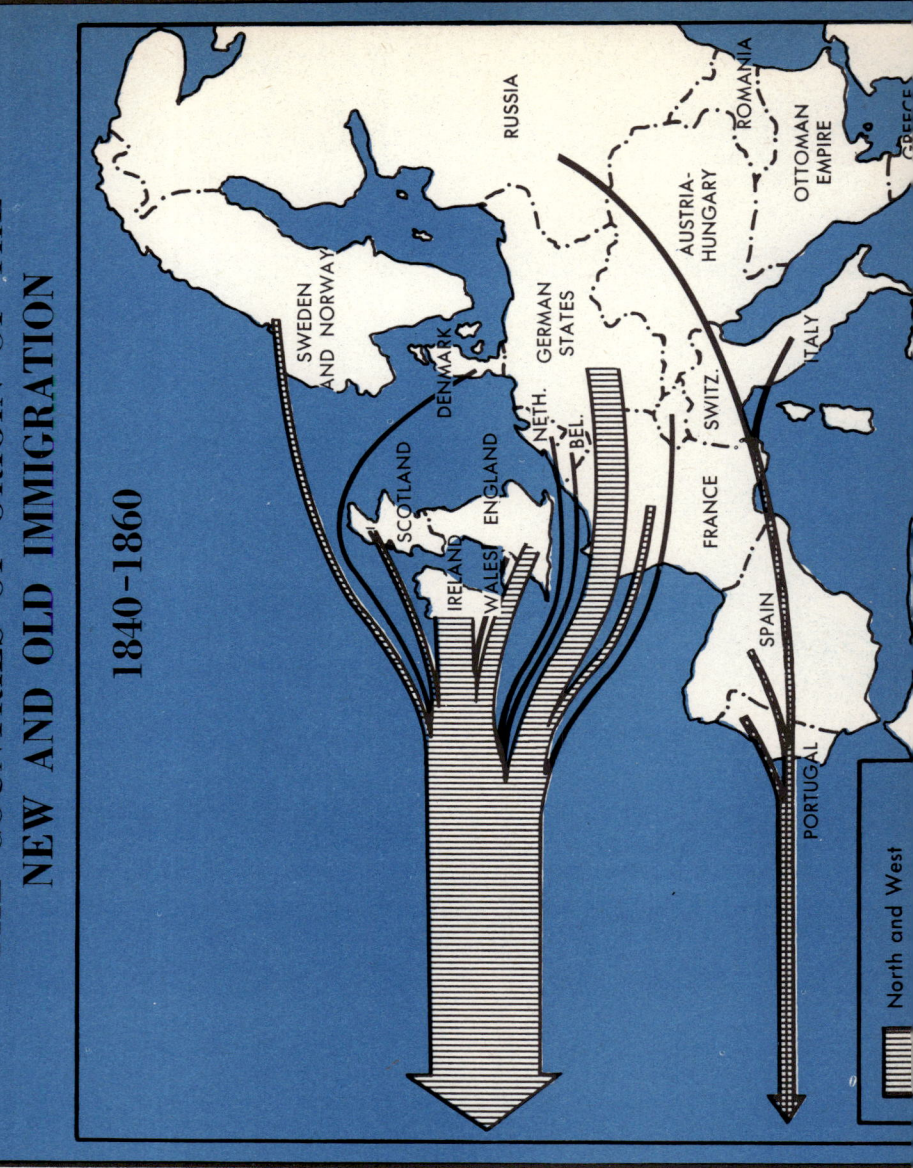

SWEDEN AND NORWAY

DENMARK

RUSSIA

SCOTLAND

IRELAND

WALES

ENGLAND

NETH.

BEL.

GERMAN STATES

SWITZ.

AUSTRIA-HUNGARY

ROMANIA

OTTOMAN EMPIRE

GREECE

FRANCE

ITALY

SPAIN

PORTUGAL

North and West

The immigrants who came to the United States before the Civil War were largely from northern and western Europe —from Germany and Ireland in particular. This "old immigration" continued on a large scale until after World War I. Meantime, however, there developed a "new immigration" from eastern and southern Europe. The "new immigration" reached its peak after 1900.

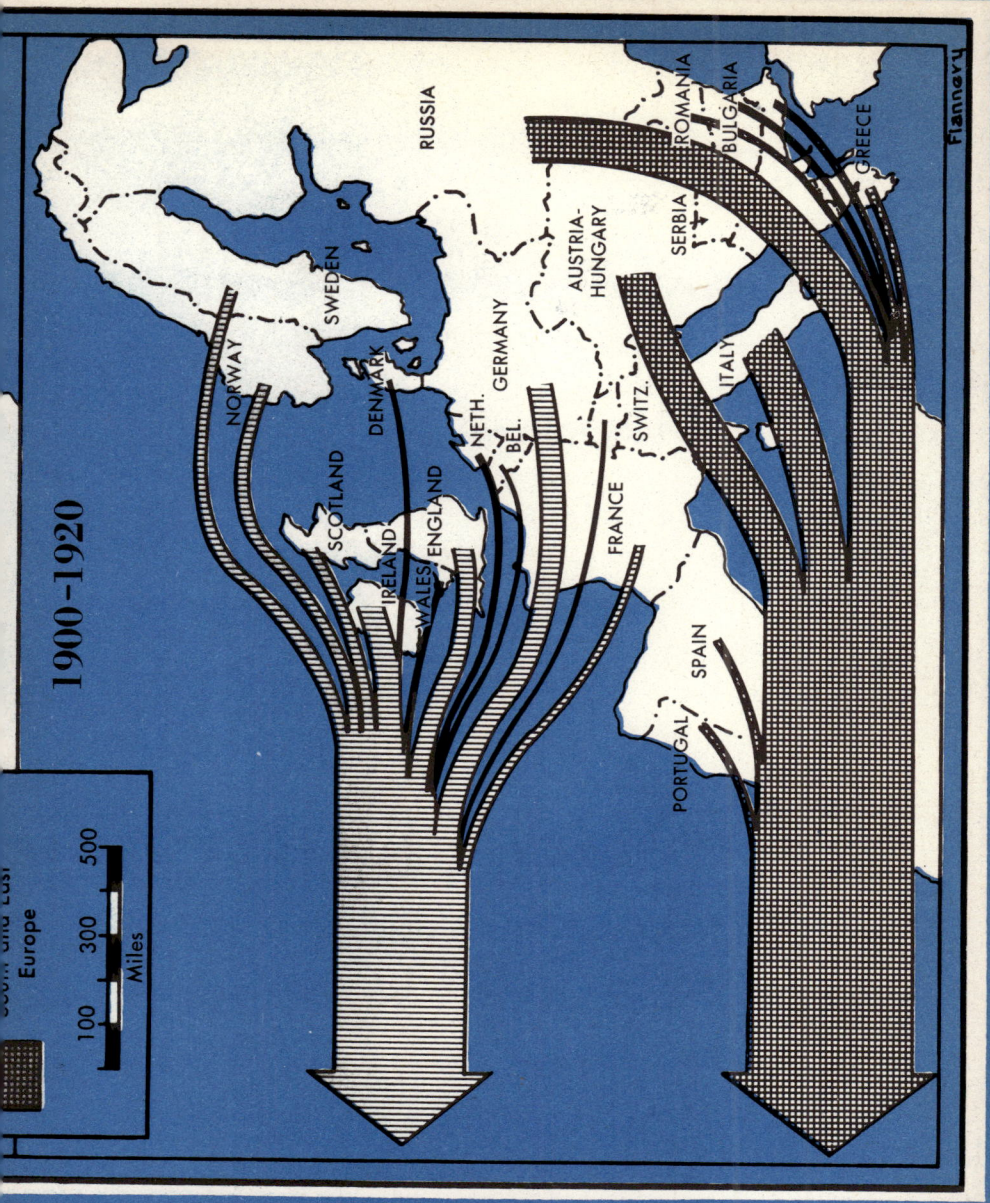

1900–1920

North and East
Europe

Miles
100   300   500

RUSSIA

SWEDEN

NORWAY

DENMARK

SCOTLAND

IRELAND

WALES

ENGLAND

NETH.

BEL.

GERMANY

FRANCE

SWITZ.

AUSTRIA-HUNGARY

ITALY

SERBIA

ROMANIA

BULGARIA

GREECE

SPAIN

PORTUGAL

Flannery

As cheap land disappeared, and opportunities for employ-ment declined, demand for im-migration restriction increased. Some restrictionists favored reducing immigration from all foreign countries. Others wanted a selective quota sys-tem, designed to favor north European countries ("old im-migration"), since most Ameri-cans were of north European stock. The immigration law of 1924 followed this line.

an increased sense of security for the working class. At the same time, many citizens of Italy, Austria-Hungary, Russia, and the Balkans found economic conditions increasingly difficult and encountered additional burdens associated with anti-Semitism and militarism (which involved conscription and new taxes). The New World beckoned to these people, promising jobs, a better standard of living, religious freedom, and peace.

Steamship lines made migration easier by opening direct connections between eastern and southern Europe and the United States. These transportation companies launched propaganda campaigns calling attention to the attractions of the New World. So did American employers who wanted cheap labor. Even more impressive were the messages which those who had migrated wrote to friends and relatives back home. These letters described America in glowing terms; and often they enclosed passage money for those left behind.

The arrival of the Poles and Czechs, Italians, Greeks, Hungarians, and Russians alarmed many native-born Americans. There had been opposition to the old immigration, too. But the north Europeans who had come in before 1890 represented a fairly advanced standard of living and a culture not essentially different from that of the United States. Save for the Irish and south Germans, the immigrants of 1840–90 had been overwhelmingly Protestant, as were most old-stock Americans. Those who came in after 1890, on the other hand, came from cultural backgrounds of a somewhat different sort. Few of the new immigrants belonged to the Protestant churches active in the United States. Instead, the newcomers were mainly Roman Catholic, Greek Orthodox, or Jewish.

Judging the new immigrants, many native Americans overlooked the significant contributions of the newcomers to the development of industry and the enrichment of American culture. The tendency was rather to criticize the new arrivals for huddling together in the slums, for retaining Old World ways, for selling their votes, for indulging in crime. Often the criticism was grossly unfair. As an example, the immigrants were attacked as clannish when they lived in their own settlements, and denounced as pushing when they tried to mix with older residents. And the critics forgot that municipal corruption, slums, sweatshops, and city crime all predated the arrival of the new immigrants.

In any case, culture conflict was inevitable. Many of the newcomers desired to become Americanized; but the process was retarded by the conditions under which they lived and by their Old World heritage of poverty, ignorance, and frustration. Too often the new arrivals took on only the superficial aspects of American culture. This resulted in psychological conflicts, which became more pronounced as the gulf widened between the first generation and their children. In school and elsewhere, the children learned that European ways were a social and economic handicap which kept them from "getting ahead." Such discoveries brought cultural disorganization, which in turn produced unhappiness and, sometimes, delinquency and crime.

The melting pot, said some Americans, no longer worked.

Restrictive Legislation

Organized labor joined in the protests against the new immigration. Immigrants accustomed to a low standard of living accepted wages that the native American worker spurned. Newcomers with peasant backgrounds failed to understand the advantages of trade unions. Some would not join even when they could (most were excluded anyway, as unskilled workers). All of this made labor leaders hostile to immigrants. The dislike increased when employers hired immigrants as strikebreakers. Finally, the few immigrants who did enter the labor movement included socialists and anarchists whom the native American workers disliked as much as they disliked employers. Many American labor leaders believed that radical immigrants deliberately provoked violence in strikes, thus setting public opinion against the whole labor movement.

As a result trade unionists early favored partial or complete exclusion of immigrants. The Knights of Labor fought for exclusion of Orientals as early as the 1870's. The American Federation of Labor stood for curtailment of immigration from the 1880's on. Many American-born workers, in the unions and out, backed the American Protective Association, the anti-Catholic, anti-immigrant organization that briefly threatened (in the 1890's) to become a strong political force.

The exclusionists won their first victories in connection with immigration from the Far East. Chinese coolies had been brought to the United States to provide cheap labor in the construction of western railways. Gradually, they had turned to other pursuits. Like the Japanese, who came later and in smaller numbers, the Chinese worked for a pittance and thus undercut native laborers. In addition, the Orientals did not prove easily assimilable in a social sense. Hence there were disgraceful anti-Chinese riots in the western states (twenty-eight Chinese were killed in the Rock Springs, Wyoming, massacre of 1885). And political agitators like the Irish-born Denis Kearney of California shouted that "the Chinese must go!"

Responding to labor and other pressures, Congress suspended Chinese immigration in 1882, and put exclusion on a permanent basis in 1902. By then feeling was developing against immigrants from other Oriental areas—a Japanese and Korean Exclusion League was organized on the west coast in 1905. To prevent the passage of further exclusion legislation, President Theodore Roosevelt worked out a gentlemen's agreement (1907) under which the government of Japan agreed to limit the emigration of laborers to America. This, though, did not satisfy the exclusionists. California and other states passed laws discriminating against Orientals. Congress followed suit, adopting legislation which specifically excluded most Asiatics in 1917, and Japanese as well seven years later.

In barring Asiatics, many Americans operated on the assumption that Orientals were not only different from Occidentals but inherently inferior. Unfounded in scientific knowledge, this view was nonetheless widely entertained. It helps explain why Asiatics were not permitted to become naturalized citizens of the United States. Obviously, such a position aroused much antagonism in the Far East; and it later enabled the expanding Japanese empire to denounce as hypocritical American statements about democratic equality.

In the 1880's, when excluding the Chinese, Congress also began to restrict immigration from Europe. In a series of statutes passed in that and the next two decades, the United States excluded contract laborers, convicts, prostitutes, anarchists, the mentally ill, and others likely to become public charges. The restrictionists wanted still more drastic measures; and in four separate years they persuaded Congress to pass bills requiring a literacy test. Feeling that illiteracy reflected lack of opportunity rather than inferiority, Presidents Cleveland (1897), Taft (1913), and Wilson (1915, 1917) vetoed these bills. The last of them, however, was passed over Wilson's veto and became law.

The passage of the act of 1917 indicated the growing strength of those who wanted to abandon the historic policy of welcoming foreigners to American shores. Riots against aliens (as in Omaha in 1915) were another sign of the changing times. So was the organization of a new Ku Klux Klan in Atlanta in 1915. The Klan, a secret society hostile to Negroes and Catholics and Jews, included in its program definite opposition to immigration.

Just before World War I an effort was made to speed up the Americanization process by a vast educational program. When this failed, many declared that the doors should be closed to outsiders, as a way of safeguarding the American way of life. The exclusionists won further converts by claiming (in the face of evidence to the contrary) that immigrants were likely to be disloyal in wartime. More telling still were claims that a flood of immigrants from an impoverished postwar Europe would threaten American standards of living. The 1920's, therefore, would see the exclusionists triumphant.

Increasing Inequalities

In the first quarter of the twentieth century millions of immigrants turned their backs on a Europe of poverty, insecurity, and religious intolerance and sought the comforts and freedom which democratic America promised. At this very same time new-rich Americans moved in the opposite direction. In an effort to increase their prestige, these social climbers frequented the fashionable resorts of the Old World and married their daughters to titled (and often impoverished) Europeans.

The United States had long known a wealthy class. Before the Civil War, however, fortunes rarely exceeded a million dollars. The post-

Civil War commercial and industrial expansion produced far greater wealth. Every large city had its millionaires and multimillionaires. In many instances the established aristocracy—those who had inherited wealth—cold-shouldered the newly rich. But the latter persevered, and they or their children or grandchildren were ultimately admitted to "society."

Even those beyond the pale seemed to like to read about the four hundred, the ones who set the social pace. Society pages reported the fabulous banquets and balls staged in princely mansions. Much ink was spilled about society at the opera, society at the summer resorts, society at the races, society abroad. Some events even made the London headlines—for example, an 1897 ball which cost the Bradley Martins of New York $369,000.

In New York City snobbery reached unprecedented heights in competition for the most favored boxes at the Metropolitan Opera House. Those eager for status spared neither pains nor dollars in efforts to trace their family lineage back to British and French monarchs. It became the height of fashion to be presented at the Court of St. James in Britain—but other courts were better than nothing. No one knows how many daughters of the rich married Old World titles. One writer estimated that by 1910 some 500 American women had taken a fifth of a billion dollars to titled European husbands.

This display of conspicuous waste defied the traditions of democracy and mocked the middle-class Americans who tried to emulate the rich. But high society mocked even more bitterly the mass of citizens who did not enjoy what economists and sociologists called the American standard of living. The increasing inequalities in the United States became ever more evident to foreign visitors who contrasted the living habits of the rich and the poor. A study of 1890 indicated that seven-eighths of the families held only one-eighth of the wealth. A later examination of estates probated in five urban and rural counties in Wisconsin confirmed these estimates. In these counties the top 1 percent owned half the property probated, whereas the bottom two-thirds had less than 6 percent. Clearly, a few Americans enjoyed luxury while many were barely able to make ends meet.

Despite these facts, Americans clung to the belief that courage, industry, and ordinary luck would produce success. The country boasted many self-made men; and the tradition of the success story as set forth by Horatio Alger had surprising vitality. Newspaper writers, educators, and public relations counsels of industrialists helped keep this cult of the self-made man alive, by way of insisting that the American system offered equal opportunities to all. The doctrine was not discredited until the great depression that set in in 1929.

Family Patterns

Although political and economic issues were highly important, most individuals were even more concerned about their family problems. The normal man was of course interested in his job, but not simply on his own behalf. Could he be secure enough to marry or to provide his children with a better chance? Women, too, were absorbed in family matters.

As has been seen, the urbanization process broke up the economic unity of the family. Wives remained economic assets among the poor, since they often worked in factories; and children also took jobs when they reached twelve or fourteen. But father, mother, and the children no longer worked together as on the farm. They separated early in the day and reassembled in the evening, so that most of their time was spent away from home. If the mother worked, small children were likely to be neglected and the older ones grew up on the streets.

In an effort to solve the problem, industrial states adopted compulsory-education laws. Most of these required children to attend school until they reached the fourteenth year. Hence even poor children gained educationally from the urban location, where schools were ordinarily better and sessions longer than in rural districts. Since city youngsters spent more time at school and less at home, the schools took over something of the family's function in the disciplining and supervising of the younger generation. Here and there municipal authorities were beginning to recognize this great responsibility by 1919 and to provide gymnasium facilities and baseball diamonds for use after school hours.

Mothers and children ceased to be direct economic assets to families of middle and upper station. Housewives took care of the home and of the children but no longer had to perform all the extra tasks required of their mothers and grandmothers on the farm. Yet household drudgery was greater around 1900 than it is now. Houses occupied by those in comfortable circumstances were of considerable size, intended for large families. Many provided a parlor used for formal ceremonies, in addition to a sitting room (the living room today serves both purposes). There was endless dusting, cleaning, and washing to be done by hand. A servant was therefore more necessary than in the present day of vacuum cleaners and electric washers.

In the South, household servants were Negroes; in the North, usually immigrants. Americans, however, were less certain of good domestic service than were Europeans in like circumstances. Europeans could count on a permanent servant class; but in equalitarian America maids demanded higher wages and were not expected to do the heavy work required of Old World servant women. Immigrant girls, moreover, took over the American hope of improving their station; so that sooner or later they or their children turned their back on domestic service. This was disconcerting to employers, who had to turn in each generation to some fresh supply of unassimilated newcomers.

Relieved of much routine, and possessing increased legal rights, the middle-class woman of 1910 fared much better than her ancestors. Better opportunities for education and employment also improved her situation. So did the trend away from the father-centered farm economy. Increasingly aware of her rights, the city woman began demanding absolute equality with men. She did not get it in this generation. She did, however, get the ballot, first in school, municipal, and state elections, finally on a nation-wide basis with the adoption of the Nineteenth Amendment to the Constitution (1920).

Divorce

Divorce had long been legal in most states, but had remained rare through the nineteenth century. Economic factors had worked against it in an age when the woman who left her husband had few job opportunities. Religious attitudes had also made divorce undesirable even for an "innocent party."

Points of view were shifting by 1910. Religious condemnation of divorce lessened among Protestants with the decline of theological orthodoxy. At the same time economic barriers were being reduced. Divorce also began to be viewed as one of the "women's rights" since the wife suffered more than did the husband in the typical unhappy marriage. Feminists condemned the old double standard in morals, which had required chastity in women before marriage and fidelity thereafter, while men were excused for their "affairs." As wives became more independent and conscious of their rights, they demanded that their husbands also respect the marital relationship. And when marriages broke up, many wives were not satisfied with an old-fashioned separation. Rather they insisted on divorce settlements which clearly established property rights and custody of the children.

Catholics and conservative Protestants and Jews continued to condemn divorce on theological or moral grounds. They pointed out that the availability of divorce tended to weaken family ties, and claimed that divorce broke down moral standards. Those who favored more liberal divorce laws recognized the problems of broken marriages, especially where children were involved. They argued, however, that the maintenance of totally unsuccessful unions was not likely to help either parents or children.

Social behavior was sometimes influenced by social status. Among certain classes of the very poor, irregular sex relations were not always taken seriously. Nor were existing legal formalities uniformly observed when a marriage was dissolved—desertion was "the poor man's divorce." On the other extreme, some wealthy families (especially of the so-called smart set) copied "Continental" manners. But the great majority of Americans, rich, poor, and in between, continued to be attached to the "middle-class virtues" of their ancestors.

Children Fare Better

Children received much attention in the first quarter of the twentieth century. Legislation in urban states required school attendance and prohibited the labor of young children. All over the country there were efforts to improve the schools. In the cities especially, but in rural districts too, the nation was becoming child-conscious.

In some respects, the trend was not new. Americans had long given their children more freedom and consideration than had Europeans. As a result, American teachers and European travelers had for years complained that American children were universally "spoiled." A nineteenth-century aspect of the situation was the elimination of brutal punishment both at home and in the schools. By 1920 physical punishment had largely disappeared in middle- and upper-class families and was forbidden by law in urban public schools.

In the home, changing times had made obsolete the old adage that "children should be seen but not heard." Youngsters were now more vocal than adults. Instead of being repressed, they were cultivated. Parents were urged to understand and befriend their sons and daughters. Schools as well as homes were becoming "child centered." Other organizations, such as the Boy Scouts and the Girl Scouts, provided training and relaxation for the younger generation. Churches also increased their concern for the young.

Had things been carried from one extreme to another—from overdiscipline to overindulgence? During the decades to follow, much would be heard about the "problem child" and the rise of juvenile delinquency. These phenomena, however, involved so many factors that it was extremely difficult to measure their relationship (if any) to the decline in parental control over children.

Nor was it easy to explain the greater consideration given children in this period. It was related, no doubt, to the growing influence of women, who undermined the old, father-centered household. The humanitarian interests of the progressive era also figured in the picture, as did the declining birth rate (with fewer children, each could receive more individual attention). Significant, too, was the rise in the city of specialists who gave their full attention to children's problems: educators, writers, manufacturers, psychologists. Physicians who specialized in child care (pediatricians) impressed on parents the importance of proper attention. So did city health officials bent on reducing child mortality. Psychological clinics for children with mental difficulties were set up in a number of universities after 1900; and a generation later special magazines began to enlighten middle-class parents along medical and psychological lines.

Changing Fashions

The most immediate needs of a people relate to clothing, food, and housing. Changes in these matters are therefore close to the life of any population.

After 1896, as before, wool and cotton were the most common materials for clothing, silk and linen being used chiefly by the prosperous. Most men's clothing, except that of the wealthy, was "ready made" in factories equipped with power sewing machines. Shoes for both sexes were now factory made, and the local shoemaker confined himself to repair work.

Styles were changing for both sexes. The vogue in feminine apparel was set by dressmaking firms in Paris. A few wealthy American women bought their dresses at the fashion capital. Many more patronized American dressmakers who followed the French styles; and housewives who made their own clothes used Paris-influenced patterns supplied by such women's magazines as the *Ladies' Home Journal*. The commercialization of women's fashions accelerated changes in style, for dressmaking concerns profited from any new look which necessitated the frequent purchase of new garments.

Hoop skirts, always impractical, disappeared after the Civil War; but dresses and petticoats remained full for a generation thereafter. During the 1880's and 1890's dresses were tight-waisted affairs, reaching to the floor and set off by an exaggerated bustle. Elaborate with buttons and bows, they revealed the same taste for the ornate that expressed itself also in the gingerbread details of interior decoration and architecture. Bustles, marble mantels, whatnots, and Gothic villas combined to create a late Victorian effect which, though ridiculed after 1910, is now sufficiently remote to appear interesting once more.

In general, women's styles of the 1890's still reflected nineteenth-century moral attitudes. A relatively prudish age had dictated that the fair sex be completely clothed from neck to ankle, regardless of convenience or safety. Long, heavy skirts were perfect devices for tripping their wearers and for sweeping the streets; and they made ladies somewhat helpless in emergencies. Seashore costumes were daring by comparison: short sleeves, knee-length skirts, long stockings.

Yet even by 1896 there were signs of change. Health reformers had long contended that women's styles were confining and unhealthy. Feminists urged that young ladies should be permitted exercise more violent than croquet. In apparent response, undergarments became less cumbersome, and the tight lacing of rigid corsets was gradually relaxed. The upper-middle-class ideal of the early 1900's was the Gibson girl, an outdoor type who was ready for yachting or tennis. There was a trend toward informal dress at resorts and summer camps after 1910; and teen-age girls would soon revolt against corsets altogether.

The costumes of working-class women were less elaborate than those affected by the genteel—a contrast related to price and practicality. (Millworkers had never worn hoop skirts, for obvious reasons.) But there were no distinctive class costumes in America. The equalitarian tradition prevented that.

Masculine costumes changed slowly. Trousers became narrow and relatively short (to the shoe tops) in the 1890's and the old wing collar and scarflike broad tie of the 1880's gave way to long four-in-hand ties and high, stiff collars. Other changes pointed toward greater simplicity and comfort. Thus, high shoes began to give way to low oxfords at the end of this period. Belts replaced suspenders, canes and detachable cuffs went out, and lightweight Palm Beach suits were introduced for summer wear.

Feminine hair styles changed frequently, as now; and the early 1900's saw such remarkable forms as the high pompadour. The male appearance underwent an even greater transformation. The full beard of the 1880's gave way to the handlebar mustache, then (by 1910) to the clean-shaven appearance of pre-Civil War days. Advertisers of safety razors and shaving cream speeded the transition, arguing that the fair sex liked men with smooth faces, and that "Adam did not wear a beard."

Until after the Civil War children were viewed as "little men" and "little women," and were dressed accordingly. Distinctive costumes for youngsters were introduced toward the end of the nineteenth century. Little girls now wore short dresses quite different from their mothers' cumbersome garments; boys shifted from miniature long pants to short trousers fitting tightly at the knees. Store clothes came in for children as well as adults, and there were vogues in children's

styles. One came when the novelist Frances Hodgson Burnett popularized the Little Lord Fauntleroy costume. For a time boys in
genteel families were arrayed in velvet blouses over which flowed long
curls. The protests of the boys themselves had something to do with
the passing of this style, which had disappeared by 1910.

Dietary Trends

Food habits, like clothing, changed more
rapidly in the city than in the country. Farmers continued the heavy
diet inherited from colonial days, with emphasis on meat and starchy
vegetables. This was marked in the rural South, where many whites
and Negroes depended largely on "hog and hominy" (salt pork, corn
meal, molasses) through the winter season.

Meantime, urban Americans were making concessions to the sedentary life of the cities. Only one meat was now served at dinner, and
there was more interest in fruits and green vegetables. This period
saw the introduction of foods unkown to or little used by previous
generations of Americans: tomatoes, bananas, grapefruit, broccoli.

The old plea for a greater use of whole wheat and green vegetables
was now reinforced by the biochemical discovery of vitamins. The
implications of this trend were important not only for taste but also
for personal hygiene and mortality rates. The advantages of a more
balanced diet were, however, largely confined to the prosperous classes.
Ignorance and poverty made a good diet less accessible to low-income
families.

Etiquette

The growth of equalitarian feeling in the
days of Andrew Jackson had led to some decline in formality in American social functions. But the rise of a new superwealthy class after the
Civil War brought with it a revival of formal etiquette. Elaborate
customs in dining and other entertainment were again introduced, in
imitation of those observed by European aristocrats. Correct usage on
this level was inculcated as a matter of habit (until it seemed inborn)
in expensive preparatory and finishing schools.

Most Americans rejected such formalism and preferred the informality traditional to the United States. Middle-class citizens did, however, buy and study the new etiquette books ("Consume soup quietly"). This was a part of their effort to "keep up with the Joneses."

Customs associated with marriage, birth, and death changed slowly. The tendency in the cities was to remove all these matters from the home, just as education and recreation were being separated from the family environment. Couples were married in church or in city halls. More and more urban children were born in hospitals; and the upper classes were turning from dependence on general practitioners to the more skilled services of obstetricians. There was a growing tendency, too, to transfer funeral ceremonies from the home to funeral parlors, operated by undertakers who now called themselves morticians. These specialists took care of every detail, and charged accordingly, more than some people could afford.

Commercialization of Leisure

As city residents enjoyed reduced hours of toil, they demanded facilities for recreation. But they did not expect the government to supply these for nothing, as ancient Rome had provided its famed circuses. The tradition prevailed that Americans must buy their own recreation or do without. Only a handful of cities built playgrounds and true recreational centers for the ordinary people. Most municipal governments confined their activities in this sphere to improving city parks and constructing parks and parkways on the edge of town. Some lower- and middle-class citizens used the trolleys to go fishing, take walks, and enjoy picnics in the outer parks and nearby country. These facilities, however, chiefly benefited the fairly well-to-do people who could afford automobiles. Ordinary urban citizens tended rather to use the commercial amusements available inside the city.

Much popular entertainment centered around music. Ragtime and the blues were becoming the folk songs of the machine age. Ground out along New York's tin-pan alley, pieces were available as sheet music and on phonograph records, and could be heard at vaudeville performances and in music and dance halls. Irving Berlin started his professional career as a singing waiter in such a resort.

Many theater owners bid for lower-class patronage, offering melo-drama, burlesque, and vaudeville at reasonable prices. There was heavy emphasis on sentimental romance and wild West themes; on girl shows; on acrobatics, juggling, magic, animal acts, and what passed for humor. Traveling companies took to the road, covering regular circuits built up by enterprising businessmen. There were chains of theaters, organized bookings, and well-advertised productions. Combination and efficiency, the watchwords of manufacturing, trade, and transpor-tation, had invaded the entertainment world.

Burlesque and vaudeville finally met their match in the motion picture. This developed from Thomas Alva Edison's kinetoscope, a peep-show machine which for a penny or a nickel revealed tiny figures dancing, tumbling, bathing, or sneezing. The introduction of the projector next made it possible for people to see moving pictures on a screen. The first commercial show exploiting this device was staged in New York in 1896. Proprietors of penny arcades began to show the new moving pictures in small, darkened back rooms. Then, in 1905, an enterprising promoter opened in McKeesport, Pennsylvania, a spe-cial movie theater, named the Nickelodeon. In no time at all there were nickelodeons in all the nation's cities.

The early movies flickered badly, and were confined to simple episodes: a man flirting with his stenographer, a thief escaping through city streets, fights with custard pies. The Great Train Robbery broke new ground by presenting a real story (1903). But the leaders of the new industry (largely owners of penny arcades) continued to put more stress on slapstick than on art.

As producers discovered the boy-meets-girl theme, the star system emerged. Movie-goers became acquainted with Pearl White and Mary Pickford, Charlie Chaplin and William S. Hart. These performers re-ceived more pay than established stage actors. Directors, producers, and exhibitors also profited, for by 1910 the movies earned more than all other types of commercialized amusement put together. No less than 10,000 theaters displayed pictures to an audience of 10,000,000 spectators every week.

From the beginning the movies encountered opposition from moral leaders and the intellectual and artistic elite. Not until D. W. Griffith produced *The Birth of a Nation* in 1915 did the critical-minded discover how effectively the movie makers could use the closeup, the fadeout, the switchback, and the flashback. It was apparent, too, that the movies had social impact. *The Birth of a Nation* dealt with Reconstruction in such a way as to nourish race hatreds.

Meantime, spectator sports were coming into their own. Professional prize fighting, long outlawed in most states, gained a limited respectability as bare-knuckled bouts gave way to contests with gloves, and as "Gentleman Jim" Corbett demonstrated that pugilism could involve skill as well as brutality. Large crowds attended fights in states which legalized this "sport." Heavyweight champions like James J. Jeffries and Jack Johnson drew substantial purses, and there were even greater profits for promoters such as "Tex" Rickard.

Most Americans, however, preferred baseball. This national pastime was played by amateurs on city sand lots and country pastures all over the land. It was also a highly organized and commercialized spectator sport. With the launching of the American League at the beginning of the twentieth century, there were two major professional organizations, the National and American leagues. The league champions staged a play-off for the "world's championship" at the end of each playing season. Minor leagues fed talent to the majors, and leading professional players like Christy Mathewson and Ty Cobb became nationally famous. Profits mounted. The 1913 World's Series, in which Connie Mack's Philadelphia Athletics defeated John McGraw's New York Giants, drew 150,000 spectators and over $325,000 in gate receipts. Organized baseball fought outside competition much as did big business combinations. When a new Federal League (1913–15) challenged the domination of the American and National leagues, the intruder was quickly forced out of existence.

Certain sports remained largely amateur, and confined mainly to the wealthier classes. This group included yachting, tennis, and golf, the latter two introduced from Great Britain in the 1870's. There was professional competition in golf and tennis, however, by the time of World War I. Horse racing, patronized by the rich, became thoroughly commercialized, with betting increasingly important.

The colleges helped build interest in spectator sports. Football, an

American adaptation of English Rugby, caught on quickly after Rutgers and Princeton played the first intercollegiate game (1869). By World War I, the game was attracting large crowds of alumni and their friends. Well-paid coaches and costly stadiums, emphasis on gate receipts and winning teams, plus talent scouting all suggested a quasi-professional outlook. At first, football was highly dangerous— there were forty-four fatalities in 1903. Protests led to rule changes, the use of better equipment, and a shift away from close-formation mass plays. The new game, though, was no less commercial than the old.

College rowing and track and field, which drew few spectators, avoided commercialization. So, also, did college basketball, which was invented at the Y.M.C.A. College at Springfield, Massachusetts, in the early 1890's. Eventually, however, basketball would also develop spectator interest, leading to the construction of huge gymnasium buildings and concern about the gate.

The Quest for Personal Security

Americans were finding the problem of security more pressing than ever before. As people moved to the cities and lost the self-sufficiency of the early farm, they found that income fluctuated with the state of business. Farmers likewise became dependent on the business cycle as they turned to money crops.

Under the circumstances it was inevitable that efforts would be made to provide families with some degree of security against major financial risks. Fraternal organizations offered some health, unemployment, and life insurance. Most such plans, however, yielded insufficient sums for large emergencies and reached few of the poorer workers who most needed protection.

Nor was commercial life insurance common until after 1890. Some companies had begun selling life policies before the Civil War; but the business had expanded rather slowly. The obstacles were partly psychological. Some men disliked taking out a policy calling for payment after their death, just as they disliked making a will. As a form of saving, a policy seemed less tangible than real estate, and was only as strong as the issuing company. To the poor, a life insurance policy appeared less certain than investment in a building and loan society, or even a hoard in the old stocking. Nevertheless, the habit of taking out life insurance gradually spread. One factor was the decline of rates, which was associated with increased business and longer life expectancy. Life insurance became safer, too, with the establishment of state supervision. This became general after the New York insurance investigations, conducted in 1905–06 by Charles Evans Hughes.

Although increasingly popular with the middle class, life insurance did not help the poor (save for burial policies, paid for with small, weekly payments). Nor did life insurance adequately protect any class against the risks of unemployment, illness, and old age. These risks became acute in urban society, for crowded city families were less able (and perhaps less willing) to care for the sick and aged than had been the patriarchal farm families of an earlier generation. The panics of 1893 and 1907 caused some progressive politicians to wonder if American states should not consider extending the insurance principle by law. European countries were doing this, Germany having adopted social security legislation even before 1880.

Early American efforts in this direction, however, were largely blocked by the opposition of business and labor to government paternalism. Humanitarian sentiment did secure laws regulating the labor of women and children in nearly forty states before World War I. This protected the health of poor families in some measure. Almost as many states required compensation for industrial accidents. But both labor and capital opposed early suggestions for unemployment insurance, on the ground that this would sap the rugged independence of workers. When social reformers urged the enactment of compulsory health insurance, the general opposition was supplemented by that of the organized medical profession, which felt that its own freedom would be threatened by any public program. A compulsory health insurance bill did pass one house of the New York legislature in 1915; but the movement went no further at this time.

Conservation of National Resources

While city families were increasingly concerned about individual security, the more thoughtful began to worry about national security. For two centuries the American people had acquired wealth by a ruthless exploitation of natural resources. Although these at first seemed endless, it eventually appeared that they could be and were being exhausted by unrestricted competition and greed. Soils, forests, and fur-bearing animals were being destroyed over large areas; and the long-run threat to the national economy was very real.

Individuals took the short-run view, in the interest of their own profits. (Why worry if Alaskan fur seals became extinct, provided one had made his pile in the process?) Only the states or the federal government could put a stop to this destruction. So said the American Association for the Advancement of Science as early as 1873, when it demanded government conservation of natural resources.

The efforts of scientists and naturalists finally made an impression on legislators. States passed fish and game laws and established forestry departments. In 1891 a forest service was set up in the United States Department of Agriculture, and a national forest reserve was organized. Theodore Roosevelt was the first President to display a marked interest in the program. He saved much public land from reckless exploitation by withdrawing it from entry under the land laws. He appointed a national Conservation Commission (1909). He also called a special White House conference on the subject. Here scientists met with politicians in the discussion of great public questions—an interesting event in the public relations of science.

The concept of conservation presently came to include human as well as natural resources. Was it not as important to save American children as to protect soil and seals? In 1909 Professor Irving Fisher of Yale and other private citizens issued a *Report on National Vitality: Its Waste and Conservation*. This volume urged the importance of public health programs and called attention to the need of the poor for more adequate medical care. The government must act, said Fisher, for it was "bad policy and bad economy" to leave protection against disease to private charity. This was a new note in the United States: sanitation was not enough, the poor as individuals must receive proper attention from physicians. In making his suggestions, Fisher may have been influenced by the German health insurance program. In any event, the *Report on National Vitality* made an impression, and reformers were soon urging state legislatures to adopt health insurance legislation.

This development was related to the remarkable progress of the medical sciences between 1870 and 1900. As long as medicine could do so little for patients, the poor had not worried greatly about inadequate medical care. They had usually preferred to stay out of hospitals at all costs. But now that doctors could promise more, the masses were worried by medical bills or by inability to get service because of inability to pay. This sense of frustration was closely tied to general financial insecurity, and eventually it would promote further agitation for health insurance measures. As the costs of more complicated medical services rose, even the middle classes found them difficult to meet; and they too began to look about for some means of assuring security in regard to medical care.

The wasting of human resources was dramatized in 1917–18, when the examination of military recruits revealed how widespread were preventable illness and remediable defects, even among young men. It was apparent that many of these youths could have been in good health had they received proper medical attention. In this case, the federal government as well as the health reformer was immediately interested, because illness reduced the man power available for military service. Thus the old humanitarian concern about the public health was supplemented by the modern motive of national interest.

9

Cultural Patterns

An "American Century"?

Who generates the atmosphere or "spirit" of a society? What basic themes and activities create such attitudes? Hard as it is to answer such questions, there seems little doubt that from ancient Greece to modern America the controlling points of view have been primarily the outgrowth of the beliefs of the more powerful groups in society. Hence, though the period 1896–1919 was one of declining living standards for a substantial part of the population, the "national spirit" reflected a warm glow of progress and prosperity. For those who set the standards in business and society, in education, religion, science, and the arts, this was a venturesome and satisfying era.

In the judgment of these community leaders, the United States had finally drawn abreast of the great nations of Europe. American restaurants, theaters, watering places, and mansions no longer suffered by comparison with those of the Old World nobility. In wealth and enrollment American colleges and universities were forging ahead faster than were European institutions. American scientists pursued their investigations with as good facilities as those available in the famous research centers of the European continent. Americans were challenging Old World standards even in painting and poetry.

Above all else, economically favored Americans had a deep confidence in the future. As Herbert Croly said in 1909, these citizens still believed that "somehow and sometime something better will happen to good Americans than has happened to men in any other country; and this belief, vague, innocent and uninformed though it may be, is the expression of an essential constituent in our national idea."

236

The great days still seemed to be ahead. The American Century was just dawning.

Improving Educational Opportunities

By 1896 the American people had committed themselves to the democratic ideal of equality of educational opportunity, with schooling of some sort for everybody. But much remained undone. The next generation witnessed an impressive expansion in education. This narrowed though it did not entirely close the gap between ideal and practice. This expansion was linked to the growing wealth of the United States and to the educational issues raised by industrialization and urbanization.

Figures told the story. In 1896 less than 47 percent of the population between the ages of five and seventeen attended school. A generation later there had been a rise to 56 percent. Meantime, the average number of school days per year had gone up from 140 to 160. The annual expenditure for each child in school had soared from less than $9 to more than $27, an impressive gain even when one considers the decline in the purchasing power of the dollar.

In total numbers, expansion was greatest in the elementary day schools. There enrollment increased more than 6,500,000 between 1896 and 1921, reaching 22,000,000 by the latter date. In percentages, there was an even more spectacular increase in evening schools for adults, immigrant and native. Barely 150 cities provided evening schools in the late 1890's. Two decades later the number approached 500, and these enrolled two-thirds of a million persons. The number of free public high schools trebled from the mid-1890's to the early 1920's. Instead of enrolling 5 percent of the boys and girls of high school age (as in 1896), the high schools of 1921 took care of about 30 percent of those in that age group.

This expansion resulted partly from the new laws forbidding child labor and requiring school attendance for a specified minimum number of years. (When Mississippi passed a compulsory-attendance law in 1918, all the states possessed such statutes.) The rapid development of the public school system of the South after 1900 also helped account for the general upswing.

No less significant was the growing recognition of the educational needs of the new industrial civilization. The immigrant invasion burdened the schools with some responsibility for "Americanizing" the children of the newcomers. The waning influence of home and church imposed new obligations on the school as a moral teacher. The crowded slums cried for new approaches, such as the conversion of the school into a community service center, a guardian of the health and hygiene of the poorer classes. Job opportunities in mills, plants, and offices stimulated the development of manual training, commercial courses, and evening classes. Finally, the humanitarianism associated with the progressive movement brought about the establishment of special classes for the handicapped—the deaf, the blind, the crippled, the feeble-minded.

In spite of increased school enrollment, opportunities remained unequal. Opportunities were better in the city than the country, better for the middle classes than for the poor, better in the North than in the South, better for southern whites than for southern Negroes. Illiteracy (inability to read and write) declined from 13 percent of the population in 1890 to 6 percent thirty years later. But the First World War revealed that many classified as literate actually possessed no adequate command either of reading or of writing. And, notwithstanding the lengthened span of years of school attendance, the average was only just above six in 1919.

The expansion of elementary and secondary education was accompanied by a great increase in the number of persons attending college. In the early 1890's, only three out of every hundred young men and women attended institutions of higher learning. By the 1920's the proportion was eight in a hundred. Financial support for the colleges increased fivefold. The western state universities improved their extension programs, thus enabling adults to attend college classes near home or to pursue university-level work through carefully supervised correspondence courses. The University of Wisconsin here led the way. The period also witnessed the beginnings of the junior college movement, first associated with the University of Chicago under President William Rainey Harper. By the outbreak of World War I over fifty such institutions provided young people who could not leave their communities with an opportunity to pursue collegiate studies for two years beyond high school.

Financing Education

All this cost money. The funds spent on education mounted to provide for the new high schools and for the modern plants needed at the elementary level. The longer terms also involved added expense, as did the gradual increase in the shamefully low pay for teachers. In 1910 the country spent slightly over $200,000,-000 on public education. A decade later expenditures reached the $1,000,000,000 level.

Most of this financial support came from local taxation, chiefly from taxes on real estate. The states also increased their contributions, especially in the field of higher education. The state universities, imbued with the ideal of service to the commonwealth, flourished as never before.

The federal government also figured in the educational picture. As before, United States funds were poured into the land-grant colleges. In addition, the central government entered the vocational education field. The Smith-Lever Act of 1914 recognized the need for specialized instruction for farmers and mechanics who could not attend college. Under this statute, the United States supplemented state funds used for disseminating knowledge of agriculture and home economics. In 1917 Congress passed the Smith-Hughes Act, which offered the states federal aid for vocational training programs in the public schools. This laid the foundation for the rapid development of a national system of vocational education unsurpassed by that of any other industrial nation.

Private funds also flowed into education. The groundwork for philanthropic aid to public education was laid in 1867, when George Peabody, a wealthy American banker residing in London, established a trust fund to promote education in the South. Thanks to this, public school systems in the larger cities were assisted until the communities and states could support them. After 1890 the Peabody Fund effectively aided teacher training. Supplementing Peabody's work was that of Samuel Slater, a New England textile manufacturer who gave money for Negro education in 1882. The Slater Fund was used chiefly to support normal schools and industrial education.

In the twentieth century others provided aid—Julius Rosenwald, for example. Rockefeller money helped public agencies improve agricultural and health programs on the secondary and advanced levels. Colleges and universities profited from liberal gifts. The Rockefeller bounties to the University of Chicago amounted to $13,500,000 by 1910. Meanwhile, Harvard, Yale, Columbia, and dozens of other private institutions used gifts from philanthropists to improve their plants and build large endowments. Also of moment was the establishment of a Carnegie fund to provide retirement pensions for professors.

The Practical Approach

The emphasis on practical education found justification in the teachings of John Dewey. Dewey, who taught at midwest universities, then at Columbia, critically examined education at all levels. As early as the 1890's he rejected the old concept of education as a matter of memorizing traditional bodies of knowledge. Instead, he insisted, students should learn how to live by meeting the conditions of life in the classroom itself. This meant project work involving the solution of problems, adaptation to new situations, working together in coöperation. Building on experiences thus acquired, children could then move naturally to the next level of learning.

As Dewey saw it, mind was an ever changing process, a "growing affair." Educators must therefore reconsider their methods and materials constantly, so that the school might reflect a changing society. Education could thus become closely related to living, to the solution of social problems, to the building of democracy. Dewey, however, disapproved of vocational education that was geared only to job training. He maintained that children who learned vocations should also understand the social and economic patterns in which the vocation operated.

Such ideas caught hold slowly. Conservatives were in opposition; and conservatives occupied most of the key positions in the educational system. As a consequence, only a few schools tried to exemplify the Dewey theories in full. But elementary education was beginning to show the influence of Dewey's ideas by the end of this period.

Higher education also was adjusting itself to the requirements of an industrial civilization. This was seen in the relaxation of the traditional liberal arts curriculum so as to permit students to choose subjects considered useful for those planning to enter the world of industry and technology. The social studies (especially economics) and the natural sciences enjoyed unprecedented popularity. So did engineering, industrialization bringing a gradual shift from civil to mechanical, electrical, and chemical engineering. There was also great interest in law—functional to the needs of corporations as well as those of justice —and the new field of business administration. The needs of a mechanized and science-minded society influenced instruction and research in agricultural colleges, too. The women's colleges, having won their uphill fight for recognition as sound educational ventures, clung to the liberal arts curriculum. So did many of the smaller coeducational colleges, and those for men alone. But by 1919, many of these institutions were beginning to follow the general trend.

The age of industry changed institutions of higher learning in other ways as well. This could be seen in the new emphasis on public relations, on efficiency of administration, on measurement of results by educational tests. Businessmen and professional leaders closely identified with business now dominated many boards of trustees. This brought money to the colleges and universities. Sometimes there were other results. Now and again trustees and administrators refused to continue on their faculties men whose social and economic ideas were at variance with those of the business community. To give just one example, the University of Pennsylvania dismissed Scott Nearing, an economist of socialist convictions.

Disturbed over such trends, a group of distinguished academicians launched the American Association of University Professors in 1914. This new organizations was to represent the "common interests of the teaching staffs" and to consider "general problems of University policy." In years to follow, the A.A.U.P. would strike many a blow for academic freedom.

Developing Interest in Science

The subjects taught in public school gave some clue to the sort of learning which society most desired. The decline in the teaching of Latin after 1900 indicated that educators no longer viewed this language as having the value once ascribed to it. On the other hand, the natural sciences were given more attention both in high schools and in colleges. By 1910 nearly every secondary school required at least one science course.

Science subjects were not always taught in such a way as to arouse interest. There was a tendency to direct experiments by set rules, or to summarize knowledge without suggesting how such knowledge was originally acquired or how it might be supplemented in the future. Hence science, alive in the laboratory, often became dead in the classroom. Many students "passed" science courses without any realization of what it was all about.

At first, therefore, the new science did not produce a general appreciation of the role of science in general society. Few nonprofessional people discussed scientific subjects; and the press did not yet view scientific discoveries as news. But by the 1930's—as the high school students of the early twentieth century came to direct the destinies of the republic—Americans would show a mounting interest in science.

Among educated people the resistance to the natural sciences involved a vague fear that science was materialistic and could never be a part of culture in the old or genteel sense. Still, there was no escaping its importance. Even those uninterested in science had to pay attention when scientific theories challenged well-established beliefs. As in the case of Darwinism.

By the turn of the century most biologists and some churchmen had come to accept the doctrine of evolution. Yet controversy persisted, as conservative clergymen used their pulpits to accuse the evolutionists of undermining Christian doctrine. Replying, the evolutionists wrote about the "warfare between science and theology," in which the former was represented as supporting and the latter as opposing the free search for truth. This debate gave science much publicity in the first quarter of the twentieth century. The evolutionists gradually gained ground, and by 1921 only the fundamentalist churches continued to fight Darwinian theory. As other religious groups accepted the new biology, those who defended Darwin found less reason to oppose theology; and the stage was set for a partial reconciliation of science and religion.

Controversies, of course, attracted attention to science in a rather sporadic manner. More persistent interest developed as Americans became aware of the close relationship between science and technology. Citizens did not change their basic values—they still prized utility more than they did "pure" research. But as basic research yielded increasingly useful results, a practical-minded people became interested.

Financing Scientific Research

Between 1896 and 1919, basic research was promoted chiefly by big business corporations and the universities. Government became interested toward the end of the period. Even then, however, and for a decade more, governmental bodies were less important in the science field than were private agencies.

Even before 1896 the electrical industry had demonstrated the relationship between science and technology. The twentieth-century leaders of that industry recognized the need for basic as well as applied science. General Electric led the way, establishing its permanent research laboratory in 1900. The Du Ponts, Eastman Kodak, the A.T. & T. were not far behind. Meantime, basic studies in bacteriology and pharmacology were being undertaken in the applied laboratories earlier established by the chief pharmaceutical houses. By 1919, it was apparent that these investments in research had "paid off"—the acid test in the business world. The ensuing years would therefore see a rapid expansion of business-supported research, both in corporation laboratories and through subsidies extended to university scientists.

As corporation laboratories multiplied, the line between basic and applied research was less sharply drawn. In 1850, scientists concerned with general principles had shown little interest in applying these principles; and the inventors of that day had been ignorant of theory. By 1920, the same man might solve a basic problem and direct its applications. What was more, even the "practical" inventor needed scientific training. Invention was becoming a systematic business on the part of men or teams of men whose names were rarely heard outside the corporation. In return for this devotion to the firm (to which they assigned their patents), they received better facilities, more coöperation, and a surer income than the earlier free-lance inventors.

The same general circumstances that encouraged research in industry also stimulated it in the universities. Attracted by the reputation of German schools, chemists, physicists, and medical men had migrated to them in growing numbers between 1870 and 1900. There they were trained in the methods and value of original research. Returning home, they maintained these interests in American universities and trained new scientists to carry on their work.

A major factor in the success of these scientists was the increasing wealth of American institutions of higher learning. Loyal alumni, philanthropists, and state legislatures provided funds on a larger scale than ever before. Except for a few corporation and foundation grants earmarked for research, the new funds were not given specifically for the natural sciences. Science professors, however, got their share. By 1896, money was becoming available for laboratories, instruction, and even (on a small scale) student fellowships.

As the importance of science became increasingly evident, trustees and presidents assigned a larger percentage of institutional funds to scientific subjects. Although much of the expansion of laboratories was requested for teaching purposes, one result was to provide facilities for research. Medicine furnishes an example. A few medical schools, including those at Harvard, Michigan, and Pennsylvania, established research laboratories as early as the 1870's. Even more interesting was the founding of a medical school at the Johns Hopkins University in 1893 for the primary purpose of advancing original investigations. Under the leadership of such men as William Osler and William H. Welch, this school did much to encourage medical research throughout the country.

Welch and other organizers of research were aided by the appearance of large private foundations. These were set up in order to channel the funds of philanthropic millionaires into science and scholarship, generally through fellowships and research grants. Of key importance was the Rockefeller Foundation, created in 1913. During the next three decades this organization was to dispense over $300,000,000 in assisting research in the United States and abroad. The chief beneficiaries were medicine and public health, where prospects for useful results were especially promising.

When the foundations were first established, they were under heavy fire. This was natural, for the money came from the very millionaires whom the literary muckrakers and progressive politicians were attacking as "malefactors of great wealth." Perhaps the donors just wished to hide their previous records of exploitation? Perhaps the whole thing was an effort to buy public approval? But, whatever the motivation of the founders, the foundations made possible a great expansion of university research activities.

Science and the Government

Although this private support of science was the dominant pattern between 1896 and 1919, government backing was also significant. State universities became major scientific centers. Though these institutions drew some support from the foundations and other private sources, their major income came from the state legislatures. Many also received funds from the federal government—notably the land-grant schools connected with the agricultural experiment stations set up under the Hatch Act of 1887. All this helped provide facilities and personnel essential for fundamental research.

Meantime, state and federal bureaus, long active in applied science, were extending their interests into basic investigational work. The United States Bureau of Fisheries did creditable work in biology. The United States Bureau of Standards achieved an excellent reputation in the physical sciences. In seeking a means to prevent Texas fever among cattle, Dr. Theobald Smith of the United States Department of Agriculture demonstrated as early as 1889 that the disease was spread by an infected tick. This discovery was basic to the control of any disease (of animals or man) which was carried by a so-called secondary host. Smith's work opened the way to later demonstrations of the manner in which mosquitoes served as carriers of malaria and yellow fever. A Cuban, Dr. Carlos Finlay, supplied the leads in the case of yellow fever. But it was Dr. Walter Reed and other members of an American military commission who provided the final proof (1901).

Such valuable findings led to conscious Congressional support of basic studies. This came in 1912, when the United States Public Health Service was authorized to "study and investigate the diseases of man." Here was a charter for engaging in fundamental studies comparable to those being carried on in the universities. The advent of such research had a peculiar significance, for federal funds provided potentially greater resources than those of the wealthiest universities and foundations.

Relations between government and science became closer during World War I. The outbreak of the war turned the attention of Congress and the President to the application of science to twentieth-century warfare. Abraham Lincoln had established a National Academy of Sciences during the Civil War as part of an effort to enlist scientific knowledge in the Union cause. The Academy had survived as a small and largely honorary body. In consequence, it was not prepared to undertake the studies needed in an age of submarines, aircraft, and poison gas. At President Wilson's request, therefore, this National Academy set up a new National Research Council in 1916.

Once organized, the National Research Council brought the ablest scientists into a planned program of turning scientific knowledge to military use. The Council's many sections coöperated with physicists, chemists, and other research workers in the universities. Scientists in the army's Medical Department and other government agencies were also brought into the picture. The results were such products as poison gas for destroying men and improved antiseptics for saving them.

Contrary to popular impression, war rarely encourages basic advances in science. Rather it concentrates on the quick application of known principles to military needs, thus actually diverting scientists from theoretic investigations. Still, the World War I experience showed Congress and the educated public how potentially useful were the fundamental studies made before 1916. The lesson was made more dramatic by the superiority of some German scientific equipment based on earlier research. Inevitably, then, there was a growing tendency of both private and governmental institutions to support theoretic as well as applied science.

Science and Society

While society was pouring money into scientific work, science was exerting an ever widening influence on society. As the achievements of science became increasingly impressive, its prestige rose accordingly. Americans therefore began to wonder if science and scientific methods might not prove effective in attacking social problems.

Was this possible? Certainly help was needed; most social problems remained unsolved. Biologists and physicians now knew how to improve food products and how to prevent many diseases; but social difficulties still made it impossible to avoid famine and epidemics in many parts of the world. Although technology had enabled men to build and supply large cities, crime and poverty persisted in those great urban centers. In the past, such matters had been dealt with in terms of moral enthusiasm rather than calm analysis. Would it not be better to try a scientific approach—to collect facts systematically, to interpret the data rationally, in attacking such problems as business depressions, divorce, and race relations?

A few persons had tried this approach in the half-century before 1896. For one thing, they had collected and published social statistics. But when it came to interpreting this material, scholars had differed widely according to their preconceived opinions or value judgments. It was fairly easy for a natural scientist to view his data on planetary orbits with impartiality. It was much more difficult for a social scientist to view with detachment the race question or the rights of labor unions.

As a consequence, social scientists developed conflicting "systems" in the second half of the nineteenth century. One group of economists defended capitalism, another condemned it. Yet the writings of this period increasingly reflected a scientific tone. The influence of Darwinism was very evident. Indeed, much of the serious literature of these years may be viewed as an attempt to adjust social thought to the implications of evolution and to the realities of the American scene.

Some defended the existing economic order. The English thinker, Herbert Spencer, saw the history of civilization as an evolution from simple societies to the complex. Modern industrialism, then, was the highest and most desirable state of society. Taking over from there, William Graham Sumner of Yale stressed the role of an unchecked struggle for existence in business competition. Sumner felt that if the government stopped this struggle, Americans would lose desirable incentives to thrift, initiative, and aggressiveness. Sumner's analysis, phrased in scientific language, was really a defense of the industrial capitalism of his day.

Others who accepted Darwinism were less happy about this domination of "ruthless," "predatory" capitalism. Were all save the masters of capital "unfit" in an evolutionary sense? Would protecting ordinary people against exploitation necessarily slow down social progress? Traditional American sympathy with the common man inspired the sociologist Lester F. Ward to defend the rights of the majority. If social evolution was an inevitable process in which the less fit must go down (as Sumner and Spencer seemed to imply), then little could be done for the masses. But Ward was convinced that man, as a free agent, could guide the evolutionary process in terms of such old ideals as the greatest good for the greatest number. Like Sumner, Ward used scientific language; but his conclusions justified future government control of business and even the more general philosophy of the welfare state.

Learned though they were, the writings of Sumner and Ward could be criticized as based on preconceived views about the types of society desired. They were rationalizations of current social debates, one way or the other. Many intellectuals felt that such partisanship was improper—that social scientists, like chemists and physicists, should stand off from their data and interpret them in a cold-blooded or objective manner. Science would simply present the evidence. Politicians or reformers could carry on from there.

This point of view was increasingly adopted by the professional social scientists after 1896. The prestige of the natural sciences was now greater than ever, and social thinkers were therefore anxious to follow scientific methods and scientific terminology ("social *dynamics*," "urban *ecology*"). American sociologists, economists, historians, political scientists came to stress objectivity, to insist on systematic observations and measurements, to discourage speculative theorizing. Particularly successful were the anthropologists, who studied so-called primitive peoples like the American Indians or Pacific Islanders. It was easier to be detached and impartial in analyzing such societies than in dealing with one of which the observer was himself a part.

As they came to stress exactitude and objectivity, some social scientists felt disdain for welfare workers and reformers. These "do-gooders," said the social scientists, still displayed emotional attitudes and worked without benefit of scientific principles. (This resembled, in a way, the aloof attitude of some "pure scientists" toward practical inventors.) Eventually, however, the two groups moved closer together. Sociologists became consultants for welfare organizations, and economists were employed by banks and by the government.

The Rise of Psychology

Related to the social as well as the natural sciences was the emerging field of psychology. After 1850 neurologists began to study the behavior of the nervous system in laboratories, observing such phenomena as sense perceptions and reflex actions. From this there evolved the notion of investigating mental behavior as a whole; and a group of professional psychologists emerged. After 1900 this work was carried into such special fields as social and educational psychology. In the spirit of science, the psychologists strove to substitute controlled and systematic observation for casual impressions, exact measurement for general descriptions.

Unlike most social sciences, psychology could often employ experimentation as well as measurement. This was true even in educational psychology. Thus one could experiment with a method of teaching arithmetic to one group, and compare the result by exact testing with what was accomplished by using another method with a different ("control") group. Even when no exact measurements could be made, something of an experimental spirit was introduced into educational methods. Normal schools and teachers colleges took over this "scientific education" with enthusiasm.

Measurements became useful in practice even before there was agreement as to the principles of the learning process. After their introduction from Europe, the Binet tests and the concept of the intelligence quotient (IQ) were gradually taken over by American public schools. When improved, these tests were very useful in rating students. They were used by the United States Army in World War I, by business later. Hence quantitative procedures, and the scientific attitude in general, were beginning to permeate education as well as the other social fields.

Another specialty in psychology dealt with abnormal or pathologic mental processes. This field, psychiatry, had had a long history as a branch of medicine. Physicians, however, had given little attention to the baffling phenomena of mental illness between 1850 and 1900. Engrossed in the strictly physical approach to disease, medical men had tended to ignore mental troubles except when they could be ascribed to some physical ailment.

Then came Freud. During the 1890's this Austrian physician associated neurotic symptoms with long-suppressed desires, particularly those of a sexual nature produced in childhood. Although social taboos or inhibitions could repress many of these thoughts, they became embedded in the subconscious, and produced tensions which caused nervous behavior. This could be cured, said Freud, by questioning the patient until he recalled the original circumstances. Once these were recognized, and memory was brought to the conscious level, the tensions and neurotic behavior would disappear.

Many medical men were skeptical, especially since experimental verification was not immediately forthcoming. But interest in Freudian theories grew. Whatever its limitations, psychoanalysis appeared to offer hope to patients who feared a nervous breakdown. Ordinary medicine seemed of little help in most such cases.

In addition, Freud's emphasis on sex aroused curiosity among the educated; and after 1910 Freudianism became almost a cult in the United States. Freudian concepts were introduced into sophisticated conversation. Talk about inhibitions and the like produced a daring feeling of escape from the prudishness of Victorian grandparents. Current literature presently reflected this attitude. The public was offered novels and plays with such titles as *Suppressed Desires.* "Realistic" writers offered amateur analyses of their characters, and the more imaginative sought hidden sex motivation in the lives of Napoleon and other historical personalities.

These reflections of psychoanalysis illustrate the influence which science was exerting on literature. This was not new; literary men had been discussing science since the days of Sir Isaac Newton. Naturally enough, interests had changed with the times. Walt Whitman, a nineteenth-century writer, had spoken of the "learned astronomer." Sinclair Lewis, a twentieth-century novelist, exploited the dramatic possibilities of bacteriology (in *Arrowsmith*). This literary treatment doubtless reached readers who would otherwise have been unaware of the growing significance of science.

Science and the Universe

While science influenced literature, it also interested historians and all others who were concerned with the broader intellectual and moral implications of scientific trends. As has been noted, some sociologists interpreted social evolution as a predetermined, inevitable process. Others held that man was a free agent who could direct evolution toward his own welfare. The divergence brought up the old problem of the freedom of the will—now presented in scientific form instead of in the earlier theological terms of predestination.

Such philosophic questions were of more than abstract interest; for the answers affected conduct. Thus a Herbert Spencer, viewing evolution as inevitable, adopted a fatalistic or indifferent attitude toward attempts to improve society. One could do nothing about it; let it alone and it would work itself out in even higher forms. On the other hand, a Lester F. Ward believed that man was a free agent. Hence he favored social reforms in the interests of the masses. This was the hopeful view, and seemed to many more consistent with democratic aspirations.

The central philosophical problem of this era was the relationship of man to the whole universe. The theory of evolution was one—but only one—expression of a continuing tendency in science to interpret things in material terms. Physicists and astronomers pictured the universe as a vast clockwork mechanism which operated in terms of unchanging natural laws. The earth was a mere speck in this endless system, and man a minute accident who was destined for extinction when the universe ran down. Even on his own tiny planet, man was not a unique creation as heretofore believed, but rather the product of a blind, brutal process of evolution from the lowest animal forms.

It was no wonder that religious leaders were alarmed at this picture. At no point was there a suggestion of divine concern about man or his destiny. Orthodox religious thinkers simply refused to accept the evidence set forth by scientists. Idealistic philosophers, such as Josiah Royce, did not deny the findings of science within its own field of operations. They insisted, however, that this field of science was one of surface appearances. Behind the natural phenomena with which the scientists dealt lay an ultimate reality of spiritual essences. Man himself was not merely an animal but was endowed with a spark of that divine principle which animated the entire universe.

The advantage of this idealism was that its advocates could accept scientific data without giving up a belief in spiritual principles and a hope in some larger destiny for man. As the English poet Tennyson wrote, in discussing the grim aspects of the biological struggle for existence:

> And yet we hope that somehow good
> Will be the final goal of ill.

He ended on the hopeful note that he could still believe in

> One God, one law, one element,
> And one far-off divine event
> To which the whole creation moves.

The American historian John Fiske wrote in similar vein. He maintained that evolution was true. But, he added, it did not deny a divine plan for the world. Quite the contrary; evolution was the process by which God had brought man into existence as the highest of His creations.

Less hopeful thinkers became completely skeptical of spiritual reality and pessimistic about human life as a whole. Some were defiant of nature; others took refuge in the old philosophy of Epicureanism. Man could at least enjoy his brief existence by cultivating the arts or the good life. *The Rubáiyát of Omar Khayyám*, which provided a beautiful expression of this outlook, had a considerable vogue in the United States. "Eat, drink, and be merry, for tomorrow you die."

In opposition both to such pessimism and to idealism, some thinkers embraced science with enthusiasm and held that it would replace religion as a guide in life. Even if it offered no evidence of God or immortality, was not science actually doing more for mankind than the old religions had ever done? So said Auguste Comte, a French thinker of the early nineteenth century. Rejecting religion and most philosophy, Comte held that, since the human mind could not answer questions about the ultimate nature of reality, all thinking along such lines was a waste of time. Philosophers should devote themselves simply to the larger questions raised by science itself. This view (positivism) was accepted by many scientists at the end of the century.

Theologians and others wrote in rebuttal. The American historian Henry Adams pointed out that science had evil as well as beneficial results. Science, he said, was cold and impersonal; and the machines which it created were not an unmixed blessing. Had not the irreversible introduction of factory techniques already destroyed the old joy of craftsmanship? Did not science provide men with weapons with which to destroy themselves? Perhaps science was a sort of Frankenstein's monster, made by man but destined in turn to dominate and to destroy him.

As new generations accepted science as a matter of course, the cosmic problem gradually became a less intense issue, and social questions became the chief subject of philosophic concern. Such intellectual leaders as William James and John Dewey felt that it was unnecessary to worry much about the problem of the universe. After all, man was a part of nature for better or for worse, and he might as well make the best of it. One should neither worship nor condemn science, but use it to improve man's lot in the world. In short, science should be directed toward social betterment—an objective similar to that of the eighteenth-century Enlightenment.

To be sure, major questions would have to be answered along the way. Men would have to decide what was good or true in order to choose their social goals. But these concepts need not be defined in the absolute terms of idealism or by the dogmas of theology. Things were true, said William James, if they were pragmatic—that is, if they worked well. If an ideal proved illusory, or a process unfortunate, it was not really good or true; and something more practical must be found.

Both James and Dewey sought to apply their principles in socially useful ways, as in the improvement of education. As a psychologist, James was interested in the nature of the learning process, and felt that an understanding of this process was basic to teaching procedures. This prepared the way for Dewey's emphasis on the child-centered school, in which subjects would be fitted to children's needs, rather than (as heretofore) the children to the subjects. As we have seen, Dewey did much to revolutionize the spirit and methods of American education. Hence, with James and Dewey, philosophy was shifting its focus from the universe to matters of a useful, social nature.

The pragmatism of James and Dewey was a logical outgrowth of American experience. From the beginning, citizens of the United States had been practical people. Practical they remained in the age of science. By emphasizing the practical or pragmatic approach, James and Dewey had caught the spirit of the land.

Money and the Arts

Among all peoples, even the most primitive, the arts have satisfied basic human needs—religious, social, aesthetic. Americans of the early twentieth century furnished no exception to this rule. As before, Old World influences were strong in the fields of music, sculpture, painting, and architecture. At the same time, these arts reflected the values and influence of the American republic's new urbanism and industrialism.

With the rise of industrial wealth, the arts obtained added financial support—individual, corporate, public. The older indifference to the fine arts, or benevolent toleration of them as dispensable frills, did not wholly disappear. But an increasing section of the middle class interested itself in these matters. Further up the social scale, the prestige value associated with liberal patronage of the arts counted for a good deal. Some wealthy persons also developed a genuine aesthetic interest in music and painting. Simultaneously, civic pride in public buildings was on the upgrade; and the economic development of the nation permitted that pride to find expression.

Some rich men and women had supported symphony orchestras and opera even before the 1890's. There was a sharp increase in the number of patrons after 1900. The very largest cities now had much good music; and symphony orchestras were organized in such smaller centers as Seattle and Minneapolis. Eager to emulate the rich, members of the middle class also cultivated music. Wives and daughters took piano lessons, providing a $75,000,000 yearly business for the piano manufacturers by 1914. Phonograph sales were even higher.

Although European classical influence remained strong, Theodore Thomas and other leaders in the music world believed that a native American music might emerge from Indian, cowboy, and Negro themes. Edward A. MacDowell, Henry F. B. Gilbert, and other composers experimented with these materials. Their efforts, though, met with only limited success. Closer to the people, and more impressive in many ways, were the developments in the popular-music field. Irving Berlin, an immigrant of Russian-Jewish background, caught the public fancy with his "Alexander's Ragtime Band" (1912), the most famous of the new ragtime songs. Meanwhile, Negro bands in New Orleans, Memphis, and St. Louis were improvising sad, lovesick blues and a pioneer form of jazz.

Besides patronizing opera, the super-rich filled their mansions with art objects. The most famous collectors included J. Pierpont Morgan, who bought ivories, bronzes, wood carvings, miniatures, tapestries, pottery, glass, statuary, paintings, rare books; Henry Clay Frick, supercollector of old masters; Andrew W. Mellon of Pittsburgh; and Henry E. Huntington of California. Money was no object with these Titans; and the value of art objects imported into the United States ran over $30,000,000 a year during the period just before World War I. Private wealth also flowed into the building and endowment of impressive art galleries. Although many of these galleries were architectural monstrosities, their collections helped develop aesthetic interests among

Americans of middle station. In addition, several museums established art schools where aspiring painters could obtain training.

Trends in Architecture

The mansions of the richest Americans were imposing and uncomfortable Romanesque or Renaissance palaces—quite out of harmony with an industrial America. The new factories, banks, and office buildings, on the other hand, suited the changing times. They used the new materials (concrete, steel, glass), and they were built to serve the purposes of modern life. Real-estate values dictated another characteristic feature, height. To save expensive space in downtown districts, structures became taller and taller. The businessmen and architects of Chicago led the way. New York and other cities followed suit, and the metropolitan skyline took on a twentieth-century appearance.

Unlike the turreted homes of the rich, the new skyscrapers expressed clearly the internal organization and uses of these business buildings. This was their strength and their beauty. So said Louis Sullivan, greatest of the new architects. Sullivan generalized the emerging trend in the slogan "Form follows function." Although he did not completely forgo decorative effects, this Chicago architect put his emphasis on substance and utility rather than on frills. The power and grace of his office and bank buildings came from the satisfying perpendicular lines and from the massive spaces of glass made possible by the steel frames.

Sullivan's student, Frank Lloyd Wright, carried functionalism still further. The Larkin Building, which he constructed in Buffalo, protected the workers from the smoke, dirt, and noise of the railways at the rear by a massive, unbroken wall. At the same time, Wright provided ample light by a generous use of glass. There were built-in files, cool, restful stairs and hallways.

Wright also tried to change the domestic architecture of the well-to-do. Beginning in the 1890's, he designed houses in the Middle West exemplifying the principle that a home should grow out of the soil and the surroundings. Every part of a house, said Wright, should be "a thing of beauty in itself as related to the whole." His clean vertical lines and jutting horizontals proved his thesis that true simplicity and functional use need not be the simplicity of the side of a barn. For the heavy bookcases and other massive pieces of the Victorian era Wright substituted built-in shelves, tables, and benches. These were integral parts of the structure and often recapitulated the shapes and proportion of the room itself.

Creative and original though Wright's work was, it took hold only very slowly. Most wealthy people preferred traditional houses that suggested a remote time or place. In the late nineteenth century they went for European-style castles. In the twentieth, they turned to American regional traditions: the colonial style in New England and New York, the Spanish mission type in Florida and California.

In public architecture, the accent was on the classical. Here a major influence was that of the Chicago World's Fair of 1893. European experts considered Louis Sullivan's frankly functional Transportation Building the only truly American structure on display. American visitors, however, were more impressed by the main features of the Fair: the glistening white classical temples of imitation marble, their domes, columns, and façades reflected in the lagoons. (The impression was heightened by the magnificent landscaping work of Frederick Law Olmsted, who also laid out Central Park in New York.) The result was that most state capitols constructed in the next generation copied classical forms and used classical allegories in their murals. So did the gigantic railway stations, conceived in the image of the Roman baths. The revamped civic design for the national capital, with geometric parkways and cold Greek and Roman façades, likewise testified to the classical triumph.

The classical style did not exclude other derivations. Gothic dominated ecclesiastical and collegiate architecture in this era. John La Farge's successful experiments with light and color in stained glass contributed to the popularity of this style. So did the work of Ralph Adams Cram, an architect with a religious devotion to the Middle Ages. The Tudor Gothic used by many academic institutions had its attractive features; but there were shortcomings, too. When applied to the library, it often resulted in reading rooms that required artificial lights even on the brightest days.

Painting and Sculpture

The classical influences that dominated public architecture also influenced painting and sculpture. Again, the Chicago Fair was important. The sculpture at this exposition (under the direction of Augustus Saint-Gaudens) reflected the classical taste. So did the painting, for the planning commission used classical murals in the classical temples. The classical triumph was so complete that the gallery of art excluded the rising French moderns—Manet, Degas, Cézanne.

Mistreated at the Fair, these French artists nonetheless had much to do with the development of American painting. In the last quarter of the nineteenth century, American artists had come under French influence. The great landscapist George Inness had changed his style as he came to appreciate the work of the French Barbizon school; James McNeill Whistler had learned much from the French impressionists. As the nineteenth century gave way to the twentieth, French leadership pointed Americans first toward realistic presentation of their industrial society, then toward experiments in abstraction.

Realistic representation of the new America at first centered around a group of Philadelphia painters, of whom Thomas Eakins was the most notable. Later, the most active artists in this category were New Yorkers. Included were Robert Henri, leader of The Eight, who publicly crusaded for the new art; Henri's pupil, George Bellows; and John Sloan. Both the New York and the Philadelphia groups found rich material in the everyday life of the cities. Some painted pictures of the new skyscrapers. Others sketched engineers at work; street urchins in alleys strewn with ash cans; crowds in public parks; barroom, pushcart, and tenement scenes. In short, they were interested in the whole of urban life, and were especially sensitive to the lot of the lowly. They painted in oils, they made etchings, they used the lithograph form. Since their appeal was broad, these new city artists found an outlet through the magazines and books as well as the art galleries. Their work was admired by discerning critics; but they were also genre painters, artists to the people.

French artists, meantime, were trying new experiments, notably geometric abstractions. Postimpressionists, cubists, futurists felt that they were discovering a more profound aesthetic experience than that revealed by traditional forms, colors, and lines. Even before World War I the trend had influenced a number of American painters (John Marin and A. B. Davies, for example) and some sculptors, including Jo Davidson. Davies, who was one of The Eight, was the major figure behind the staging of the spectacular Armory Show of 1913. This New York exhibition introduced Americans to European and native painters who were working with symbols and abstractions.

As might have been expected, the first reaction was one of surprise and horror. Conservative critics denounced the efforts of the cubists and expressionists as "anarchistic," "undisciplined," "chaos." The bewildered public was inclined to agree. There was no "picture" here; one could not even tell what the artist was trying to do. But perhaps the abstraction and distortion, the defiant lines and broken colors were no more confusing than other aspects of the new industrialism. And in any case, this "modern art" had come to stay.

Literature

In the field of letters, the popular demand still ran to the sentimental, the romantic, the conventional. Victorian taste was very evident in the enormously popular "molasses fiction" of Mrs. Gene Stratton-Porter (*Freckles, A Girl of the Limberlost,* and three other Stratton-Porter novels sold more than a million copies each). Equally proper and equally popular were the sentimental and sermonized melodramas of the Reverend Harold Bell Wright (*Shepherd of the Hills; Winning of Barbara Worth*). But not all best sellers were conformist. Zane Grey introduced a note of brutality into some of his wild West novels, which sold 15,000,000 copies; and Elinor Glyn's wretchedly written *Three Weeks* became a best seller because it dealt with sex.

Historical novels were very popular at the beginning of the twentieth century. Some of these dealt with Old World themes. An increasing percentage, however, touched on the history of the United States. This was natural enough, in view of the upsurge of patriotic sentiment during the War with Spain (1898) and the general pride in the new world power of the United States. Hence readers eagerly

devoured sugar-coated history. One could read about the colonial days
(Mary Johnston's *To Have and to Hold*), or the American Revolution
(*Richard Carvel*, by Winston Churchill), or the Civil War (Stephen
Crane's *Red Badge of Courage*). Crane's book, incidentally, was an
exception to the general rule that historical novels were both poor
history and poor literature.

While most writers were turning out escape literature, a few were
trying other paths. At the end of the nineteenth century, Henry
James, William Dean Howells, and Samuel L. Clemens (Mark
Twain) were pointing the way toward realism. Several leading American authors were influenced by French and Russian naturalists, who
tried to describe actualities in life just as scientists described what
they saw under the microscope. But, for all the European influence,
the end product remained distinctively American.

Several of the ablest of the new writers were women. Edith Wharton, a disciple of Henry James, wrote of the New York elite. Willa
Cather, who was reared in Nebraska, told of immigrant pioneers on
the prairie, concealing neither their heroism nor their insecurity. Some
of Ellen Glasgow's Virginians were uncouth, some genteel; nearly all
were poor.

Many of the new authors stressed the faults of the new urban and
industrial civilization. Frank Norris, who was much influenced by the
French novelist Zola, wrote about the monopolistic railways and the
ruthless speculators (*The Pit, The Octopus*). Jack London, impressed
with Darwinism, turned out popular adventure stories about the struggle for survival on the last frontiers (*Call of the Wild*). He also developed the themes of class struggle in industrial society, in *The Iron
Heel*. Much more effective was Upton Sinclair's widely read *Jungle*,
which dealt in gory detail with the horror, the filth, the ruthlessness
of Chicago meat-packing concerns. Intended as a plea for socialism,
this novel failed in that particular; but it did swell the growing public
demand for effective meat-inspection legislation.

Among the new writers who treated unpleasant aspects of industrial
civilization, Theodore Dreiser deserves special notice. Careless about
style and inclined to use too many words, Dreiser nonetheless showed
great power in laying bare the bewildering and planless character of

much of urban life. He had great difficulty finding a publisher for *Sister Carrie*, the tale of a village girl in the city; and critics denounced or ignored this novel. There followed *The Financier* and *The Titan* (the second virtually suppressed by the publishers), two novels that portrayed the corrupt capitalist in realistic fashion. *The American Tragedy*, most powerful of Dreiser's novels, dealt with problems associated with the traditional American struggle to get ahead.

Many writers of this era were less extreme in their criticism of the evils of their day. Booth Tarkington, for example, viewed the struggle for business success with less cynicism than did Dreiser. Tarkington, however, did attack political corruption, in an effort to advance the progressive cause. So did the historical novelist Winston Churchill, who wrote fiction about corruption in high places (*Mr. Crewe's Career*), and himself entered politics in New Hampshire. Many others took up their pens in the same fight.

Poets, too, turned their attention to social problems. In "The Man with the Hoe," Edwin Markham touched on the plight of exploited labor. William Vaughn Moody warned against the new slavery to materialism and the machine. Carl Sandburg celebrated in Walt Whitman fashion the strength and dignity of the common man in the midst of urban confusion and smoke. Vachel Lindsay's "ragtime rhythms" suggested the new popular music, and caught the spirit of the social gospel and of the humble and the poor. All this helped provide background and support for progressive reform.

Magazines and Newspapers

There were magazines for every taste— professional and trade journals, religious and literary organs, periodicals devoted to science, to humor, to romance, to detective and wild West fiction. In terms of circulation, the giants were Edward Bok's *Ladies' Home Journal* (2,000,000 copies) and George Horace Lorimer's *Saturday Evening Post*. Not far behind were such others as *Munsey's, Collier's, McClure's,* and *American*. The "quality" magazines (*Harper's, Scribner's,* and the like) also showed an increase in sales.

There were several factors in the circulation increase. One was price—*Munsey's* led the way in the 1890's by cutting to a dime. New printing and distributing techniques made mass circulation possible. So did advertising. More attractive format, better pictures, and more lively stories helped both the popular leaders and the special magazines. Finally, *McClure's*, the *Ladies' Home Journal*, and other leading periodicals won new readers by stressing "literature of exposure" after 1900, attacking corruption in government and business. This meant profits, except when advertisers were offended; and it advanced the progressive cause.

With the improvement of news-gathering agencies, newspaper readers obtained information sooner than before. News coverage was also better than in earlier decades—these years, as an example, saw an increase in the amount and quality of foreign news. What was more, a good many newspapers joined the progressive novelists and magazine writers in exposing fraud. Much good was done by such journalists as Joseph Pulitzer of the New York *World* and St. Louis *Post-Dispatch*.

That, however, was only one side of the picture. On the other side, there was a continuing trend toward standardization and sensationalism. The old ideal of the editor as an individual molder of public opinion retreated before the new concept of journalism as a big business dominated by the profit motive. This involved deferring to advertisers, with editorial writers instructed not to alienate any important group or firm. It also meant catering to the public taste—playing down discussion of issues and building up the feature sections. The new newspaper put emphasis on women's pages, with household recipes and shopping hints and advice to the lovelorn; on comic strips; on sports coverage; on romantic serials. Some of this was slanted toward local interests. But as time went on, newspaper chains and feature syndicates spread the same fare all over the nation.

Religion: Church Membership

Although this was not an age of religious revival, church membership increased about as rapidly as did the population. Certain Protestant denominations added substantially to their following; and both the Roman Catholic and the Jewish churches made spectacular gains.

In terms of total numbers, the Baptists and Methodists led the Protestant procession at the beginning and at the end of this period. The Presbyterians, the Lutherans, the Disciples of Christ, the Episcopalians, and the Congregationalists followed. Several smaller groups grew at a more rapid rate than did the larger bodies. The Mormons (who abandoned polygamy in 1896) remained dominant in their Utah stronghold and gave evidence of missionary vitality in surrounding states and even in foreign lands. The Christian Scientists also made an impressive advance, with the founder, Mrs. Mary Baker Eddy, providing leadership until her death in 1910.

Equally interesting was the appearance of new Protestant sects. More than a dozen began their careers in these years. Many of them were holiness or pentecostal groups organized among the rural poor. In the main, the new bodies represented a protest against the older denominations. The established sects, it was said, were "settling down," were abandoning revivalism and were substituting an educated clergy for the more exciting leaders of yesteryear. The new denominations were bent on recapturing the emotional spirit of the circuit rider and camp-meeting days.

The Roman Catholics gained rapidly in the generation after 1896. By 1919, the Catholic Church claimed about a third of the church members in the country, substantially its percentage of 1950. (This does not mean, of course, that the Catholics numbered a third of the population. Nearly half of the persons who considered themselves Protestant had no formal church connection. Hence in 1919 and afterward approximately one-sixth of the inhabitants of the United States were Catholic.) The major factor in the rise to this level was the arrival of Catholic immigrants. Able leadership, as of Cardinal James Gibbons, was also in the picture.

As the Catholic population increased, new dioceses were formed at the rate of about one a year. More and more religious orders were set up; and there was a large increase in the number of and enrollment in Catholic educational institutions. The growth was especially marked on the elementary (parochial school) and college levels.

Although some Protestants viewed these trends with alarm, there was less organized anti-Catholic activity in this period than in the

years before and after. Having failed in its bid for influence in the
Republican party, the anti-Catholic American Protective Association
was fading out by 1896. Two decades later, in 1915, the Ku Klux Klan
would be organized as an anti-Catholic, anti-Negro, anti-Semitic, antiforeign society; but the Klan would not reach its peak of influence
until after 1919.

The Catholics were not alone in profiting from immigration between the 1890's and the 1920's. Some Protestant bodies (the Lutherans in particular) obtained reinforcement from this quarter. In
addition, the new immigration brought in a substantial number of
Jews, many of them refugees from persecution in Russian Poland and
elsewhere. The number of Jewish congregations in the United States
doubled in the fifteen years after 1890, and doubled again in the next
decade and a half. In a few cities, notably New York, the Jews made
up a considerable fraction of the population by 1920. But in the
country as a whole, the Jews remained a very small part of the total
population—less than 4 percent in 1919, fewer still if one counts
only actual communicants.

Religion and Social Problems

As in the preceding generation, a major
problem of religious leaders was adjustment to industrial civilization.
Critics put the churches on the defensive by charging that clergymen
and leading laymen ignored the social and economic evils of the
time and were tied to an exploitative capitalism. Yet in fact the
churches were doing more than before to meet the challenge of
the age.

Just what was accomplished? One by one leading Protestant groups
followed the earlier example of the Episcopalians in giving official
recognition to labor—the Congregationalists in 1901, the Presbyterians in 1903, the Methodists in 1908, and so on. Ministerial associations in the larger cities showed a quickening interest in the problems
of the working class. Some even sent delegates to central trade-union
councils.

The literary trend was unmistakable. Protestant clergymen read and
praised such books as *Christianity and the Social Crisis*, by Walter

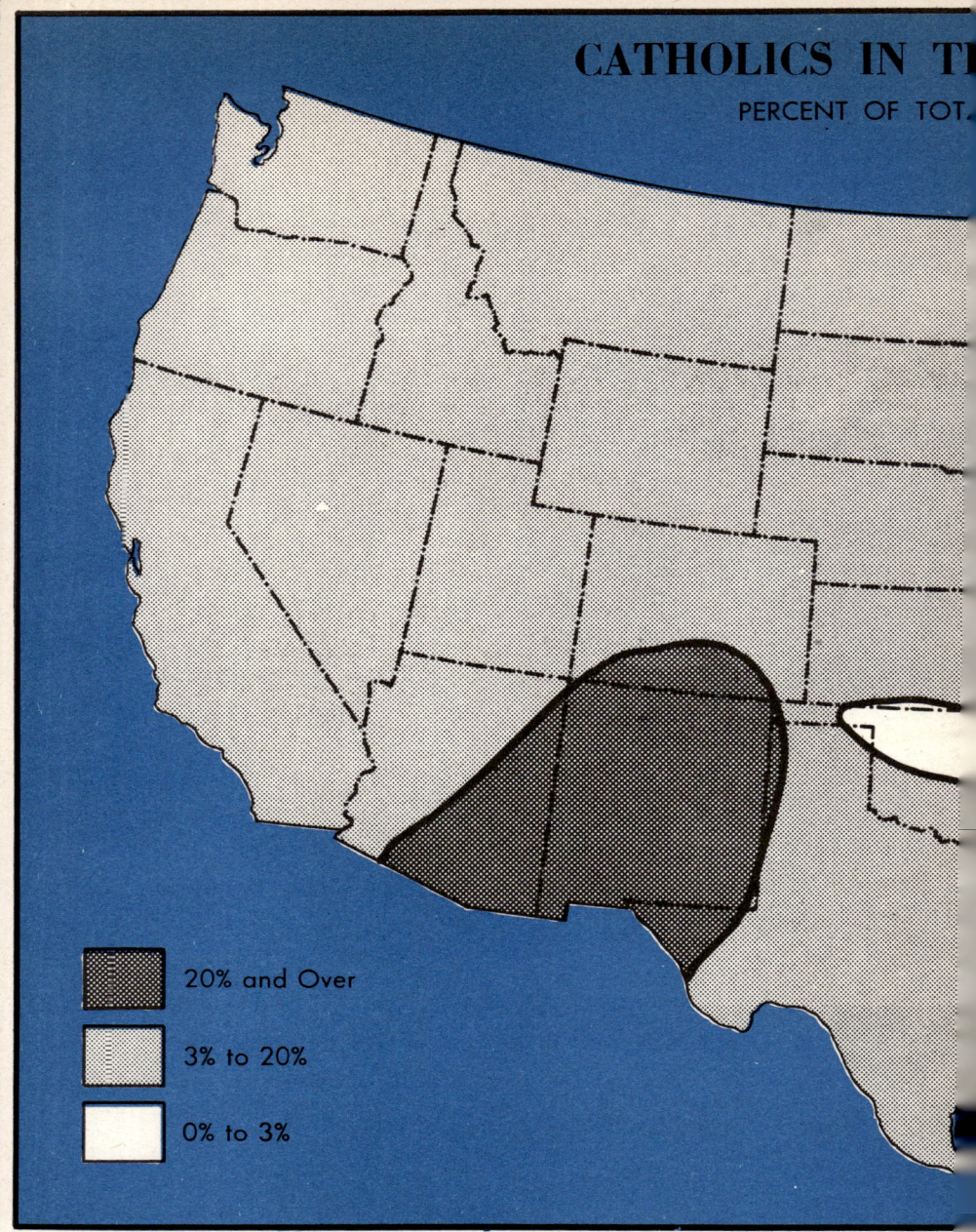

20% and Over

3% to 20%

0% to 3%

In 1850, five out of every hundred Americans were Catholic; in 1950, sixteen out of every hundred. The Catholic increase is closely related to the history of immigration. Hence the southern states, which attracted few immigrants, have a very small percentage of Catholics even today. (Louisiana, first settled by the French, furnishes an exception.)

The Catholic Church in the United States has been stronger in urban than in rural areas. Many German Catholics settled in Middle West farm communities in the nineteenth century; and twentieth-century Mexican

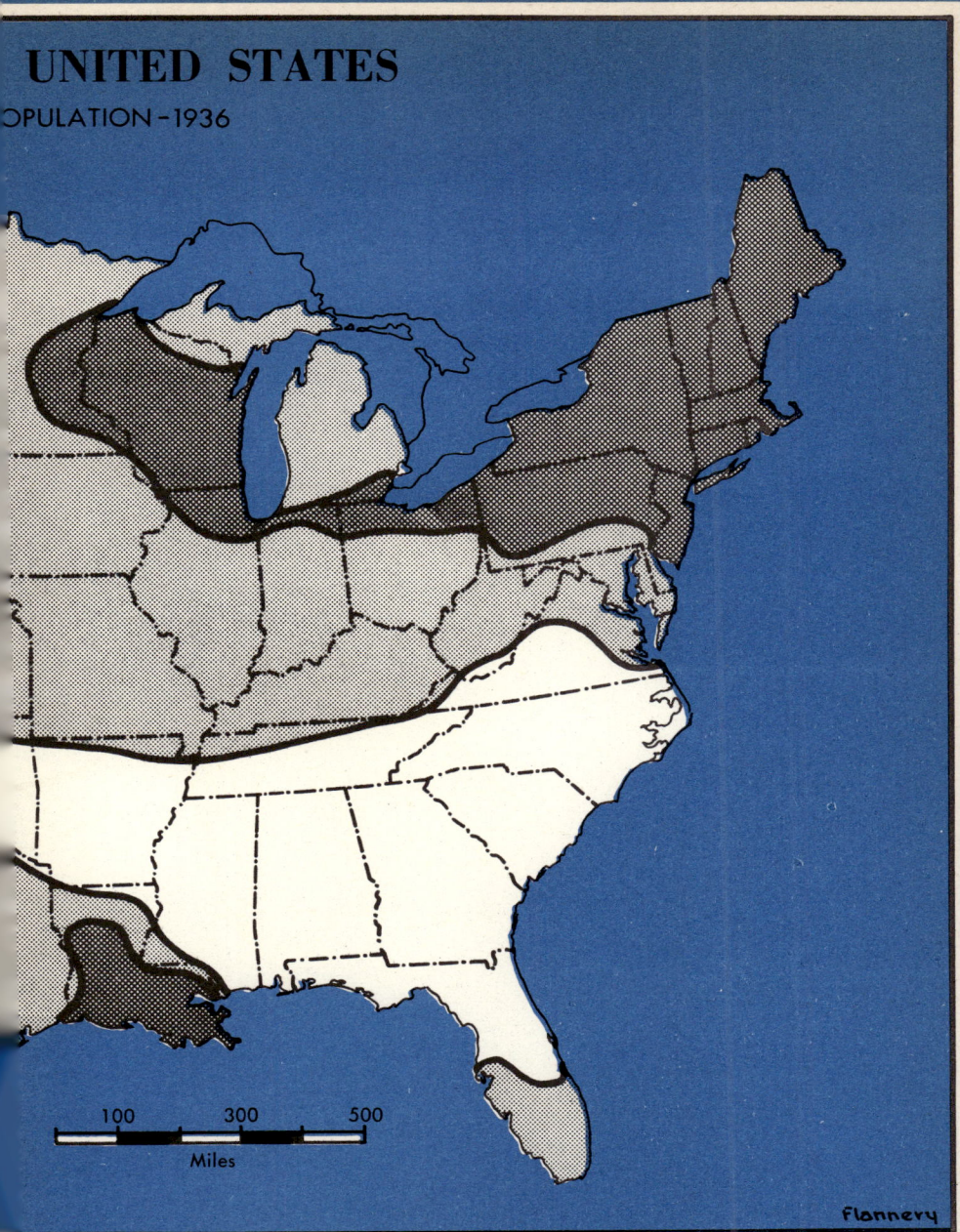

UNITED STATES

OPULATION - 1936

100	300	500

Miles

Flannery

immigrants have also been employed in agricultural regions. (Americans of Mexican background bulk large in the Catholic population of the Southwest.) In the main, however, Catholic immigrants settled in urban districts. The Irish, who arrived from the 1840's on, located in and around the northeastern cities. So did the Italians, the Poles, and the French Canadians, all of whom came in in large numbers after 1880. Economic factors were more important than religious ones in this situation, for non-Catholic immigrants followed the same pattern.

Rauschenbusch of the Rochester Theological Seminary, a leading figure in the social gospel movement. In this book, Rauschenbusch eloquently called on the churches to coöperate with forward-looking forces in the creation of a more humane social system. The general public showed an interest in the same approach when it made best sellers out of Winston Churchill's *Inside of the Cup*, and *That Printer of Udell's*, by Harold Bell Wright. Popular plays used similar themes; and Street and Smith, the pulp publishers, found a good market for paper-backed volumes with such titles as *Would Christ Belong to a Labor Union?*

An important force in the new movement was the Federal Council of Churches of Christ in America. Organized in 1908, the Council represented thirty-three Protestant bodies with 17,000,000 communicants. From the beginning it endorsed the social gospel, adopting a platform which stressed the moral and social obligations of Christianity to work for legislation in the interest of the laboring class, and for a more equitable distribution of the profits of industry.

The Protestants who wanted to implement the social ideals of religion had support from other groups. Judaism, especially its liberal wing, actively extended its historic interest in charities by cultivating closer affiliation with the working people. Among Catholics, the encyclical *De Rerum Novarum* of Pope Leo XIII (1891) pointed toward social reform. One Catholic prelate who did active work along that line was Kentucky-born Archbishop John L. Spalding, whom President Theodore Roosevelt named as one of the arbitrators of the anthracite coal strike in 1902. Another was Father John Ryan, who published a spirited book, *A Living Wage*, in 1910.

Strong though it was, the movement toward social reform did not affect all churchmen. Many Catholic prelates, Jewish rabbis, and Protestant clergymen were definitely not interested. Those who advocated the social gospel found the going especially difficult in the rural areas. There interest in social issues was likely to be confined to one problem: the liquor question. Granting the importance of this matter, the fact remained that concentration on it tended to turn attention away from other questions that also merited serious consideration.

The Liquor Question

Long in the field, the foes of alcohol were much better organized than were those interested in other social problems. Until the 1890's, the most effective work was done by the Woman's Christian Temperance Union. Organized on a national and international basis, this society was run by Frances Willard from the late 1870's until her death in 1898. In her day many rural and small-town areas "went dry"; and, with Kansas leading, there was launched a new movement for state prohibition legislation.

During the 1890's, the Anti-Saloon League entered the fight. The new association soon became the spearhead of a nation-wide drive to ban the sale of liquor. The League was backed financially and politically by nonurban Protestants. Important as a propaganda agency, it was even more effective in the lobby field. It fought with vigor. It forced newspapers to give it space. It enlisted the aid of pulpits. (Billy Sunday the revivalist was of great aid to the cause.) It won over employers of labor. It browbeat and converted legislators through its competent lobbyists. Wayne B. Wheeler, the League's kingpin "legislative representative," was one of the ablest lobbyists in American history.

Although the Anti-Saloon League encountered opposition in the cities, it won many victories in village and rural local-option contests. Then it worked at the state capitals; and bit by bit state prohibitory laws were enacted. By the time of World War I, a very substantial part of the United States was dry, though the industrial Northeast still held out. War brought a need for the conservation of grain, adding a patriotic argument to the many already employed by Wheeler and his cohorts. At the end of 1917 Congress adopted a proposed Eighteenth Amendment to the Constitution, banning the manufacture, transportation, and sale of intoxicating beverages. When approved by three-fourths of the state legislatures, this became effective (1919); and the United States began its experiment in national prohibition.

Interdenominational Activity

The new era of cities and factories stimulated an effort to combine some of the 150 separate Protestant bodies. Economy and efficiency dictated the reunion of some of the fragments into which Protestantism had split. As doctrinal quarrels subsided, the possibility of combination or coöperation increased. Meantime, the need for it was becoming acute. In rural areas depleted by migration to the city, financial necessity pointed toward union or some form of interdenominational activity. The repeal of Sabbath-observance laws and the increase in secular interests (as in motoring) also thinned church attendance, reinforcing the movement for coöperation or unity.

Under all these pressures, many small towns and farm areas formed community churches. Several rival groups within the larger sects joined hands. Others discussed union, paving the way for such later combinations as that of the Methodists. In addition, interdenominational coöperation advanced with the work of the W.C.T.U., the Anti-Saloon League, the Y.M.C.A., the Y.W.C.A., the Home Missions Council. The new tendency was to divide foreign mission fields, rather than to insist on overlapping and competition. In some cases the traditional denominational management of church colleges gave way to interdenominational control. Finally, the establishment of the Federal Council of Churches of Christ in America in 1908 provided a clearing house for the evangelical churches. Some Protestant groups did not join—the Lutherans, for instance, and the southern Baptists. Even so, the Council had contact with the great majority of Protestants and promoted unity of thought through joint study of problems.

There were efforts, too, to promote religious coöperation on a broader basis. The World Congress of Religions at the Chicago Fair in 1893 represented an attempt to bring together all religious-minded people. Somewhat the same end was served by the developing interest in comparative religion among American scholars. Protestants, Catholics, and Jews coöperated in many causes, as in denouncing Russian persecution of the Jews early in the twentieth century. Suspicions remained. Many Protestant clergymen looked with disfavor on the growth of Catholic strength; and most members of the Catholic hierarchy were very cautious about coöperating with Protestants. Jewish-Christian coöperation was also difficult to arrange. But those who tried achieved some success, which testified to the continuing vigor of the American tradition of toleration.

Modernists and Fundamentalists

There were doctrinal controversies in all the churches, despite a strong tendency to deëmphasize theological disputation in the secular age. Orthodox Jews believed in the strict observance of the dietary laws and other age-old religious customs. Reformed Jews felt that many of these traditional beliefs had outlived their usefulness. Conservatives took a position in between. Catholics differed among themselves on such questions as coöperation with Protestants, and as to how far doctrine should be adjusted to fit the changing times. Addressing the American hierarchy in 1898, Leo XIII felt called upon to condemn a tendency to modify traditional beliefs.

The Protestants, meanwhile, continued to be plagued by the modernist controversy. Liberal Protestants kept on trying to reconcile Biblical criticism and the new science with the essence of Christian teachings. On the whole, they were successful, and won victory after victory. A major factor in these triumphs was the influence of leading theological schools, notably the Chicago Divinity School and New York's Union Theological Seminary.

Yet the modernists did not sweep all before them. In the rural areas of the West and South, conservatives held to the old doctrine and denounced the liberal tendencies of the urban preachers. In 1909 these champions of the historic position of the Christian churches organized to oppose the new trends. During the year that followed they issued a booklet entitled *The Fundamentals, a Testimony to the Truth*. Here they set forth their firm belief in the literal truth of the Bible, the divine birth, the bodily resurrection, the imminent second coming of Christ.

The fundamentalists were not to be ignored. Theirs was a powerful voice in every large Protestant denomination. They had influence in theological seminaries, they had many votes at annual conventions. In the southern states they controlled a majority of the pulpits in this period. And they had mighty champions: William Jennings Bryan was one; and this great commoner was ever willing to lend his eloquence and moral fervor to the cause. Another effective advocate was William A. ("Billy") Sunday, who turned from professional baseball to evangelism. Sunday's racy preaching and his athletic behavior in the pulpit attracted huge crowds (80,000,000 altogether, was Sunday's estimate). He and other traveling revivalists covered country districts and pitched their tents in the cities as they carried on their fight against skepticism and sin, liquor and liberalism.

The fundamentalists won some victories in the World War I decade, and would win some more in the 1920's. But even in 1910, when *The Fundamentals* appeared, most of these conservatives knew that they were fighting a last-ditch stand; and not a few suspected that their cause was already lost.

10

The Progressive Movement

From Populism to Progressivism

In the 1890's, it was the Populists and the Bryan Democrats who carried the banner of reform. When Bryan went down in the presidential contest of 1896, some felt that his defeat would indefinitely postpone any possibility of reform. Actually, reform came soon after 1896, reaching a climax in the progressive movement of 1901–17.

The progressive movement, however, was somewhat different from the agrarian crusade of Bryan and the Populists. For one thing, the progressives had urban as well as agrarian leadership. For another, most progressives were disinclined to follow Bryan's 1896 condemnation of urbanization and industrialization. (The progressives tended rather to accept the new city-and-machine civilization as a fact, and to try to make it serve the average citizen to best advantage.) Finally, the progressives included many persons who had considered Bryan and the Populists dangerous radicals. Conservative in outlook, these individuals came to see moderate reform as a means of satisfying the common people and keeping them from turning to political extremists.

Profits and Politics

Among other things, the progressive movement was a protest against political corruption. To be sure, the last dozen years of the nineteenth century did not witness any federal scandals comparable to those of the Grant era. Corruptionists had

270

learned how to be discreet. But there was much of the sordid in national politics. Votes were openly purchased in such key states as Indiana, Connecticut, and West Virginia during the 1888 campaign, in which John Wanamaker, the Philadelphia department store magnate, passed the hat among leading industrialists. Bribes were used throughout the 1890's to secure federal land grants for private individuals and corporations.

On the state level, governors sold pardons, used the military to break strikes in plants of friendly industrialists, vetoed social legislation distasteful to the well-to-do contributors to party campaign funds. This carried on into the next century. In 1907, for example, Pennsylvanians were disturbed to find that millions in public money had been squandered by corrupt deals between the legislature and the contractors who built the new state house.

Conditions were worst of all on the local level. Schools, roads, public health, law enforcement all provided a paradise of peculation in the nation's 3000 counties. Corruption was standard in the cities. Contractors and politicians found ample opportunity for profitable deals in the ever-increasing need for urban and suburban transportation, gas and electricity, sewage disposal, paving, and public buildings. Profit-minded contractors were willing to pay political bosses for franchises certain to yield a handsome harvest. Hazen S. Pingree, reform mayor of Detroit, was offered a trip around the world by one group of franchise hunters, a $50,000 bribe by another. The press was bought to insure secrecy. "Keep the newspapers on your staff as well as the city officials," a speaker told the Ohio Gas and Light Association in 1896. A judicious division of stock, he went on, was a cheap price for a friendly press.

A chief source of political corruption was the regulation of public morals. In administering legislation against prostitution, gambling, and the liquor traffic, the politically controlled police levied tribute on the underworld and shared the loot with those to whom they owed their appointments and promotions. A legislative inquiry directed by State Senator Clarence Lexow in 1894 revealed that appointments to the New York police force were openly sold, and that officials exacted a percentage of the profits of streetwalkers, pickpockets, gunmen, gamblers, saloonkeepers, and bawdy-house managers. Just before World War I, a Chicago vice commission estimated that the police received 20 percent of the city's $15,000,000 taken in annually by prostitutes in that city.

Although the unholy alliance between profits and politics was not limited to America, no leading Western nation had a more unsavory reputation for malfeasance in public office. For this there were many reasons. The cumbersome separation of legislative, executive, and judicial powers opened the gates to corruption by division of responsibility, and the multiplicity of boards, bureaus, departments, commissions, and offices responsible to no central control invited a chaos well suited to corruption. The election of hundreds of different types of officials imposed a burden on the voters that they could not possibly handle well. The complicated nature of the American elective machinery thus invited the lush growth of political machines which exercised the power theoretically in the hands of the voters.

Other circumstances also contributed to political corruption. The very richness of American natural resources presented a vast opportunity for profit from irregular activities. The rapidity of industrialization and urbanization made regulation all the more difficult. So did the magic growth of great consolidated industrial enterprises, which possessed enormous political influence. These organizations functioned smoothly in a culture that attached great prestige to wealth and great value to getting things done quickly.

Yet there was resistance, too. Some came from agrarian reformers, who continued to oppose monopoly and special privilege. Some came from labor leaders who threw their weight behind reform. Some came from well-to-do citizens with a sense of civic decency, liberal clergymen, professional leaders, small businessmen and the members of women's clubs. When the facts about political corruption became known in a community, many rose in righteous indignation. So, too, did citizens respond when they were made aware of the social needs of depressed groups. Quite evidently, the Puritan-Quaker sense of individual responsibility for community well-being was not dead.

Reforming Mayors

Middle-class influence was very much apparent in the election of reform mayors. These were chosen in scores of cities in the two decades after 1890. Some were Republicans. Some were Democrats. Some were independents, who ran on nonpartisan or fusion tickets. Nearly all were earnest men of better-than-average income. Their effort was to cleanse the Augean stables and then to establish good government. A number stressed municipal home rule, in hopes of breaking the stranglehold of state bosses on local politics. Others put the emphasis on civil service, so as to increase government efficiency. Still others concentrated on breaking corrupt alliances between private interests and city officials.

Many of the most famous reform mayors were well-to-do businessmen. Hazen S. Pingree, a prosperous shoe manufacturer, was elected mayor of Detroit in 1889. He used his office to insure competition among private interests bidding for public favors and franchises. He also tried to regulate utility rates and to establish a municipally owned electric plant; and he helped the poor by providing vacant lots for potato patches. Samuel ("Golden Rule") Jones, who was elected mayor of Toledo in 1897, was a machinery manufacturer who had introduced democratic and coöperative methods in his own plant. As a city official, he established civil service for policemen and water works employees. In addition, he vetoed renewals of trolley franchises to a private corporation. Seth Low, a wealthy tea importer and president of Columbia University, won a mayoralty race in New York in 1901, defeating the Tammany machine. He then checked patronage excesses by extending the merit system of appointment.

Most spectacular of all the reform mayors was Tom Johnson of Cleveland. A trolley magnate and iron manufacturer, Johnson became a political crusader after reading Henry George. Elected mayor of Cleveland in 1901, he held tent meetings to educate the citizenry in municipal affairs. He then overhauled the city government and promoted municipal ownership and operation of the consolidated street railroad services. At the same time he lessened the grip of state machine politics by fighting for municipal home rule.

These were four of many. In Minneapolis a grand jury uncovered a graft ring and forced prosecution of the culprits. In Jersey City Mark Fagin led a movement to free the city from the coils of utilities, railroads, and spoilsmen politicians. In St. Louis Joseph W. Folk, while circuit attorney, exposed corruption and prosecuted many bribery cases. It was much the same in many other municipalities.

The movement for municipal reform was aided by the National Municipal League, by municipal research bureaus, and by the commission form of government. The National Municipal League, founded in 1894, fought for definite improvements in city government: simplification of governmental machinery, full publicity of accounts, protection against franchise grabbers, administration by experts, municipal home rule. The research bureaus (modeled after one established in New York in 1906) trained administrators and studied ways and means of improving city government. The commission form of government came into being in Galveston, Texas, after the great flood of 1900. It substituted an elected commission of five men for the old and cumbersome mayor-and-council plan. The five commissioners enacted ordinances, made appointments, and awarded contracts in open meetings. Four of them ran city departments; the fifth (a mayor-president) coördinated the work of his colleagues. With many variations, this scheme had spread to over 200 cities by 1912.

Frequently reform administrations ended in defeats at the polls, the old gang of politicians regaining control. Even when the reformers hung on, the bosses and their allies often found new methods of getting what they wanted. Nonetheless, there was more competence and decency in municipal government in 1919 than there had been in 1896. That much at least had been accomplished by the reforming mayors, the militant prosecuting attorneys, the aroused citizens.

Progressive Governors

While progressive-minded citizens were succeeding on the city level, reformers were also active in state politics. There was in fact no sharp dividing line between the two fields. After four terms as mayor of Detroit, Hazen Pingree was twice elected governor of Michigan. In like fashion, Joseph W. Folk began as a reform politician in St. Louis, fighting bribery and corruption. Then he became reform governor of Missouri, securing anti-lobby and utility regulation laws, the initiative and referendum, the state-wide primary, compulsory education and child labor statutes, and appropriations for highways ("Get Missouri out of the mud").

There were some reforming governors in the last dozen years of the nineteenth century. John Peter Atgeld of Illinois and James S. Hogg of Texas are examples among the Democrats, Theodore Roosevelt among the Republicans. But the great era of state reforms came after 1900. In the first decade of the new century there were progressive governors in every section. In the Republican party, there were Robert M. La Follette of Wisconsin, Albert B. Cummins of Iowa, Charles Evans Hughes of New York, Hiram Johnson of California, and many more. The Democratic reform governors included Folk of Missouri, Hoke Smith of Georgia, Woodrow Wilson of New Jersey.

Many of the progressive governors centered their attention on the improvement of political methods and devices. The first and most important victory in this field was achieved before 1900, with the adoption of the secret official ballot. In earlier years parties had printed and distributed at the polls their own lists of candidates. This meant that voters had little chance to express their preferences with any privacy. Massachusetts changed the situation in 1888 by requiring secret, uniform, and officially printed ballots. Within a decade the reform had been adopted in all but four states. Although vote buyers continued to operate, and pressure was still exerted on citizens at the polls, the Massachusetts ballot marked a major step toward the removal of corruption from politics.

Also important were state laws regulating the use of money in elections. In 1890 New York adopted such a statute; and before the end of the century sixteen states had followed her example. Three states expressly prohibited corporations from contributing to political campaign funds. It was possible to evade the prohibitions laid down in these laws; but this corrupt-practice legislation had some effect.

The revolt against political bossism found further expression in the direct primary movement. In 1903 Governor Robert M. La Follette persuaded Wisconsin to adopt the direct primary. The idea was to have party nominees chosen by the voters rather than by machine-ridden conventions. All the states had adopted the direct primary in some form by 1915.

In some respects the movement proved a disappointment. Bosses controlled the primaries much as they had controlled the party conventions. Still, the primary did on occasion serve democratic ends— as when it helped bring victory in the fight for direct election of United States Senators. Under the Constitution, United States Senators were chosen by the state legislatures. More times than not, the legislators ignored popular sentiment in choosing Senators. Sometimes the choice hinged on bribery; and the general tendency was to select machine politicians or men of enormous wealth. Taking advantage of the new direct primary, a number of states allowed voters to indicate their preferences as to senatorial nominees. Legislators were then bound to respect these views. Finally, in 1912, the United States Senate reluctantly joined the national House of Representatives in submitting to the states a proposed constitutional amendment providing for the popular election of Senators. A year later, the necessary three-fourths of the states had approved, and the Seventeenth Amendment had been added to the Constitution.

The direct primary and the popular election of Senators did not exhaust the political program of the progressives. Noting the practice of the Swiss cantons, American political reformers agitated for the initiative and the referendum. Under the initiative, a small percentage of the electorate could force the legislature to consider a measure. The referendum made it possible for a similar group to compel the submission of a measure to the people in a general or special election. A Populist-Democratic regime in South Dakota enacted this program as early as 1898. Four years later William S. U'Ren, an unobtrusive but effective progressive, persuaded Oregon to do the same. Within a decade, fifteen more states accepted the initiative and referendum.

Meantime, in 1908, Oregon had adopted the recall on a state-wide basis. Colorado and other states followed suit. This made it possible for dissatisfied citizens to challenge the right of an office holder to continue in office. If enough voters were interested, the official could be forced to submit himself and his policies to the test of a new election.

Many states tinkered with their constitutions in the first two decades of the twentieth century. In some cases changes were limited to amendments. In others whole new constitutions were submitted to the electorate. Quite a few of the new constitutional provisions curbed the power of the legislature, which was suspected of being the seat of corrupt and partisan influence. The changes also increased the power and responsibility of the executive. Administrative functions were generally expanded with the establishment of commissions of nonpartisan experts for regulating railroads, insurance companies, and utilities. Under La Follette's progressive leadership, Wisconsin made wide use of this type of machinery, which was a central aspect of the so-called Wisconsin Idea.

In a number of cases the constitutional changes included the extension of suffrage to women. In 1910 the state of Washington followed the example of Wyoming, which had granted votes to women back in territorial days. California then climbed on the bandwagon, as did other western states—a dozen, all west of the Mississippi, by the time of World War I.

The proponents of woman suffrage argued that women were as competent as men to share in the making of public decisions. Denial of the ballot, they continued, was a contradiction of the democratic principle. Political reformers and labor leaders further felt that women voters could help check corruption and secure social legislation in the interest of the working class. This very point led some conservatives to take the other side. Joining them were men and women who saw in the movement a threat to the family and the home. But the objectors gradually lost ground. The National American Woman Suffrage Association, led by Carrie Chapman Catt, pressed Congress for action. Success came in World War I. Congress submitted a proposed amendment to the states; and in 1920 the Nineteenth Amendment gave votes to women all over the land.

Social and Economic Reforms

Many progressives were relatively conservative middle-class citizens who wanted honesty in government. Allied with them were humanitarians who backed political reform as a means of securing economic and social benefits for the plain people.

Moderate reformers rather than left-wing radicals, these ministers, teachers, social workers, and writers all owed much to the social gospel. As they saw it, industrialization and urbanization had brought a social crisis, and right-thinking people could not ignore the challenge.

Making contact with the labor movement, the new humanitarians began a spirited crusade to raise the standard of living of the poor. They repudiated the age-old idea that every individual in the struggle of life is rewarded according to his worth. They refused to believe that the poor must always be numerous, and that national well-being rested on the accumulation of wealth by the competent few. In the eyes of humanitarians both knowledge and wealth are created, not individually, but socially. In consequence, society has a responsibility toward those handicapped by misfortune, by illness, or by an unfavorable environment.

Strong in character, lofty in ideals, the humanitarian reformers were also practical. They saw that organization was essential if they were to win. They knew that propaganda was a must. They recognized that sustained and determined pressure on legislatures, courts, and executives was the most necessary of all. These men and women therefore hired lobby agents and publicity managers. They organized many effective associations, including the National Consumers League, the Association for Labor Legislation, the National Housing Association, the National Association for the Advancement of Colored People. At first the most conservative pillars of society regarded the ideas of this vanguard as dangerous. In time, the humanitarian program came to be accepted in widening circles.

The humanitarians operated in many different ways. Such clergymen as Washington Gladden and Josiah Strong developed the social gospel in their preaching and writing. Lester F. Ward, the pioneer sociologist, did much to publicize the idea that knowledge and wealth, being socially created, must be socially shared. The government, he said, must be the instrument to this end. A notable group of economists, including Richard T. Ely and Thorstein Veblen, undermined the classical economic theory of laissez faire, and as experts helped frame laws regulating private enterprise in the public interest. Meantime, such novelists as Frank Norris, Upton Sinclair, and Jack London advised the people of the need for reform.

Jane Addams, Lillian Wald, and other pioneer social workers played a leading role in the humanitarian agitation. These individuals developed social settlements in the slums (Lillian Wald also organized nursing service for country districts). At the same time, the social workers demanded reforms that would eliminate slum conditions and help solve the problems of the poor. Florence Kelley, who did social settlement work in Chicago, also performed valiant service in enforcing Illinois factory inspection acts. In addition, she organized consumers and secured improved labor legislation.

These and many other citizens (including labor leaders) worked for tax reform; for factory legislation to protect the lives and health of workers; for insurance against sickness, accidents, and unemployment; for old-age pensions; for maximum hour and minimum wage laws; for the regulation of tenements; for the public development of playgrounds; for public health clinics and the improvement of public education. As they labored for these reforms, the humanitarians obtained political support on city, state, and national levels. Some politicians came into the movement because of their own humanitarian sympathies. Others saw that the newspapers and the public were becoming interested, and that it would be politically unwise to resist the rising tide.

A substantial body of social legislation was the result. Massachusetts enacted a factory inspection law as early as 1867. Within the next decade, that same commonwealth extended this type of legislation, and limited the working day for women to ten hours. By 1907 nearly half the states had statutes reducing the working day for miners and others engaged in dangerous pursuits. Virtually all the industrial states were regulating working conditions in mines and factories in the interest of the health and safety of employees. And the voters of New York took a further step when they endorsed a constitutional amendment authorizing accident insurance legislation.

These and other laws reflected the growing conviction that private interests must submit to some measure of government control in the public interest. Many of the new laws, however, were not carried out effectively; and quite a few were declared unconstitutional by the courts. Such developments in turn gave strength to the movement to nationalize the local and state reform impulse.

The Muckrakers

The extension of the reform movement to the national political stage owed a great deal to a group of magazine writers whom Theodore Roosevelt disparagingly christened "muckrakers." Henry Demarest Lloyd had anticipated the muckrakers with his *Wealth Versus Commonwealth* (1894), an exposure of the methods by which Standard Oil crushed small competitors. B. O. Flower had also paved the way with his work as editor of *The Arena*. But the great era of muckraking began in 1902, with the appearance in *McClure's Magazine* of Ida Tarbell's history of the Standard Oil Company. The public displayed interest; and *McClure's* published detailed and sensational exposures of the techniques of railroad executives, insurance companies, and city bosses. The series on bosses was done by the engaging and gifted Lincoln Steffens, whose *Shame of the Cities* laid bare the corrupt dealings of politicians with franchise seekers.

Impressed with the success of *McClure's*, other magazines joined the parade. *Everybody's* increased its circulation by a series on stockbrokers ("Frenzied Finance"). *Collier's* had Samuel Hopkins Adams expose patent medicine frauds, and David Graham Phillips attacked the United States Senate in *Cosmopolitan*. In due time, there were series on the antisocial behavior of banks and packing houses and distilleries, on the immoral traffic in women and the tragic effects of child labor, on the exploitation of the Negro.

The muckrakers were specific in their accusations, sparing no names. Though sensational, the exposures were substantially accurate, as the relatively few libel suits indicated. In time, the movement died down. The public tired of reading all the sordid details; and advertisers used pressure to curb the literature of exposure. But, while it lasted, the muckrake crusade increased public interest in political reform and made possible much progressive legislation.

The National Scene

As the muckrakers gained strength, it was apparent that the progressive movement was taking on a national character. This could be seen in the activities of leading reformers. Many young progressives were seeking and obtaining seats in Congress:

George W. Norris of Nebraska, Miles Poindexter of Washington, Albert J. Beveridge of Indiana, to name only a few. Such reforming governors as La Follette of Wisconsin and Cummins of Iowa went from their state capitals to the United States Senate. Joseph W. Folk, who had begun as a municipal reformer in St. Louis, and had then entered the state arena in Missouri, ended his public career as a federal officeholder. And two men who had sponsored progressive legislation while in state politics (Theodore Roosevelt and Woodrow Wilson) became Presidents of the United States.

For this nationalization there were several precedents. The federal government had been involved in reform more than once during the nineteenth century. The Jeffersonian and Jacksonian movements furnish examples. So do the national appeals of the Populists and Bryan. The obvious inability of the states to control railroads led in 1887 to the passage by Congress of the Interstate Commerce Act. Likewise, the failure of the states to check monopoly in business led the federal government to adopt the Sherman Antitrust Act in 1890. In emasculating these laws, the United States courts merely inspired reformers to agitate for more effective national legislation and, if need be, amendments to the Constitution. Moreover, the tendency of the higher courts to hold state social legislation unconstitutional reinforced the conviction that the next great battle must be fought on the national stage.

The progressives were ready for the battle. The advocates of various reforms had taken care to organize national associations of like-minded people. The exposures of the muckrakers appealed to a national audience. And the reform victories in the cities and the states provided experience and publicity useful in carrying the progressive movement into national politics.

The American progressive crusade was far from unique. It was, rather, a part of a world movement. Many states of the United States modeled their reform legislation on English and German statutes providing for factory inspection, compensation of injured workingmen, and the protection of women and children in industry. The British Parliament was expanding control over business and industry and was revamping the tax structure in the interest of such enlarged social services as slum clearance, public health, and old-age pensions. France, Germany, and the Scandinavian countries were taking similar steps, and New Zealand and Australia were in many respects leading the world in social improvements under government auspices. Returning from a round-the-world trip, William Jennings Bryan declared in 1906 that citizens everywhere were demanding that the government be brought closer to the people, and exert itself vigorously in their behalf. Hence Americans were in step with world trends when they looked to the central government to take up the movement begun in the cities and the states.

In national as in state politics, the progressive movement cut across party lines. Reforms were sought by progressive Democrats like William Jennings Bryan and Woodrow Wilson, by progressive Republicans like Robert M. La Follette and Theodore Roosevelt. The opposition, too, found adherents in both major parties. Conservative Republicans who opposed change—men like Senator Nelson Aldrich of Rhode Island—frequently found themselves working hand in hand with conservative Democrats who clung to doctrines of states' rights and laissez faire.

Although grounded in economic factors and in a desire for political success, progressivism also possessed a strong moral appeal. Most political reformers of the early twentieth century subscribed to the doctrine of progress, long a part of the American creed. This fired the sponsors of reform with an optimistic faith in their cause. At the same time it tied progressivism to a long-cherished folk belief, thus strengthening the hand of progressive politicians. The reformers and their followers fought with a will, assuming that the future was on their side, that an aroused opinion and sustained effort would surely bring victory.

The progressives also identified their measures with Americanism. That is, they appealed to the cluster of patriotic beliefs that identified Americanism with the well-being of the common man. Throughout the nineteenth century Americans had believed in a basic law of right, to which human institutions had to conform. This higher law provided the standard of action, the goal of endeavor. Nineteenth-century Americans held such beliefs with an almost evangelical enthusiasm, as is seen in reform movements from abolitionism and temperance to greenbackism and Populism. The progressive crusade was, in a way, heir to these doctrines, all embedded in the American faith.

Another factor in the situation was the gain in Socialist strength. Brought into the country by immigrants in the post-Civil War years, Socialism at first had little appeal for old-stock Americans. Then, at the turn of the century, there appeared a new group of leaders, including Eugene V. Debs of Indiana and Victor Berger of Wisconsin. These men showed that it was possible to put Socialism into the American idiom and attract a large-scale following. In the presidential election of 1904 Debs polled over 400,000 votes. Eight years later the same Socialist candidate mustered almost a million supporters at the polls—7 percent of the total vote. The Socialists showed great strength in Schenectady, New York, in Reading, Pennsylvania, in Milwaukee, Wisconsin, and in other cities; also in some western wheat and mining states.

Many Americans were disturbed by the rise of the Socialists. The Socialist doctrine of class war repelled both conservatives and progressives, as did the Socialist demand for public ownership of the means of production and distribution. Defenders of the existing economic order were still more frightened by the I.W.W., which fashioned its platform after that of the French syndicalists and openly preached sabotage, violence, and revolution.

What to do about this situation? Faced with a similar problem, Bismarck and other European conservatives had made concessions to the workers. That is, European defenders of the *status quo* had backed reform to please the workers and keep them from turning radical. The same thing might work in the United States. Thus thoughtful conservatives joined the humanitarians after 1900, supporting progressive legislation as a means of opposing radicalism.

From McKinley to Roosevelt

In the election of 1896, the major-party candidates stressed the currency issue. The hard-money forces won, with the Republican William McKinley defeating the Democratic

William Jennings Bryan. As President (1897–1901), McKinley supported legislation designed to aid the groups which had elected him. The Wilson-Gorman Tariff of 1894, passed in Grover Cleveland's second term, was replaced by the highly protective Dingley Tariff of 1897. The currency question was settled in a manner calculated to satisfy the hard-money forces, with the passage of the Gold Standard Act of 1900.

The general public was more interested in other matters. One was the war with Spain, fought and won in 1898. Victory in this popular conflict added greatly to McKinley's prestige. At the same time, there was a revival of business activity, and the United States pulled out of the depression that had followed the panic of 1893. This meant jobs for workers; and, as gold poured in from Alaska, farm prices rose.

The result was general satisfaction with the incumbent Republican administration. Also in the picture was the personal popularity of President McKinley, who was a kindly, soft-spoken, religious man. Inevitably, then, McKinley was renominated by the Republicans in 1900. Just as naturally, he was victorious at the polls. His most effective slogan in the 1900 contest was "the Full Dinner Pail," a term that called attention to the prevailing good times. Prosperity enabled McKinley to hold the states that he had won in 1896, and to add half a dozen states west of the Mississippi.

As in 1896, McKinley's Democratic opponent was William Jennings Bryan. In the campaign of 1900, Bryan continued to advocate free silver. He also set himself against imperialism, opposing retention of the Philippine Islands, which McKinley had acquired from Spain. But, as the campaign proceeded, Bryan put more and more emphasis on opposition to monopoly. This antitrust issue did not bring the Democrats the victory; but it did call attention to what would be a key demand of the progressives.

Although the Bryan Democrats publicized the antitrust campaign, quite a different group of politicians pressed the issue into service. For, after 1901, the fight against the trusts was taken up by Theodore Roosevelt, a Republican. And Roosevelt, not Bryan, was to be the central figure in the national progressive movement for the first dozen years of the twentieth century.

Theodore Roosevelt came from a long-established New York family. Being well-to-do, he could have coasted through life. Instead, he chose to be unceasingly active. With grim determination, he transformed a weak body into a strong, athletic one. He cultivated the manly sports, took up ranching in the Dakotas, established a reputation as a popular writer of western history. Fascinated by politics, he served an apprenticeship as an assemblyman in the New York legislature. Although defeated for mayor of New York City (running third behind Abram Hewitt and Henry George), he secured various appointive jobs: United States Civil Service Commissioner; New York Police Commissioner; Assistant Secretary of the Navy under McKinley. He then led a highly publicized group of "Rough Riders" in the Spanish-American War. His military reputation helped win him election as governor of New York in 1898.

Finding Roosevelt hard to control, New York's Republican bosses had him "kicked upstairs." That is, they had him nominated for Vice-President in 1900 (McKinley's running mate of 1896 had died in office). The vice-presidency was generally regarded as a political graveyard. But not this time. Soon after McKinley was inaugurated for his second term, the President was shot by a fanatic. When McKinley died in September, 1901, Theodore Roosevelt became President of the United States. Elected in his own right in 1904, Roosevelt occupied the White House from 1901 to 1909.

Only forty-three when he took office, the new Chief Executive was a man of bursting energy, with a magnetic, buoyant personality. Roosevelt possessed the gift of turning phrases, of making timeworn platitudes seem fresh and full of meaning. Despite his upper-class origin, this President knew how to express the yearnings of the great middle class. He also knew how to dramatize himself. His vehemence and bluster, his intensity and gaiety kept him always in the limelight. Dramatic speaking tours helped, as did striking newspaper interviews; and T. R. was publicized as no preceding President had been. This enabled him to use his office as one of leadership. For Roosevelt believed that a President could do anything in the public interest not specifically prohibited by the Constitution.

To thoughtful humanitarians and resolute reformers, Theodore

Roosevelt seemed a somewhat superficial individual, a compromiser who lacked spiritual insight and did not understand economics. Conservative Republicans, on the other hand, regarded the new President as too much on the impulsive, reforming side. Yet Theodore Roosevelt managed to get on pretty well with both groups. He cultivated the support of such progressive Republicans as Albert Beveridge, and at the same time remained intimate with Republican conservatives, including Henry Cabot Lodge and Nelson Aldrich. Personality, political acumen, and a willingness to compromise made possible this double association.

In the White House years inherited from McKinley (1901–05), Roosevelt proceeded cautiously in championing the reform measures long advocated by Bryan and others. Then, in the presidential contest of 1904, Roosevelt won an overwhelming victory, defeating an undistinguished Democratic candidate, Alton B. Parker. Parker carried only the solid South. Thereafter (1905–09) Roosevelt moved more vigorously along the path of reform. In doing so, he helped nationalize a progressive movement already strong and popular on the municipal and state level.

Trust Busting

Of the crucial issues that presented themselves to Theodore Roosevelt, none was more important than the rapid growth of monopoly. In 1900 a Congressionally appointed Industrial Commission revealed that ninety-two great business combinations had been organized in the preceding year. These included Standard Oil of New Jersey, a Rockefeller holding company with far-flung properties. Soon after this there appeared the billion-dollar United States Steel Corporation, followed by the International Harvester Company, which was made up of the five leading units in the industry. Organized by profit-minded bankers, many of the new trusts were fantastically overcapitalized, with consequent ill effects on the purchasers of securities. Some of the new combinations engaged in practices definitely against the public interest. (The sugar trust cheated the government out of millions of dollars by tampering with customs scales and by diverting water from public reservoirs through secret, unmetered mains.) Popularized by the muckrakers, such revelations of the Industrial Commission aroused middle-class Americans to great indignation.

Sensitive to the mounting public criticism of monopolies, President Theodore Roosevelt determined to enforce the long-neglected Sherman Antitrust Act of 1890. He therefore ordered his Attorney General to start proceedings against the Northern Securities Company. This holding company was a creation of J. Pierpont Morgan and James J. Hill. The intention was to combine the railroads of the Northwest—the Great Northern, the Northern Pacific, the Chicago, Burlington and Quincy. In 1904, by a bare majority, the United States Supreme Court upheld a lower court in declaring the merger a violation of the Sherman Act. The judges then ordered the Northern Securities Company dissolved.

Although the Northern Securities decision had little practical effect, many hailed it as the herald of a new day for the people. In the next year the Supreme Court handed down a decision against the beef trust; and by 1909, when Roosevelt left the White House, the Department of Justice had prepared twenty-five indictments against trusts.

For this record, Theodore Roosevelt was acclaimed as a "trust buster." But, as the President himself recognized, no number of anti-trust suits could unscramble the omelet of modern monopoly. Roosevelt himself refrained from an all-out attack on big combinations, by insisting that some trusts were "bad," some "good." The Supreme Court took much the same line. In the Standard Oil case of 1911, the learned justices set forth the rule of reason. Under this rule, they held that monopoly itself was not necessarily undesirable, and that the government could break up trusts only when the companies involved were pursuing policies that were clearly unfair and unreasonable. Unreasonable, that is, in the eyes of the judges.

In addition to the suits against the trusts, the Roosevelt administration sponsored legislation establishing a Bureau of Corporations. Set up in 1903, the Bureau had power to investigate and publicize the practices of big business. Within these limits, the new agency represented an extension of public interest into the field of private enterprise.

Theodore Roosevelt also played an important part in pushing Meat Inspection and Pure Food and Drug acts through Congress (1906). These laws provided for the regulation in the public interest of the products of packing houses and patent medicine firms engaged in interstate commerce. Although the measures did not go as far as many reformers thought they should, they were important steps in advancing the doctrine of control of business for the public good.

Regulating the Railroads

Closely related to the problem of curbing the antisocial practices of big business was the widespread demand that railroads be brought under effective public control. In 1903 Congress grudgingly bowed to a White House demand that the Interstate Commerce Commission be given increased power. Striking at the rebate evil, the Elkins Act of that year specifically prohibited variations from published freight rates, and provided fines for shippers as well as for carriers. Hoping for release from the necessity of favoring large shippers, many railroads approved of this statute.

Then came demands for further action. Congressional reformers led by Senator La Follette insisted that the Interstate Commerce Commission be empowered to fix rates on the basis of fair earnings on the actual investment railroads had made in their lines and equipment. The House of Representatives passed such a bill in 1906, but it met with vigorous opposition on the part of the old guard in the Senate. Much to the disgust of La Follette, President Roosevelt compromised. The resulting Hepburn Act increased the power of the Interstate Commerce Commission by requiring that the railroads, rather than the Commission, initiate litigation testing the validity of the Commission's orders in rate matters. The Hepburn Act also brought express and sleeping car companies within the jurisdiction of the I.C.C.; and it banned free passes, a notorious source of political influence. The I.C.C. was further authorized to prescribe uniform accounting methods for all railways. This made it difficult for carriers to conceal expenditures for bribery and other improper activities.

In the same year, 1906, Congress also passed an Employers' Liability Act. This statute, recommended by President Roosevelt, required the railroads to compensate employees injured in the course of duty. Although the Supreme Court declared this law unconstitutional, a similar act of 1908 was upheld.

Roosevelt did relatively little in the general field of labor; here problems were left to the states. But T. R. did favor a "square deal for labor," and did seek the labor vote. This led him to intervene in the coal strike of 1902. His intervention was quite different from that of Grover Cleveland in the Pullman strike of 1894. President Cleveland had used federal troops to help the employers break the strike. President Roosevelt used his influence to effect a compromise settlement between John Mitchell's United Mine Workers and the Morgan-connected coal operators. Plainly, the government's relation to business was changing.

Conservation

Theodore Roosevelt's most notable contribution to the movement for controlling private property in the public interest was in the conservation field. He began at once, in his first annual message to Congress in 1901. This message called attention to the need for conserving such natural resources as forests, coal, oil, water sites, and the soil itself.

The demand for conservation was not new. Such scientists as John Powell, founder of the United States Geological Survey, had long warned the nation that the chaotic policy of wasting natural resources would exhaust this priceless heritage within the predictable future. The remarkable achievements of the German conservationists, featured at the Chicago World's Fair of 1893, brought home the lesson to those ready to learn. Roosevelt took up this movement and gave it support and direction. He worked directly and through such able lieutenants as Gifford Pinchot, who had studied forestry in Germany. State governors also helped, as did a Roosevelt-appointed National

Conservation Commission, which made an inventory of the natural resources of the nation.

The first concrete achievement was the Reclamation Act of 1902, providing for construction by the federal government of irrigation projects. The financing was to come from proceeds of public land sales. The new Reclamation Service established under this act initiated a series of significant projects, including, ultimately, the Roosevelt Dam in Arizona, the Boulder Dam on the Colorado River, the Grand Coulee project on the Columbia. As a result, millions of acres of arid land were reclaimed for cultivation. Nor was that all. In due time, new sources of hydroelectric power were made available, flood control was promoted, reforestation advanced. Lands useless by reason of swampy conditions were also reclaimed; and the conservation program further included the development of inland waterways in the interest of cheap transportation.

Besides these long-range projects, President Roosevelt withdrew from sale tens of millions of acres of public land. Here he worked closely with Gifford Pinchot, director of the Forest Service; and he acted under the authority of a hitherto little noticed Forest Reserve Act of 1891. Roosevelt withdrew further lands from entry when his National Conservation Commission recommended that the government retain (and lease for limited periods) all public lands containing phosphates, natural gas, oil, and coal. Congress at first refused to confirm the retention by the government of mineral and water-power sites; but the conservationists won their point during the presidency of Roosevelt's successor, William Howard Taft.

Theodore Roosevelt's contribution to the conservation movement went far beyond the laws and executive orders of his administration. By dramatizing the need for a new policy, T. R. made the public conservation-minded. Ordinary citizens came to feel that private monopolies must not be allowed to sequester and exploit what remained of the natural resources on the public domain. Instead, the national and state governments should take hold. The advocates of ruthless exploitation would win further victories. But at long last, after three centuries of reckless waste, the American people were begininng to see the need for conservation.

Then Came Taft

Roosevelt's talent for combining crusade and compromise enabled him to control the Republican party machinery all through his presidency (1901–09). In consequence, he could easily have obtained the party nomination for President in 1908. But, after winning in 1904, Roosevelt had announced that he would not be a candidate in 1908 for what in effect would be a third term. Adhering to this promise, T. R. resisted pressure that he run again, and persuaded his party to nominate William Howard Taft of Ohio.

Progressive Republicans were somewhat surprised at Roosevelt's choice for the succession. Charles Evans Hughes, the liberal governor of New York, would have been a logical selection. Taft had shown conservative tendencies as a judge during the 1890's, before his appointment as Commissioner in the Philippines and Secretary of War under Roosevelt. What was more, Taft obviously lacked Roosevelt's energy—he was an easygoing, genial, bulky man weighing 350 pounds. Roosevelt, however, believed that his cabinet officer was loyal and would continue the Roosevelt policies. Besides, the President did not care for Hughes.

In the campaign of 1908, Taft sounded like a progressive. He was 100 percent for the Roosevelt record. He was against monopoly. He was for conservation. He was even for tariff reform (Roosevelt had avoided the tariff issue as politically dangerous).

This in public. In private, Taft seemed to side with conservative Old Guard Republicans, and to favor slowing down the impulsively reformist crusades of T. R. Taft was progressive, he insisted, largely to prevent the radicals from taking hold. "If the tyranny and oppression of an oligarchy of wealth cannot be avoided," he said, in denouncing the money trust, "then socialism will triumph, and the institution of private property will perish."

Having failed with the relatively conservative Alton B. Parker in 1904, the Democrats in 1908 turned again to William Jennings Bryan, the "peerless leader." In his third presidential campaign, Bryan denounced the protective tariff—the "mother of trusts," the "cause" of the steady rise in the cost of living. Bryan demanded government ownership of the railroads. He asked for the elimination of the injunction in labor disputes; he favored the income tax and the direct election of United States Senators. Long a favorite in rural districts, Bryan now gained labor support as well. Specifically, he won the official backing of the American Federation of Labor, which had never before endorsed a presidential candidate.

But Bryan lost, as he had lost before. This time he made his poorest showing, carrying only three states outside of the South. Taft swung middle-class votes by insisting that his Democratic foe was "irresponsible," that a Bryan victory would mean the unjust punishment of the rich. Besides, times were fairly good, in spite of the minor panic of 1907. Prosperity and Roosevelt's popularity saw Taft through to victory, and to one term in the White House (1909–13).

Republican Divisions

One commentator said that shifting from Roosevelt to Taft was like changing from an automobile to a horse-drawn carriage. Unlike his predecessor, Taft stressed the legalistic restrictions on the powers of the executive; and, more than Roosevelt, Taft worked with the conservative Old Guard Republicans. He was close, for instance, to reactionary Senator Aldrich of Rhode Island, and to Joseph G. Cannon of Illinois, the autocratic Speaker of the national House of Representatives.

Even so, Taft did a good deal for the reform cause. Operating in a quiet, undramatic way, he kept pushing the Roosevelt program. He persuaded Congress to grant authority for the withdrawal from private entry of coal lands on the public domain; he withdrew petroleum property from private exploitation. He added great stretches of timberland to the national forests. In one term under Taft the Justice Department instituted almost twice as many antitrust suits as it had in Roosevelt's two terms. Railroad legislation was extended. The Mann-Elkins Act of 1910 gave the Interstate Commerce Commission authority over telegraph and telephone lines, and facilitated the immediate execution of Commission orders for rate reduction.

Taft also struck out in new directions. He urged Congress to submit to the states a proposed constitutional amendment enabling the federal government to impose an income tax. (This resulted in the Sixteenth Amendment, which became effective just before Taft left the White House in 1913.) The Taft administration also saw the steady progress of the movement which resulted, just after Taft's retirement, in the Seventeenth Amendment, providing for the direct election of United States Senators. And, with Taft's approval, Congress also enacted legislation limiting expenditures in Congressional campaigns and requiring publication of such expenditures.

Despite such accomplishments, the Taft regime was a failure, and was so regarded by both progressive and conservative Republicans. The President was unable to get all party members to work in harmony. Such Republican progressives as George W. Norris broke party ranks to join the Democrats in curbing the arbitrary power of "Uncle Joe" Cannon, the conservative Republican Speaker of the House (1910). In this revolt, the Speaker was shorn of his power to appoint committees and to dominate the process of legislation. The result was pleasing to reformers but disturbing to Republican party managers.

The rift within Republican ranks was still more evident in the tariff situation. The party platform of 1908 called for tariff revision, which Taft interpreted to mean revision downward. This view was shared by western Republicans (mostly progressives), who felt that the Dingley Tariff of 1897 favored eastern industrialists. A House bill therefore cut many schedules. But the Old Guard took over in the Senate. Senator Aldrich, a wealthy New England industrialist, introduced over 800 amendments, most of which increased duties. Republican progressives—La Follette, Cummins, Beveridge, William E. Borah of Idaho, and others—joined the Democrats in opposing the Aldrich proposals. There followed one of the most hotly contested tariff controversies in three generations.

In this situation, the administration had the balance of power. Puzzled, Taft at first lent support to the progressives. Then he switched, and threw his weight to the conservative Republican protectionists. This gave Aldrich the victory, embodied in the Payne-Aldrich Tariff of 1909.

In its completed form, the Payne-Aldrich bill contained many commendable features: a Tariff Commission to gather facts on relative costs of production at home and abroad; a flexible clause enabling the President to raise or lower duties in response to discriminations of a foreign country; a one percent tax on corporation earnings above $5000. Basically, however, the measure was a standard high protective tariff, in a class with the McKinley Tariff of 1890 and the Dingley Tariff of 1897. Its passage represented a victory for the conservative Republicans. But, since the tariff was unpopular in the country as a whole, its enactment actually strengthened the progressives. Taft found this out when he defended the Payne-Aldrich measure as the best tariff ever enacted. This statement brought withering criticism from the Middle West, which considered the bill a betrayal of the promise to lower tariff schedules.

Hoping to regain lost ground, the President sponsored a tariff-cutting reciprocity treaty with Canada (1911). This, however, failed to yield the desired result. The proposed treaty provided for the admission of Canadian farm produce into eastern markets previously dominated by agricultural goods from middle western states. In return, American industrialists would receive favorable treatment in Canada. Middle western voters, naturally, were far from pleased. And to make matters more embarrassing for Taft, the Canadian government rejected the treaty, fearing that it would mean domination of Canada by the United States.

Republican difficulties were increased by the Ballinger-Pinchot controversy. This involved the conservation movement launched by Roosevelt. When he became President, Taft replaced Roosevelt's Secretary of the Interior by Richard A. Ballinger of the state of Washington. Ballinger reflected the western desire to use natural resources now; and he regarded Roosevelt's withdrawal of land from private entry as wanting in legality. Hence Ballinger restored to private entry valuable timber and water-power sites. Which, of course, brought criticism from Roosevelt conservationists.

Then came more serious charges. A Land Office field investigator, Louis R. Glavis, claimed that Secretary Ballinger was blocking investigation of allegedly fraudulent corporation claims to Alaskan coal lands. President Taft authorized the dismissal of Glavis, who publicized his sensational story in *Collier's*. Glavis was then supported by

Roosevelt's friend Gifford Pinchot, who still headed the Forest Service in the Department of Agriculture. When Congressional investigators found Ballinger innocent of the Glavis-Pinchot charges, Taft dismissed Pinchot for insubordination. To clear the air, Ballinger also resigned. But the progressives insisted that Taft had betrayed the conservation cause.

The Bull Moose Campaign

Dissatisfied with Taft, the progressive Republicans planned to capture the party machinery and make sure that a progressive received the Republican presidential nomination in 1912. La Follette was obviously the logical man; and in 1911 a National Progressive League entered the field to forward his cause. The League stood for direct election of Senators, preferential primaries, the initiative, referendum, and recall, corrupt-practices acts, and the control of big business in the public interest. The nation, said League spokesmen, should follow the lead of La Follette's home state of Wisconsin. There progressives had revised the tax structure, had tightened regulation of railroads and insurance companies, had pioneered in social legislation to benefit farmers and workingmen.

At this point Theodore Roosevelt reëntered the political arena. After bowing out as President, he had gone to Africa to hunt wild game, and to Europe to visit leading dignitaries. How would he stand in the progressive-conservative struggle within the Republican party? Would he support his protégé Taft, who had lined up with the conservatives? Or would he go with the La Follette crowd?

When Roosevelt returned to the United States in 1910, it was soon apparent that he and Taft were less friendly than before. The Ballinger-Pinchot row was one factor in the situation. Roosevelt's exclusion from the inner councils of the Taft administration was in the picture. So was Taft's unwillingness to be dominated by his overbearing predecessor.

Tying in with all these points was the trend of the times. Progressive strength was rising. Taft was inclined to be cautious, to resist rapid change. Roosevelt, on the other hand, tended to go along with the tide of reform. Soon after he returned to the United States, he spoke out for the initiative, for the referendum, and for the recall of judicial decisions. He moved sharply to the left in a speech at Osawatomie, Kansas, in 1910, when he tried to balance the old individualism of free enterprise with the movement for social control. He would allow a man to gain wealth, he said, "only so long as the gaining represents benefit to the country." This, he added, "implies a policy of a far more active governmental interference with social and economic conditions in this country than we have yet had, but . . . such an increase in governmental control is now necessary. . . . The man who wrongly holds that every human right is secondary to his profit must now give way to the advocate of human welfare, who rightly maintains that every man holds his property subject to the general right of the community to regulate its use to whatever degree the public welfare may require."

Terming this philosophy the "new nationalism," Theodore Roosevelt favored increasing the power of the federal government. The government could then control corporations, abolish child labor, introduce unemployment insurance, old-age pensions, minimum wages, workingmen's compensation.

Thus Roosevelt was lining up with the progressive Republicans. Would he, then, support La Follette for the Republican presidential nomination in 1912? Or would he himself seek the Republican designation, despite his 1904 renunciation of a third term? Gradually, and after some hesitation and contradiction, Roosevelt made it clear that his own hat was in the ring. La Follette was understandably irked at this, and the progressive Republicans went into the 1912 campaign divided.

There were other troubles ahead. When Roosevelt tried to get the Republican presidential nomination, he found that Taft controlled the party machinery. Roosevelt won convention delegates in states which had presidential preference primaries; but Taft won elsewhere. The Taft forces controlled the nominating convention; and they nominated the President for a second term, rejecting Roosevelt's bid for consideration. The progressives were also ignored in the platform, and Taft ran as a conservative.

Terming these results a machine victory, Roosevelt's supporters called a separate convention. Amid much evangelical fervor and hymn singing, the delegates created a new Progressive party. Theodore Roosevelt was nominated for President, with Hiram Johnson of California as his running mate. The bull moose became the symbol of the new organization, as the elephant was the emblem of the Republicans.

The Progressive platform of 1912 called for the democratization of political machinery, social legislation, monetary reform, control of big business in the public interest. There were prolabor planks, too. The American Federation of Labor, however, withheld endorsement, perhaps because the Bull Moose party was heavily supported by George Perkins, a wealthy industrialist who had been a J. P. Morgan partner.

Meantime, the Democrats also adopted a progressive platform. They demanded tariff reform and the strict enforcement of the Sherman Antitrust Act. They asked for new laws to check such business practices as the watering of stock, price discrimination, interlocking directorates, the monopolistic suppression of free competition. The Democrats also advocated rural credits and a flexible banking system in the interest of the farmers, and, to please the workers, legislation against injunctions in labor disputes. After a long and heated contest for the nomination, William Jennings Bryan threw his support to Woodrow Wilson, progressive governor of New Jersey. On the forty-sixth ballot, Wilson was named the Democratic candidate for President.

Southern-born, of strict Presbyterian background, Woodrow Wilson had been a professor of political science and president of Princeton before he entered politics in 1910. His conversion to progressivism came late; in the early years of the century he was anti-Bryan, anti-union, a defender of property rights who said much that was pleasing to big business. But as governor of New Jersey (1911–13) he opposed machine politics and fought for measures intended to curb big business and benefit the working class.

During his campaign for the presidency in 1912, Wilson presented the country with a political philosophy for which he was in part indebted to the brilliant Boston lawyer, Louis D. Brandeis. This philosophy Wilson called the "New Freedom." Differing from Roosevelt's New Nationalism in approach rather than in essence, the New Freedom aimed to restore the older freedom of competition which corporate wealth had all but eliminated. Roosevelt proposed using a strong central government to advance the public well-being, and stressed the need of distinguishing between good and bad business combinations. Wilson leaned toward the states as vital instruments in advancing social reform; and he was inclined to feel that bigness in itself was dangerous, whether in business or in political administration. Still another difference was in tone. Roosevelt bitterly attacked the policies and even the integrity of President Taft. Wilson maintained a high, impersonal level in his speeches.

In dividing their votes between Taft and Roosevelt, the Republicans threw the election to Wilson. The Democratic candidate received 6,000,000 votes; Roosevelt 4,000,000; Taft 3,500,000; Eugene V. Debs, the Socialist, just under 1,000,000. Carrying forty states,[1] Wilson had a large majority in the electoral college; and his party won control of both houses of Congress. Wilson was, however, a minority President. What was more, he polled fewer votes than Bryan had obtained in any of his three unsuccessful campaigns.

For all of that, the Wilson program unquestionably represented the views of most Americans. The conservative Republican candidate, Taft, carried only two states, Utah and Vermont, and polled a smaller percentage of the total vote than any other major-party nominee since the Civil War. The voters flocked rather to the banners of the protest candidates, Wilson, Roosevelt, and Debs. The country was in a reform frame of mind.

Wilson and the New Freedom

Planning his presidential policies, Wilson at first considered departing from normal patronage patterns. Instead of giving jobs to deserving Democrats, he would surround himself with experts and use his appointive power to convert the Democratic party into a truly progressive instrument. But Colonel

---

[1] Forty-eight states participated in this election. The wholesale admission of western states in 1889–90 had raised the total to forty-four states. Utah was admitted in 1896, Oklahoma in 1907. New Mexico came in during January, 1912, Arizona one month later.

Edward M. House of Texas, who had played an important part in getting Wilson nominated and elected, persuaded the incoming President that he must play ball with party managers if he wished to get his bills through Congress. In consequence, Wilson straddled. He appointed to his cabinet both professional politicians and nonpolitical experts. He shocked party politicians by ignoring many of their requests; but in the end he permitted the Democratic bosses to control a large share of the jobs.

Was this wise? It is hard to say. One of Wilson's political appointees was that of William Jennings Bryan as Secretary of State. The idea was to reward the Great Commoner for helping Wilson get the presidential nomination and to make sure of the support of Bryan's western and southern followers. And Bryan was in truth a tower of strength when it came to pushing Wilson's reform program through Congress. At the same time, Wilson's surrender to the bosses resulted in his appointing conservative as well as progressive Democrats to office and dismissing some progressive Republicans. On jobs, Wilson helped a party rather than the progressive cause.

Wilson was more firm in adhering to his views on presidential leadership. Early in his academic career he had become impressed with the merits of the British constitutional structure. In a book, *Congressional Government*, and in other writings, he had urged that the United States borrow certain features of the English system. Specifically, Wilson felt that Americans had put too much stress on the separation of powers, and that legislative leaders had acquired too much power. In Wilson's view, a President should be virtually a Prime Minister. That is, he should not only administer the laws but also play a leading role in the lawmaking process. Wilson's views were in line with those of progressive constitution-makers who had enlarged the governor's power in the states; and, on the national scene, Theodore Roosevelt had built up presidential prestige.

Wilson carried this trend further. Breaking a century-old precedent, he delivered his message to Congress in person. And when his proposals met with opposition—as in the fight over tariff revision in 1913 —Wilson himself acted as party whip. He continued to assert presi-

dential leadership for the greater part of his two terms in the White
House (1913–21).

The first Wilson administration (1913–17) witnessed the triumph
of the most significant reform program since the American Revolution. As Wilson himself admitted, the legislative achievements of this
period were not merely Wilsonian and Democratic. Rather they represented the culmination of a generation of reform effort. When he
advocated domestic reform, Wilson was generally supported by progressive Republicans as well as by his own Democratic followers. The
President also counted on the support of the bulk of American farmers, laborers, small businessmen and white-collar workers.

Wilson lost no time in getting started. In his inaugural address he
appealed to "all honest men, all patriotic, all forward-looking men."
Help him, he asked, "abolish everything that has even the semblance
of privilege or any kind of artificial advantage."

This appeal caught hold. Wilson had given the public an emotional
lift. "It seemed as if we had climbed mountain heights," said the great
liberal Louis Brandeis, in recalling the Washington of 1913, "and
entered into a purer, more rarefied atmosphere." (Brandeis, incidentally, had an important influence on Wilsonian legislation. In 1916,
over conservative objections, the President appointed him to the
Supreme Court.)

The Underwood Tariff

Wilson began with the tariff. Calling
Congress into special session in 1913, the President demanded repeal
of the Payne-Aldrich Tariff of 1909 and the substitution of a measure
that would abolish special privilege and reduce the cost of filling a
market basket. When Democratic protectionists pleaded the cause
of special interests, Wilson used his control of patronage to bring
them into line. When lobbyists attacked tariff reform, Wilson exposed their activities and called on the public to take note and take
action. The President, therefore, deserved much of the credit for the
passage of the Underwood Tariff of 1913.

This was not a free-trade measure. It modified instead of junking
the protective principle. But the act shifted hundreds of items from

the duty to the free list. Among these were such important products as wool, paper, steel rails, lumber, wood pulp, sugar. In addition, there were reductions averaging 10 percent for nearly a thousand other products.

The country as a whole greeted the Underwood Tariff with approval. As the public well knew, tariff reform was long overdue. Had the period been a normal one, the new measure might have had significant long-range influences on American overseas trade. But the outbreak of World War I in Europe in 1914 dislocated normal channels of trade; and it was never possible to judge the effect of the Wilsonian tariff cuts.

The ratification of the Sixteenth Amendment in February, 1913, enabled Congress to add an income tax clause to the new tariff act. The tax ranged from 1 percent on annual earnings over $3000 (with a further exemption for married men) to 6 percent on income above $500,000. These rates were very moderate. Still, the introduction of the graduated income tax marked a turning point in American financial history. Traditionally, the federal government had relied on tariff revenues, excise taxes, and income from the sale of public lands. After 1913, the whole tax structure would be overhauled; and there would be heavy reliance on the income tax, with the highest rates applying to those best able to pay.

Banking and Monetary Reform

Even before the Underwood Tariff reached its final stages, Wilson asked Congress for banking and monetary reform. After the panic of 1907, even conservatives admitted the need for greater elasticity than was provided by the old national banking system and under the Gold Standard Act of 1900. A commission headed by conservative Republican Senator Aldrich therefore recommended the establishment of a centralized national banking system controlled by private financiers. Conservative Democrats approved this recommendation. There was opposition, though, from Bryan Democrats and progressive Republicans. These groups were heirs of the old Jacksonian and Populist fears of centralized banking. Besides that, they were impressed with the findings of the Pujo

Committee, which had reported the existence of a money trust in the United States. Would not a privately owned centralized banking system be dominated by this combination of New York financiers?

After consulting Brandeis, Wilson swung over to the progressive side. The result was a compromise. The Federal Reserve Act of 1914 deferred to Bryan's opposition to a centralized system. Instead of one national institution, there were to be twelve Federal Reserve Banks. A measure of centralization, however, was achieved by the creation of a Federal Reserve Board to supervise the whole system.

Bankers and other citizens were pleased to see that the new organization could expand or contract the currency in relation to the country's need. Yet thoroughgoing reformers felt that the Federal Reserve Act did not go far enough. State banks could still remain outside of the system; and the legislation of 1914 did not prevent officers of some national banks from speculating recklessly with deposit money. Even so, the Federal Reserve law had enormous importance. It increased business efficiency, and did so without undue concentration of power in the hands of one group of financiers.

Regulating Business

Having taken up the tariff and banking questions, President Wilson turned next to business practices. Like Theodore Roosevelt, Wilson took care to state that he was not the foe of legitimate business; rather, he favored reform as an efficient safeguard against revolutionary change. Wilson disapproved of government ownership; he wanted no monopoly, government or otherwise. Suspicious of bigness, he hoped to curb the largest combinations, restore competition, and see that business was regulated in the public interest.

The Wilson program found expression in the Clayton Antitrust Act of 1914. The Sherman Antitrust Act of 1890 had been little more than a general prohibition of combinations in restraint of trade. The Clayton Antitrust Act was much more specific. It forbade interlocking directorates of competing financial corporations capitalized at more than $1,000,000. Also forbidden were price discriminations designed to lessen competition, and tying contracts under which manufacturers forced dealers to handle only one line of goods. The Clayton Act made corporation officials personally responsible for failure to observe the rules.

Closely tied to the Clayton Act was a Federal Trade Commission Act, establishing a board of five members, to be appointed by the President. Inheriting the investigative functions of the old Bureau of Corporations, the Federal Trade Commission was able to publicize dishonest business practices. It could also issue cease-and-desist orders to firms violating antitrust legislation or engaging in unfair competition in interstate trade. The commissioners were further empowered to follow up court decrees in antitrust cases and to report findings to the Attorney General. Although the Federal Trade Commission failed to realize all expectations, it did a good deal in its early years to eliminate unfair business practices.

Labor and the Farmer

All this legislation was intended to benefit the small businessman and the consumer. In addition, the New Freedom conferred important benefits on workingmen. The Clayton Antitrust Act contained a section which declared that strikes, peaceful picketing, and boycotts were not violations of federal law. The statute also exempted unions from the provisions of the Sherman and Clayton Antitrust acts. This exemption was set down because of the antiunion record of federal courts.

Finally, the Clayton Act limited injunctions in labor disputes to cases in which there was danger of irreparable injury to property rights. As it turned out, this provision did not help the unions very much. By seeing grave danger in almost any strike, conservative judges were able to issue injunctions much as before. Not until 1933 was legislation passed to close this loophole.

The prolabor record of the Wilson administration included other acts. One set up a cabinet-level Department of Labor; another provided for the mediation of railway labor disputes (both 1913). Confronted with the possibility of a nation-wide railway strike in 1916, the President persuaded Congress to pass the Adamson Act. This conceded the eight-hour day to railway employees whose work touched interstate commerce. In these years Congress passed two child labor acts, both later declared unconstitutional by the Supreme

Court, and the La Follette Seaman's Act, which improved working conditions in the merchant marine.

There were also special concessions for the farmers. A Farm Loan Act of 1916 supplemented the Federal Reserve Act by setting up a system of federal land banks authorized to extend long-term loans to farmers on terms more favorable than those prevailing in private banks. The Smith-Lever Act of 1914, to promote agricultural extension work, and the Smith-Hughes Act of 1917, for vocational education, both helped farmers face twentieth-century problems. So did the new federal system of matching state road-building funds.

End of the Progressive Era

The domestic reforms of Wilson's first term helped him win a second term. The Republicans ran only one candidate in 1916, the Taft conservatives and Theodore Roosevelt progressives uniting behind Charles Evans Hughes. Wilson's reform record, however, brought him the backing of many citizens who normally voted Republican, also some who had voted for the Socialist Debs in 1912. Friction in Republican ranks (particularly a misunderstanding between Hughes and Hiram Johnson) also helped the Democrats; and Wilson was chosen for a second term (1917–21).

The victory was a narrow one. Wilson lost the three most populous states—New York, Pennsylvania, and Illinois. But he swept the South, picked up Ohio and New Hampshire, and carried eighteen of the twenty-two states west of the Mississippi. This gave him the victory in the electoral college, 277–254. The popular vote stood at 9,000,000 to 8,500,000. Thus the margin of triumph was small. But one could look at the figures in another way. Wilson drew a much larger percentage of the total vote in 1916 than he had obtained four years before—a larger percentage of the total vote than had been obtained by any Democratic candidate since before the Civil War.

When he won reëlection in 1916, Wilson had virtually stopped pressing for domestic reforms. His pace-forcing on progressive legislation had begun to slow down before the end of 1914. The President had then told a friend that he could not continue the reform crusade with anything like the intensity and success that had marked his efforts that far.

Why? Well, for one thing, it was difficult to keep Congress under control for a long period of time. Second, Wilson was himself a moderate who did not want to go "too far." Finally, the war in Europe was turning attention to world affairs. So the liberal drives of the New Freedom days came to an end.

In some areas, the progressive trends were actually reversed. Supreme Court decisions emasculated the labor gains of the Clayton Antitrust Act; and child labor laws were pronounced unconstitutional. The Federal Trade Commission lost its initial energy and became increasingly pro-business. Even before the United States entered World War I, Wilson brought businessmen into his administration; and in Republican ranks liberals lost ground to the conservatives. The progressive era was grinding to a close.

Assessing the Progressive Movement

Despite this, the reform movement had been important. The Wilson record demonstrated that traditionally states'-rights Democrats, with a Jeffersonian tradition of as-little-government-as possible, could enlarge the scope of the central government in the interest of the public welfare. In other words, the final doom of states' rights had been pronounced by Wilson, a southern-born advocate of individualism. From this time forth, American reform movements would function primarily on a national basis.

By 1916, the progressive urge was slackening. But what had once been done could be done again. The Wilson achievements were not forgotten. Equally important, liberal leaders had been trained in public service; many would reappear in a new era of reform after 1929.

Nor were the practical accomplishments unimportant. The plan of federal grants-in-aid to the states (highways, agricultural education) remained a significant feature of the American system. The banking reforms were important, as was the establishment of the Federal Trade Commission. Labor received legislation on which it could build later; and the farmer obtained more than that. The progressives had not worked in vain.

11

The Expanding Nation

A New Manifest Destiny

It was decreed by fate that the great United States should be greater still. So thought Americans as they pushed their country's frontiers outward, to the Gulf of Mexico and the Rio Grande, the Columbia River and the Pacific Ocean. In the process, they created a whole philosophy of expansion, summed up in the term "Manifest Destiny." By the 1850's, Manifest Destiny had become part of American patriotism, American literature and folklore, political philosophy and ideals.

The sectional crisis of the mid-nineteenth century turned attention away from diplomacy; but the crisis strengthened the foundation on which expansion concepts rested. In defending territorial gains, Americans had used the arguments of nationalism; and the Civil War was a great triumph for the nationalists. The prophets of expansion had always pictured Americans as a chosen people, guided toward conquest by the hand of the Almighty. An accurate description, thought most Northerners when their armies had humbled the Confederates. Surely the Lord of Hosts had stood guard over the fortunes of the Union when it was tested under fire.

The new Darwinian theories also added strength to the expansionist philosophy. Darwin had shown that the fittest would survive in the biological struggle for existence. By the 1880's, John Fiske and other American popularizers of Darwinism were applying this formula to world affairs. They claimed that through natural selection the United States had become a superior nation, and that Americans, having shown themselves to be more fit, would naturally and logically rule feebler, less fit peoples.

306

Thus the expansion flames still burned. But the interests of the United States were changing. Down to the 1850's, American expansion had been largely an agricultural enterprise. The aims had been protection and new lands for the farmer, and outlets for farm products. After mid-century, the agrarian expansion urge had become less strong. Having acquired California and Oregon, the United States had spanned the continent. Canada still beckoned, but could not be won without a costly fight with Great Britain. Down to the 1860's, southern planters had been interested in Cuba, northern Mexico, and Central America. But defeat in the Civil War had reduced their influence, and, with slavery dead, the planters were less interested in territorial additions.

As the drive for agrarian expansion lost its vigor, another outward impulse took on new importance. This was the urge for an overseas expansion in which businessmen would figure more than would the farmer. The old Manifest Destiny had pointed to the acquisition of nearby regions suitable for farming operations. The new imperialism looked far afield, and sought commercial and strategic rather than agricultural opportunities. Farm expansionists had insisted on outright ownership. The advocates of commercial expansion, planning no mass migration, were often satisfied with influence or control.

Efforts to build trade were not new. Back in the eighteenth century, Federalist foreign policy had featured efforts to aid the merchant marine. After 1800 the Jeffersonians had fought the Barbary pirates to protect American trade in the Mediterranean and had used the diplomatic machinery to get new markets for American farm products. President John Tyler had sought commercial agreements with Germany and China. Congressional subsidies had helped the Collins steamers compete with the British Cunard line for passenger traffic on the Atlantic in the 1840's and 1850's.

Though important, this was of secondary interest to a people more concerned over domestic developments and agrarian expansion. But the second half of the nineteenth century brought a major change in attitudes. From 1850 on, Americans turned more and more toward manufacturing; and the pressure for overseas expansion increased with the emergence and development of an industrial economy.

The Turn of the Trade Balance

The trade balance provides a key to the new imperialism. For a century after independence the United States had an import or "unfavorable" balance of trade. That is, the country bought more products than it sold—a natural situation for a young and growing agricultural nation. It was in the 1870's that the pattern changed. By the end of that decade the republic was selling more than it purchased. This was a fundamental change, for the United States has retained an export or "favorable" trade balance to the present time.

When the balance turned, American foreign commerce was increasing by leaps and bounds. Imports soared, exports went up still more rapidly. The character of the trade also changed. In earlier years the nation had imported manufactured products and had exported raw materials (chiefly farm products like wheat and the all-important cotton). Trade continued in these lines; but the rise of industry brought new trends. Export lists began to show more manufactured articles—textiles, farm implements, machines, railroad equipment. Imports included proportionately fewer finished goods, proportionately more raw materials like wool and sugar, copper and petroleum, coffee and rubber. Such items were demanded by the factories and by the growing urban population tied to the new industrialism.

Expansionists: Exporters

The shift in trade did not change foreign policy immediately; merchants and manufacturers of the 1870's and 1880's still concentrated on domestic problems. Gradually, however, they gave more attention to the international scene. The National Association of Manufacturers, when organized in 1895, devoted half of its ten-point program to the expansion of American foreign trade.

By that time, export-conscious producers were turning to the government for aid in locating and capturing markets overseas. Those who wanted raw materials from abroad had come to feel that the United States should have influence at the source of supply. Activity of European competitors had increased the demands for action, notably with reference to the tropics, the so-called "backward areas" of Latin America, Asia, Africa, and the Pacific. There one could get needed raw materials. There, too, were great potential markets for manufactured goods.

In urging the government to be more active overseas, American businessmen did not insist on territorial acquisition. Rather they stressed trade promotion. They asked for (and in 1906 obtained) reorganization of the traditionally inefficient consular service. They wanted the government to collect trade information, fight discrimination against American products, subsidize the merchant marine, dig and control an Isthmian canal. Many felt that business expansion overseas could be promoted by strengthening the navy; and there was growing sentiment among exporters for reciprocal trade agreements. Those who favored reciprocity maintained that the United States had outgrown industrial infancy and could afford to reduce tariff rates without losing the home market. Cuts, then, could be used to get tariff concessions abroad, forcing open needed foreign markets.

Expansionists: Shipowners

Industrialists and other exporters were not alone in planning a broad future for the American republic. Shipowners had the same idea, saw in expansion an opportunity to revive the faltering American merchant marine. Back in the era of clipper ships the United States had been a power in the carrying trade. Then came decline, as wood gave way to iron, sail to steam. Britain led in the new construction, for she had a well-established iron industry, and her coal and her iron ore were near together, and both close to the sea. The British government assisted English shipping interests, whereas the American subsidy system collapsed in the 1850's. The next decade brought the Civil War, with Confederate privateers sinking some Union vessels and causing others to shift to foreign registry. This flight from the flag was permanent, for when war ended in 1865, Congress refused to allow these ships to transfer registry back to the United States. So the decline continued until, in 1900, less than 10 percent of the foreign trade of the United States was carried in American bottoms.

Aware of their poor competitive position, American carriers went after government assistance. They finally obtained some aid, in the Ocean Mail Subsidy Act of 1891. This was not enough to restore the merchant marine to its old-time glory. Still, the lobbying and publicity activities of the merchant marine group increased public interest in overseas affairs.

In a few cases, shipowners had an even more apparent influence on expansion. As an illustration, the rise of American power on the Isthmus was linked to steamship companies. During gold-rush days, the United States did not rely exclusively on covered wagon and pony express routes to California. Mail, express, and passengers normally were routed by steamer from the eastern United States to Panama and Nicaragua, then by land and inland waterways across to the Pacific, and by steamship up to California. William H. Aspinwall, whose Pacific Mail Steamship Company dominated the Pacific part of this traffic, added to his profits by constructing a railway across Panama; and from the 1850's on, this American-owned Panama Railroad helped the United States to dominate the destiny of this region.

While Aspinwall worked into Panama, Cornelius Vanderbilt gave his attention to Nicaragua. Starting a steamship line to Nicaragua, the aggressive Commodore soon set out to control the transit route across the Central American republic. This took Vanderbilt into Nicaraguan politics and brought him into conflict with long-established English interests. When bloodshed followed, the United States Navy backed American interests, destroying Greytown, the center of British influence in Nicaragua (1854).

Shipowners also promoted American expansion in the Pacific. During the Reconstruction era, an American named William H. Webb started steamship service from San Francisco to Australia. New Zealand gave the enterprise some help; but Webb, as a shoestring operator, also needed the support of the United States. To get it, he set out to interest the Washington government in Samoa, one of his chief ports of call. Webb's steamship venture collapsed before he could land a subsidy; but out of his efforts came notice for Samoa, especially in naval circles. And in 1889 the United States moved into Samoa to stay.

Expansionists: Investors

Closely associated with the carriers were those who invested money abroad. In many "backward areas," influence and investment went hand in hand. Recognizing that fact, the State Department eventually developed a system of dollar diplomacy, using financial strength to build diplomatic power. The big deals came in the twentieth century, when industrial profits created large surpluses of capital and when declining interest rates in the United States tempted financiers to look for openings abroad. But even before 1900, American promoters were interested in special opportunities overseas. In general, the well-established bankers held back. They were willing to let the ground be tested by newcomers and shoestring promoters. If the wildcatters failed, what of that? If they succeeded, the conservative financiers could step in later and work with or replace the pioneers.

Some of the schemes were too ambitious for immediate realization. Hinton Rowan Helper (of *Impending Crisis* fame) failed in his efforts to promote a Three-Americas Railway from Chile to Alaska. Less ambitious projects, like that of the Panama Railroad, brought profit to investors and influence to the United States. The work of Minor Keith is a case in point. Unknown when he began building Costa Rican railroads in the 1870's, Keith gained fame when he planted bananas to provide freight for his lines. Within a generation he had laid the foundations for the politico-economic empire of the United Fruit Company. This concern, organized in 1899, did much to make the northern part of Latin America a sphere of influence for the United States.

While Keith worked on banana culture, the Guggenheims acquired copper and silver mines in Canada, Mexico, and South America. Other Americans developed sugar plantations in Spanish Cuba. The United States government did what it could to help, securing a treaty which gave Americans better commercial chances in Spain's colonies (1887). Sugar was also in the picture in Hawaii. A reciprocity agreement of 1875 tied that Pacific kingdom to the United States, thus stimulating American investment in the islands and helping to determine Hawaii's future.

The United States remained a debtor nation until World War I. That is, there was more European capital invested in the United States than American capital invested overseas. But the American stake abroad grew rapidly, especially after 1900. Americans put money in Mexican oil lands and Argentine packing plants. American banking houses lent money to foreign governments. They provided funds which helped Japan defeat Russia in the Russo-Japanese War (1904–05). They took over the foreign debt of the Dominican Republic and several Central American countries. Each such step increased American diplomatic influence abroad.

Expansionists: Missionaries

Backing up the economic interests were powerful religious groups. From its early days, Christianity has been a missionary religion. The first white settlers of the New World tried to convert the Indians; and at the beginning of the nineteenth century, American Protestants started sending agents into Asia. From 1850 on, mission work was the chief American enterprise in much of the Near, Middle, and Far East. Missionary boards thus obtained large influence with the State Department.

Missionaries created interest in expansion by writing books and articles about distant lands. They pushed American influence into faraway areas by demanding rights of trade and residence in regions closed to foreigners. They increased trade by teaching Asiatics and Pacific Islanders to use and desire goods from the United States. They called for American political influence, as preferable to European imperialism or the misrule of native despots. Some religious leaders, like the Reverend Josiah Strong, took an even bolder view. In his best seller, *Our Country* (1885), Strong asserted that the Anglo-Saxon was the favored child of destiny, picked by the Lord to control, Christianize, and guide the backward peoples.

It was a missionary-diplomat, Peter Parker, who in the 1850's arranged to have Americans seize Formosa. Superiors, however, chose to let China keep the island. Four decades later, Dr. Horace N. Allen, another missionary turned diplomatist, obtained for Americans railroad, mining, and other concessions in the kingdom of Korea. Meantime, missionary-founded Robert College in Constantinople became a center of American influence in the Near East. In Hawaii, missionaries served as royal advisers, and did much to prepare the way for the absorption of the islands by the United States. And the American Asiatic Association, organized in 1898 to build American influence in the Far East, had missionary as well as commercial backing.

Expansionists: The Navy

The new navy—launched with the construction bills of 1883 and 1890—was both product and cause of American expansion overseas. As the nation's foreign interests grew, there came demands for fighting ships to protect the American stake abroad. The navy in its turn found that it helped itself by working for economic expansion. The navy bills, by requiring the use of domestic materials, started the manufacture of armor plate and big-gun forgings in the United States (1887). These enterprises, once launched, became centers of big-navy and expansion sentiment.

One effective advocate of American sea power was young Theodore Roosevelt, whose *Naval War of 1812* (1882) argued for a larger navy. More important were the writings of Captain Alfred T. Mahan, who in 1890 began publishing his studies of the influence of sea power on history. In Mahan's view, national power and national welfare depended on naval strength. In the early days Americans had been satisfied with a navy designed for coast defense. But, having become a major exporting nation, the United States now needed a world fleet built around modern battleships. The prestige and power of these new fighting vessels would help make American commerce greater than it had ever been before. To assure success, the republic would need such coaling stations as Pearl Harbor in Hawaii, Pago Pago in Samoa. Also an Isthmian canal, said Mahan. Americans had set out on the path of destiny, and on that path there could be no turning.

Mahan explained, others executed. They worked along the lines of Commodore Matthew Perry, who in 1854 had used naval might to force the hermit country of Japan to deal more actively with the Western world. The Perry trick was duplicated in Korea by Commodore Robert Shufeldt (1883). At that same time the navy showed its growing interest in diplomacy by improving its attaché system, assigning naval officers to watch trends in the chief diplomatic centers. Action tended to be more direct in such out-of-the-way places as Haiti, Samoa, and Hawaii, where actual force was used to build American influence.

Expansionists: Politicians

The expansion movement left its mark on politics. It is the job of politicians to reflect the interests which they represent, to carry out and even to anticipate the wishes of their constituents. In the second half of the nineteenth century, business had much influence on politics. Politicians, therefore, sought to satisfy the expanding needs of manufacturers, traders, and financiers.

Besides, like other Americans, political leaders were affected by the swelling tide of nationalism. Many politicians were active in religious groups and sympathized with missionary views. Others saw expansion issues as good campaign material. Increased activity in many areas meant competition with the British. This afforded opportunities to catch Irish votes by twisting the lion's tail. Politicians in the State Department and on diplomatic missions stood to gain more by urging expansion than by maintaining the *status quo*. If things stayed as they were, there would be little publicity. Expansionist activity, by contrast, might catch the public fancy and help the politician to improve his position.

Opposition to Expansion

Although strong, the expansionists were not able to persuade the government to adopt their program until the last years of the nineteenth century. Even then, those who wanted to increase American influence overseas ran into difficulties of many sorts.

The most serious problem was indifference. Having long concentrated on domestic affairs, Americans knew and cared little about diplomacy. Nor was it easy to learn. The foreign news coverage of the American press was woefully inadequate, and American educational institutions paid little attention to current international developments.

Even interested parties found it difficult to concentrate on the subject. For example, most of the manufacturers who ,wanted foreign markets sold the bulk of their product in the United States. It was necessary, therefore, for them to give most of their time and energy to domestic sales. Foreign problems were neglected until companies began assigning special officers to give their full attention to such matters (generally after 1890).

In addition, overseas expansion was specifically opposed by a certain number of Americans. The peace societies provided a part of the opposition. Pacifists were quick to see the tie between expansion and naval construction, and to denounce both. These enemies of war also noticed that European powers were expanding. Inevitably, then, an increase in American activity would bring the United States into conflict with Germany or Britain, France or Russia.

Weakened by the Civil War, the peace movement was anything but strong when expansion agitation was gathering force in the 1880's. By 1900, however, the pacifists had registered important gains, especially among religious leaders, educators, and other intellectuals. Successful international peace congresses, the partial success of the government-sponsored Hague peace conferences (1899, 1907), and the establishment of the Nobel Peace Prize all added to pacifist strength. Meantime, increased financial support (as from Andrew Carnegie) enabled the peace organizations to publicize their views on militarism, expansion, and other matters.

Besides the pacifists, the foes of expansion included many public figures who feared that overseas adventures would hurt the United States. Some (the Populists, for example) wanted to concentrate on domestic reform. Others found that acquisition or control of tropical areas would present difficult race problems. (This helped explain the Senate's rejection of President Grant's proposal to annex the Dominican Republic in 1870.) There were humanitarians who held that expansion always resulted in the mistreatment of "subject peoples." (Among the most active anti-expansionists were officers of the Indian Rights Association, and Moorfield Storey, an organizer of the National Association for the Advancement of Colored People.) And many citizens, including Grover Cleveland, Carl Schurz, and Thomas B.

("Czar") Reed felt that the control of distant areas would strike at the principle of self-government and thus adversely affect democratic institutions in the United States.

Some economic groups set themselves against expansion. Growers of sugar cane and sugar beets opposed annexation of tropical areas where sugar cane could be grown cheaply. Tobacco farmers also feared competition. Farmers in general could not see how they would gain if the United States became active overseas. The new imperialism centered in tropical regions, where American farmers could neither sell goods nor settle to advantage. Agrarian spokesmen like Bryan therefore tended to be critical of expansionist activity.

The new Manifest Destiny also encountered opposition in labor ranks. Conservative labor leaders like Samuel Gompers and left-wing spokesmen like Eugene V. Debs both denounced imperialism. Gompers and Debs were anti-navy and anti-militarist, partly because they feared the use of the military to break strikes. Like many socialists, Debs was a pacifist, and felt that expansion would aid Wall Street but not the workingman. Gompers stressed other matters. As he saw it, United States control of colonial areas would not help American workingmen; moreover, such acquisitions might result in flooding the United States with immigrants who would take jobs away from American workers.

Pierce, Seward, Blaine

The war with Spain in 1898 brought the expansion issue to a head. But when the war came, the expansionists had already prepared the ground. Their work is seen in the activities of President Franklin Pierce and Secretaries of State William H. Seward and James G. Blaine. All three popularized the new Manifest Destiny in the half-century before 1898; and all three focused attention on the key areas of Latin America and the Pacific.

Franklin Pierce linked the old, agrarian expansion with the new, commercial kind. In his presidential administration (1853–57) a final scrap of territory was added to the United States, the Gadsden Purchase of 1853. Three years later Congress authorized Americans to take possession of uninhabited guano islands (guano being used for fertilizer). Under this statute, the United States obtained its first overseas possessions, including such islets as Navassa in the Caribbean and Baker and Howland in the Pacific. In the Ostend Manifesto of 1854, diplomats chosen by Pierce demanded that Spain transfer Cuba to the United States. During that same year, American naval forces reduced British influence in Central America by bombarding British-controlled Greytown in Nicaragua. Meantime, Perry was forcing the Japanese to trade more actively with the outside world; and, also in 1854, the United States negotiated a treaty of annexation with Hawaii. But the Senate rejected the treaty, and domestic difficulties (notably in Kansas) prevented Pierce from carrying out his expansion program.

Sectional complications also restrained William H. Seward, who was Secretary of State under Presidents Abraham Lincoln and Andrew Johnson (1861–69). A New York politician who worked well with business, Seward looked forward to American economic and military domination of the Caribbean and much of the Pacific. By opposing French designs in Mexico, the Secretary added to his country's influence in Latin America; but he failed to whip up enough enthusiasm to put over his program of annexing the Danish West Indies, Haiti, and the Dominican Republic. He was also unsuccessful in Pacific Ocean projects which involved Hawaii and Korea. He did, however, snap up the little Midway Islands; and in 1867 he bought Alaska from Russia for $7,200,000.

Though some Americans thought Alaska worthless ("Walrussia," "Seward's Folly"), most citizens decided that the area was worth the purchase price. Russia, too, recognized that Alaska had real value. For that very reason, the colony was likely to tempt enemies of Russia. It seemed better, therefore, to sell to the friendly United States than to lose Alaska to some European power. Hence Russia opened the negotiations. Snatching at the opportunity, Seward signed a treaty, which the Senate then approved. For various reasons, the House appeared reluctant to vote the purchase money; but it did so in 1868, after the Russian minister in Washington had invested some cash in publicity and bribes.

Active as were Pierce and Seward, it was James G. Blaine who best represented the new expansion. Although he considered the annexation of Hawaii, Puerto Rico, and Cuba as inevitable, Blaine was less interested in territorial acquisition than in trade promotion. "It is not an ambitious destiny for so great a country as ours to manufacture only what we consume," he asserted, "or produce only what we can eat." As Secretary of State (1881–82, 1889–92), he pushed exports in many ways, his efforts gaining wide attention by reason of his business ties and his prominence in politics.

Blaine's most celebrated project was the first Pan-American conference, held in Washington during the winter of 1889–90. Studying trade statistics, Blaine found that Latin America sold to the United States twice as much as she bought from this country. That is, the republics to the south marketed much of their sugar, wool, coffee, and rubber in the United States, then used the proceeds to buy European goods. To change this situation, Blaine proposed forming an organization that would include the United States and the Latin-American nations, but not the European states or their New World possessions. As the one industrial country in the Pan American group, the United States would be in a favored position as against Old World competitors.

The conference was a limited success. Blaine pleased his guests with banquets and a tour of American industrial establishments. The delegates responded by forming what in time became the Pan American Union, with headquarters in Washington. The conference also adopted resolutions calculated to develop the economic side of inter-American relations.

That was a start; but little more. Trade, investment, and tradition linked Latin America to Europe, and those who lived south of the Rio Grande had long viewed the United States with suspicion. To many Latin Americans, Blaine seemed more foe than friend. For, good will notwithstanding, the Secretary of State used a heavy hand in dealing with Central America and the island republics. Again, United States interference in local politics, and a drunken brawl involving sailors from the U.S.S. *Baltimore* brought Chile and the United States close to war (1891). Although hostilities were averted, the bullying technique of Blaine and President Harrison increased

Latin-American doubts as to the desirability of accepting leadership from the United States.

Pan-Americanism was only one aspect of Blaine's expansion program. During Blaine's second period as Secretary of State, the United States gained its first foothold on Samoa (1889). The Navy Bill of 1890 reflected developing ambitions, as did the Ocean Mail Subsidy Act of 1891, designed to aid the merchant marine. Also in 1891, Congress protected export markets by empowering the President to retaliate against European countries which discriminated against American meat products. And the McKinley Tariff, passed a year earlier, contained so-called reciprocity provisions, aimed at increasing American exports to Latin America.[1]

Taken together, Pierce, Seward, and Blaine accomplished a good deal. But when Blaine left the State Department in 1892, the major period of American expansion lay ahead. In the quarter-century before American entry into World War I (1892–1917), the United States would acquire a colonial empire, build a sphere of interest in the northern part of Latin America, and abandon traditional isolation to become an important factor in the world balance of power.

Acquiring a Colonial Empire

By 1892, the United States had already begun to annex colonial possessions: Alaska and Midway (1867); the guano islands (1856–80). In 1889, the Samoan Islands came under

---

[1] The President could impose penalty duties against countries not providing satisfactory openings for goods from the United States. This brought concessions but (since the United States gave nothing in return) also built ill will. The program died when the Democrats repealed the McKinley Tariff in 1894. Back in power in 1897, the Republicans put reciprocity provisions in the Dingley Tariff. The steel manufacturers and others approved—they had little need for tariff protection, and wanted to get into foreign markets. But there were objections from small manufacturers (toys, jewelry, etc.). As a result, Congress let the President cut duties on only a few items, e.g., tonka beans. When J. A. Kasson negotiated broad reciprocity agreements, the Senate rejected them. President McKinley supported reciprocity until he died, saying that American manufacturers must give concessions in order to win foreign markets. But the National Association of Manufacturers, pressed by small manufacturers, withdrew its endorsement of reciprocity; and President Theodore Roosevelt, save in Cuba, did not press the point. Franklin D. Roosevelt would revive the subject in 1934.

the joint control of Great Britain, Germany, and the United States. Besides that, the United States had a special position in the kingdom of Hawaii, including (as of 1884) the right to use Pearl Harbor as a naval base.

These were the beginnings. In 1898 Hawaii—now a republic—was annexed outright by the United States. So were Puerto Rico, Guam, and the Philippine Islands, all of which had belonged to Spain. In 1899 the American republic obtained permanent possession of part of Samoa. Four years later the United States acquired complete control (but not full ownership) of the Panama Canal Zone. One more acquisition followed in 1917, when the United States purchased the Danish West Indies, or Virgin Islands, for $25,000,000. Meantime, the United States had leased naval bases in Cuba, and the Corn Islands off the coast of Nicaragua.

These territorial additions affected the American republic in several ways. For one thing, they provided economic openings. Trade between the United States and most of her new possessions was restricted to American vessels. There were new investment opportunities for American capitalists; and the tropical islands provided the United States with sugar, tobacco, copra, and other important products. Strategic factors were equally significant. No longer were American defenses based on the Atlantic and Pacific coasts. Instead, the new United States Navy thought in terms of Alaska and Hawaii, Panama, Puerto Rico, and Cuba. The annexation of overseas possessions also changed the outlook of many Americans, made them aware that their country was a world power, with world influence and world responsibilities.

Hawaii

The reciprocity treaty of 1875 made the Hawaiian Islands an economic dependency of the United States. Hawaii could send sugar to the United States below the normal tariff rates; and American products received special treatment in the Pacific kingdom. As a result, nearly all of Hawaii's foreign trade was with the United States. What was more, Americans invested in Hawaiian sugar lands; and when reciprocity was renewed in 1884, the United States also obtained control of Pearl Harbor.

Then the situation changed. The McKinley Tariff of 1890 transferred sugar to the free list and voted a subsidy to sugar growers within the United States. Americans who owned plantations in Hawaii (a foreign country) could not qualify for the subsidy. Nor did reciprocity assist them now. With sugar duty-free, they no longer had any advantage in the American market over planters from Spanish Cuba, Haiti, and other sugar-producing regions. At the same time, Queen Liliuokalani, who believed in Hawaii for the Hawaiians, set out to reduce American influence in her kingdom.

Disturbed, the Americans in Hawaii revolted, early in 1893, much as the Americans in Texas had revolted in 1836. The most prominent of the Hawaiian rebels was Sanford B. Dole, whose family represented both missionary and business interests. He and his fellow insurrectionists received support from the United States minister to Hawaii, John L. Stevens. Stevens, a Blaine man and a pronounced expansionist, summoned American marines to Honolulu. Theoretically, the marines were landed to protect United States property. Actually, their presence in Hawaii helped persuade Queen Lil to give way to a Hawaiian republic, headed by Dole.

This republic, naturally enough, petitioned for annexation to the United States, just as the American-dominated republic of Texas had done six decades before. Republican President Benjamin Harrison was coöperative, and tried to rush an annexation treaty through the Senate. But, having been defeated for reëlection in 1892, Harrison was a lame duck when he took up the Hawaiian question. He was unable to effect annexation before he left the White House in March, 1893; and his successor, Grover Cleveland (1893–97), withdrew the treaty from the Senate. As a Democrat and as an anti-imperialist, Cleveland disapproved of the methods used by Republican Minister Stevens.

Annexation efforts were renewed by President William McKinley in 1897. When it proved impossible to get the two-thirds vote needed for Senate approval of an annexation treaty, the administration brought forth a joint resolution. This device, used in the case of Texas a half-century before, made it possible to effect annexation with only a majority vote in each house. The required votes were obtained in June, 1898, and Hawaii belonged to the United States.

The Cuban Question

When Hawaii was annexed, the United States was engaged in a war with Spain (April-August, 1898). This was a curious conflict. Although it added materially to the colonial possessions of the United States, the war of 1898 was not originally a territory-grabbing venture. Although it yielded results which pleased businessmen, it was not at first desired by business leaders. And although victory over Spain would help William McKinley win re-election, the President long delayed asking Congress for a declaration of hostilities.

The war centered around Cuba. After five centuries of Spanish rule, the residents of the "ever faithful isle" were clamoring for independ-ence. It took Spain a full decade to put down one revolt (the Ten Years' War of 1868–78). Then came a new insurrection, in 1895–98.

With few exceptions, citizens of the United States sympathized with the rebels. There were several reasons. Spain was a traditional enemy and was to many Americans the symbol of monarchy and absolutism. Being weak, the Cuban insurrectionists won sympathy as underdogs. More important, the Cubans were fighting for goals which most Americans approved: independence, republicanism, liberty, self-government.

Other factors made special groups of Americans enthusiastic about Cuba's fight for freedom. American religious leaders felt that mission-ary activities could be expanded if Cuba broke away from Spain. Businessmen guessed that Cuba libre would be a better customer than a Cuba controlled from Europe. The cause attracted humanitarians impressed by propaganda which the Cubans circulated in the United States. Some politicians saw political opportunity in the question; and a number of expansionists felt that intervention in Cuba would make the United States expansion-conscious.

All these groups were brought together by sensational journalists who increased circulation by backing the popular Cuban cause. Wil-liam Randolph Hearst of the New York *Journal* and Joseph Pulitzer of the New York *World* were two of many leaders in this field. Mixing appeals for liberty with stories about Spanish atrocities, these news-papermen turned American sympathy for Cuba into a crusade to save the Cubans. By 1897 aroused citizens were contributing money, volunteering for service in the Cuban forces, and petitioning Congress and the President to take action against Spain.

Grover Cleveland was in the White House when the Cuban insurrection broke out in 1895. Although opposed to annexing overseas possessions, Cleveland nonetheless believed in extending American influence. So he demonstrated in his endorsement of the Olney Doctrine. This was set forth by Cleveland's Secretary of State, Richard Olney, in 1895. Intervening in a boundary dispute between Venezuela and British Guiana, Olney demanded that Britain arbitrate the dispute, and stated flatly that the United States proposed to be dominant in the northern part of Latin America. In supporting his cabinet officer, Cleveland took expansionist ground. The President, however, would not go so far in the case of Cuba. He refused to support interventionist schemes.

McKinley, who succeeded Cleveland in 1897, was also indisposed to act. McKinley was at heart a cautious and peaceful man. Moreover, he was backed by Mark Hanna and other business leaders who did not want war with Cuba. Business did desire expansion; but it preferred peaceful methods. War, it was feared, would bring inflation. Business had gone to some pains to defeat Bryan's inflationists in 1896. Why, then, have war and get inflation anyway? The depression was lifting in 1898, and business was content to leave well enough alone. Americans with money invested in Cuba inclined to the same view. These individuals prized law and order (essential for successful economic operations), and felt that a Spanish-dominated Cuba was likely to be more peaceful than one run by Cubans.

Despite these business attitudes, McKinley eventually swung over and asked Congress to declare war against Spain. As a religious man and a humanitarian, the President was impressed by the anti-Spanish views of religious leaders. As a professional politician, he was aware that the people wanted war. This was notably the case after the De-Lôme letter and the destruction of the *Maine*. The letter was a foolish private communication from the Spanish minister in Washington, denouncing McKinley. When published, it increased anti-Spanish sentiment in the United States. Even more important was the sinking of the *Maine*, an American warship blown up while visiting Havana. Although the explosion remains a mystery to this day, Americans generally felt that the Spaniards were responsible, and called for war.

In a last-minute effort to head off conflict, Spain offered major concessions. But the offer came too late; the whole United States burned with the war fever. In April, 1898, McKinley asked and obtained a declaration of hostilities. The President's appeal stressed humanitarian motives; and, in the Teller Amendment, Congress asserted that the United States intended, not to annex Cuba, but to set the island free. (Teller, incidentally, was from the beet sugar state of Colorado, which preferred to keep sugar islands outside American tariff walls.)

War with Spain

Before war was declared, American businessmen feared that a Spanish-American conflict would wear on for a long time and force the United States to adopt inflationary measures. They were needlessly concerned. Beating Spain proved an easy and relatively inexpensive job. Congress took care of some of the expense by voting a few war taxes (an inheritance tax, stamp duties on legal documents, sales taxes on chewing gum and patent medicine). This brought in $100,000,000 the first year. The government also floated one war loan, for $200,000,000. Despite the fact that this bond issue carried only 3 percent interest—half the Civil War rate—subscriptions were seven times the amount requested.

The popularity of the war also made it easy to raise troops. There was no need to resort to a draft, for President McKinley obtained without difficulty all the volunteers that he desired (200,000). The government also increased the size of the Regular Army and Navy; and this sufficed to win the war.

Latter-day critics of the policies of 1898 were to make much of the military errors of the United States. The American republic had possessed the largest standing army in the world in 1865. This had been broken up in a demobilization that was almost complete; the army in 1898 was small and poorly supplied. On top of that, the War Department had not bothered to acquire up-to-date weapons and the new smokeless powder. Soldiers were sent to tropical Cuba wearing the heavy, hot blue uniform of Civil War days; and they were given rations improper for the tropics. Medical and sanitary needs were woefully neglected; fourteen-fifteenths of the 5000 enlisted men who lost their lives in this war died of disease.

In addition, the armed services were shot through with politics and petty strife. Theodore Roosevelt, a young Republican, obtained a good command and became a military hero; William Jennings Bryan, a young Democrat, had to be content with a Nebraska state commission, and served out the war in Florida. W. T. Sampson and W. S. Schley, ranking naval officers, spent much of the war, and years thereafter, deciding which should get the credit for winning the battle of Santiago. (Neither deserved very much.) Nelson A. Miles, the ranking general, used the war as a political sounding board; he was ready to accept a presidential nomination from either the Republicans or the Democrats. (All he got was a feeler from the Prohibitionists.)

Nor were operations carefully planned. The United States assembled troops in Tampa, Florida, a town served by a one-track railroad. War had been a possibility for two long years. Yet neither the army nor the navy had planned movements with any care. Having failed to consider the transportation and supply problems, the military was able to transport to Cuba only a small fraction of the soldiers assembled in Florida. This expeditionary force was landed clumsily on an exposed beach; only Spanish weakness prevented heavy loss.

Although justified, such criticism should not conceal the fact that the United States won a quick and smashing victory. Commodore George Dewey overwhelmed Spain's Pacific fleet at Manila Bay in the Philippines. Sampson and Schley crushed the enemy's Atlantic squadron off the coast of Cuba (battle of Santiago). Spanish Guam surrendered without a struggle, and General Miles took Puerto Rico by marching across the island. Working with the Cuban rebels, General William R. Shafter defeated the Spaniards in Cuba. Meanwhile, American soldiers and Filipino insurrectionists took the city of Manila. Spain then asked for an armistice, and, in August, 1898, hostilities came to an end.

In the sixteen weeks of action, the United States had made many blunders. Mistakes are to be expected, however, in the opening months of any war. Had the conflict lasted longer, the American forces would have developed greater efficiency. Even as it was, the American republic had accomplished its mission, with much to spare. The United States could, in fact, have beaten a much stronger foe.

The most striking feature of the conflict was the ease with which the newly constructed United States Navy had established complete control of the approaches to the Spanish islands. As military observers were quick to note, the United States had become a great naval power. And in sea power, the United States held a key to further overseas expansion.

The Peace Settlement

Only a few Americans had urged the war with Spain as a means of acquiring territory. But when the war enlarged horizons, opinions changed. Businessmen who had been disinclined to favor a declaration of hostilities now felt that the United States should get as much as possible out of the struggle. Religious leaders—Lyman Abbott, for example—favored annexation projects as a means of broadening their zone of action. The expansion cry was taken up by enthusiastic journalists, including Whitelaw Reid of the New York *Tribune* and Henry Watterson of the Louisville *Courier-Journal*. A. T. Mahan and other naval spokesmen pointed out the need for coaling stations. Enthusiastic young politicians like Theodore Roosevelt, Henry Cabot Lodge, and Albert J. Beveridge called for empire, as did older Republicans who felt that the acquisition of the Spanish islands would increase McKinley's chances for reëlection in 1900.

Under the circumstances, territorial additions seemed inevitable. The armistice agreement of August, 1898, specified that Spain would cede to the United States the islands of Puerto Rico and Guam. The final peace settlement, signed at Paris at the end of the year, also transferred the Philippine Islands to the United States. Spain did not want to make this cession, and argued that the Americans occupied only a tiny part of the islands. The question was finally settled when the American negotiators agreed to pay Spain $20,000,000.

The peace treaty further specified that Cuba was to be set free.

Americans affected by the new Manifest Destiny would like to have added the island to the United States. Here, however, the Teller Amendment blocked the way. So the Cubans were allowed to set up a republic. But United States troops occupied Cuba until 1902; and when they left, the island was a protectorate of the United States. Cuba granted land to the United States for a naval base. Besides that, the United States secured the right to intervene in Cuba to maintain order. The Platt Amendment, which set forth this right of intervention, was incorporated in American law, in the Cuban constitution, and in a Cuban-American treaty. Ties were made closer still by a special reciprocity agreement of 1902, which gave Cuban sugar special advantages in the United States and enabled American manufacturers to dominate the Cuban market.

While expansion sentiment was rising in the United States, the anti-expansionists were also forming their lines. An Anti-Imperialist League organized in 1898 had as vice-presidents Samuel Gompers of the American Federation of Labor; such farm spokesmen as Herbert Myrick; humanitarians like Jane Addams and Moorfield Storey; Mark Twain and other intellectuals; such anti-imperialist Democrats as Grover Cleveland; and anti-expansionist Republicans like "Czar" Reed, who disliked seeing the Republican party falling into the hands of Lodge, Roosevelt, and other young imperialists. Coöperating closely with the League was William Jennings Bryan, who controlled the Democratic party machinery.

For tactical reasons, the anti-imperialists raised no objection to the annexation of Puerto Rico and Guam. They concentrated rather on opposing the acquisition or retention of the distant and populous Philippine Islands. Opponents of expansion felt that it would be impossible to give the Philippines statehood—doing so would give the Filipinos the balance of power in the United States. Annexing the Philippines without giving them statehood would involve denying Filipinos the right of self-government, which would undermine the whole structure of American democracy. Further, Filipino laborers and goods would compete with the workingmen and products of the United States.

Rallying their forces, the anti-imperialists tried to defeat the ratification of the treaty of peace with Spain. They came close; the Senate approved the treaty in February, 1899, with just one vote to spare. Two factors influenced the result. Bryan, though anti-imperialist, urged ratification so that the Philippine question could be threshed out in American political circles rather than in diplomatic discussions. And just at this time armed conflict broke out between American troops in the Philippines and Filipinos under Emilio Aguinaldo. Many Senators felt that approval of the treaty was necessary to give the McKinley administration support against Aguinaldo.

Undaunted by defeat, the anti-imperialists tried again, in the presidential election of 1900. In that contest McKinley, the Republican candidate, sought reëlection on an expansionist platform. Bryan, the Democratic candidate, ran as an opponent of expansion, with the special endorsement of an anti-imperialist convention. The diplomatic issue was only one of several in the campaign. Still, McKinley's triumph was a victory for the expansion cause.

Retreat from Empire

The imperialists, then, had won all along the line. Having come out on top, they might well have clamored for more colonies. In fact, however, they did not. Although the United States later picked up the Canal Zone, the Virgin Islands, and some naval bases, the Philippines were the last large-scale addition of territory by the American republic.

Why so? Partly, it seems, because of competition. The United States was late to enter the imperial scramble; European powers had grabbed most of Africa and Asia before the American republic became a competitor. Going after what was left would involve greater naval expenditures and graver diplomatic risks than most Americans were willing to take.

More significant, perhaps, was the experience of the United States with the colonies which it did acquire. When shouldering the "white man's burden" in 1898, Americans generally believed that the returns would justify the effort. Puerto Rico and the Philippines were considered worth having for their products, as areas for investment, and because of their strategic locations. In addition, the Philippines were thought of as a distributing center, a gateway to the China market. Some of this reasoning was correct; the new possessions did provide agricultural products, investment opportunities, and naval bases. But the investment openings helped only a few Americans. Farmers within the United States became increasingly aware of competition from the islands. On the strategic side, it gradually became apparent that the Philippines were as much liability as asset (an "Achilles heel," admitted Theodore Roosevelt). Nor did Manila become a second Hong Kong; and the whole China market expanded more slowly than had been anticipated.

The Filipino insurrection was an even greater reason for discouragement. For three long years (1899–1902), Aguinaldo's Filipinos waged guerrilla warfare against the United States. Putting down the rebels took more time and cost more men and money than had the war with Spain. In fighting the Filipinos, American commanders found it necessary to resort to concentration camps and strong-arm tactics—the very things that Spain had used in Cuba. Thus a movement that had started as an effort to liberate the Cubans ended in a drive to subjugate the Filipinos. Meanwhile, Congressional investigations were uncovering corruption and inefficiency in the armed services. As a consequence, imperial operations seemed less glorious than before. Many Americans wanted no more of overseas possessions.

At the same time, American imperialists were changing front. These expansionists were coming to feel that the annexation of colonies was an inefficient method of building American influence abroad. Cuba, which was not annexed, brought the United States more profit and less trouble than the Philippines, which were acquired outright. Might one not conclude, therefore, that control was preferable to ownership? This did not mean abandoning expansion. Quite the contrary. The United States would continue to push outward in trade and investment fields, would continue to seek diplomatic influence and strategic control. But the American republic would stop short of actually annexing overseas areas.

From 1900 on, the United States would follow the new policy, would stress influence and control rather than territorial additions. Existing colonies were retained; but there was little effort to work out a well-coördinated colonial policy. Alaska was handled by the Department of the Interior. Samoa and Guam were under the Navy Department, and the Canal Zone (after 1903) was controlled by the War Department. Hawaii, Puerto Rico, and the Philippines were under no cabinet official; and each was governed by a separate set of officers.

In the Insular cases (1901–03), the Supreme Court gave Congress virtually a free hand in dealing with the newly acquired possessions. Holding that the Constitution did not necessarily follow the flag, the justices said that Congress could withhold constitutional guarantees from the colonies and if it chose could force the islanders to pay tariff duties. Uncertain as to what to do, the legislators at first charged 15 percent of the Dingley Tariff duties on goods coming in from Puerto Rico (Foraker Act, 1900). Then, in 1902, these duties were dropped. But in that same year, Philippine goods were required to pay three-fourths of the Dingley rates. Seven years later, these charges were wiped out, although there were restrictions as to sugar and tobacco trade until the passage of the Underwood Tariff of 1913.

Stirred by humanitarian motives and by anti-imperialist criticism, McKinley and his successors tried to create model governments in the new insular possessions. Despite a painful lack of overall plans, the effort was partially successful. Most administrators sent to the islands were honest and well-meaning, and quite a few were efficient. Schools were established, disease was reduced. Natives were brought into the administration, and local voters were given a measure of home rule.

But problems remained. A substantial part of the wealth of the colonies was controlled by outsiders, notably by American business-men. Then, too, there was a continuing desire for self-government. In Hawaii and Alaska, both settled largely from the United States, the cry was for statehood. In both cases the low population was an obstacle; but ultimately, after World War II, global strategy added strength to the statehood movements.

The Spanish-speaking Puerto Ricans and Filipinos were more interested in independence. During World War I, President Woodrow Wilson, an anti-imperialist, tried to work out a solution. One Jones Act, passed in 1916, promised the Philippine Islands eventual independence. A second Jones Act, adopted the next year, made Puerto

Ricans citizens of the United States and gave them increased powers of self-government.

Wilson's successors had little liking for the Jones acts; and the trend toward home rule was arrested. It was resumed after the crash of 1929. The ensuing depression made American farmers and laborers protection-minded; they wanted to exclude all competitors for their markets and their jobs. Beet sugar, cane sugar, tobacco, hemp, and dairy farmers joined the American Federation of Labor in urging that the Philippines be given independence and put outside American tariff and immigration walls. These economic groups accomplished what humanitarian anti-imperialists had been unable to do. A Tydings-McDuffie Act, passed in 1934, gave the Filipinos political independence as of 1946.

With Philippine independence a reality, the empire of 1898 seemed to be breaking up. In 1947, the United States Congress increased home rule in Puerto Rico—among other things, the local citizens were permitted to choose their own governor. By then some Americans, including President Harry S. Truman, were indicating that they might be willing to allow the Puerto Ricans, like the Filipinos, to become independent.

Here was evidence that the United States had moved away from emphasis on colonies. There were other indications along the same line—for example, the refusal of the United States to take territory, even on a temporary, mandate basis, at the close of World War I. This was not a matter of withdrawing from the scene. The United States was much more of a world power after the world wars than before. But the weight had shifted from territorial to economic, strategic, diplomatic, and even moral factors.

The Far East

It was apparent as early as 1899 that the United States was shifting from annexation schemes to projects for economic and strategic control. The decade and a half that followed would see the American republic more active in diplomacy than ever before. The activity would involve all sections of the globe; but a great deal of emphasis would be on Latin America and the Far East.

Nineteenth-century annexations had given the United States strong positions in the Pacific. To begin with, there was Hawaii, with its great Pearl Harbor base. This was the key to the mid-Pacific. To the north was Alaska; to the south, Samoa; to the west, the Philippines; to the east, the Pacific coast states and, presently, the Panama Canal.

This looked secure enough, in 1900. Naval officers, however, felt that their position would be strengthened if they could have a base or two on the Asiatic mainland. They therefore had the State Department ask China for a naval base in that empire (1902). The request was denied, largely because of opposition from Japan.

At that time, Americans tended to underrate the Japanese. Shortly, however, Japan won a major victory in the Russo-Japanese War (1904–05). In the process, Japan demonstrated great naval strength; and she followed up the war by taking control of south Manchuria and Korea (another place where American naval leaders had tried to secure a base). Thereafter, American concern over Japan's naval strength increased. This could be seen in the pronouncements of Congressman Richmond P. Hobson of Alabama, the navy spokesman in Congress; the Navy League (organized in 1902); west coast labor leaders who led the fight to exclude Japanese immigrants; and the Hearst newspapers, much worried about the "yellow peril."

American Far Eastern policy depended more largely on economic than on strategic factors. American textiles, cigarettes, and kerosene had a good sale in the Orient at the end of the 1890's, and Americans were getting interested in Chinese railroads. American manufacturers and financiers, organized in an American Asiatic Association, hoped for even better business in the future. Their efforts centered on the Chinese Empire. China, however, was very weak. Taking advantage of that weakness, Japan and the European powers were marking out spheres of interest. Given the normal policies of great powers, it seemed likely that the United States would be squeezed out of China's economic life, and that American missionaries, too, would have hard going.

In an effort to protect the future, McKinley's Secretary of State, John Hay, issued the Open Door Notes in 1899. The notes plainly indicated that the United States hoped that China would remain territorily intact. But even if the empire was divided into spheres, the United States still wanted equal economic opportunity.

Despite some support from the British, Germans, and Japanese, Hay failed to gain general acceptance of his proposal. Yet the Open Door Notes were not without result. They marked a turning point in American diplomacy; the United States would hereafter play a more active role in world affairs. The notes also set a pattern for the future; American diplomats would soon be demanding equal economic opportunities all over the world. Finally, the notes improved American relations with commerce-minded Britain and with the grateful Chinese.

The following year, 1900, saw the rise in China of the antiforeign Boxer movement. Backed by government officials, this movement resulted in great loss of life and property among the foreign residents of China. When the legations in Peking were besieged, Japanese, American, and European troops invaded China and crushed the Boxers. In this crisis, American missionaries suffered heavily. The United States, however, made few demands for punishment. Rather the American emphasis was on maintaining Chinese integrity—essential for American trade and investment, for missionary work, and for the Asiatic balance of power. Like the other nations, the United States accepted monetary damages from China. Later, the United States returned the greater part of this Boxer indemnity, thus earning the good will of China and starting a heavy flow of Chinese students to the United States.

Investment projects featured the next decade of American relations with the Far East. At first American financiers, traders, and diplomats felt that they could coöperate with the Japanese. Japan, after all, was allied to Great Britain, and claimed to favor the open door. Certainly the Japanese were less obstructionist than the Russians, who consistently opposed American enterprise. In the Russo-Japanese War, therefore, Wall Street joined the English bankers in helping to finance Japan. Being pro-Japanese and anti-Russian, President Roosevelt and the American people generally approved of this development.

Presently, however, coöperation broke down. American traders encountered difficulties in Chinese areas under Japanese control. E. H. Harriman found himself blocked by Japan when he tried to buy into Manchurian railroads (he saw these as a link in his projected round-the-world transportation system). Japan also wrecked a J. P. Morgan-sponsored Anglo-American financial project and joined Russia in defeating an American proposal for international control of Manchurian development (the neutralization proposal of Philander Knox, Taft's Secretary of State, 1911).

Despite such rebuffs, the United States continued to try to work with Japan, partly to please Britain, partly because President Theodore Roosevelt was pro-Japanese. A secret Taft-Katsura understanding of 1905 specified that Japan had no designs on the Philippines and that the United States would give Japan a free hand in Korea. The Root-Takahira agreement of 1908 half-recognized Japan's "special interests" in Manchuria.

Unable to make headway against Japan and Russia in north China, American financiers did somewhat better in central and southern China. Here the bankers had the enthusiastic backing of President Taft, who knew that diplomacy and finance were closely connected. Taft used his influence as President to get Americans a share in the Anglo-French-German Hukuang Railway project (1909). Later he helped create the first consortium. This was an international combination of government-supported bankers, who proposed to lend money to China and supervise currency and other reforms. But the overthrow of the Manchu dynasty in the Chinese Revolution of 1911 prevented the consortium from being very effective.

When Woodrow Wilson became President in 1913, he roundly condemned the policies of his predecessors. In particular, he disapproved of Taft's support of the consortium. In Wilson's view, Taft was helping the money trust—the American group in the consortium was dominated by the house of Morgan. Besides that, the consortium had monopolistic aims, and seemed more interested in controlling than in helping the Chinese government.

When Wilson announced that he would not support Wall Street in China, the American group withdrew from the consortium. But this, as the President soon discovered, weakened American influence without helping China. With the United States inactive, and with Europe engaged in World War I, Japan increased her influence. Wilson did what he could through diplomatic channels. He tried to persuade Japan to soften her Twenty-One Demands against China

(1915). He tried to work with Japan, and granted that the Japanese had "special interests" in China (Lansing-Ishii agreement, 1917). Since this helped neither China nor America, Wilson eventually went back to dollar diplomacy. At the end of World War I, Wilson's Secretary of State invited the house of Morgan to organize a second consortium.

Latin America: The Panama Canal

In the Far East, the expectations of 1898 were not realized in the years that followed. In Latin America, by contrast, the early part of the twentieth century saw an enormous increase of American influence, especially in the northern countries. Part of the time the emphasis was on strategic considerations (as under Theodore Roosevelt and during World War I). Again, as in the Taft administration, economic approaches were stressed. Either way, influence soared.

Much of the story involved the Panama Canal. Mahan and other naval writers had long demanded an Isthmian canal, either through Panama or through Nicaragua. So had American merchants, who hoped to increase trade with western South America. The war with Spain dramatized the strategic need—the U.S.S. *Oregon* had to go all the way around South America to join the American fleet off Cuba. After the peace settlement, therefore, the American government moved ahead.

First, Secretary of State John Hay took care of the British. Under the Clayton-Bulwer Treaty of 1850, the United States and Britain had agreed to approach the canal problem together. By the end of the century, however, Britain was willing to let the United States go ahead alone. The first Hay-Pauncefote Treaty (1899) canceled the Clayton-Bulwer agreement; but it specified that the United States could not fortify an Isthmian canal or adjust rates so as to favor American ships over British vessels. When the Senate objected to the terms, the British gave way on the fortification question (second Hay-Pauncefote Treaty, 1900), and the matter was settled. A decade later, Congress attempted to aid American shipowners by passing a Panama Canal Tolls Act in apparent violation of the 1900 treaty. President Wilson was able, though, to secure repeal of this statute before the canal was opened in 1914.

Having decided to dig a canal, the United States government had to choose between Panama and Nicaragua. The Panama route was shorter; but it was also more rugged. In either case, it was a job for public rather than private enterprise. An American private company had tried and failed in Nicaragua. There had been a similar failure in Panama, where Ferdinand de Lesseps' French Panama Canal Company had been unable to overcome promotional and geographical difficulties, not to mention yellow fever. But the French company had maintained its organization, and hired William Nelson Cromwell of New York as lobbyist.

Cromwell's job was to persuade the United States government to buy the rights and property of the French company. The lobbyist did his work extremely well, fully earning his $800,000 fee. First of all, he helped persuade United States officials that the Panama route was better than the one through Nicaragua. Second, he finally obtained a high price ($40,000,000) for the French company's franchise and assets.

Meantime, the United States had been dealing with the republic of Colombia, which owned Panama. President Theodore Roosevelt and Secretary of State Hay offered Colombia $10,000,000 and an annual rental for a Canal Zone (proposed Hay-Herran Treaty, 1903). This was rejected by the Colombian government, which wanted more money. The United States was left with several alternatives. Roosevelt and Hay could raise the offer, turn to Nicaragua, put off the whole project, or use force. The first two possibilities seemed most logical. But Theodore Roosevelt, irritated with Colombia, chose to make no concession whatsoever. Instead, he took matters into his own hands. ("I took the Canal Zone," he said later.)

It was almost as crude as that. The French Panama Canal Company helped organize and finance a Panama secession movement. The movement was supported by Panama patriots who had long desired home rule. If left alone, Colombia could have crushed the revolt with ease. Roosevelt, though, sent United States naval vessels to the Isthmus, and they gave support to the revolution. This made it possible to organize a republic of Panama.

The new state was at once recognized by the United States. Immediately after that, a canal treaty was negotiated (the Hay-Bunau-Varilla Treaty, 1903). The United States secured full rights in the Canal Zone; and a canal was dug (opened in 1914). Panama became a protectorate of the United States, rights of intervention being similar to those stated in the Platt Amendment in the case of Cuba.

Roosevelt's high-handed policy won general approval in the United States—after all, the President did get canal rights. What was more, the administration claimed to have acted legally, under a Colombian-American treaty of 1846, which gave the United States the right to intervene to protect the Isthmian transit route. But, in bullying Colombia, the United States won the animosity of many Latin Americans. United States diplomats encountered more opposition than before; American businessmen found it difficult to get economic concessions. Finally, in 1921, the United States gave Colombia $25,000,-000. Although the sum was not accompanied by apologies, it was plain that the United States was asking the Colombians to forget the Panama affair—and consider Americans for oil concessions. All this might have been avoided if Theodore Roosevelt had been less impulsive, or more generous, in 1903.

Intervention as a Policy

From this time on, the Canal Zone loomed large in the foreign policy of the United States. The Canal, when opened in 1914, helped turn the trade of western South America from London to New York. No less important were strategic factors. Through the centuries, Great Britain had been the dominant naval power in the West Indies. The rise of American naval strength and the acquisition of the Canal Zone by the United States changed this age-old pattern. Recognizing the new situation, the British in 1906 broke up their Caribbean fleet. This strengthened Britain against Germany in European waters; and it made the United States unchallenged master of the New World.

Constant vigilance was necessary to protect the new position. Theodore Roosevelt felt that even that was not enough. It was necessary, he said, to make a great display of strength. Quoting an African proverb, he claimed that it was wise to "speak softly and carry a big stick." Actually, Roosevelt rarely spoke softly. But he did favor a big navy; and he did use force and the threat of force as an arm of foreign policy. On the broad international front he called attention to American power by sending the United States Navy around the world (1907). In Latin America he used naval strength to develop the intervention policy which centered around the Roosevelt Corollary to the Monroe Doctrine.

Under the Roosevelt Corollary the United States claimed the right to intervene in a Latin-American republic to prevent the intervention of an outside power. Only in this way, said Roosevelt, could the United States defend the approaches to the Panama Canal, protect American rights, and carry out the responsibilities of world power.

Roosevelt was concerned even before the acquisition of the Canal Zone—as in 1902, when Great Britain, Germany, and Italy used pressure to collect debts from Venezuela. Two years later, Roosevelt moved into the Dominican Republic, taking over the collection of customs. At the time, the Dominicans were deep in debt to European creditors; and Roosevelt (who was anti-German) feared that Germany might intervene if the United States did not. Once in control, the President had American bankers take over the Dominican foreign debt. When the Senate failed to approve a treaty providing for a financial receivership, Roosevelt carried on under executive authority. The Senate finally gave way in 1907. Despite United States supervision of revenues, political turmoil remained constant in the Dominican Republic; and in 1916 American troops occupied the republic. The armed intervention lasted for eight years.

By then, Theodore Roosevelt had sent troops into Cuba, under authority of the Platt Amendment. Inexperienced in government, the Cubans had moved into an era of political chaos after the end of the first American occupation (1902). Since Cuba was an American protectorate, Theodore Roosevelt felt that the United States was obliged to see order maintained in the island republic. In addition, the President was again concerned about Germany. General Enoch Crowder was in charge of the occupation, which lasted for four years (1906–10).

Roosevelt's successors continued his policies. William Howard Taft and his Secretary of State, Philander Knox, placed great reliance in dollar diplomacy—the use of financial influence to determine diplomatic policy. Many Latin-American treasuries depended heavily on tariff revenues. Those who controlled the customs, then, controlled the country. Taft therefore felt that American banks should lend money to Latin-American governments, and that, to assure repayment, they or the State Department should get control of the customs.

Some Americans objected to this close coöperation between Wall Street and Washington; and the United States Senate refused to agree to financial receivership treaties which Taft and Knox negotiated with Honduras and Nicaragua. But, even without the treaties, the bankers and the State Department made the necessary arrangements.

In defending dollar diplomacy, Taft said that it meant more trade for Americans; and that using financial power was better than using military force ("Dollars not bullets"). Yet the Taft-Knox program led to the employment of troops. In 1909, the United States Navy helped overthrow the Zelaya regime in Nicaragua. Three years later, American marines moved in. Save for a few months in the 1920's, they were to remain until 1933.

As a Democrat and anti-imperialist, Woodrow Wilson roundly condemned the interventionist policies of his predecessors (as in his Mobile speech of 1913). In practice, however, Wilson continued and extended the intervention program. Although he disapproved of Wall Street bankers, he found that financial influence helped him control such republics as Nicaragua. Although he was antimilitarist, the President was gravely concerned about a possible German threat to the Panama Canal. The Canal, in fact, came to be of great importance in his thinking.

Wilson therefore kept the marines in Nicaragua. Then he had the State Department negotiate an agreement that made Nicaragua virtually a United States protectorate. (This was the Bryan-Chamorro

Treaty of 1914, which gave the United States exclusive canal rights and permission to build Atlantic and Pacific naval bases.) Wilson tightened control over the Dominican Republic by sending in troops. He also had Haiti occupied by American naval forces, thus inaugurating an armed intervention that lasted until 1934.

All these developments took place during World War I; and Wilson felt that he was protecting the approaches of the Panama Canal against possible German moves. In the same spirit, the United States acquired the Virgin Islands from Denmark (1917), for the high price of $25,000,000. Germany, it was thought, might coerce her neighbor Denmark into ceding the islands to her, for a submarine base.

Wilson followed much the same line in Mexico. The Mexican Revolution of 1910 had been followed by an age of turmoil, involving difficulties for foreign capital. This disturbed Wilson, who also disapproved strongly of the most powerful Mexican politician, Huerta. Refusing to recognize Huerta, Wilson would not let that dictator buy arms in the United States; arms could, however, go to Huerta's foe Carranza. A minor incident concerning American sailors at Tampico led to the occupation of Vera Cruz by American naval forces in April, 1914. Again, the Germans were in the picture; the occupation prevented Huerta from getting arms from German sources. The ABC countries of South America (Argentina, Brazil, Chile) then arranged a sort of compromise, with Huerta going into exile and the United States withdrawing from Vera Cruz. Carranza, whom Wilson had supported, became President of Mexico.

More troubles followed. In 1916 Pancho Villa, a bandit-politician, slaughtered Americans in Mexico and across the border in New Mexico. Since Carranza was unable to catch Villa, Wilson sent General J. J. Pershing and 15,000 troops on a punitive expedition into Mexico. Pershing did not catch Villa; and the whole affair embittered Mexican-American relations. In a constitution of 1917, the Mexicans made new attacks on Americans who owned oil properties south of the Rio Grande. On the American side, Wilson became convinced that the Mexicans were under German influence; and at the end of World War I the American President saw to it that Mexico was not invited to join the League of Nations.

UNITED STATES

GULF OF MEXICO

M E X I C O

VERA CRUZ

BRITISH HONDURAS

GUATEMALA

HONDURAS

EL SALVADOR

NICARAGUA

COSTA RICA

⬭ U.S. Possessions and
Leaseholds

▨ U.S. Protectorates and
Occupied Areas

100   300   500
Miles

Flannery

The United States acquired a few guano islands even before the Civil
War, Navassa being the first of these. Congress, however, rejected
presidential proposals for the annexation of the Virgin Islands (Danish
West Indies) and the Dominican Republic in the Reconstruction era.

After the war with Spain in 1898 the United States annexed Puerto
Rico, secured a naval base at Guantanamo, and a protectorate over
Cuba. During Theodore Roosevelt's administration, the United States won
control of the Canal Zone (1903), with a protectorate treaty covering all
Panama (1903-39). Roosevelt set up a "financial protectorate" over the

THE UNITED STATES
IN MIDDLE AMERICA
1898-1918

THE BAHAMAS

CUBA

GUANTANAMO   HAITI

JAMAICA   NAVASSA IS.

PUERTO RICO   VIRGIN IS.

DOMINICAN REPUBLIC

CARIBBEAN   SEA

CURAÇAO

IS.

TRINIDAD

CANAL ZONE

PANAMA

VENEZUELA

COLOMBIA

Dominican Republic (1905-41, there being armed intervention, 1914-24). Occupation of Nicaragua (1912-33) began under Taft, who also tried to arrange a financial protectorate of Honduras. Wilson continued the intervention policy, occupying Haiti (1915-34), holding Vera Cruz briefly (1914), leasing the Corn Islands from Nicaragua (1914), and purchasing the Virgin Islands from Denmark (1917).

Finding that force diplomacy brought resentment and opposition in Latin America, the United States abandoned the direct intervention method after 1930.

All in all, the intervention policy of 1900–20 fell short of complete success. True, the United States obtained the Canal Zone; and these years saw an enormous increase in American influence in the northern part of Latin America. United States trade, investment, and naval power rose sharply. Diplomatic influence went up, too; and when the United States entered World War I in 1917, several Latin-American states followed suit. (Not only such United States-dominated states as Cuba, but also the larger republic of Brazil, which depended on the United States for its coffee market.) But, along with the rise of influence, there was a rise in animosity toward the United States. During the generation to follow, citizens of the United States would find that abandonment of the intervention policy would increase American effectiveness in the Western Hemisphere.

Europe: Isolation Fades

When the United States declared war on Spain in 1898, most Americans still believed that their republic should steer clear of European quarrels. But even then, the old isolation ideology was breaking down. By 1914 the United States would be very close to Europe's quarrels.

There were many aspects to the new trend. Greater wealth and improved transportation facilities caused large numbers of well-to-do Americans to visit Europe. These travelers were frequently regarded with contempt by European intellectuals; and the Americans in turn sneered at European culture (see Mark Twain's *Innocents Abroad*). Still, the closer contact made many realize that American and European cultures were closely related. European-trained American scholars had even more influence; and the same end was served by the gradually improved foreign correspondence of American newspapers. In the International Copyright Act of 1891, Congress eliminated book pirating, and to that extent cut the circulation of European books in the United States. At the same time, the statute indicated that the United States was at last recognizing its responsibilities in international cultural relations.

Simultaneously, the economic and naval expansion of the American republic brought all sorts of new commitments. As early as 1865, the United States joined European nations in maintaining the Cape

Spartel lighthouse near the Strait of Gibraltar. From the 1880's on, the American government took part in many international conferences. Some concerned areas far from the United States—the Congo, Morocco, Spitzbergen. Others dealt with subjects which the United States would not earlier have considered to be matters of international concern: the slave trade; the liquor traffic; patents and trademarks; weights and measures; sanitary regulations; peace, disarmament, and international arbitration; the rules of war. In 1900, American troops served as part of an international military force in China; and in the Boxer Protocol that followed, the United States joined other nations in determining the fate of China. Beginning with the 1880's, the United States signed many multilateral agreements and joined a number of international organizations, including the Universal Postal Union and the Pan American Union. There was semiofficial and unofficial activity, too, as in the case of the China consortium agreements; when Congress chartered the American Red Cross (associated with the International Red Cross); and when, from 1896 on, Americans took part in the international Olympic games.

Presidential Influence

Presidential power increased as the United States became more active in diplomacy. The Chief Executive had broad constitutional powers in the international field: the right to appoint diplomats; control over recognition of foreign governments; power to negotiate treaties; and authority as commander in chief of the nation's armed forces. Twentieth-century Presidents used these powers to the full, as when Taft sent marines to Nicaragua, and when Wilson determined Mexican policy by withholding recognition from Huerta.

Not stopping there, Presidents added to their authority. Theodore Roosevelt acted as a kind of mediator at the end of the Russo-Japanese War. Normal diplomatic appointees (ambassadors, for instance) required Senate confirmation. But Presidents could and did by-pass the Senate by using executive agents, responsible only to the President. The peace treaty with Spain in 1898 was handled in this fashion. Presidents could also get around the constitutional requirement that the Senate approve treaties, by making executive agreements which were not submitted to the Senate. Several important Far Eastern commitments fell into this category: the Boxer Protocol; the gentlemen's agreement with Japan on immigration; the Taft-Katsura, Root-Takahira, and Lansing-Ishii agreements. The Taft-Katsura understanding, worked out in Theodore Roosevelt's time, was not submitted to the Senate, and was kept secret from the public. Moreover, it was negotiated by an executive agent, who was not confirmed by the Senate. And yet, apparently, the terms bound the United States.

Under the circumstances, the personal attitude of the President was bound to influence the diplomatic alignments of the United States. It is significant, therefore, that Theodore Roosevelt, Taft, and Wilson, despite their differences, agreed on many points of diplomatic policy. All felt that the United States must have increasing influence overseas. All believed in presidential leadership in the diplomatic field. And all were enthusiastically pro-British.

Anglo-American Friendship

The four decades before World War I saw a great upsurge of nationalism in Europe, a new interest in imperialism, an enormous increase in armaments, and the formation of new alliances. Being part of one world, the United States was involved at every point. Nationalism was a mighty force in the United States. The American republic sampled imperialism, and became a great naval power. Only in the matter of alliances did Americans seem much different from Europeans. Even there the difference was not as great as it appeared at first glance, for in the generation before 1914 the United States became the informal partner of Great Britain.

Anglo-American friendship developed slowly. Old claims-and-boundary difficulties were removed in the Treaty of Washington (1871). Some controversies remained, as over fisheries; and the United States and Britain continued to be strong commercial rivals. But, as earlier quarrels subsided, Americans and Englishmen became increasingly aware of their ties of blood and language, their similarities of government, their common cultural heritage. These bonds were keenly felt by such Britishers as Joseph Chamberlain and Rudyard Kipling, by such Americans as Hay and Roosevelt and Wilson.

Diplomatic trends also affected the result. With the rise of Germany, Great Britain came to feel the need for friends. She therefore built new alliances, with Japan, France, and Russia. Before any of these had been arranged, the British government approached the United States, suggesting an Anglo-American combination in the Far East (1898). President McKinley replied that the United States had a tradition against alliances. But that, of course, did not rule out friendly coöperation.

Britain made every effort to effect that coöperation. When Cleveland's Secretary of State Olney scolded Britain in the Venezuela boundary dispute of 1895, British diplomats restrained themselves, and did what the United States desired. Britain took the American side in the Spanish-American War, and told the European powers that they could not intervene to save Spain. By that time, Britain was working with the United States in Samoa. Soon afterward, Great Britain advanced American canal ambitions by voluntarily giving up most of her Isthmian rights in the Hay-Pauncefote treaties (1899–1900). When Canada and the United States became involved in a dispute over the Alaska boundary, a British arbitrator sided with the Americans against the Canadians, giving the United States the victory (1903). Three years later, the British withdrew their fleet from the West Indies, thus turning strategic control of the Carribbean over to the United States.

There were those who felt that the United States gave little in return. Despite pro-British sentiment in the White House, Anglophobia remained strong in the Senate, especially among Senators with Irish-American constituents. In Cleveland's day and again in Taft's, the Senate rejected Anglo-American arbitration treaties. Anti-British sentiment figured in the rejection of the first Hay-Pauncefote Treaty and in the passage of the Panama Canal Tolls Act. Twisting the lion's tail was still a favorite political sport in the United States, one that paid off in Irish-American and German-American districts. And some progressives were suspicious of the British because of the close relations between Wall Street and British bankers.

Despite all this, Anglo-American coöperation did become a reality. Hay's Open Door Notes of 1899 were drafted by a Britisher. The United States, Great Britain, and Japan worked together during the

Russo-Japanese War, against France and Russia. At the Algeciras Conference of 1906, the Americans worked with the French and British against the Germans. And on both sides of the Atlantic, citizens were saying that war between Great Britain and the United States was unthinkable, and that the English-speaking nations would stand together in the years to come.

By 1914, Britain was allied to France, Japan, and Russia. Franco-American relations were improving at the time, partly owing to French efforts to win American friendship. Japanese-American relations, traditionally good, were taking a turn for the worst. There was even greater friction between Russia and the United States. Fairly friendly in the nineteenth century, these two nations ran into difficulties in the twentieth. There were economic clashes in northeast Asia, where the United States favored and Russia opposed the open door. No less significant was Tsarist persecution of Russian and foreign Jews. Russian unwillingness to give passports to American Jews finally resulted in the termination of a Russian-American commercial treaty in 1911.

Conflict with Germany

Though sometimes irritated with Britain's allies, most Americans emphatically preferred the Anglo-Russian-French entente to the opposing alliance (Germany, Austria-Hungary, Turkey, the Central Powers). During the nineteenth century there had been much pro-German sentiment in the United States. Some of this was associated with immigrants from Germany, some with Americans who had studied in German universities. But the unification of Germany had changed the pattern after 1870. The new German empire was aggressive, belligerent, efficient; and Americans were concerned.

Friction developed at several points. Government-subsidized German firms captured Latin-American markets which Americans desired to control. Americans ran into German competition in Samoa and China. Germany plainly preferred Spain in the Spanish-American War of 1898. After that conflict, the German empire bought Spain's remaining islands in the Pacific and thus secured potential naval bases close to America's Pacific strongholds. In addition, citizens of the

United States were alarmed by the violent public statements of Kaiser Wilhelm II and were impressed by the anti-German views of leading Britishers.

Quite evidently, then, the United States was moving toward Britain and away from Germany. To most Americans, this trend did not matter much, one way or the other. Actually, it was exceedingly important. As a great power, the American republic had great influence. And in a world that would soon be torn by war, few facts would be more telling than the American alignment with Great Britain.

12

In World War I

America and the War in Europe

On April 6, 1917, the United States declared war on Germany. By that action, the American republic became officially involved as a belligerent in the First World War.

Americans had mixed in European wars since before the days of Louis XIV. Normally, however, they had confined their participation to the "American phase" of these Old World conflicts and had felt relatively little interest in European battles and campaigns. And on most occasions European diplomats had regarded the Americans as of minor importance in the balance of power.

In 1917–18 the picture was very different. The industrialized United States was now a great world power, strong enough in men and materials to play an active role in determining the course of the war and the peace settlement to follow. What was more, the American people came to be deeply concerned about the conflict, in Europe as well as outside. There was a general feeling that triumph of the Central Powers would be a major blow to democratic institutions throughout the world, whereas a victory for the Allies and the United States would aid democracy and promote the cause of the self-government of peoples everywhere.

If one accepted these conclusions, total involvement became logical if not inevitable. Economic participation quickly became complete, the whole industrial and agrarian economy of the United States being geared to war production. And American armed forces were sent across the Atlantic Ocean to wage war in the European theater of operations.

Why did the United States go to war in 1917? At the time, the reason seemed entirely clear. President Wilson and most other Americans felt that their republic had been called on to save democracy, to crush autocracy as represented by the German Kaiser, Wilhem II. Eminent historians supported this position, pointing out that Germany had broken treaty obligations by invading neutral Belgium and had offended further by taking American lives with the new submarine weapon.

Postwar disillusionment brought forth other views. Revisionists were especially active in the middle 1930's, when Americans were concerned about the possibility of a second world war. Historians then suggested that the United States had been drawn into war in 1917 by British propaganda, or by American bankers who had lent money to the Allies and who feared the effects of German victory, or because trade with the Allies gave the United States a strong economic stake in Allied victory.

Later, there was still another change in attitude. World War II caused some writers to reconsider their revisionist views. Books appeared defending the earlier view that the declaration of war in 1917 was a matter of defending the interests of democracy.

Basic Sympathy for Allies

Despite the conflicting interpretations, certain points are fairly well established. First of all, it is clear that the basic sympathy of most Americans was with the Allies. This was the case from the beginning of hostilities in 1914. The United States was bound to one of the Allies, Great Britain, by strong ties of blood and culture. Americans spoke the English language, read and appreciated English literature, had a government and society based in large part on British institutions. Trade and investment further linked the English-speaking nations and notably connected Canada and the United States. Finally, a generation of diplomatic trends had pointed toward Anglo-American coöperation.

Relations with the other Allies were less intimate. There was, however, a tradition of Franco-American friendship, dating back to the American Revolution and symbolized by the French gift of the Statue of Liberty to the American people (1886). In contrast, the leading Central Power, Germany, was regarded with suspicion by many citizens of the United States. Particularly disturbing were the Kaiser's saber rattling and German-American competition in Latin America and the Orient.

During the years of American neutrality (1914–17), sympathy for the Allies and distrust of Germany sharply increased. Military developments were in part responsible. Being well organized for war, the Germans scored heavily at the start, occupying most of Belgium and smashing into France. Meanwhile, Germany's partner, Austria-Hungary, was going after little Serbia. All this aroused the traditional American fondness for the underdog, the more so since Belgium had been neutralized by international agreement.

Americans were also influenced by the German use of the U-boat, or submarine. Though strong on land, the German empire could not match the British fleet. But the Germans could and did challenge British sea power by using submarines to sink merchant vessels bound for British shores. Striking without warning, the U-boats took a heavy toll in ships and lives. The dead included women and children as well as men, neutrals as well as belligerents. Many Americans thereupon concluded that undersea warfare was improper, and that the Germans were breaking the rules of international law and fair play.

Propaganda, Trade, Finance

News treatment tended to support this position. The Central Powers had no way to send information quickly to the United States. (Britain cut German-American cable connections early in the war, and the radio was not yet a very satisfactory medium.) Germany did try to reach the American public by establishing a propaganda unit in the United States, under Dr. Dernburg. But the job was bungled, and, in any case, Americans were not receptive to the German point of view.

With the Allies, it was another story. The British had access to the transatlantic cables, and censored news as it went through to the United States. To this they added an active publicity campaign, skillfully directed by Sir Gilbert Parker. British propaganda placed heavy emphasis on German activities in Belgium ("Hun atrocities"), and on the "inhumanity" of the U-boat campaign. Use was made of names well known in the New World—Rudyard Kipling and James Bryce, for instance. Americans, already partial toward the Allies, were further impressed by this material.

Economic trends provided another link to the Allies. The British blockade prevented American trade with the Central Powers; hence the United States had no economic stake in German victory. Trade with the Allies, on the other hand, increased enormously during the three years of neutrality. This growing commerce headed off a threatened economic depression in 1914 and gave a large measure of prosperity to American farmers and industrialists. Some citizens felt that this association with the Allied cause was unfortunate, especially in so far as it involved munitions. But the great majority of Americans approved of the trend, because of their pro-Ally attitudes and because of the resulting profits.

To finance these purchases France, Great Britain, and the other Allies floated loans in this country. Altogether, they borrowed more than $2,000,000,000 from private American investors by 1917. Citizens who bought French and British bonds were of course already pro-Ally—many were businessmen who were selling goods to Britain. In all probability, however, their bond purchases increased their concern for Allied victory. Worried over this, neutral-minded Secretary of State William Jennings Bryan refused to allow the belligerents to float bond issues in the United States in 1914–15, although he did allow banks to extend short-term credit. But when Bryan left the State Department, in 1915, long-term loans were authorized.

Concerned over American aid to Britain, the German government filed protests. When this approach proved ineffective, German agents in the United States turned to other methods. They tried to organize strikes along the water front, to delay loading of ships bound for Britain. They entered the market through dummy corporations, seeking to corner key raw materials. Under the direction of Franz von Papen, the German military attaché, they even tried direct action— blowing up munitions plants. Being poorly organized, these activities did not materially affect American production. They did, though, influence public opinion. Anti-German sentiment increased when

Americans learned about sabotage operations; and there was talk of the "enemy within."

The friends of Britain operated through many channels. Some of their most effective work was done through the League to Enforce Peace. Organized in 1915, this association aimed at building sentiment for a postwar League of Nations. But the League to Enforce Peace was also, and emphatically, in favor of the Allied cause. This League and other pro-Ally organizations received good publicity in most newspapers (the Hearst chain being an exception). In addition, Germany was condemned in pulpits and classrooms, in business, farm, and labor periodicals, and in a great flood of pro-British books.

The Other Side

Though general, the anti-German sentiment was not shared by all in the United States. German-Americans were highly critical of the Allies and did what they could to keep America from aiding the opponents of the Central Powers. So did the Irish-Americans, who cared little for Germany but harbored a deep hatred for the English. Many middle-western agriculturalists were also affected by Anglophobia. Farm leaders who had long disliked the tie-up of Wall Street with British finance now noted that J. P. Morgan and Company was the Allied purchasing agent in the United States. The Socialists and the I.W.W. condemned both sides in this "imperialist" war; and pacifists opposed any step likely to take the United States into battle.

Had they pulled together, these groups might have had an important influence. But they did not coöperate; and, working separately, they were ineffective. It was easy for the opposition to dismiss the pacifists as visionary cranks, to call the Socialists dangerous radicals, to denounce the immigrant groups as disloyal. In 1916 both President Wilson and ex-President Theodore Roosevelt were attacking citizens of Irish and German ancestry as "hyphenated Americans."

By then, the American people were overwhelmingly anti-German. Still, few desired to go to war. A popular song of the period was "I Didn't Raise My Boy to Be a Soldier." In the presidential campaign of

1916, Wilson's managers found that the voters gave the President little credit for his anti-German utterances but were definitely interested in the slogan, "He kept us out of war." The American people were not neutral "in thought," as Wilson had advised them to be in 1914. They definitely sided with the Allies. But, for all that, there was little of the "get-in-the-fight" feeling that had swept the country in 1898.

Wilson and Neutral Rights

Nonetheless, the United States did get in the fight. As early as 1915, President Wilson took a firm stand on German violations of neutral rights. At the time, Germany yielded. When she changed her policy early in 1917, Wilson severed diplomatic relations with Germany; and war soon followed.

Actually, both sides interfered with neutral rights. The British interfered with the United States mail; seized American property under doubtful interpretations of the international rules of contraband and continuous voyage; limited trade between the United States and Europe; prepared black lists of United States firms suspected of trading with Germany. Although the United States protested against these practices, the Wilson administration considered them less serious than the acts of Germany. Why so? Partly because Wilson and his chief advisers were pro-British. Also, apparently, because the British interference with property rights seldom resulted in loss of life. German submarine activity, on the other hand, cost over 200 American lives.

Under international law, belligerent warships are supposed to give notice before they sink enemy merchant ships. The German U-boats sank without warning, which made for heavy losses on the vessels that went down. Defending their practice, the Germans said that submarines were frail. If they came to the surface to give warning, they could be rammed, or destroyed by fire from an armed merchant vessel's deck guns. To avoid trouble, neutral citizens should travel on neutral ships.

Some Americans agreed with this point of view—Bryan among the Democrats, La Follette among the Republicans. In 1916, Congress very nearly passed the Gore-McLemore resolution, which was designed to keep Americans off vessels belonging to belligerents. But the resolution was defeated, by administration pressure. In Wilson's opinion, it was improper to yield on this question. ("Once accept a single abatement of right," he said, "and other humiliations will follow.")

The first submarine crises came in 1915. In that year the Germans sank several Allied ships on which Americans were traveling. The most famous case was that of the *Lusitania*, an English merchant vessel sunk off the Irish coast. Of the thousand passengers who lost their lives, 128 were Americans, nearly half of these being women and children. The *Lusitania* was a belligerent vessel traveling in a war zone; and it was carrying contraband (cartridges). But the vessel was unarmed and was not carrying troops.

As might have been expected, the *Lusitania* affair created a great furor in the United States. Notwithstanding or perhaps because of this, Secretary of State Bryan felt that Wilson should go very slowly, and that if the United States protested German actions, it should at the same time crack down on Britain's violations of neutral rights. When the President insisted on a firm stand against Germany, Bryan resigned from the cabinet. Wilson thereupon gave the State Department post to Robert Lansing, a pronounced Anglophile.

Having overruled Bryan, Wilson told Germany that U-boat commanders should safeguard American lives, even on Allied ships. Not desiring to have the United States enter the war, the Germans gave way, and stopped unrestricted submarine warfare until February, 1917.

Knowing Wilson's stand, the German government well understood that the resumption of unrestricted submarine warfare might lead to a break in German-American relations. Germany, however, finally took the risk; on February, 1, 1917, she set out to sink all belligerent and neutral vessels heading for the British Isles or France. The hope was to bring Britain to her knees before the United States could give effective aid to the Allies.

Woodrow Wilson was definitely pro-British. In 1916 he permitted his personal agent Colonel House to intimate to Britain that, under certain circumstances, the United States might join the Allies against Germany. Yet the President really hoped that the United States would not have to take up arms. As late as the end of 1916 he talked of settling the war by compromise ("peace without victory"). At the beginning of the new year, when the Germans announced resumption of unrestricted submarine warfare, Wilson gave the German ambassador his passports. But even then the Chief Executive hoped against hope that a declaration of hostilities would not be necessary.

Declaring War

The nation, however, rapidly moved toward war. In February and March, 1917, German submarines sank Allied ships with United States citizens aboard, and sank American vessels, too. Wilson thereupon asked Congress for authority to arm merchant craft, only to run into a Senate filibuster led by Senators La Follette and Norris. Denouncing the filibusterers as eleven "willful men," the President had the ships armed anyway, under authority of a statute of 1797.

Just at this time—March, 1917—the British turned over to the United States an intercepted German message to Mexico. This Zimmermann note proposed a German-Mexican-Japanese alliance in case war broke out between the United States and Mexico. Germany would help Mexico (how, was not clear), and Mexico would regain her "lost territory" of Texas, New Mexico, Arizona. When set before the American public, this astounding dispatch inflamed opinion against Germany and took the United States closer to war.

In this same month there came news of the overthrow of the Russian czar in the March Revolution. Eight months later, the Provisional Russian government would be overthrown by the Communists; but in March, 1917, it seemed that Russia would have an American-type republican government.

Now, at long last, it was possible to state that all the Allies believed in democracy, and that World War I was a conflict between democracy and autocracy. So Wilson felt; and so he said when, early in April, 1917, he asked Congress to declare war against Germany. The House and Senate quickly responded, 373–50 and 82–6. The votes roughly reflected public opinion. Although some Americans held back, most citizens of the United States had come to regard entry into the war as inevitable.

Economic Conversion to War

American industry was relatively unprepared for war in 1917. This is not surprising, for the United States had fought no major war for a half-century. Then, too, modern war calls for ordered collectivity, involving governmental supervision of economic life. Despite the progressive reforms, American business still generally regulated its own affairs in 1917. In some industries control was in the hands of a few monopolists. In other fields there was sharp competition. Either way, businessmen ran the show, and prized freedom from the governmental control that is essential in periods of military crisis.

During the years of neutrality (1914–17), a few leaders urged industrial preparation for the possible demands of war. They were largely unsuccessful. In 1916—rather late—President Wilson created a Council of National Defense. This Council was made up of cabinet officers, with an advisory committee of business and labor leaders. By April, 1917, the Council had made a number of suggestions. Most of these, however, had been disregarded, by both business and the government.

Such preparation as there was stemmed from the Allied war orders, which were channeled through the house of Morgan. Between 1914 and 1917 Britain and her partners bought $3,000,000,000 worth of supplies in the United States; and American industry expanded to meet the demand. To some degree, this increased the ability of the United States to produce war goods. Much of the Allied purchasing represented cotton, wheat, and other agricultural products. A good deal of the balance was made up of semifinished manufactures and parts, rather than complete implements of war.

In consequence, American entry into World War I made necessary a tremendous industrial reorganization. Businessmen could not effect the reorganization by themselves; hence government controls, quotas, and administered prices came in overnight. Later in the century, such phenomena would be familiar to all Americans. But they were strange in 1917, and came as a shock to the business community.

The difficulties of conversion to war production were linked to the complexity of twentieth-century warfare. A new airplane engine or artillery weapon required months of planning and thousands of blueprints to check every detail. Besides that, new machines needed to make the parts might call for an equal amount of consideration. Solution of these problems left still unsolved questions of labor, materials, and transportation. Allied purchasing in the neutrality period had brought Americans close to full employment. As a result, the diversion of man power to war production meant abandoning some civilian activities. This in turn necessitated government-directed allocation of materials, capital, and labor.

Confusion reigned all through 1917. The Council of National Defense established a War Industries Board in July, 1917, but failed to give the Board sufficient power. Priorities were established with little regard to time schedules or the quantity of goods available. Raw materials delivered to processors ahead of schedule were left on sidings in freight cars, while those cars were urgently needed elsewhere. Army and navy, American and Allied priorities were in conflict with each other, and no one had final power to control allocations.

The transportation situation was worst of all. Too many contracts were let in areas where traffic was overcongested. The thirty-two major railroad systems, held apart by the Sherman Antitrust Act, could not unsnarl the tangle. Conditions became worse each month, as shippers routed orders through bottleneck port areas, particularly New York. By the end of 1917 the jam of freight cars and cargo boats in that city was threatening to halt the movement of supplies to Europe.

Would inefficiency mean defeat? Fearing that it might, President Wilson gradually began to exercise the sweeping war powers conferred on him by the Constitution and by acts of Congress (e.g., the Lever Act of August, 1917, and the Overman Act of May, 1918). In December, 1917, he seized the railroads and coördinated them into one vast government-administered system under Secretary of the Treasury William G. McAdoo. In January, 1918, Wilson took over the telephone and telegraph lines. Two months later he gave the War Industries Board mandatory control over prices and allocations, and vested power and responsibility in its chairman, Bernard Baruch. By the summer of 1918, America at last had a smoothly functioning war machine.

Coördinating War Production

During the progressive era many public figures had attacked big business. War changed this, for industrial productivity depended on the very men whom the progressives had denounced. In 1917 and 1918, leading capitalists were recruited for government service, many of them as "dollar-a-year men." Examples are Daniel Willard of the Baltimore and Ohio Railroad; Julius Rosenwald of Sears, Roebuck; and Charles M. Schwab of Bethlehem Steel. The presence of these men in the government gradually changed the whole tone of the Wilson administration.

The key man in the structure was Bernard Baruch, a successful member of the New York Stock Exchange. Baruch's War Industries Board leaned heavily on manufacturers' trade associations and on the United States Chamber of Commerce. These organizations were asked to report on who could make what and how soon. Some effort was made to reach medium-sized and even small producers. But, since drawing up many contracts was difficult and time-consuming, the tendency was to rely most heavily on the industrial giants. Wilson, long a foe of bigness, was to help make the largest producers larger yet.

During the first year of American war effort, the War Industries Board had to negotiate prices with suppliers. After the passage of the Overman Act rates were often set arbitrarily. To insure maximum supply, the government set prices high enough to cover costs of production in inefficient plants. Inevitably, then, the larger, more efficient companies made huge profits. Nevertheless, profits for business as a whole were lower in 1917 than in 1916, and lower still in 1918 (after the imposition of excess-profits taxes). War was less rewarding than neutrality.

The most serious wartime shortage was in ships. Sinkings far exceeded launchings in the early part of 1917, when the German submarines were most effective. To take care of the problem, the United States and Britain worked out antisubmarine devices. The United

States seized and pressed into service enemy and neutral cargo ships. Meantime, new construction was pushed as rapidly as possible.

High freight rates had stimulated American private building even before the United States entered the war. A third of a million gross tons had been completed in 1916. This total was doubled in 1917. But, given the U-boat toll, it did not come close to being enough. The United States government therefore encouraged shipbuilding concerns to move faster, and provided government loans to make possible the adding of new ways.

Knowing that still more was needed, the Wilson administration also went directly into business. The Shipping Board established a government-owned Emergency Fleet Corporation and authorized it to construct freighters. Government shipyards such as Hog Island, south of Philadelphia, were rushed to completion. But building ships is a slow job. The government was just getting into production when the war came to a close (November, 1918). The building program was continued for a time after the armistice; and by 1921 the United States had acquired 9,000,000 gross tons of slow, uneconomical freighters, for which there was little peacetime use.

Raw materials also presented pressing problems. Food and fuels were placed under control of federal administrators during the summer of 1917. These administrators, like Baruch of the War Industries Board, bought at prices high enough to bring out maximum production. As an illustration, Food Administrator Herbert Hoover announced that his Grain Corporation would pay $2.20 a bushel for all wheat produced in 1917, and $2.26 for the 1918 crop. In 1913, the price had been 97¢.

Encouraged by price trends and by government appeals for top production, farmers expanded their planting operations. Wheat acreage in 1919 was 20 percent above any previous year. (For various reasons, however, the total yield was below that of 1915, the only billion-bushel year before World War II.) Unfortunately, much of the land added to cultivation was marginal or submarginal—not likely to show a profit in times of peace. A good deal of this acreage was bought and cultivated with funds borrowed from government Farm Loan Banks;

and the war boom was too short to give the farmer a chance to pay back the money.

Efforts to control civilian consumption were on a voluntary basis. Price fixing and rationing measures were not applied directly to the consumer. Automobiles, tires, and gasoline went unrationed, although motorists were asked to avoid unnecessary driving. There were wheatless, meatless, and heatless days. Enforcement, however, was limited to individual action and the force of community opinion.

Paying for War

American banks and investors played a large part in financing the Allied cause all through the neutrality period (1914–17). With American entry into the war, the United States government assumed this function. During and immediately after the war the American Treasury advanced almost $10,000,000,000 to the Allies. Including these war loans, the direct cost of World War I to the United States from April, 1917, to June, 1920, was about $32,000,000,000.

Although these sums seem large, it is worth noting that war costs approached a quarter of the national income only in 1918. Had Congress imposed high taxes immediately after the declaration of hostilities, the United States could have financed World War I on a pay-as-you-go basis. Doing so would have spared the aged and the salaried groups the economic distress that came with postwar inflation. But, though some economists and a few politicians urged high taxes, Congress paid little heed. Pay-as-you-go would have been politically unpopular, might have discouraged business, and would certainly have reduced enthusiasm for the war.

Rejecting pay-as-you-go, the House and Senate voted moderate taxes in the spring of 1917. These were increased during the year, and again in 1918. Heavy reliance was placed on income and excess-profits taxes. Income taxes were increased, the government taking over three-quarters of 1918 incomes above $1,000,000. Tobacco and liquor taxes, inheritance duties, and postal rates were stepped up, and the government secured revenue by taxing express and railroad, telephone and telegraph charges, automobiles and insurance, theater admissions and club dues, and all sorts of "luxury" items (yachts and cosmetics, jewelry and chewing gum and sporting goods). The total yield, however, was only about $11,000,000,000 for 1917–20, approximately one-third of the cost of the war.

Two-thirds, then, had to be obtained by borrowing. This reënacted the early history of the Civil War—but with a difference. In the Civil War, it had been necessary to resort to greenbacks. The establishment of the Federal Reserve System just before World War I enabled the Wilson administration to raise money by selling short-term certificates and bonds directly to the banks. Although inflationary, this was not as psychologically upsetting as issuing unsupported paper money.

To retire the certificates held by the banks, the Treasury set out to sell long-term bonds to the general public. Each new issue of Liberty Bonds was marketed at local rallies and movie houses, and advertised in giant poster campaigns. Bonds were sold through employers and in door-to-door canvasses; and war savings stamps were purchased by children in the schools. Subscription was made a patriotic duty, and volunteer committees exerted pressure on those who were reluctant to coöperate. In this way the government netted $21,000,000,000 in four Liberty Loans and a post-armistice Victory Loan.

The smaller bonds ($100 and less) were bought largely from savings. The larger denominations were purchased by the banks, which then created deposits to the government's account, or by businessmen who used the bonds as security for loans. These operations did not represent real savings, and were inflationary in effect. Here was a basic cause for the 85 percent rise in living costs between 1916 and 1920.

Civil War inflation had hurt the workers. Organization and labor shortages made the World War I situation somewhat better for the workingman. For all workers taken together, wage increases nearly kept pace with the rise in the cost of living through 1918, and forged ahead in 1919–20. White-collar workers and those living on savings and annuities were less fortunate. Living costs nearly doubled between 1916 and 1920; but clerical salaries advanced only 25 percent, and teachers' pay remained virtually stationary. Citizens living on pensions or fixed salaries lost nearly half their purchasing power.

While this was going on, war profits were adding to the wealth of the more fortunate. In 1910 the top tenth made 34 percent of the national income, the bottom tenth 3½ percent. Ten years later, the figures were 38 percent and 2 percent. Looked at in another way, the average member of the top group received ten times as much income as the average in the bottom group in 1910, and nineteen times as much a decade later. World War I had made the rich richer, the poor relatively poorer.

Labor and the War

President Samuel Gompers of the American Federation of Labor became a member of the Advisory Commission to the Council of National Defense even before the United States entered the war. He lost no time in pledging labor's coöperation in the war effort. A.F. of L. unions would not strike. Workers would buy Liberty Bonds, and they would stick to the job, not drift casually from plant to plant. In return, Gompers hoped that employers would not interfere with organization drives.

On the whole, results were satisfactory. There was some antilabor sentiment, as is indicated by the passage of work-or-fight laws in half a dozen states. In addition, the federal Espionage Act was used to imprison radical labor leaders. But special commissions and a national War Labor Board kept the peace in most manufacturing centers. Workers set new production records; many employers agreed to bargain collectively and abandon the nonunion shop. Most important of all, perhaps, was the general establishment of the basic eight-hour day (overtime extra). The new standard was applied to the railroads by the Adamson Act of 1916. Later, the principle was extended by the application to war contracts of a 1912 statute which had fixed eight hours as the working day for individuals employed by the government.

During the period of hostilities, Gompers and his chief lieutenants thought it best to refrain from pushing hard to unionize the most vital war industries (steel, motors, chemicals). In consequence, union membership increased moderately, about 25 percent, between 1916 and 1918. After the armistice, in November, 1918, organizational and strike activities were increased. Union strength went up 50 percent in

1919–20. Some 4,000,000 workers went on strike in 1919—a larger number and a higher percentage of all workers than in any other year in America's history. Some strikes were unsuccessful, the great steel strike being an example. Others succeeded; and the work of 1919 raised labor's real wages to a new high. The new level would prevail through the 1920's, despite the relative inefficiency of labor leadership in that postwar decade.

The People Move

Though brief in time, American participation in World War I influenced every aspect of society. On the most obvious level, it quickened and accentuated the characteristic American tendency to keep moving. Two million young American men crossed the Atlantic, and almost as many more moved about within the United States, from cantonment to cantonment. It is impossible to measure the effect of this on provincialism, sectional peculiarities, and class barriers; but personal horizons certainly broadened, and, for a time, the comradeship of camp and trench promoted the ideal of social democracy.

Job opportunities in war plants lured hundreds of thousands of rural citizens to urban centers. Wages were high, even in terms of soaring prices; and they stayed high. It could hardly have been otherwise, considering the drain of man power to the armed forces, and the virtual cessation of immigration (except from Mexico). So the shops and factories acted like magnets.

No aspect of the country-to-city migration was more dramatic than the movement of southern Negroes to southern and northern industrial centers. This movement began before World War I and continued long afterward; but the war brought the trend to a climax. From 1914 on, the word spread of fantastic wages available in the nation's industrial cities. Southern whites tried to discourage Negro migration, lest they lose their cheap labor supply. But the movement continued.

Many Negroes who left the soil went to nearby southern cities. Others took the longer trip north. In doing so, they sought not only good pay but also the social freedom and cultural opportunities that the North was said to offer. ("I would like Chicago or Philadelphia," wrote one prospective Negro migrant in 1917, "but I don't care where so long as I go where a man is a man.")

The results were impressive. The 1920 census, as compared with that of 1910, showed a proportionate decrease of colored population to total population in almost all the southern states. There was a corresponding gain in such northern industrial states as Illinois, Michigan, Pennsylvania, and New York.

But all did not go well. The Negro migration to the cities presented the usual problems of adjustment of rural people to urban ways. In this case, the difficulties were heightened by bad conditions in the crowded slums into which the Negroes necessarily moved. There was discrimination, too, in the North as well as in the South, marked by bloody race riots in East St. Louis and Chicago. Disheartened, some Negroes went back home.

But the great majority stayed. Opportunities were limited, both North and South. Negroes could not get into the labor unions. They met with discrimination in employment (last hired, first fired). Even the prosperous and educated Negro could not buy a house in the better residential areas, be he in the South or the North. Most clubs and restaurants were closed to him. But, both in northern and in southern cities, educational and economic opportunities were better than on share-crop farms. The political outlook was better, too. Negroes were allowed to vote in some southern and all northern cities; and they had substantial influence in the latter.

Women and the War

In opening jobs to women, World War I gave American mothers, wives, and daughters an enhanced sense of freedom and power. Social workers pointed to the undesirable effects on children of the disruption of home life occasioned by working mothers; but the pull was too great to be denied. To begin with, the work paid well, in this period of labor shortage. On top of that, employment gave women a feeling of independence. Finally, it was considered patriotic to work in a war plant, as a million women did.

By demonstrating the capability of women in industry, the war emphasized the absurdity of denying the vote to this half of the population. The point was the more clear in view of the government's claim that this was a war to make the world safe for democracy. Suffragettes, while shouldering their full share of war duties, at the same time made it plain that they expected the vote as soon as the shooting stopped. Among their converts was President Wilson. Earlier, Wilson had believed in leaving this matter to the states. Now he decided that the nation must act. In September, 1918, he announced that the successful prosecution of the war required the ratification of the proposed woman-suffrage amendment. Thanks to his prodding and other influences, the Nineteenth Amendment became a part of the Constitution soon after the armistice.

The C.P.I.

All the belligerents in World War I early discovered the importance of controlling public opinion and building enthusiasm for the war effort. The need was very evident in the United States. For one thing, a substantial number of Americans had opposed the entry of their country into war. Many more, though willing to accept Wilsonian leadership, thought of the conflict as something remote, little related to their lives. Volunteering lagged in the early months of American participation. The government therefore adopted conscription; and it also set out to sell the war to the people.

The result was the Committee on Public Information, which was directed by a picturesque and able journalist, George Creel. The C.P.I. spared no effort to promote hatred of the enemy. Creel engaged 75,000 volunteer speakers who gave short patriotic talks at every sort of public meeting. The audience total for these "four-minute men" was nearly a third of a billion. The C.P.I. also enlisted the aid of artists, who prepared huge posters depicting the brutality of the "Hun" foe and the idealistic nature of the Allied cause. Journalists, clergymen, and university professors aided the Committee by writing pamphlets detailing German war atrocities and stressing the baseness of the enemy's aims. A hundred million of these pamphlets reached the public. Creel also had a variety of handouts for daily and weekly newspapers; and the movie industry coöperated by turning out such films as *The Beast of Berlin* and *Wolves of Kultur.*

This whipped-up, steam-roller propaganda did contribute to the efficiency of the war effort. It also excited the popular emotions to such an extent that Americans considered it disloyal to read or speak German, to play German music, to retain German place and family names. Many colleges and most schools dropped German from the curriculum. Distinguished musicians of German background lost their posts or had to endure public insults—Fritz Kreisler, for example. Intellectuals suspected of entertaining sympathy for anything German experienced ostracism or persecution.

In other words, the war spirit made it difficult to distinguish between patriotism and disloyalty, liberalism and treason, indifference and crime. This carried on into the postwar period. It helped create the antiradical, antiliberal, antilabor Big Red Scare of 1919–20; and in the 1920's, it helped supply the background for the ultranationalist, nativist, antiminority crusades of such organizations as the Ku Klux Klan.

The vast majority of Americans did everything possible to advance the war effort. Virtually all the immigrants from enemy countries wholeheartedly supported their adopted land. So did the overwhelming majority of native Americans, including those who had been active in the peace movement. Such dissidents as there were, a tiny minority of the population, hardly justified the widespread hysteria. Nor did it excuse the tendency to single out for condemnation any lukewarmness or considered opposition to the most sweeping aspects of war emotionalism.

Opposition to the War

Who opposed the war effort? Among others, a few pacifists. This question came to the fore when religious objectors were called in the draft. About 4000 refused, on grounds of conscience, to put on the uniform. Nearly nine-tenths of these finally agreed to serve, e.g., in the Medical Corps. Those refusing any sort of service, or refusing to obey military orders after induction, were tried and sent to federal prisons. Some were given cruel treatment; and nearly all were kept behind bars for years after the war.

In addition, there was some opposition to the war from left-wing labor. A Socialist party convention declared that the conflict stemmed from capitalist and imperialist exploitation; but Upton Sinclair and other prominent leaders, as well as many rank-and-file Socialists, resisted the convention action. There was prowar feeling even among the Industrial Workers of the World. The I.W.W. leaders, however, condemned Wilsonianism and would not join the A.F. of L. in taking Gompers' no-strike pledge. Rather the Wobblies saw the war as a chance to undermine the capitalist system. But when they fomented strikes in western copper and lumber camps, they met with determined opposition from local officials and an enraged citizenry. A Montana crowd lynched an I.W.W. leader; and Wobbly strikers in Arizona were forcibly deported beyond the state line.

Some moves against opponents of the war were spontaneous. Others were worked out in coöperation with the federal government. Wilson's Justice Department sponsored an organization known as the American Protective League. Membership was made up of 250,000 volunteers. These patriots watched their neighbors, ostracizing, insulting, or reporting those deemed insufficiently ardent in their support of the war.

As for legislation, Congress in 1917 adopted an Espionage Act, fixing fines and imprisonment for those guilty of inciting disloyalty or interfering with recruiting. Later in that year came a Trading-with-the-Enemy Act, which, among other things, broadened Wilson's censorship powers. The next year brought Sabotage and Sedition acts, the latter authorizing severe punishment of anyone using disloyal language or in any way attacking the government, the Constitution, the flag, the uniform, or the war effort. When first proposed, these measures were labeled unnecessary and unconstitutional by some progressive Congressmen. But war passions ran high. The bills were quickly passed, and the laws were vigorously enforced by the executive and upheld by the courts.

In enforcing these and similar statutes, the government arrested some 2000 persons. In most cases, the charges collapsed of their own weight, and the individuals were discharged. Yet several dozen citizens were sentenced to prison for long terms. One was Eugene V. Debs, the Socialist leader. Nearly a hundred I.W.W. organizers were convicted after a sensational trial before Judge Kenesaw Mountain Landis; and their whole movement was broken. Meantime, the Postmaster General barred from the mails some Irish-American and German-American periodicals, and such Socialist publications as Victor Berger's Milwaukee *Leader*. Berger was also convicted under the Espionage Act; and when Wisconsin voters elected him to Congress at the end of the war, he was not allowed to take his seat.

Religion, Education, Literature

Although a few religious leaders took pacifist positions, the great majority endorsed World War I as a holy crusade. Yet, curiously, the war brought no great religious revival. The stress of the times, the imminence of death, the strength of Wilsonian idealism turned some people to the churches; but religious leaders found the results generally disappointing.

Education, like religion, rallied to the war effort. Colleges and universities opened their doors to officer-training units; and a Student Army Training Corps was being set up in 500 institutions at the time of the armistice. The SATC came too late to help win the war. What was more, it was disliked by most of the military men who controlled it and the professors who provided instruction. Still, the program saved some colleges from bankruptcy and provided experience useful in later crises.

Much more important was the contribution of scholars to the war effort. Many professors rushed off to jobs in Washington; others did military research on their campuses. With the new National Research Council playing the role of coördinator, scientists searched for substitutes for scarce materials; experimented with antisubmarine detectors and new aeronautic devices; worked with poison gas. Medical men improved military surgery and applied psychiatry to war neuroses. They also launched an army campaign against infection, thus breaking down public resistance to open discussion of venereal disease. Psychologists used the new mental tests to determine aptitudes. Academicians from every field engaged in intelligence work, and helped Colonel House prepare data for the peace conference.

The schools, too, did their part. Teachers sold war savings stamps and used C.P.I. materials in their classrooms. The schools and school children were mobilized to sell the war to parents: to persuade them to buy more bonds, to accept the war aims, to observe meatless and wheatless days. Children saved tin foil and increased the food supply by working in school and home gardens.

Besides contributing propaganda pieces, artists, composers, actors, and authors entertained soldiers in camp. They also tried to interpret the war to the public. This effort brought forth some stirring military marches and some popular war songs ("Pack Up Your Troubles in Your Old Kit Bag"). Soldiers' narratives had a brisk sale; and Joyce Kilmer and others wrote moving war lyrics. Yet neither in music nor in literature did the war bring forth much of enduring merit. The more impressive work came later, in the era of postwar disillusionment. Then deglamorized accounts of war would be presented by such writers as Ernest Hemingway (*Farewell to Arms*); John R. Dos Passos (*Three Soldiers*), Maxwell Anderson and Laurence Stallings (*What Price Glory?*).

America and the Allies

In entering the war against Germany, the United States did not declare war on the other Central Powers. To Wilson, German Kaiserism was the great threat. The American republic did, at the end of 1917, declare war against Austria-Hungary, doing so because one of the Allies, Italy, was in need of help. The United States also broke relations with Turkey. Here, though, there was no formal declaration of hostilities (such a declaration would have hurt American missionary interests in the Turkish Empire). Diplomatic relations with Bulgaria were maintained all through the war, providing a useful listening post and channel of communication with the Central Powers.

In the light of these developments, it could be said that the United States was not an all-out participant in World War I. Along the same line, the United States did not become one of the Allies. To have done so would have irritated citizens who were attached to the old no-alliance principle. Nor could America have become an Ally without raising the question of the secret treaties, which provided for postwar division of enemy territory. Preferring to postpone discussion of the problems of the peace, Wilson was content to have the United States called an Associated Power.

This did not mean that the United States was uncoöperative. Far from it. Wilson appealed to neutrals everywhere to join in the crusade against Germany. Many did—China, Liberia, Brazil and other Latin-American countries. The United States also set aside isolation notions to insist that all the foes of Germany work together, instead of competing with each other for control of money, munitions, and transportation. Americans also had much to do with the creation in 1918 of an overall (Franco-British-American) command on the western front, under the French Marshal Foch.

Yet there were many quarrels between America and the Allies. John J. Pershing, who commanded the American Expeditionary Force (A.E.F.) in France, disliked trench warfare, which the English and French had come to regard as necessary. Pershing also differed from his Anglo-French colleagues in his high rating of the rifle and his low rating of the machine gun. The British had felt the same way until the battle of the Somme (1916). Thereafter, they had developed a caution that irritated the offense-minded commander of the A.E.F.

French and British military leaders also felt that the inexperienced American troops should be worked into veteran Allied units. This would provide a reinforcement which the English and French badly needed. It would train the Americans more quickly than would otherwise be possible and at the same time reduce United States casualties. (Trench-wise English and French soldiers could guide the newcomers.)

National pride made Pershing and his superiors unwilling to accept these suggestions. The French and British had separate parts of the western front; let the United States have its own sector, too. It might take a little longer to train the Americans that way; but they would be more effective in the long run, when the war reached its decisive stage (late 1919, estimated the Americans, or 1920).

Winning the War

In fact, the crisis of the war came some-
what sooner. Having gained victories to the east and south, against
Russia and Italy, Germany in 1918 put her full weight into a drive
against the western front. As the French and British lines bent back,
Pershing offered to set aside his demand for a separate sector. This
made it possible to rush American troops into the lines. Green though
they were, these units from the New World helped stop the German
offensive in the second battle of the Marne.

When the Germans had been stopped, the Americans were finally
given a separate part of the western front. In the first distinctly American operation of the war, Pershing pinched out the St.-Mihiel salient
(September, 1918). Other engagements followed, in the Meuse-
Argonne, as Americans joined the British and French in a general advance that resulted in German surrender (November 11, 1918).

What was the American contribution to victory on the western
front? At first, relatively little; later, a great deal. President Wilson
was not converted to preparedness until 1916, and the United States
was not ready to fight in April, 1917. It took many months to raise,
equip, and train an American army and to transport it to the Old
World. Only 300,000 reached France in the year that followed American declaration of war against Germany. But after that, American
troops poured in at the rate of nearly 300,000 a month. All in all,
2,000,000 got to France; and if the war had lasted on into 1919, the
American republic could have added at least that many more. This reinforcement boosted sagging Allied morale and turned the tide on the
battlefields of France. When Germany's 1918 offensive failed, the
German High Command knew that their cause was lost. They were
reaching the bottom of their man-power barrel, whereas the Americans were just coming into action. The Germans thus saw little use in
fighting on; and they surrendered before Germany was invaded.

In the main, this war was fought on land. Americans heard more of
General Pershing than of Admiral W. S. Sims. Yet World War I was
also won at sea. One important factor was the Allied blockade of
Germany, established before United States entry into the war. Ger-

many's surface fleet failed in its one attempt to break the blockade (battle of Jutland, 1916). The U-boats also failed to cut Britain's supply lines. The submarines were most effective during 1917, and for a time the British cause was in grave danger. Then, with the development of antisubmarine devices, the United States and Britain reëstablished control of the Atlantic. Triumph was complete before the end of the war, as is indicated by the transportation of 2,000,000 American troops across the ocean without loss.

Besides the campaign on the Atlantic and the struggle along the western front, the United States had small numbers of fighting forces elsewhere. American vessels operated in the Mediterranean, and a few troops were sent to Italy, to help that limping Ally. Another handful went with Allied forces to north Russia in the summer of 1918, under the mistaken theory that such an operation might help the White Russians overthrow the Bolsheviks (who had seized power in November, 1917, and had made peace with Germany). This north Russian intervention lasted until after the armistice, and was closed out in the spring of 1919. Still another contingent of Americans served with Allied forces in Russian Siberia, down to January, 1920. In this case, the main purpose of the United States was to see to it that the Japanese did not seize territory on the Asiatic mainland.

All the operations of World War I proved clearly that the United States was a more efficient fighting power than before. The United States Navy had done well in the war with Spain. It did an even better job in World War I, making good use of its up-to-date equipment and showing a willingness to try new ideas. The army, too, made a good record. Army blunders in the war with Spain had led to a general overhauling, much of which took place while Elihu Root was Secretary of War under Theodore Roosevelt. A feature of this reorganization was the creation of a General Staff. In 1916 there were further changes. The old state militia system, now known as the National Guard, was fitted into the national military pattern. Inefficiency still reigned in many military bureaus; but the mistakes were not to be compared with those of former years.

The new strength of the armed forces was not entirely owing to military improvements. Modern war depends heavily on equipment—on ships and tanks and trucks and airplanes, on the power of infantry and artillery weapons, on the supply of food and clothing and medicine. Starting slowly in 1917, the United States did not make a good showing in all lines of production. American aviators had to use European planes; Americans had to rely on British transports. But by war's end, the United States was in full military production and was turning out more and better goods than any other belligerent. The American manufacturing economy was, clearly, a major factor in the world military picture.

No less interesting was the medical picture. In 1898 the military had failed to make sufficient use of what was generally known about medicine and sanitation. During the next two decades, the armed forces caught up with scientific findings and helped extend medical knowledge. Army research in Cuba aided in the conquest of yellow fever; military application of these findings saved countless lives during the construction of the Panama Canal (1903–14). The army's medical experts were ready for World War I; and their showing was remarkably good. Despite an influenza epidemic in the closing months of the war, only 60,000 men died of disease during the conflict—less than 2 percent of those mobilized. Forty thousand were killed in battle, losses being heavy in the few battles in which Americans were engaged. But improved methods of treatment saved six out of seven of the 200,000 who were wounded, an exceptionally high ratio.

While fighting World War I, the United States also carried on a propaganda campaign. George Creel's Committee on Public Information, which whipped up war excitement in the United States, also functioned in foreign lands. It explained American views in areas controlled by the Allied and Associated Powers. It developed anti-German sentiment in neutral countries. It functioned behind enemy lines. Here the aim was to separate the German government and the German people, to persuade German soldiers and civilians that they could avoid postwar punishment if they overthrew the Kaiser and sought peace. Such propaganda appears to have contributed to the breakdown of morale in the Central Powers, and the collapse of morale hastened the end of the war.

Peace Planning

Before the United States entered the war, the Allies had worked out plans for an old-fashioned peace, with the Central Powers to cede territory and pay a huge indemnity. Wilson stated different objectives in a fourteen-point peace plan of January, 1918. The Central Powers would have to get out of Belgium and restore territory earlier taken from France (Alsace-Lorraine). In general, though, the emphasis was to be on national self-determination rather than on punishment. Subject peoples in the Turkish and Austro-Hungarian empires would have the right of self-government; and those who lived in German colonies would be consulted with reference to their future. A just peace, Wilson indicated, would also establish complete freedom of the seas; would end secret diplomacy; would reduce tariff barriers and provide for disarmament. As the capstone of the structure, there would be a League of Nations, to enforce the just peace and point the way toward a better future.

The Fourteen Points were well received in the United States, by members of both major parties. The reception was not so good in the Allied countries. Wilson seems here to have made a tactical mistake. Back in April, 1917, when the United States entered the war, the President could have insisted on Allied acceptance of his postwar plans. If the Allies refused, Wilson could then have threatened to withhold money or goods or men. Wilson, however, had thrown the full weight of the United States into the cause without exacting any promises. This reduced his bargaining power when he did take up the question of the peace.

When the German offensive of 1918 failed, the men who took control of Germany sought peace on the basis of the Fourteen Points. Britain, though, insisted on dropping the point relating to freedom of the seas. France asked for the inclusion of a reparations clause. That done, the armistice agreement of November, 1918, was concluded.

During the formal peace negotiations that followed, other Wilson points were dropped. The President himself stopped insisting on open diplomacy, and worked out the Versailles Treaty of 1919 in secret meetings with Lloyd George of Great Britain, Clemenceau of France, and Orlando of Italy (these being the Big Four). The point about removing economic barriers was pretty well forgotten. Disarmament was to be confined to the defeated nations. Instead of asking colonial peoples what they wanted, the Big Four assigned colonies to the victors, under the mandate system. Wilson's central demand for national self-determination found expression in the creation of such states as Poland and Czechoslovakia; but the peace settlement put Austrians in Italy, Germans in Czechoslovakia and Poland, Hungarians in Rumania. Japan was given control of Shantung in China. Wilson's original desire was that the German people be treated kindly after they had disposed of the Kaiser. But Germany was required to accept war guilt, and to pay reparations to the Allies; and the Central Powers were not invited to join the League of Nations.

Though disappointed in the Versailles Treaty, Wilson felt it the best that could be obtained. The settlement did recognize the principle of national self-determination; and it did set up the League of Nations. Remaining problems could be threshed out in the League. The President therefore asked the United States Senate to approve the Versailles Treaty and take the United States into the League of Nations (July, 1919). But, to Wilson's sorrow, the Senate rejected the treaty and kept the United States out of the League.

The Senate and the League of Nations

In his first four years as President (1913–17), Wilson had shown himself to be a competent political manager. As he turned his attention to world affairs, he seemed to lose touch with domestic developments. This was important, for Wilson had won reëlection in 1916 by the narrowest of margins. Hence if neglecting home affairs meant losing a bit of ground, it meant losing control of Congress and the country. This is just what happened.

When the United States entered World War I in April, 1917, the declaration of hostilities was supported by both major parties. War measures were supported by Republicans as well as by Democrats. Wilson, however, refused to set up a bipartisan war cabinet; and in the fall of 1918 (just before the armistice) he asked the people for a Democratic Congress. Wilson's Republican opponents seized the opportunity to accuse the Democratic President of playing politics in the midst of war.

The attack apparently swung some votes. More shifted because of general dissatisfaction with the government's wartime controls over economic life. Leadership was involved, too. Will Hays, as chairman of the Republican National Committee, healed wounds within his party, persuaded progressives and conservatives to work in harmony. Success crowned his efforts. The Republicans won the Congressional elections of 1918 and obtained control of both houses of Congress.

This meant, of course, that the peace treaty would go before a Senate controlled by Wilson's opponents. Realizing this, Wilson would have been wise to have allowed the Republicans to share in the peacemaking process. That is, he should have put a leading Republican like Elihu Root or ex-President Taft on the commission to negotiate the Versailles Treaty. Instead, Wilson headed the commission himself, and took with him to Paris his Democratic Secretary of State Robert Lansing and his Democratic adviser Colonel House. One obscure Republican was appointed to the commission, and Wilson made other minor concessions to the Republicans. But it was Wilson's treaty; and, as the Republicans well knew, its acceptance by the Senate would be a Wilsonian and Democratic victory.

Only fifteen of the ninety-five United States Senators (one vacancy) opposed the Versailles Treaty and the League of Nations outright. These were the irreconcilables, many of them progressive Republicans who had long regarded Wilson with distrust (La Follette, Norris, Hiram Johnson, William E. Borah of Idaho). The other eighty Senators favored the treaty and the League. Half of the eighty were Wilson Democrats who wanted the treaty as it stood or with Wilson-approved amendments. John Sharp Williams of Mississippi and Gilbert M. Hitchcock of Nebraska were prominent members of this group. The other forty were Republican reservationists, like Frank B. Kellogg of Minnesota. Though friendly to the League, they insisted on tacking on Republican reservations, so that their party could get some of the credit for the treaty.

With eighty for and fifteen against, victory for the treaty seemed probable. But it was the fifteen irreconcilables who had their way. For this, there were several reasons. One was the position of Henry Cabot Lodge, Republican chairman of the Senate's Foreign Relations Committee. Formerly a League man, Lodge swung his weight to the irreconcilables, partly for political reasons and partly, it seems, because of his personal dislike for Wilson. Another factor in the situation was a popular anti-League campaign, financed by Henry Clay Frick and Andrew W. Mellon. Above all else, the treaty ran into party politics. Republican reservationists who wanted the League felt that, for party reasons, they could not accept the Versailles Treaty as it stood, or with Wilson-sponsored amendments. They therefore joined the irreconcilables in voting against the treaty in those forms. The Wilson Democrats were just as unwilling to yield to their political opponents; so they voted against the treaty with Republican amendments. And in consequence, the treaty and the League were beaten all around.

Hoping to save the League, Wilson appealed to the people. This was an old method of his, and it had worked before. But the President broke down when on his 1919 speaking tour; and he was an ineffective leader in the last year and a half of his presidential term.

He might have failed in any case. For the people, though moderately pro-League, were anything but enthusiastic. During the war Americans had come to feel that beating Germany would save the world for democracy. But when the war was over, citizens of the United States felt let down, disillusioned, tired of crusades. With the war excitement gone, France and England seemed less attractive partners than before. The Kaiser was defeated; but there were new dangers to democracy. The Communists had taken hold of eastern Europe. The Japanese were rising in the Orient. Distress and want haunted the Western world. International problems, apparently, were less simple than they had seemed to George Creel's four-minute men and to those who had written pamphlets for the C.P.I.

While discouraged over international developments, Americans were also busy with domestic affairs. In 1919, when the League issue was under discussion, citizens of the United States were concerned over rising prices, over the rash of strikes, over rumors that there might be revolution in the republic. These matters all tended to turn attention away from the Versailles Treaty and to make the average man indifferent to the fate of the League of Nations.

Campaign of 1920

The lack of interest in the Versailles Treaty was quite apparent in the presidential campaign of 1920. In that contest, the Democrats nominated for President James M. Cox, who had made a progressive record as governor of Ohio; for Vice-President, Franklin D. Roosevelt of New York, who had a magic name and had been an efficient Assistant Secretary of the Navy. Cox and Roosevelt ran on a pro-Wilson, pro-League of Nations platform. Although they campaigned aggressively, they won little backing. The voters seemed tired of Wilson, tired of the Democrats, tired of the talk about the peace treaty and the League.

If Theodore Roosevelt had been alive, he would probably have been the Republican presidential nominee in 1920. His death in 1919 left the field wide open. After some jockeying, the political managers arranged in a smoke-filled room to give the nomination to Senator Warren G. Harding of Ohio. The second place on the ticket went to Governor Calvin Coolidge of Massachusetts, who had achieved some notice for opposing a Boston police strike.

Harding staged a quiet ("front porch") campaign, quite in the McKinley tradition. His Republican managers stressed opposition to the Wilsonian war controls and asked for a "return to normalcy." On the League, the Republicans straddled. Harding had an anti-League, Coolidge a pro-League record. Both made confusing statements during the campaign; and their supporters added to the general uncertainty. Some Republicans, including Hiram Johnson, were sure that Harding was anti-League. Others, like Taft and Herbert Hoover, announced that they considered the Republican candidate pro-League. Take your choice.

The campaign of 1920 ended with a smashing victory for Harding and Coolidge; the Republicans returned to power after eight years on the outside. Most League supporters found the result disheartening. They hastened to state, however, that the election really proved nothing, in view of Republican hedging on the League question. But that

conclusion was not altogether right. If the citizens of the United
States had really wanted the League of Nations, and had considered
the issue important, they would have gone to Cox. The Harding victory did not show that Americans hated the League; but it did indicate that they did not take the matter very seriously.

Still a World Power

When Harding was sworn in as Presi-
dent, in March, 1921, the League issue was dead in the United States.
A few Wilsonians did keep up the fight; but only a few. Most of the
politicians who had favored the League of Nations in 1919–20 conceded defeat and turned to other things.

Rejection of the Versailles Treaty by the Senate meant that the
government of the United States would not form close political relations with the major European powers. Much the same decision was
made when other issues came to the fore. Wilson proposed, and the
Senate rejected, an Anglo-French-American alliance. The Senators
also refused to consider having the United States take mandate control
over Armenia; and they would not approve of the United States'
joining the World Court (Permanent Court of International Justice),
even though this was favored by Wilson and his three Republican
successors.

For all of this, the American republic was not abandoning its world
power position. For some time after 1920 the United States would
steer clear of alliances and would be suspicious of international organizations. But the United States would remain a great military nation and, on the economic side, would push outward more vigorously
than before.

Part III

Contemporary America
(Since 1919)

 *The period since World War I has brought a succession of crises. After a decade of prosperity in the 1920's there were ten desperate years of depression (1929–39), during which the whole American economy seemed to be on trial. Then came a half-dozen years of American involvement in global war. The collapse of Germany and Japan brought an uneasy peace, featured by a "cold war" between the United States and Soviet Russia.*

At mid-century, the United States was the wealthiest nation that the world had ever known. Most Americans enjoyed a high standard of living, and there were indications that it would be higher still. But, living in a troubled world, many citizens found it difficult to avoid a feeling of confusion and uncertainty. In three and a half centuries, Americans had accomplished a great deal. Plainly, however, much more remained to be done.

13

Corporate Business

The American Economy

Depression and war divided the years after World War I into three parts. From 1919 to 1929 life seemed to be resuming many of its nineteenth-century patterns. But under the surface new forces were gathering. After the stock market crash of 1929, these welled up in a tidal wave of disorganization and confusion in the depression of the 1930's. The outbreak of World War II in 1939 inaugurated a third period, which covered the war (1939–45) and its aftermath.

Developments in the third period (after 1939) seemed to reëstablish the pattern of ordered prosperity. Yet Americans well knew that their world had changed. All ranks of society now saw what a handful of intellectuals had noted in the 1920's—the many subtle problems of urban life, the general insecurity associated with an industrial economy, the all-pervading uncertainty as to social goals and directions.

Fearful of a world that nobody really understood, men and women groped for certainty rather than for new adventure. College graduates came to hope for comfortable and secure lives rather than the opportunity to get rich. Established businessmen accepted security at the expense of both salary and profits. And workers, enjoying the highest standard of living in history, demanded the additional assurances of state support in old age and adversity. Fear of atom bombs merely symbolized the deeper fear of the ruthless impersonality of an urban industrial society.

The Business Cycle

The Western world had long been disturbed by the ups and downs of the business cycle. As problems became increasingly acute after World War I, citizens sought a major economic philosophy that would explain the perplexing trends. The result was a sweeping acceptance of the policies, if not all the reasoning, of the British economist John Maynard Keynes (later Lord Keynes).

Immediately after the armistice in November, 1918, there was a sharp upswing in the American economy. Then came a collapse, caused mainly by panicky overbuying of inventories (stocks of material for manufacture or sale). After 1921, the United States settled down to seven relatively prosperous years. Real per capita income rose about 13 percent from 1923 to 1929. There was suffering because of technological unemployment, and because of depression in farm areas and in a few declining industries. Most Americans, however, shared in the gains.

In contrast with earlier booms, the upswing after 1923 did not result in efforts to expand production and transportation faster than the savings of the country would allow. Everything in the productive area of the economy seemed to stay in fairly even balance. Wholesale prices and long-term interest rates scarcely rose. Wages remained steady; and until 1927 there was no great boom in the stock market.

Then came peculiar developments. Beginning in 1927, there was a slowing down of activity in fields that had done much to support prosperity: building construction, automobile sales, foreign lending. Yet simultaneously the stock market boomed. Had a depression come in 1927, it might have been moderate. The unsound stock market boom of 1927–29 led ultimately to more serious difficulties. In earlier decades, unstable prosperity had been prolonged by land booms. Now, speculation in stocks did the same thing.

Meantime, the changing character of the American economy was influencing the business cycle. In the first quarter of the twentieth century, such products as automobiles, radios, and electric refrigerators had become increasingly important. These new consumers' goods had an indefinite length of life. If times were good, householders would buy new models, this process being easier because of the new installment-purchase plans. If times were bad, the old car or household appliance could be repaired and kept in use. All of which meant that the advent of depression would cut production (and employment) more than in earlier periods. Once begun, the downward spiral was bound to affect all commodities. Hence heavy consumer buying of durable goods had introduced a highly explosive element into the American economy.

The depression that set in after the stock market crash of 1929 was complicated and increased by a host of European difficulties. The cost of World War I and the maze of debts and reparations claims had never been adjusted in a way that would permit a general return to prosperity. The whole Old World economy was held up in the 1920's by American loans—that is, by foreign bond issues floated on Wall Street and sold to private American investors. When the New York stock market crash of 1929 stopped the flow of money from America to Europe, Old World nations suspended international debt payments. This in turn upset trade relations; and by the middle of 1932 the entire Western world was in a desperate economic situation.

A Keynesian Revolution

At this juncture Lord Keynes gained new followers. This British economist saw the problem in classical economic terms, in the relationship between new investment and savings. If savings were invested in new labor-employing ventures, prosperity was possible. If this investment lagged behind savings, there would be unemployment and depression. In such a situation, the government could and should redress the balance by investing in public works.

Putting it another way: Keynes felt that the poor (who had to spend their income) received too little, and that the rich (who could save) received too much. Thus savings accumulated, instead of going into new labor-employing ventures. The way out, said Keynes, was to get rid of the savings of the rich by heavy taxation of upper-bracket income. The proceeds could then be distributed among the poor as payments for relief or for work on government construction projects. Nor did Keynes stop there. Government spending, he felt, would stimulate business activity in general. It would therefore encourage private capitalists to invest what savings they retained in new ventures, which would mean more jobs.

Closely related to these points was the belief that the national debt could be used as an economic stabilizer. During depression, the government could resort to deficit financing—increase the debt and spend extra money on relief and public works employment. During prosperity, the debt could be paid off by higher taxation. In sum, the economy could be stabilized by proper government financial policies.

Keynes was, of course, merely providing a theory that fitted the practical situation. In spite of the old conviction that revenue and expenditures should be roughly equal, government budgets of the 1930's were unbalanced all over the world. President Herbert Hoover (1929–33) deplored deficits, but had them just the same. His successor Franklin D. Roosevelt (1933–45) was less bothered by mounting governmental debts; and his advisers gradually taught him the Keynesian language. But neither F. D. R. nor his chief lieutenants ever entirely approved of the new doctrines.

Nor were results spectacular. In spite of large-scale government spending, unemployment and economic stagnation lasted for a full decade (1929–39). Only with the outbreak of World War II (1939–45) did full employment and prosperity return.

But then came victory for the advocates of Keynesian views. World War II left the United States with what an earlier generation would have regarded as a managed economy. Price supports for farm commodities were continued from the prewar depression. In addition, the whole level of federal government spending for defense, European recovery, veterans' benefits and administration was very high—so high that prosperity appeared to depend more on government policies than on those of any segment of business.

Scarcely realizing it, most American legislators had now accepted the major tenet of Keynes: that government financial policy could regulate the economy. Many American politicians and economists deplored the trend; but Keynesianism had become orthodoxy in the British Empire and Europe and an accepted fact in the United States.

Without admitting conversion to the new doctrines, the United States Congress applied them when an economic recession threatened in 1949. The House and Senate increased appropriations, unbalancing the budget by a record peacetime sum. Spurred by the promise of federal outlays exceeding taxes by $5,000,000,000, business and the stock market started upward.

Such a policy of acquiring debt might profoundly alter the nature of capitalism in the United States. But it might also help the nation avoid the widespread unemployment and deep depression which had plagued Americans in the decade before World War II. What was more, the trend seemed to commit the American republic to an active role in international affairs. Government spending on public works within the United States might compete with private business. There was no such competition when it came to spending on armaments and on loans or gifts to foreign countries. There was, therefore, an increasing preference for such expenditures, which linked American prosperity more and more to the world economy. American planners would have to think in global terms; the comfortable isolation of the nineteenth century was gone for good.

The Quest for Normalcy

The new age of government subsidies, Marshall Plans, and atom bombs was not anticipated by the business and political leaders of 1919. Like men in all ages, they looked back to what seemed a pleasant bygone day and strove to recapture the past.

The first step in that direction was the termination of World War I price controls, priorities, and contracts. The United States Army was reduced to a low peacetime level within a year; and Congress sharply cut back naval construction plans. Government employment agencies were closed; and the Transportation Act of 1920 ended government administration of the railroads. It could be said, therefore, that save for shipping and aviation, World War I brought few changes in the size or functions of the national government, or in its relations with business. In 1914 there had been 485,000 federal civilian employees; in 1922 there were only 530,000.

The year and a half after the armistice saw a world-wide scarcity in manufactured goods and in certain raw materials. To a degree that is hard to understand, businessmen bid against each other for commodities, piling up inventories, placing duplicate orders, and in general acting as though high prices and shortages would continue indefinitely.

They should have known better. For one thing, the fantastically high exports of 1914–19 were bound to decline. With the fighting over, Europe came back into normal production. As the shipping crisis eased, European countries could buy from such distant areas as Australia and Argentina as easily as from the United States. At the same time, the credit situation was taking a turn for the worse. Although the United States Treasury did lend the Allies nearly $2,000,-000,000 in 1919, such government operations were drawing to a close. European countries, already deeply in debt, were reluctant to float more long-term loans on Wall Street. American exports in 1920 were therefore carried by banks on short-term loans. As bank reserves dipped toward the legal minimum in the summer of that year, the process of lending began to slacken. The prices broke suddenly.

The resulting stock market panic and depression of 1921 hit manufacturers and farmers alike. But the very rapidity of the price break raised real wages; and the physical volume of American consumer purchases kept on expanding. Business confidence returned by 1922, and business leaders congratulated themselves on the return of "normalcy." Trade was increasing. Except for service on the war debt, government expenditures were not much above their prewar level. Trade unionism was on the wane, the Republicans were in power, and the foreign outlook was promising.

Finance in the Golden Twenties

Despite appearances, the leaders of the 1920's could not reënact the "good old days." Nowhere was this more noticeable than in banking and in the stock market. The Liberty Loan drives had put securities in the hands of many people who had never before purchased stocks or bonds. When patriotic ardor cooled, many of these investors decided to exchange their government bonds for something paying a higher rate of interest and offering more chance of a rise in value. This situation helped create the best market for securities in the world's history. Before World War I, the yearly market for stocks and bonds in the United States rarely exceeded $2,000,000,-000. By 1929 the annual sales of corporate securities stood at five times that figure.

The desire of American investors for new issues had unfortunate repercussions on business and banking. Commercial banks hastened to follow the lead of the Chase and National City banks, New York institutions which had established security-selling affiliates before World War I. Young salesmen from these agencies and from countless brokerage firms successfully sold securities from door to door in the more prosperous neighborhoods. As sales mounted, dealers ran short of good domestic issues representing solid capital investment. They then resorted to highly speculative stocks and weak foreign bonds.

Ambitious financiers were quick to see the possibilities of such an apparently insatiable demand. The result was the meteoric rise of the pyramided holding company. This corporate device depended on the fact that one could control a corporation with a majority or less of the voting stock. Thus a first-level holding company (B) could control an operating company (A) by owning half A's stock. A second-level holding company (C) could control B by buying half its stock. Company C could then control A with an investment equal to only one-quarter of the value of A's stock.

That was only the beginning. The process went on through five or six levels of holding companies, with the amount needed for control of the whole structure growing ever smaller. Using bank loans, bond issues, and nonvoting stock as well, the smart operator could control a billion-dollar railroad or public utility empire with an investment of a few hundred thousand dollars. The whole process depended on the willingness of the public to buy the securities of the intermediate companies; and in the 1920's investors fought for the privilege.

The investment trust also served to put corporate controls into the hands of financial operators. Small buyers who could not study the market themselves turned their savings over to investment trusts. By pooling the savings of many citizens, these trusts had large sums at their disposal and could secure control of large corporations. Sometimes the power was used for the benefit of the general stockholder, sometimes to further the aims of insiders. The results would become apparent during the depression; but while the boom lasted, holding companies and investment trusts were market favorites. And since no outsider could tell what their stocks were really worth, only the blue sky seemed to be the limit.

Meanwhile, big business was expanding operations at a moderate rate. Traditionally, new working capital for most companies had been obtained through bank loans. Now practice changed, because of the ease of raising money by issuing securities. The banks themselves encouraged and participated in the trend; and bank assets shifted from thirty- to sixty-day commercial paper to "demand loans" backed by stock. Few dreamed that all stocks would fall so fast that the banks would be unable to cover their largest loans.

Although urban banks expanded their business in the flush days of the 1920's, the banks in depressed farm regions had hard sledding. In 1921 there were about 10,000 banks in the Federal Reserve System and twice that many state banks on the outside. By 1929 failures and mergers had reduced the latter group by more than 20 percent; and many of those that survived were in weak condition. A large number of rural banks would go down after 1929, their failures being associated with advances made on nonliquid, declining agricultural assets. These country banks were joined in failure by city institutions that had made large, uncollectable loans on stocks.

Growing Industries

Over the whole span of history down to the nineteenth century, agriculture, handicrafts, and trade gave individuals a fair degree of stability in expectations. Industrialism, by contrast, has meant continuous change, and has offered lasting security to neither manufacturer nor financier nor employee. Each manufacturer competes with all others for the consumer's dollar. Technological changes produce a continuous assault upon apparently secure positions. In the best times of peace and prosperity, some industries gain greatly in size and profits while others languish and die.

In the period between the world wars, automobiles and associated industries (oil, rubber, glass, concrete) forged ahead in an amazing fashion. American civilization was readjusted to the needs, physical and cultural, of automotive transportation. Far behind, but still important in their growth, were electrical appliances for home and factory, chemicals, and processed foods.

World War II did not change these trends. Save for ships and munitions, war needed the same types of goods as were produced for the peacetime economy. Automobile companies turned from passenger cars to airplanes, tanks, and other military vehicles. Electrical companies developed new electronic devices, many of which would be useful in peace. The chemical industry produced munitions and expanded its production of plastics and synthetic fabrics. Food manufacturers found new methods of processing. And when peace came in 1945, the prewar industrial leaders resumed their growth on a still larger scale.

The auto industry had begun to change American life in the years before World War I; but the central period of the automotive revolution was 1919–29. At the end of the First World War there was one passenger car for every sixteen people. A decade later there was one for every six. With some crowding, all Americans in 1929 could have ridden simultaneously in automobiles. (Often, on Sundays around the big cities, it seemed as though they were trying to do so.) Meanwhile, trucks increased fourfold and by 1929 were nearly half again as numerous as all types of railroad cars.

This great sales expansion in autos and other expensive durable goods was made possible by general use of installment credit. Families with middle incomes cut down on food and clothing to keep up payments on new or used cars. But once the installment market had been thoroughly exploited (as in the late 1920's), a limit to easy expansion had been reached. And the depression after 1929 would bring wholesale defaults.

The weaker automobile companies were unable to endure the collapse of sales after the stock market broke in 1929. By 1932 only the big firms remained. The industry had settled into a fairly stable competitive pattern, with General Motors the largest concern and Ford and Chrysler the leading competitors. These three companies steadily produced 80 to 90 percent of all passenger cars. The remaining business was divided among a half-dozen smaller concerns.

Some of the smaller firms would have gone down if General Motors, Ford, or Chrysler had set out to eliminate competition by price wars similar to those of Standard Oil in the 1870's. But if that had been done, the Antitrust Division of the Department of Justice might have prevented the victors from reaping the full reward of conquest. Consequently, a policy of live-and-let-live was pursued by the managers of the big companies.

Although the mechanical features of automobiles were fairly uniform, competition was active in styles and advertising. That is, differences were more aesthetic, rhetorical, and sentimental than physical. Up to 1925 all patents had been pooled. From then on companies controlled the results of their own research. It was difficult, however, to keep trade secrets in a mass production industry where all novelties had to be thoroughly tested before application. What was more, it was so costly to introduce important changes in machinery that no company sought any major advantage from technologic advance. And in any case, the pioneer era of fundamental development was over by the 1930's. The eight-cylinder, enclosed car with a rigid steel top, four-wheel brakes, and low-pressure tires was altered only in minor details from then on until after the middle of the century.

Representing 8 percent of the value of all finished commodities in 1929, the manufacture of automobiles had become the leading American industry; and Detroit, the auto center, had become one of the major manufacturing cities of the nation. But car manufacture was only one aspect of the auto age. The new machines transformed street and highway construction, relocated shopping and residential areas, consolidated schools, affected advertising, recreational activities, and a host of service industries. America had become a nation of concrete highways and roadside markets and eating places.

Not until World War II did Americans realize how much their world had changed. Then, when rubber and other shortages forced the rationing of gasoline, the whole pattern of American life was thrown out of adjustment. Millions of employees could reach their jobs only by automobile. Still larger numbers found that almost all their recreation required the use of a car. City deliveries and short-haul freight traveled chiefly by truck. Buses provided most urban passenger transportation and took rural children to school. Airplane travel was essential to the business of winning the war. King Cotton had never attained the imperial control of King Gasoline; and even the tightest restrictions could reduce gasoline consumption no more than a third.

Household electrical equipment joined the automobile in the expanding world of individual possessions. The vacuum cleaners, electric heaters, and electric irons of pre-World War I days were just a slight forerunner of the later flood of costly electrical appliances. Radios, electric phonographs, refrigerators, and washing machines came by the 1930's to represent 10 per cent of all consumer expenditures for durable goods. The radio led the group in sales. By World War II nearly every family had at least one radio; and the slightest rumor (true or false) could be spread in a few minutes from the Atlantic coastal cities to prairie farms and mountain ranches.

Down to 1914 Westinghouse and General Electric—the dominant electrical equipment companies—had dealt largely with commercial users. By the 1930's, every housewife knew these names. By then, however, the dual monopoly of the two leaders in heavy electrical machinery had given way to competition in the field of household gadgets. Since it took relatively little capital to manufacture radios, dozens of small companies tried their luck. Refrigerators and the other large machines fitted the pattern of the automobile industry; hence subsidiaries of the motor firms went into production. This tended to knit the manufacturers of the new durable consumers' goods together into what might be called a major industrial group, producing everything from table radios to limousines. Certainly all companies within the group competed with each other for the same consumer dollar. A new television set bought from General Electric probably postponed the purchase of a new car from General Motors.

The growth of the chemical industry was also geared to the new consumer economy. American chemical firms had begun to grow rapidly in the late nineteenth century. Still greater expansion came with the seizure of the German patents during World War I and the rise of synthetic fibers and plastics in the postwar years. Allied Chemical and Dye, Union Carbide, and Du Pont led in the threefold increase of chemical production between 1914 and 1939.

Of all the new products, rayon was probably the most important. This synthetic was first used in women's wear. Later it was tried elsewhere, as in cords for automobile tires. As it grew, the rayon industry struck heavy blows against domestic cotton and Japanese silk. The important addition of nylon in the 1940's heralded the day when synthetic fibers, made with just the qualities desired, might replace natural threads and yarns. This would pose problems for the southern cotton states.

The other major area of industry that grew phenomenally from 1919 to 1949 was processed food. Flour and packed meats, of course, are types of manufactured food products as old as America. The nineteenth century added canned goods and prepared cereals; the twentieth, dehydrated and frozen products.

The upward trend in food manufacture after 1919 depended on more than new processes. Small urban families wanted to avoid cooking. They were also being educated to eat more fruits and vegetables. Food processors took great pains to capture this market for millions of little orders of out-of-season commodities. Long-distance shipments (even by air), fancy packaging, and brand advertising all played a part. Canners offered a wider variety and better quality. And after the early 1930's frozen foods of all kinds offered the upper-income family a variegated menu that needed no preparation beyond heating.

There was sharp competition in the food industry; but there was combination, too. Some was at the retail end, as in the growth of the great food chains like the A & P (the Great Atlantic and Pacific Tea Company). Mergers at the producing end resulted in the creation of such giants as General Foods, which spread across many fields.

Declining Industries

Textiles, coal, and general construction were principal areas of industrial decline between the world wars. Some textile manufacturers were hit by the shift from cotton and silk to rayon. All were affected by the declining bulk in men's and (particularly) women's clothing. This was partly the consequence of urban living and improved heating, partly a matter of style. The Gibson girl of the Theodore Roosevelt era wore several wool or cotton petti-

coats, long underwear, a slip, a corset, and other paraphernalia, total-
ing three to five pounds of textiles. The undergarments of the young
woman of the Franklin D. Roosevelt era, on the other hand, represented only a few ounces of material. As a result, there was a steady
readjustment in the textile industry that depressed both wages and
profits.

Seeking a way out, some factory managers shifted location. Textile
factories were moved from New England to the South and from New
York and Philadelphia to nearby coal areas where they could employ
miners' wives and daughters. But the cutting and stitching of outer
garments remained a city industry, centered in New York.

The coal industry suffered most from increased efficiency in fuel
utilization. Electric power stations cut their use of coal per kilowatt-
hour by half in the decade following World War I. In addition, other
sources of heat and power were substituted for coal. Homeowners
shifted from coal to oil or gas furnaces. Some factories switched from
coal to hydroelectric energy (water power). Petroleum products were
even more important, fuel oil superseding coal for heating and hauling. In the middle 1940's the steam railroads—the backbone of the
demand in the coal industry—began a rapid conversion to oil-burning
Diesel engines. By 1949 one major southern road operated no coal-
burning engines. Anthracite and bituminous coal production in 1947
was about the same as in 1920, whereas hydro-, oil- and gas-generated
electric power had more than doubled, and oil production had
quadrupled.

Between the wars, building construction spurted for a decade, then
lapsed into a dozen years of low activity. For the period as a whole
the industry consumed only about 3 percent of the national income
as against 7 or 8 percent in the late nineteenth and early twentieth
centuries. Quite apart from depression, a slower rate of physical expansion and restricted immigration limited the demand for new building. And although many Americans were poorly housed, national,
state, and local governments were reluctant to enter this field.

During the depression years of the 1930's, the United States government helped owners save and repair their homes; but Franklin D.
Roosevelt's New Deal was less active in housing than in many other

fields. Most of the government-financed World War II housing construction (1939–45) was of an emergency and temporary nature. Hence, after a decade and a half of lagging activity, Americans ran into a severe housing shortage in the postwar years. Since times were good in the late 1940's, private building boomed. Prices were high, but credit was available to most middle-class citizens. Banks and loan companies did an active business; and the United States government underwrote many loans, especially for veterans. It seemed likely that the construction boom would last for many years.

A New Pattern of Transportation

Highways, automobiles, trucks, and airplanes were added to railroads as basic elements in the transportation system. The mileage of surfaced roads increased more than fourfold between 1919 and 1949. Four-lane concrete highways, sometimes having over- and under-passes for crossroads, connected metropolitan centers. Cities from New York to Los Angeles built throughways to their central sections; and outlying parkways avoided the suburban towns. The speed of motor traffic on such routes nearly equaled that of fast passenger trains, and trucks easily outdistanced slow freights. Still more important was the fact that cars could go to places never served by the rail networks. By mid-century, hard-surfaced roads were penetrating the tiniest villages, were connecting the most isolated mountain farms with the whole outside world.

Government-owned, the new highways and byways were built and maintained with income from license and gasoline taxes. The need for work relief during the depression stimulated construction during the 1930's. World War II was an interruption; but large-scale federal, state, and local building was resumed immediately after the cessation of hostilities. The average rate for the whole period was about $1,000,-000,000 a year. Since no private industry steadily attracted capital in such quantities, it could be said that gasoline transportation socialized the most important single segment of American investment.

Aviation also looked to the government. Without public airports, beacons, and mail subsidies, civilian flying would have remained a rich man's sport. Private companies paid rent for the use of airport facilities, and all private plane owners paid license fees. But the fact remained that the two new transportation devices of the twentieth century were closely tied to government spending.

American commercial aviation for mail and passengers began at the end of World War I. It grew very slowly until the Air Mail Commerce Acts (1925–26) provided for the general granting of mail contracts on a subsidy basis. Soon after that, in 1927, Charles A. Lindbergh's flight from New York to Paris increased public confidence in air travel. Thereafter air-line transportation boomed; and at the end of the 1920's nearly fifty companies were flying 30,000 miles of route.

Like other luxury services, air transportation suffered heavily in the depression. In addition, the air lines had to contend with shifting government policies. A Republican-sponsored statute of 1930 gave the Postmaster General broad powers over the creation of air-mail routes and the granting of postal subsidies. Four years later the Democrats accused favored lines of corrupt political bargains and canceled all contracts. The army was then called in to fly the mails. Unaccustomed to night and instrument flying, and given no time to plan operations, the military aviators suffered heavy losses in the three months that followed. Then, after the private companies had dropped certain officials, the Post Office Department awarded new mail contracts.

In response to the need for permanent arrangements, Congress in 1938 passed a new Civil Aeronautics Act. This vested regulatory powers in a six-man Civil Aeronautics Board; and mail rates were to be set by negotiation. Meantime, Congress was increasing the authority of the Interstate Commerce Commission. Originally designed for railroad regulation, the I.C.C. had been given supervisory power over pipe lines and express companies. Later (notably in the Motor Carrier Act of 1935), the Commission's jurisdiction was extended to cover bus lines, interstate truckers, and certain water carriers. Thus all long-haul transportation was under the jurisdiction of government commissions.

World War II brought a boom in commercial aviation. The rush of war business pushed passenger travel to heights scarcely dreamed of in the 1930's. Frantic study and experiments with bomber designs also improved transport planes; and the trend toward air travel continued after the war. Although air passenger travel had fallen to half its wartime peak two years after World War II, the total was still six times that of 1940. Schedules for coast-to-coast flights reached a 300-mile-per-hour average, and fares dropped to approximately the level for Pullman travel. As a result, passenger-miles reached 15 percent of the railroad total. At the same time, air freight and express, insignificant before World War II, became a major part of the business.

In the face of auto and air competition, the railroads ceased to expand as rapidly as the rest of the economy. Trucks made small branch rail lines unprofitable, and when regulatory authorities would permit, these tracks were torn up or abandoned. For the first time in a century, no important new routes were opened.

Still, there was progress. Main-line track was improved and extended to accommodate more and faster traffic. Increase in speed went hand in hand with economies in operation. By the end of World War II, the railroads were doing half again as much business as in 1920 with a third fewer employees. In the same period, passenger-miles declined slightly, and the trend was continuing downward. Freight, however, had increased 60 percent, and operating revenues had grown about a third. The railroads were less important than formerly in the nation's economic life; but there was no reason to believe that they would soon be superseded for long-haul freight and many types of passenger business.

All through this period, railroad policies were under close government supervision. The lines, however, were owned and run by private interests. The government took over during World War I; and some believed that this would set the pattern for the future. A Plumb Plan, for continued government operation, was endorsed by the railway brotherhoods. Congress, however, rejected the Plumb Plan and returned the railroads to private ownership (Transportation Act of 1920). When the owners ran into trouble during the depression, the government helped by extending loans through the Reconstruction Finance Corporation (RFC). But the railroads remained in private hands, through the depression and through World War II.

Opposition to government ownership was seen in ocean shipping, too. Total tonnage for the American merchant marine engaged in foreign trade climbed from 1,000,000 tons at the outbreak of World

War I to eleven times that much in 1921. Most of the new vessels were government-owned, built in connection with the wartime effort to construct a "bridge to France." Unfortunately, the ship construction program had stressed quantity rather than quality; American ships were slow by comparison with their European competitors. Vessels owned in the United States did carry nearly half the American foreign trade of 1920, as against less than 10 percent six years earlier. But then came reversals, and the figure dropped to about one-third.

Being devoted to private enterprise, those who controlled Congress after World War I decided to sell the government vessels to private owners (Jones Act of 1920). Sales were at bargain rates, credit was extended liberally, purchasers were given special tax consideration. Even so, the ships moved slowly, and a tenth were never sold at all. Raising postal subsidies (1928) did not help materially, and in 1936 Congress found it necessary to direct the new United States Maritime Commission to hand out direct subsidies for construction and operation.

A survey made at that time showed that the American merchant marine was in sad shape. American shippers did well enough where they enjoyed a monopolistic position—in the Great Lakes ore trade and in coastwise shipping, including commerce between the east and west coasts, through the Panama Canal. But in competitive areas America lagged far behind.

Had it been an economic matter only, the United States might have given up the struggle. Shipping, however, has military as well as commercial value. Strategic considerations played a part in the passage of the Merchant Marine Act of 1936; and with the coming of World War II the United States again turned to construction on a large scale. As a result, the American republic emerged from the war with the largest ocean-going merchant fleet in the world (over 25,000,000 gross tons). Yet there was little evidence that Americans had learned how to fit their vessels into an efficient peacetime economy.

The Role of Technology

The changing place of various economic activities in American life depended largely on advances in technology. The automobile did not revolutionize transportation until it was mechanically perfected to a point of cheapness and dependability. The new position of the chemical, electrical, and food industries obviously reflected scientific and engineering progress. Technology gave new goods to the consumer; and it altered the means of production and distribution.

On the whole, the tendency was toward larger and larger plants. As an example, the post-World War I continuous strip mill for the manufacture of sheet steel was so large that one unit cost at least $50,000,000. One-piece-stamping machines for automobile bodies were similarly gigantic.

Nevertheless, the trend was not all in one direction. Concrete highways, pipe and power lines divorced plants from the need to be near coal-carrying railroads; and in some industries, decentralization of operations became possible and profitable. Technology helped here, too, by enabling officials to manage many plants from one central office. The railroad, telegraph, and telephone all figured in this type of business empire; so did the punch card, the teletype, telephotos, and microfilm. The top executives could be close to the financial and trade resources of New York or Chicago, whereas the plants were scattered through low-cost rural areas.

Changing technology usually altered the demand for labor. New machines threw men out of work in one industry and created opportunities elsewhere. The adjustment was far from automatic. Often the displaced worker had the wrong skills or experience for the new type of job. Similarly, it was hard for the unemployed head of a family in New York to take advantage of opportunities in California. An active federal employment service would have helped; but prejudice against federal power and government activity stood in the way. Technological unemployment therefore remained a definite social problem.

Business and the Market

Although improved technology made bigness economical and efficient, better control of the market remained the strongest incentive to merger and growth. By 1929, less than 1000 companies did a majority of the nation's business in manufacturing, transportation, and finance. In manufacturing and transportation, a bare 200 accounted for half the output. And in both prosperity and depression, the big firms continued to grow faster than the small.

Plenty of middle-sized and small concerns remained in the field. There were no less than 200,000 manufacturing companies in 1920, and half again that many three decades later. A census of 1939 showed that 97 percent of these companies had less than 250 employees. This 97 percent employed less than half the workers engaged in industrial pursuits and turned out less than a third of the product.

Small enterprise was most successful in trade and service. There little capital was needed; and the energy, frugality, and personal appeal of the owner-manager could compensate for the operating economies of the big distributor. The tiniest neighborhood shops in the poorest districts were able to compete with department stores and chains. Furthermore, an increasing emphasis on service opened new fields for small business (catering, diaper service, radio repair).

In the nineteenth century, it had been generally assumed that prices should be set in a free market, and that price warfare was the heart of the competitive system. After 1900 this view gradually gave way to the much older—indeed, medieval—doctrine of a just price based on costs and a reasonable profit.

The shift away from price competition was approved and encouraged by the trade associations. There were a thousand-odd of these, one or more for each industry. The trade associations became strong in World War I, when they helped Bernard Baruch's War Industries Board regulate production. After the war, the trade associations tried to maintain uniform prices by exchange of information among member firms. This practice, known as open price policy, was endorsed by Secretary of Commerce Herbert Hoover (1921–28), and was not wholly condemned by the United States Supreme Court.

Being organized on a voluntary basis, the trade associations could not require their members to work together. After 1929, therefore, the depression brought desperate price cutting in competitive lines of business. This convinced many business leaders that something stronger than open price policy was needed to protect profits. The Franklin D. Roosevelt administration responded with the National Industrial Recovery Act of 1933, which permitted agreements for uni-

form prices (the NRA codes). Although the Supreme Court killed
the NRA in 1935, the price-maintenance idea remained important.
Many states passed "fair practice" statutes, designed to maintain
prices Congress extended the state systems under certain conditions
to trademarked articles in interstate commerce (Robinson-Patman
Act, 1936, and Miller-Tydings Act, 1937).

The biggest businesses needed neither trade associations nor acts of
Congress for regulation of prices. In industries like steel, motors, glass,
and cigarettes—where a few companies turned out most of the product
—prices were maintained by informal agreements. A leading company
set prices, and the others followed, knowing that warfare would be
futile and self-destructive. Or a few executives met informally and
agreed on price policies. Such arrangements proved effective even in
the depression. In industries dominated by a few firms price declines
rarely exceeded 20 percent. In other fields the drop was sometimes
twice that much, or even more.

Was it wise to hold up prices? Had there been no effort to do so,
production might have been maintained during the depression at low
wages and prices. To maintain prices and pay union wages it was
necessary to cut production—which meant reducing employment.
Rigid price policies therefore tended to shift the major force of depression from prices to unemployment.

Depression and war brought the government into the picture, adding the rigidities of government supports and regulation to the existing rigidities of union wages and controlled prices. How this would
all work out was difficult to tell at the beginning of the 1950's. It was
plain, however, that the American economy was not likely to move
back toward old-fashioned price competition.

Advertising

In 1900 total advertising outlays in the
United States were less than $100,000,000. By 1929 they had risen
to more than ten times that figure. After a dip during the depression,
the upward movement was resumed; and the nation's annual advertising bill was $2,000,000,000 during the boom that followed World
War II.

Everybody advertised, both big companies and small. The giants came out better in the deal. An advertising budget that was moderate for a big firm would be ruinous for one a tenth that large. And big business used advertising both to protect its share of the market and to prevent interlopers from invading the field.

In advertising as in other matters, the automobile was a major force. Even before World War I the automobile joined drugs, cosmetics, and liquor as a mainstay of national periodical revenue. Mass driving also gave a new importance to outdoor displays; and auto sales demonstrated beyond question the business value of advertising expensive consumers' goods. Manufacturers of household appliances took the hint.

As business mounted, advertising agencies improved their techniques. Their experts studied psychology and learned the art of appealing to the emotions. George Creel's C.P.I. taught them a great deal; and they picked up more as they experimented with new methods. No longer was the citizen urged to buy mouthwash because it was a good product; rather he was told that bad breath might cost him his girl or his job. Talented artists and photographers were hired to supply illustrations. Consumer buying habits were studied; and after 1913 periodicals were forced to allow regular audits of their circulation.

From 1922 on, the radio was the important new element in advertising. Money spent on broadcasts was small until 1929, perhaps $25,000,000 a year. Then, during the depression, radio advertising increased while expenditures for other media fell to about half their former level. In 1943, when advertising as a whole had regained its pre-depression position, radio advertising stood at eight times the 1929 figure.

Public-relations and institutional advertising also assumed new importance during and after World War I. Busy with war production, many companies had little to sell to the general public from 1917 to 1919. It seemed wise, however, to insure future markets by advertising the social utility of the product. Consequently, United States Steel publicized the contribution of steel to American welfare. When the war was over, some large companies found that it paid to continue this tactic.

Much of the advertising designed to create favorable public opinion took the form of articles and news releases. Advertising agencies kept newspapers supplied with items showing their client's company or industry in a favorable light. Some editors threw this material into the wastebasket. Others, knowing that their papers needed advertising, published some of the releases. A public relations expert wrote that on a given morning in the 1920's he could trace to an institutional source 90 percent of the news on the front page of a leading New York paper. Again, many editors toned down or suppressed news that might offend their principal advertisers. ("It is neither fair nor businesslike to take a man's money for an advertisement," said an advertising agent, "and then use the reading columns of the paper to destroy the value of his investment.") Under such guidance, many journals became virtual branches of the public relations offices of business firms.

Managerial Enterprise

The new interest in public relations was only one indication of the changing position of the large business corporation. While public relations officers were selling big business to the public, management was taking control of corporations away from the owners. In practically all of the 600 companies that by 1940 carried on a majority of American corporate business transactions, 95 percent of the owners had been divorced from any control of the property. The company officials were running the company, and those who owned the stock had become passive investors with the conventional privilege of sharing to some extent in net profits.

This situation had been shaping up for a long time. Even before 1900, the ownership of stock in many companies was widely scattered, making it difficult for the owners to act in harmony. But very large stockholders sat on the board of directors; and the board was still the governing body of the corporation.

In time, the original owners died and their stock was divided among numerous relatives. There was then no important concentration of personal ownership. In this situation control often went to the Wall Street bankers who marketed the company's stock. Finance capitalism remained significant through the first two decades of the twentieth century, a period when big businesses were expanding rapidly and needed banker aid in raising new capital.

Then conditions changed again. In the 1920's, the great debt-free industrial companies had less need for Wall Street aid or advice. These companies had ample funds for expansion, or could obtain money easily from the investing public. Banker influence further declined during the depression, when the United States government divorced investment from commercial banking, and when the RFC lent money to big companies in distress. By the 1940's, some industrial companies had no bankers and no large stockholders on their boards—only salaried officials representing management.

Now and then the managers of big companies were challenged by the stockholders or the financiers. But, like reform in politics, a fight for control of a company cost money, and was not lightly undertaken. In general, therefore, the managers ruled about as they pleased. ("The management of this institution is in the hands of the . . . directors. . . ." said one New York executive in 1950. "The stockholders have no right to intervene.")

The typical professional manager cared relatively little about paying large dividends to thousands of unknown stockholders. He was interested rather in building personal power and prestige by creating a successful concern. This meant holding or improving the company's position in the market, and keeping labor, suppliers, consumers, and fellow officers reasonably content. Managers were more likely to strengthen the organization with reserves than to pay out large dividends to owners. Dividends were only about 35 percent of earnings in manufacturing corporations in 1947.

Since profits meant prestige, security, and high salaries, management was profit-minded. As a rule, though, managers were more interested in avoiding risks than in seeking enormous returns. In consequence, business put less emphasis than before on pioneering and radical change.

Running Big Business

As business units grew larger, they required more and more administrators. By the 1940's, General Motors had over a hundred top executives, each the head of a large organization with its own officers and top-level managers. Running such an enterprise was more difficult than directing a small government. Hence business developed new techniques to handle the task—techniques that stressed administrative efficiency rather than democratic control.

Serious study of managerial problems had barely begun before World War I. A great increase in university-level schools of business heightened interest in such matters during the 1920's; and personnel studies, cost accounting, and social psychology all came to the aid of the overburdened chief executive. But the difficulties remained great. The business hierarchies of the twentieth century turned out few hard-driving individualists of the empire-building sort. Success went rather to the agreeable conformists who accepted routine practices.

In any company, only a few reached the top. Keeping the rest satisfied became an important goal of top management. One approach was the company magazine, designed to indoctrinate minor executives and employees below that level with company aims and policies. Organized social activities also made employees feel a common bond in working together in the company.

Protecting Free Enterprise

With their new alertness to morale and public approval, managers began to see stockholders in a new light. Owners of stock might not set policy; but they could be important as public friends. The ownership of even a few hundred dollars' worth of utilities stock made citizens critical of public regulation. Many companies, therefore, instructed branch managers to seek more local stockholders. In this way A.T. & T. by the early 1930's had acquired a total of over 700,000 owners.

Not content with numbers alone, many companies set about winning the loyalty of their owners. Presidents signed letters welcoming new members of the stockholder family. Annual reports grew into illustrated booklets which made the stockholder feel that he was a recognized member of the organization.

While wooing stockholders, managers appealed to the general public through advertisements and speeches. The response was good in the prosperous 1920's. Business became more popular than ever before in American history; and Bruce Barton (an advertising and public relations expert) won acclaim when he interpreted Jesus Christ as a businessman, in *The Man Nobody Knows.*

Severe depression changed public attitudes after 1929. The prestige of business declined when the stock market collapsed. It went down still more when Congressional investigations revealed evidence of recklessness and moral laxity among industrial and financial leaders. The breakup of Samuel Insull's holding-company-based utilities empire left Americans gasping. So did the trial and conviction of Richard Whitney, who had been president of the New York Stock Exchange and had talked about business honesty.

Plainly, the prosperity formulas of the 1920's had lost their magic. If business leaders hoped to regain the confidence of the American people, they would have to do more than talk about the long-run virtues of private industry and free enterprise. Yet no new approach seemed to be forthcoming. After a decade of depression (1929–39), prosperity returned in the 1940's. Its return, however, did not bring back the old public confidence in business leadership. A few businessmen admitted as much after the presidential election of 1948.

What, then, of the future? For good public relations, business obviously needed deeper and stronger roots in the community. In 1950 there were about 6,000,000 stockholders in the United States— scarcely more than in 1929. This made an average of only one stockholder to every six families. Since well-to-do families usually included several investors, the true figure might be one stockholder to every ten or twenty families. To broaden the popular base, brokers favored selling stock more widely. Some academic champions of business doubted that this could be quickly accomplished, and suggested that companies reach the people at once by including labor and community representatives on their boards of directors. But management was not sure that it wanted to move in that direction.

14

The General Welfare

The Standard of Living

The nation as a whole enjoyed great prosperity during two of the three decades after World War I. This, however, tells little about the welfare of any particular group of Americans. Nor does a rising standard of living necessarily mean a more pleasant life. Fear of war may rob a citizen of the feeling of security in the midst of a boom era.

Certainly any overall calculation of material welfare after the 1920's must take into consideration the psychological effects of the depression of 1929–39. Here was an experience difficult to forget. At least a third of the population of the United States lost so much in security and self-respect that a decade of prosperity could not bring back the pre-1929 sense of well-being. Even those who had stayed at work during the 1930's remembered the suffering of less fortunate friends and relatives; remembered pay cuts; remembered worrying about how long their jobs would last or how long they could stave off bankruptcy; remembered seeing their children grow up with scant hopes of employment. World War II brought better times, without erasing the memory of the dark days.

The most convenient measure of the general welfare is found in the figures for real income—dollar income adjusted in line with the changing value of money. This shows purchasing power of the pay check, a good starting point in any analysis of living standards.

In broad outline, labor and the self-employed gained most in the "good times" of the 1920's and the 1940's, while the salaried middle class relatively speaking lost ground. In the depression years of the 1930's, it was the other way around. Citizens on salary fared well in the depression, if they could hold their jobs and if their employers could keep their heads above water. Meantime, workingmen and the self-employed had a hard time.

Back in the nineteenth century, clerical employees had earned much more than manual workers. The spread in income was still substantial (about a third) in the early 1920's. But by the middle of the twentieth century, much of this difference had disappeared. In 1948, hand book-keepers, the best-paid office workers, received about $60 a week in the larger cities, whereas manual workers employed in automobile assembly plants averaged four dollars a week more than that. On the lower end of the scale, the poorest-paid clerical workers, class B file clerks, were paid $30 per week, 20 percent less than the lowest-paid manual group (workers in tobacco factories). To compensate, white-collar employees had a little more prestige than manual laborers and were a little less likely to be dropped overnight. But even here the difference was not so great as in former years.

In this shift, real wages for clerical workers had not declined—they were about as high in the early 1950's as they had been three decades before. Meanwhile, however, the real income of manual workers had increased sharply. Using 1939 dollars as its yardstick, the Bureau of Labor Statistics estimated the earnings of the average workingman in manufacturing as $18 at the end of World War I, $20 in 1929. After a depression dip to $17 in 1932, the figure rose to $25 eight years later and went above $30 in 1948. Thus the average factory worker had nearly two-thirds more purchasing power at mid-century than in 1919. Although the laborer of 1950 had to pay some of his increased earnings in taxes, he was definitely ahead of the game as compared with the workingman of a third of a century before.

In this picture, price changes played less part than did other factors. Prior to World War I, increases in real wages had generally been caused largely by declines in prices. When prices had advanced (1843–57, 1897–1918), wages had lagged or had barely kept abreast of the cost of living. But after 1919, union activities and government policies —collective forces outside the sphere of "natural economic laws"— had been the most important factors in increasing the worker's share of the national income.

While the worker gained greatly in wages, he also acquired leisure through a shorter working week. The chief impetus in this direction came from the great depression. The average work week had remained close to fifty hours after World War I, through the prosperous 1920's. The mass unemployment and low business activity of the early 1930's had led to a sharp decline. Share-the-work and spread-employment appeals played a part; and thirty to thirty-five hours became the rule. When World War II provided full employment after 1941, the United States government aided the unions in maintaining forty hours as the normal week, with extra hours classified as overtime. Since overtime meant pay-and-a-half or double pay, forty hours became standard for workers after the war.

Labor could thus look back on very substantial gains over three decades. With real wages up 70 percent and hours down 20 percent, America appeared to be fulfilling its promise of a better life for the common man.

Life in the Machine Age

But average hour-and-income calculations are often deceptive. Happiness depends to some degree on relative money income; but it depends on many other things as well. And in some of these other aspects of life the middle of the twentieth century had produced problems without providing solutions.

Urban concentration was one point. In the thirty years after World War I 20 percent more people came to live in cities. By 1950 half the people of the United States—two-thirds of those not directly engaged in farming—lived in metropolitan centers of 50,000 or more inhabitants. Most of these centers shared the problems of unattractive and inadequate housing, too many automobiles for their roads or parking places, and living quarters remote from places of work.

By the late 1940's, government planning and financing was bringing some improvement. Nevertheless, there seemed no way of restoring the old-fashioned town community. Newspapers, radio, and television all operated increasingly on a national rather than a local scale. People read about or were entertained by, not flesh-and-blood people whom they knew personally, but national celebrities who had the mythical or symbolic qualities of characters in low-grade fiction. A citizen could have some importance in the local sphere of the store, the club, and the church; but in the remote world that provided his general information and relaxation he was utterly insignificant.

Psychology was not yet able to assess the social results of this situation, any more than psychologists could spell out the effects of fear of Russia and the atom bomb. But taken together, such matters produced an America of new contradictions. At a time when wages and employment were at all-time highs, when the government stood ready to take care of the unfortunate, many Americans talked in terms of insecurity and distrust of the future. Youth no longer seemed so confident of its own or of the American mission. Industrialism appeared to have produced change more rapidly than man's social organisms could adjust to it.

A Shifting Population

One cause of weak community relations was as old as America itself. This was the continuous movement of population. The second quarter of the twentieth century saw people shifting from one area to another, from one type of job to a new one promising better opportunity. Although the frontier was gone, Americans moved as often as in earlier generations. And, thanks to the automobile, they moved farther and faster than before.

Immigrants ceased to arrive in vast numbers after the emergency quota act of 1921; and immigration was further reduced by the restrictive acts of 1924 and 1929. Native Americans, however, continued to move west. In the three decades after World War I, California nearly trebled in population, and rose to be the second most populous state. The population of Oregon practically doubled; that of Washington and Texas increased by one-half. In each of these areas growth came primarily from new industrial activity. With total farm population tending downward, the western agricultural states grew slowly. East of the Mississippi only Michigan and Florida expanded rapidly, one from automotive workers, the other from retired couples and vacationers.

The great depression moved people from one occupation or area

to another with ruthless disregard for sentimental ties and attach-
ments. Farmers from the southern states moved to California in quest
of work as migratory agricultural laborers. Office workers became road
builders, city laborers tried subsistence farming. New occupations
created by World War II continued this gigantic shuffling of population, and postwar uncertainties brought still further movements.

While the people moved, they changed their occupations. The
generation after World War I brought a spectacular decline in the
number of domestic servants. Equally striking, and more important
for the country as a whole, was a reduction of the number of workers
in rural areas. The percentage of farmers and hired agricultural laborers in the nation's working force was cut in half between World
War I and 1950, and stood at only 13 percent of the total. These years
saw a great increase in the number of persons gainfully employed in
the United States; but not in farming. Ten million men made a living
by raising agricultural products in 1920; only 7,000,000 at the end of
the 1940's.

Meantime, there were increases in other fields. The percentage of
clerical and sales employees in the total working force rose by a third;
the fraction of the working population in the upper reaches of business
and the professions grew two and a half times. The professional
people, proprietors, and managers now outnumbered the farmers and
farm workers by over 3,000,000; and they were nearly as numerous as
the clerical and sales employees. Looking at it another way, the urban
upper middle class was the fastest-growing element in American
society. Next came the middle class as represented by sales and clerical
forces.

As these changes occurred, family (father-to-son) patterns were
disturbed more frequently than ever before. Millions of citizens were
working at jobs remote from their early training and experience.
Added to displacement caused by depression and war were the great
government-subsidized programs of military and veterans' education
designed to fit men and women into new careers. The process put
many people into jobs and places where they felt strange and uneasy.
Sometimes, too, government funds trained young people for fields

where there were too few employment opportunities. At the same time, it could be maintained that the whole cycle of change was in keeping with the spirit of democracy.

The Decline of Trade Unionism

Many traditional institutions proved poorly adapted to the new world of mass production industrialism. One such institution was the specialized craft union, the organization of workers according to their skill. In the nineteenth-century factory system it had been quite proper to organize workers according to their skills; men were carpenters or boilermakers, cigar makers or glass blowers. Then subdivision of labor and the new assembly line techniques eliminated skills. All through the twentieth century the truly skilled were steadily decreasing in number, as machines replaced specialized hand labor. It was absurd to try to maintain the old type of union organization in the automobile or steel or rubber or electrical equipment factories. Most men in these plants had no specialized skill; and organization along craft lines would leave out most workers altogether.

The obvious solution was industrial organization—putting all the auto workers into one union, the rubber workers into another, and so on. But there were obstacles. One was the power and the antiunion point of view of manufacturers in the mass production industries— the Detroit auto makers, for example. Equally difficult was the attitude of certain American Federation of Labor craft unions, which were determined to oppose industrial unionism. When the Carriage Workers tried to organize the workers in the auto factories, there were complaints from many craft unions, although these unions had been unable to make much headway in the car industry. When the Carriage Workers went ahead anyway, the A.F. of L. ordered them not to cut into the jurisdiction of existing craft unions (1913). Specifically, the order was not to organize workers who might be classified as painters, blacksmiths, upholsterers, sheet-metal workers, patternmakers, metal polishers, machinists, carpenters, or electrical workers. Five years later, the Carriage Workers were expelled from the A.F. of L. Had they been encouraged rather than denounced, they might have made Detroit a union area. As it was, the region remained nonunion until the depression.

During and immediately after World War I, union membership increased to nearly 5,000,000 workers. The increase was largely in such older areas of union strength as the building trades, printing, and railroads, and in war-stimulated industries that would soon be doomed to inactivity—shipping, for instance, and the metal trades. Even at their peak, the craft unions inside and outside the A.F. of L. failed to gain a secure footing in the expanding mass production industries. President Gompers of the A.F. of L. did give half-hearted support to an effort to organize the steel industry; but this campaign broke down after the spectacular and unsuccessful steel strike of 1919.

In line with historic trends, union membership had grown during wartime prosperity; and it declined during the postwar depression of 1920–22. The decline, however, was more than merely cyclical. It was definitely associated with a national employer-backed campaign against the closed shop. Trouble began with President Woodrow Wilson's Industrial Conference of 1919. Called to plan industrial peace, the meeting soon demonstrated the inevitability of conflict. Employer representatives refused to accept the closed shop; and labor representatives withdrew.

Then and later, employers throughout the country formed industrial associations and organized local clubs and civic bodies to fight for the open shop as "the American way." No one should be denied the right to a job because he refused to join a union. The arguments were similar to those used in the antiunion drives a generation before; but the methods were more comprehensive. To the speeches and advertisements of an earlier day the participants now added labor spies to report on and confound organizers; trade association agreements specifying the open shop; banker pressure on employers of union labor; letters to stockholders urging them to help.

The success of these antiunion measures was increased by the red scare of 1919–20. The rise of communism in Europe and the use of bombs by one group of extremists in the United States led many Americans to fear that revolution was at hand. Playing on this fear, employers called attention to the great increase of strikes and the presence of a few radicals in the labor movement. Since antiforeign sentiment was rising in America, labor leaders were also denounced as foreigners.

Nor was that all. From 1919 on, the federal government showed its sympathy with employers. Although the war was over, wartime legislation was used to end the coal strike of 1919. A number of states passed laws prohibiting the closed shop or forbidding strikes. Federal and state courts granted injunctions to prevent strike action.

Considering the antiunion movement and the downward trend of the business cycle, it was natural that American Federation of Labor membership should drop from its top of over 4,000,000 to below 3,000,000 by 1923. More disheartening was the failure of the Federation to come back during the next six years of prosperity. In 1929 the membership totals for A.F. of L. and independent unions were about the same as for 1923, although the nation's labor force had grown by more than 10 percent. The only significant gains in the decade were in company unions, which doubled and came to have a membership half as large as that of the Federation. Many of these company unions departed from the craft approach and organized on an industrial basis. To this degree they represented the needs of the new manufacturing economy. But, since company unions were influenced or controlled by management, they helped little in wage and hour disputes.

Unable to gain during prosperity, the craft unions in the A.F. of L. suffered heavily after the stock market crash of 1929. In the three years that followed, Federation unions lost nearly a quarter of their members. By 1933, at the bottom of the depression, the A.F. of L. represented only 4 percent of the national labor force. All labor's organizing efforts of a half-century seemed to have been in vain.

The New Labor Movement

In the late nineteenth century and again after World War I, the government had helped employers to check the growth of organized labor. During World War I and again in the 1930's, the government took the other side, and actively aided the union organizers.

The labor policy of the Franklin D. Roosevelt administration (1933–45) seems to have had three major aims: (1) to redistribute national income through higher pay for shorter hours of work, (2) to encourage organization and concerted labor action, and (3) to pro- mote the peaceful settlement of labor disputes. This program first found expression in 1933 in Section 7a of the National Industrial Recovery Act, which stated that employees had the "right to organ- ize and to bargain collectively through representatives of their own choosing."

Protected by this legislation and by a short-lived National Labor Board, unions regained within two years the strength they had lost during the depression. But company unions—also recognized as bar- gaining agencies—grew even faster. By 1935 the strength of company unions was about two-thirds that of the other unions. The National Labor Relations (or Wagner) Act of that year checked the spread of the company union. This was done by prohibiting employers from using coercion or giving financial support to company unions and by specifying that the employer must bargain with the union represent- ing the majority of his employees.

The Wagner Act, which established a permanent National Labor Relations Board, was the cornerstone of New Deal labor policy. Employers regarded the statute as a complete victory for labor; and many were reluctant to abide by it. Most of them did so, however, after the Supreme Court upheld the constitutionality of the legisla- tion (Jones and Laughlin Steel Corporation case, 1937). Even before that decision, the Wagner Act had added notably to union strength and had helped effect a major improvement in wages and working conditions.

Opportunity to organize the mass production industries under the protection of federal law clearly pointed to the desirability of setting up industrial unions. Convinced of this, John L. Lewis of the United Mine Workers and a few other A.F. of L. leaders organized a Com- mittee for Industrial Organization and began recruiting rank-and-file workers on an industry-wide basis (1935). This action was roundly condemned by craft-minded Federation leaders, including William Green, who had succeeded Gompers as president of the A.F. of L. As this group saw it, Lewis was crossing jurisdictional lines; and in 1938, the Committee for Industrial Organization was expelled from the Federation. The expelled officials promptly called a national convention and established the Congress of Industrial Organizations, with John L. Lewis as president.

When formed, the C.I.O. had as members several old A.F. of L. unions, including the United Mine Workers and Sidney Hillman's Amalgamated Clothing Workers. The greatest strength, however, came as the C.I.O. organized the mass production industries, winning victories in steel, motors, rubber, and textiles.

Warfare between the A.F. of L. and the C.I.O. harassed labor leaders, government officials, employers, and the public. Yet the competition was responsible for heroic organizing efforts. To defeat its younger rival, the Federation remodeled many of its unions along industrial lines. This put a final stamp of approval on the industrial idea; and it brought in many members. Racing neck and neck, the A.F. of L. and the C.I.O. increased total union membership from 4,000,000 in the middle 1930's to four times that number at the end of the 1940's. About half of these belonged to Green's A.F. of L., one Federation union (Daniel Tobin's International Brotherhood of Teamsters) claiming more than a million members. Two C.I.O. unions, the United Steelworkers of America and the United Automobile Workers, had just short of a million members each; and Philip Murray, who headed the C.I.O., had 6,000,000 followers. The other 2,000,000 union members were in independent unions—the railway brotherhoods, for instance, and the United Mine Workers, which John L. Lewis took from the A.F. of L. to the C.I.O., then back to the A.F. of L., then out of both major combinations.

Compared with the figures of 1933, these numbers were enormous. Some observers noted, though, that a great deal remained undone. Organizing drives were more successful from the mid-1930's to the mid-1940's than they were thereafter; membership went up very slowly after World War II. Yet of the more than 40,000,000 workers in manufacturing, the union share was far less than half.

The union victories were not achieved without difficulty. In the middle 1930's, employers used company unions, propaganda, and even force ("service" units) against the organizers. Sixteen workers were killed when police and strikers clashed in the Republic Steel strike of 1937. Die-hard employers tried the Mohawk Valley formula to beat strikes—close the factory, ship away machinery, hint that operations would be suspended forever.

But labor won. United States Steel, traditionally antilabor, gave in without a strike. Others resisted, but, with or without conflict, the old nonunion industries granted recognition to the unions. Detroit the auto town became a union center. The unions carried the electric and rubber industries. They organized government and office workers, they penetrated antiunion districts of the South.

In the main, the labor leaders used traditional weapons. Now and then, however, they tried something new. As when, in 1936, they used the sit-down strike. The first determined application of this method came in a strike against the Goodyear Rubber Company. Instead of going "out" on strike, the workers stayed in the plant, while their wives and fellow unionists brought them food. For labor, the sit-down had the advantage of preventing operation of the plant by strikebreakers; and it forced company officials to resort to violence if they wanted to expel the strikers. Those who opposed the new technique claimed that the sit-down was an improper invasion of property rights. Those who favored it held that it demonstrated the worker's vested right to his job. While the debate wore on into 1937, Governor Frank Murphy of Michigan protected sit-down strikers at Flint (Fisher Bodies and Chevrolet); and General Motors eventually negotiated contracts covering its major plants. Later, in the Fansteel case, the Supreme Court held the sit-down strike illegal. But by sustaining the Wagner Act and the rulings of the National Labor Relations Board, the judges made such forceful tactics unnecessary.

Not until after World War II was there a reaction against labor. The postwar era brought a swing toward conservatism. Franklin D. Roosevelt's successor in the White House, Harry Truman, took an antilabor attitude when a national railroad strike was threatened in the spring of 1946. Thereafter, President Truman moved toward labor. But the fall of 1946 brought Republican victories in state and

Congressional elections; and the nation's lawmakers became less favorable to union growth.

The most important new statute was the Taft-Hartley law of 1947, passed over President Truman's veto by Republicans and conservative Democrats. This act imposed sweeping restraints on unions. While the union or preferential shop was permitted, the shop definitely closed to nonunion workers was prohibited. A worker could stop paying dues and still keep his job. Unions could be sued for breach of contract. Unions could be forced to pay for damages suffered through jurisdictional disputes, as when C.I.O. and A.F. of L. unions fought for control of the same plant. Labor organizations were also to be held accountable in cases of secondary boycott—say, the refusal of workers to handle the products of a firm involved in a labor dispute. A sixty-day negotiating period was required between the calling and start of a strike. Union funds could not be used for political purposes; and to preserve their legal bargaining rights, union officials had to sign oaths that they were not Communists.

This sudden reversal of government policy from extreme friendliness toward labor to severely restrictive legislation symbolized the reaction of nonunion groups to labor gains of the preceding dozen years. Postwar labor scarcity and low man-hour productivity in many lines had brought this resentment to a climax. Although there was a swing toward labor in the 1948 election, the unions were unable to secure quick repeal of the Taft-Hartley law. But labor still retained its rights of collective bargaining, as established under the Wagner Act of 1935. It retained as well many other gains dating from the New Deal era—wage and hour legislation of 1938, and the beginnings of a social security system.

Organizing Office Workers

Among the new fields invaded by union organizers was the field of office work. In earlier days clerical employees had hoped to advance to executive positions; and because of the "opportunity for rapid advancement" they had accepted low initial salaries. But adding machines, card sorters, and other new devices eliminated skills and contradicted the old theory that clerks needed more education and more brains than plant or road employees. Almost any youngster of the 1920's had enough education for most office work. And by then many clerical positions were "dead end," rather than steps on a ladder. Many of the jobs went to women, who would not in any case be considered for the better executive posts.

Despite these underlying changes, clerical workers enjoyed a number of advantages before 1929. Since paper work goes on even in slack times, the office staff could count on year-round employment. Though their real income advanced little between 1890 and 1929, white-collar workers consoled themselves with the thought that they had paid vacations, and more security, higher social status, and better opportunities than manual workers.

Then came the great depression. Office staffs, overexpanded in the 1920's, were cut almost as drastically as factory employees. Many of those who kept their jobs were forced to take payless vacations and deep salary cuts. Time and motion studies were introduced into offices to increase the efficiency of machine operators. Stenographic pools and dictating machines eliminated much secretarial work; and "opportunity for rapid advancement" disappeared altogether.

The situation beckoned to the labor leader. The Newspaper Guild led the way in the early 1930's; and organizers soon invaded many other fields. Government workers were organized. A Teachers Union sought members in the unorganized calling of education. Draftsmen and clerks, stenographers and office boys joined unions and engaged in collective bargaining.

Although many office workers were reluctant to join up, the white-collar unions grew steadily. The price inflation of the 1940's increased discontent; as usual, the salaries of office employees lagged behind the cost of living. In this postwar era, the organized manual workers gained pensions and paid vacations—privileges hitherto confined to the office. In addition, social distinctions were slipping away. To gain higher pay, young people with good education often took factory jobs in preference to clerical positions. The trend seemed to foreshadow the disappearance of a sharp class line and the spread of organization to all types of nonexecutive employees.

The growth of clerical and manual unions was a world-wide feature of industrialism. Nowhere had a more satisfactory solution for employer-employee relationships been found. But union rules still further diminished the flexibility and buoyancy of the enterprise system. When backed up by a strong union, wage rates became as rigid as monopolistic prices and made labor costs an important element in discouraging new ventures. When employment declined, seniority rules forced the retention of tired, conservative old workers and the firing of vigorous young ones. Inside the unions, leadership tended to become entrenched, conservative, and autocratic. For these reasons, unions joined bureaucratic management, controlled prices, and high taxes in fostering the rigidity that was creating deep uncertainties as to the future of the traditional economic system.

The Self-Employed

Although most Americans were employees, the self-employed proprietary group (including farmers and tenants) remained as numerous as the white-collar workers. Within the ranks of the self-employed, farmers declined by more than 1,500,000 between the early 1920's and late 1940's. Other proprietors, however, increased by approximately an equal amount.

Outside of farmers, the largest group of owner-managers was that of the retail merchants, who made up about a third of the remaining self-employed. Only slightly smaller—and growing steadily—was the group of people who performed "services." Included here were hotel owners, repairmen, lawyers, physicians, and the like.

Taken together, these two groups of self-employed citizens influenced America beyond the weight of their numbers. In villages and the smaller cities, the successful lawyers and doctors, insurance agents, merchants, and restaurant owners made up the core of the community. They ran the local clubs, selected the local politicians, spoke for the "people." Often, too, they set the tone in state and national politics, for small city and country areas were more heavily represented in Congress and the state legislatures than were metropolitan districts.

The self-employed had less social uniformity in the large cities than in the smaller towns. Retailers and those who provided service were, on the average, too small and insecure to be regarded as members of the upper middle class. (Many, in fact, were poorer in net income than the manual workers.) Large proprietors and successful professional men occupied social positions dependent upon their incomes, personalities, and origins. Leadership in big-city affairs, however, was largely in the hands of professional politicians, journalists, and the top executives of the big companies.

The self-employed were much affected by economic fluctuations. Good times and rising prices brought substantial fees or profits; falling prices and poor business meant reduced income. Many went bankrupt. But the self-employed could also hope for wealth, if they struck on the right location or product or clientele. The self-employed thus differed from the manual workers and white-collar employees in their hopes for the future. They were, in a sense, the spiritual descendants of the optimistic boomers of an earlier America.

In spite of the changing character of the American economy, there was little reduction of the citizen's opportunity to go into business for himself. The first two decades of the twentieth century saw 7,500,000 new firms founded (banks, railroads, and professional enterprises not being counted in this total). The next two decades, the period between the world wars, saw the launching of 8,500,000 new enterprises, and this despite ten years of depression. The biggest companies were getting bigger; great economic power was held by a relatively small number of Americans. But because of the rise of service activities, the small operator remained in the field, and the number of ventures kept pace with the population.

Although a large percentage of small businessmen were trained in somewhat similar family ventures, many citizens took chances in unfamiliar fields. A young man took whatever job he could get; and when he had saved a little money, he set out on his own. The process bore a resemblance to that of children leaving the old family farm and setting up in farming for themselves. This testified to the continuing desire of many an American to be his own boss.

Little capital was needed to make a start in retailing, service, or certain lines of manufacturing. Some began with no capital at all, by securing credit from landlords, wholesalers, and finance companies. An investment of more than $5000 was rare. In garment making, leather or woodworking, silk manufacture or printing, one could rent machinery and operate on a small scale. The median personal investment of fifty Paterson, New Jersey, silk manufacturers who began operations between 1926 and 1936 was only $611.

The mortality of these shoestring enterprises was high. A study of retail ventures in Illinois during the prosperous 1920's indicated that a man entering such business had a two-to-one chance of surviving two years, and only two chances in five of lasting for three years. Well-financed and well-managed businesses that escaped such infant mortality generally kept going for a decade or more; but the average life for small enterprise was less than seven years. This was not a new development, for much the same situation had obtained a century before.

Why the many failures? Lack of capital, for one thing. New Jersey bankruptcy records for 1929–30 showed that only 18 percent of the original capital of the average company had been provided by the owner. The rest had come from friends, relatives, banks, and wholesalers; and there was little margin in case of an emergency. Inexperience and incompetence were other causes of failure. Men without business education, sometimes with little general education, were lost in the intricacies of bookkeeping, cost accounting, inventory valuation, and market forecasting.

The real degree of insecurity, though, was not so great as the figures indicate. The shoestring operator often risked only the savings of two or three years. If he failed, he could take a job and save enough to try again. "Failure" might mean simply a reorganization with new loans, a new location, perhaps a new partner. Dishonest entrepreneurs might fail profitably by selling off their stock and concealing the proceeds from their creditors. And, at all events, there were plenty of men and women willing to assume the risks and to work far harder for less income than at a salaried job. In return, there was the excitement of directing one's own enterprise, and the hope of substantial profits.

Paradoxically, these risky small businesses, taken as a whole, constituted the most stable and unchanging part of the American economy. Service and trade continued to be conducted much as they had been for many years. In spite of superficial changes in store fronts, displays cases, dentists' offices, or hotel lobbies, the same essential activities were still performed by human beings for human beings. Technologic revolution through super markets and mechanized self-service did not yet dominate the nation.

The Motorization of Agriculture

In many ways the factory, the store, and the office of the 1950's were basically similar to those of the World War I era. But in these years, the American farm went through a profound technological transformation.

In 1918 the average commercial farm still represented nineteenth-century patterns of work and leisure. Most farmers had not yet bought automobiles. Few had electricity. The radio and the consolidated school were still experiments. On more than 6,000,000 farms there were only 85,000 tractors. Save for a few Fords, the country was still the quiet habitat of horses and mules, weekly journals, home amusements, kerosene lamps, muddy roads, and antiquated clothes, manners, and speech.

By 1950, successful commercial farming was a mechanized business sometimes conducted by men who spent much of their time in cities. Almost every extensive farm had a tractor, and only the poor farmers in depressed areas lacked electricity or automobiles. In the corn and wheat states 90 percent of the acreage was cultivated with tractors. The horse was becoming as rare as on the city streets. As a result of motorization, better machines, and advances in agricultural science, a third fewer farmers and hired hands, using about the same number of acres for crops, were turning out half again as much product as before. One man in the wheat lands could do the work that had required three before World War I.

Changes went beyond equipment and production. Aided by government subsidies and price supports, the average farmer with cash receipts of about $5000 had become a prosperous middle-class citizen, scarcely distinguishable from his city neighbors. Concrete highways, radios, movies, and even television kept him in close touch with the urban world. His clothes, schooling, housing, and household equipment had become like those of the suburbs.

This attractive picture did not cover all the nation's agriculture. There were depressed areas even in the prosperous 1940's—hill sections of the South, cutover areas in the North and West, submarginal properties in New England. There was suffering on rich lands, too. The cotton belt had not yet solved its problems of a single crop, debt, tenancy, and race conflict. And in the boom times of 1950 even the most successful farmers could not help remembering the troubled 1920's and the calamitous 1930's. Would such times come again?

Farm Problems

The new tractors, combines, and cultivators made it possible to expand wheat and corn acreage at small extra cost. At the same time, the machines displaced horses and mules, both important consumers of grain. Before the coming of the tractor, over a fifth of the grain raised had been fed to work animals on the farm, at no cost for shipping and marketing. Now the farmer had to sell the grain and buy gasoline in return. This made him more dependent than ever on markets and on the price of nonagricultural commodities.

Besides the declining demand on the farm itself, those growing grain after World War I had to contend with shrinking national and world markets. Prosperity, urban living, and better knowledge of diet caused Americans to eat more dairy products, fruits, and vegetables, and less grain, potatoes, and meat. The new demand brought profit to farmers who were well located and had the capital to enter these lines. Many cereal farmers, however, could not manage the shift. The decline of foreign markets after 1925 (partly owing to competition from Argentina, Canada, and Australia) brought still heavier pressure against domestic grain prices. The price of wheat therefore tumbled downward, falling more than 50 percent between 1925 and 1930.

The same difficulties accompanied the other major American market crop, cotton. Poor yields in the years immediately after World War I led to an average price of nearly 29¢ a pound in 1923, which encouraged a 25 percent increase in acreage. Then everything went wrong. Rayon began to displace cotton at home. Egyptian and Indian cotton undersold American in the export market. Production mounted, prices fell. By 1930 the average price was under 10¢ a pound, and in 1931 the biggest cotton crop in United States history brought an average price of 5.7¢ a pound.

Farmers with money to buy the new machines and acreage enough to put them to efficient use made a fair living in the late 1920's. So did some agriculturalists who had sufficient capital and skill to diversify their crops. But 60 percent of American farms had less than 100 acres in 1925; and their owners lacked cash or credit. Many larger farms were in the semiarid parts of the plains and mountain states, where growing seasons were uncertain, mortgages common, and transportation costs high. Their owners could do well enough when wheat brought $1.25 a bushel. It was a different story when the price was half of that, especially with those who had purchased land at the high figures prevailing during and after World War I.

Some commentators took a philosophic view of the agricultural trends, and said that the inefficient producers would presently be eliminated. But, efficient or inefficient, the farmer did not propose to give up the struggle. Instead, he pressed his case through political channels. Economists and businessmen might hold that the trouble lay in too many small farms. But these critics offered no workable plans for moving farmers to other occupations; and the small farmer had enough political strength to resist liquidation.

Conservative politicians like President Calvin Coolidge (1923–29) hoped that coöperative marketing might be a cure for farmers' ills. There was hope, too, that farmers could act as a unit to capture foreign markets (under the Webb-Pomerene Act of 1918, the Sherman and Clayton Antitrust laws did not apply to combinations for export purposes). But these approaches did not work. Overseas markets dwindled away; and, save for certain perishable commodities, marketing coöperatives added little to the farmer's net return.

Agriculturalists therefore demanded something else. Working through farm lobbies—especially the American Farm Bureau Federation—they created a bipartisan farm bloc in Congress in the 1920's.

TENANT FARMERS
PERCENT OF ALL FARMERS

1880

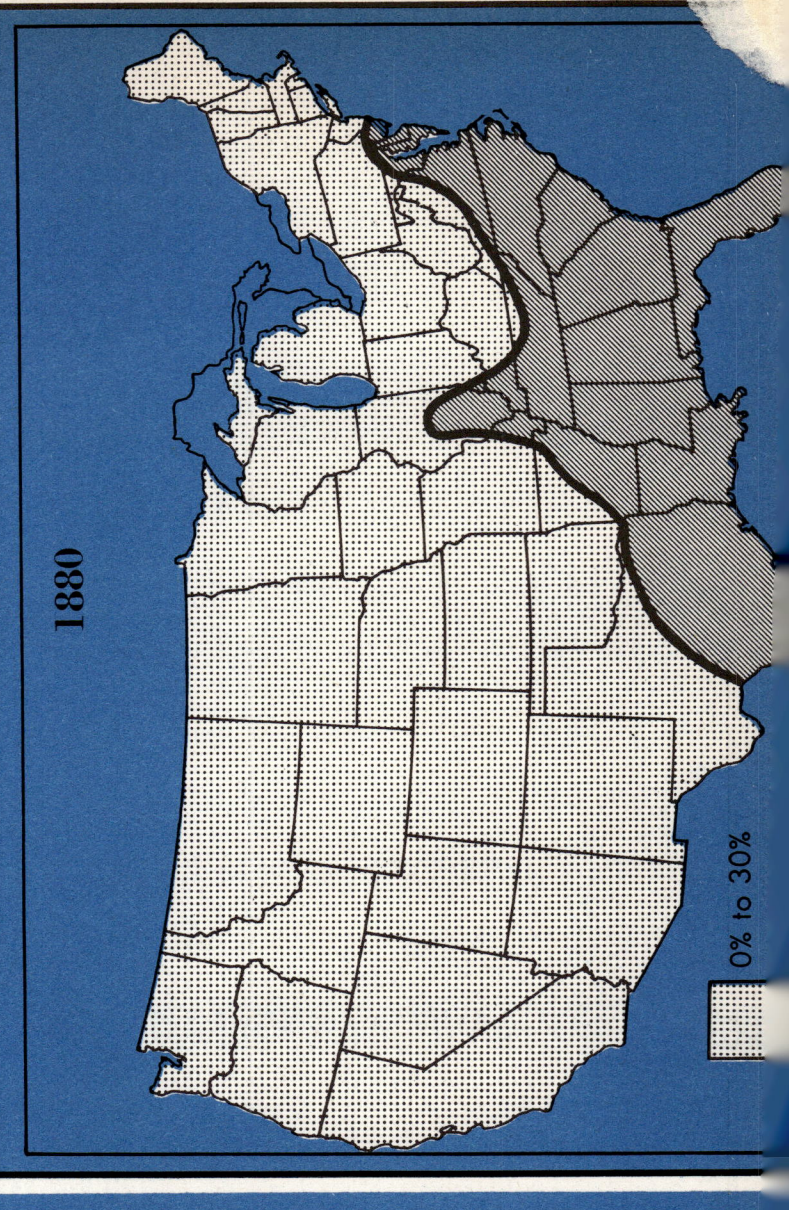

0% to 30%

The pattern of farm tenancy was well established by the end of the Reconstruction era. The heaviest concentration was in the cotton belt, where white and Negro sharecroppers accounted for most of the tenant population.

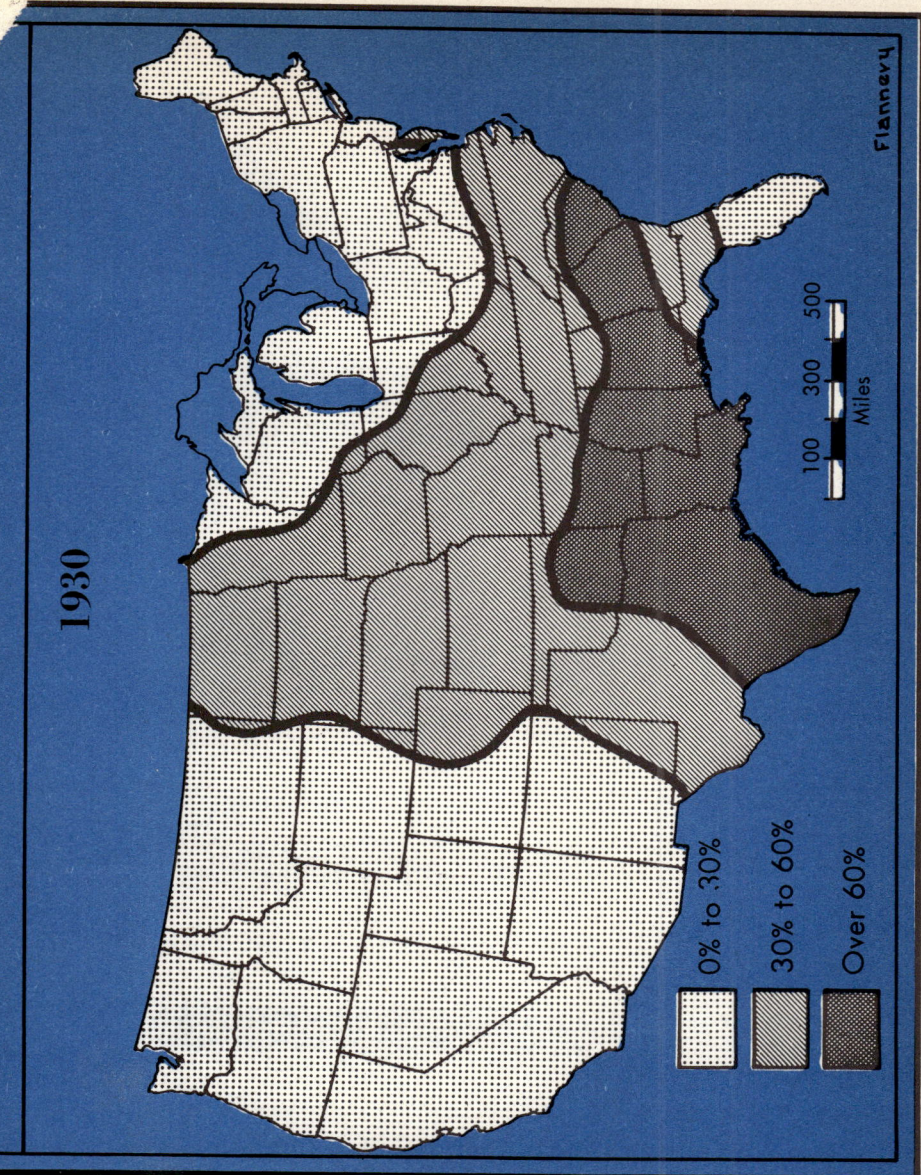

1930

0% to 30%

30% to 60%

Over 60%

100 300 500
Miles

100 300 500
Miles

Flannery

In the half century between 1880 and 1930, tenancy increased in every section. In the cotton belt, more than three-fifths of the farmers were tenants by 1930. Meanwhile, there had been a heavy increase in tenant farming in the cash grain areas of the middle section of the country.

Although some tenant farmers obtained good returns (in the Middle West especially), the average tenant was in an unenviable position. His plight would become worse during the depression; yet the government would do less for tenant farmers (and for migratory farm workers) than for other depressed groups. After the late 1930's, however, there would be a trend away from tenancy, because of better times and the changing character of American agriculture.

Pressure resulted in the establishment in 1923 of Federal Intermediate Credit Banks. Farmers could go to these institutions for loans running from three months to five years. (Loans for shorter terms were available through the Federal Reserve System; and long-term credit could be obtained through the banks set up by the Federal Farm Loan Act of 1916.) The farm bloc also pushed McNary-Haugen bills through Congress in 1927 and 1928. These were complicated measures under which the government would have paid farmers compensation for the protective tariff rates on other commodities. But President Coolidge killed the proposal each time with a veto.

The Farmer and Depression

Barely able to make ends meet during the 1920's, farmers ran into serious trouble after 1929. To begin with, the crash caused over 1,000,000 unemployed workers to leave the cities and return to the land. In addition, town workingmen who had done farming on the side turned entirely to agriculture when they lost their factory jobs. Southern agrarians and a few Northerners (including Franklin D. Roosevelt) spoke hopefully of this "return to the soil." Actually, it worked out badly. Farmers who were having trouble were burdened with the extra task of supporting relatives. The movement of population to the country increased farm production, cutting prices below their already low levels. And the migration added to the number of farms that were too small to support families even in good times.

As their income dwindled, hundreds of thousands of farmers found it impossible to pay their taxes or the interest on their part of the $8,000,000,000 farm mortgage debt. Foreclosures followed, and owners became tenants of banks and insurance companies. By the mid-1930's, managers or tenants operated over half the farm acreage. This created acute dissatisfaction in many areas; and not infrequently farmers took over foreclosure sales, forcing those in charge to sell to the old owners at a low figure. Here were reënacted scenes played out in the days of Daniel Shays, a century and a half before.

Calamity was piled on calamity in the dark days of the early 1930's. Town and county governments in rural districts went bankrupt. Relief payments and public works employment were impossible. Schools were closed; roads fell into disrepair. Farmers talked of desperate measures to restore prices. Dairy farmers organized milk strikes—refused to send milk to market and used road blocks to enforce coöperation from their neighbors. But, lacking national organization, these protesting groups were generally unsuccessful.

Government Policy

Just as the depression began, the presidential administration of Herbert Hoover (1929–33) established a Farm Board. The idea was to raise the prices of staple crops by lending money to marketing coöperatives. The coöperatives could store surpluses and release them only in times of scarcity. Had abundance and scarcity alternated frequently, the Hoover plan might have worked. But scarcity never came in the depression years; and the Farm Board used up all its funds vainly trying to support a sinking market.

When Franklin D. Roosevelt became President in 1933, his New Deal administration set out to raise farm prices. This was to be done by limited inflation and by planned scarcity. Under the Agricultural Adjustment Act of 1933, farmers were offered payments for cutting acreage, the money to be raised by taxes on the processing of farm goods. In addition, one government agency refinanced farm mortgages at a lower rate of interest (4½ percent). Another offered to help the most unfortunate farmers move to better locations.

Some of these measures did some good; others were less successful. The whole program was threatened in 1936, when the Supreme Court held the processing tax feature of the AAA unconstitutional (Hoosac Mills case). Congress hastily passed a Soil Conservation and Domestic Allotment Act; but this failed to develop much restrictive force.

Meantime, nature entered the picture, temporarily restoring a better balance between production and consumption. In 1934, the prairie and plains states suffered a drought even more severe than that of the late 1880's. Crops dried up, and western Kansas, Oklahoma, and Texas became a vast dust bowl. One third of the nation's grain crop was lost, and "Okies" abandoned their burned-out Oklahoma farms to seek work picking fruit in California. Although the following year brought some rain, 1936 was almost as bad as 1934. As a result of these short crops, farm prices rose, and by early 1937, real farm income was about as high as in the late 1920's. But the next year saw bumper corn and wheat crops and a return to the problem of general overproduction.

To meet the situation, the government initiated a long-run program in the Agricultural Adjustment Act of 1938. The plan was based on two major ideas: (1) fitting production to market demand and (2) insuring a constant supply of major commodities by government storage of surpluses. Marketing quotas would be imposed on certain basic crops if two-thirds of the producers agreed. Farmers who conformed to designated acreage quotas and planted soil-conserving crops on their remaining land would receive federal payments. (This was an effort to avoid constitutional objections to direct subsidies.)

The main controls, however, were in the marketing arrangements. The administration set a "just" or parity price for major crops, based on the relation of farm to industrial prices in a prosperous agricultural era (1909–14). If market prices fell to less than 75 percent of these arbitrary levels, the farmer who had conformed to his quota would have the difference restored by parity payments. If he did not want to market his crop, he could store it in a government warehouse and borrow half to three-quarters of the parity price. If he did not redeem this no-interest loan, the government merely took over the produce.

With the establishment of the permanent AAA program in 1938, farms were added to railroads, shipping, and public utilities in the area of the economy that was partly government controlled. At first farmers were somewhat disturbed by the curtailment of their freedom of enterprise and denounced the measures that boosted their living standards. In the Middle West especially, the late 1930's saw the farm vote shifting away from the Democratic sponsors of the AAA.

But as time went on, the arrangements became routine and customary. By the late 1940's, a large number of farmers had come to accept AAA, and to support government aid policies with their ballots. It appeared unlikely that farmers as a whole would voluntarily relinquish government support. For it was clear that under the new regulations they were getting more security and a larger share of the consumer's dollar than ever before.

War Brings Boom Years

In the early stages of World War II (1939–41) the American farmer benefited from increasing domestic prices and consumption. After Pearl Harbor (December, 1941) things were better still. Large shipments of food to wartime allies from 1942 to 1945, and to post-war friends thereafter, insured the farmer a market for record-breaking crops. In 1944, for the first time since 1915, American farmers produced over 1,000,000,000 bushels of wheat. This crop went at the high price of $1.40 a bushel. More billion-bushel years followed, with prices soaring above $2.00 a bushel. Corn-and-hog farmers fared even better. In 1931 the entire corn crop had brought its growers less than $1,000,000,000. Returns exceeded $5,000,000,000 in each of the two immediate postwar years and approached that figure in 1948 and 1949. Drastic acreage restriction allowed even cotton growers to share in the boom. Production remained well below the level of the 1920's and 1930's; but prices soared to more than 30¢ a pound, as against less than a fifth of that sum during the depression.

Land prices, of course, responded to the good times. All through American history, farmers had seen the value of their land appreciate. After World War I there came a change. From 1920 to 1933 the value of farmland declined (and by 60 percent). Economists began to talk of heavily taxed land losing its value altogether. But by 1948 farmland had regained its record-breaking price level of 1920.

There was, meanwhile, some shift in the nature of crops planted. The increasing demand for plastics and other synthetic products opened new markets for agriculture. The cultivation of soybeans, used for oil and in plastics, jumped from 200,000 acres in the early 1920's to fifty times that much (10,000,000 acres) in 1949.

In this era of expansion, the farmer relied on the machine rather than on human labor. The city people who had flocked to the country during the depression hastened to return to urban centers as soon as the job market made that possible. The demands of military service further cut the available supply of agricultural labor; and those who were willing to be farm hands wanted better pay and better living and working conditions than before. The owners of farms therefore speeded up the mechanization process, so as to reduce their dependence on labor. While agricultural production rose 20 percent in the 1940's, the number of workers on the land decreased.

The Advance of Science

The 50 percent increase in the productivity of agricultural land and workers after World War I stemmed from better knowledge of soils, greater use of lime and fertilizer, new varieties of seed, scientific breeding and feeding of animals, and new machinery. Soil analysis improved, especially after the translation from the Russian of Glinka's findings (1927). Scientists discovered some of the effects of rare minerals and microörganisms, adding to the older chemistry of the soil an equally important biology. Patient research workers developed new types of wheat, corn, cotton, and other crops with greater yields and more resistance to disease. Ceres wheat and hybrid corn removed many of the farmers' problems associated with climate, fungi, and insects, while at the same time these varieties grew faster and more luxuriantly.

There were improvements in every field. Veterinary medicine reduced hog and cattle disease such as cholera and tuberculosis, protecting both raiser and consumer. Better nutrition and selective breeding added as much as 50 percent to the weight of hogs and cattle and the milk yield of dairy cows. Even the barnyard chicken changed its form through confinement in "chicken hotels" and breeding for meat or eggs rather than legs and wings. Farm machinery had, of course, been evolving for a century; but small, reasonably priced tractors gave a new incentive to mechanization. Multiple-row corn cultivators, field hay-bailers, farm elevator equipment, and numerous new devices increased productivity per worker for those who could afford the capital investment. Mechanical cotton pickers were proving successful on some cotton lands by the end of the period, a fact of great social significance in the South.

This rapid evolution of agriculture into a scientific, mechanized industry threatened the small and inefficient farmer. The spread became greater between the well-equipped operator on 400 acres and the hand worker on 40. During the first half of the 1940's the total value of farms between 30 and 99 acres rose only half as fast as that of farms between 100 and 499 acres. With the favorable prices after World War II, even small farmers were doing fairly well; but leaner years and further mechanical and scientific advances would renew the economic pressure for their elimination.

The farm problem was not solved. Once again the government might have to face the question of whether inefficient men should be kept on farms because farming is a desirable way of life, or whether the agricultural working force should be limited to its economically valuable members. The answer to this, in turn, might depend upon the level of employment in industry.

The General Welfare: A New Conception

As they entered the second half of the twentieth century, American citizens worried about their economic future. But along with this concern went a sort of confidence in the government. For now at last Americans believed that they could rely on the intervention of government to prevent dire distress for any major part of the population. Certainly this seemed true for the farmer, and for most of those who received wages and salaries. Whether similar aids would come to the rescue of the business proprietors or independent professional men remained to be seen.

All groups recognized that government had become the central mechanism in economic stability. A drastic reduction in government spending would undermine prosperity, whereas old-style depressions seemed unlikely if government activities were rapidly expanded. Very evidently, the clause of the Constitution giving Congress power to "provide for the common Defense and General Welfare of the United States" had come to have a meaning far broader than the founders could have dreamed. Welfare now seemed to mean the personal welfare of each citizen, not merely the welfare of the nation as a political abstraction. Similarly, common defense now appeared to include not only the American people but a large part of the people of the world.

The immediate limits of these concepts were still in doubt in 1950. But the trend toward a continually greater responsibility of the state for the welfare of each group of citizens seemed to be established.

15

Social Reactions

Population Trends

The makeup of the American population changed rapidly after World War I. Birth and death rates declined sharply, causing shifts in age groupings. Americans continued to move about, justifying their reputation as the world's most mobile people; and immigration virtually ceased.

Immigration

Immigration was very heavy between 1880 and World War I; and most of the newcomers came from eastern and southern Europe. These two facts and the decline in opportunities in the United States caused some citizens (including children and grandchildren of foreign born) to speak out in alarm. Would the American people and American culture be swamped by foreigners?

Those who expressed concern noted that immigrants were coming in at the rate of nearly 1,000,000 a year; the total for 1900–17 exceeded the population of the country as of 1830. Through most of the nineteenth century the bulk of the immigrants had been of British, Irish, and German stock. Such people had a cultural background similar to that of native white Americans and were assimilated without too much difficulty. But by 1920 most of the foreign born were from eastern and southern Europe. (In 1880, the foreign born included 2,000,000 of German origin, less than 50,000 of Italian. Four decades later, there were 1,700,000 Germans, 1,800,000 Italians.) Many considered the new groups difficult to assimilate because their cultural traditions were dissimilar from those of the older American stocks. The problem was aggravated by the fact that most Italian, Slavic, and French-Canadian newcomers tended to congregate in urban neighborhoods, where their own culture persisted in "islands" surrounded by native areas. Although the older Americans did not want the newcomers in *their* neighborhoods, they at the same time claimed that the immigrants were holding aloof; that the melting pot no longer worked.

Such fears had been expressed before. But circumstances now increased the effectiveness of opposition to immigration. World War I strengthened the labor unions that opposed the influx of low-wage workers. The war increased nationalist feeling, which added to suspicion of foreigners. And some citizens who sympathized with the hopes of newcomers felt that the immigration process must be slowed down if assimilation was to be made effective.

In response to pressures of this sort, Congress passed several acts which sharply reduced immigration. Emergency quota laws of 1921 and 1922 were followed by permanent legislation in 1924. This cut total annual immigration to 150,000; and it favored northern Europeans over persons from southern and eastern Europe. From 1924 to 1929 the annual immigration from each country was limited to 2 percent of its immigrants who had been living in the United States in 1890. Since the foreign born of 1890 were predominantly north Europeans, this formula favored immigration from that area, as against other parts of Europe. The national origins system used after 1929 operated in much the same fashion. Average immigration from northern Europe in the years just before World War I had been 175,000. Under the quota rates of 1929, the limits were set at the slightly lower figure of 130,000. But eastern and southern Europe, which had averaged just short of 700,000 before World War I, were now cut sharply to 20,000. Asiatics were treated even more severely, most of them being barred altogether.

Canadians and Latin-Americans were exempted from these restrictions. So were residents of American insular possessions. Seeking opportunities in unskilled labor, thousands of Puerto Ricans crowded into New York City slums; and some 45,000 Filipinos entered the country during the 1920's. Many Mexican laborers also crossed the border, as employers in the Southwest continued to seek cheap labor. By the time of the depression their numbers had reached 1,500,000.

Despite the entry of these special groups, and a very small amount of smuggling, the new restrictive statutes were generally effective. The coming of the depression after 1929 reduced immigration below what the quotas would have allowed. Under the legislation, the executive was authorized to exclude anyone likely to become a public charge. This could cover anybody in the dark days of the 1930's. Such an interpretation cut the flow of immigrants to the merest trickle (35,000 in 1935, as compared with 800,000 in 1921). Emigration exceeded immigration in the early 1930's, for the first time in American history. When business improved, after 1939, World War II prevented the movement of peoples. The trend was upward after the war but was held within narrow limits by the quota system. After 1920 there was a steady decline in the percentage of foreign born in the population of the United States.

In closing the door to most immigrants after 1929, Congress reversed a long-standing American tradition. For three centuries, since the first settlements had been made, the practice had been to welcome newcomers. Exceptions there had been, as when the slave trade in Negroes was stopped (1809), and when the Chinese were excluded (1882). But the mass movement of Europeans went on unchecked, providing needed labor and satisfying the American desire to help the poor and oppressed.

By 1920, however, basic needs and attitudes had permanently changed. Although the country was still capable of supporting greater numbers of people, there was no longer an urgent need for additional farmers or laborers. Employers still wanted cheap labor; but employers could not determine all national policies.

By 1929, therefore, a great historic experiment in blending the peoples of many lands had come to an end. Unless policy is changed soon again (which seems unlikely), the United States will develop in the future a population based on that which existed here before 1930. This means a people who are, in greatest part, descended from British, Irish, Scandinavian, and German forebears. British stock (including the Scots-Irish) made up just short of half the total population. A sixth of the total had German background, a ninth Irish. Americans of African background were about as numerous as those with Irish ancestors. Eastern and southern Europeans, on the other hand, furnished very little of the total: Poles 4 percent, Italians slightly less.

Of greater significance was the fact that the customs and outlook— the whole cultural pattern—of Americans would be related to the north European background. Americans from other parts of Europe, and from other parts of the world, would make valuable contributions to national life. But, in the main, they would be assimilated into the earlier tradition.

Migrations Within the United States

Down to the time of the Civil War, the most persistent and significant internal migration was the westward movement—inland across the coastal plain, over the Appalachians into the Mississippi Valley, and on to the Pacific coast. This continued after 1865, as the farther reaches of the Valley, the Rocky Mountain area, and the Pacific coast were partially filled in by settlement. There was a heavy movement into Texas, Oklahoma, and the western plains just before World War I, and to California during and after the depression of the 1930's.

Nonetheless, the westward movement had slowed down by the twentieth century, as the more desirable regions had become well occupied. Despite the growth of total population between 1910 and 1940, the number of eastern born who lived west of the Mississippi declined, from a little more than 5,000,000 to a little less. Meantime, a reverse movement back to the East gained momentum. In 1910, 700,000 western born had lived in the East; by 1940 this had risen to nearly 2,000,000.

While many Americans moved east or west, almost as many migrated north or south. Northern businessmen, teachers, and white-collar workers had long found opportunity in southern towns. Many had gone south during Reconstruction days; and their numbers increased slowly after 1890, as industrialization in Dixie stimulated the growth of cities. The twentieth century saw a continuation of this trend; and by 1940 there were more than 2,000,000 Northerners resident in the South. This movement was facilitated by declining opposi-

tion of Southerners toward Yankees, as memories of the Civil War
receded. Such memories lingered in rural areas but largely disappeared
in growing cities, which now aspired to be as much as possible like
northern centers.

More striking and extensive was the movement of Southerners to
the North. The chief motive, among both professional people and
laborers, was to escape the poverty that followed the Civil War. As
early as 1870, more than 1,000,000 southern born were located in the
North. The movement was given a further impetus in World War I,
when war industries in northern cities created a demand for skilled
and unskilled workers. By 1940 there were nearly 3,500,000 southern-
born citizens living in the North. Many of these were white people
from the southern hill country, where the birth rate was high and
where economic opportunities were limited.

In addition, there was a growing migration of southern Negroes to
such cities as Chicago, Detroit, New York, and Philadelphia. These
Americans made the move for higher wages and to escape the worst
features of the southern segregation system. Movement was heavy in
both world wars; and by 1950 a third of the nation's Negroes lived
outside the South.

More important than intersectional migration was the movement
of citizens from rural to urban areas, from small towns to large cities.
This phenomenon, well under way by 1850, had been accelerated by
the industrial expansion that followed the Civil War. Despite the advantages which technology bestowed on rural life (telephones, automobiles, radio), the urban trend continued through the first half of
the twentieth century. By 1940 more than half the population of the
United States was in towns of over 10,000 population.

Migration to the cities sometimes involved long distances, as when
Negroes went North or Middle Westerners retired to California. Except during war years, however, the greater part of the influx into
large centers came from the surrounding territory. The rate at which
people moved was not continuous, nor was the migration entirely one-
way. Some families went back to the farms and small towns; and the
balance of the ebb and flow was largely determined by comparative
opportunities in rural and urban areas at any one time. Prosperity in-

creased the flow to the cities; depression sent people back to the farm. But in only two years between 1910 and 1950 was migration to rural areas greater than that to the cities. There was no mistaking the long-run trend.

One of the factors that encouraged all internal migration was improved transportation. The spread of the railway network up to about 1910 was followed by the advent of the moderate-priced automobile and the resulting improvement of highways. A considerable part of the population took to the roads, not only for short rides but also for vacation touring. During the 1920's, hundreds of thousands of Easterners motored to the South for winter vacations; and a speculative boom ensued in Florida real estate. Florida lots could be bought from roadside offices as far north as New England. The artificial inflation of real-estate values was reminiscent of earlier land booms. The Florida bubble burst even before the stock market crash of 1929; but winter migration south was only temporarily checked. In addition to the seasonal movement, some moved to Florida or California for good. Growing numbers of elderly people (now more numerous because of the declining death rate) preferred a warmer climate during the years of retirement.

Meanwhile, a reverse flow of peoples moved northward for summer vacations. New England advertised itself as Vacation Land. Other northern areas shared in the business, as longer vacations and the growing popularity of sports took more and more people out of doors. Summer camps as well as summer hotels shared in the profits. New England even cultivated a minor opportunity as a winter resort, with the advent during the 1930's of a vogue for winter sports. It was a rare show at the movies thereafter which did not display either mermaids in Florida or skiers in New Hampshire or Sun Valley, Idaho.

Migration to California was in a class by itself. Thousands of retired midwest farmers were lured to the Los Angeles area by its climate and took up permanent residence there. Besides that, large numbers of poor farmers moved to California during the 1930's, desperately seeking jobs of any sort. These people were driven from their farms on the plains by low prices, exhausted soils, and dust storms. They reached the west coast in dilapidated Fords, destitute and at the mercy of fruit ranchers who exploited their casual labor. The tragedy of these Okies was dramatized for the public in John Steinbeck's memorable novel, *The Grapes of Wrath*.

Migratory labor on the farms was no new thing. For many years, gangs of agricultural laborers had moved with the wheat harvest in its seasonal course from Kansas north to the Canadian plains. Migratory workers were also employed in northwest lumber camps; on sugar beet farms; even, in a less systematic fashion, on truck farms near eastern cities. Living arrangements among the families of such workers were temporary and low grade, shocking from the point of view of any normal standards. Child labor persisted here, after it had been largely eliminated in the cities. Conditions like these bred social bitterness, and the whole situation seemed inconsistent with American living standards and ideals.

As travel by auto became widespread, the railroads were aroused by this competition to a belated improvement in their own services. Schedules were improved and streamlined trains were introduced on main routes. This action dated mainly from the 1930's, when low-fare buses were cutting deeply into railroad passenger service. By then the major bus networks (that of the Greyhound Lines, for instance) rivaled those of large railway systems. In the 1940's the commercial air lines entered the competition, challenging both the railroads and the steamship companies for control of first-class passenger service. The net result of these developments was to provide unexcelled travel facilities to the American public.

Overseas travel greatly expanded after 1920. Steamship lines had long done a big business in bringing immigrants to the United States, and in returning some of them to the old countries. After the Civil War, increasing numbers of American tourists also used the improved steamer services for vacation trips abroad. When quota laws cut off most immigration in the 1920's, steamship lines turned to American tourists as their chief source of passenger revenue. Bigger and better luxury liners were provided—Britain's Cunard Queens, for example.

The depression years after 1929 limited the number of American tourists, and many of the liners were lost in World War II. But during that struggle some 2,000,000 young Americans were in service overseas, and saw more of foreign parts than would have been possible through private travel. After the war tourist business revived rapidly. By 1950, over 1,000,000 Americans were spending summer vacations in Europe, and steamship companies were taking up the winter slack by conducting special tours in Latin-American waters. Travel to Asia, which had reached considerable proportions before 1939, was delayed after the war by disturbed conditions in the Orient. But even here there was some revival by 1950. Travel agencies flourished. European nations had come to look on the tourist business as a chief source for needed American dollars; and the adjacent countries of Canada and Mexico benefited in the same manner.

Important though foreign travel was, most Americans confined their trips to the United States. Here one could move about over an enormous and picturesque land without worrying about passports, baggage inspection, and changing currencies. Americans formed the travel habit, for business and for pleasure; and as they moved about, their horizons broadened, and they tended more and more to think in national terms.

Postwar Nationalism

The upsurge of nationalism in the years following World War I was not without precedent in American history. Earlier periods had witnessed a comparable glorification of American institutions and the identification of Americanism with conservative ideas. But never before had such nationalism been so intensified and so efficiently organized; and never had it been so strongly supported by government action.

Involved in the new nationalism was the repudiation of Wilsonian internationalism and the restriction of immigration to north Europeans—peoples considered racially superior to Orientals and residents of southern and eastern Europe. In the name of 100 percent Americanism, some citizens turned against all radicals and all liberals, on the assumption that they were plotting to extend the Bolshevik Revolution from Russia to the United States. Simultaneously, aliens, Negroes, Catholics, and Jews were made the special targets of intimidation and discrimination. Opposition to these minority elements was led by a new Ku Klux Klan, which justified its actions as necessary to keep America safe for "true Americans." Safe, that is, for native white Protestants who rejected radical or liberal philosophies.

Here was reaction against a deep-rooted American tradition of liberalism. Here was departure from the spirit of tolerance and adaptability to change, essential parts of the American creed.

One factor in the situation was the war. World War I accustomed Americans to rely on force rather than reason. The war also developed propaganda techniques for mobilizing emotions. During the years that followed, these same techniques were exploited by pressure groups interested in swaying public opinion.

The wartime propaganda put out by Wilson's Committee on Public Information had stressed the possible disloyalty of left-wing labor and of immigrants from central Europe. This had created feelings of suspicion and insecurity. It was natural that the fury against the Germans should be transferred to fury against the Bolsheviks, whose revolution seemed to threaten the family, religion, democracy, and private property. As the anti-Bolshevik excitement replaced the anti-German excitement, it seemed logical to regard all American radicals and liberals as advance agents of the world revolution emanating from Moscow.

America was not alone in these trends. The war intensified nationalism everywhere. In Italy it helped bring Benito Mussolini's Fascists to power. A feverish chauvinism developed in the Balkans. Japan, India, and even China stirred with a new nationalism. As always, the United States was affected by world movements. In addition, American prosperity aroused envy and resentment in war-impoverished Europe. Struggling to rebuild their shattered economies, the Allies expected the United States to cancel war debts and otherwise aid in the rehabilitation of the Old World. When the United States did not do so, America was denounced as selfish, materialistic, and grasping. Such attacks on "Uncle Shylock" served to intensify the nationalistic reaction in the United States.

Labor disturbances also contributed to the postwar troubles. Leaders of organized labor had no intention of losing in the peace the gains they had made during World War I. Postwar inflation and the determination of management to make no more concessions caused a wave of strikes in 1919, involving 4,000,000 workers. Americans already worried about the possibility of revolution looked on these strikes with grave concern.

Early in 1919, the nation's eyes were focused on Seattle, Washington, where the walkout of 30,000 shipyard workers led to a general strike. Mayor Ole Hanson advertised the affair as an effort to overthrow the government and organized society. The strike was broken; and Mayor Hanson wrote a book entitled *Americanism Versus Bolshevism*. He also toured the country, telling audiences how he had turned back the Red tide. His speeches and writings attacked labor leaders, demanded exclusion of eastern and southern Europeans, and labeled the advocate of internationalism as "one who sympathizes with the bolshevistic tendencies of our time."

The same year, 1919, brought a dramatic effort to organize the workers in the steel industry. The organizing drive was sponsored by Samuel Gompers, the anticommunist and antisocialist president of the A.F. of L. But the drive itself was led by William Z. Foster, a left-wing labor organizer who had been a syndicalist and would soon announce his conversion to communism. In the fall of 1919, a third of a million steel workers left their jobs in plants around Chicago and Pittsburgh. Partly because of Foster's leadership, and partly because of the temper of the times, much of the nation's press portrayed the strike as a Bolshevik plot. Many citizens accepted this interpretation when they heard of the high proportion of recent immigrants among the strikers and when they read news reports of violence and bloodshed in strike areas. There was general satisfaction, therefore, when martial law was proclaimed, and when the strike collapsed, early in 1920.

After the strike was over, there was some shift in public sentiment toward the steel workers. This was in part owing to an investigation by the Interchurch World Movement. In a published report, the investigators stated that, despite Foster's presence in the picture, the strike was not Bolshevik controlled, nor was it designed to overthrow the government. It was, basically, an effort to improve the lot of steel workers, many of whom toiled twelve hours a day, seven days a week,

under unenviable conditions. Much of the violence associated with
the strike was employer connected. Company officials broke up union
meetings and promoted bad feeling between Serbian and Italian workers. Negro strikebreakers were brought in, which caused riots; and the
steel companies organized a gigantic publicity campaign against the
strikers.

The month that saw the beginning of the steel strike—September,
1919—also brought a walkout of most of Boston's policemen. The
pay and conditions of work were admittedly unsatisfactory; but the
strike immediately concerned the suspension of leaders of a unionization drive. Left without effective protection, Boston suffered property
loss. Public sentiment was strongly against the police. President Wilson called the strike a "crime against civilization"; and Governor Calvin Coolidge found himself a national hero when he belatedly sent
state troops to patrol Boston. ("There is no right to strike against the
public safety," said Coolidge.) This police strike helped Coolidge get
the Republican vice-presidential nomination in 1920. It also confirmed
many Americans in their conviction that revolution was around the
corner, and that the forces of law and order had to be upheld at all
cost.

Next came the Palmer raids, organized by A. Mitchell Palmer, Wilson's Attorney General. Palmer suspected a nation-wide Bolshevik
plot to murder public officials who had offended labor. There was
reason for alarm, for packages containing bombs had been addressed
to several government officials; and Palmer's own house was bombed.

Determined to deal summarily with the unknown criminals, the
Attorney General proceeded with a minimum of regard for constitutional guarantees. (If one used ordinary legal methods, Palmer insisted, the radicals would get away.) Agents of the Federal Bureau of
Investigation raided meeting places and private homes, arresting several thousand persons presumed to be members of left-wing groups.
Most of these were subsequently released; but a few hundred were
deported. Some 250 Russian-born radicals were sent to Soviet Russia
at the end of 1919, though many were long-time residents of the
United States, and not a few were anti-Bolshevik.

In violating civil liberties, Palmer had gone too far and had alarmed Americans who had no sympathy for radicals. In 1920, therefore, there was a reaction against the wholesale raid technique. The Department of Labor refused to give Palmer full coöperation in his deportation plans. Some prisoners were then released. Others were given counsel and, after fair trials, were set free. Members of Congress severely criticized Justice Department methods; and President Wilson stated that suppression was not the answer to America's problems. Palmer failed in a bid for the Democratic presidential nomination in 1920 and slid into political oblivion.

On the state level, the reaction against radicalism expressed itself in a number of ways. Many states passed criminal syndicalist laws which forbade writing or speaking words that might imply revolutionary intent. The effect was to outlaw membership in left-wing parties. Socialists, anarchists, I.W.W. organizers, Socialist Laborites, and Communists all suffered. The New York legislature expelled five Socialist legislators, on the ground that no Socialist could be a loyal American.

Sometimes there was bloodshed, as in the I.W.W.-American Legion clash at Centralia, Washington. The Legion was an organization of World War I veterans, set up to work for pension legislation and to protect the republic against radical ideas. (Theodore Roosevelt, Jr., and other founders of the Legion had the anti-Bolshevik goal very clearly in mind.) The I.W.W., of course, was frankly anticapitalist and had been opposed to the war effort. On Armistice Day, 1919, Legionnaires attacked an I.W.W. meeting hall at Centralia, Washington. In the ensuing riot, four Legion men were killed. Mass arrests of Wobblies followed; and the I.W.W., already declining, practically ceased to exist.

Somewhat different in character was the case of Nicola Sacco and Bartolomeo Vanzetti, Italian immigrants of anarchist views. Sacco, a shoemaker, and Vanzetti, a fish peddler, were charged with a robbery and murder that took place in South Braintree, Massachusetts, in April, 1920. The evidence was contradictory; and many felt that the court was unduly influenced by emotional prejudice against the political views of the defendants. After a long judicial contest, the men were electrocuted (April, 1927), amid a storm of protests. By then the case had become a world symbol of the bitter conflicts between conservatives and radicals.

When Sacco and Vanzetti were executed, the Big Red Scare had run its course. By the end of 1920, it was apparent that the Bolshevik Revolution was not coming to America. Communism, in fact, had failed to take hold outside Russia, despite temporary gains elsewhere in Europe. After a Wall Street explosion of September, 1920 (costing thirty-eight lives), there were no more bomb outrages. American radicals, and some liberals, too, had retreated into silence; and conservatives were reconsidering their positions.

Was repression really wise? In attacking the expulsion of the Socialists from the New York legislature, Charles Evans Hughes (a Republican and no radical) said that this was not the proper way to protect American democracy. New York's Governor Alfred E. Smith (a Democrat and no radical) took much the same position when he vetoed repressive legislation proposed by the witch-hunting Lusk Committee. On the national scene, conservative President Warren G. Harding (1921–23) released Socialist Eugene V. Debs from prison; and this Chief Executive seems to have advised the steel industry that one way of combating radicalism was to get rid of the twelve-hour day.

As excitement died down in the middle 1920's, the liberals and radicals again spoke out freely. These groups were very vocal in the 1930's; and, as before, some conservative groups raised the cry of revolution. This was done when World War I veterans marched on Washington to demand their bonus money (1932–33); when a general strike paralyzed San Francisco (1934); and when workers tried the sit-down. The public, however, did not become alarmed until the late 1940's, when, in the years after World War II, strained relations between Russia and the United States raised disturbing questions.

Treatment of Minorities

The anti-Bolshevik drive of 1919–20 reflected a sense of insecurity which was a relatively new phenomenon in America. That sense of insecurity was especially marked among members of the lower middle classes—persons hit hard by post-World

War I inflation. Rural Protestants blamed their woes on the cities, saw American culture threatened by urban communities which contained Catholics, Jews, foreigners, and radicals. Native white laborers North and South saw the Negro and the foreigner as their competitors. A swimming-beach incident unleashed pent-up emotions in Chicago in 1919, leading to a virtual race war in which three dozen citizens were killed and over 500 wounded (the Negroes suffering more than the whites). There were other race riots in Omaha, Tulsa, and elsewhere. All of which provided a background for the rise of the Ku Klux Klan.

Founded at Atlanta in 1915, the Klan remained unimportant until 1920. It was in effect a revival of the nativist Know-Nothing party of the 1850's and the anti-Negro Ku Klux Klan of Reconstruction days. But the new Klan differed from its predecessors in its high degree of organization and commercialization. Ten-dollar memberships were sold all over the nation, proceeds being divided among local, state, and national officers (called Kleagles, Goblins, and the like).

Many of the citizens who joined the Klan did so to find escape from village boredom in the hooded processions, the secret rituals, the burning of great wooden crosses on hilltops. Many also found in the bigoted and prejudiced exclusion of aliens, Negroes, Jews, and Catholics the emotional satisfaction that comes from the sense of being of the elite. Klan hoods gave protection to the brutally inclined. According to exposures in the New York *World*, the Klan in 1920–21 was guilty of two murders, two mutilations, forty-one floggings, twenty-seven tar-and-feather outrages.

In some states, notably in Indiana, the Klan became a political power. But influence faded fast when Indiana's Klansman governor, David C. Stephenson, went to prison for murder. (He was not released until 1950.) By 1926 the power of the Klan everywhere was on the wane. But the prejudice which the Klan reflected remained a part of American life.

In most southern states the Ku Klux Klan was primarily anti-Negro; in the North and West, chiefly anti-Catholic. Only incidentally was it anti-Semitic. These years, however, did see various attacks on the Jews. Immediately after World War I, Henry Ford's Dearborn *Independ-*

ent waged a campaign against the Jewish "money power," Jewish "radicals," and Jewish "monopoly" of the professions. The paper even professed to believe in the long-discredited "Protocols of the Elders of Zion," a forgery purporting to be an agreement for Jewish subjugation of the Gentiles. Although Ford publicly repudiated anti-Semitism, these articles did much harm.

The 1930's saw the rise of Adolf Hitler and his brutal treatment of the Jews in Germany. Most Americans were shocked, and many stated their views in protests and by boycotting German goods. But Hitler's anti-Semitic propaganda also found ears in the United States. Part of this was owing to the depression situation; job competition tends to increase discrimination. In addition, some of those who attacked the Jews were pro-Nazi and favorable toward dictatorship—Fritz Kuhn of the German-American Bund, for example, and William Dudley Pelley of the Silver Shirts. Anti-Semitism was also voiced in the 1930's by Father Charles Coughlin, a Detroit radio priest with a large following. (Coughlin was ultimately silenced by superiors; and most Catholic leaders, including the Pope, severely condemned anti-Semitism.) Anti-Semitism persisted even in the 1940's, in the midst of war against the race-persecuting Nazis.

Other minorities also suffered. When Japan attacked Pearl Harbor in December, 1941, Japanese citizens in the United States were very badly treated. So were Americans of Japanese descent. Those located along the Pacific coast were forced to wind up their business affairs at once, generally at great sacrifice. Then they were sent inland, to government camps. This mass uprooting of tens of thousands of persons was associated with the shock Americans felt after the Pearl Harbor disaster, and with the fear of espionage and sabotage along the Pacific coast. But it is also evident that Americans who had long been anti-Japanese used the occasion to get rid of Japanese and Japanese-Americans. In other words, the evacuation of 1942 was a logical sequel to the California land laws of the World War I era, which prohibited aliens from owning land; a logical sequel, too, of the United States immigration law of 1924, which barred Japanese from entering the United States.

It could be said, then, that minority groups fared badly at the hands of many Americans in the twentieth century. At the same time, it should be added that other citizens criticized the hate campaigns and did all they could to combat mistreatment of minorities. Furthermore, it is apparent that most minority groups in the United States were in a better position at mid-century than they had been a generation earlier.

Attacks on discrimination and intolerance never ceased. Through its whole active career, the Ku Klux Klan was denounced, not only by radicals, but by liberals too, and by many conservatives, including conservative Southerners. Although many politicians were glad to have Klan support, few would admit as much or acknowledge being Klansmen. The Klan was strong; but anti-Klan sentiment was always stronger. This was very evident when bigots tried unsuccessfully to revive the Klan in the 1940's.

In like fashion, anti-Semites of the 1930's drew little backing from the public. When Charles A. Lindbergh made a statement critical of Jews at an America First rally just before American entry into World War II, that utterance did the America First cause substantial damage. Even during World War II many Americans criticized the manner in which the Japanese-Americans were treated. An even friendlier gesture toward a minority group was seen in the repeal in 1943 of the Chinese exclusion legislation. This made Chinese-born residents of the United States eligible for citizenship; and it ended Chinese exclusion, putting China on the quota list. This meant the admission of only a handful of Chinese each year (105, to be exact); but it was an important gesture of good will.

Still more significant was an antidiscrimination movement which gained force after World War II. States passed fair employment practice laws and took steps to enforce them. Efforts were made to reduce discrimination against minorities in federal employment. Scholars, novelists, movie makers turned to antidiscrimination themes. Laura Z. Hobson's *Gentleman's Agreement* (dealing with anti-Semitism) sold well as a novel and was an effective moving picture. The same could be said for William L. White's *Lost Boundaries*, which dealt with the Negro question. Radio and school programs were aimed at the elimination of discrimination.

Among other things, the trend toward better treatment of minorities reflected humanitarian sentiment. Involved, too, were intellectuals who believed in cultural pluralism and who therefore stressed the contributions of minority groups to American culture. Rather more important was a mounting conviction that the United States would be judged abroad partly by its treatment of minorities at home. Finally, thoughtful Americans were concluding that if minority groups were treated well they would be unlikely to be interested in extremist views.

Negro Americans
These were important years in the history of American Negroes, who composed a tenth of the population of the United States. For one thing, this was an era of Negro migration, from southern farms to southern and northern cities. At the same time, it was a period when Negro leaders became more outspoken, more insistent on the constitutional and human rights of the members of their race. And, despite the Ku Klux Klan and other obstacles, the Negroes made substantial gains in these decades.

Not that all was well. It most emphatically was not. The segregation system survived in the South; and poverty and restrictive real-estate covenants kept northern Negroes jammed into urban slums. There was friction between Negroes and whites in northern schools and factories, and on the streets. But the Negroes had come to stay. Negro physicians and lawyers, journalists and clergymen became more prosperous, more militant, and more effective in northern cities. At first politicians paid little attention to the Negro vote, which was solidly Republican (the party of Abraham Lincoln). During the depression, however, many Negroes shifted to the Democrats. As the Democrats tried to hold, and the Republicans to regain, Negro support, the Negro vote became increasingly important. Negroes were elected to Congress from New York and Chicago; and little by little their race obtained greater consideration from city, state, and national officials.

What the Negro wanted was elimination of discrimination in public and private employment, in education, housing, and other fields. Striking victories were achieved after 1920, and especially after 1945. These included the adoption of state anti-bias and fair employment practice

THE NEGRO IN THE UNITED STATES

DISTRIBUTION OF NEGRO POPULATION
PERCENT OF TOTAL POPULATION 1940

In the twentieth century, as in slave days, most American Negroes lived in the southeastern part of the United States, and especially in the cotton-producing states. It will be noted, however, that whites outnumber the Negroes even in the states of the deep South. (Negroes make up most of the population in many lowland cotton-growing counties, but the hill counties are predominantly white.)

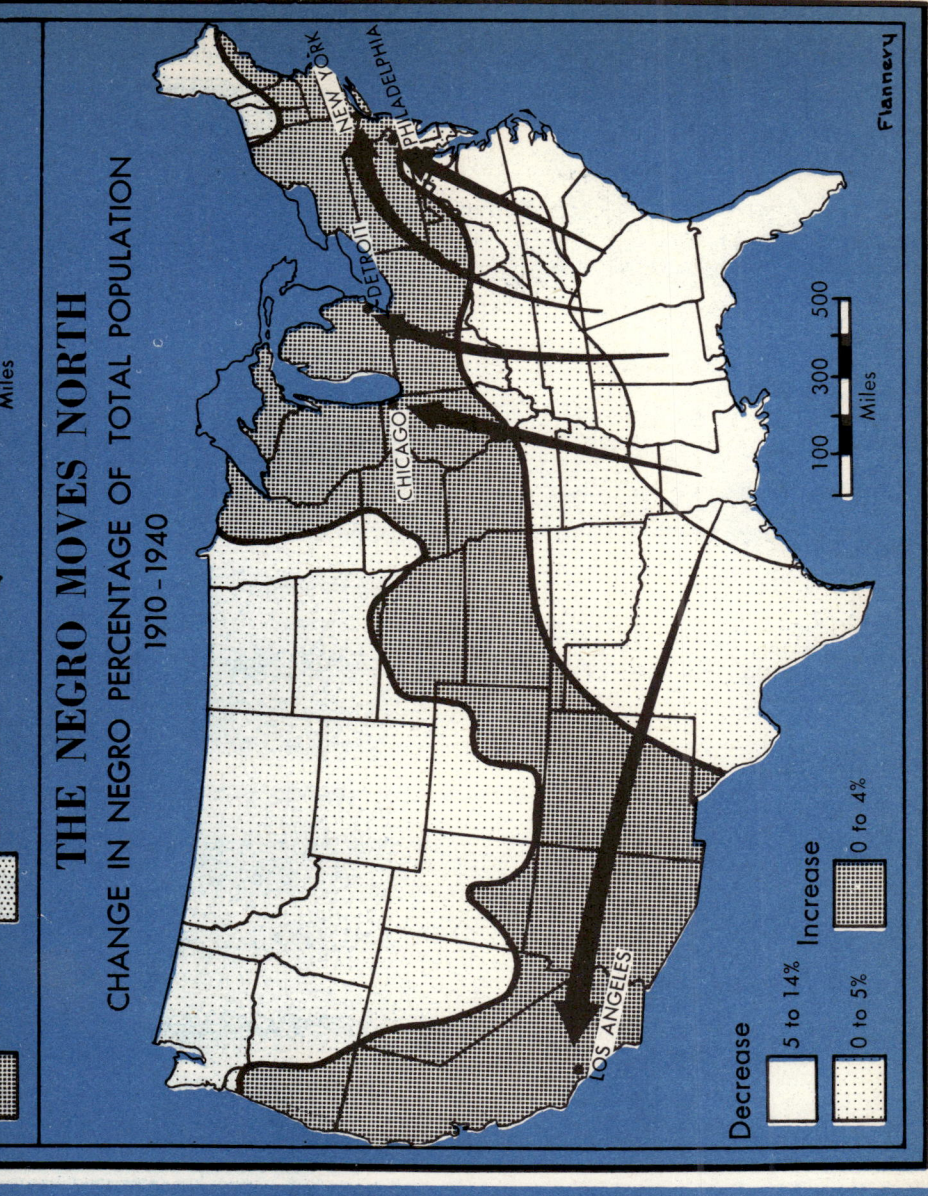

THE NEGRO MOVES NORTH

CHANGE IN NEGRO PERCENTAGE OF TOTAL POPULATION
1910 - 1940

6 to 25%

Less than 1%

100 300 500
Miles

100 300 500
Miles

Decrease

5 to 14%

0 to 5%

Increase

0 to 4%

NEW YORK
PHILADELPHIA
DETROIT
CHICAGO
LOS ANGELES

Flannery

Although most Negroes remained in the South, many were dissatisfied with their role in the southern plantation economy. Some therefore migrated to southern and border cities—Atlanta, New Orleans, Birmingham, St. Louis, Baltimore. Others moved to northern or far western industrial centers. As a result, the Negroes made up a smaller percentage of the southern population in 1940 than in 1910. In like fashion, Negroes formed a larger percentage of the northern population in 1940 than in 1910.

It will be noted that the Negro showed a greater tendency to leave the deep South than the border states, and that the Negro, a farmer in the South, did not move into northern farm areas. The Negro population of the wheat states showed a relative decline in this period.

acts; an increase in opportunities for Negroes in federal government service; the espousal of national fair employment legislation by President Harry Truman and by leading Republicans; the partial breakdown of segregation in the armed services after World War II; the admission of Negroes to organized baseball (when Jackie Robinson joined the Brooklyn Dodgers in 1948); the slightly less unfriendly attitude of labor leaders toward Negroes; the decision of leading newspapers to stop giving undue attention to crimes committed by nonwhites; the appointment of Negroes to high positions (as in the case of Ralph Bunche of the United Nations); the popularity of books and moving pictures dealing with race discrimination (Richard Wright's *Black Boy; Kingsblood Royal,* by Sinclair Lewis; and many more). Although any number of problems remained acute in the early 1950's, the Negro had come a long way in two generations.

The Negro had moved ahead in the South as well as in the North. The old tenancy system continued to prevail, except where white and Negro sharecroppers were thrown off the land to make way for large-scale production. (Croppers then became farm laborers, if they were employed at all.) The segregation system persisted; and when depression came, Negroes on relief received less consideration than did the unemployed whites. But the situation did get better, all the same. There was some increase in the number of Negro landowners. And, humble though they were, the Negro sections of the southern towns provided opportunities for Negroes to rise in the economic scale and become merchants, dentists, realtors, lawyers, bankers, and insurance salesmen.

Gradually, too, dents were made in the old segregation system. In a series of decisions (notably Nixon *vs.* Herndon, 1927, and Smith *vs.* Allwright, 1944), the United States Supreme Court upheld the right of Negroes to vote in Democratic primaries—the only important elections in most southern states. There followed a sharp increase in the number of Negro voters in the old slave states. In other decisions (as in the Ada Sipuel case of 1948), the Supreme Court ruled that, in fields where there were no adequate educational facilities for Negroes, the southern state-supported "white" institutions had to admit qualified Negroes. By 1950 a handful of Negroes had been admitted to the medical and law colleges of the state universities of such southern states as Arkansas. By then the judges were beginning to question the legality of agreements designed to keep nonwhites out of certain residential neighborhoods (as in the District of Columbia Covenant cases of 1949).

Disapproving of such developments, some southern whites tried to stop the tide. Southern state legislators attempted to rewrite restrictive and segregation laws so that they would hold up in court. Some conservative states'-rights Southerners went so far as to break with the national Democratic party in 1948 and run a separate (Dixiecrat) presidential candidate. But, though the movement for Negro rights gained slowly, it nonetheless did continue to advance, in all parts of the nation.

The Indians

According to census figures, there were forty Negroes to every Indian in the United States. Despite a slow increase in population during the twentieth century, the Indians numbered less than 400,000 at mid-century—about one-quarter of one percent of the total population. Many persons with some Indian blood were not included in this figure; but even their inclusion would not have made the total large.

Before the Civil War, government policy had been to drive the Indians west and herd them into reservations. Theoretically, reservation lands were granted in perpetuity; in practice, the whites continually cut down the Indians' share of the national domain. The Dawes Act of 1887, designed to prepare the Indian for citizenship, did not do that job very well. (Citizenship rights were not extended until 1924.) The Dawes Act did, however, lead to the breakup and loss of much tribal land. Contrary to popular belief, only a very few Indians profited from oil strikes on their property. The bulk of the red men remained extremely poor; the Indian had lost the old ways without picking up the new. An Indian Reorganization Act of 1934 proposed to keep remaining reservation lands intact and to improve these properties through long-range planning. This did some good. But some reservations were too small or barren, too eroded or overgrazed to be redeemed. In 1948 the American public was shocked to hear of widespread malnutrition among the Navahos. The news was the more impressive in that it came just when the United States was getting ready to help foreign nations through the Marshall Plan. Congress hastily voted emergency funds; but it was necessary to admit that three full centuries had not sufficed to solve the Indian problem.

Perhaps, however, time would provide a solution. Many an Indian had left the reservation by 1950, had cast off tribal culture and become absorbed in the general population. And, despite efforts to preserve and revive Indian arts, the reservations also felt the impact of the white man's ways. Absorption in blood and culture seemed the long-run outlook for the Indian.

Prosperity and Depression

During the middle 1920's many Americans came to believe that prosperity was both universal and permanent. The great financial crash of 1929, therefore, came as a sickening shock; and the shock helps explain the turmoil and confusion of the 1930's. As if domestic woes were not enough, the same decade saw the rise of totalitarian fascism in Europe—a challenge to the American way of life.

All this time, Americans faced problems associated with technologic change. New sources of power transformed the farm and factory and affected every aspect of life in the United States. Most Americans welcomed the new machines as keys to comfort; but few saw the dislocations caused by the machine age. Men change their values slowly. Hence there was little planning of the social and economic adjustments called for by mechanization. Machines gave control over time and distance. At the same time they made men more interdependent, thus robbing the old individualism of much of its meaning. Machines brought leisure; but they also threw the economic system out of gear by producing more than could be consumed under prevailing patterns of income and distribution.

The economic recession of 1920–22 was followed by a half-dozen years of prosperity. This prosperity was shared unequally by the urban classes and only slightly affected the farmer. Yet there was a substantial increase in real per capita income. Most citizens accepted the thesis that this expansion of the nation's wealth proved the soundness of big business, mass production, and scientific management. Champions of the new order in the 1920's claimed—and few Americans doubted—that production and consumption would continue to expand in a never ending prosperity. Provided, of course, that government continued to be friendly to big business, and so long as radicals were kept from upsetting the applecart.

In support of this general view, it was noted that citizens in the lower-income brackets were buying automobiles, radios, and other mechanical gadgets. In 1919 there were fewer than 7,000,000 automobiles in the whole country. As mass production lowered costs, the number more than trebled in one decade. As early as 1923 two out of every three families in the typical small city of Muncie, Indiana ("Middletown"), owned cars. The sums spent for radios increased by 500 percent between 1923 and 1929, when every third home in the land had a set. Equally spectacular were the increases in sales of cigarettes, rayon clothing, and cosmetics.

But there was another side to the picture. In the prosperous 1920's wage earners received a slightly smaller proportion of the total value of goods produced than they did in 1900. Even at the end of the 1920's most city homes lacked electric refrigeration, and many had neither electric lights nor furnace heat. A substantial fraction of the car owners of Muncie, Indiana, lived in shabby houses without bathtubs. Great sections of textile workers and coal miners suffered from the chronic depression that plagued these industries; innumerable tenant and sharecrop farmers enjoyed few of the luxuries of the prosperity decade. In some industries, workers over forty-five years of age had difficulty holding jobs. Besides that, new machines threw perhaps 2,000,000 men out of work each year.

Figures told the story. In the 1920's, 7,000,000 families had less than $1500 annual income. An additional 15,000,000 received less than $2500. None of these families enjoyed what government experts regarded as an adequate standard of living; but they included most of the population of the United States. At the same time, many citizens were very wealthy. In 1929 two percent of the population owned three-fifths of the nation's wealth. Clearly, the prosperity of the 1920's was shared unequally.

Moreover, much of the prosperity rested on insecure foundations. Paper fortunes, "made" in Florida real estate and on the New York stock market, melted away as quickly as they had been won. Billions of dollars were spent in advertising electric gadgets, cosmetics, and other luxuries. High-pressure salesmen appealed to the citizen's desire to look young, attractive, and prosperous. Installment buying reached the $7,000,000,000 mark in 1929, or 15 percent of retail purchases. It should have been clear that if installment buyers suffered a shrinkage of income or lost their jobs, the economy would sustain a serious blow. But mass advertising, success stories in the magazines and movies, and the pronouncements of business and government leaders reassured the people. Prosperity had come to stay; every American was to enjoy an increasingly high standard of living. A chicken in every pot, said Herbert Hoover; two cars in every garage.

A few questioned these statements and assumptions—liberal journalists, some social workers, a few politicians, and spokesmen of the submerged left. Some novelists painted a dark picture of the republic. In *Main Street*, Sinclair Lewis satirized the parasitic relationship of the midwest business community with neighboring farmers. Ring Lardner's racy stories described the frustration of suckers who fell for get-rich-quick schemes, and the victims of the highly commercialized sports world. The chaos of the times, the dependence of men and women on forces they could not understand provided the themes for John Dos Passos in his *U. S. A.* trilogy.

Others also issued warnings. The dangers and inconsistencies of prosperity were set forth by social scientists in such studies as *Recent Economic Trends* and *Recent Social Trends*. John Dewey, the leading educator and philosopher, insisted that machines controlled rather than served mankind; it should be the other way around. Some pointed to the less attractive social features of the automobile: the decline in church attendance; the quick getaway for criminals; the appalling accident toll (30,000 fatalities in 1929). But all these notes of warning were overshadowed by the general optimism of the decade.

The crash of 1929 and the ensuing depression gave the critics of the

1920's a larger audience. For a brief period in the 1930's, Americans listened to Howard Scott and other advocates of technocracy. The technocrats favored turning control of the economy over to a managerial-engineer elite. The Marxists enjoyed a longer period of influence; but they too failed to win more than a small proportion of Americans. Most citizens remained attached to capitalism, and rejected the argument of those who said that only under socialism could a machine economy function in the interest of the people. Others, including the Southern Agrarians, reacted to the depression by repudiating the whole technological basis of modern society and by advocating an impossible return to an idealized agrarian culture.

While rejecting such points of view, the majority of Americans refused to continue to accept business leadership. Citizens who had allowed Henry Ford, Samuel Insull, and other big businessmen to set the philosophic as well as the economic patterns of the 1920's now turned to other models. The greatest number took up the thesis behind Franklin D. Roosevelt's New Deal (1933–38). According to this thesis, Americans could work out a way of life mid-point between the old rugged individualism of an uncontrolled big business economy and a European-type collectivism. The economy might be held in proper balance by moderate state subsidies and controls. In other words, the machines would produce for a public capable of buying its products, once purchasing power was restored and extended.

Was this goal achieved during and after the 1930's? Not entirely. The New Deal was based on compromise as well as principle; and after 1939 world crises made it difficult to concentrate on domestic problems. The postwar years (after 1945) still saw the great majority of Americans badly housed and unable to afford many of the comforts created by modern science and technology. Productivity increased both on the farm and in the factory; and the economy was still capable of turning out more product than could be absorbed easily by normal domestic peacetime consumption.

By mid-century, however, the average citizen fared better than in the booming 1920's. Farmers and laborers had made substantial advances. In 1929 every third family had a radio. Two decades later nearly every family had one, and the average was two. Few farms and city residences lacked electricity; and an increasingly large percentage of working-class Americans were thinking in terms of electric refrigerators and washing machines.

Crime

In the decade of the 1920's, the accent was on conservatism and order. Such an age might have been expected to produce reverence for traditional values and for obedience to the law. But it did not. The scandalous corruption of highly placed officials during the presidential administration of Warren G. Harding (1921–23) was paralleled by misdeeds in the states and cities. Never a notably law-abiding people, Americans outdid themselves in the 1920's, flouting laws distasteful or inconvenient. The homicide rate was sixteen times that of England. Theft cost Americans a quarter of a billion dollars a year, little being recovered and few culprits apprehended. More serious still, crime came to be organized in an efficient manner. The organizers—men like Al Capone and John Dillinger—received much newspaper space and were half-admired by many law-abiding citizens.

One feature of the crime wave was violation of the Eighteenth Amendment to the Constitution. This amendment prohibited manufacture, transportation, and sale of intoxicating beverages. Prohibition stemmed from the old temperance movement, which was associated with evangelical church endeavor and with rural opposition to the encroachment of urban folkways in country districts. For decades before World War I, restrictive legislation had been demanded by religious and women's organizations; by white Southerners who said that drink made Negroes "hard to handle"; by employers who felt that liquor reduced the efficiency of employees. Then World War I, with its need for grain conservation, put the movement over, in the United States and many other countries.

After the adoption of the Eighteenth Amendment, Congress passed the Volstead Act and other enforcement measures. These never worked well, chiefly because of the determined resistance of millions of urban Americans. Neither cities nor states nor the federal government provided adequate enforcement machinery—if, indeed, any machinery could have been adequate under the circumstances. Americans who had seldom touched liquor were intrigued with the desire to do what the law prohibited. Others, accustomed to drinking, did not propose to stop. Some brewed and distilled in their cellars and bathrooms. Others patronized speak-easies and bootleggers. Supplies came partly from industrial alcohol channels; partly from rumrunners who smuggled in liquor from Canada, Mexico, and the West Indies; partly from farmers who produced corn and grapes, wheat and hops directly for the illicit liquor manufacturers, small and large.

Bootlegging became a big business, yielding profits that equaled those of all save the largest legitimate enterprises. To protect these profits, the liquor interests paid protection to the police, and corrupted journalists and legislators. Using machine guns and armored cars, they forced their goods on retailers and crushed their rivals in gang warfare.

As they gained power, many bootleg gangs expanded their empires, bringing under their control betting establishments, gambling houses, brothels, even such respectable small businesses as garages and laundries. The helpless proprietors were required to pay substantial sums in return for the "protection" of their establishments against hoodlums in the employ of the gangs. When appealed to, the police tended to throw up their hands in utter helplessness.

Not until the depression hit was the trend reversed. Then came repeal of the Eighteenth Amendment, by the adoption of the Twenty-First Amendment in 1933. This came as a result of widespread recognition of the failure of enforcement efforts, also a depression-inspired desire to raise money with liquor taxes. When prohibition died, some bootleg gangs went out of existence. Others shifted their attention to different enterprises. Gambling was a favorite: slot machines; the policy racket; betting halls that quoted odds on horse races, prize fights, basketball games, and elections. Some bootleggers tried politics. Others wormed their way into small business. Still others managed to get into labor unions.

Gradually, however, the public became aroused. The press printed stories about the doping of race horses and the fixing of prize fights; about the beating of restaurant owners and furriers who would not pay protection; about the tie-up between politics and crime. A series of kidnapings (notably that of the son of Charles A. Lindbergh) shocked the public into action. As a result, new laws were passed. Improved federal and state law-enforcement agencies coöperated in efficient fashion, using science and technology to track down criminals. The Treasury Department closed in on Al Capone for non-payment of income tax. Government agents (G-men) from J. Edgar Hoover's Federal Bureau of Investigation in the Justice Department took the place of racketeers as folk heroes of young Americans. Local prosecutors like Thomas E. Dewey and William O'Dwyer in New York built reputations as racket-busters. O'Dwyer, a Democrat who had been a policeman, broke up "Murder, Incorporated" in Brooklyn. Dewey, a Republican, put behind bars the notorious "Lucky" Luciano, and also Jimmy Hines, a Tammany politician with underworld connections.

Although the results were impressive, this was no job that could be done and laid aside. When one criminal was killed or caught, others took over the work. World War II saw officials selling influence, and criminals penetrating into war production. Then and in the postwar period there was an alarming increase in juvenile delinquency, featured by wars between youthful gangs. Americans were also disturbed to learn that foreign spies could operate within the republic. Concerned also with the operations of leading gamblers, Congress launched an investigation of such persons in 1950. By then, with the coöperation of sports officials and labor leaders, businessmen and schoolteachers, government officials were making real headway in the long fight against crime.

The Jazz Age, and After

The defiance of prohibition was in line with other trends of the jazz age. In the 1920's the younger generation (and many older citizens as well) took pleasure in defying conventions. The new code called for women to emancipate themselves by smoking cigarettes, wearing their hair in "boyish bobs," taking to the new short dresses that barely reached the knees, and talking freely about sex. It was "smart" to look down on such traditional values as respect, reverence, and propriety; to appear cynical and disillusioned about "ideals"; to defy the old double standard of morals by open displays of affection and by drinking bootleg liquor in mixed gatherings. Dancing became a matter of intimate embraces to the tune of syncopated jazz rhythms. The popular songs stressed sex and pseudo-sophistication.

Many writers of the 1920's echoed the sentiments of the jazz age. One example was Ernest Hemingway, who wrote hard-boiled stories about drinking, bullfighting, and sex. But the real voice of the era was the *American Mercury*. Edited by H. L. Mencken, this organ poked cynical fun at country yokels and city boobs, at pretentious and superficial politicians and businessmen. It belittled religion and conventional morality and set forth a gospel of an emancipated, sophisticated elite. Not until the depression years did Americans realize that Mencken's approach was essentially negative, destructive rather than constructive; that he sneered at reform as well as at reaction.

Many rural areas and many urban citizens did not capitulate to the jazz age. Yet it cut a wide swath. It made its impact felt on many college and university campuses. F. Scott Fitzgerald overdrew the picture in *This Side of Paradise*, a novel that pictured the reckless gaiety and dissipation of well-to-do college students. It must be admitted, however, that many undergraduates took their studies lightly in the 1920's, paid little attention to public issues, and assumed they would automatically make big money once their college days were over.

The depression that set in after 1929 cut short many of the excesses of the jazz age. In the 1930's fewer college students had time or money to spare. It was necessary to economize, to find odd jobs, to rely on the help provided by the government's National Youth Administration. Confronted by harsh realities, many of those seeking higher education showed concern over social, political, and economic problems.

What was true of college students was likewise true of large segments of middle-class Americans. Gone were the days of easy money. A new seriousness characterized the American mood. There was an upswing in sales of "proletarian novels," dealing with the struggles of working people. *Tobacco Road,* a play concerning southern poor whites, broke records on Broadway. John Steinbeck's book about migratory workers, *The Grapes of Wrath,* became a best seller, rivaling the detective mystery stories and the escape-into-the-past historical novels. Even Hollywood experimented cautiously with serious themes.

Some aspects of the jazz age lasted on into the depression and beyond. Women and girls continued to spend a good deal on cosmetics and at beauty parlors. Smoking habits persisted, as did frankness of speech and informality of manner. Skirts became longer, but women refused to return to the confining garments of their grandmothers. Jazz and the movies remained permanent parts of the American system.

When the depression lifted in the late 1930's, there was some effort to recapture the reckless and carefree spirit of the jazz age. For a time, during World War II, the attempt seemed to be successful. But, though Americans enjoyed prosperity in the postwar years, the atmosphere was different from that of the 1920's. Chastened by the depression, concerned about the atom bomb, citizens could not let themselves go as they had before. Mencken cynicism did not fit the age of the cold war. Besides, what had seemed sensational in the 1920's now appeared routine and commonplace (scanty bathing costumes, for example, and frank discussions about sex). In their day, the flask-toting "flaming youth" of the jazz age had considered themselves sophisticated and daring. But the young people of the 1940's would have thought them superficial and naïve.

The Triumph of Sports

At mid-century, old-timers looked back on the 1920's as the golden age in sports. Was it not the age of Babe Ruth in baseball, Jack Dempsey in boxing, Bill Tilden in tennis, Bobby Jones in golf, Red Grange in football? And, whatever the quality of its headliners, it was certainly the decade of big gates. More than 100,000 people paid over $2,500,000 to see Gene Tunney defend his heavyweight championship against Jack Dempsey in 1927. Newsreels, sports magazines, and radio made Americans more sports-conscious than ever before. And, although gate receipts dropped during the depression, the trend was upward again during and after World War II.

Under the circumstances, commercialization and professionalization inevitably increased. College and high school football and basketball became more and more commercialized. So did amateur tennis and golf, even track-and-field events. Professional football, relatively unimportant before the 1920's, became profitable at the end of that decade. Organized baseball, with a livelier ball calculated to produce exciting home runs, did so well that owners could pay $50,000 bonuses to exceptionally talented teen-age boys. Professional basketball, professional hockey, professional tennis, professional auto racing all became profitable to leading participants, and especially to big promoters. Horse racing and dog racing became tremendously popular, especially after depression-haunted state governments permitted the installation of betting machines (the state's cut generally going for relief or for the aged). Professional wrestling degenerated into farce; but it was professional, profitable farce. Interest declined only in six-day bicycle racing, which did not appeal to people-in-a-hurry.

As sports became big business, many took on a monopolistic character. The key to this was the reserve clause, which bound an athlete to play with one club until he was dropped or traded ("sold"). It was difficult to challenge the Madison Square Garden control of big prize fights. It was all but impossible to buck organized baseball, which was presided over by a powerful commissioner, aptly called "czar." The years after World War II brought an effort to unionize big-league ballplayers. Though unsuccessful, this attempt did help the players get a pension system. Meantime, National League control of professional football was challenged by an All America conference. But after four years of competitive (and expensive) bidding for talent, the new circuit was merged with the old.

Interest was not limited to spectator sports. Thanks to new municipal courses, golf and tennis were no longer for the rich alone. Motoring, swimming, and boating were also within the reach of ordinary people. Every village had its ball teams; and there was a steady increase in the number of fishing and hunting licenses sold by the states.

Business profited as a result of these activities: sporting goods manufacturers, auto and boat makers, owners of resort hotels.

Where would all this lead? One could not make a living writing poetry in the United States; but one could make ends meet as a billiard champion, or as a professional golfer, or as an "amateur" in certain sports. The more critical called this unfortunate, said Americans were trying to escape from the grim realities of the 1920's. Defenders answered by saying that, thanks partly to sports, Americans were the healthiest people in the world. Moreover, the growth in sports did not prevent a simultaneous increase in interest in good literature and music. Sports enthusiasts further insisted that international athletic competition (as in the Olympic games) made sports fans more international-minded than other Americans.

Changing Family Patterns

Like all other institutions, the family was affected by the continuing advance of urbanism and industrialism. In many ways, these basic changes weakened traditional family patterns. As commercialized leisure-time activities multiplied, recreation became less focused in the family. Other functions, such as canning, laundering, sewing, and dressmaking, declined with the advent of processed foods and commercialized services. Even child care moved in part into the multiplying nursery schools.

Some women used their new leisure at country clubs, movies, and bridge luncheons. Others tried civic uplift. More found jobs. Throughout the 1920's the middle-class circles buzzed with the question: Should it be marriage, a career, or both? More and more frequently, the answer was both. Before and after marriage, women worked in department stores, beauty parlors, souvenir shops, tearooms, and business offices; and a few entered the professions. Factory employment was most important of all.

The experience of World War I contributed to the employment of an increasing number of women. The good times of the 1920's continued the trend. When both husband and wife worked, the extra income enabled the family to enjoy the new comforts and luxuries.

Along with economic independence came political opportunity. The long struggle for woman suffrage ended in 1920 with the ratification of the Nineteenth Amendment. But the predictions of both friends and foes of woman suffrage proved ill grounded. Politics changed very little. Women's groups did fight for legislation to improve standards of health and well-being, especially for children; and such groups worked for honest government on the local level. But relatively few women entered politics, and women rarely voted as a bloc. Voting by women did not wreck the home; nor did it make the world much better.

The divorce rate, which was advancing before World War I, continued to rise thereafter. In 1914, statistics showed that one marriage out of ten was ending in divorce. Twenty-five years later, it was one in six; in 1945, one in four. The divorce rate did go down a little in the early days of the depression (though not as far or as fast as the marriage rate). The sharp rise after World War II was due partly to hasty and ill-considered war marriages. Largely, however, it reflected the long-range trend. Although many deplored the situation, it received less notice at mid-century than it had thirty years before.

The birth rate declined through the prosperous 1920's and the depressed 1930's. The restriction of immigration was one factor in the change—immigrant families ran large. Increased interest in birth control was even more important. The Catholic Church continued to oppose the use of contraceptive devices; and in Massachusetts and Connecticut, where the church was especially influential, it continued to be illegal even for physicians to disseminate information about birth control. Some Protestant groups agreed with the Catholics. But in most parts of the United States, family limitation was taken for granted by 1950, in public discussion as well as in practice.

When the birth rate dropped to a record low in 1933, some predicted that the population of the United States would soon become stationary. But the curve turned sharply upward during and after World War II, as the marriage rate reached an all-time high. (The rate in 1946 was more than double that of 1932.) The birth rate climbed back to World War I levels; and the schools faced overcrowding in the 1950's.

The depression of the 1930's had a profound influence on the family. Women were the first to lose their jobs when employment fell. Back in the home, many tried to economize by reviving the household arts of baking, canning, and sewing. But on the whole the hard times still further weakened family patterns. Many families disintegrated during depression-caused migrations. Friction developed when two or more families were forced to double up in one home; and the whole atmosphere of the depression sharpened personal antagonism.

World War II brought new problems, with husbands away in service, or working overtime on war jobs. Wives found employment in record numbers; and sometimes children were neglected. Many war marriages could not be well established, despite efforts of wives to follow their husbands from one military camp to another. Once the war was over, the housing shortage subjected family life to still other strains. Alarmists expected disaster; but the institution of the family came through very well. The tendency toward early marriages, the high birth rate, the permanence of the great majority of unions all pointed to that conclusion.

Religion

In the 1920's the "smart set" sneered at religion. Yet there were fewer indications of militant agnosticism than in the late nineteenth century, when Robert Ingersoll stumped the country with his agnostic lectures. The American Association for the Advancement of Atheism, founded in 1925, attracted only the merest handful of members. Polls suggested that the great majority of Americans gave at least lip service to basic religious belief. In 1927, for example, a sampling of newspaper readers indicated that 91 percent believed in God, 89 percent in the divinity of Jesus Christ. Church membership grew in that decade. (It would decline in the depression, but come up again in the 1940's.) Radio took sermons to many who did not attend church.

There were evidences, however, that religion was losing ground in this secular age. The collapse of prohibition was a bitter blow to the prestige of the Protestant leaders who had supported that experiment.

The decline of missionary activities in many parts of the world, together with the rise of antireligious totalitarian movements in Europe, indicated loss of influence. Church officials complained that, even when membership was rising, golf and the automobile kept people away from services on Sundays.

All through these years many religious leaders felt that they were on the defensive. This was reflected in the drive for interdenominational unity in Protestantism. The several Lutheran bodies drew closer together in 1931, and the Congregational and Christian churches were joined in that same year. Another union established the Evangelical and Reformed Church three years later; and in 1939 a great merger brought together 8,000,000 Methodists. Religious leaders of many sects coöperated in the peace movement; Protestants, Catholics, and Jews worked together on such problems as unemployment and bigotry.

The churches had hard sledding during the depression. Revenues fell off, almost to zero in some cases; and the national crisis led many clergymen to reconsider their views on social questions. The revitalization of the social gospel was reflected in a poll of 20,000 ministers (1934). Almost three-fifths advocated a "drastically reformed capitalism," and nearly a third declared in favor of socialism. In the prosperous 1940's the stress was shifted from economic to spiritual matters; but many clergymen continued to advocate reform.

In Protestant ranks these years saw one of the last rounds in the battle between the rising urban modernists and the declining rural fundamentalists. The modernists reconciled the Bible with modern scientific thought by using figurative interpretations. The fundamentalists insisted on literal interpretation of Scripture. When several southern states passed laws prohibiting the teaching of the doctrine of evolution in publicly supported schools and colleges, many regarded the move as a last-ditch confession that the tide had turned the other way.

In the summer of 1925 the attention of the nation was turned to the trial in Dayton, Tennessee, of John Scopes, a young high school biology instructor who admitted having taught evolution in violation of state law. Noted liberal lawyers, including Clarence Darrow, defended Scopes, while William Jennings Bryan supported the prosecution. A jury composed of rural Tennesseeans found Scopes guilty (a higher court threw out the case on a technicality). But the public in general felt that Bryan's showing had been less than effective. The fundamentalists kept up the fight, even founding a William Jennings Bryan University in Dayton. The modernists, however, seemed to be gaining ground.

As always, there were new religious groups. The years after 1920 saw a notable increase in the number and strength of Churches of God, Pentecostal Assemblies, Evangelical Associations, and other groups that used emotional appeals no longer stressed by the older sects. Most of the rising churches appealed primarily to the lower-income groups; but the Oxford or Buchmanite movement tried to fit the evangelical approach to the needs of upper-class citizens.

With the virtual cessation of immigration, the Roman Catholic Church grew less rapidly than before. The decade of the 1920's, which brought immigration restriction legislation, also brought the anti-Catholic Ku Klux Klan movement. There were additional attacks when a Catholic, Alfred E. Smith, ran for President in 1928.

Despite such difficulties, the Catholic Church continued to grow, and consolidated its position in a growing system of parochial schools and other institutions. By the 1930's and 1940's, Catholic leaders were increasingly outspoken and active. Among other things, Catholics launched a campaign to "clean up" the movies; and their Legion of Decency became a strong influence in Hollywood. Members of the hierarchy, and Catholic laymen as well, attacked writings deemed hostile to their cause. The *Nation* was barred from New York City high school libraries because of a series of anti-Catholic articles by Paul Blanshard. By mid-century, Catholic spokesmen were demanding increased government aid to parochial schools, as for bus transportation to school and for health services. At the same time, Catholic officials were giving more attention to small towns and rural areas, where Catholicism had been feeble in the past.

16

Learning and the Arts

Education

Education experienced unprecedented expansion in the decades after World War I. By the mid-1920's half of the nation's children of high school age were in school; and almost everywhere legislative action had lengthened the school year and extended compulsory-attendance requirements through the sixteenth year. Institutions of higher learning enrolled one-eighth of the young people of college age by the middle 1920's, a fourth after World War II. Illiteracy steadily retreated, though draft and military records of the 1940's indicated that many persons whom census takers counted as literate should not have been so classified.

In addition to the expansion of formal education, the second quarter of the twentieth century witnessed an impressive development of adult education. This was evidenced in the growth of a workers' education movement under the auspices of the more progressive unions and a few universities. Forums, discussion groups, and lecture series expanded, as did vocational schools. Educational radio programs were no less important; and there was an enormous growth in the sale of books designed to give the public a taste of mathematics or philosophy, etiquette or history.

Notwithstanding all these gains, the equality of educational opportunity remained an ideal in 1950. In rural sections, especially in the South, many young people did not attend high school because of economic pressure or the lack of adequate educational facilities. And, because of low salaries, many grade school classes were taught by substandard teachers. At the higher level, the phenomenal expansion

of colleges still left millions of competent young men and women outside the educational fold.

Some saw a remedy in the substantial increase of federal educational
subsidies to the states. After World War II, President Truman urged
such action. The question bogged down, however, first over states'
rights and segregation, then over the parochial school issue.

The vast growth of the educational enterprise was a matter of
legitimate pride. Yet the increase in attendance raised many problems. Some said that the stress on mass education put a premium on
mere accumulation of credits. A number of educators felt that the
solution lay in deëmphasizing traditional subjects in the primary and
secondary schools and stressing vocational and social education designed to equip the next generation for work, marriage, and citizenship. The influence of John Dewey's learning-by-doing and learning-
for-living was unquestionably great. Even more important in effecting
the change were the requirements of industrial society, and recognition of the fact that most high school students would not go on to
college.

On the college level, many were dissatisfied with curriculums which
reflected the pressure for specialization. A few small colleges, such as
Bennington, adopted individualized programs that stressed student
initiative and the project approach. Under the leadership of Robert
Hutchins, the University of Chicago moved away from the elective system. Rejecting the idea that one subject was as good as another,
Hutchins insisted that there is a core of knowledge indispensable to
every educated person, a core that could be acquired partly by studying the great books of Western civilization. Other institutions tackled
the problem in other ways. By the 1940's, many were experimenting
with some form of "general education," especially for freshmen and
sophomores. The elective system, however, held its own. So did the
trend toward specialization. This was natural in view of the job-con-
sciousness of students during and after the depression and World
War II.

The depression of the 1930's hit education very hard. Many schools
could not pay their teachers, and closed their doors. In any number of

areas the school year was shortened. Outworn equipment was not repaired; and teachers' salaries, never high, sank to ever lower levels. Research suffered in many centers of higher learning.

There were, however, some bright points. Students were more serious than before. National Youth Administration subsidies enabled many high school and college students to continue their studies; and enrollment mounted. It kept on going up when prosperity returned after 1939; but from 1940 on, the draft cut into college totals. During World War II, institutions of higher learning kept their doors open by teaching women students and by inaugurating specialized military training programs subsidized by the federal government. The regular job was resumed at war's end, but under difficulties, as veterans subsidized under the G.I. Bill of Rights doubled college and university enrollment overnight.

By 1950 the veteran load was leveling off. There were indications, however, that college enrollment would in the long run increase. Nineteenth-century Americans had come to consider a grade school education as desirable. Early in the twentieth century the thought was to extend high school opportunities on a broad basis; and by 1950 more and more parents and employers were considering college training a must. Opportunities were increasing, with the establishment of many additional public institutions—municipal four-year and junior colleges, state university extension centers, and the like.

On the graduate and professional level American education made remarkable progress after World War II. Public support and private philanthropy made possible the great expansion of graduate schools, the enrichment of libraries, the construction of laboratories, the addition of personnel. In most fields it was no longer necessary for Americans seeking specialized training to go abroad. The totalitarian onslaught on higher education in Germany and the impoverishment of higher institutions in all war-torn European countries brought hundreds of outstanding scholars to the United States. This still further enhanced the prestige of American colleges and universities. European, Latin-American, and Oriental students now came to study in American institutions.

The atomic age posed serious problems for scholars in the United

States and elsewhere. As an example, the need for secrecy limited the free exchange of scientific information. Less tangible, but no less real, was the problem of preventing all-important specialization from undermining a broad humanistic approach to man and his environment. Most serious of all was the necessity for continuing to expand frontiers in a period of crisis, continuing to keep alive the spirit of inquiry, continuing to use the knowledge gained for the freedom and well-being of mankind.

While higher education was wrestling with such problems, the secondary and primary schools were facing immediate and pressing difficulties of space and personnel. Depression, the declining birth rate, and World War II all kept school construction at a relatively low level from the early 1930's to the middle 1940's (though the federal government did help with its public works programs). In addition, many teachers left the field because of the poor pay. The great increase in the birth rate created a crisis by the late 1940's. Despite a reluctance to raise taxes, and despite general disapproval of teacher strikes, citizens in all sections decided that something must be done. Teachers' salaries were gradually increased—not fast enough, unfortunately, in view of the price inflation—and new school buildings were constructed. The trend was toward rambling, one-story construction, with an emphasis on light and air.

Philanthropy and the Arts and Sciences

By the 1920's, the United States had become the wealthiest nation of all time. This led some individuals to boast about their riches, as a result of which Americans acquired abroad the reputation for being money-minded. Yet no nation displayed a greater generosity in supporting good causes of all kinds. Both the wealthy and the middle classes contributed to churches, schools, and welfare organizations; and those who could afford it supported the arts and sciences. Generosity often overflowed the national boundaries and poured millions of dollars into stricken areas abroad. This was the case during the Japanese earthquake of 1923, and again after World War II, when Americans sent C.A.R.E. packages to those in want in Europe.

Pricr to World War I, wealthy Americans had lavished fortunes on the fine arts; but this had been done largely by purchasing the works of European masters. Certain millionaires, operating through dealers, acquired valuable collections which now enrich the country's permanent holdings. But their extravagant spending raised the price of rare books and paintings; and Europeans resented the loss of their treasures to Yankee plutocrats. What was more, collecting did little to foster creative art in the United States. The situation was similar in the sciences, where the importation of ready-made European knowledge had done little to stimulate original contributions on this side of the Atlantic.

After World War I the zeal for private collecting gave way to interest in supporting art and science for the public benefit. Wealthy men continued to play the chief role. Despite earlier efforts to regulate business, there was still little control of profits in the 1920's; and this prosperity decade was the heyday of great fortunes. In 1914 there had been fewer than 5000 millionaires in the United States; by 1926 there were at least 11,000. Although many gave little for cultural purposes, the total gifts greatly increased. Motives varied: social conscience, a desire for public reputation, personal interest in particular enterprises, a desire to avoid income taxes.

Large gifts were now made to art institutes, museums, symphony orchestras—institutions calculated to improve public taste and encourage native contributions. Sometimes large single gifts were involved, as when Mrs. Curtis Bok founded the Curtis Institute of Music in Philadelphia in 1924 with a donation of $12,000,000. Again, much support was extended in a manner that was difficult to measure, by annual contributions or the meeting of recurrent deficits. Leading businessmen also used their influence to secure municipal aid for orchestras, libraries, and museums. Thus the city government assumed the upkeep of the main building of the New York Public Library, an institution made possible by the earlier merger of three great private collections.

Colleges and universities also received support. Earlier gifts to institutions of higher learning had been motivated by piety, by a nostalgia for Alma Mater, or by an enthusiasm for education in general. During the 1900's, however, there was increasing interest in the encouragement of original scholarship and science within academic halls. Gifts were made to expand libraries, and to finance laboratory programs that had no direct relation to teaching. A further indication of this trend was the growth of private foundations, which channeled a large part of their income into university research.

Private gifts were not the main funds for higher education. Most college and university income came from government (as in state and city schools) or from tuition fees. The ratio of endowment income to total funds declined after 1920, falling to 12 percent by the 1940's. But the percentage is not an accurate measure of significance. A large part of the private funds went to universities well equipped to do basic research work. Between 1920 and the late 1930's Harvard and Yale secured $300,000,000 from private sources. Forty-nine leading institutions received during the same period a total of over $800,000,-000.

The expansion of foundations was almost as spectacular as that of the universities. In 1900 there had been practically no large private funds devoted to subsidizing research or welfare work. Forty years later there were 150 such organizations in the fields of medicine, education, welfare, the natural sciences, the humanities and social sciences. Medicine and public health led the way.

Many foundations specialized. The Rosenwald Fund was concerned with welfare and educational work among Negroes; the Twentieth Century Fund supported investigations of economic and social trends. The giant was the Rockefeller Foundation, which by 1940 had handed out nearly a third of a billion dollars. This foundation was notable for the wide range of its interests and for the amounts which it spent abroad as well as at home. About 40 percent of its grants went overseas, to aid medical education and many other activities in Europe, Asia, and Latin America.

At first foundation support was accepted with surprise and enthusiasm. Later, criticism arose. Some felt that foundation officers were not always well informed, and on occasion played favorites. Others feared that foundations might exercise too much influence over universities. Scientists complained about the short-term character of grants. But, whatever their mistakes, foundations did stimulate research and welfare work between 1910 and 1940, when large-scale government aid was not yet available.

Science and the Government

The depression of the 1930's underscored the need for increased government activity in the welfare field. Foundations could not meet mass emergencies; indeed, their income fell during the depression, because of declining return on investments. The states, too, were in financial straits; hence the tendency to turn to Washington. This was logical anyway, since some federal government bureaus had set a high standard in applied research even before World War I.

During World War I, a National Research Council had directed public and private investigations. After the armistice in 1918, the Council continued operating as a quasi-public body. It avoided dependence on government funds, however, in order to maintain freedom from bureaucratic control. By 1940 its membership represented chiefly the national scientific societies, but also included men from federal agencies appointed by the President. The Council established a fellowship program for training scientists; and it initiated special research programs which were subsidized by the foundations. In other words, it coördinated the natural science research interests of federal bureaus, corporations, and the universities. Somewhat similar work was done in the humanities by the American Council of Learned Societies, in the social sciences by the Social Science Research Council.

When the business crash of 1929 forced the federal government to take stock of all possible means of recovery, the resources of science naturally came into the picture. In 1934 President Franklin D. Roosevelt appointed a Science Advisory Board made up of more than a hundred scientists and engineers. This body prepared the first report ever made on the whole relation of science to the government in the United States. Although federal government appropriations for research had doubled in a decade, it was noted that less than one-half of one percent of the budget was devoted to research. There was also much duplication of effort. The report urged that funds be increased and coördination improved; but it declared against centralized control, such as had already been set up in Russia. In this respect the scientists reflected the general outlook of a free society. They wished to strike a happy mean between confusion and regimentation.

From this time forward, government research appropriations increased rapidly. By 1937 more than 120 federal agencies made some claim to research activities; and the total federal costs for research reached an eighth of a billion dollars a year. This was more than the amount available for research from foundations or in universities, though not as much as was expended by corporations.

The greater part of federal funds was spent on applied science, and more than two-thirds of it on natural science and technology. The Department of Agriculture continued to maintain the largest research program among federal agencies, receiving about a third of all federal appropriations earmarked for scientific investigations. A Bankhead-Jones Act of 1935 authorized the department to set up regional laboratories and to match state funds for the development of state experiment stations. No less than 7000 projects relating to the improvement of farming and animal husbandry were undertaken in these stations the following year.

Were these government funds well spent? Some feared that results were not in proportion to the outlay, that bureaucratic red tape reduced efficiency. But government scientists made impressive records; and excellent results were obtained when government and university scientists worked in coöperation.

Science and World War II

The outbreak of World War II focused attention on the application of science to military technology and medicine. Basic science had suffered in Germany under Nazi controls and persecution, but engineering skills had remained high. German inventions and techniques were ahead of those of Britain and the United States in certain respects, as in the development of jet planes, guided missiles, and supersubmarines. Much depended on whether Americans and their allies could meet or outdo these German achievements. It was immediately realized—more clearly than in 1917—that science was a central factor in the whole war effort. Indeed, a comparison of the ways in which the federal government turned to scientists in the successive emergencies of 1861, 1917, and 1941, shows a growing recognition that national survival itself may turn on research.

Girding for combat, federal agencies turned to the research councils for assistance. The Social Science Research Council aided by preparing a roster of needed scientific personnel. The American Council of Learned Societies developed a program for training in "unusual languages" which the armed services would need to know (Japanese, Siamese, Arabic). But the brunt of demands fell on the National Research Council. When it became apparent that the job was too vast for this organization, President Franklin D. Roosevelt appointed a new National Defense Research Committee to direct war research in the physical sciences and technology, and a Committee on Medical Research to coördinate studies in that field. Combined, these two committees were known as the Office of Scientific Research and Development (O.S.R.D.).

Though made up primarily of civilian scientists, the O.S.R.D. included army and navy representatives and received direct government appropriations. The research itself was done in university, corporation, and government laboratories, the O.S.R.D. providing grants to cover actual costs. A very large proportion of the nation's scientists were used in the program.

Most war research involved physics and its applications. The army needed more potent artillery and better communications equipment. The navy desired new detection devices and aids to navigation. The air services called for improved planes, armaments, and explosives. Even the training of personnel demanded experimentation, involving psychology as well as physics. Out of the resulting studies emerged such products as improved tanks, "walkie-talkies," radar, the proximity fuse, fast fighter planes, giant bombers.

While the physical scientists were producing weapons with which to destroy the enemy, medical men were seeking better methods for saving the lives of American troops. These were partly preventive (e.g., insecticides like D.D.T., and more reliable vaccines). Remarkable advances were also made in medical treatment, as in the large-scale production of penicillin and the isolation of blood derivatives for the handling of shock and hemorrhage. As a result of such progress, the army death rate from disease declined from the 1917 figure of 14 per thousand to .6; and this though many troops served in the tropics. Of wounded men who received medical attention and who did not die almost instantly, 97 percent survived, an amazing record.

It was more difficult to handle the large number of troops who became mental casualties as a result of the strain of combat or even of camp service. Their type of illness was more clearly recognized in World War II than before, and some progress was made in psychiatric treatment of the milder forms. Serious cases, however, had to be assigned to veterans' hospitals, where many linger as tragic reminders of the horrors of war and present inability to cure the so-called psychoses.

In World War II, as in earlier conflicts, most of the research consisted of applying known principles of science to military needs. Hence applied science was greatly speeded up; but at the same time men were diverted from the basic research necessary for the applications of the future.

This was true even in the case of the most spectacular technologic achievement of the war—the production of the atomic bomb. The principles of atomic fission, upon which this was based, had been worked out before World War II. There ensued a race between the physicists on both sides, to determine which could first apply these principles to the manufacture of a super bomb. Here Americans, aided by Allied scientists, had two advantages: (1) their old flair for engineering stages of development, and (2) their unique resources in both money and materials. Some $2,000,000,000 was spent by the supersecret Manhattan Project on a vast coördinated development which involved many scientific teams. As a result, atomic bombs were exploded over Hiroshima and Nagasaki, Japan, in August, 1945, with terrifying results. Over 150,000 persons were killed by these two blasts.

The A-bomb affected the American public more profoundly than any earlier scientific event. The prestige of science rose at once, even among those who feared the threat of destruction. Physicists involved in the bomb research acquired a prestige greater than that enjoyed by big businessmen in the 1920's and commanding generals during war. ("The 'absent-minded professors' with their theories. . . ," said one writer, "shed their black alpaca coats and overnight donned the tunic of Superman.") Americans had always admired those who could get results; and in this case, the most abstract physics produced the most practical consequences. The atom bomb certainly "worked." Basic science might be feared; but it could never again be disdained.

Actually, of course, the bomb only accentuated a popularizing process already under way. Cumulative advances in research and their rapid application to technology had made a strong impression on the public after World War I. Newspapers began using science reporters in the mid-1920's; and citizens read more and more about the "wonders of modern science." The movies and the radio helped, too; millions saw such motion pictures as *The Story of Louis Pasteur* and *Madame Curie*. Then the achievements of war research further impressed the public. Everyone heard of radar and penicillin, as well as the more spectacular bomb.

Advances in Physics and Chemistry

In the three decades after World War I, Americans became aware of developments in physics through the appearance of practical inventions: commercial radio, the talkies, television. Some inkling also reached the public of a revolution in theoretical physics, a new principle of "relativity" in the relations of space, time, energy, and matter. The chief figure in this thinking was the German physicist Albert Einstein, who fled to America from the Nazi regime during the 1930's. It testified to the growing awe for basic science that this leader became something of a popular hero here, among millions who could not possibly comprehend his technical theories.

It could be vaguely understood, however, that physics was no longer chiefly concerned with the relatively superficial behavior of bodies of matter and forms of energy like heat and electricity. Nor was chemistry concerned only with the relationship of atoms in chemical combinations, or of molecules in the physical combinations of solutions. Research had invaded the interior of atoms, where a whole new microcosm was revealed. Atoms, it was found, were made up of charged electrons and other particles; and these moved within a minute universe of their own. The seeming solidity of bodies disappeared, since they were all made up of these largely empty atomic units. Whether the electrons or other atomic particles were to be viewed as points of matter or as electrical charges was hard to say; the old distinction between matter and energy was breaking down.

So, too, were the distinctions between physics and chemistry. By redistributing particles in the atoms of one element, scientists could actually transfer it into another element—a miracle of which the alchemists had dreamed centuries before. It was the ability to tamper with the internal universe of the atom which made possible the atomic bomb. This universe within the atom was held together by a tremendous amount of energy, far greater than that which bound together the whole atoms in the molecules of a chemical combination. Hence when a single atom was split apart, as in the bomb, it released a far greater force or explosion than could be produced by splitting (recombining) chemical substances. Obviously, there were vast possibilities here for the production of energy useful in peace as well as in war. No other source of energy promises so much for the power engines of the future. It will take time, though, before this greatest force in existence—locked up in the smallest bodies—can be safely harnessed to industry and to other uses.

In chemistry proper, the most notable advances were those in synthetic research. After 1900, this field became even more promising than the earlier analytic work. It now was possible to put together compounds unknown to nature, taking over, as it were, where nature left off. Thus the German Paul Ehrlich developed innumerable arsenic compounds until, in 1910, he found one (salvarsan) that provided a specific remedy for syphilis.

Dealing with the hydrocarbons that make up the food and structure of living organisms, organic chemists were able to make whole series of dyes and other articles. Down to World War I, this was largely a

German story; but Americans played a leading part after wartime seizure of enemy patents. The American chemical leader, Du Pont (formerly a powder-making concern) became one of the world's greatest producers of chemical products. By mid-century these included everything from paint to textiles, for creative chemistry was unfolding a whole new synthetic world of plastics.

Genetics and Medicine

In the biologic fields, the most remarkable advances of the twentieth century were in genetics (the science of heredity) and in medicine. Genetics came into its own when, at the turn of the century, students gave their attention to the earlier findings of Mendel, an Austrian. Mendel had discovered that certain qualities in crossed species were inherited according to an exact pattern in the descendants. Experimenting with fruit flies, the American biologist Thomas H. Morgan demonstrated that hereditary characteristics such as eye color depend on certain factors (genes) in the germ cells. As a result, it became possible to predict in some measure the qualities of specific combinations. Plant and animal breeding began to be relatively exact, applied sciences.

Medical research had developed vaccines against some infectious diseases (e.g., typhoid fever) even before 1910. But no bacteria were found responsible for other infections, such as influenza and yellow fever. Presently it was discovered that these diseases were caused by minute organisms known as viruses. Since viruses could not be cultivated outside the animal or human host, it was difficult to prepare vaccines against them. Except in the case of syphilis, the search for effective drugs (chemotherapy) was also discouraging. Whatever would kill the disease would also kill man.

From 1915 to 1935, therefore, the advance against infectious diseases seemed to be stalled. Then, in the late 1930's, new synthetic drugs coming out of German laboratories—the sulphonamides, or "sulfa drugs"—proved useful against such infectious diseases as the common forms of pneumonia. Shortly thereafter, another type of drug, the antibiotics, suddenly displayed great promise. These involved a principle recognized by Pasteur, that one organism could be set against another. English scientists found that a certain mold produced a substance destructive to many dangerous bacteria. This substance, penicillin, had an advantage over sulfa drugs in that it would combat more infections and seemed less toxic in its aftereffects. The war period also saw the development of vaccines against such virus diseases as influenza and yellow fever. Thus both preventive and curative medicine had resumed their advance before mid-century.

Other vistas were opening elsewhere. Biochemists traced serious malnutritional diseases, such as pellagra (widespread in the South), to a lack of certain vitamins. Prevention or cure was possible if the vitamins were supplied. No less important was the growing knowledge of the physiology of ductless glands. The hormone substances produced by certain glands are extremely potent; their absence or excess in the blood causes serious illness. In the case of diabetes, it was found that the patient could be maintained in health by use of insulin, a product of the same glands in cattle. Pernicious anemia appeared when the blood-forming organs failed to produce needed substances. It was learned that this could be kept under control by the feeding of liver or liver extracts.

Over against such progress must be set the fact that no reliable means were discovered for preventing or treating most of the degenerative or chronic diseases. As infectious diseases came more under control, average life expectancy increased, and more people survived into old age. Since cancer and heart conditions take their greatest toll in the later years, the incidence and mortality of these steadily increased. There was even some evidence of an absolute increase of these diseases within given age groups, perhaps as a result of unrecognized conditions or stresses in modern living. At the present time, therefore, medical research workers are concentrating much of their attention on degenerative disorders. The problems are very complex, and research has been handicapped by lack of clear knowledge of causative factors.

Although progress in dealing with these diseases has been limited, the general picture of scientific advance was most promising at the end of World War II. The public was interested; and there was a widespread demand that research should not be allowed to decline with the return to peace. Congressmen, for example, were wide-eyed in their appreciation of what the wartime Office of Scientific Research and Development had accomplished, both in making victory possible and in providing discoveries useful for peacetime purposes.

Since the O.S.R.D. record had been made possible by government funds, many felt that its program should be carried on by a new federal agency. Private support of science, unaided by government, could hardly be expected to maintain the recent tempo of scientific advance. Congress consequently began to discuss the possibility of creating a National Science Foundation. But various disagreements delayed the adoption of plans. One difficulty was the old fear of federal interference with the freedom of science. Another was the question of defining fields which should be assisted. For example: should the social as well as the natural sciences be included?

The Social Sciences

When it was proposed that the government support social science research, some objected on the ground that the social disciplines were not really sciences. Besides, they dealt with controversial themes such as immigration and race. On the other hand, it was evident that the general tone of social research had become scientific in spirit as early as World War I. Professional social scientists in the universities prided themselves on the objectivity of their investigations. There was a growing use of statistics and the calculation of probabilities, of case studies, questionnaires, and systematic interviews. It became possible to predict, within limits, the average number of paroled prisoners who would "go straight" under certain circumstances, or the average number of marriages that would not be broken. Prediction of individual behavior remained unreliable (as of the weather, in physical science), but overall averages were often predictable.

Down to 1930, basic work in the social sciences had little application to practical social problems. University men did not wish to be confused with the politicians, administrators, and welfare workers who actually directed social policies. Professors wished to follow the example of natural sciences in developing pure research; and for some time they were too busy laying down principles and improving methods to give much heed to immediate social issues.

Gradually, however, principles were applied to practice. Government and business employed social science specialists, especially after the stock market crash of 1929. Economists advised banks, industries, and labor unions. Sociologists were consulted by courts and prison officials. Experts were taken into government (Franklin D. Roosevelt's brain trust, for example). In applying principles to social practice, social scientists played a part analogous to that of the natural scientists who had been taken into twentieth-century industrial corporations. Business leaders found it worth while to spend money both on science laboratories and on business research (studying production, marketing, advertising).

The influence of social scientists on the courts, on parole boards, and on welfare organizations was one of objectivity and exactitude. Such attitudes tended to replace well-intentioned but uncritical enthusiasms. Instead of citing horrible examples of the need for reform, social scientists marshaled their statistics and appealed to reason. In this manner they sought to overcome popular superstitions or prejudices in social matters, much as natural scientists had earlier overcome suspicions about nature.

Most social scientists believed that an individual's environment exerted more influence on his behavior than did his heredity. The majority of citizens, however, felt that men were "just made that way," that some races or individuals were inferior, or criminal, or what not. Both these views were deterministic, since people were made what they were by nature (heredity) or by nurture (environment). Determinism was inconsistent with the free-will belief that men could improve themselves by individual effort. But the social science outlook was, on the whole, optimistic. It seemed easier to improve man's surroundings than to control biologic inheritance.

Trends in American social science had few counterparts abroad. Social thought in Europe continued to be largely of the armchair, philosophic sort, which had flourished in America also before 1900. The Europeans were preëminent as theorists. Their writings molded general outlooks and contributed to social controversies, as in the debate over Marxism. But many Europeans neglected, even disdained, to check theory by systematic and controlled observations. Their work, therefore, had little value for the actual direction of business or governmental administration. Hence, when west Europe faced severe economic and social difficulties after World War II, leaders found few systematically trained experts to handle these problems. By 1950, however, a number of nations had set up social science institutes so as to produce the needed personnel.

Some Europeans still view American social science as another scheme for getting merely practical results. But in social science, as in certain natural sciences, American research was by 1950 equal to or in advance of that in most European countries. It would be a mistake to exaggerate this statement out of national pride; Europeans retained leadership in many scientific fields. But the United States had several key advantages. Not the least of these was the availability of relatively large funds for research—an important point as scientific work became more and more expensive. After three centuries of colonial dependence on European leadership, the American republic had finally become an outstanding country in science as well as in technology.

Cultural Maturity: The Fine Arts

Nor was progress limited to the natural and social sciences. In architecture and sculpture, in painting, music, the dance, and literature, the United States forged ahead after World War I. In some fields (as in abstract art) Americans continued to follow Old World styles. At the same time, many New World figures created in an independent spirit. Europeans as well as Americans acknowledged that the United States had at last come into its own in the creative arts—that American cultural achievements indicated a new sense of national maturity and power. By mid-century, few disputed the place of America as the cultural center of Western civilization. Involved in the pattern was the return home of expatriates (no longer able to live abroad on American remittances); the coming of distinguished artists seeking haven from totalitarianism; the devastating blight of war and poverty that held back Europe.

Some themes ran through all the years after World War I: notably, the artist's reaction to the machine age. In addition, each decade saw special political, economic, and social currents reflected in the fine arts. The prosperity and standardization of life in the 1920's made possible a widespread patronage of the arts and led also to much satirizing of materialism and conformity. The depression decade of the 1930's brought expatriates home and led many intellectuals to discover for the first time the historic richness and promise of America. These years also saw the first major effort of the government to support the arts.

In architecture the classical tradition continued to enjoy support. The new government buildings of the 1920's and the 1930's followed the Greco-Roman form. But even classical structures reflected (especially in the interiors) the conviction that form must be related to function. No one could fail to recognize that the functionalist school, represented by Frank Lloyd Wright, William Lescaze, and others, was making steady gains.

In domestic building, the modern style found much favor among the adventuresome rich, and, after World War II, increasingly among the middle classes. Factories and hospitals adopted it. So did the Nebraska state capitol, with its imposing shaft, which—unlike the classical dome—provided office space. The simplicity, the clean lines, the emphasis on light and utilization of space, the consideration for the purposes to which a structure was dedicated all made modern architecture catch hold.

The popularity of the classical style before World War I owed much to the Chicago World's Fair of 1893. New expositions reflected changing attitudes. The Chicago Century of Progress (1933) and the New York World of Tomorrow (1939) featured the dominance of machine civilization, presenting curious-shaped but functional structures, boldly painted and admirably lighted. San Francisco's Golden Gate Exposition of 1939 rejected the machine motif for that of Maya, Inca, and Malay themes; yet its buildings, too, were experimental and influenced by function.

The idea of efficient use found expression in city and state planning. Planners developed highways that connected the hearts of cities with suburban areas and the surrounding country. Zoning restrictions became general. Slum clearance was discussed in many cities and tried in a few. Highways were broadened and improved; and a few areas experimented with roadside parks and anti-billboard drives.

Meantime, the skyscraper was modified, in line with changing conditions and ideas. To insure sufficient light on crowded thoroughfares, New York in 1916 required that the upper reaches of skyscrapers be set back from the street. This led to a variety of designs which relieved the boxlike regularity of lines. Here was variation both functional and attractive.

As the years passed, a reaction set in against the tendency to increase the height of skyscrapers. New York City's Empire State Building reached a hundred stories; but such gargantuan structures yielded less return on investment that did more modest buildings. As traffic became congested and transportation systems overloaded, many planners proposed a decentralization of business activities in the interest of convenience. One result was the development of suburban shopping centers.

The quarter-of-a-billion-dollar Rockefeller Center in New York was only one of many building units to adopt mural decorations in the modern manner. Thomas Hart Benton's murals for the New School for Social Research suggested the objectives of the institution. During the depression, when the government put up federal buildings as part of relief and pump-priming efforts, well-known artists were employed to decorate these structures. The painters, who included Rockwell Kent and Boardman Robinson, chose themes reflecting the new social consciousness: bread lines, mobs, dust bowls, erosion. Much the same tendency was apparent in the work of the needy painters supported by the Federal Arts Project after 1935.

Sculpture also responded to the new tendencies. The Rockefeller Center forecourt featured an Atlas modern in technique and spirit. Chicago's Field Museum commissioned Malvina Hoffmann to model dozens of heads and figures to show variations among ethnic groups of the human race. Many younger sculptors, defying classical precedents, followed the modernist painters in striving for angular lines, distorted figures, and the power, bewilderment, and despair which they considered characteristic of modern life.

Regionalism presented a variation on the functional theme. In painting, regionalism was partly a reaction against the international abstractionist school, with its emphasis on geometric design and symbolic meanings. The abstractionists continued to be strong; the revival of nonobjective art was the most notable trend after World War II. Even before that, many leading artists worked in that vein; others, like Georgia O'Keeffe, owed much to it. For that matter, the regionalists themselves often adopted the bold colors and sinuous lines which the modernists favored. But the regionalists also made their work comprehensible to the average man.

Most of the regionalists chose homely themes and stressed social significance. Part of this represented the choice of themes—eroded hillsides, ramshackle farmhouses besmirched with dust storms, impoverished sharecroppers. Some critics claimed that the regionalists reverted to European genre painting and failed to catch the meaning of the machine age. But there was something genuinely American in the simplicity and strength of Grant Wood of Iowa, Thomas Hart Benton of Missouri, John Steuart Curry of Kansas and Wisconsin. The regionalists increased popular interest in painting. Museum directors coöperated, changing the art gallery from a morguelike hall into a dynamic agency for community education.

Composers of music were very active in this period. Working in the classical tradition, Deems Taylor achieved acclaim with his opera *The King's Henchman.* Jerome Kern and Sigmund Romberg carried on the Victor Herbert tradition of light opera; and Richard Rodgers and Oscar Hammerstein 2d introduced a definitely American note in their musical shows.

The music world differed on the merits of jazz. Some champions hailed its various phases (hot jazz, swing, and the like) as contributions to serious music. Paul Whiteman won favorable notice from some critics when he took his jazz band to Europe in the 1920's, and when he presented a New York program in 1924 with all the trappings of a classical concert. The program included George Gershwin's *Rhapsody in Blue,* which at once kindled interest. In other works, Gershwin made interesting use of Negro themes.

The interest in native compositions did not make Americans indifferent to the classics, or to the works of Europe's modern composers. In operatic and symphonic circles, American music received far less attention than did Old World compositions. European musicians were welcome in the United States, whether as visitors or as refugees from totalitarian states (Bruno Walter, Arturo Toscanini). The sale of classical records increased enormously, partly because of better music training in the schools. Partly, too, because of the availability of good music on the radio, though this was often drowned out by commercials.

The depression accentuated the economic problems of musicians. Unfortunately, the crash of 1929 coincided with the coming of talking pictures, which enabled movie exhibitors to get along without "living music." At the same time, night clubs closed for lack of patronage. Restaurant owners dropped their orchestras; and hard times made it difficult for some philanthropists to support symphony organizations. The federal government finally stepped in with a Federal Music Project. Under the auspices of this relief agency hundreds of orchestras gave free concerts; and thousands of Americans heard good music at first hand. Musicians also collected and recorded American folk songs and ballads from old people whose children did not sing these forms.

The dance, like music and painting, reflected the trends of the times. Public interest grew, not only in a great variety of popular forms, but also in more serious efforts. In the World War I era, Isadora Duncan sponsored a sort of classical revival. In the generation that followed, there was increasing interest in the modern dance, as developed by Martha Graham and others. Here were seen many of the influences present in modernist paintings and sculpture.

Cultural Maturity: The Theater and the Movies

The movies cut into the theater even before World War I. With the coming of talking pictures in the late 1920's, many predicted death for Shakespeare's stage. "Opera houses" which had presented plays for generations were made over into movie palaces. Promising Broadway actors were snapped up by Hollywood;

and when depression struck in 1929, playwrights found difficulty getting backers.

The theater, however, showed real vitality. Untroubled by the censorship problems that beset Hollywood, those who wrote plays could deal frankly with current problems. The stage retained prestige, and established movie actors added to their reputations by appearing in Broadway productions. Friends of the drama were, however, worried about the decline in road business: would the theater become merely a New York institution?

There was reason for concern, but there were hopeful signs as well. The depression-inspired Federal Theater Project gave Americans everywhere a chance to see stage plays, many with social significance. As depression lifted, there was a definite upswing in summer stock, with repertory companies performing plays in small New England towns. Colleges all over the land improved their play-directing work; and some sponsored regional drama programs. This work may be compared with that of the regional painters. In both cases, decentralization meant greater interest and progress.

Far greater, however, was the influence of the motion picture. This was the great entertainment medium of the American people, rivaled only by the radio, motoring, and sports. The movies influenced fashions and speech, molded ideas about history and diet, morals and diplomacy. In peace or war, prosperity or depression, America went to the movies. Attendance did drop during the hard times of the early 1930's—dropped in spite of frantic efforts of exhibitors (reduced rates, double features, bank nights, free dishes). But recovery brought even bigger numbers than before.

On the technologic side, the movies improved rapidly after World War I. Of key importance was the shift from silent to talking pictures. Important, too, was the coming of color films. There were all sorts of improvements in camera techniques, in costumes and make-up and sets, and in acting and directing.

Less can be said on the story side. The movie magnates aimed their product, apparently, at children and adults with twelve-year-old mentality. Stress was on spectacle and glamour rather than high-quality performance. Hollywood seemed to fit all products into a few standard plots, though this often meant distorting history or rewriting literary classics. Concern over government and unofficial censorship made producers afraid of offending anybody, with insipid results. But Hollywood did do well in certain fields, such as comedy and suspense; and by the 1940's some producers were tackling adult themes.

All through these years producers adjusted their product to the temper of the times. During World War I they worked with the C.P.I. on anti-German films. In the gay 1920's they produced pictures about flaming youth. One favorite of that decade was Clara Bow, the girl with "It" (i.e., sex appeal). Escapist movies were popular during the depression; but eventually, Hollywood turned toward social themes, as in *Tobacco Road* and *Grapes of Wrath*. Early in the 1930's, when the public opposed involvement in European affairs, there were many antiwar pictures, such as *All Quiet on the Western Front*. As opinion against Germany developed in the later 1930's, Hollywood turned out a flood of anti-Nazi films, mostly spy-and-suspense. In World War II, the industry helped maintain morale, and among other things made movies praising America's allies (*Mrs. Miniver*, which dealt with England, and *Song of Russia*). During the postwar years Hollywood joined the antidiscrimination crusade, turning out some excellent movies on the Negro question and on anti-Semitism. Meantime, the cold war with Russia brought forth anticommunist films.

Cultural Maturity: Literature

The literature of this era was richly varied. There were significant developments in technique: boldly free forms of verse; the camera-eye method of description; the lean, hard impressionism of the rising young novelists. In the 1920's many writers stressed sex and disillusionment with traditional values. The decade of the 1930's revived the earlier literature of social protest. The 1940's brought treatments of the fascist threat, the war, the communist challenge to capitalistic democracy. And at mid-century, literary people—like philosophers and plain citizens—were searching for certainty, for definite values, for something-to-count-on in a bewildering world.

In letters, as in painting, there was a trend toward regionalism. Active throughout the period, this trend was promoted by the depression era's Federal Writers Project, which collected folklore and prepared state guides. Among the more important regionalists were Robert Frost and Edwin Arlington Robinson, poets who described a decaying New England. But the real center of literary regionalism was the South. Many wrote romantically of slavery days (Margaret Mitchell, for example, in her fabulously successful *Gone With the Wind*). Allen Tate and other Southern Agrarians, working in a sophisticated mood reminiscent of the intellectualism of T. S. Eliot, belittled machine civilization and idealized bygone southern agrarianism.

More telling was the work of other Southerners. William Faulkner and Erskine Caldwell, for instance, wrote with skill of poor whites and Negroes, of commercialism and decay. Negro writers also entered the field. As an illustration, Richard Wright's *Native Son* described the prejudice and oppression that warped the personalities of many colored people. Such writings were in sharp contrast with the older, nostalgic regional presentations of Negroes in the stories of Joel Chandler Harris.

Many American writers of the 1920's were influenced by behavioristic psychology and Freudian psychoanalysis. In *Winesburg, Ohio* and other writings, Sherwood Anderson shocked many readers with his frank revelations of sex in its normal and abnormal expressions. F. Scott Fitzgerald caught the escapist drives of "lost" individuals in *The Great Gatsby*. Ernest Hemingway, a leader of the hard-boiled school, used quick, vernacular dialogue to describe the violence and the excesses of near-derelicts (as in *The Sun Also Rises*). Thomas Wolfe wrote powerful though uneven autobiographical novels of restless seeking and frustration.

In drama, the most notable exponent of this psychological orientation was Eugene O'Neill. His *Emperor Jones* described the mental collapse of a dictator who succumbed to his own neurotic fears. In *Strange Interlude*, he had his characters reveal hidden thoughts through the old melodramatic device of the aside. *Mourning Becomes Electra* dealt with incest in the tradition of the Greek tragedies.

Among poets, Edna St. Vincent Millay defied convention with her sensual lyrics, and Robinson Jeffers somberly expressed Freudian concepts in violent verses about frustration, mutilation, sexual aberrations, and death.

While dealing with individual psychological reactions, many of these writers were expressing their dissatisfaction with the business-minded decade in which they lived. Other authors did the same without the psychological trappings. Sinclair Lewis won a large reading public when he used the novel form to indicate his objections to commercialism in American life (*Main Street, Elmer Gantry, Dodsworth*). H. L. Mencken did much the same thing in the nonfiction field as editor of the *American Mercury*.

A much stronger condemnation of the machine age was expressed by the poet T. S. Eliot in *The Waste Land* (1922). Erudite and technically original (and hard to understand), Eliot found the America of his day mechanical, commercial, vulgar, and intellectually barren. Expatriating himself, Eliot went to England, where he espoused monarchy, Anglo-Catholicism, and classicism. Another expatriate poet was Ezra Pound, who repudiated American democratic capitalism altogether and became a World War II propagandist for Mussolini's fascism. (Being declared insane, he escaped trial for treason in the postwar years.)

The depression of the 1930's wrought a profound change in American letters. It no longer sufficed to talk as F. Scott Fitzgerald did of the disillusioned individual. Nor could one follow T. S. Eliot in giving way to fashionable despair. Rather the emergency called for action, for examination of social and economic problems. The worldly-wise intellectuals of the 1920's suddenly discovered that there were things worth fighting for in their land and elsewhere.

In many cases the transformation was extraordinary. Ernest Hemingway, who had led the chorus of disillusionment in the 1920's, found values worth defending when fascism threatened Europe. Hemingway expressed his new faith in *For Whom the Bell Tolls*. Edna St. Vincent Millay shifted from erotic verses to protests against economic ills. Sinclair Lewis turned from satirizing business to treating social welfare work (*Ann Vickers*) and warning against the evils of dictatorship (*It Can't Happen Here*).

In the prosperous 1920's, many intellectuals felt discouraged. The depressed 1930's brought them hope, for it reaffirmed their belief in democracy. Among poets, Archibald MacLeish and Carl Sandburg asserted the positive values of a new social democracy. Sandburg's *The People, Yes* praised the common man in an impressive fashion. The migratory workers in John Steinbeck's *Grapes of Wrath* suffered almost unbelievable hardships. Yet they did not give way to despair in the Fitzgerald-Eliot manner. Rather they were looking forward in spite of every difficulty. And their creator, Steinbeck, rejecting the aloof attitude of Eliot and Mencken, looked on his humble characters with compassion and a touch of admiration.

World War II brought the inevitable crop of war books. Several were distinguished: *A Bell for Adano*, in which John Hersey wrote of military government in Italy (even more telling was Hersey's reportorial account of the A-bomb, *Hiroshima*); Norman Mailer's *Naked and the Dead*, a vulgar, hard-hitting, and vivid book about the war against Japan; *Mr. Roberts*, in which Thomas Heggen wrote engagingly of the noncombat side of the Pacific war. Also important were James Gould Cozzens' *Guard of Honor* and Stefan Heym's *Crusaders*; not to mention Bill Mauldin's cartoons, which caught the spirit of the average G.I.

Most of these books were marked by realism, and by a deep and all-pervading democratic spirit. The same spirit could be seen in the great flood of postwar books about discrimination against Negroes and other minorities. It was impressive, too, to see writers who had earlier used Marxian approaches announce their rejection of these, and their desire to work within the main stream of American democratic reform (John Dos Passos, for example, and Richard Wright).

At mid-century, many writers were uncertain as to their goals. There was a revival of interest in T. S. Eliot and F. Scott Fitzgerald, authors who dealt in symbols of disillusion and despair. Authors who refused to succumb to such views generally headed the other way, and sought certainty. *Peace of Mind* (by a rabbi) and *Peace of Soul* (by a Catholic churchman) were high on the nonfiction best-seller lists; and novelists too were seeking firm ground in the atomic age.

American Culture and the Rest of the World

How did non-Americans regard the twentieth-century United States? Down to World War I, American imports of European capital, labor, techniques, and bodies of knowledge were more impressive than America's tangible influence beyond the national boundaries. In the years that followed, the situation gradually changed. By the middle of the twentieth century, many had come to regard the United States as the economic, military, and cultural center of Western civilization. The shift inevitably altered the images of America in the minds of peoples in other lands.

American military and naval power impressed Europeans and Orientals even before World War I. Alfred T. Mahan's writings on sea power received wide attention in Great Britain, Germany, and Japan; and the naval construction program of the United States also caused the powers to take notice. The American reinforcement of the Allies in 1917–18 led many to conclude that the United States had become the most powerful nation on earth. At the same time, the disruption of the European economy in World War I caused Old World observers to call America the nation of the future.

Great powers are more likely to be admired than loved; and debtors seldom like their creditors. Uncle Sam was not now pictured as a peace-loving and tolerant Yankee tinkerer. Rather he was drawn as Uncle Shylock, laden with moneybags and machine guns. The United States government and people contributed generously to postwar relief, even in Soviet Russia. But Europeans were in no mood to be grateful. They felt that the American republic was wrong to insist on repayment of war debts of the Allied governments to the United States Treasury. These should be canceled, thought Britain, France, and Italy, and charged up as an American contribution to the winning of the war. Hence it became common to denounce the United States as selfish, mercenary, and materialistic.

This tendency increased when it became clear that the United

States was going to do little to implement Woodrow Wilson's idealistic program for a postwar world of national autonomy, peace, and plenty. The Treaty of Versailles disillusioned many. Then the American Senate's rejection of the League of Nations disappointed European idealists who wanted a disinterested United States to provide leadership in the world fight for peace and justice. Again, American legislation reducing immigration aroused deep resentment. The United States had always welcomed immigrants. This had relieved population pressure in Europe; and the emigrants had strengthened European economies by sending money back across the Atlantic. Now Europe's impoverished men and women had no place to go. America was big and rich, they said—and exclusive.

This was the frame of mind in which Europeans spun their images of American civilization in the 1920's. Educated visitors to the United States took back reports of religious bigotry and Ku Klux Klan persecution of minorities. They pictured a drably monotonous machine culture lacking in spiritual depth or richness. They described the bankruptcy of the American home—a home in which women reigned and youth ran wild. They told of debauchery, of widespread defiance of the prohibition laws, of crime waves and gangsters, and of riotous spending.

Travelers were not the only sources of information. Europeans encountered denunciations of United States civilization in the writings of American authors, including F. Scott Fitzgerald, Sinclair Lewis, and John Dos Passos. American movies, technically outstanding, circulated widely in the Old World. To many Europeans, these Hollywood films afforded new "proof" of the character of Americans as degenerate, comfort-loving people, excessively conscious of sex and sports, preyed on by corrupt politicians and ruthless gangsters. The millions of American tourists who traveled overseas after World War I struck many Europeans as wasteful, crude, and patronizing, incapable of appreciating Old World culture. All these images of American civilization encouraged the Italian Fascists and the rising German Nazis to assert that the United States was soft and corrupt, and would fall as Rome had fallen before the new vigor of a hard, aggressive Europe.

But even in the 1920's there was another side to the image and impact of America abroad. While intellectuals belittled the civilization of the United States, they admitted that the new American writers had to be taken seriously. American jazz, fashions, and sports intrigued millions. On a more serious level, American technology intrigued the perceptive business leaders of western Europe and the secretive men in Moscow. Recognizing the superiority of American "know-how," manufacturers invited American efficiency engineers to reorganize their antiquated plants. The Russian government commissioned 120 American firms to help modernize Russian industry, and employed 1500 American technicians to accelerate the goals of the first Five-Year Plan. Here the idea was to adopt American technology without adopting the capitalism in which this technology had developed.

Sharing the general view of European intellectuals, Latin-American writers continued to berate Yankee imperialism, commercialism, and materialism. This image of the United States prevailed even after Presidents Herbert Hoover and Franklin D. Roosevelt abandoned the older type of Caribbean imperialism in favor of a Good Neighbor Policy. Nazi and Communist propagandists who worked in Latin America did what they could to keep suspicions alive.

Many Chinese and Indian intellectuals also regarded the United States as a young nation intoxicated by success and power. But American influence on China was nevertheless marked. For a century American merchants and missionaries had helped Europeans undermine the old Chinese culture and economy. Chinese students who studied in the United States from 1872 on took back to China American concepts of individual freedom, of the emancipation of women, of vocational and technical education; also something of modern medicine, industry, and technology. These returned students (together with many trained in Europe) attacked traditional Chinese conceptions of a feudal economy and a patriarchal family. The "new" China of the 1920's made some show of modeling its educational system on the ideas of John Dewey. And American missionaries, educators, physicians, and businessmen in the Far East continued to picture the United States as a land more powerful through a technology which China needed and must imitate. Japan had already shown the way, for the Japanese had gone to school to America . . . and now threatened American policies in the Orient.

Though the depression of the 1930's was world-wide, it seemed to some to vindicate Soviet and fascist indictments of American inadequacy. The economic isolationism of the early New Deal appeared to indicate that the United States did not mean to challenge the outward march of totalitarianism. But the militancy and relative success of American reform measures encouraged liberals who had despaired of the conservative America of the 1920's. The Tennessee Valley Authority especially excited the imagination of peoples in economically backward areas. Foreign governments sent technical missions to study the program; and TVA became almost a legend in many parts of the globe.

Once the danger of American involvement in World War II became apparent, the administration of Franklin D. Roosevelt bent its energies toward dispelling the suspicion and hostility of Latin America toward the United States. The already active Good Neighbor Policy was broadened in 1938 by the development of a cultural relations program—one of the first formal efforts of the Washington government to use cultural relations as an instrument of national policy. American libraries were established in Central and South American capitals. Visiting scholars, artists, musicians, and educators from the United States served to correct the old view of the Yankee republic as a cultural desert.

The beginnings thus made were expanded when the country became fully engaged in the world struggle. The Office of War Information stressed the idealistic aims of America. Radio broadcasts, continued after the war (the Voice of America), outdid the propaganda efforts of the Creel Committee in World War I.

Besides noting the attractive features of American culture, it was necessary to combat enemy images of the United States. These included the pointed stress on American racial segregation and discrimination. Sometimes Americans abroad helped the foe by manifesting toward darker people a feeling of superiority ill fitting to nationals whose government claimed to be combating Nazi racism. But in the postwar years, more and more Americans were recognizing that what Americans did at home and abroad affected the reputation of their country overseas.

Victory in World War II heightened the prestige of the United States. In the postwar years American historians journeyed to the universities of Latin America, Australia, India, and Europe to tell the American saga to eager ears. American literature, art, music, and science enjoyed a reputation comparable to that of Europe in the years before World War I. American books, magazines, movies, and comic strips publicized the United States as never before. Few doubted that the American republic had become the cultural center of the Western world. Her technology in particular achieved a reputation little short of miraculous. In 1948 some 50,000 foreigners journeyed to the United States to learn at first hand the secrets of American "know-how."

Tending to concentrate on military and economic programs (e.g., the Truman Doctrine and the Marshall Plan), Congress was somewhat reluctant to vote funds for the Voice of America and the cultural relations activities of the State Department. Even so, these activities continued to be important and were sufficiently effective to alarm the Russians. Money realized by the sale of surplus war equipment enabled the United States to provide Fulbright awards, under which scholars presented the nation's cause abroad. In 1949, President Harry Truman called for appropriations to step up a long-active program of technical assistance to so-called backward areas. By 1950 Congress seemed disposed to provide appropriations for the Point Four program.

Still, the preëminence America enjoyed was precarious. Soviet Russia and her Communist disciples everywhere spared no pains to publicize a false image of the United States. That image resembled Nazi pictures of an America temporarily prosperous but destined to collapse. The Soviet propaganda view made much of the denial of full equality to American Negroes, and the power of business and the military. The United States was further charged with an imperialistic design to keep much of the world in bond to Wall Street. This, the Communists cried, was the meaning behind the military aid programs

(Truman Doctrine, Atlantic Pact) and the Marshall Plan for economic aid.

The Soviet image of America enlisted many adherents in Asia and even in the Marshall Plan countries of Europe itself. A survey of opinion in these countries in 1948 indicated that, although most people opposed Communism, many also opposed capitalism of the United States variety and were unhappy about American criticism of socialist experiments in western Europe. The survey further revealed that perhaps one-third of the people believed the United States was "too changeable" to guide the world effectively toward prosperity and peace, and a half of those approached felt that America was "too materialistic" and too much dominated by big business. All this was a far cry from nineteenth-century days, when liberals and radicals everywhere looked to the United States as a model.

17

Politics: The 1920's

End of the Progressive Era

In American political history, the major parties have often shown a tendency to move in the same direction. As the public shifts position, as special interest groups change front, the political leaders take note. Then, slowly, they adjust themselves to the needs and desires, the prejudices and yearnings of the day.

From the middle 1870's to the middle 1890's, both the Republican and the Democratic parties were controlled by conservatives. Republicans like Benjamin Harrison and Democrats like Grover Cleveland opposed each other at the polls; but both had the same outlook on many matters. Both tended to be pro-business and anti-labor, to favor hard money, to avoid the farm question, to steer clear of reform.

After the rise of William Jennings Bryan the major parties shifted. Republicans and Democrats alike espoused the progressive movement between 1900 and World War I. Such Republicans as Theodore Roosevelt joined such Democrats as Woodrow Wilson in advocating laws calculated to aid the farmer and the laborer and to curb the excesses of big business. Both these men, and other progressives too, felt that the best way to fight radicals was to take the wind out of their sails by improving the capitalist economy. Satisfied Americans would never listen to extremists.

With World War I, the parties changed again, turning from the progressive movement to a more conservative position. This shift set the pattern for the period from 1917 on, until the stock market crash of 1929 brought new demands for progressive legislation. Few reform laws were adopted in the dozen years after American entry into World

War I. What was more, this period saw few reform mayors and governors, fewer reform Congressmen, and no reform Presidents. The farmers and laborers, who had been courted by the progressives, were looked on with less favor than before. The corporations that had been attacked in the progressive years were now treated much more gently. The progressives had headed off radicalism by pushing reform laws; the new technique was to denounce and prosecute members of the left wing.

Postwar Reaction

Republicans occupied the White House during most of these years (Warren G. Harding, 1921–23; Calvin Coolidge, 1923–29; Herbert Hoover, 1929–33). Many, therefore, associated the new trend with Republican leadership. Actually, both major parties were involved. The progressive movement ended, and the period of conservative ascendancy began, during the latter part of the administration of the Democratic Woodrow Wilson (who was President from 1913 to 1921). The reform measures summed up in the New Freedom were placed on the statute books during Wilson's first term (1913–17). In his second term (1917–21), this Democratic Chief Executive concentrated on the problems of war and peace. This resulted in the neglect of domestic matters; and progressive legislation cannot be achieved without careful planning.

Nor was that all. To win the war, Wilson brought into the government any number of high-ranking businessmen. Such appointments were bound to change the tone of the administration. Meantime, the influence of the Bryan progressives had declined, with Bryan's departure from the cabinet in 1915 and his disagreement with Wilson on foreign policy. After 1917, the necessities of war production forced the government to set aside the antitrust laws and to promote rather than oppose coöperation among the industrial giants.

Simultaneously, war feeling and Russia's Bolshevik revolution turned most Americans against radicals, who were regarded as pacifists or revolutionaries or both. In the excitement, many citizens also turned against liberals and against labor and against the whole progressive tradition. Of great importance in this situation was the general dis-satisfaction with wartime government controls. The progressives had long urged the importance of government activity in the economic field; but the unpopularity of war controls brought a reaction against such activity.

At the end of Wilson's administration, therefore, the Democratic party was shifting away from progressivism. By this time the Demo-crats had lost control of Congress, as a result of Republican gains in the election of 1918. But the Democrats still controlled the executive arm; and here the influence of Bryan progressives was giving way to that of antilabor Democrats like Attorney General A. Mitchell Palmer of Pennsylvania. Conservative Southerners like United States Senator John Sharp Williams of Mississippi were also increasingly powerful in administration circles.

There had been a similar shift among the Republicans, who domi-nated the legislative branch of the government in 1919 and thereafter. Under the leadership of Theodore Roosevelt and Robert M. La Fol-lette, progressives had figured largely in the councils of the Republican party during the first dozen years of the twentieth century. The party split of 1912 saw the conservatives recapture control of the regular Republican machine. This they retained even after the Theodore Roosevelt progressives returned to the Republican fold in 1916. Roose-velt himself, like Wilson, seems to have lost much of his interest in progressive reform during the World War I era (he died in 1919).

Some progressive Republicans kept up the fight for party influence and progressive legislation—La Follette, for example, and George W. Norris. A number of these men, however, were suspect in the party and with the public because of their opposition to American entry into World War I. Many were getting old and discouraged; and, given the temper of the times, they had difficulty attracting young recruits to carry on their work.

Back in the progressive era (1901–17), the Supreme Court of the United States had gradually come to reflect the spirit of the day. In the Northern Securities decision of 1904, the judges had given support to Theodore Roosevelt's trust-busting program. In later cases, the

Court upheld the constitutionality of state social legislation, as in Muller *vs.* Oregon (1908) and Bunting *vs.* Oregon (1917), both concerning laws limiting the hours of labor.

Then came a shift. By the end of World War I, the Supreme Court justices, like major party politicians, were taking conservative ground. The Court showed a definite unwillingness to break up big business combinations. In the United Shoe Machinery case of 1918 and the United States Steel decision two years later, the judges held that trusts should be judged, not by their intent to monopolize, but by their effects on the economy. In other words, the courts would decide whether a specific combination was desirable or undesirable. Such rulings, and others, served to break down the enforcement of the Sherman and Clayton Antitrust acts.

The courts also aided business by adopting an attitude hostile to labor activity. Despite the Clayton Act's supposed prohibition of injunctions in labor disputes, a federal district court broke a nation-wide railroad strike in 1922 by one of the most sweeping injunctions in American history. Court decisions in close sequence showed that the antitrust laws would be enforced against unions under circumstances where they would not be upheld against business. (Compare Industrial Association of San Francisco *vs.* U. S., 1925, with Bedford Cut Stone Co. *vs.* Journeyman Stone Cutters Association, 1927.)

Nor was that all. The courts struck many a blow against social legislation. On two separate occasions, the Supreme Court wrecked Congressional efforts to eliminate child labor. In Hammer *vs.* Dagenhart (1918), the judges held unconstitutional a law prohibiting interstate commerce in the products of child labor. Four years later, in Bailey *vs.* Drexel Furniture Company, the Court threw out a statute levying a prohibitory tax on articles produced by children. Along a somewhat similar line, the justices declared unconstitutional a Congressional act fixing minimum wages for women and children workers in the District of Columbia (Adkins *vs.* Children's Hospital, 1923).

The decisions were rarely unanimous. There were liberal judges on the bench, just as there were progressive politicians in the major parties. Oliver Wendell Holmes, appointed by Republican President

Theodore Roosevelt, was one; Louis Brandeis, appointed by Democratic President Wilson, was another. But control rested with the conservatives—with Democrats like J. C. McReynolds, a Wilson appointee, and with Republicans like ex-President William Howard Taft, whom Harding made Chief Justice in 1921.

Party History: Republican Triumph

Conservatism remained the dominant note in both major parties right through the 1920's. This could be seen in the campaigns, in the executive policies, and in the legislation of the decade. Nowhere was it more apparent than in the presidential contests and the attitudes of the occupants of the White House.

As Wilson's administration drew to a close, the Republicans organized for victory in 1920. There was a sharp contest for the presidential nomination, for it was generally assumed that this nomination meant election. Money was spent freely. W. C. Procter, the soap king, and others backed General Leonard Wood (the presumed heir of Roosevelt) to the tune of more than $1,500,000; and nearly a half-million was spent on another hopeful, Frank O. Lowden of Illinois. Among the other candidates was one progressive, Hiram Johnson, the Californian who had been Theodore Roosevelt's running mate in the Bull Moose campaign of 1912. But this was no day for progressives; the Republican convention turned instead to a conservative, Warren G. Harding of Ohio.

The Republican candidate was not a well-known politician. He had been a small-town editor and businessman, then an average sort of United States Senator. He was brought forth by conservatives, including Senators Reed Smoot of Utah and Henry Cabot Lodge of Massachusetts. To run with Harding, the Republicans selected Governor Calvin Coolidge, of Massachusetts. Coolidge was also conservative, and was known on the national scene chiefly for his opposition to the Boston police strike.

Under the direction of party managers, Harding and Coolidge staged a quiet campaign, doing little stumping and avoiding the ticklish League of Nations issue. On domestic matters, though, they did take a stand. Here their slogan was "Back to Normalcy." Back to normalcy meant, of course, a relaxation of wartime controls. It did not, however, mean a return to the prewar progressive era of domestic reform. The accent was rather on a return to the McKinley days, when the United States government had given some help to business but had otherwise tried to avoid interfering with economic trends.

With the Republicans taking such a stand, the Democrats could have featured a progressive program. Their selection of candidates seemed to point in that direction. After a long and bitter convention struggle, the party named for the presidency James M. Cox, who had a reform record as governor of Ohio. For the second place on the ticket, the delegates picked Assistant Secretary of the Navy Franklin D. Roosevelt, a cousin of T. R. The family name suggested progressivism; and young F. D. R. had shown some interest in reform as a New York State senator in the days before World War I. But, instead of attempting to revive the progressive movement, Cox and Roosevelt chose to put their emphasis on the League of Nations question. This was in accord with the wishes of President Wilson. It was also in accord with party policy; the Democratic platform of 1920 called for few reforms.

Those who wished to concentrate on domestic reform had to turn to the third parties. There was a new Farmer-Labor party, which ran P. P. Christensen of Utah for President. In addition, the Socialists again nominated Eugene V. Debs, though he was in prison for violation of the Espionage Act. The Farmer-Labor ticket did poorly, save in the state of Washington. Debs did better, polling the largest vote of his five campaigns. But his percentage of the total vote was less than in 1912; the Socialists, apparently, were heading downhill.

Cox also made a disappointing showing. This indicated that the public cared little for the League of Nations issue; that citizens were tired of the war, tired of war controls, tired of Wilson; and that voters were inclined to blame the Democrats for the hard times of 1920. Harding won by a landslide, polling nearly twice as many votes as his opponent (16,000,000 against 9,000,000). The Republicans carried all the Northeast, the Middle West, the mountain states and the Pacific coast; and they cut into the normally Democratic South, carrying Maryland, Oklahoma, and Tennessee.

Government to Help Business

President Warren G. Harding (1921–23) felt that there should be "less government in business and more business in government." By this he did not mean that the government should be inactive with respect to the private economy (laissez faire). Rather he believed the government should deëmphasize control and punishment, and should stress assistance to business. He and his successors in the 1920's therefore sought to aid business (big business especially) by tax and tariff legislation, by encouragement of trade associations, by promoting export of goods and capital. For almost a decade the system seemed to work; and businessmen enjoyed a sense of political security they had not experienced since the preceding century.

In pushing this "help business" policy, Harding did not altogether neglect labor and agriculture. At the end of his administration, Congress created the Federal Intermediate Credit banks for farmers; and federal highway appropriations also helped rural sections. In addition, Harding asked the steel industry to cut the working day; and he favored immigration restriction, which was desired by workingmen. But the President and those about him gave much more attention to helping business. The theory was that if business prospered, workers and farmers would profit, too.

During the Harding regime, the Fordney-McCumber Tariff (1922) restored the high rates that had been a Republican tradition since the days of Abraham Lincoln. The Hawley-Smoot Tariff of 1930 would raise duties further still. The only marked departure from the high-tariff policy—the Underwood Tariff of 1913—had never been tried over a substantial peacetime period. The Fordney-McCumber law therefore marked a return to a long-established pattern of high protection.

High tariff duties did not help all producers. American manufacturers of electrical equipment, machine tools, and motors could have held their domestic markets had there been no tariff rates at all. Lower duties would have increased foreign commerce and thereby would have widened export markets for such efficient manufacturers (also for farm products). Other producers, however, depended on tariff protection for survival. But for high duties, foreign products would have hurt Americans engaged in making woolen clothing, shoes, sugar, and handmade luxuries. Americans active in these industries were too well represented in Congress to permit tariff reduction.

Among the "help business" features of the Fordney-McCumber Tariff of 1922 was the sharp increase in duties on chemicals, dyes, laces, and toys. Formerly purchased from Germany, these articles were now produced in the United States by war-created "infant industries," many of which operated under confiscated German patents. The rates here were virtually prohibitive.

The Fordney-McCumber law also extended the principle of flexibility, which had figured incidentally in earlier tariff acts. On recommendation of the Tariff Commission, the President could raise or lower duties by as much as 50 percent, when this was considered necessary to equalize differences in production costs here and abroad. The trend of the times can be seen in the recommendations of the Tariff Commission and the action taken by President Harding and his successor. Duties were lowered on less than half a dozen items, all minor (quail and paintbrush handles, for example). Rates were raised in over thirty cases, involving such major items as chemicals, pig iron, and dairy products.

Designed as a measure to aid industry, the Fordney-McCumber Act was in some respects disappointing. European countries raised their rates in reprisal, established quota systems, and otherwise discriminated against American products. American exporters, therefore, had difficulty building trade. Yet when the crash of 1929 brought a new crisis, Congress still further increased rates (Hawley-Smoot Tariff, 1930). This in turn would bring new reprisals and force a general reconsideration of the question.

The "help business" program of the 1920's concerned finance as well as trade. Prior to World War I the United States had been a major debtor. A surplus of exports had helped meet debt payments.

Then the war had suddenly made the American republic a great international creditor, European nations having borrowed heavily from private American investors and from the United States Treasury.

In the long run, these war debts could be paid only in gold or goods Since gold was scarce—and largely in America—payment had to be in goods. But such payment would mean a surplus of imports over exports. With protectionists in the political saddle, it was hard to see how this could be arranged.

The answer was found in more lending. The United States Treasury stopped lending to foreign governments soon after World War I. American citizens, however, bought foreign bonds and invested in economic enterprises overseas. Europeans and Latin Americans used part of the money thus provided to make interest payments on earlier loans. Another part was used to buy products from the United States. This was a strictly temporary arrangement, and it raised serious questions. What would happen to American trade when Americans stopped lending money abroad? And how could foreign governments repay old loans when new lending became impossible? But in the 1920's few Americans asked these questions. Foreign bonds yielded a good return, and served to stimulate the sale of goods abroad. Most citizens were willing to let it go at that.

United States government policy fitted in with the general attitude. The $10,000,000,000 in war debts owed by the Allies to the United States Treasury presented the first problem. Arrangements were made for very gradual repayment over periods of about sixty years. Except for Great Britain, the rate of interest was made negligible. Under this plan, debt payments to Washington would interfere only slightly with the ability of foreign nations to make payments on new private loans. European central and local governments were thus encouraged to float bond issues on Wall Street and buy American goods with part of the proceeds. The result, it was thought, would be profit for American investors and American exporters.

In promoting investment abroad, the United States government did not stop with the war debt policy. During the Harding period and afterward, Department of Commerce agents scoured the earth in search of opportunities for American traders and investors. Herbert

Hoover, who was Secretary of Commerce from 1921 to 1929, pushed the policy with vigor. Simultaneously, the State Department, under Charles Evans Hughes, offered advice to bankers on Latin-American issues. The implication was that, in Central America at least, the United States government would look after the safety of the investment.

On this basis Wall Street financiers urged loans on weak foreign governments. The result was misuse of the money, leaving already poor nations with large debts and few improvements. After the crash of 1929, many of these loans would go into default. But Americans would retain valuable properties acquired in the 1920's. An example of these direct investments was an oil empire in the Near East, obtained by American companies with the assistance of the State Department.

Domestic financial policies were also geared to the assumed needs of capital investment. Andrew W. Mellon, whose vast business empire included the Aluminum Company of America, presided over the United States Treasury Department from Harding's inauguration in 1921 until the dark days of 1932. With one exception (Albert Gallatin), this was the longest cabinet tenure in American history. An elderly man, Mellon believed firmly in the doctrines that had been evolved in the rapidly expanding economy of the nineteenth century. In particular, he felt that businessmen should be allowed to accumulate large sums. (This money would then go into new enterprises and contribute to the national welfare.) He accordingly urged and obtained the reduction of taxes on corporate profits and large incomes.

Since government expenses were kept low, even the sweeping tax reductions voted by Congress failed to prevent annual surpluses in the 1920's. The national debt was cut from $24,000,000,000 to $16,000,000,000. Any possible deflationary effect from such repayment was obviated by a more than equal increase in state and local borrowing for highway and sewer construction, and other aids to economic development.

Still further aid to business was provided through Herbert Hoover's Commerce Department. Hoover gathered information on economic conditions and gave useful advice to businessmen. He also urged industrialists to standardize sizes, types, and measures, so as to reduce the varieties of paving blocks, milk bottles, typewriter ribbons, and hundreds of other items. Finally, he encouraged the formation of trade associations to maintain uniform prices and business practices. This represented his belief in ordered and stabilized, rather than completely free competition. At first the Supreme Court ruled that much trade association activity ran counter to the Sherman Antitrust Act. But by 1925, as in the Maple Flooring Manufacturers' Association case, the judges were taking a kindlier view of industrial coöperation through trade associations.

The Harding Scandals

The pro-business program was the most important aspect of government policy in the 1920's. The news headlines, however, more commonly concerned the prohibition experiment, the crime wave, and the Harding scandals. The scandals broke soon after Harding died, in August, 1923; and the revelations continued to make news through much of the remainder of the decade.

President Harding was a handsome, friendly man, popular with the public because of his amiable, easygoing manner. Long in politics, the President knew how to handle himself in most political situations. But he was no student and no statesman. He lacked a penetrating mind; and he was lamentably weak in judging his associates. When guided by party managers, he selected able men for key positions—Taft, Hughes, Mellon, Hoover. Frequently, however, Harding was steered and betrayed by close personal friends. This President liked informality, enjoyed poker games and small talk with political cronies. Unfortunately, many of these White House intimates were greedy for money and for office, and used their influence with the President to fleece the government.

The resulting scandals were strikingly like the post-Civil War scandals of the Grant era. At the center of the stage was an Ohio gang, operating under the direction of Harry M. Daugherty, a corruptionist whose friendship with Harding brought appointment as Attorney General. Alcohol permits were illegally sold through Daugherty's Justice Department. The Alien Property Custodian, Thomas Miller, and the director of the Veterans' Bureau, Charles Forbes, both went to prison for misusing their positions.

Most spectacular of all was the Teapot Dome scandal. Government oil lands at Teapot Dome, Wyoming, and Elk Hills, California, were leased to favored individuals without proper bidding. The favored oil magnates, Edward L. Doheny and Harry F. Sinclair, "lent" large sums to Secretary of the Interior Albert B. Fall, who arranged the leases. (Fall, like Daugherty, was one of Harding's personal friends.) A Senate investigation under Thomas J. Walsh of Montana uncovered the shocking facts; and eventually Fall and Sinclair went to jail, for short terms.

Had Harding lived on into the campaign year of 1924, his party might have found Teapot Dome a heavy load to bear. But Harding died before the scandals reached the public ear. He was succeeded by his Vice-President, Calvin Coolidge, who served out Harding's term and one of his own (1923–29). Coolidge was not connected with the Harding scandals; and it was hard to blame him for the faults of his predecessor. Harder when Coolidge eased suspected persons out of government positions, and said that the guilty should be punished. This, combined with general public indifference, saved the Republicans.

Keeping Cool with Coolidge

Although not the ablest of the accidental Presidents, Calvin Coolidge was a highly competent politician. A native Vermonter, Coolidge was a taciturn and cautious man who had slowly but surely edged his way forward in Massachusetts politics. He was short on personal magnetism and was anything but a crusader. He was, in fact, no leader. But, since he took care not to make enemies, he was "available," a good compromise candidate. Thus he rose from the Massachusetts legislature to the governorship, and on to the vice-presidency and the White House.

As President, Coolidge displayed his lifelong caution. He often spoke in platitudes, as in endorsing thrift and progress and tradition. On other occasions, he said nothing whatsoever, earning the nickname "Silent Cal" and building the slogan "Keep Cool with Coolidge." The

President's solemn face was frequently in the papers, for he was willing to oblige the news photographers by posing any way they wished, even in cowboy clothes and Indian costume. However absurd, these pictures served to draw attention away from the Harding scandals.

Nor did Coolidge lack a policy. Even more than Harding, he developed domestic and foreign policies that aided big business. National prosperity, in Coolidge's view, was related to the success and leadership of industrialists and financiers like Secretary of the Treasury Mellon and Coolidge's college classmate, Dwight Morrow, a Morgan partner whom the President sent on a diplomatic mission to Mexico.

To protect business, Coolidge opposed anything that smacked of government ownership or regulation. He killed with a pocket veto Senator Norris' resolution for government development of the water-power resources at Muscle Shoals, Tennessee (1928). He wrecked chances for subsidies to farmers by vetoing the McNary-Haugen bills (1927, 1928). At the same time, he helped business by his executive appointments. He appointed friends of big business to commissions which were supposed to investigate and regulate big business—the Tariff Commission, the Interstate Commerce Commission, the Federal Trade Commission. But for Senate opposition, he would have given the Attorney Generalship to Charles B. Warren. The Attorney General has charge of enforcing antitrust legislation; and Warren was a businessman apparently hostile to such legislation. Under William E. Humphrey, a Coolidge appointee, the Federal Trade Commission shifted emphasis from investigation of unfair business practices to the support of business combinations through the trade associations.

Coolidge took somewhat the same position in the foreign field. Like his predecessor, he favored American investment overseas. He also made it plain that he would protect American lives and property anywhere on earth. When Mexico began cracking down on foreign oil and mining interests, Coolidge and his Secretary of State, Frank B. Kellogg, refused any sort of compromise. They showed clearly that the United States would use force if necessary to protect every interest of every American investor. Mexico thereupon backed down (1927).

On the whole, Coolidge seems to have approved of the stock market speculation of the 1920's. At the end of the decade, his administration helped keep this speculation going by an easy credit policy (that is, by holding the Federal Reserve System's rediscount rate at a low level). Meantime, however, Coolidge favored economy in government, and sometimes spent less than Congress appropriated. The President's Yankee frugality was involved here—Coolidge managed to save part of his own presidential salary. Then, too, stress on economy paid off in politics by providing a good contrast with the waste and corruption of the Harding regime. Finally, economy in government made it possible to put through Mellon's program of cutting taxes on upper-bracket incomes.

Since the public was generally pro-business in this prosperity decade, Coolidge's policies were well received. The President also made some effort to woo workingmen and farmers. He pleased labor by signing the restrictive immigration law of 1924. He favored highway appropriations partly in the interest of farmers; and, though he opposed farm subsidies, he stood for high protective duties on agricultural products.

The La Follette Campaign

The Republicans of course gave Coolidge their presidential nomination in 1924. His running mate was Charles G. Dawes, a Chicago financier. In a way, Dawes symbolized the prosperity decade's admiration for men of wealth. In other periods, nominating a banker for high office would have been politically unwise; but in the 1920's, doing so strengthened the ticket.

As in 1920, the Democrats could have challenged their opponents by naming an anti-big-business candidate. The Democratic party, however, was badly split, wet against dry, North against South, urban against rural. In the 1924 convention there was a bitter fight between the factions, which were headed by Alfred E. Smith of New York and William Gibbs McAdoo of California. After 103 weary ballots, the delegates turned to John W. Davis. Originally a West Virginian, Davis had become a conservative New York corporation lawyer; later, he would be known as the legal representative of the house of Morgan. There was a lingering suggestion of progressivism in the nomination of William Jennings Bryan's brother Charles as Davis' running mate.

But the Democrats, like the Republicans, had taken the conservative side.

The major-party trend toward business leadership deeply dissatisfied old progressives from the major parties; also certain farm and labor groups. After the collapse of the Farmer-Labor party of 1920, the railway brotherhoods led in the formation of a Conference for Progressive Political Action. After two years of preparation, this group launched a new third party in 1924.

For President, the Progressives nominated a Republican, Robert M. La Follette; for Vice-President, a Democrat, Senator Burton K. Wheeler of Montana. The La Follette forces counted heavily on the farm vote—on rural voters who had been Farmer-Laborites, or supporters of the Nonpartisan League or the earlier progressive movement. Labor was also in the picture. The American Federation of Labor set aside its tradition of not endorsing presidential candidates to throw its weight behind the Progressives. La Follette also had the backing of the Socialists, who ran no candidate of their own in this campaign. But the Progressive nominee specifically repudiated an offer of Communist support.

In his campaign, Senator La Follette used many of the old progressive battle cries and some new ones. He attacked monopoly, proposed curbing the power of the courts, favored government ownership of the railroads and of water power. He demanded more rights for farmers and for workers, called for tariff reduction, opposed the Mellon program of reducing taxes on high incomes.

Considering the difficulties, La Follette did fairly well. But somehow his campaign lacked the fire of the old progressive contests. This was in part a matter of age. A large percentage of the progressives of the first decade of the century had been young in years as well as spirit. Many of the Progressives of 1924 were old and tired; their leader, La Follette, would die soon after the election. Attitudes were no less important. Back in the Bryan-Roosevelt era, the progressives had optimistically looked forward to total victory. They had expected to usher in the golden age. World War I and its aftermath had brought disillusion to some; and it was difficult for a progressive to be optimistic in the business-dominated 1920's.

Calvin Coolidge won the 1924 election. The general prosperity, the President's personal popularity, the weakness of the opposition brought the Republicans a smashing victory. Except for Wisconsin, which went to its native son, La Follette, Coolidge carried every state outside the solid South. He lost Tennessee and Oklahoma, which Harding had carried in 1920; but he won in Kentucky. He carried nearly three-quarters of the electoral votes and had a clear majority of the popular total (54 percent, against 29 percent for Davis, 17 percent for La Follette).

Another Republican Victory

La Follette's campaign had been waged largely as a personal battle; the Progressives had a minimum of machine organization. In consequence, this third party collapsed immediately after the election and was never revived. Some observers prophesied disaster for the Democrats as well. Certainly the Democratic party had done dismally. Although it controlled political machines in northern cities, it could not carry northern states. Laboring men, who had flocked to Wilson, no longer showed much interest in the Democratic organization; and the farmers who had followed Bryan now voted Republican. Lacking issues and effective candidates, the Democrats seemed politically bankrupt.

Coolidge's successes led many Republicans to hope that the President would run again in 1928. Democrats and progressive Republicans objected, on the ground that this would violate the third-term tradition set by Washington, Jefferson, and Jackson. Regular Republicans replied that another term would not be Coolidge's third; he had served out half of Harding's time but had had only one term of his own. The President resolved the problem by saying that he did not "choose to run." A draft-Coolidge move fell flat, and the Republicans then named Herbert Hoover of California for President in 1928. Senator Charles Curtis, a conservative Kansan, was nominated for Vice-President.

Like Coolidge, Hoover fitted in with the prosperity decade. A self-made man, he had become a successful mining engineer and promoter, much of his wealth and reputation being made overseas. World War I saw him directing relief in Belgium, then serving as Food Administrator in the United States. His pro-business policies while Secretary of Commerce gave him reputation and prestige and made him a logical candidate for President. Some progressive Republicans complained that Hoover was too conservative. Some professional politicians said that Hoover was a political amateur, who would blunder if placed in the White House. Others felt that Hoover lacked popular appeal, was stiff and colorless and an indifferent speaker. But in the end, Hoover won.

In the campaign that followed, the Republicans presented Hoover as a great engineer, humanitarian, and businessman. They also tried to humanize their candidate, pointing out that he liked fishing and detective stories. The basic stress, though, was on prosperity, which was ascribed to the Republican policy of not interfering with business. Hoover's term was "rugged individualism," suggesting a connection with the American traditions of individualism and liberty. Under business leadership, Hoover said, the United States could expect continued prosperity, which would benefit not only the capitalist but also the laborer. (There would be a chicken in every pot, and two cars in every garage.) As for the farmers, Hoover would have them combine for marketing, somewhat as other businessmen had combined through trade associations.

In this 1928 campaign the Democrats gave their presidential nomination to Governor Alfred E. Smith of New York. There was opposition to Smith, and it centered in the area where the Democrats were strongest—the solid South. Rural dry Protestant Southerners objected to Smith as a city man, as a Northerner, as a Catholic, as a wet (anti-prohibition). Some found Smith's Tammany connections objectionable; others disliked his harsh voice and pronunciation. But Smith had drawing power in New York and other industrial states. This was important, for it was evident that the Democrats could not regain office without northern city votes. So Smith was nominated; and the ticket was "balanced" by giving the vice-presidential nomination to Senator Joseph T. Robinson, who was Protestant and dry, and came from the southern and rural state of Arkansas.

As governor of New York, Al Smith had frequently backed pro-

gressive measures. As presidential candidate in 1928, he did not emphasize this line. Instead, he adopted a pro-business line. Smith did
favor some governmental activity in the utility field. This, said Hoover,
was the road to "state socialism." But Smith replied, and with some
reason, that business had nothing to fear from him. Was not his campaign manager, J. J. Raskob, a Wall Street financier?

Once more, therefore, the major parties were pursuing a like course.
This time, though, there was no Progressive opposition in the field.
The most important protest organization, Norman Thomas' Socialist
party, was extremely feeble. It drew only 270,000 votes, less than 1
percent of the total. Debs had polled more than three times that many
Socialist votes in 1912, when the total vote was less than half that cast
in 1928. Plainly, this leftist group had gone into decline. War and
postwar repression had weakened the Socialists. So had divisions, secessions, and purges; and, after Debs' death, the party had no leader
with his popular appeal. In Europe, labor endorsed socialism; in America, the leading unions were antisocialist. And the general prosperity
of the 1920's made other citizens reluctant to consider any major reorganization of the economy.[1]

The 1928 campaign closed with a resounding Republican victory.
Smith made a good showing in the popular vote but carried only eight
states out of forty-eight. Hoover won the North and West, and cut
more deeply into the Democratic South than had any Republican
since Grant. Florida, Texas, North Carolina, and Virginia all went Republican in a presidential race for the first time since Reconstruction.
They did so, apparently, because of Smith's religion and his opposition to prohibition (which Hoover labeled a noble experiment). The
normally Democratic border states all supported Hoover: Maryland,
Kentucky, Tennessee, Oklahoma. On the other hand, Smith's urban

---

[1] Even feebler than the Socialists were two other left-wing parties: the old and militant (but microscopically small) Socialist Labor party, which traced its origin back to
Daniel DeLeon; and the Communists, who called themselves Workers in 1924 and
1928. The American Communists had broken away from the Socialists in the World
War I era. Unlike the Socialists, the Communists were unwilling to put much faith in
the ballot; and, unlike the Socialists, the Communists looked to Soviet Russia for leadership. The Communist presidential candidates—first William Z. Foster, then Earl
Browder—gained votes from 1924 to 1932, then declined. In their peak year as an independent party, 1932, they polled about one-fourth of one percent of the total vote.

and Catholic connections and his wet views brought him the electoral votes of the usually Republican states of Massachusetts and Rhode Island.

The Democrats, however, lost New York—mainly, perhaps, because of prosperity. Smith had tried very hard to carry his home state. To strengthen Democratic chances there, he had insisted on the strongest possible candidate for governor, Franklin D. Roosevelt. Nevertheless, Smith lost the state. But his friend Roosevelt squeaked through to victory, winning the governorship by the narrowest of margins and setting the stage for a broader political future.

Having scored a mighty triumph, the Republicans looked forward to further victories. But, as it happened, the Republican party had won its last major victory for many years to come. Soon after Hoover was inaugurated as President, the speculative bubble burst; and in the ensuing depression, and after, the Republicans would suffer any number of humiliating defeats.

Political Techniques

All through the 1920's public-spirited citizens complained that the people were losing interest in politics. A few observers felt that Americans were disgusted by scandals in national, state, and local governments. Some thought that it was a matter of competing attractions, including sports, motoring, and the movies. Others noted that the new guiding star was business; that citizens now looked at the financial pages before they read the political news. It could be further stated that until 1929 there was no crisis to force men to turn to government. Nor were the major parties enough different from each other to arouse the public. When interesting issues did appear—the Ku Klux Klan, Teapot Dome, prohibition—most politicians ducked, sidestepping the question or meeting it with weasel words.

In some ways the American public was better informed than before. Political news came over the air and through the movie houses as well as in the press. Radio took Americans inside convention halls; the interminable Democratic convention of 1924 was a turning point in radio history. As Franklin D. Roosevelt would presently demonstrate, a "radio voice" was a great political asset. Newsreels and improved newspaper photography gave citizens a chance to see the country's leaders. The automobile and the sound truck enabled candidates to hit every hamlet when they took to the road. Simultaneously, state governments required primary and secondary schools to introduce civics courses, so as to teach young people about government; and political science became an important part of collegiate instruction.

Even so, interest lagged. Which meant that control often rested with political machines and pressure groups. There was little to praise in the conduct of city machines, whether they were run by the Republicans (as in Philadelphia and Chicago) or the Democrats (as in Jersey City, New York, and Kansas City). Local bosses took bribes, protected gambling and the liquor traffic, rigged assessments to reward friends and punish enemies. A few candidates for local office were able; more were incompetent or corrupt. Tammany's dapper Jimmy Walker got by on his looks and wisecracks (not much of a mayor, the politicians said, but what a candidate!). Chicago's Big Bill Thompson tried superpatriotism, announced that he intended to keep British influence out of Illinois. Campaigns for higher office were sometimes waged with enormous slush funds.

At the state and national capitals, public indifference gave great influence to the lobbyists. Of these, the business representatives were strongest. Few Americans had as much political power as Joseph Grundy of the Pennsylvania Manufacturers' Association. William B. Shearer, who represented munitions makers, helped wreck disarmament negotiations. The prohibitionists were also strong; right through the 1920's, Wayne B. Wheeler of the Anti-Saloon League cracked the whip over Congressmen from rural areas. No less powerful were the representatives of the war veterans. The American Legion was never so strong as the G.A.R. had been in the late nineteenth century; but it persuaded Congress to pass a soldiers' bonus bill over a Coolidge veto in 1924, and a measure providing for immediate payment of the bonus over Franklin D. Roosevelt's veto twelve years later. Even more significant was the development of a strong farm lobby. Though largely unsuccessful in the 1920's, this group was ready for decisive action in the next decade. Labor's lobby helped put over immigration restriction in

1924; but it too was less powerful than it would be after the crash of 1929.

The Central Government

The progressive era and World War I had seen trends toward executive leadership and the centralization of political power. The first of these trends was reversed after 1919; the second continued to prevail. Despite discussion of state and local rights, despite reduction in federal expenses, the central government retained its position of influence.

The 1920's saw a shift from regulation to encouragement of business. But the encouragement, like the regulation, came from Washington rather than the state capitals. Thanks to Wilson's New Freedom, the federal government had increased its activities in finance, in agricultural education, in highway building. Coolidge economy did not end this work. Meantime, federal power increased in the law-enforcement field. Prohibition was one factor. The automobile was another, for, under the Dyer Act of 1920, federal officers could enter a case if a suspect drove a stolen car across a state line. The changing pattern was indicated by the increasing reliance of state and local officials on the fingerprint files and scientific laboratories of the FBI.

Presidential Influence Declines

The Constitution of the United States calls for the separation of executive, legislative, and judicial powers, but with the various branches related to each other through a system of checks and balances. Within this structure, Congress had asserted its influence in the years after the Civil War. But after 1900, legislative influence had given way to the executive. Presidential power had increased rapidly under Theodore Roosevelt and Wilson, popular Presidents who provided leadership in the progressive era and World War I. These Chief Executives had not been content to administer; they had also proposed new legislation and had used their control of patronage to advance their ideas. In addition, Congress delegated vast powers to the President during World War I.

Beginning in 1919, there was a sharp reaction against White House power. It was partly a matter of a Republican Congress checking a Democratic President (as in the Senate rejection of the League of Nations). Also in the picture was Wilson's illness during his last two years in office, and a natural desire of Congressmen to regain lost prestige.

The presidential campaign of 1920 furnished a clue to what was coming. Lodge, Smoot, and other Senators specifically selected Harding as Republican nominee because they considered the Ohioan a second-rater whom they could control. Legislation followed the same line. In 1921, while establishing the budget system, Congress specified that the Comptroller General (an accounting and auditing official) could never be discharged by any President. This was in sharp contrast to the wartime delegation of powers to the Chief Executive.

Once in the saddle, the House and Senate refused to be dislodged. No longer did Congress wait for the President to propose policy. Instead, the legislative bodies went ahead on farm, tariff, and veterans' legislation. The Presidents could veto bills if they desired—as Coolidge did with the McNary-Haugen measures. But the White House did not provide the leadership of earlier years.

In former days, presidential ineffectiveness had often been related to control of Congress by the opposition party. Harding and Coolidge, however, were Republican Presidents in a decade of Republican Congresses. Yet neither could control the legislative branch. Coolidge, the more capable of the two, met with many defeats at the hands of Congress. The House and Senate passed bills and resolutions which Coolidge did not like, and refused to enact legislation which the President desired. On occasion, Coolidge vetoes were overridden and presidential appointments were turned down. In the case of Charles B. Warren, Coolidge was so irritated by Senate rejection that he resubmitted the appointment. The Senators thereupon rejected Warren by a larger margin.

When Hoover became President in 1929, he showed some signs of developing executive leadership. Congress followed to the extent of accepting some Hoover farm proposals, in the Agricultural Marketing Act of 1929. The House and Senate, though, would not listen to the President on tariff. Instead, they passed the spectacularly high Hawley-

Smoot Tariff of 1930, which Hoover disapproved (though he did sign the bill). As depression deepened, Hoover lost prestige, and his efforts to control Congress were thus further weakened. Then, after the election of 1930, the Democrats won control of the House of Representatives; and they, of course, showed little disposition to follow the lead of a Republican Chief Executive. Hence presidential power remained low—until another Roosevelt burst on the national scene.

18

Politics: The New Deal

The Great Depression

Operating under the two-party system, Americans have rarely gone to extremes. It has usually been a case of a little more or a little less. Only major crises have produced rapid change.

Such a crisis came when the New York stock market broke in the fall of 1929. Though unexpected and spectacular, the crash did not at first seem very serious. Presently, however, it became apparent that stocks would not make a quick recovery. Instead, they sagged to new lows. Business was dull. Wages and farm prices fell. Exports dropped because of depression abroad. Unable to sell their goods, manufacturers reduced production; and unemployment soared. In 1931, the economy of central Europe collapsed. International payments went into general default. The New York bond market then broke, and banks throughout the United States began to fail. Americans found themselves in the worst depression of their history.

There could be no doubt as to the seriousness of the crisis. By 1932 industrial production and national money income stood at barely half the 1929 levels. Yet interest due on long-term debts (mortgages and bonds) had fallen less than 5 percent; and state and local taxes had increased. As a result, taxes claimed a third of the national income in 1932; and the claims of creditors erased corporation profits and drove property owners to the wall.

Meantime, prices and production had fallen so unevenly that the whole economy was out of balance. By cutting production 80 percent, farm machinery companies had been able to keep prices near the 1929

521

level. But farmers, who were unable to curtail production, saw their prices drop some 60 percent.

The human aspects of the situation were most serious of all. By early 1933, the jobless exceeded 15,000,000, or about a third of all normally employed workers. Many of the unemployed took to wandering in quest of work, piling their worldly possessions on their antiquated automobiles. Tens of thousands lived, if that is the word, in wretched tent-and-shanty camps ("Hoovervilles") on the fringes of American cities. Others doubled up in already overcrowded tenements or added to the desperate farm problem by returning to the land. Evicted farmers, refugees from the dust bowl, bankrupt small businessmen, and professional people who could not find work swelled the ranks of the jobless.

Private charity could not handle such a load; the soup-kitchen approach was simply not enough. The support of the unemployed therefore fell on the state and local governments. These governments, however, could not or would not assume the full burden. With taxes in arrears and revenues drying up, some cities went bankrupt and failed even to carry on normal functions. In Atlantic City the courts suspended civil suits because they lacked money to pay jurors. Los Angeles put its zoo up for auction. Chicago discontinued many municipal services and failed to pay its schoolteachers. Under such circumstances, it is not surprising that many destitute citizens received as little as four cents' worth of food a day. Some were given nothing at all.

Proposed Solutions

At first, businessmen, economists, and politicians denied that anything was wrong. After all, a major collapse was outside the range of American expectations. Just a few years earlier, Calvin Coolidge, Herbert Hoover, and others had been talking about permanent prosperity and the abolition of poverty. But by 1932, citizens were beginning to wonder just what was ahead. "This is not a cycle of hard times from which we shall return to build bigger panics . . . ," said so prominent a businessman as Henry Ford, late in

1932. "This is not a breakage to be patched up so that we can resume our reckless course again. This is the ending of an Era."

In spite of unemployment and deep distress, the Socialists and Communists gained very few adherents. Weak leadership in the leftist parties was one explanation. More important was the traditional American rejection of Marxist approaches. Even in times of crisis, long-held philosophies of life are not lightly cast aside.

In like fashion, the overwhelming majority of Americans refused to listen to suggestions from the extreme right. There was little response when *Vanity Fair*, an upper-crust monthly, and *Liberty*, a mass-circulation weekly, suggested editorially that President Hoover assume dictatorial power. Few paid attention to the editor who proposed that Congress abdicate in favor of twelve "Dictators of the Nation." Nor did the public respond favorably when Lawrence Dennis, William Dudley Pelley, Fritz Kuhn, and other fascist-minded "leaders" raised their banners. The only substantial success in this category was that of Huey Long, who established something like a dictatorship while governor of Louisiana. Moving to the United States Senate, Long launched a national share-the-wealth movement, complete with dazzling slogans ("Every Man a King"). But Long had made relatively little headway when he was assassinated in 1935.

In general, Americans preferred less extreme proposals. There was passing interest, but no more, in technocracy, a half-thought-out scheme under which engineers were to solve the problems of society with money representing productive energy. Elderly people became interested in Dr. Francis E. Townsend, who favored large pensions for "senior citizens." (This would help the aged, Townsend said, and bring recovery by forcing money into circulation.) As in the days of Bryan, inflation attracted farmers who were burdened by low prices and fixed debt payments. Senator Elmer Thomas of Oklahoma, a greenbacker, was their principal spokesman. Senator Burton K. Wheeler, from Montana, tried to revive the free-silver crusade. That is, he favored inflation-through-bimetallism. The idea was to raise prices and to confer special benefits on the silver-producing states, including Wheeler's own. From urban Detroit, Father Coughlin also

attacked gold, which he associated with Wall Street and international
bankers. Meanwhile, labor spokesmen favored share-the-work proposals, including the thirty-hour week. Gerard Swope of General Electric and the United States Chamber of Commerce proposed attacking
the problem through the trade associations, by setting aside the antitrust laws, and by letting industry eliminate competition and arbitrarily increase prices.

The Hoover Policies

Like most Americans, President Herbert
Hoover failed to foresee the severity of the economic disturbance
when the stock market broke in 1929. His first effort, therefore, was
to assure the public that all would soon be well. This was a speculative
downturn, Hoover announced; the nation's "fundamental business" of
production and distribution remained sound. Other administrative
officers were equally optimistic, and claimed that prosperity would be
back in thirty or sixty or ninety days. Later, foes of Hoover would
publish a collection of such statements as a book entitled *Oh, Yeah?*

Soon after the crash, the President turned to the industrialists and
financiers with whom he had coöperated during the prosperous 1920's.
Walter S. Gifford, Henry Ford, and other business leaders were called
to the White House and urged to maintain wages and continue production and construction. This, Hoover felt, would reassure the public,
end hoarding, and cushion the shock of reduced purchasing power.
But it did not work. Businessmen felt that cutbacks were necessary;
and the public was in no mood to be reassured.

As the depression deepened, Hoover tried other methods. His Federal Farm Board bought farm surpluses in a vain effort to hold up
prices. The Federal Reserve Banks pumped money into the financial
markets by buying United States bonds from the banks and other
investors. The administration also tried to stimulate recovery by an
extensive public works program, which included the Boulder (then
Hoover) Dam on the Colorado River.

Taken together, these measures went beyond all earlier government
efforts to end depressions. But in years of world collapse this was not
enough. Hoover and Congressmen of both parties decided that fur-

ther steps were necessary; and in 1932 they created the Reconstruction Finance Corporation. During the rest of Hoover's term, the RFC extended loans of nearly $2,000,000,000; and it continued in subsequent years to be the established agency for federal loans to business.

In the Hoover period most RFC loans went to banks and railroads. In the President's judgment, such loans would protect the economy at key points; and the benefits would penetrate down to the people by a kind of percolator process. Hoover approved of a law that established home loan banks to lend money on household mortgages. But he was against direct aid to agriculture and labor. Too expensive, he said; and for the same reason, the United States could not take over the relief burden from local communities. Even without such expenditures, there were mounting deficits; and Hoover was convinced that a balanced budget was a necessity.

The Hoover program, then, heavily stressed government coöperation with business. In the 1920's, such coöperation had struck Americans as logical and desirable. With the coming of depression, citizens were not so sure. The public was turning against business leadership as it became evident that bankers and industrialists were as confused as other Americans. And the trend was accelerated when the Congressionally sponsored Pecora and Black investigations examined business practices in the old progressive manner.

Seizing their opportunity, the Democrats launched an effective smear-Hoover campaign. This was under the direction of a capable publicist, Charles Michelson. Michelson wrote speeches for Democratic Congressmen, prepared material for radio, fed copy to the daily and weekly press. In this copy, Hoover was blamed for the depression. He was blamed for failing to propose reform of the financial exchanges. He was blamed for the Hooverville shanty towns. Above all else, the President was accused of favoring the rich and neglecting the poor. He was denounced for proposing a sales tax, which would bear most heavily on low-income groups. He was attacked for using troops to disperse veterans who had come to Washington demanding immediate payment of the bonus voted back in the Coolidge period.

Replying, Hooover partisans said that the Democrats were engaging in a demagogic quest for votes, were "playing politics with human misery." Administration spokesmen rightly asserted that Hoover had been active, that he, first among Presidents, had recognized the government's direct responsibility for the national economic welfare. (This would be a cornerstone of future federal policy.) But Hoover had acted slowly and reluctantly, had done too little, too late. And, since the Republicans had claimed credit for prosperity, the public quite naturally gave them blame for the depression.

Presidential Election of 1932

With recovery still unrealized, it was clear that Hoover would be defeated for reëlection in 1932. The Democratic nomination thus seemed tantamount to election. There was, in consequence, a scramble for the job. Al Smith wanted to run again; John Garner of Texas and Cordell Hull of Tennessee were other hopefuls. The nomination, however, went to Franklin D. Roosevelt.

A well-to-do member of a famous family, Roosevelt had been educated on two continents. After serving as Assistant Secretary of the Navy under Wilson, he had been defeated for the vice-presidency in 1920. Soon afterward, he was crippled by poliomyelitis. Nonetheless, he remained in politics, and succeeded Al Smith as governor of New York. His gubernatorial record included a run-in with Tammany, which strengthened him throughout the country. His cause was further advanced by an able political manager, James A. Farley; and Roosevelt's name helped, as did his location in a strategically important state. The Hearst-Garner forces came in when Garner was offered the vice-presidential nomination; and Roosevelt was named for President.

In later years, F. D. R. would be known for his striking personality, his bold experimentation, his aggressive leadership. But these factors did not figure in the 1932 campaign. During that canvass, it was hard to find any sharp divergence in policy between the Republicans and the Democrats. Roosevelt talked persuasively, but rather vaguely, of a "New Deal." He promised to be less bound by precedent than Hoover, less afraid to expand the power of the federal government, more of a humanitarian. He spoke against prohibition (Hoover hedged), he endorsed tariff reciprocity, and he talked of cutting government expenses. On the whole, though, he confined his efforts to attacks on the incumbent administration.

That was enough. Voting against Hoover, rather than for Roosevelt, the people gave the Democrats a solid victory. The popular vote was 23,000,000 against 16,000,000. Roosevelt carried the whole South and West and much of the East as well. Hoover led in only half a dozen states—Pennsylvania, Delaware, and four states in New England.

Franklin D. Roosevelt, President

When Franklin D. Roosevelt was inaugurated as President in March, 1933, he seems to have had no strong convictions regarding long-run policies. His was a trial-and-error approach, involving experiments with new uses of federal power. "It is common sense to take a method and try it . . . ," he said. "Above all, try something."

As Roosevelt moved into action, he was basically influenced by the apparent needs of the economy. His policies were radical in their departure from nineteenth-century precedents. They were not radical, however, in the sense of threatening the overthrow of capitalism. First and last, F. D. R. believed in the capitalist economy. He saw his New Deal as a program of protecting, preserving, and improving the existing economy, so that Americans would not turn to extreme measures.

Specifically, Roosevelt and his brain trust of 1933 favored immediate relief. This involved feeding the hungry and seeing to it that citizens did not lose their homes, their farms, their businesses. Beyond that, the need was for recovery measures. Roosevelt's advisers felt that business and agriculture were stranded on the rocks of capital overhead, during an ebbing tide of purchasing power.

In earlier depressions, the normal practice had been to cut down the rocks—liquidate bonds and mortgages through bankruptcies and foreclosure action. Roosevelt preferred to raise the level of purchasing power. This could be done, he felt, by distributing relief payments to the unemployed and to farmers, by promoting public works, and by raising prices through trade agreements and currency management. The government could then turn its attention to reform, so that the economy would not again face so serious a crisis.

The Banking Crisis

Before any Roosevelt policies could be tried, the country was faced with a complete collapse of the banking system. Confidence in banks, already shaken by spectacular failures, was further weakened by revelations of the Senate Banking Committee in the winter of 1932–33. Committee hearings indicated that many leading financiers had been more interested in profits for their companies than in the safety of the funds entrusted to their care.

The record was rather dismal. Operating through security companies affiliated with their banks, officers had sold questionable stocks and bonds to depositors. Worse yet, the financiers had brought their own institutions into the picture. Overconfident of the stability of speculative securities, many bankers had granted loans on stocks and bonds, as well as on land mortgages and business paper. When the bottom dropped out of the market, the securities could not be sold for enough to cover the loans. The banks were forced to keep the stock, extend the loans, and slip into a position where the claims of the depositors could exhaust the total assets of the bank and still leave a deficit.

As the public lost confidence in the banks, depositors withdrew their savings, often in the form of gold, and hoarded their money in safe-deposit boxes and closets. The weakened banking structure could not stand the strain. Beginning with Nevada in October, 1932, state authorities declared bank "holidays," during which payments to depositors were suspended. With the suspension of Detroit's banks on Lincoln's birthday, 1933, the creeping paralysis turned into an acute crisis. In the early morning of March 4, 1933, the day of Roosevelt's inauguration, the governors and the incoming President coöperated to extend the bank holiday to cover all banks in the nation.

Later the same day, Roosevelt said in his inaugural address that "the only thing we have to fear is fear itself—needless, unreasoning, unjustified terror which paralyzes needed efforts to convert retreat into advance." This struck a note that explained the rapid action of the following weeks. Conservatives were too disturbed by the crisis to resist innovation. For a hundred days, all but die-hards gave way before the Roosevelt leadership. Had the President believed in the socialism favored by western European Social Democrats, he could perhaps have had his way. As an example, he could probably have nationalized the banks. But instead, Roosevelt developed a relief-and-recovery program, based on meeting the immediate emergency rather than overhauling the economy.

First on the agenda was the banking problem. Acting under extraordinary powers voted him by Congress, Roosevelt looked into the affairs of all closed banks. Solvent institutions were permitted to reopen. After the passage of the Glass-Steagall Banking Act of June, 1933, individual deposits were guaranteed by the government, through a Federal Deposit Insurance Corporation (FDIC). To curb speculation, security affiliates were divorced from commercial banks. Hoarding of specie was prohibited, citizens being required to sell their gold to the Treasury.

The Hundred Days

These were but a few of many measures adopted from March to June, 1933. Roosevelt moved quickly to provide relief for the needy. A Federal Emergency Relief Administration (FERA), under Harry Hopkins, took relief out of the hands of state and local governments. A Civilian Conservation Corps (CCC) gave jobs to a quarter-million young men from relief rolls and a few veterans of World War I. The Public Works Administration (PWA), under Secretary of the Interior Harold Ickes, was also expected to provide employment. So were the NRA (National Recovery Administration) codes, which were based on the shorter-hour, spread-the-work concept.

Relief for the farmer came in several ways. The Emergency Farm Mortgage Act enabled farmers who faced foreclosure to have their mortgages taken over by the federal government. To facilitate all lending operations, the government's farm loan agencies were brought together in a Farm Credit Administration (FCA), first headed by

Henry Morgenthau, Jr. The AAA (Agricultural Adjustment Administration), directed by Secretary of Agriculture Henry Wallace, also provided farm relief, by paying for immediate reduction of output. After 1933, cuts were to be achieved by reducing acreage under cultivation. But, since land was already planted when the program began in 1933, the first-year cuts involved plowing under cotton, and even killing little pigs.

There was relief for other groups as well. The Home Owners' Loan Corporation (HOLC) offered relief for hard-pressed owners of residential property, and for mortgage holders, too. An expanded RFC (Reconstruction Finance Corporation), now headed by Jesse Jones, kept large and small businessmen from going to the wall. Depressed mining areas were benefited by a silver-buying program and by higher prices for gold.

Besides providing relief, the legislation of the Hundred Days was directed toward economic recovery. Often the goals overlapped. Payments to the unemployed (FERA) and to farmers (AAA) were designed both for relief and to increase the purchasing power necessary for recovery. PWA construction projects meant employment. Their more important purpose, though, was to stimulate recovery. The theory was that government spending would prime the pump, set things going in iron and steel and in the building industry. And Roosevelt took the United States off the gold standard partly in hopes of recovering foreign markets (countries with depreciated currencies are at an advantage in international trade).

These moves were important; but Roosevelt put even greater emphasis on raising prices. This, in fact, was the central feature of the New Deal's recovery program. The crop-reduction plan of the AAA was, basically, an attempt to boost farm prices. The price-fixing provisions of General Hugh Johnson's NRA codes were designed to do the same in the industrial and merchandising field.

Monetary policy aimed in the same direction. F. D. R. definitely disapproved of all-out inflation. Although authorized to issue unsupported greenbacks, under AAA legislation, he did not use these powers. To please the mining states—strong in the Senate—he had the Treasury buy huge quantities of silver at a price above the market value.

Yet he refused to endorse bimetallism, or free-silver inflation. He did, however, favor a controlled type of inflation, through reduction of the gold content of the dollar. During 1933 he used authority granted him by Congress to change the price of gold at frequent intervals. This was in accordance with the advice of Professor George Warren of Cornell University, who maintained that prices could be controlled by such a policy. But results were somewhat disappointing, and in 1934 Roosevelt pegged gold at just over 59 percent of its old value.

Republicans and conservative Democrats disapproved of Roosevelt's monetary experiments. On the whole, though, these groups grudgingly accepted the legislation of the Hundred Days. Even the most conservative farm leaders had to admit that the AAA helped agriculture during a desperate crisis. Conservative businessmen found much of the NRA acceptable (the whole scheme closely followed proposals of the United States Chamber of Commerce and of General Electric's Gerard Swope).

In those early New Deal days, criticism came rather from the left. Socialists and some reform-minded members of the major parties felt that Roosevelt had erred in not taking advantage of his opportunity to inaugurate government ownership (say of banks and railroads). Many more complained that the laws passed in the Hundred Days pointed to no permanent solution of the problems of the capitalist economy. In other words, by stressing relief and recovery, Roosevelt had neglected reform.

Answering such criticisms, the President's supporters said that first things must come first, and that relief and recovery legislation did contain important elements of reform. Most notably, the new statutes established for all time the vital principle that the government would supply all needed aid in an emergency. The CCC advanced the cause of reforestation. The PWA supplied irrigation dams and needed highways. The NRA eliminated child labor in industry, banned unfair business practices, and (in Section 7a) guaranteed workers the right to organize. The AAA pointed toward better agricultural planning, as in taking submarginal lands out of production. The establishment of the FDIC was an important step forward. The separation of banks from security affiliates was another reform; and a new Securities and

Exchange Commission (SEC) gained some control over Wall Street.

One creation of the Hundred Days stood entirely alone. This was the Tennessee Valley Authority (TVA). During World War I, the government had built a great plant for the chemical fixation of nitrogen, at Muscle Shoals on the Tennessee River. After the war, the plant was no longer used; and Senator George W. Norris, a progressive Republican, strove perennially to convert it into a government-run electric power plant. Twice he succeeded in getting the necessary legislation through Congress, only to meet presidential vetoes. In rejecting the Norris program, Presidents Coolidge (1928) and Hoover (1931) held that the proposal was socialistic. So, in a sense, it was. Roosevelt, however, gave Norris his support.[1] He did this, not because of doctrine, but because of the immediate practical gains which he felt would come from a TVA program.

Linked to a rural electrification drive, TVA did a great deal to aid the inhabitants of the Tennessee Valley. Since it was limited to one region, advanced the cause of conservation, and helped depressed farmers, the program aroused less controversy than might have been expected from so fundamental a deviation in policy.

Still, there was strong opposition, from conservative politicians and businessmen, and especially from the utilities (notably Wendell Willkie's Commonwealth and Southern). Many were disturbed when Norman Thomas called TVA the first flower of American socialism. Roosevelt nevertheless went ahead, and talked of launching Columbia and Missouri and Arkansas Valley authorities. In fact, however, these extensions of the program were postponed; and TVA remained unique to the end of the Roosevelt era.

The Opposing Forces

During the Hundred Days, F. D. R. sought support from everyone—business, labor, and agriculture, producer and consumer, conservative and radical. But, as time went on, the administration's more conservative support melted away. Business-

---

[1] Norris also fathered the Twentieth ("lame duck") Amendment, added to the Constitution in 1933. Before this, federal officeholders defeated in November had served until March. Now they leave office in January.

men and professional people began to worry about government deficits and about the growth of the federal bureaucracy. Equally disturbing was the increase in the number of forms to be filed with numerous and conflicting government agencies. Did this not mean increasing regulation and loss of freedom?

There were innumerable special complaints. Many small businessmen did not like the NRA codes, many of which were drawn up by big business. Financiers viewed the President's monetary policy with disfavor, and felt that the SEC (by checking speculation) would impede recovery. Utility spokesmen were alarmed about TVA, and the administration's opposition to holding companies. Industrialists disapproved of Roosevelt's prolabor attitude, and believed that the New Dealers were doing too much for the farmer.

While business drifted away from the administration, Roosevelt picked up support from other quarters. Though puzzled and uncertain about the new government-directed agriculture, farmers in every state recognized that they were being helped by AAA. Labor leaders were enthusiastic about the New Deal, for Section 7a of NRA ended the decline in union membership. The improved relief situation led lower-income groups to regard Franklin D. Roosevelt as their great champion. Most radicals remained critical, but liberal and progressive journalists and politicians generally endorsed the Roosevelt policies.

These trends, of course, influenced the character of the administration. Conservative advisers and officeholders faded out of the picture. Roosevelt no longer took suggestions from the United States Chamber of Commerce. Lewis Douglas, a businessman whom Roosevelt had appointed Budget Director, quit because he disapproved of deficit financing. Conservative brain trusters like Raymond Moley were eased out and became critics of the New Deal. General Hugh Johnson, administrator of the business-inspired NRA, stayed on until the Supreme Court killed his agency; but he was unhappy to see business and government drifting apart. So were other conservative officials, including Vice-President Garner and James A. Farley, who was both Postmaster General and chairman of the Democratic National Committee.

Meanwhile, Roosevelt was turning more and more to liberal advisers. These individuals told the President that he would fare best if he relied on labor and agriculture rather than on business, and if he gave as much attention to reform as to recovery. This advice came from many different persons: from young brain trusters like Thomas Corcoran and Benjamin Cohen; from long-time friends like Secretary of Labor Frances Perkins and Henry Morgenthau (who moved from FCA to the Treasury Department); from Harry Hopkins, who headed government relief and later became confidential White House adviser; from Secretary of Agriculture Henry Wallace; from Senators like Hugo Black and Robert Wagner.

As the months rolled by, conservative opposition to the Roosevelt administration became increasingly well organized and active. Business associations and metropolitan newspapers became critical of the New Deal. Most of these stressed the theme of individual liberty *versus* government control. A good many also argued against Rooseveltian legislation on the ground of states' rights. Similar in tone were the statements of the National Association of Manufacturers, now well backed by big business. The Du Ponts and other wealthy individuals also joined such anti-administration Democrats as Al Smith in a so-called Liberty League. The politicians in this combination talked of states' rights and called themselves Jeffersonian Democrats. Most of them, though, were close friends of big business. Criticism of Roosevelt also mounted in the South, where conservatives were worried about Roosevelt's relationship with the labor and the Negro vote. Eugene Talmadge of Georgia and many another southern politician also complained that F. D. R. was building a national machine; that federal grants and federal officeholders would soon make it impossible for local politicians to run their state machines.

If one judged by the newspaper and radio, by news magazines and the business periodicals, the Roosevelt administration was a menace to American tradition. The average citizen, however, was less worried than were the well-to-do about unbalanced budgets and government control of the economy. Nor were most Americans impressed when the N.A.M. and the Du Ponts talked about the threat to liberty and freedom. To millions of citizens, freedom in the depression meant freedom to look for jobs that did not exist, liberty to do without the wonderful things that modern science had created. Not a few were willing to exchange a little of their freedom for a bit of security. Besides, who could tell? Depriving businessmen of some of their liberty of action might result in greater individual freedom for the bulk of the people.

A Second Term

The results could be seen at the polls. In 1934, Roosevelt's Democratic party carried the Congressional and gubernatorial elections by a wide margin. In 1936, the administration did even better. That year saw the Republicans nominating Governor Alfred M. Landon of Kansas for the presidency, and Frank Knox, a Chicago publisher, for the vice-presidency. Landon was an oilman who had favored economy in politics. Thus he could be called the "Kansas Coolidge." He and his running mate were, however, quite devoid of popular appeal; and their platform echoed that of the opposition. A few disgruntled Democrats, including Al Smith, gave Landon their support; and the Liberty League poured money into his campaign. But Roosevelt and Garner won by a landslide.

With 27,000,000 votes, Roosevelt ran 11,000,000 ahead of his opponent. Landon could carry only Maine and Vermont, an interesting pair in view of the old adage: "As Maine goes, so goes the nation." Forty-six states went for Roosevelt. This was the most striking electoral-college victory of a century—indeed, the most striking since the introduction of popular voting into presidential contests. Local and Congressional races went the same way. In both the House and the Senate, the Republicans reached their lowest level since the Civil War, with barely a fifth of the membership.

Roosevelt's triumph over Landon was in many ways a victory of lower-income groups over the well-to-do. During the campaign, the *Literary Digest* polled a sample group of citizens who owned automobiles and telephones. The result was overwhelmingly pro-Landon; whereupon the editors predicted Roosevelt's defeat. This bad prediction helped kill the *Digest* after the election (it was limping anyway). Had the magazine also polled Americans who owned neither cars nor phones, they would have found a different current running in the land.

Noting the class division, some foes of Roosevelt said that the President, a rich man, had become a "traitor to his class." Others saw real peril to the republic in an alignment of rich against poor. Yet the 1936 result was no triumph for radicals. Roosevelt had consistently and vigorously defended the existing economic system. The Socialists, the Communists, the Socialist Laborites all refused to support the Chief Executive, and nominated tickets of their own.

Others, too, felt that Roosevelt had not gone far enough: Gerald L. K. Smith, who had taken over the remnants of Huey Long's share-the-wealth movement; Dr. Townsend of the old-age Townsend Plan; Father Coughlin and his "Social Justice" cohorts; and many farm inflationists. Combining, the Smith-Townsend-Coughlin groups nominated for the presidency Congressman William Lemke, a North Dakota Republican who had been active in the Nonpartisan League.

Citizens who felt that Roosevelt had not gone far enough could vote for Lemke (Union), or Norman Thomas (Socialist), or Earl Browder (Communist), or Aiken (Socialist Labor). But Lemke received fewer than 900,000 votes, less than a thirtieth of Roosevelt's total. The Marxist parties fared even more poorly, all doing less well than in 1932. While spurning Liberty League conservatism, Americans even more decisively rejected those who wanted to go beyond the New Deal.

The Court Fight

Victory at the polls did not bring final triumph to the New Deal. There remained the troublesome problem of the judiciary. By 1936 the voters had ousted a very large percentage of the Congressmen and administrators of the pre-1929 era. But the Supreme Court remained unchanged. The justices who had ruled against labor and against social legislation and for big business in the 1920's had appointments for life. Most of them still clung to office in the following decade.

As late as 1936, when Roosevelt carried all the states but two, a majority of the Supreme Court mirrored the anti-Roosevelt sentiment of successful business and professional people. A liberal minority felt that much of the legislation passed in the Hundred Days and after could be declared constitutional (Justices Louis D. Brandeis, Harlan F. Stone, Benjamin N. Cardozo, and Chief Justice Charles Evans Hughes). The majority disagreed, and maintained that most New Deal legislation was unconstitutional (Justices J. C. McReynolds, Willis Van Devanter, Pierce Butler, George Sutherland, Owen J. Roberts). Since the Supreme Court had expressed a variety of views through the years, there were plenty of precedents on both sides. It all depended on the social philosophy of the particular judge.

Decisions were not all adverse. The Supreme Court upheld Roosevelt's monetary legislation, including the act of 1933 that voided the clause in private contracts calling for payment of debts in gold (Gold Clause cases, 1935). In U. S. vs. Curtiss-Wright Export Corporation (1936), a case that involved arms embargoes, the Court ruled that Congress could delegate sweeping powers to the President in the foreign relations field. And the judges stated, in the Ashwander decision of the same year, that it was constitutional for TVA to sell electric power.

Meanwhile, however, the Court declared unconstitutional several major New Deal statutes. The decisions often stressed the limitations of the power of Congress under the interstate commerce clause of the Constitution. In 1935, the justices threw out two statutes passed the preceding year—a Railroad Retirement Act and the Frazier-Lemke Farm Bankruptcy Act. In addition, the Court curbed the President's power to discharge members of independent commissions. (Roosevelt had dismissed the ultraconservative William E. Humphrey, Coolidge-appointed chairman of the Federal Trade Commission.) Then, in a unanimous decision in the Schechter Poultry case, the judges ended the NRA codes, on the ground that Congress could not delegate lawmaking powers to the President.

The following year, 1936, saw the Court invalidate a Municipal Bankruptcy Act and overthrow the administration's farm program. In the latter instance, six justices held, in the Hoosac Mills case, that the AAA processing taxes interfered with the rights of states. Yet the Court checked state action, too. The Morehead decision of this same year invalidated a New York law establishing minimum wages for women and children. As President Roosevelt bitterly remarked, there seemed to be a "no man's land," a "twilight zone" in which neither the federal nor the state governments could legislate.

How could the administration meet this problem? Partly by re-writing laws to meet the objections of the Court majority. New rail-road-pension and farm-mortgage acts ultimately survived judicial ex-amination. But the Guffey Coal Act, an NRA-type statute rewritten in hopes of satisfying the judges, was declared unconstitutional in 1936.

Other possibilities remained. Roosevelt could wait until some of the conservative judges died. Four of the five were over seventy. But to a man of action, waiting is not easy. Besides, judges often live to a ripe old age; all these five lasted until late in 1939, and two outlived Roosevelt. And the President, encouraged by his great victory of 1936, felt strong enough to move against the "horse-and-buggy" justices.

Theoretically, F. D. R. might have denounced the whole doctrine of judicial review and the right of any court to overthrow legislative acts by 5-to-4 decisions. But Roosevelt had little interest in abstract doctrine. He was interested rather in quick, practical results. He there-fore turned early in 1937 to the method used during Abraham Lin-coln's day—increasing the size of the Court so that the administra-tion, by new appointments, could have a favorable majority. But Roosevelt did not approach the matter directly. Instead, he indicated that he felt that elderly judges were inefficient. Then he asked Con-gress for authority to make an additional appointment (up to a total of six) when any Supreme Court justice over seventy refused to retire.

Since the Democrats had complete control of both houses of Con-gress, the President expected victory. But there was unexpected op-position; and the Senate Judiciary Committee reported adversely on the President's proposal. In the years since the Civil War, Americans had developed a great respect for the Supreme Court. This was true of the legal profession in particular—and most members of Congress are lawyers. But this was not the entire story. Republicans who had been casting about for an issue denounced "court packing" with en-thusiasm. Conservative Democrats who had long disapproved of Roo-sevelt, but had been bound to him by patronage, now ventured to sound off against the White House program. Elderly liberals were offended by the accent on age. (Was not the liberal Brandeis the oldest of the justices?) The opposition also included many Congressmen who felt that the executive branch of the government had grown too strong. If Congress now yielded, the executive would gain still more influence. If the legislative branch resisted, it might regain some of its lost prestige, while protecting the judiciary.

Before the issue was decided, the judges themselves swung into action. After many months of voting against New Deal statutes, the Court began upholding such measures. In National Labor Relations Board vs. Jones & Laughlin Steel Corporation (1937), the Supreme Court affirmed the constitutionality of the Wagner Act of 1935, which had reasserted and extended the labor guarantees of Section 7a of NRA. At the same time, in the West Coast Hotel Company case, the justices approved of a Washington state law fixing minimum wages for women and children. This reversed the Morehead ruling of the year preceding; and it reversed also the old Adkins vs. Children's Hospital decision.

These striking changes owed much to one man. Down to 1937, Justice Roberts voted with the older conservatives, enabling them to strike down New Deal legislation, 5–4. In 1937 Roberts shifted, and laws were now upheld, 5–4. The new situation, of course, made many feel that judicial reorganization was now unnecessary.

As finally passed, the Judiciary Reform Act of 1937 contained little of what Roosevelt desired. The statute did, however, raise retirement pay for Supreme Court justices. Under its provisions, one conservative resigned in 1937, one in 1938, one in 1939. Roosevelt replaced them with liberals. With Roberts' shift, this meant that the Court now vigorously upheld New Deal legislation. The justices, in fact, put a very heavy emphasis on "presumption of constitutionality," and overthrew Congressional legislation only on the rarest of occasions. The Court retained its importance, especially with reference to civil rights; but it no longer stood in the way of social legislation.

Roosevelt partisans said that the President, though whipped in battle, had won the campaign. Nonetheless, the Court fight represented a real setback for the occupant of the White House. The economic recession of 1937 was a further surprise and disappointment;

and many said that F. D. R. had passed his peak and was headed downhill.

Stung by such statements, and irritated by the Court episode, Roosevelt announced a purge of some of the Democratic members of Congress who had fought the administration. That is, he tried to prevent the renomination in 1938 of such conservatives as Senators Walter George of Georgia and Millard Tydings of Maryland. But the purge was a dismal failure. Much as they liked Roosevelt, Democratic voters did not want to have him interfere in state contests. And the purge, like the Court plan, looked to many like an effort of the executive to dominate another branch of the government.

The Permanent New Deal

By 1938, the year of the purge, the New Deal had taken on its permanent form. The legislation of the Hundred Days in 1933 had been hastily framed. In the next few years it was reconsidered, modified, and extended. As early as 1935, the President had said that the basic program to which he was pledged had now reached "substantial completion." A "breathing spell" had come —"very decidedly so." This statement proved somewhat premature, for the Court fight and the recession spurred Roosevelt on to new action. But 1938 would see the end of the advance.

The administration's approach to relief changed gradually after 1933. The direct-relief method of the FERA met the needs of the emergency, then gave way to the more generally accepted work-relief philosophy. When the PWA failed to furnish as many jobs as anticipated, Harry Hopkins organized a Civil Works Administration (1933–35), for jobs-in-a-hurry. Since many CWA projects were trivial, there were widespread complaints about leaf-raking and other "boondoggling." In 1935, therefore, both PWA and CWA gave way to a Works Progress Administration, which lasted on into World War II. WPA had interesting sidelights, including white-collar and fine-arts projects and aid for students (National Youth Administration). Basically, though, it was a construction agency which built roads, post offices, and the like. The liquidation of WPA (and NYA and CCC) in 1944 did not rule out the possibility of relief-through-public-works

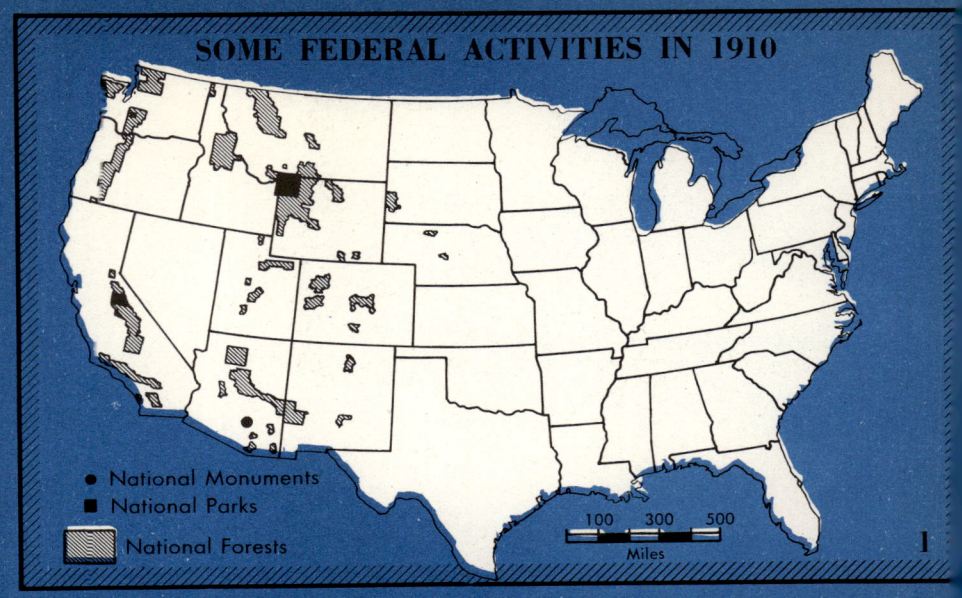

SOME FEDERAL ACTIVITIES IN 1910

- ● National Monuments
- ■ National Parks
- ▨ National Forests

100   300   500
Miles

1

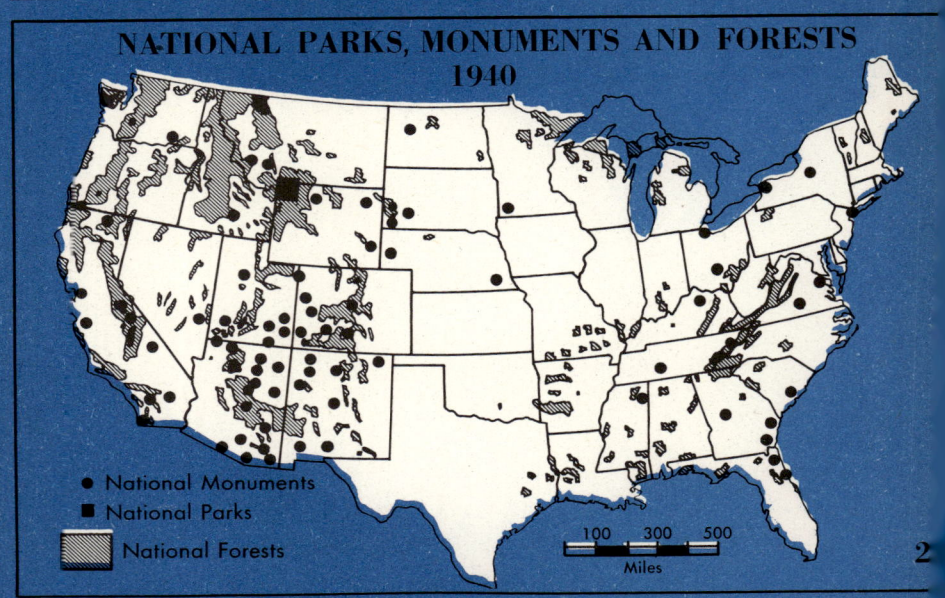

NATIONAL PARKS, MONUMENTS AND FORESTS
1940

- ● National Monuments
- ■ National Parks
- ▨ National Forests

100   300   500
Miles

2

These maps indicate a few of the fields in which the federal government now operates. By 1910, Presidents Theodore Roosevelt and Taft had launched a conservation program (Map 1). This program was greatly expanded in the years that followed, Franklin D. Roosevelt having particular interest in the national parks, monuments, and forests (Map 2).

The United States highway program was begun in Wilson's administration, with grants to the states. This development came into its own in the

UNITED STATES HIGHWAYS IN 1950

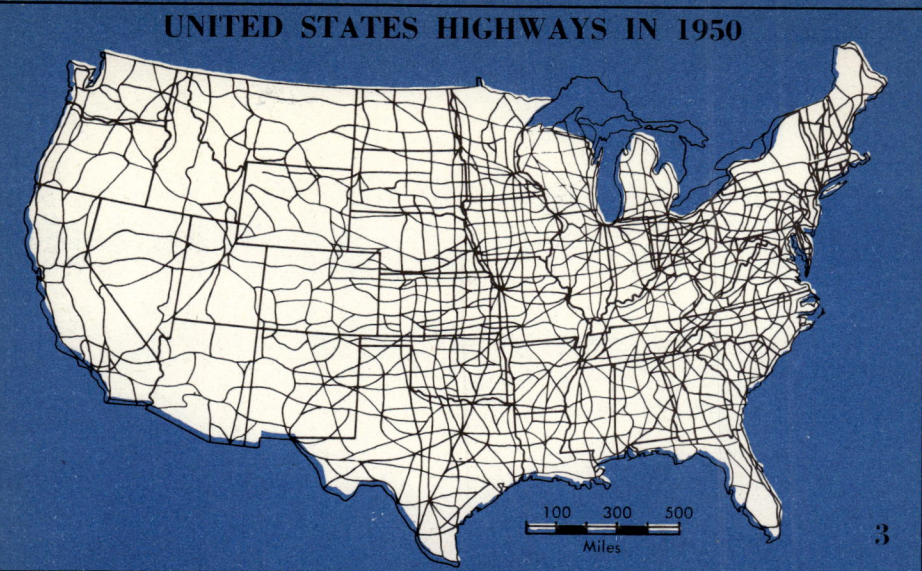

100 300 500
Miles

3

FEDERAL DAMS AND IRRIGATION PROJECTS
1948

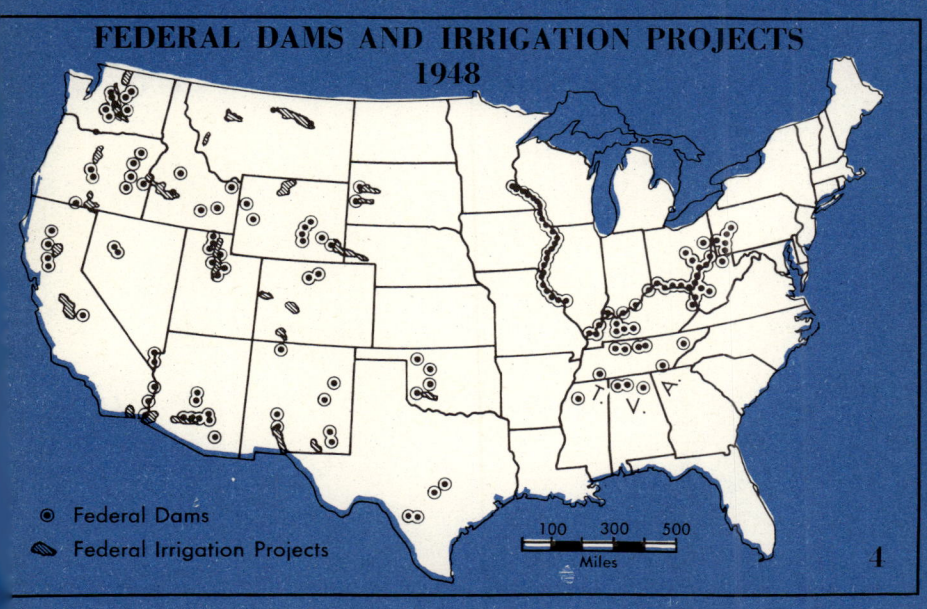

◎ Federal Dams
◈ Federal Irrigation Projects

100 300 500
Miles

4

1920's, and was further extended during the depression, under Hoover and Roosevelt (Map 3). Federal interest in irrigation began in the early days of the century, expanding after small beginnings. Since the 1920's, the national government has also constructed dams for flood control, notably in the Mississippi Valley. Finally, the creation of the Tennessee Valley Authority in 1933 saw the United States using dams for power purposes.

in later emergencies. It was hoped, however, that social security would reduce the need for this approach.

Public works expenditures reduced but never eliminated the need for direct relief. This was gradually turned back to the states and localities, with the federal government providing assistance. Two interesting experiments were the school-lunch program and the food-stamp plan. The latter enabled families on relief to obtain supplies of surplus commodities, say citrus fruits, thus enriching their diet and at the same time relieving overproduction.

These were temporary projects. The social security system, set up in 1935 and expanded in 1938, was designed to be permanent. It provided federal grants for old-age assistance, mothers' and orphans' benefits, and aid to the handicapped. Social security also comprised unemployment insurance and retirement programs, handled through the states and financed by employee and employer contributions. Amounts were small, and coverage was limited largely to industrial workers. Still, it was a beginning. And it involved recognition of the duty of the government to prevent acute distress, to help the least fortunate, and to do a bit toward providing a measure of security in an age when many found less individual opportunity than before.

Recovery was a major aim of the monetary legislation of the Hundred Days, and the NRA, PWA, and AAA. In 1934 the administration took another step in the same direction, passing the Reciprocal Trade Agreement Act. This authorized the President to negotiate agreements with foreign countries. American tariff duties could be cut as much as 50 percent, in return for concessions abroad. The plan was to promote exports, thus contributing toward domestic recovery, and, by building international commerce, to aid world recovery. Government loans to foreign countries, through the Export-Import Bank, fitted into the same pattern.

World crisis prevented these measures from getting much of a trial. For a time, however, it looked as though the domestic recovery program would work. Prices, production, and employment rose from 1933 to 1937. Pleased, Roosevelt began to feel that the recovery job was done, and that he could have a balanced budget. Disabused by the 1937 recession, the President then turned to new recovery efforts.

These included the establishment of minimum wage rates for labor, under the Fair Labor Standards Act of 1938; new legislation to raise farm prices, the permanent AAA of 1938; increased WPA activity; and some federal aid for housing construction. The last came through the United States Housing Authority, set up in 1937 to promote slum clearance. (A Federal Housing Authority, launched three years before, aided middle-class residential building.)

For a time, Roosevelt also considered stimulating competition as a means of reviving business activity. This was the exact opposite of the 1933–35 NRA principle of coöperation and elimination of competition. Here the President was influenced by William O. Douglas and Thurman Arnold and by the findings of the Congressionally appointed Temporary National Economic Committee, which investigated the concentration of economic power after 1938. Pushing along this line, Roosevelt launched antitrust suits against some of the largest combinations.

All these things yielded less return than was desired. At the end of the decade, more than ten years after the crash of 1929, there were still 7,000,000 unemployed. It would take defense orders to restore full employment and full production. But one point at least was established by the recovery efforts of the New Deal. It was apparent that the United States government would not again let the business cycle operate uncontrolled; that those in charge would attempt to pull the country out of economic depressions.

In the Hundred Days of 1933, the New Dealers had put relatively little stress on reform. They had, however, increased government influence on the economy. Following this up, they tightened government control over the stock market in 1934, enabling the Securities and Exchange Commission to protect the public against fraud and uncontrolled speculation. The following year a new Banking Act gave the Federal Reserve Board power to regulate stock market margins. A Public Utility Holding Company Act of 1935 forbade the pyramided holding companies through which Samuel Insull and other financiers had controlled great power empires with relatively small investments.

Regulation reached into many other fields. A Federal Communications Commission was set up in 1934 to regulate radio and allied fields. A United States Maritime Commission (1936) and a Civil Aeronautics Board (1938) also increased government control of economic life; and the I.C.C. was given new authority, as over buses, trucks, and water carriers. The old pure food and drug legislation was extended—in the cosmetics field, for instance; and the federal government stepped up its regulation of advertising. Other legislation was designed to help independent merchants against the chain stores. The Miller-Tydings Act of 1937, as an example, specified that state-sponsored agreements against price cutting were not to be considered violations of the federal antitrust laws.

While tightening regulation of business, the New Deal also increased taxes on higher-level incomes. Roosevelt was slow to take up the taxation question. By 1935, however, he was moving toward a "soak-the-rich" position, partly, no doubt, because of the response to Huey Long's share-the-wealth movement. Late in 1935, Congress increased levies on high incomes and on the profits of large corporations. The antitrust activity that came later in the decade fell into the same pattern.

In planning for agriculture, Roosevelt had at first aimed chiefly at raising farm prices. At the same time, the President (like his cousin Theodore) was deeply interested in conservation. This was seen in the CCC program; also in Roosevelt's campaigns against erosion and for flood control. When the Supreme Court invalidated the first AAA in 1936, Roosevelt brought in Soil Conservation and Domestic Allotment, a plan for paying farmers for improving their land. This in 1938 gave way to a permanent AAA, which stressed conservation of the soil as well as high-level farm prices (the latter to be achieved through crop loans and a price-support system). Crop insurance for wheat, and later cotton, was another feature of the new system. No less important were improved credit facilities and the work of the Rural Electrification Administration.

President Roosevelt was also interested in the plight of farmers on submarginal land, and the difficulties of sharecroppers and other tenants, as well as agricultural laborers. A few were helped through the TVA. The Bankhead-Jones Act of 1937 was designed to aid some tenants and farm hands on the path toward ownership. A variety of experiments with resettlement, subsistence homesteads, and coöperative agriculture were brought together under the Farm Security Administration in 1937. This agency, however, met with tremendous criticism, was always starved for funds, and was killed altogether in 1947. Unquestionably the New Deal did help agriculture; but the help was least striking among those who needed aid the most.

From 1933 on, Roosevelt and his advisers became increasingly labor-conscious. The success of organization drives under NRA and the Wagner Act made organized labor an increasingly important element in the community; and labor voted for Roosevelt. The President was disturbed by jurisdictional conflicts (A.F. of L. versus C.I.O.). He was doubtful about the sit-down strike; and he had his troubles with John L. Lewis. Yet F. D. R. remained consistently pro-labor. His legislative record in the field came to a climax with the passage of the Fair Labor Standards Act of 1938, which fixed minimum wages and maximum hours.

End of the New Deal

Several important New Deal acts were passed in 1938: the new AAA; the Fair Labor Standards Act; improved social security. That, however, was the end of the advance of Franklin D. Roosevelt's New Deal. Much remained undone, as the President himself admitted; but the movement slowed down and stopped.

Some wondered why. Partly, perhaps, because Roosevelt was a moderate, and felt that after the successes of 1938 he should go easy for a time. Partly, too, because the President received a serious setback when his attempted purge failed in 1938.

More important, though, was the international crisis. This was the year of the Munich settlement in Europe, the year before the outbreak of World War II. Concerned over world developments, Roosevelt turned his attention away from domestic problems, much as Wilson had a generation earlier. In diplomatic affairs, Roosevelt needed the support of the southern Democrats, who were more likely to render aid if the White House deëmphasized domestic reform. Roosevelt was also anxious to win some backing from Republican politicians and businessmen in the Northeast; and they too were anti-New Deal. Needing the backing of industrialists for war production, the President was unable to continue his antitrust campaign. Needing efficient executives in government, F. D. R. turned to, and came to work with, big business administrators.

So the New Deal era ended. What had been accomplished in those exciting years? Certainly many Rooseveltian efforts had failed. The administration had been unable to produce full employment in peacetime by currency management and moderate government spending. Nor had Roosevelt solved the problem of an increasing national debt ($3,000,000,000 added yearly during the 1930's). He had not checked the growth of big business or greatly altered the business system. He had only slightly alleviated urban and rural slum conditions.

On the positive side, the New Deal established federal unemployment relief and old-age pensions. It insured small savings and curbed speculation and the defrauding of unwary investors. It set precedents for government aid to and regulation of agriculture, and government subsidies for housing and conservation. It made the government a guarantor of many mortgages, and stimulated home building and ownership. Roosevelt's support of collective bargaining changed a weak labor movement into one of the world's strongest. And, most important of all, the force of events during these years established the principle of federal responsibility for the general economic welfare as an accepted part of the American political system.

A Third Term and a Fourth Term

The New Deal was standing still when Franklin D. Roosevelt ran for his third and fourth presidential terms in 1940 and 1944. In these years, Roosevelt's thoughts were primarily about foreign policy. Yet the New Deal, as a record, was the leading factor in both contests.

After some hesitation, or appearance of hesitation, Roosevelt agreed to run for a third term in 1940. Some who opposed this were concerned about the tradition against a third term, or the danger of entrenched executive power. Others were thinking of their own presidential ambitions. Still other opponents of the move were con-

servatives who disliked Roosevelt's New Deal and wanted to see the
Democratic party led by a conservative. Among Democrats critical of
the third-term idea were James Farley, John Garner, and, for a time,
Cordell Hull—all conservatives hostile toward much of Roosevelt's
domestic program. Backing Roosevelt for a third nomination were
such New Deal Democrats as Harold Ickes, Harry Hopkins, and
Henry Wallace; also machine Democrats who considered F. D. R. the
candidate most likely to win. The association of the 1940 ticket with
the New Deal was further seen in the vice-presidential nomination.
At Roosevelt's insistence, this went to Wallace, Garner having decided not to run again.

In the 1940 campaign, the Republicans gave their presidential
nomination to Wendell Willkie of Indiana, formerly a Democrat
and a relative newcomer to politics. As a businessman who had fought
TVA, Willkie was backed heavily by the utility interests. But he also
was popular with the Republican rank and file, which had long been
looking for a fresh and buoyant personality.

Willkie and Roosevelt agreed fairly well on foreign questions (both
were internationalists). The campaign, therefore, was centered on
domestic issues. Roosevelt was known for the New Deal. Willkie was
known for his opposition to it. Nevertheless, the Republican nominee
indicated approval of most Rooseveltian measures, insisting, however, that the Republicans could do the same thing much more efficiently.

A good campaigner, Willkie picked up midwest farm support and
made a bid for labor backing (he got John L. Lewis, but little more).
The returns showed Willkie running 5,000,000 votes ahead of Landon's 1936 total, while Roosevelt dropped a half-million. This cut in
half the margin between the Democrats and the Republicans. But it
left Roosevelt ahead, 27,000,000 to 22,000,000. The President carried
five-sixths of the electoral vote. Willkie carried ten states, adding
eight midwest states to faithful Maine and Vermont.

Again the voters had expressed confidence in Roosevelt. There
were many factors in the victory: the President's personality and political skill; the effectiveness of the Democratic machines; the critical international situation. Above all else, however, the continuing support

for F. D. R. seems to have been associated with a fairly general approval of the President's domestic record.

There were new elements in the situation in 1944, when Roosevelt sought his fourth term. By this time the United States was a belligerent. During wartime, a President assumes new stature as Commander in Chief; and citizens are naturally reluctant to change leadership in a military emergency. Roosevelt had other points of strength in 1944. With the leveling off of the New Deal, conservative Democrats (as in the South) were less hostile than they had been in previous years. Further to placate this group, the President dropped Vice-President Henry Wallace from the ticket and substituted Senator Harry S. Truman of Missouri. Truman had voted for New Deal measures and was approved by labor; but, unlike Wallace, he was not viewed with suspicion by conservatives. The conservatives, however, did not dominate the Roosevelt party. An important element in the F. D. R. strength was the Political Action Committee (P.A.C.), a labor-sponsored agency.

To oppose Roosevelt the Republicans turned to Governor Thomas E. Dewey of New York. Like Willkie, Dewey took care not to attack the aid-to-labor, aid-to-agriculture approach of the New Deal. He did, however, carry on a spirited campaign, and made a reasonably good impression on the electorate. Roosevelt's total dipped a million and a half, to below 26,000,000 (partly because state laws made it difficult for many of those in uniform to cast votes). With 22,000,000, Dewey polled substantially the same vote as Willkie four years before—a little more in the South and Far West, a little less in the Middle West and East. Save for Michigan, Dewey carried all the states that had gone for Willkie; and he added Wisconsin, Ohio, and Wyoming. But Roosevelt won, carrying over four-fifths of the electoral votes. Again the public had backed the father of the New Deal.

19

World Horizons

An Expanding Nation

Early in the twentieth century, Americans had come to accept the fact that the United States had become a world power. Manufacturers and financiers paid increasing attention to opportunities abroad. A reorganized State Department helped these businessmen locate and secure influence in all quarters of the globe. Military power went hand in hand with economic might. The United States built one of the world's great navies and secured strategic control of the Caribbean and much of the Pacific. Reluctant to form alliances with major powers, the American republic nevertheless did develop an informal entente with Great Britain. At the same time, the United States established close ties with lesser states in Latin America, notably with Cuba and Panama. Ideologically, too, Americans pushed outward. The whole world became acquainted with such American doctrines as sea power, dollar diplomacy, and the open door. Americans became active in the world peace movement, and American engineers carried their technology all over the earth.

The Wilsonian Experiment

Given these trends, American participation in the European phase of World War I was, if not inevitable, at least logical. It was the extent of participation that was surprising. On the military side, the United States threw its navy into the balance and poured 2,000,000 troops into the European combat area. On the economic side, the American economy was geared to war production; and the United States Treasury loaned $10,000,000,000 to the Allies. As to diplomatic commitments, the United States preferred not to become an Ally, but worked closely with France and Britain, and insisted on a joint approach to every problem of the war.   .

Nor were ideas neglected. George Creel's Committee on Public Information publicized the Wilsonian creed on six continents—from China to Chile to Canada, in neutral Spain and Allied France, in revolutionary Russia and behind enemy lines. According to Wilson and the C.P.I. the United States believed in national self-determination and international organization, and was convinced that a threat to peace in any part of the world was a threat to democracy everywhere.

In advancing such views, the World War I President was running ahead of public opinion in the United States. Popular attitudes are not changed overnight. It generally requires at least a generation to bring about a major transformation of national feelings. Hence, though Americans recognized the world-power position of their republic, they were not yet aware of the full meaning of their situation. Neither Creel nor Wilson could persuade them that developments in distant lands necessarily affected the domestic pattern of the United States.

For this and other reasons, there was a reaction against Wilsonian internationalism when it was discovered that the armistice of 1918 meant problems as well as triumph. The reaction was a sharp one, and covered many different fields. On the diplomatic front, the Senate rejected the League of Nations and refused to consider a Wilsonian proposal for an Anglo-French-American alliance. The Senators also refused to take the United States into the Permanent Court of International Justice (World Court), although membership was favored by Presidents Wilson, Harding, Coolidge, and F. D. Roosevelt.

Withdrawal involved military as well as diplomatic moves. Congressional and popular pressure persuaded the administration to bring American soldiers and sailors home as soon as possible. To put it in another way: the average American and the average legislator did not feel that the strategic interests of the United States necessitated active participation in the occupation of the Central Powers, or the working out of postwar European boundary lines.

In like fashion, few citizens of the United States approved of the

Allied and American intervention in north Russia and Siberia (1918–20). Though strongly anti-Soviet, the ordinary citizen of the United States thought of Archangel and Vladivostok as very distant, and of little interest to Americans. Similarly, the Senate flatly rejected Wilson's proposal that the United States take on an Armenian mandate. Doing so would have involved building a strategic interest in the eastern Mediterranean, far beyond the American zone of security as defined by most military and political authorities.

As generally viewed after World War I, the American security zone centered on the Panama Canal. It included much of the Western Hemisphere, but not Europe, Africa, or the mainland of Asia. The line from Alaska to Hawaii was considered important; but most strategists wrote off the Philippines as difficult to defend and of decreasing importance in view of the failure of the United States to develop a large trade with China. Thus defined, American strategic interest did not call for a large army or for the completion of Wilson's plan for a navy second to none. Congress therefore reduced military appropriations. The army was cut almost to zero, and the United States became a leading exponent of naval disarmament.

Unwilling to assume burdens in the diplomatic and strategic fields, the United States also retreated on the ideological front. The C.P.I. was closed out after World War I, and it had no immediate successor. In so far as American ideas were set forth overseas, it was mainly through private channels (books, movies, statements of businessmen and engineers).

To Wilsonians, the withdrawal of the United States from the world scene seemed complete. Americans had scrapped Wilson's world diplomacy, his world strategy, his world ideological campaign. Wilson's successors even quarreled with America's old partners, France and Britain, over war debts and oil. In addition, those who succeeded Wilson set aside the concept of self-determination by announcing that Philippine independence was to be postponed.

Return to Economic Emphasis

In fact, however, the United States had not turned its back on the world. From the 1880's on, the growth of American influence overseas had been closely tied to economic expansion. Though important, strategic considerations, diplomatic commitments, and ideological patterns had at first been subordinate to commercial and financial factors.

Then came Wilson. In the days before he became President, Wilson viewed much economic expansion with suspicion (dollar diplomacy, for example). Wilson's judgments were based on moral rather than economic grounds. He felt, therefore, that economic matters should be relegated to secondary place, and that the accent should be on right and wrong; on ideas and principles like democracy and self-determination; and on the military force and diplomatic arrangements needed to support principles.

On rejection of the Wilsonian program, the economic note again became predominant in American expansion. It remained so through the prosperous 1920's and on into the decade of depression. Finally, in the World War II era, an effort would be made to reconcile and combine economic expansion with the Wilsonian program of international organization, world strategy, and American ideological leadership.

World War I raised American agricultural and industrial exports to a new high. The conflict also stimulated private and public investment overseas. In the process, Americans gained prosperity at home and influence abroad. It was natural, therefore, that postwar policy should try to keep the formula in operation.

There were certain difficulties. One was the fact that much of the war exporting had been financed by the United States Treasury, which stopped lending money to foreign governments soon after the peace negotiations. Another problem was foreign competition. During World War I, the United States had captured Latin-American markets which Britain could not supply. After the war, the British (and the Germans, too) came back into the market. Along the same line, the wartime shipping crisis had led the Allies to buy meat and grain from American producers rather than from distant countries like Argentina and Australia. After the armistice it was the other way around. Exchange complications, associated with American high-tariff policy, made it more convenient for Europe to buy from countries other than the United States.

Notwithstanding the problems, the United States managed to keep

exports at a high level during the first postwar decade. Under the
Webb-Pomerene Act of 1918, American manufacturers and farmers
were allowed to combine for foreign operations without running into
conflict with the antitrust laws. Nor did the government object when
General Electric, Standard Oil, and other American concerns made
deals with foreign monopolies, associating with international cartels.
The State Department did object, however, when the British and
Dutch used their monopolistic position in southeast Asia to run up
the price of natural rubber. In this case, American diplomats assisted
Henry Ford and Harvey Firestone in their rather unsuccessful efforts
to develop new rubber plantations in the Brazilian Amazon and in
Liberia.

The government, in fact, was willing to help nearly any American
who wanted to invest money abroad. Defending this policy, State
and Commerce Department officials said that investments would
bring profit to Americans, a laudable objective. Besides, money sent
abroad would furnish dollars with which foreigners could buy American products. Finally, investments would increase the diplomatic
influence of the United States.

Investments overseas had great variety. There were many sales and
service plants—for Johnson & Johnson drugs, Otis elevators, Singer
sewing machines, Underwood typewriters, International Harvester
farm equipment. The State and Commerce departments maintained
large staffs to gather information useful to these firms and helped
them in many other ways as well. Western Union and the foreign
arm of A.T. & T. invested in cables and land communications in the
Pacific and the Mediterranean. Branch factories for manufacture or
assembly were built in Canada, Germany, Brazil, and elsewhere by
General Motors, Goodyear, General Electric, and many other American concerns. (Often the foreign branch was started to get around
laws discriminating against manufactured products shipped from the
United States.)

After the creation of the Federal Reserve System, national banks
were allowed to have branches abroad. Many did, and these developed
great influence. Meantime, Americans invested in the British movie
industry and tightened their hold on meat packing in Uruguay and

Argentina. Mellon's aluminum combine became interested in distant bauxite properties. Besides their interest in copper, the Guggenheims tried to revive the Chilean nitrate industry. American diplomacy helped the United Fruit Company carve out a banana and sugar, coffee, railroad, and steamship empire in Central America and the West Indies. Secretary of State Hughes used extreme pressure to get American petroleum companies into Near East oil. Congress voted a large sum of money to make Colombia forget the Panama affair and grant concessions to American as well as British oil companies. The United States government subsidized Juan Trippe's Pan American air lines, and employed diplomatic influence to help Trippe beat out the Germans.

American investments overseas also involved loans to foreign governments. That is, investment bankers floated foreign bond issues on Wall Street and sold the bonds throughout the United States. This added to the trade, prestige, and diplomatic influence of the United States abroad. Frequently, however, the money was loaned to unsound governments, which meant ultimate loss to American investors. Often, too, the loans supported antidemocratic regimes, like those of Machado in Cuba and Leguia in Peru. The United States government could have discouraged such lending, for the investment bankers kept the State Department advised of latest developments. But Washington officials encouraged loans, and ruled against only two issues. One of those disapproved was for the valorization of Brazilian coffee, which would have raised prices to American consumers. The other was to aid the Czechoslovakian brewing industry (this was the prohibition era in the United States).

When American traders and investors ran into trouble overseas, the government lent immediate aid. Gunboats helped Standard Oil and other American companies during the Chinese civil war, in which Nationalists ultimately triumphed, in the mid-1920's. The State Department used pressure when France discriminated against American products, in retaliation for the high duties of the Fordney-McCumber Tariff. Even greater insistence finally helped American corporations land Arabian oil concessions, despite the efforts of the English and French to exclude the United States.

There were many other examples. Both Harding and Coolidge took the firmest of stands when Mexico launched campaigns against foreign investors; and the Mexicans were forced to back down. (Anti-Mexican feeling in the United States was increased by the hostile attitude of the Mexican government toward the Roman Catholic Church.) Marines remained in Nicaragua and Haiti, partly to protect investments, largely to protect the approaches to the Panama Canal. The Nicaraguan venture took a bad turn in the 1920's, when an anti-Yankee politician, Sandino, led a guerrilla campaign against the marines. But, though unable to catch Sandino, the United States remained in occupation.

These foreign economic activities formed but a small percentage of the total trade and investment of Americans. In the 1920's, as before and since, the bulk of American capital and commerce was associated with domestic consumption. Yet for many firms the foreign deals meant the margin of profit, or the difference between a small gain and real prosperity. Besides, an investment that seemed small on Wall Street might give control of a substantial part of the economy in a small foreign country. Often foreign investments had strategic as well as economic importance—as in the case of oil. And no one could deny that the whole history of Germany between the wars was affected by Wall Street loans and investments. During the 1920's, American money enabled Germany to pay reparations to the Allies and to reconstruct her shattered economy. And when the money stopped pouring in, after the New York stock market crash of 1929, Germany was plunged into the depression in which Hitler seized power.

Depression Diplomacy

When the stock market broke in 1929, American investors stopped buying foreign bonds. This created crises in many foreign countries, where governments had grown accustomed to meeting old obligations by borrowing additional sums. Areas producing raw materials—southeast Asia and Latin America, for instance—had been hit by a reduction of orders even before the stock market collapsed. The result was widespread distress. Governments fell.

Trade dwindled; the foreign commerce of the United States declined by two-thirds. Exchange controls became universal, and Americans with funds abroad found that they could not transfer them to the United States. Foreign bonds went into default, an important factor in the New York bond market collapse of 1931, which was followed by bank failures.

Governmental debts formed part of the same pattern. When depression struck, Germany could no longer obtain funds from Wall Street. She could not, therefore, meet reparations payments to the Allies. The Allies, in turn, could not pay war debts owed to the United States. President Hoover arranged a one-year moratorium on both reparations and war debts in 1931. This Hoover moratorium, however, came too late to save the sagging economy of central Europe; and it covered too short a period. By 1932 it was evident that payment on reparations and war debts could not be resumed. The Allies therefore canceled German reparations and hoped that the United States would do the same with the war debts. When the American government refused, the war debts went into general default.

In this depression crisis, some Americans felt that their country should pay little attention to developments abroad, and should concentrate on domestic matters. Such an attitude helps explain the Hawley-Smoot Tariff of 1930. The intention here was to protect the home market, no matter what happened overseas. The result, of course, was increased discrimination against American goods in foreign countries. The voting of independence to the Philippines in the early 1930's also reflected the desire of many Americans to wash their hands of overseas operations and keep home opportunities exclusively for continental Americans.

This spirit continued strong after Hoover gave way to Roosevelt. F. D. R. broke up the World Economic Conference at London in 1933, when he sent word that he could not coöperate in international efforts to stabilize the currency. The important thing, said Roosevelt, was that he be free of international controls, so that he could meet the domestic crisis by adjusting prices as he chose.

Something of the same outlook was seen in the early AAA. Several sponsors of this farm-planning agency felt that American agriculture could no longer rely on foreign markets and would have to cut acreage so as to readjust production in line with home consumption. In defense of this, it was said that hemispheric self-containment would be a good thing anyway, as it would remove the United States and its nationals from the zone of future war. While some discussed withdrawal from world trade, others favored getting out of international finance. The Johnson Act of 1934 prohibited war debt defaulters from borrowing money in the United States.

Despite sentiment for economic isolation, the Roosevelt administration never officially endorsed this approach to the problems of the depression. Rather, there were determined efforts to recapture lost markets and to find some solution for the world financial tangle. For, whether Americans liked it or not, their economy was inextricably associated with world economic patterns.

One way to increase foreign markets was to build good will. By 1929 it was apparent that the United States was losing as much as it was gaining by its use of strong-arm methods south of the Rio Grande. President Hoover and his Secretary of State, Henry L. Stimson, therefore decided to move away from force diplomacy. Hoover made a good-will tour of Latin America while President-elect (1929). After his inauguration he announced the scrapping of the Theodore Roosevelt Corollary of the Monroe Doctrine, which sought to justify intervention practices (Clark Memorandum, made public in 1930). Finally, marines were withdrawn from Nicaragua at the end of the Hoover term.

Roosevelt and his Secretary of State Cordell Hull continued and extended this good-will policy. Roosevelt coined the "Good Neighbor" term, and pushed Good Neighbor propaganda, by press, speech, and radio. He withdrew troops from Haiti. He abrogated the Platt Amendment, which had given the United States special rights of intervention in Cuba. He agreed to cancel similar rights in Panama. Roosevelt personally attended a special Pan-American conference at Buenos Aires in 1936. At this conference the United States agreed that the Monroe Doctrine, which had long been a United States policy, should become a general American policy, run by and for all the New World republics.

The Hoover-Roosevelt approach did not mean an abandonment of American interests in Latin America. Rather it was an effort to build greater interests by befriending the people south of the Rio Grande. When crises arose, the United States was still able to handle the situation, by using economic pressure instead of military might. Thus, when a Cuban government under Dr. Grau San Martin set out to confiscate foreign properties in 1933, the United States talked sugar quotas, instead of sending in marines. Since Cuban prosperity rested on sales of sugar to the United States, the Grau government fell, and the confiscation program stopped.

There was a more serious crisis in Mexico, when President Cárdenas took over foreign holdings, including English-owned railroads and American-owned oil wells (1937). The United States reduced purchases of Mexican silver, then insisted that Mexico pay a fair price for the expropriated properties. This was less vigorous than the Coolidge policy of forcing Mexico to back down; less vigorous than Britain's policy of severing diplomatic relations with Mexico. Roosevelt's position represented his desire to protect American interests without hurting a reform-minded Mexican administration. American officials also feared that an anti-Cárdenas approach might drive Mexico into the arms of the fascists or Communists.

However useful, a good-will program would not in itself restore American foreign trade. The United States therefore used other methods, too. One was depreciation of the currency. England here led the way, going off the gold standard in 1931. The United States followed suit in 1933, Roosevelt's 40 percent devaluation of the dollar being designed to raise domestic prices and at the same time improve prospects for sale of American goods abroad. The establishment of a Stabilization Fund also enabled the government to enter the international money market and prevent discrimination against American finance and trade.

As another contribution to the fight for foreign commerce, Congress passed the Reciprocal Trade Agreements Act in 1934. Under this statute, several times renewed, the President was authorized to reduce tariff duties by 50 percent or less, in return for concessions abroad. When a concession was given to one foreign country, that concession was extended to all nations with which the United States had most-favored-nation agreements. In turn, the United States expected foreign nations to give American goods all the advantages given to products from any other nation. Secretary of State Hull, the main sponsor of this measure, hoped that it would break down tariff barriers and, by increasing world trade, contribute to the peace of the world.

Finance being as important as trade, the United States government also established the Export-Import Bank system. During depression, American investors were in no position to lend money abroad. Yet foreign countries needed funds; and if they had them, they might buy goods from the United States, or unfreeze American credits in foreign lands. The United States government therefore proposed to enter the lending picture, to extend credit to foreign countries through official channels.

Meantime, the United States stepped up its aid to aviation and to the merchant marine. And recognition of Soviet Russia in 1933 was a further attempt to locate new commercial opportunities.

In time, trade would revive—after the outbreak of World War II. During the 1930's trade recovery was painfully slow; and finance limped even more than did commerce. Currency depreciation brought no permanent advantage, for Nazi Germany and other countries went far beyond the United States in the manipulation of exchange. While the good-will offensive did yield some return, one could not eliminate overnight the prejudices of generations. On top of that, countries that had been badly burned on Wall Street loans were reluctant to borrow further, either from New York financiers or from the Export-Import Bank. The reciprocal trade agreements worked, but only within relatively narrow limits. For one thing, the administration was reluctant to make far-reaching concessions, for fear of offending special interests. Besides, the extremely high Hawley-Smoot Tariff remained in effect. Even with substantial cuts, the rates were still heavy.

Each of these factors had importance. More significant still were the disturbing effects of the rise of the Axis nations, Germany, Italy, and

Japan. The bids for power made by these fascist states complicated every economic, strategic, and diplomatic question and produced a situation which ended with American participation in a new world war.

Working with France and England

When World War II broke out in 1939, Americans were sympathetic with the British and the French, as they had been in World War I, and earlier. Anglo-American-French association and coöperation therefore emerge as long-range facts of tremendous importance in twentieth-century history.

Not that all went well on every occasion. Far from it. After World War I, the close coöperation of the war era gave way to serious conflict. French intellectuals joined Latin-American scholars in attacking the United States as a nation without a soul. There was bad feeling when the American republic insisted that France and Britain arrange for payment of their war debts. France developed a quota system directed especially against products from the United States. France joined the British in trying to squeeze American companies out of Near East oil. British and American concerns competed vigorously for world trade. (The Prince of Wales, later Edward VIII, made a good-will tour through Latin America to advance British sales; Charles A. Lindbergh did the same in the interests of American enterprise.) There was sharp competition in money markets, and London bankers bitterly resented hearing Americans say that New York had become the financial center of the world. Americans responded with vigor; some leading journalists asserted that Britain was a nation in decay.

On the surface, American-French-British conflict seemed very serious. Underneath, the conflict was less bitter. Traditional friendships were kept alive by travel, by exchange of students and scientific information, by literary and fine-arts bonds, by the work of international veterans' organizations and such groups as the English-Speaking Union. More basic was the fact that all three of these powers were satisfied nations, with large interests to defend: colonies or spheres of influence, and established world trade and investments. No one of the three felt the need for further territory. All were "have" nations, with every reason to hold back the nations that felt dissatisfied with the World War I peace settlement: Germany, Soviet Russia, Italy, Japan.

In the light of this fundamental situation, it was often possible for the United States, France, and Britain to work out common solutions. This was apparent in the Far East, where these three nations were rivals, but were agreed in suspicion of rising Japan. At the end of World War I, all three joined Japan in sending troops into the Vladivostok area. The English, French, and American forces were sent partly to make sure that the Japanese did not establish themselves permanently in eastern Siberia.

After the war, the Japanese question figured largely in the Washington Disarmament Conference of 1921–22. In the long run, this conference did little to preserve world peace. At the time, however, it seemed to represent a victory for the nations interested in maintaining the existing strategic and territorial situation. Japan sought but did not obtain the right to have strength in capital ships equal to the battle strength of the United States and Britain (the final ratio was 5:5:3). The Japanese were persuaded to sign a Nine-Power Treaty recognizing the open door and guaranteeing Chinese territorial integrity; also a Four-Power Treaty (United States, Britain, France, and Japan) calling for consultation in case of aggressive action. The twenty-year-old Anglo-Japanese alliance was terminated, as was the five-year-old Lansing-Ishii agreement, in which the United States had unwittingly recognized Japanese special interests in China.

At this same conference, France put up a show of opposition to Italy's bid for naval power. France, however, was far more interested in guarding against the rise of her old enemy, Germany. Here France's chief reliance was on the Versailles Treaty, which had disarmed Germany, and the League of Nations. In addition, France joined Britain and others in working out the Locarno system, specifically designed to prevent future German aggression. Although the United States did not sign the Locarno treaties, it did join France in working out the Kellogg-Briand Peace Pact, which was signed by most of the nations in the world in 1928. The signatories pledged themselves not to wage aggressive war; that is, the treaty was in line with the thinking of France,

Britain, and the United States, nations interested in maintaining the territorial *status quo*.

The Russian Question

In their concern over threats to peace, France, Britain, and the United States all were worried over Soviet Russia. French, British, and American political leaders had expected the Bolsheviks to collapse soon after the Revolution of November, 1917. But they did not; and through the next decade the Soviet Union was regarded with grave suspicion in Paris, London, and Washington. France and Britain did not welcome the Russians into their League of Nations; and American Presidents, who had the recognition power, pointedly refused to have diplomatic relations with Moscow.

Anti-Russian sentiment, strong in the United States in tsarist days, became stronger still after 1917. It flared high in 1919–20, when many Americans talked about the possibility of a revolution in the United States. Dislike for communist Russia persisted after these fears subsided; and the average American approved of White House refusal to recognize the existence of the Soviet Union, from 1917 to 1933.

Recognition was urged by a few businessmen, by some intellectuals and liberal politicians (notably Senator William E. Borah of Idaho), and by the Socialists and Communists. By the 1920's, most financiers and manufacturers were opposed to recognition. One factor was the ideological conflict between communism and capitalism; another was Soviet refusal to assume the debts of earlier Russian regimes. Also against diplomatic contacts were Catholic and other church groups, disturbed over the antireligious aspects of communism. Nonrecognition was further approved by labor leaders, who followed in Gompers' anti-Marxian tradition and were concerned about communist infiltration into American labor organizations.

Attitudes changed somewhat during the depression. There was little objection when President Franklin D. Roosevelt extended recognition to the Soviet Union in 1933. With foreign trade at disastrous lows, the Russian market beckoned to exporters. The Russian attitude on debts seemed less serious, now that dozens of other countries were in default.

And Russia appeared, for the moment, to be concentrating on domestic developments rather than on foreign conquests. She thus seemed less menacing than did Japan, Italy, and Germany, which were pushing outward with great vigor. The Russians, in fact, indicated a willingness to join Americans, Britishers, and Frenchmen in maintaining the *status* quo.

Notwithstanding these trends and attitudes, Russia and the United States did not become friends in the 1930's. During that decade, Communists all over the world offered to coöperate with Socialists and liberals in antifascist "popular fronts." Such combinations were formed from France to Chile; but not in the United States, where there was deep and continuing doubt as to Russian motives. The Norman Thomas Socialists refused to work with Earl Browder; and President Franklin D. Roosevelt repeatedly stated that he wanted no aid from Communists. Nor was dislike one-sided. Soviet agents everywhere spared few words in attacking American capitalism and the American government.

Rise of the Axis Powers

In the 1930's, then, most Americans viewed Soviet Russia as a continuing threat to the American system; and the Russians looked on American capitalism with real enmity. But Russian-American relations did not then hold the center of the stage. Instead, attention was focused on the rise of the fascist states.

Germany, Italy, and Japan were dissatisfied even before the downward economic turn of 1929. Depression made dissatisfaction acute; and the political leaders of these three nations set out to improve their positions. Like the United States and Britain, those who controlled Germany, Italy, and Japan put much effort into trade promotion ("We must export or die," said Adolf Hitler, who came to power in Germany in 1933). In addition, Italy and Germany carried on active propaganda drives in Europe and South America, while Japan did the same in the Orient.

Along with trade and ideology came force. Japan invaded China's Manchurian provinces in 1931, establishing the puppet empire of Manchukuo. Then she pressed on into adjacent provinces, and in

1937 carried war into the heart of China. Meanwhile, Mussolini had added to Italy's African possessions by conquering the kingdom of Ethiopia (1935). The Italian dictator then joined Hitler in helping the rebel leader Franco to win the Spanish civil war of 1936–39. Simultaneously, Hitler tore up the Versailles Treaty, reoccupied the demilitarized Rhineland, and began a heavy armament program. By 1938 he was ready to annex Austria, and to demand that Czechoslovakia cede her German-speaking Sudeten territory to Nazi Germany. After this was done, in the Munich settlement of 1938, Hitler took over all of Czechoslovakia (1939). By then the three chief fascist powers were moving closer together, forming what would become a formal Berlin-Rome-Tokyo Axis in 1940.

President Hoover and Secretary of State Stimson were profoundly disturbed when Japan invaded Manchuria in 1931. But just what could they do? Outside of the Pacific coast states, Americans had little interest in the Orient; less now, with the depression absorbing their attention. Hoover's ability to act was limited by his political weakness (he had lost control of Congress). Japanese occupation of Manchuria meant loss for some American concerns. Even so, few businessmen wanted to boycott Japan. That would mean loss of America's best Oriental customer; and times were already bad. The United States Navy, cut by international agreement and economy drives, was not ready for action. But few Americans wanted to use military pressure in any case, especially after France and England indicated that they did not propose going beyond protest.

So protest it was. The United States government announced that it would not recognize territorial changes achieved by force. This Hoover-Stimson doctrine had the weight of tradition behind it; Wilson, Bryan, and Lansing had used it in the Orient during World War I. The policy was, of course, a recognition of weakness, an admission that the United States would employ neither economic nor military force against Japan. But the announcement did represent American leadership of a sort in an international emergency. And it drew the United States closer to Britain and France, and to the League of Nations, which endorsed the nonrecognition principle.

Such expressions of disapproval displeased but did not stop Japan.

American and other businessmen—and missionaries, too—found it increasingly difficult to operate in areas under Japanese control. Reasonably coöperative at the London Naval Conference of 1930, the Japanese government would thereafter agree to no limitations. On the contrary, Japan entered into a naval armament race with Great Britain and the United States. On the propaganda front, Japanese agents used racial arguments in appealing to the native peoples of the Far East. American exclusion of Orientals, and Anglo-French mistreatment of the darker races, made such arguments effective.

Meantime, Nazi Germany was rising. Hjalmar Schacht, Hitler's Brooklyn-born financial wizard, used barter deals and special currency to cut into United States markets in Latin America. Hand in hand with the economic problem was the strategic; German pilots were flying German planes for German-dominated air lines within easy striking distance of the Panama Canal (in Colombia, for instance). And Hitler's extensive propaganda campaign was directed in part against the United States.

"Stay Out This Time"

By the middle 1930's, a great many Americans had come to feel that there would be a second world war. Lines of sympathy were already formed, with Hitler generally condemned. Sentiment against the Japanese and Germans was rising rapidly; and there was more and more sympathy for the victims of fascism, including the persecuted Jews of Germany and the Chinese and the Ethiopians.

But neither sympathy nor antipathy was the predominating note. Above all else, Americans wanted to stay out of war. Public opinion polls indicated this clearly. So did surveys of the nation's press and the speeches made in Congress. *All Quiet on the Western Front* and other pacifist movies were popular; so were history books that condemned American entry into World War I. The public also approved Senator Gerald P. Nye's investigation of the munitions industry. The Nye group presented munitions makers as merchants of death, and suggested that Wall Street bankers had tricked the United States into declaring war in 1917.

The desire to "stay out this time" resulted in the adoption of the neutrality laws of 1935–37. Under this legislation, belligerents were forbidden to raise money in the United States, directly or under guise of humanitarian activity. American vessels were prohibited from entering war zones. Citizens of the United States were warned against (later prohibited from) traveling on belligerent ships. The statutes also barred sale of arms and ammunition to belligerents. Sale of other articles was permitted, but, for a time, was limited by a cash-and-carry clause. That is, purchasers had to pay "cash-on-the-barrel-head and come-and-get-it." All provisions applied with equal force to any and all belligerents.

Sponsors of this legislation maintained that it would prevent the associations and incidents that had led American entry into World War I. Had the legislation of 1935–37 been in force twenty years earlier, it would have prevented the munitions trade which had bound American industry to the Allied cause. It would have prevented the Wall Street loans that had tightened ties with Great Britain and France. It might have prevented American involvement in the submarine controversy, since citizens of the United States could not have traveled on such vessels as the *Lusitania*.

Those who favored the neutrality legislation of 1935–37 generally classified themselves as noninterventionists, or defenders of neutrality. Their opponents more commonly called them isolationists. In the main, those who were enthusiastic about the neutrality laws were opposed to American participation in international organizations. Some were anti-British; a very few were pro-German. Most, however, were favorable to Britain and hostile to Germany—but anxious to avoid close friendship or conflict with either side.

The noninterventionists included most of the pacifists. As a whole, however, noninterventionists were antipacifist, for it was felt that an isolated America would need powerful defenses. Isolationist Congressmen therefore voted for steadily increasing naval appropriations in the 1930's. They also tended to favor close relations with Latin America, since they saw isolation as hemispheric rather than merely national.

Though strong throughout the country in the middle 1930's, the noninterventionists were particularly influential in the Middle West. Their most effective spokesmen were United States Senators: Nye from North Dakota; Robert M. La Follette of Wisconsin (son of the old progressive); Burton K. Wheeler of Montana; Robert A. Taft of Ohio; Arthur H. Vandenberg of Michigan; Bennett Champ Clark of Missouri. Of these, Wheeler and Clark were Democrats, the others Republican.

The Roosevelt Position

Opposing isolationism were citizens called internationalists by their friends, interventionists by their foes. Very weak in the early 1930's, the internationalists gained strength during the decade, especially in the South and on the Atlantic and Pacific coasts. The internationalists, or interventionists, maintained that for economic, strategic, and moral reasons, the United States could not avoid choosing sides in the world struggles of the 1930's. Specifically, they felt that American coöperation with England and France might cause the Axis states to back down. And if war did come, coöperation with the Anglo-French group was essential to prevent Axis domination of areas vital to the American economy, and to American defense and democracy. Gaining strength year by year, this view ultimately won the support of prominent Republicans, including Henry L. Stimson (Hoover's Secretary of State), Frank Knox (Republican candidate for Vice-President in 1936), and Wendell L. Willkie (Republican presidential nominee in 1940). On the Democratic side, support was stronger still, for it included Secretary of State Cordell Hull and President Franklin D. Roosevelt.

Back in the World War I period, Franklin D. Roosevelt had been an active Wilsonian internationalist, a pro-British advocate of the League of Nations. Practical politics later caused him to shift his ground a little. Thus, while seeking his first presidential nomination in 1932, Roosevelt announced that he did not favor American membership in the League of Nations. When he became President the next year, he refused to coöperate with other nations in the London Economic Conference. He favored but did not actively insist on

American membership in the World Court. He endorsed the pacifist-and-isolationist-sponsored Nye investigation. He signed the neutrality laws of 1935–37 and asked that they be extended to cover the Spanish civil war.

In these matters, Roosevelt seemed to be standing with the non-interventionists or isolationists. Gradually, however, he made it clear that he stood on the other side, with those who favored close co-operation with the French and British. As early as 1934 he took the United States into an international organization, the International Labor Office (by Congressional joint resolution). More striking was his developing program of working with France and Britain against the Axis states.

Particularly impressive were the economic aspects of coöperation. Acting under authority of the Reciprocal Trade Agreements Act of 1934, Roosevelt made reciprocal trade agreements with Britain and France, with British dominions and with such allies of France as Czechoslovakia. In addition, agreements were made with Latin-American nations, partly as a means of fighting Hitler's barter deals. But no reciprocity agreements were made with the Axis states. Negotiations with Italy were terminated by the United States when Mussolini invaded Ethiopia. Because of discrimination against American trade, Japan was denied most-favored-nation treatment in American markets; and, for the same reason, products from German and German-controlled countries were placed on a penalty level. When the reciprocal trade agreement system was authorized, in 1934, Cordell Hull had said that it would develop trade everywhere and contribute toward world peace. Presently, however, the program became a device to strengthen the Anglo-French combination for a showdown with the Axis.

Along the same line, Roosevelt arranged an Anglo-American cotton-for-rubber swap; and the United States persuaded the Latin-American republics to condemn Nazi trade methods (Lima Declaration, 1938). Finance came into the picture, too. Export-Import Bank loans were used to fight Hitler exchange deals. The United States also made use of its $2,000,000,000 Stabilization Fund, established in 1935. As Secre-

tary of the Treasury Morgenthau admitted, this fund was employed
to tie the dollar to the pound and the franc—but not to the mark, or
lira, or yen.

Strategic considerations also received attention. As hopes for limitation of armaments faded, a great arms race ensued. In 1934, Japan
gave notice of the end of the Washington naval treaty of 1922. At a
London conference of 1935–36, Japan and Italy refused to sign any
agreement. France, Britain, and the United States therefore joined
in a treaty which, though weak in most respects, did draw these three
states closer together, and paved the way for exchange of naval information. As this type of coöperation improved, the gulf between
America and the Axis widened, as in the Western Hemisphere, where
Pan-American Airways and the United States government managed to
force German interests to yield control of strategically important
routes.

By the late 1930's American diplomats were working in close cooperation with British and French agents. Roosevelt worked with the
British and French during the Ethiopian crisis of 1935, when the
League of Nations unsuccessfully experimented with the use of economic sanctions against Italy. When Japan bombarded unfortified
Chinese cities after 1937, the United States, France, and Britain sent
identical protests. The American government also supported the
Anglo-French policy of nonintervention in the Spanish civil war.[1] At
the Evian conference, called at Roosevelt's suggestion, American
diplomats worked with delegates from France, Britain, and other
countries in unsuccessful efforts to solve the problem of Jewish and
other refugees from the fascist states. In the Munich crisis of 1938,
Franklin D. Roosevelt backed French-English policy again. This
meant appeasing Hitler, in line with the views of British Prime Min-

---

[1] The hope here was that if Britain, France, and America refrained from aiding the
Loyalists, the Axis states might reduce aid to Franco. But Hitler and Mussolini kept on
helping Franco, who won. Since Russia gave some help to the Loyalists, and since some
Loyalists were Communists, the situation was complicated by the issue of communism.
Another factor was the support Franco received from the Vatican, which disliked the
anticlerical record of the Loyalists. In backing nonintervention, Roosevelt followed his
basic policy of working with Britain. He also satisfied isolationists who wanted the United
States to steer clear of all foreign disputes. Finally, he pleased those Catholic Church
officials and laymen who opposed any plan involving support of the Loyalists.

ister Neville Chamberlain. As subsequent events would demonstrate, appeasement had grave defects. To Roosevelt, however, the choice was not between appeasing and challenging Hitler. It was a matter of supporting or abandoning the French and English in their efforts (however ineffective) to hold back the Axis states.

Roosevelt had defined his position early in his term as President. He was against aggression, which he defined as the crossing of frontiers. As he came to doubt the effectiveness of paper promises, he publicly suggested that peace-loving nations take specific action against aggressors (quarantine speech, Chicago, October, 1937).

Although he signed the neutrality laws of 1935–37, President Roosevelt did not altogether approve of those statutes. In his opinion, the legislation should have authorized the President to discriminate between aggressors and the victims of aggression, to bar the sale of war materials to attacking nations while permitting such trade with the attacked. Feeling that such discrimination might take the United States into war, Congress insisted that the prohibitions be levied against all belligerents.

The laws did, however, require a presidential proclamation before the provisions could be effective. Roosevelt issued such a proclamation in the Italo-Ethiopian conflict of 1935. Since the United States traded little with Ethiopia, the President reasoned that enforcement of the Neutrality Act would do little harm to that victim of aggression. The prohibitions would, however, reduce commerce with the aggressor, Italy.

Two years later, when Sino-Japanese hostilities were resumed, Roosevelt issued no proclamation; and the neutrality legislation did not go into effect. By not applying the statute, the Chief Executive made it possible for Japan to buy oil and scrap iron in the United States. But he also enabled hard-pressed China to buy desperately needed American supplies, and to obtain credits in the United States.

Many isolationists were distressed by Roosevelt's refusal to apply the neutrality legislation to the Sino-Japanese war. Their fears mounted when, at the end of 1937, a Japanese military force made a deliberate and unprovoked attack on the *Panay*, a United States gunboat in Chinese waters.

Four decades before, the destruction of the *Maine* had caused Americans to cry for war, though the facts of the *Maine* affair were far from clear. In 1937, moving pictures and other evidence clearly established the guilt of the Japanese military. Yet there was no demand for war. This was partly owing to the fact that the civilian-dominated government of Japan immediately offered apologies and damages. The chief point, though, was that Americans did not want to be drawn into war.

Noting this sentiment, anti-interventionist Congressmen pressed for adoption of the Ludlow Amendment. Louis Ludlow, an Indiana Democrat, wanted to change the Constitution so as to require a nation-wide referendum before Congress could declare war. (In case of actual invasion of the United States, the referendum would not be required.) Long buried in legislative pigeonholes, Ludlow's proposal was brought forward during the *Panay* crisis and was very nearly adopted. It was defeated only because Roosevelt threw all the power of his administration into the fight.

Roosevelt's triumph here strikingly resembled Wilson's success in defeating the Gore-McLemore Resolution of 1916. Then, as in the Ludlow case, Congressmen were indicating opposition to the foreign policy of a pro-British Chief Executive. In both cases, key resolutions were voted down; and administration policy ultimately prevailed.

World War II Begins

For a time, Soviet Russia coöperated with Britain, France, and the United States against the Axis powers. The masters of Russia regarded the relatively inactive capitalist democracies as less of a menace than the aggressive fascist powers; and London, Paris, and Washington considered Hitler a more immediate danger than Stalin. Coöperation was limited, however, by mutual suspicion. Moscow disapproved of the appeasement policy and did not like being left out of the Munich negotiations. And many of the policy makers in Britain, France, and America felt that it would be both improper and dangerous to trust the Russians.

Then the situation changed. Hitler and Stalin came to terms in the summer of 1939, signing what was called a nonaggression treaty. As a result, Hitler invaded Poland on September 1, 1939, the plan being to divide that country with the Russians. As Poland's allies, Britain and France declared war against Germany. World War II had begun. It would last six years, until 1945.

This time the United States would get in sooner and stay in longer than in World War I. This time, the American republic would become so far involved that Americans would be unable to confine postwar activities to the economic field. Now at last, the United States would be forced to recognize what had long been a fact: that growth had made the United States a world power, not only in the economic sense, but also in political and diplomatic, military and cultural definitions.

When World War II ended, in 1945, the world spotlight would be on the United States. But in the early stages of the conflict, the American republic played only a minor role. The United States stood by when Hitler used his blitzkrieg (lightning war) technique to overwhelm Poland in September, 1939. Nor did America act when Russia received part of conquered Poland and snapped up the little Baltic republics of Estonia, Lithuania, and Latvia. Russia then demanded key positions from Finland; and when the Finns refused, the Red Army invaded the Baltic republic (winter of 1939–40). Despite heroic resistance, Finland was quickly beaten, and forced to cede the territory that Russia desired.

Meantime, all was quiet on the western front. Britain and France were wedded to the defensive; and Hitler was not yet ready to strike. So little happened that some called the whole thing a "phony war." The inadequacy of this description soon became apparent. In the spring of 1940, Hitler's Nazi legions turned to the West. First, they overran such northern neutrals as Norway, Denmark, and the Netherlands. Then they smashed through Belgium and Luxembourg and into France. A dramatic evacuation at Dunkirk saved a substantial British force; but in June, 1940, France fell.

Hitler occupied most of the republic, and could easily have occupied it all. He chose, however, to leave a fragment of the country under French officials at Vichy. Complete occupation would have caused the French colonies to break away. The Dutch colonies did this, refusing to obey orders from the Nazi-occupied Netherlands and tying in with a Dutch government-in-exile in London. German officials hoped that a Vichy government could control the French colonies and fleet, perhaps in the interest of the Axis.

Having humbled France, Hitler turned next to the British Isles. The fall and winter of 1940–41 saw the unfolding of the battle of Britain. German bombers hammered at factories and cities, the plan being to reduce British efficiency and break British morale, thus setting the stage for an invasion across the English Channel. Simultaneously, German submarines tried to cut Britain's vital trade lines. Though suffering heavy loss, Britain held up under attack. The small Royal Air Force did amazingly well; and Prime Minister Winston Churchill provided outstanding leadership in the emergency.

As France fell in the summer of 1940, Italy entered the war on Germany's side. Mussolini then attempted to secure control of the Mediterranean, by driving into Egypt from Italian Libya and by invading Greece. (He had conquered Albania just before World War II began.) Italian weakness and determined Greek resistance made these operations less successful than those organized by Hitler. Ultimately, in the spring of 1941, the Germans helped their faltering Italian partners, smashing into Greece and establishing control of Yugoslavia. Since Hungary, Bulgaria, and Rumania were coöperating with Berlin, Germany controlled Europe from the Aegean Sea to the Norwegian Arctic, and from Poland to the Pyrenees, beyond which was friendly Franco Spain.

Under the circumstances, it would have been logical for Hitler to consolidate his gains and concentrate his attack on Britain. Instead, the German dictator chose to terminate Nazi-Soviet coöperation and to invade Russia (June, 1941). Hitler and his generals well knew the danger of fighting on two major fronts at once. But victory makes for overconfidence. Hitler felt that he could smash the Soviet Union, then turn back and conquer Britain. This was his major miscalculation of the war.

When Germany drove into Russia in June, 1941, Japan was in the fourth year of her war with China. Fighting both Nationalists and Communists, Japanese forces had penetrated far into the interior.

Initial conquest was less difficult than occupation, which was marked by quiet resistance and by guerrilla operations. Japan nonetheless hoped to complete her victory in China, and also to secure other areas of value. When France fell, the Japanese moved into French Indo-China. Even more tempting were the markets, the oil, tin, and rubber of British Malaya, the Netherlands East Indies, the French Pacific islands, and the American Philippines. Those who ruled in Tokyo decided that these regions could be occupied more easily if the United States Navy were out of the way. Consequently, Japan attacked the American fleet at its Pearl Harbor base, at Honolulu in the Hawaiian Islands, on December 7, 1941. After this, the United States became a full-fledged participant in the war.

Helping Britain

Between September, 1939, and December, 1941, the United States was not a belligerent. Neither, however, was America neutral, in attitude or in the strict legal sense. From the moment when Hitler invaded Poland, the government in Washington threw its weight into the scales on the anti-Nazi side.

To be sure, President Roosevelt did proclaim neutrality after war was declared in Europe. He announced further that the neutrality legislation was in effect, that Americans could not lend money or sell arms to belligerents or travel on belligerent ships or take their own vessels into war zones. The American republic continued to maintain diplomatic relations with all the belligerents. On top of that, the United States joined Latin America in a Declaration of Panama, which established a 300-mile neutrality belt around the American republics. Belligerents were ordered not to fight within this zone, which was to be protected by a Neutrality Patrol. The American nations also agreed to plan economic coöperation among New World neutrals.

These assertions of neutrality did not prevent the United States from helping Britain and France. At the request of President Roosevelt, Congress in the fall of 1939 modified the neutrality legislation of 1937 so as to permit the sale of arms and ammunition to belligerents. The sponsors of modification maintained that they were strengthening, not weakening, neutrality. Defending this position, they pointed out that the British and French had placed large orders in the United States before the outbreak of war. The fascist powers, on the other hand, were buying almost nothing from American aircraft and munitions manufacturers (because of administration pressure, and because businessmen, like other Americans, were predominantly anti-fascist). Prohibiting arms sales would thus help one side and hurt the other. It would be more "neutral" to permit sales.

Such arguments concealed the basic reasons for modification of the Neutrality Act of 1937. They were as follows: (1) The White House exerted pressure. As in the fight over the Ludlow Amendment, Roosevelt used party influence to swing votes. (2) Times were good in the United States in 1939, for the first time in a decade. This was due partly to a great domestic rearmament program, partly to foreign sales. If these were curtailed, the United States might again plunge into depression. (3) The Nazi-Soviet pact and Hitler's shockingly quick conquest of Poland had a sobering effect on Americans. Citizens of every section began to feel that a Nazi triumph, or a Nazi-Soviet triumph, would hurt American trade and investment; would threaten American security; would constitute a challenge to American ideals and values. The overwhelming majority of Americans wanted to keep their country out of war. Some therefore felt that the United States should cut all ties with the Old World and so strengthen home defenses that no one would venture to attack the Western Hemisphere. Others, an increasing number, felt that the best way to stay out of war was to make it possible for the British and the French to check the totalitarians. This view helped bring about the 1939 modification of neutrality legislation.

In the first winter of the war (1939–40), Americans were more anti-Soviet than anti-Nazi. For the moment, the German armies were not moving; and Russia was attacking Finland. This brought to the surface all of America's traditional anti-Russian and anticommunist sentiment. The situation also called forth sympathy for the underdog; and there was a special fondness for Finland, as the one European nation that had continued to make payments on her governmental war debts. Finnish heroism increased enthusiasm for her cause. There were con-

certs and dances and benefit performances for Finnish relief; and
Congress discussed aid measures. But it was a case of too little, too
late. Finland went down before Russia.

Hitler's spring offensive in 1940 brought the first great crisis of the
war. This time President Roosevelt acted without waiting for Congress. He begged France to keep on fighting, promising aid from the
United States. He transferred rifles to the British in anticipation of a
Nazi crossing of the English Channel. (To maintain the appearance
of neutrality, the rifles were transferred to a private company, then to
Britain.) The United States joined the Latin-American republics in
announcing that no European colony in the New World could change
hands (Declaration of Havana, summer of 1940, authorizing the
United States Navy to prevent such transfer). Roosevelt also set out
to coördinate the defense plans of the United States (technically a
neutral) with those of Canada (a belligerent).

In the fall of 1940, as the battle of Britain was getting under way,
the United States and Britain worked out the destroyer deal. Acting
on his executive authority, Roosevelt transferred to the British fifty
World War I destroyers, still serviceable and useful for convoy duty.
In return, Britain gave the United States permission to build naval
and air bases on British possessions in the New World (Newfound-
land, for example, and Jamaica). Simultaneously, though not as a
part of the deal, Prime Minister Churchill announced that if the
British Isles fell, His Majesty's Navy would not surrender but would
continue the fight in the Western Hemisphere.

The destroyer deal had many points of interest. It marked an enormous departure from—perhaps the end of—traditional American neutrality. Furthermore, Roosevelt acted on rather doubtful constitutional authority, in the middle of a presidential campaign. The
opposition candidate, Wendell Willkie, approved the terms of the
agreement but denounced the method. Roosevelt, however, lost little
if at all by reason of this act. The average American approved the aid-
to-Britain principle, recognized that neutrality was not what it had
been, and approved of the acquisition of the bases. The bases, incidentally, represented another step in a long road. In 1900 Britain had

withdrawn from the Panama area. In 1906 she had taken her Caribbean fleet home. Now she gave the United States strategic control even of British possessions in the New World.

At this same time—during the presidential race of 1940—Roosevelt brought Congress into the picture again by asking for a peacetime draft. Congress responded with some reluctance by voting conscription, service being for one year only and limited to the Western Hemisphere. The time limit was extended, however, before the year ran out. On the draft, as on other foreign-policy matters, the divisions crossed party lines. Some Democrats refused to back the President's proposals, and some Republicans came to Roosevelt's assistance.

Deciding Foreign Policy

So far, a majority of people and the politicians had gone along with Roosevelt. But there was opposition, which became more bitter every day. Granting that it was wise to help the British, had Roosevelt gone too far and too fast? Would the President's policy result in American involvement in war?

Opposition to the President came from many different quarters. Included were political foes of Roosevelt, who were distressed to see the Chief Executive gain power in the crisis. Many of these persons were conservative businessmen. They were joined by liberal Democrats and Republicans and by Norman Thomas Socialists, all of whom wanted the administration to concentrate on domestic reforms rather than on foreign ventures. Farmers, laborers, and businessmen who produced for local markets were sometimes drawn into the movement. Anti-British sentiment survived among some Irish-Americans and German-Americans, and with midwest reformers who associated Britain with Wall Street money men. Some Italian-Americans were sorry to see the United States take an anti-Italian stand. American fascists, of course, wanted to support rather than to oppose Hitler; and American Communists dropped their anti-Nazi crusade when Stalin signed with Hitler in 1939. (They would pick it up again when the Russo-German pact was broken in 1941.)

Many organizations presented the noninterventionist point of view. Of these the most prominent was the America First Committee, which operated in 1940 and 1941. America First claimed that it did not want pacifists or Communists or fascists; that it favored large military expenditures, close relations with Latin America, and some aid for Britain. But not commitments that would lead to American participation in war. Heading the group was General Robert E. Wood, a West Point graduate who had become an anti-Russian businessman (president of Sears, Roebuck). Under Wood's direction, the Committee held public meetings, especially in the East and Middle West; sent out a great deal of printed matter; and organized an active lobby in Washington. America First claimed several million members. Perhaps the total was a good deal less; but America First certainly spoke for many Americans.

Of the organizations on the other side, one stood out: the Committee to Defend America by Aiding the Allies. Better known as the White Committee, this group was at first headed by William Allen White, the well-known Kansas journalist. Avowedly pro-British, this Committee went beyond the President in favoring aid for European countries that were fighting against Germany. Many of those active in the group hoped that by helping Britain the United States could avoid participation in the war. Others came to believe that American entry was inevitable and should not be delayed. Like America First, the White Committee maintained an active lobby and tried to reach the public through public meetings, pamphlets, and the press. Results were good, since the bulk of the newspapers and radio commentators inclined toward this side; and Hollywood's movie makers, turning away from pacifist themes, began playing up the Nazi menace.

The advocates of full aid to Britain were as fervent as their foes. In the group were financiers and businessmen who had interests in London, or had lost trade and investments in Nazi-occupied territory. Working with them were southern cotton growers and other farmers who thought in terms of world markets, and laborers employed by industries that sold a great deal overseas. Also involved were politicians who saw this as the coming issue, and liberal Democrats and Republicans who felt that reform at home could not proceed until international conditions improved. Artists and intellectuals who had ties with England were in the picture. So were many members of immigrant groups: Polish-Americans, Scandinavian-Americans, Czech-Americans, Greek-Americans, Serbian-Americans. All of these blocs had special reasons for hating Hitler. In addition, many German-Americans and Italian-Americans were anti-Nazi and antifascist. Religious leaders in the United States were disturbed by Hitler policies: Jews especially, Protestants and Catholics as well. And Americans in general were affected by reports of Japanese and German outrages and tyranny.

The relative strength of the opposing sides was never clearly tested in a Congressional or presidential campaign. Both presidential candidates in 1940 favored the draft, the destroyer deal, and aid to Britain. Both, however, felt it necessary to hedge a little in the interest of vote-getting. As election day approached, for instance, President Roosevelt gave his pledge to the mothers of America that their sons would not fight in a foreign war.

Lend-Lease and the "Shooting War"

After Roosevelt's election, the battle of Britain reached a critical stage. Among other things, the British were short of credit in the United States. In World War I they had raised the necessary funds by private loans. This was impossible in World War II. Britain could not float loans on Wall Street because she was in default on her World War I debt (Johnson Act, 1934) and because she was a belligerent (Neutrality Act, 1937). Prime Minister Churchill therefore proposed that the United States government provide the necessary aid.

Adopting the idea, Roosevelt asked Congress for a Lend-Lease bill. This was actually a proposal that the United States subsidize the cause of Britain and other foes of Germany. America must aid Britain, Roosevelt said. If the United States became an "arsenal of democracy," the republic might stay out of war. Opponents replied that it was just the other way around, that acceptance of Lend-Lease was a step toward American involvement in war.

Feeling that this was the decisive issue, America First and other non-interventionist groups threw their full weight into the contest. And lost; Lend-Lease was adopted by Congress in March, 1941. Aid was immediately extended to Great Britain; and after Hitler's invasion of

Russia in June, 1941, goods were dispatched to the Soviet Union, too. Before the end of the summer, Lend-Lease assistance was also flowing toward China.

After the adoption of Lend-Lease, other commitments followed naturally. In accepting the arsenal-of-democracy idea, Congress had decided that Britain must be given the goods needed to resist Germany. But many of these goods did not reach the British Isles, because of the activity of German submarines. It seemed logical, then, that the United States should see to it that the products got across the ocean. Which brought in the convoy question.

Roosevelt began convoying British ships soon after Lend-Lease was passed. At first, protection was limited to waters close to the American coastline—the zone covered by the so-called Neutrality Patrol. By the summer of 1941, American troops had taken possession of Greenland and Iceland, islands theoretically under the king of Nazi-occupied Denmark. This enabled the United States Navy to protect British vessels on the North Atlantic route to Britain. By fall of 1941, American naval vessels were convoying British merchant ships all the way to the British Isles and were actively helping the British navy in the anti-submarine campaign. By then, Roosevelt had frozen German and Italian credits in the United States (June, 1941). In November the President persuaded Congress to scrap part of what was left of the Neutrality Act of 1937, so as to permit American merchant vessels to enter war zones, that is, to deliver goods to Britain.

As might have been expected, there were incidents. An American merchantman, the *Robin Moor*, was sunk as early as May, 1941. In September of that year, the *Greer*, a United States destroyer, exchanged fire with a U-boat (the destroyer was pursuing the submarine). The following month duels between submarines and American destroyers saw nearly a dozen American sailors killed on the *Kearny* and a hundred lives lost when the *Reuben James* went down. As a leading member of the administration said, the United States was in a "shooting war" on the Atlantic.

By late fall, 1941, then, the American republic was close to all-out war with Germany and was deeply committed to the British cause. As in World War I, there were basic economic, strategic, and sentimental ties that bound the United States to Britain. In addition, there was a heavy and expanding trade as in World War I, linking aid-to-Britain to American prosperity. In World War I, American citizens lent huge sums to the Allies. In World War II, the American government (affecting all citizens) invested even larger amounts in the struggle. Of great importance in both wars was the pro-British, anti-German attitude of the Americans in high office. Propaganda seems to have intensified attachment in both conflicts.[2] And in both cases the incidents associated with the war (ship sinkings, for example) influenced both policy and public attitudes, dramatizing the strategic conflict between the United States and Germany.

The Atlantic Charter

In August, 1941, President Roosevelt met Prime Minister Churchill at sea. Problems of coöperation were discussed, and the meeting also resulted in a peace plan, the Atlantic Charter. It was strange, perhaps, for the head of a belligerent government to join the President of a nonbelligerent in preparing a document of this kind. But, as all knew, the United States was neutral only in name, and was committed to the defeat of the Axis states.

As a document illustrating Anglo-American coöperation, the Atlantic Charter was a success. As a peace plan, it was less impressive than Wilson's Fourteen Points. There was little stress on the League of Nations idea. Roosevelt and Churchill seemed to favor an Anglo-American peace, with the disarmament of aggressor nations. There was no emphasis on neutral rights. National self-determination was endorsed, and the Charter called for increased international trade and attention to social welfare. The Charter approved two of the four freedoms set forth by Roosevelt a half-year earlier (freedom from fear

---

[2] A British Library of Information in New York did effective work; and British control of the cables remained important in the radio age. The speeches and articles of Chinese publicists also had some influence, as did the work done by representatives of the Czech, Polish, Dutch, and other governments-in-exile. But propaganda did no more than tighten existing bonds. It had no effect when it ran counter to preëxisting prejudices. Thus the Germans, in World War II, avoided the propaganda errors of 1914–17. A German Library of Information in New York turned out striking documents in colloquial English; but this Nazi effort had no effect on the general public.

and freedom from want), but ignored the other two (freedom of religion and freedom of speech).

Pearl Harbor

Though interested in the Atlantic Charter, Roosevelt and Churchill were much more concerned about the war than about the peace. Among other things, they discussed the situation in the Orient. Both felt that conflict was possible at any time, that the Japanese might turn against the Far Eastern possessions of Britain and America, France and the Netherlands.

By this time Roosevelt had decided that further appeasement of the Japanese would merely encourage the Tokyo government to make new demands. He had therefore frozen Japanese credits in the United States (July, 1941). This had ended Japanese-American trade. A month later, the United States began extending Lend-Lease aid to China. On the diplomatic front, the United States sent sharp notes to Japan in August and again in November, urging the Japanese to abandon their policy of aggression and to withdraw from areas already conquered. Japan replied by asking the American government to stop backing China—and by getting ready to strike.

A special diplomatic mission to the United States acted as a cover for final preparations; and on December 7, 1941, the Japanese attacked Pearl Harbor. The attack inflicted heavy damage on the American base, which was inexcusably ill prepared. But it also united Americans behind the government, as the United States formally declared war on Japan and on Japan's allies, Germany and Italy.

20

War and a Troubled Peace

After Pearl Harbor

The year after the Japanese attack on Pearl Harbor was one of humiliation and defeat for the United States. But it was also a year of preparation. At the end of 1942, the tide of battle was turning; and by 1945 America and her allies had won the war. The cessation of hostilities, however, brought a troubled peace. At home and abroad, Americans had to wrestle with the problems of reconstruction. More serious still was the fact that the end of World War II saw not one world, but two. Soviet Russia and the United States, having joined to defeat the Axis, faced each other as rivals in the postwar world.

Producing for War

In December, 1941, the United States was inadequately prepared for large-scale warfare on a global basis. Still, the American republic was further along the road of preparation than she had been at the time of the declaration of hostilities against Germany in 1917. The President and Congress had been building a big navy since 1933. Land armaments had been increased after September, 1939, when Roosevelt had proclaimed a "limited national emergency"; and the program had been speeded up when, in May, 1941, the Chief Executive had announced an "unlimited state of national emergency." Congress had voted a draft in the fall of 1940, and there were 2,000,000 men in uniform at the time of the Pearl Harbor attack.

In organizing defense production before December, 1941, the administration had made several key decisions. One was to bring businessmen into the government to help do the job. Another was to work closely with big business, which would handle the bulk of the war contracts (General Electric, General Motors, Ford, Du Pont, United States Steel, etc.). This involved stopping the antitrust activities which Roosevelt had begun to stress in the late 1930's. It also meant using the cost-plus system, which was designed to overcome business suspicion of the administration and guarantee substantial profits.

Authorities made use of government facilities for defense production (TVA, for instance) and were ready to finance construction of plants and ships and pipe lines and emergency housing. The accent, however, was on private enterprise. Government plants were run by private companies. Operation by the government, it was feared, would raise the cry of "socialism," and make many businessmen reluctant to work with the administration.

The same policy prevailed after Pearl Harbor, on into the postwar years. In World War I, the government had taken over transportation and communication. In World War II it did not. And when the war was over, the government set out to dispose of the war plants and housing which it had built during the conflict.

In planning war production, the government followed World War I precedents—without, however, profiting from the mistakes of 1917–18. Instead of establishing centralized control at the start, the President and Congress created a confusing number of overlapping agencies in 1940–41. When an agency failed to function well because of weakness of personnel or lack of authority, a new organization was created, often without eliminating the old one.

The need for unified control was all too apparent by the end of 1941. As a consequence, the War Production Board was created, under Donald Nelson of Sears, Roebuck. This was roughly the equivalent of Bernard Baruch's War Industries Board of World War I. Nelson had the job of supervising production; and he proceeded in coöperation with representatives of the various industries involved in war work.

The WPB did get results. The greater part of the industrial structure of the United States was converted to war production. Output lagged at first, but figures were impressive by 1944. Thus, the armed services had about 8000 military airplanes in December, 1941; some 120,000 at the end of the war. Production was not merely for American units. Factories in the United States also turned out a great quantity of arms, ammunition, and other supplies for America's allies, these being handled through the Lend-Lease administration (headed in the vital years 1941–43 by Edward R. Stettinius, Jr., formerly of General Motors and United States Steel).

At best, however, Donald Nelson was no Bernard Baruch. As criticism mounted, he was eased out of his key position—and sent to China (1943). Nelson's authority, and more, was given to James F. Byrnes, who headed a new Office of War Mobilization after May, 1943. Byrnes was a politician, not a businessman; he had been Senator from South Carolina and a Supreme Court justice. As Director of War Mobilization he had powers so extensive that he was labeled "Assistant President." It may be noted, however, that this desirable concentration of authority came rather late.

Meantime, there had been many quarrels inside the administration. Most dramatic was a public dispute between Vice-President Henry Wallace and Jesse Jones of the RFC. Jones, who held the purse strings, criticized as unbusinesslike the methods used by Wallace's Board of Economic Warfare (which, among other things, obtained raw materials from Latin America). Reorganizations followed, leading eventually to the creation of the Foreign Economic Administration (FEA).

Certain pressing problems called for special efforts. An Office of Defense Transportation under Joseph Eastman wrestled with the railroad problem, and avoided some of the tangles of World War I. A War Shipping Administration headed by Admiral Emory S. Land took on the even more serious task of providing the ocean transportation needed in this global conflict. Despite submarine sinkings, the American merchant marine more than trebled during the war era; and the United States emerged from the war as the largest shipping nation on earth.

Another substantial accomplishment was in rubber, where the most important figure was Rubber Administrator William Jeffers (of the Union Pacific Railroad). Japanese conquest of southeast Asia shut off the supply of plantation rubber immediately after Pearl Harbor. To protect America's small rubber stock pile, the government resorted to tire and gasoline rationing, and a thirty-five-mile speed limit for automobiles. A synthetic-rubber program helped see the nation through.

From beginning to end, the administration relied mainly on the business giants. At the same time, there was an effort to give small producers a part in the program. Here the purposes were two: to achieve maximum production and to win popular support for the war. A Smaller War Plants Corporation operated in this field.

In general, organized labor gave full support to the war effort. Sidney Hillman of the C.I.O. occupied high positions in the government (though his influence was substantially less than that of the industrialists in the administration). Most problems arising during the war were ironed out amicably, some through a War Labor Board. To assure efficient operation of war plants, some key workers were exempted from the draft; and Paul McNutt's War Manpower Commission froze men on the job. Strikes ("work stoppages") persisted, however, and Congress finally adopted a get-tough policy, passing the Smith-Connally War Labor Disputes Act over a presidential veto in 1943.

As in World War I, the government encouraged farmers to go into full production, thus reversing the cut-production trend of the depression decade. The selective service coöperated, allowing some workers to stay on the farm. The results were spectacular. Wheat production went above a billion bushels in 1944, for the first time since World War I (and stayed up thereafter). The price of farmland increased rapidly.

War Finance

As could be seen from the beginning, World War II was phenomenally expensive. Mechanization had greatly increased the cost of any modern conflict. This one was waged on a world front. And the United States, besides financing her own activities, helped her allies. Lend-Lease cost more than $50,000,-000,000. Reverse Lend-Lease, aid to the United States, came to less than a sixth of that figure.

The totals were unbelievably high. In one fiscal year, 1944–45, the

United States government spent more than $100,000,000,000. The overall cost of the war to the United States exceeded $300,000,000,-000, roughly ten times the total for World War I. Later expenditures for interest, pensions, and the like would make the final total much higher.

Naturally, the national debt soared. It went up at a rate of fifty billions a year after Pearl Harbor, and reached $250,000,000,000 at the end of the war. This was nearly $2000 for every man, woman, and child in the land. Yet there was little public complaint. The conservatives who had grumbled about $3,000,000,000 deficits during New Deal days had little to say against war deficits fifteen times that large. Alarmists who had seen government bankruptcy in a $40,000,000,000 debt in the 1930's seemed less concerned about a debt six times as large.

Perhaps the new figures were too large for comprehension. Perhaps, too, citizens had become accustomed to deficit financing. Of greater importance, however, was patriotic sentiment, plus the fact that business was doing well in the 1940's, and was working with rather than against the government.

Government income increased along with government expenditures. In World War I, the government had met only a third of the bill out of taxes. In World War II, the figure was two-fifths (nearly a half in 1944). Taxes were increased sharply on individual and corporation incomes. A new withholding system made the former seem a little less unpalatable. An excess-profits tax of 90 percent was designed to (but did not altogether) eliminate war profiteering. And there were all the usual wartime taxes on luxuries, with some new ones besides.

Borrowing was not difficult; the banks could provide all the money the government required. This type of financing, though, was inflationary, since it increased the amount of money in circulation. Bond buying by individuals would tend to have the opposite effect, reducing the amount of money in circulation and keeping prices from rising rapidly. It was also felt that the purchasing of bonds would increase patriotic zeal. Consequently, the government made every effort to sell bonds and stamps through the radio and movies, churches and schools, and through pay-roll deduction plans. In most communities, however, there was less pressure on the individual than in World War I.

In spite of strenuous efforts, only about a fifth of the bonds went to small investors; and over two-thirds were purchased by banks. It was necessary, therefore, to take other steps to check inflation. Among these was Roosevelt's hold-the-line proclamation of April, 1943, which was intended to freeze prices, rates, wages, and jobs. The day-by-day work was done by the Office of Price Administration, which set up and administered a system of rationing, with ceiling prices for rents and for consumers' goods.

Although there was much evasion of OPA regulations, the agency did manage to hold prices down to reasonable levels. One reason for success was the general willingness of consumers to coöperate. Another was the Congressional system of subsidizing processors. Finally, OPA was run in a fairly efficient manner by national and state officials, and by local ration boards. Three different persons took on the difficult job of running the agency, the third administrator (Chester Bowles) being the most successful.

Civilians and the War

Some administration leaders (among them Undersecretary of War Robert Patterson) felt that the civilian economy should be cut to the bone in wartime. Roosevelt and Congress decided otherwise. The reasoning was partly political: most voters were civilians. In addition, Washington officials felt that too severe a cutback would reduce farmer-labor-business incentive for full production. Hence it was decided that civilians would have to make sacrifices in the interest of the war effort but that civilian needs and desires would not be totally neglected.

Production for the armed forces and America's allies came first. Consequently, there were many shortages. Civilians found it almost impossible to get automobiles or radios, apartments or Hershey bars or nylon hosiery. There were restrictions on house construction and driving, on heating fuel and intersectional sports events. It was hard to get hold of a physician or a repairman. Cigarettes and steaks, toys and can openers were in short supply, and it was often necessary to accept low-grade (but high-priced) substitutes. Citizens were asked to reduce pleasure travel and to buy bonds instead of squandering money. Yet it was possible to get the necessities and most of the comforts of life. Golf courses did a gigantic business. So did restaurants and sports arenas and motion-picture theaters, though the fare they offered was below peacetime standards.

Most civilians were anxious to make some contribution to the war. They could do so, of course, at their jobs, and by paying taxes and buying bonds. In addition, many contributed to the USO (United Service Organizations), giving cash or time, serving doughnuts and the like. Others worked for the Red Cross, or served without pay on draft and ration boards. At the beginning of the war, when there was talk of an Axis invasion, an Office of Civilian Defense organized volunteers to serve as plane spotters and air-raid wardens. This sort of work lost much of its appeal after the enemy was thrown on the defensive.

As always in wartime, the normal freedom of the press was curtailed. The Director of Censorship, Byron Price, was a newspaperman with a preference for voluntary methods. Much military information was necessarily and properly kept from the public. Unfortunately, army and navy officials sometimes went far beyond security needs in withholding statements from the public.

There was also an Office of War Information, headed by the author and radio commentator Elmer Davis. The OWI did effective work abroad, though it never became as important as George Creel's CPI. For this there were several reasons. To begin with, Davis was less aggressive than Creel. Then, too, Congress limited the domestic operations of OWI, for fear it would be a publicity agency for President Roosevelt. Finally, the CPI had helped break down German morale in World War I by offering Germany an easy peace (the Fourteen Points). This was not possible in World War II, for Roosevelt insisted on the unconditional surrender of Germany.

Immediately after Pearl Harbor, Japanese-Americans were driven from the Pacific Coast states. Most of the evacuees were citizens, and there was no sound ground for this violation of their rights. Otherwise, the government's civil rights record in World War II was better than in World War I. As was natural and necessary, individuals dangerous to the republic were put under restraint. Saboteurs sent in from Germany were executed after a legal trial, complete with an appeal to the Supreme Court. Some German Bundists lost their citizenship. A few American fascists were jailed, a few fascist-type journals barred from the mails.

There was no wartime witch hunt. Conscientious objectors were treated better than in World War I. The harsh policy toward Japanese-Americans was modified during the war. As early as 1942, Roosevelt announced that non-naturalized Italian-Americans were not to be considered enemy aliens. Such attitudes were possible because there was less opposition to the war than in 1917–18; perhaps also because Americans had developed more maturity of judgment.

A good many civilians gave up that role for the duration. Following Britain's lead, the government accepted women volunteers, not only for nursing positions, but also for a wide range of noncombat jobs. Some 200,000 women went into uniform, as Wacs (army), Waves (navy), Spars (coast guard), or marines.

The army and navy jumped from 2,000,000 at the time of Pearl Harbor to 12,000,000 at the end of the war. The great majority of these came in through the selective service system, which was headed by General Lewis B. Hershey. Selective service ultimately enrolled all males from eighteen to sixty-five, though the older age groups were not called. The standards of acceptance and rejection varied from time to time, according to the needs of the services. In addition, there were regional variations, partly because of the difficulty of interpreting orders from national headquarters, partly because of the original decision that the draft should be decentralized.

From the beginning, it was understood that the government had certain obligations to those whom it called to the colors. One was support of dependents. By the end of the war, the wife of a private was allotted $50 a month ($22 of this being from the private's $50 pay), plus $30 for one child, $20 for additional children. Soldiers were also guaranteed their old jobs when they returned from service. The passage of the G.I. Bill in 1944 provided additional benefits for veterans with special needs: better veterans' hospitals; unemployment compensation for a year; aid in finding a job (through the United States Employment Service); loans for business or residential housing; educational subsidies, for tuition, supplies, and subsistence, at college, vocational school, or in a job-training program.

The United Nations

American participation in World War I had been limited. The United States had declared war on only two of the Central Powers, and had refused to become an Ally. World War II furnished a sharp contrast. This time the United States declared war on all three major Axis powers (December, 1941); later also on Axis satellites. The American republic also entered a formal alliance with other anti-Axis states when the United Nations came into being in January, 1942.

In this hour of crisis, the creation of the United Nations alliance struck Americans as essential and therefore desirable. There was comparatively little discussion of the far-reaching character of the decision. In fact, however, this was the first alliance of the United States with a major power since the French alliance of 1778–1800. It was a military alliance, binding the United States to Great Britain, Russia, China, and lesser nations. It was also an alliance for postwar purposes, for the United Nations agreed to work together on the peace settlement.

The formation of the United Nations indicated one thing more— the growing influence of the United States in Latin America. Most of the republics south of the Rio Grande quickly followed the United States into the war against the Axis. This reflected the strength of economic ties between Latin America and the United States; also, a feeling of insecurity in the air age. Besides that, it seemed to show that the Good Neighbor Policy of Hoover and Roosevelt had yielded some returns.

The Big Four of the United Nations were the United States, Great Britain, Russia, and China. There were special meetings to work out coöperation among these major belligerents. Churchill and Roosevelt met frequently, as at Washington immediately after Pearl Harbor, at

Casablanca in 1942, Quebec in 1944. Roosevelt, Churchill, and Chiang Kai-shek met at Cairo in 1943 (Russia was not yet formally involved in the Far East war). Stalin, Churchill, and Roosevelt met at Teheran, in Iran, in 1943, and at Yalta in the Russian Crimea early in 1945. Besides these headline meetings, there were dozens of special missions, involving both lesser-known and famous individuals (among Americans, Wendell Willkie, Henry Wallace, Harry Hopkins). Even more important were day-by-day contacts of diplomatic and military leaders all over the world.

Everything considered, coöperation was quite successful. It was, however, far from perfect. American, British, and Soviet leaders neither regarded nor treated China as an equal partner. In the case of Russia, this was tied up with the fact that Russia did not enter the Pacific war until after the collapse of Germany. Also, Moscow looked with favor on the Chinese Communists, who held part of China and were bitter foes of the Nationalist government of Chiang Kai-shek. Britain and America regarded Chiang with greater favor but did not consider Chinese fighting forces strong enough to make much contribution to the winning of the war. Hence British and American strategists rarely consulted China on either major or minor matters.

The United States, Great Britain, and the Soviet Union did not underrate each other; but coöperation was imperfect. The Russians were glad to get Lend-Lease aid from America but were reluctant to supply the United States and Britain with exact information, or to let observers visit their front lines, or to provide facilities for shuttle-bombing operations. On the other side, the British and Americans made vital decisions without consulting the Russians. Churchill in particular made no secret of his anti-Russian views, and his fears that the Soviet Union would emerge from the war as master of much of Europe.

Two of the Big Four worked well together. Despite disagreements, the United States and Britain became and remained close partners. The long tradition of Anglo-American coöperation made this possible. The intimate personal relations between Churchill and Roosevelt made for top-level harmony. No less important was the work of such other officials as the American Chief of Staff, General George C.

Marshall, and such organizations as the Joint Chiefs of Staff, which functioned both during and after the war.

When Anglo-American coöperation had been established early in the century, Britain had been the stronger member of the combination. The British navy had overshadowed that of the United States, the British merchant marine had been incomparably larger than the American. London's money market had controlled more funds than New York and Washington. The United States had passed Britain in population and in coal and iron production; but American concentration on the home market had left Britain as the greater international power.

The pattern had changed by World War II, and it would change still more before the cessation of hostilities. Great Britain and the United States still worked together, and more closely than before. But it was now America that had the stronger navy and the larger merchant marine. In industrial production and exports, in finance and man power, the United States had become definitely the stronger partner.

Only gradually did Americans realize their position. At the beginning of the war, President Roosevelt was inclined to defer to Churchill not only in matters touching the British Empire (India, for instance) but also in questions involving many other areas, including the Mediterranean, Italy, the Balkans, and the Near East. But as time went on, the British themselves made it plain that leadership had passed to the United States. America supplied the bulk of the fighting force in the Anglo-American offensives of the war; and American officers had the top commands. American strength and the comparative weakness of Britain made it impossible for the United States to turn Mediterranean questions over to the British after the conquest of Italy; and when it came to Pacific problems, Britain's own dominions, Canada and Australia, often tended to look to Washington rather than to London.

The new relationship irritated many Britishers, who did not like to see their nation playing a secondary role and feared that the United States lacked the experience and responsibility necesssary for leadership. Many Americans were equally puzzled and disturbed. Some felt that the United States was being "taken in," that Britain was using the United States, that the whole thing was a device to save British soldiers and British taxpayers. Nevertheless, the trend continued through and after the war.

American leadership also became more significant in the New World. A Rio de Janeiro conference, held immediately after Pearl Harbor, indicated that most of the Latin-American nations were prepared to coöperate with the United States. Save in the case of Argentina, relations became closer still during the war. The United States provided Latin-American governments with Lend-Lease aid. In return, the republics south of the Rio Grande routed out Axis agents, supplied the United States with airfields, and increased their production of raw materials required in the war. The State Department was unable to solve the Argentine question, or to remove general Latin-American suspicion of the United States. There were complaints, too, that Lend-Lease supplies strengthened dictators, and thus operated as an antidemocratic force. But the end of the war saw close coöperation on economic, military, and diplomatic levels, a coöperation that would carry over into the days of peace.

Days of Defeat (1941–42)

Over 3000 American servicemen lost their lives when the Japanese attacked Pearl Harbor. As a consequence, many Americans felt that the United States should concentrate on defeating Japan. Certain Senators endorsed this view. Roosevelt, however, continued to feel that Hitler was the major foe and that the Pacific war was of secondary importance. Master plans therefore called for giving chief attention to the European theater.

Everything went badly at the start. With the striking power of its navy greatly reduced by Pearl Harbor losses, the United States was unable to offer effective resistance when the Japanese moved into the Philippines. It was possible neither to reinforce nor to supply the Filipino and American forces which tried to defend the islands. These troops fought valiantly, under Douglas MacArthur until that general was ordered to Australia; then under General Jonathan Wainwright. Surrender became necessary on the Bataan peninsula in April, and on the island of Corregidor in May, 1942. Meantime, the Japanese had

taken over British Hong Kong and Singapore, had overrun Burma
(where American General Joseph Stilwell took a "hell of a beating"),
had occupied Malaya and the British, French, and Netherlands East
Indies. In June, 1942, Japan invaded the Aleutian Islands.

The news from Europe was no better. The United Nations were
unable to establish any base in western Europe or to organize large-
scale bombing operations. To the east, the Nazis were driving far into
Soviet Russia. To the south, German and Italian troops under Field
Marshal Erwin Rommel were extending control over the Mediter-
ranean, threatening the Suez Canal and the Arab oil fields beyond.
And on the Atlantic, the submarine campaign was so effective that
some experts felt the United States would be unable to deliver the
Lend-Lease supplies so desperately needed by the Russians and the
British.

Taking the Offensive (1942–44)

At the end of 1942 the situation gradu-
ally changed. Antisubmarine measures became more effective; and
supplies and troops got through to the zones of combat. Huge Russian
armies stopped the Germans at Stalingrad and began rolling back the
Nazi tide. The forces under General Bernard Montgomery held in
Egypt at El Alamein, then drove Rommel back across Italian Libya
and into French Tunisia. Allied bombers began to step up their operations over the Continent.

November, 1942, saw Anglo-American forces under General
Dwight D. Eisenhower landing in French North Africa. The Russians
wanted the United States and Britain to invade western Europe and
relieve German pressure on Russia by establishing a "second front" on
the Continent. Churchill and Roosevelt, however, decided that they
were not yet ready, that a landing in France would cost many lives and
might not serve the desired military purpose. They therefore operated
further south, using 850 vessels to land 400,000 troops in the Algiers-
Oran-Casablanca region.

The landing was successful. The French resisted for a time, then
capitulated. The area was under the Vichy government of Marshal
Henri Pétain; and official orders were to resist invasion. But Admiral

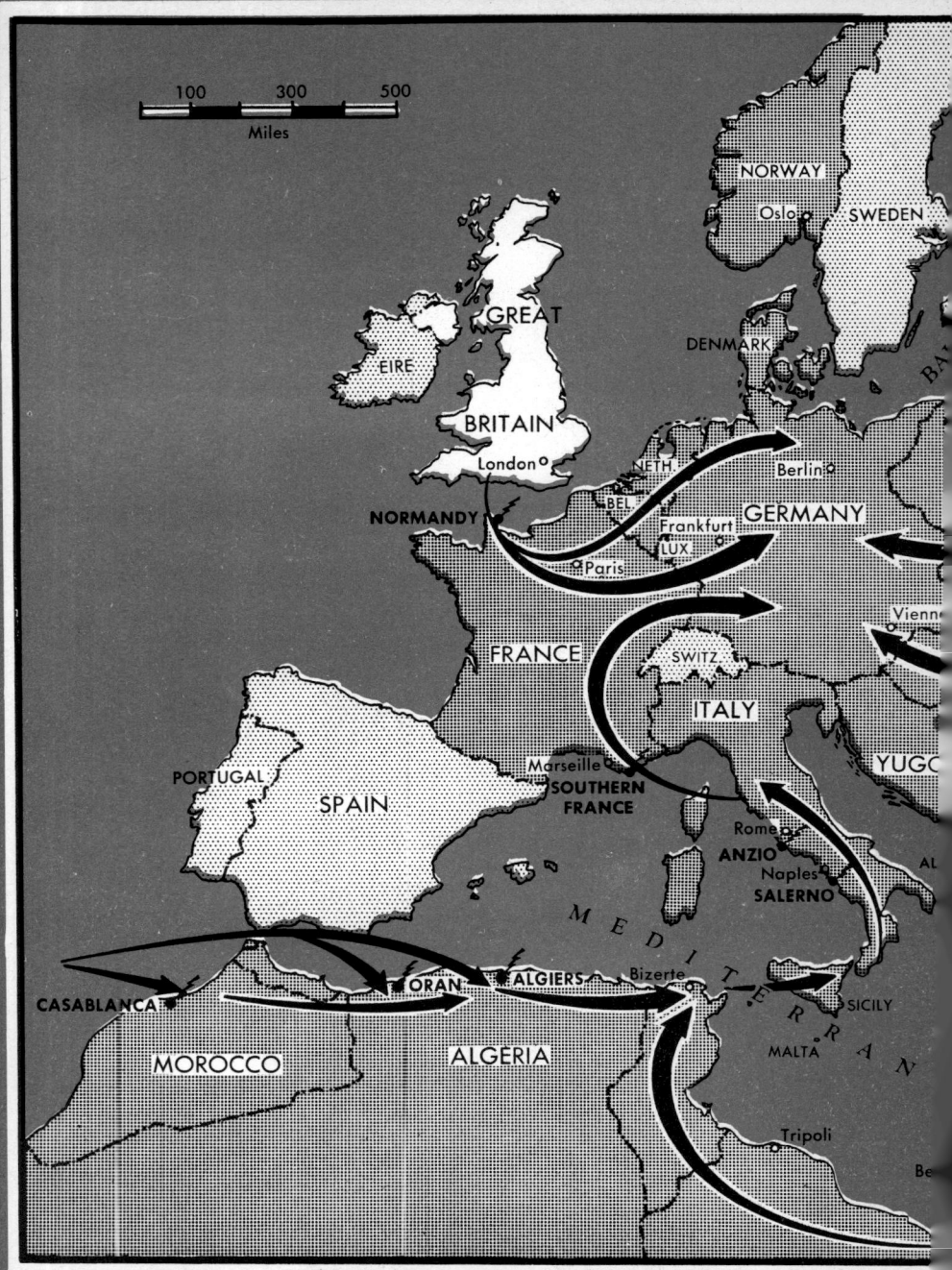

Hitler had conquered much of western Europe in the two years before Pearl Harbor (December, 1941). In 1942 the Germans extended their control, driving far into Russia and making gains in the Mediterranean. But by the end of 1942, the tide had turned. Russia held at Stalingrad, Britain at El Alamein; and American troops landed in North Africa. In 1943, while Russia pushed the Nazis westward, the Anglo-American allies took Sicily, and landed on the Italian mainland. The King of Italy sued

DEFEATING THE AXIS POWERS
1942–1945
THE EUROPEAN THEATER

FINLAND

Leningrad

ESTONIA

LATVIA

LITHUANIA

Moscow

U. S. S. R.

Warsaw

AND

Stalingrad

CASPIAN SEA

ROMANIA

BLACK SEA

BULGARIA

TURKEY

GREECE

SEA

	Area Under Axis Control In Early 1942
	Neutral States
	Area Under Allied Control In Early 1942
←	Allied Advances
—··—··— 1939 Boundaries	⬤ Beach Heads

El Alamein

Cairo o

EGYPT

Flannery

for peace; German troops, however, fought on in Italy. Churchill favored moving north from the Mediterranean. Roosevelt, though, decided on a cross-channel invasion. The D-Day landing in Normandy (June, 1944) and the landing in southern France opened the last phase of the war. After a final thrust (Battle of the Bulge, winter of 1944-45), the German armies collapsed. Aerial bombardment of Nazi territory and Anglo-American control of the seas hastened the end.

Jean Darlan, the ranking official on the ground, came to terms with Eisenhower. Since Darlan and many of his Vichyite followers were tarred with the brush of fascism, some Americans and Britishers felt that this was practically dealing with the enemy. Eisenhower and Roosevelt, however, felt that the act was defensible on several grounds: (1, and most important) it made the French stop fighting, which saved American lives; (2) it freed American troops for action against the major enemy, Germany; (3) it was easier to negotiate with Darlan (and Henri Giraud, who took over when Darlan was assassinated) than with Charles de Gaulle, the difficult and unbending leader of the Free French, who opposed compromise with Vichy.

Established in French North Africa, the American forces pushed eastward, while Montgomery drove westward from Egypt. Pressed from both sides, the Axis forces put up a vigorous fight in Tunisia. Beaten in a last-ditch stand at Bizerte in the spring of 1943, they then gave up in Africa. Although Germany held on in the Balkans, Montgomery and Eisenhower had reduced the chances of a Nazi drive into the Middle East, important for oil, because of the America-to-Iran-to-Russia supply line, and because of India.

The conquest of North Africa did not end Axis power in the Mediterranean. With the Germans in France and Italy and Germany, the United Nations could not make effective use of the Suez-and-Mediterranean trade routes. The summer of 1943, therefore, saw the British and Americans invading Sicily (July) and the foot of the Italian boot (September, at Salerno; with another landing further up the coast at Anzio in January of the next year).

When Sicily was invaded, King Victor Emmanuel of Italy tried to take his country out of the war. Announcing Benito Mussolini's resignation, His Majesty designated Marshal Pietro Badoglio as Premier. This posed a problem somewhat similar to that of Admiral Darlan in Africa. Should Americans deal with an Italian government that contained many persons who had been associated with fascism? Should the United States have traffic with a monarch who had helped elevate Mussolini to power and had coöperated with that aggressive dictator?

Again, the military joined top civilian officials in deciding to negotiate. As before, it was decided that this approach would save the lives

of American soldiers, and that the great enemy was, not Italy, but
Germany. The United States and Britain would not guarantee the
continuation of the Italian monarchy, which was, in fact, voted out
after the war.

Badoglio and the king could not, however, deliver Italy to the Allies.
The Germans stayed on, and bitterly contested the Allied advance.
Progress was painfully slow. Rome was finally taken in June, 1944; but
the Italian campaign dragged on into 1945.

Meanwhile, Allied bombers had been carrying the fight to Germany and German-occupied territory. Round-the-clock bombing began in the summer of 1943, the Americans hammering targets by day,
the Royal Air Force by night. These raids did not knock Germany out
of the war but did make it impossible for Hitler to expand industrial
production. Morale, too, was affected, leading Germany to launch an
all-out air offensive against England early in 1944. When this failed,
the United Nations had complete control of the skies. The Germans
would try rockets in a last effort to save the situation. But, with Russia
pounding in from the east, the days of Nazi power seemed to be numbered by the spring of 1944.

In the Pacific, too, the foe had been forced onto the defensive by
1944. The first American offensive—James Doolittle's Tokyo raid of
April, 1942—was of little military value, though it may have helped
Allied morale. But in the next month, the southward movement of
the Japanese was checked in the battle of the Coral Sea. This was a
new-style naval engagement. The blows were all struck by aircraft; the
surface vessels did not sight each other. A month after that, land- and
carrier-based planes inflicted heavy damage on the Japanese in the
battle of Midway. This was a turning point in the Pacific war. Thereafter, though slowly, the United States moved forward, under the
direction of Admiral Chester W. Nimitz, whose first base was Hawaii,
and General MacArthur, at first stationed in Australia.

It was hard going, because of shortages of men and material, and
because of the distances, the terrain, and fierce Japanese resistance.
Nonetheless, army, navy, and marine forces moved ahead, pounding
garrisons from the air, attacking Japanese supply lines, landing on
beaches, fighting through jungles. Marines moved into Guadalcanal,
in the Solomon Islands, in the summer of 1942—and held on, despite

the arrival of Japanese reinforcements. By February, 1943, the army had completed conquest of the island; and American forces were on their way to Tokyo.

Late in 1943, while Allied troops were digging in in southern Italy, American troops invaded the Gilbert Islands. In spite of preliminary air bombardment, there were heavy losses when the marines hit the beaches at Tarawa; but again the Japanese were routed out. With bases in the Gilberts, the United States was in a position to move against islands which the Japanese had held before Pearl Harbor—the Marshalls, Carolines, and Marianas—and to bid for repossession of such former American possessions as Guam and the Philippines.

Victory in Europe (1944–45)

As the United Nations gained the offensive, they began to lay plans for the final campaigns. But there was a sharp conflict as to what should be done. Winston Churchill felt that the Americans and the British should operate from the Mediterranean, strike the "soft underbelly" of the Axis by advancing through Italy and the Balkans. This, among other things, would give the Anglo-American combination something to say about the postwar fate of southeast Europe.

Stalin took another view. As before, he wanted the United States and Britain to land in western Europe. This would strike the Germans at a vital point. It would draw more Nazi soldiers away from the eastern front. It might bring victory sooner; and it would leave Russia dominant in the Balkans.

With two members of the Big Three at odds, it was up to the third to cast the deciding vote. This President Roosevelt did, when he ruled in favor of Stalin's plan. Although Roosevelt did want to please the Russians, advice from his own military leaders was the decisive factor. That is, invading Germany from the west looked easier than a movement from the south, across rugged country. Roosevelt, Churchill, and Stalin reached agreement at the Teheran Conference, and on June 6, 1944 (D-day), came the landing, in Normandy.

This was a tremendous undertaking, the largest military operation in American history. General Eisenhower, as supreme commander, had nearly 3,000,000 men available, mostly American and British (including Canadian). He had 4000 ships, more than 15,000 planes. After air bombardment, troops were landed along a sixty-mile beachhead.

Fearing a second landing elsewhere, the Germans did not throw their full weight against the landing forces. But there was bitter fighting along the shore, and more as the Allied troops moved inland. Using the cover afforded by the hedgerows of Normany, the Germans contested every inch of ground. But the summer brought victory in France, as troops under the British General Montgomery and the American Generals Omar Bradley and George S. Patton, Jr., forced the Germans back. Paris was liberated, partly owing to the efforts of the French underground forces; and another landing in southern France wound up the job.

With the Russians reaching Prussia by the fall of 1944, many felt that the war was almost over. Then German Field Marshal Karl von Rundstedt counterattacked in the Belgian Ardennes sector, throwing 300,000 men at a weak point in the Allied line (battle of the Bulge, December, 1944–January, 1945). This engagement cost the United States a dozen times as many casualties as the attack upon Pearl Harbor. But it was the dying gasp of the Nazi cause. By March, 1945, American troops had crossed the Rhine; and in May, 1945, after Hitler's suicide, Germany surrendered.

Victory in the Pacific (1944–45)

When the Germans surrendered, Japan was also near the end of the line. In the summer of 1944, the United States obtained a foothold in the Marianas, after a bloody battle on Saipan. Guam was reoccupied before the summer's end. In the fall, Americans moved into the Philippines, where Admiral William F. Halsey smashed Japanese naval power. American troops landed first on Leyte, then (early in 1945) on Luzon. Manila fell in February, 1945.

By then, the United States was moving on Iwo Jima, a gateway to Japan's home islands. The Americans suffered heavy loss there and on Okinawa (invaded in April, 1945). These victories, however, enabled the United States to begin saturation bombing of the Japanese mainland.

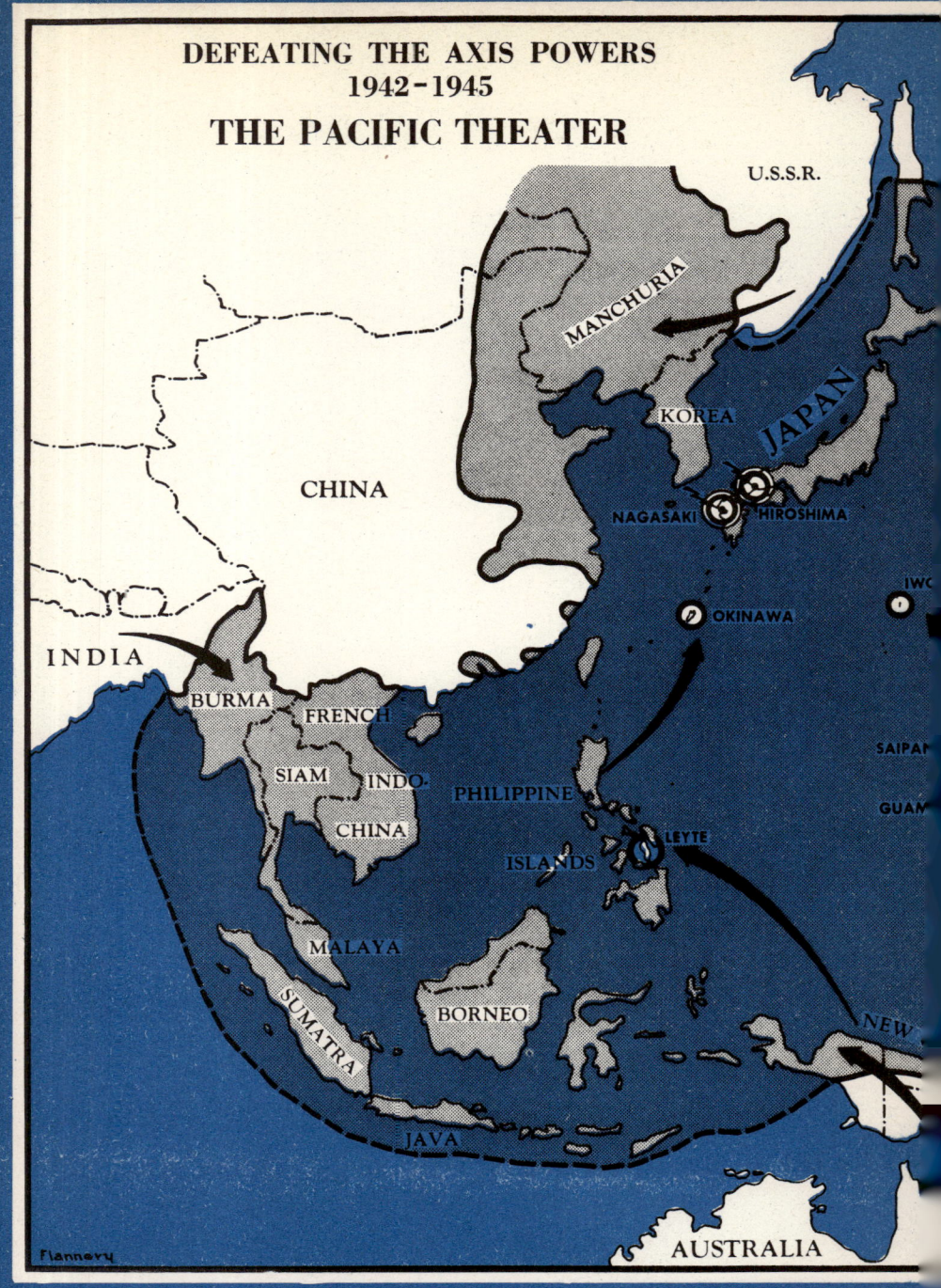

DEFEATING THE AXIS POWERS
1942-1945
THE PACIFIC THEATER

U.S.S.R.

MANCHURIA

CHINA

KOREA

JAPAN

NAGASAKI HIROSHIMA

INDIA

OKINAWA

IWO

BURMA

FRENCH

SIAM

INDO-

CHINA

PHILIPPINE

SAIPAN

GUAM

ISLANDS LEYTE

MALAYA

SUMATRA

BORNEO

NEW

JAVA

AUSTRALIA

Flannery

In Europe, Anglo-American advances were aided by Russian pressure from the other side; but Russia did not enter the Far East war until the very end. China kept many Japanese troops engaged, but was not effective on offense. Since European operations had priority, allied forces in the Pacific were short of men and supplies, especially in the early part of the war. Moreover, the distances were greater than in Europe.

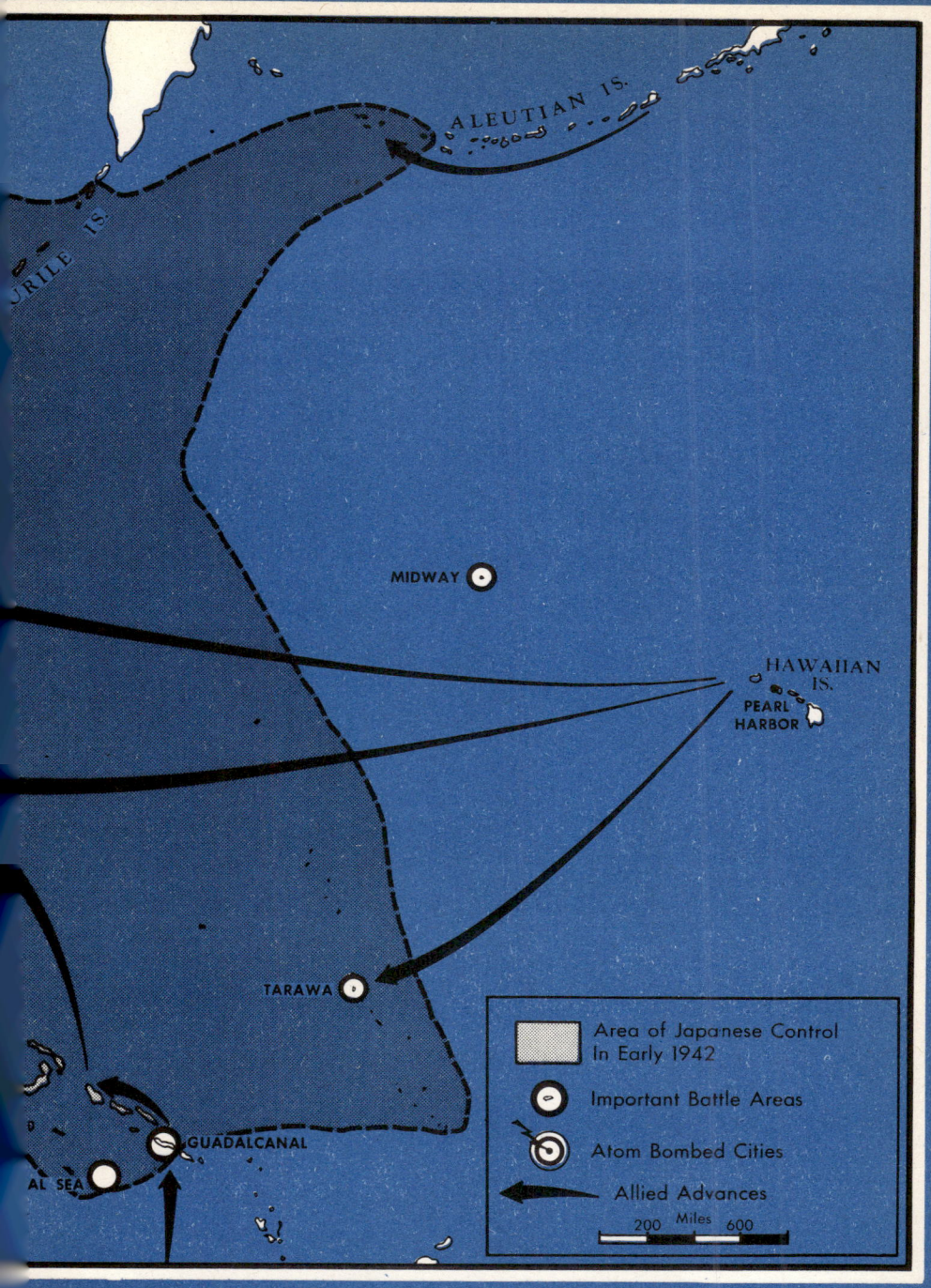

ALEUTIAN IS.

KURILE IS.

MIDWAY ⊙

HAWAIIAN
IS.

PEARL
HARBOR

TARAWA ⊙

GUADALCANAL

AL SEA

Area of Japanese Control
In Early 1942

⊙ Important Battle Areas

◉ Atom Bombed Cities

Allied Advances

200   Miles   600

Nevertheless, Americans checked Japan in 1942 (Coral Sea, Midway),
then began the long push to Tokyo. Guadalcanal was invaded in 1942,
Tarawa in 1943, Saipan, Guam, and Leyte (in the Philippines) in 1944,
Iwo Jima and Okinawa in 1945. By 1944-45, the United States and her
allies were moving back into Burma. The use of the atom bomb against
Japan (August, 1945) then brought the war to a close.

At the same time, Allied forces under Stilwell were reoccupying Burma. And, as Germany fell, Russia prepared to attack Japanese positions in Manchuria and Korea. It had been understood from the beginning that Russia would enter the Pacific war as soon as Germany went down. The American government wanted Russian help; military men judged that it would save the United States hundreds of thousands of casualties. Roosevelt, Churchill, and Stalin made the arrangements at the Yalta Conference of February, 1945; and these were confirmed by Roosevelt's successor Truman at the Potsdam Conference in July. In return for her aid, Russia was to receive the Kurile Islands, southern Sakhalin, and strategic control over Manchuria. Russia entered the war on August 9, 1945.

As it turned out, the United States did not need Russian aid in the Far East. The atomic bomb, developed in the war years, was tested in Los Alamos, New Mexico, on July 16, 1945, one day before the opening of the Potsdam Conference. Three weeks later, on August 6, an atomic bomb was dropped on Hiroshima, Japan; another on Nagasaki on August 9.

Near defeat even before the bombs were dropped, Japan now offered to surrender. She stipulated, however, that Emperor Hirohito should retain his crown. Since Japan had gone to war in December, 1941, under an imperial rescript, dealing with Hirohito was like dealing with the king of Italy. Again, however (as also in the use of the atomic bomb), a major consideration was the saving of lives of American soldiers. In addition, a quick conclusion of the war might check Russian advances. So, without giving assurances that Hirohito could continue permanently as emperor, the United States accepted the Japanese offer. The formal surrender was signed on the battleship *Missouri* on September 2, 1945; and the fighting phase of World War II had come to a close.

Truman, Postwar President

Franklin D. Roosevelt was not alive when World War II ended; worn out by years of service, he died in April, 1945, and was succeeded by Harry S. Truman. Roosevelt's death came as a surprise and shock to the American people. Contemporaries differed as to the New Deal and the Roosevelt foreign policies. Later generations would differ, too, in their interpretations of F. D. R. But all would recognize that Roosevelt had been a strong President who has set his stamp on the times.

After Roosevelt, any Chief Executive might have seemed less than forceful and effective. Citizens tended to regard the new President with sympathy rather than admiration. Little was known about Truman in 1945. He was described as a self-made man who had fought in World War I, had failed in business, and had become a Democratic politician out in Missouri. Ability, plus ties with Kansas City's Pendergast machine, had taken him to the United States Senate in 1934. There he had voted with his party, supporting the New Deal and Roosevelt's foreign policy. During World War II he had received some notice for investigating war plants; and when Henry Wallace had been dropped from the Roosevelt ticket in 1944, Truman had been named for Vice-President. Machine backing and support from labor and from Roosevelt had won him the post.

As Senator, Truman had made few broad statements. As a consequence, few people knew whether he was a liberal or a conservative. Nor was it easy to tell when Truman took up residence in the White House after Roosevelt's death in 1945. The new President surrounded himself with fellow Missourians and personal friends, without much regard to their social philosophies.

There was some evidence in 1945 and 1946 that Truman was more conservative than Roosevelt—more conservative, anyway, than the prewar Roosevelt. Truman picked a good many conservative advisers; and Roosevelt New Dealers left the administration. (Ickes, Secretary of the Interior since 1933, resigned in irritation in 1946.) Truman favored universal military service; and he took an antilabor attitude in the railroad strike of 1946.

Such policies were not unpopular. They were, in fact, in tune with the times, for postwar trends were to the right. Truman, however, seemed offhand and ineffective in his first years in office. After seeming to oppose the continuance of wartime controls, he fought for OPA in 1946. When Congress refused to coöperate, the President vetoed one unsatisfactory bill, then accepted a similar one. When this statute worked badly, Truman ended price ceilings, save for rental properties. Prices then rose rapidly.

Truman's apparent ineffectiveness helped the Republicans win the Congressional election of 1946. Another factor in the situation was the general dislike for wartime government controls (as in the "back-to-normalcy" sentiment after World War I). The Republican-controlled Eightieth Congress (1947–49) therefore took a conservative line, refusing to extend social security or to do much for the farmers, and passing the Taft-Hartley Act, which put certain curbs on labor.

As Congress shifted right, Truman moved left, took his stand with labor, and for aid-to-farmers; talked of expanding social security, providing federal help to housing, and assuring civil rights for Negroes. All this he would eventually term the Fair Deal. As finally stated, the program represented the conviction that the public did not really want to go back to the old days but preferred to have the government take an active role in economic life.

The Election of 1948

Meantime, the President's political techniques improved. Democratic managers, however, considered Truman a weak presidential candidate. Several, therefore, tried to have him set aside in the Democratic nominating convention of 1948. Most active here were the Americans for Democratic Action, including some persons who had been Roosevelt New Dealers. But the A.D.A. was short of practical politicians and could find no suitable candidate. As a consequence, Truman was nominated for President, with Senator Alben Barkley of Kentucky as his running mate.

Few felt that Truman could win. For one thing, his own party managers gave him little backing, but concentrated on local campaigns. Besides, the President displeased many southern Democrats, who considered his civil-rights position a challenge to states' rights and white supremacy. Some of these southern Democrats stayed with Truman; others ran their own Dixiecrat presidential candidate in 1948, Governor J. Strom Thurmond of South Carolina. On the other side, Henry Wallace, an original New Deal Democrat, ran on a Progressive ticket. Wallace wanted to push domestic reform faster than did Truman; and he disapproved of Truman's policy of getting tough with Russia.

This division among Democrats seemed to spell Republican victory in 1948. After a spirited contest, the Republican presidential nomination went to Governor Thomas E. Dewey of New York, who had opposed Roosevelt four years before. In 1944 Dewey had waged a vigorous campaign. In 1948 he felt so sure of victory that he avoided almost every issue and confined himself to platitudes. Substantially his only pledge was to preserve existing foreign policy.

Threatened with defeat, the hitherto ineffective Truman became a different person. He toured the country, seeing the people and meeting them as an "average man" (Dewey was stiff and formal). Seeking the farm and labor vote, the President denounced the Eightieth Congress and declared for welfare legislation. Oddly enough, the secessions from the Democratic party helped Truman in a number of states. The Thurmond opposition made many voters feel that Truman was a real liberal, not a Dixiecrat reactionary. Wallace's candidacy led many to conclude that the President was no radical, and that he could be trusted.

Straw votes taken by pro-Dewey pollsters indicated that the Republicans would come out on top. Actually, Truman won. Dewey's spiritless and Truman's active campaigning helped explain the result. Equally important was the weakness of the Thurmond and Wallace movements. The Dixiecrats did carry four states—South Carolina, Louisiana, Alabama, Mississippi. Most southern Democrats, however, were reluctant to break party lines to support a regional ticket that had no chance of winning national success or national patronage. Wallace started strong, then faded fast. Unlike La Follette in 1924, Wallace accepted Communist support. Communists and fellow travelers therefore crowded into the Progressive organization. Others left, and voters generally concluded that the Wallace party was Communist-influenced if not Communist-controlled. In the final count, Wallace received 1,150,000 votes—less than the Dixiecrat Thurmond. The Wallace showing was only a little better than that of Lemke, the forgotten Union candidate of 1936. Wallace made his strongest race in New York, where he took enough votes away from Truman to give the state to Dewey.

Strong labor and farm backing enabled Truman to carry several states which Roosevelt had lost to Dewey in 1944. Of these the most important were three midwestern states—Ohio, Iowa, and Wisconsin. Labor remembered that a Republican Congress had passed the Taft-Hartley Act over Truman's veto. The farmers knew that the Democrats were more committed to farm support than were the Republicans. Many citizens approved of Truman's support of welfare legislation and remembered him as an active though ineffective champion of price controls.

Truman's victory was a narrow one. Dewey carried most of the industrial Northeast. Not since 1916 had a victorious presidential candidate run so few votes ahead of the other major-party nominee (2,000,000 in a total of 49,000,000). Not since 1888 had a victorious presidential candidate received so small a majority in the electoral college. Only once before in presidential history (1916) had a victor lost the two most populous states, New York and Pennsylvania. Truman had barely squeaked through. His victory seemed like a great triumph only because the experts had predicted a Dewey landslide.

Yet in a way the outcome was impressive. For the fifth straight time, the Democrats had beaten the Republicans in a presidential contest. In doing so the Democratic party had demonstrated that most farmers and organized workingmen had become "normally Democratic." In most states, Democratic candidates for state office ran ahead of the President, giving the party a majority of the governorships and control of both houses of Congress. As for the presidential race, Truman had won even while losing over a million Democratic votes to Wallace and to Thurmond. And after the election many of the bolters returned to the fold. Senator Glen Taylor of Idaho, Wallace's running mate in 1948, climbed back on the Democratic band wagon. So did many job-conscious Dixiecrats. In 1950 Wallace himself broke with the Progressive party, when he backed the efforts of the United States and United Nations to drive the North Koreans out of Southern Korea.

Political Trends

Given this Democratic strength, how could the Republicans ever win a national election? Some Republican managers said that Landon, Willkie, and Dewey had erred in echoing the New Deal Democrats. Victory might come, in other words, if the Republicans dropped the "me, too" policy, and became a frankly conservative organization, under such a leader as Senator Robert Taft of Ohio.

By 1950, many Republicans were following this line, were calling the Truman administration socialist, and were charging that Roosevelt and Truman had allowed Communists to hold public office. The McGraw-Hill publications launched an active campaign against what they called the "creeping socialism" of an administration that was intent on expanding social security and providing government support for housing, education, and power development. The American Medical Association threw its full weight against candidates who approved of President Truman's proposals for national health insurance.

A number of Republican leaders, including Governor Earl Warren of California, disapproved of the conservative approach. As they saw it, the public had many times endorsed the New Deal reforms. Although it might be possible to oppose socialized medicine (many Truman Democrats had their doubts about national health insurance), opposition to housing legislation and the like would spell disaster.

At mid-century, the conflict within the Republican ranks was not resolved. But neither were the Democrats in perfect shape. The party found it easier to win elections than to agree as to a legislative program. Time after time, conservative southern Democrats joined conservative northern Republicans to defeat presidential proposals. Unfriendly critics charged that Truman, having won public backing by proposing reforms, did not care much whether or not Congress adopted his proposals. Others felt that the President tried hard enough but was an ineffective political manager. Friends of the President pointed out that Roosevelt, too, had had trouble handling Congress, except in such emergencies as the bank and Pearl Harbor crises;

and that with continued Democratic victories at the polls the Fair Deal would in time be enacted into law.

In the whole of American history, minor parties had never been weaker than in 1950. Although the Dixiecrats had an organization of sorts, it was obvious that the overwhelming majority of southern Democrats planned to work inside the regular party (and to keep the southern Democrats conservative: Fair Dealers like Claude Pepper of Florida and Frank Graham of North Carolina were defeated in the senatorial primaries in 1950). Wallace's Progressives, weak in the 1948 campaign, were weaker still thereafter. The once-powerful Socialists were so feeble that Norman Thomas proposed that the party cease making presidential nominations. The old Socialist Labor party and a relatively new Socialist Workers (Trotskyite) party had no real strength in any state. Communist party membership, never very large in the United States, declined sharply as anti-Communist sentiment increased after World War II. By 1950 the Communist organ, the New York *Daily Worker*, was in financial straits. The Prohibitionists gained some strength after World War II, but remained far from strong.[1] It was clear that the political future of the United States would be decided within the framework of the major parties.

Bipartisan Foreign Policy

Through the long course of American history, Americans have tended to pay greater attention to domestic than to foreign policy. On the whole, this continued to be true after World War II. But there were indications that the public was more interested in foreign policy than before. International news was given far more space in the newspapers. Labor unions and other groups that had neglected diplomatic issues now gave attention to these problems. A large part of the public found foreign questions baffling, and wished that the United States could steer clear of overseas commitments. But more and more it was assumed that the American re-

---

[1] The antiliquor crusade showed some signs of reviving by mid-century, mostly, however, outside the Prohibition party. Many southern counties were voting dry in local-option elections, as were some small government units elsewhere in the country. The drys carried a state-wide referendum in Oklahoma in 1950.

public would be involved in all world problems, be they military or diplomatic, economic or ideological, American or African, European or Asiatic.

When the United States became involved in World War II, many administration leaders feared a repetition of the World War I pattern, with the American republic pulling out of Europe in the postwar era. To guard against this eventuality, Franklin D. Roosevelt developed a bipartisan approach to foreign policy and took leading Senators into his confidence. (Wilson had offended the Republicans by working only through the Democrats, and had irritated Senators by ignoring them on most occasions.)

Roosevelt's bipartisan approach was evident as early as 1940, when two leading Republicans were taken into the cabinet. Henry L. Stimson became Secretary of War, Frank Knox Secretary of Navy. Republican as well as Democratic votes were needed to put through the draft, the repeal of the neutrality legislation, and other administration proposals. Later, Roosevelt officially sponsored a world tour by Wendell Willkie, his opponent in the presidential contest of 1940. Even more important was the bipartisan agreement to keep foreign policy out of the wartime presidential campaign of 1944. Dewey, the Republican candidate, worked this out with Secretary of State Hull.

The crisis, of course, came at the peacemaking stage. Here Roosevelt used a method successfully employed at the Washington Conference of 1921–22. He had United States Senators participate in the negotiations, and was careful to have both sides represented. Thus Senator Tom Connally of Texas, the Democratic chairman of the Foreign Relations Committee, was joined by Senator Arthur Vandenberg of Michigan, ranking Republican member. In addition, the Roosevelt and Truman administrations relied heavily on John Foster Dulles, as an adviser and negotiator. Dulles was a logical choice, for he had studied postwar problems as chairman of a Committee on a Just and Durable Peace, a group organized by the Federal Council of Churches. Besides that, Dulles had the merit of being a leading Republican.

Taken together with the growing recognition of America's world position, the bipartisan approach paid off handsomely. The Senate raised no objection to American membership in the United Nations in 1945. Moreover, Congress provided funds for European relief and recovery (the United Nations Relief and Rehabilitation Administration, 1943–46; the Marshall Plan after 1947); for economic aid to America's chief ally, Britain (a special loan of 1947); for military aid programs (Greece and Turkey, the Truman Doctrine, 1947; the Atlantic Pact, 1949); for postwar propaganda (the State Department's Voice of America); and for an overseas development program (technological aid, Point Four, 1950). Diplomatic issues were played down in the 1948 campaign, except for Henry Wallace, who opposed the anti-Russian attitude of both major parties.

The bipartisan program did not always work smoothly. Senators— Republican Senators especially—complained that the executive made basic decisions without consulting the Senate, as at Teheran, Yalta, and Potsdam. What was more, agreements among the Big Three were not submitted to the Senate for approval. Republicans said that the administration should, but did not, consult them before announcing such new policies as the Truman Doctrine and Point Four. That is, the Democrats made the policy and asked the Republicans to endorse it. Nor could Republicans be expected to go along when the President changed policies, as he did on the Palestine question. The Democrats, in turn, said that their opponents tried to make political capital out of questions involving national interest. Some independent voters complained that the bipartisan policy gave the public little voice in foreign policy, that everything was decided by a handful of politicians in Washington.

At mid-century, there was some evidence that bipartisan foreign policy might break down. When Truman put forth the Point Four program as his personal policy in 1949, Republicans claimed that the President was trying to make political capital out of what should be a bipartisan measure. Republicans who were calling the Truman administration "socialistic" were increasingly reluctant to vote Marshall Plan funds for socialist governments in western Europe. The conquest of China by the Chinese Communists in 1949 led some Republicans to criticize the administration for not having given enough help to the Nationalists.

In 1950, Republican Senator Joseph McCarthy of Wisconsin brought the question to a crisis by making sensational charges as to Communists in the State Department. Since McCarthy offered accusation without proof, many Republicans were reluctant to support him, the more so since the Truman administration was strongly anti-Communist. Others backed the Wisconsin Senator, because they believed some of his statements, or saw an opportunity to embarrass the administration, or desired to break the bipartisan foreign policy.

Occupation Policy

Several problems had to be met immediately after the cessation of hostilities. The Allies agreed on a general policy of coöperation. In most areas, however, the actual job of occupation was assigned to one power. Germany and Austria, for example, were divided into French, English, American, and Russian zones. North Korea was to be occupied by Soviet Russia, South Korea and Japan by the United States.

Soviet Russia had a definite policy with reference to areas under her control. First, she obtained needed goods—machinery from Manchuria, mineral products from eastern Germany. Second, she remodeled the government and economy of each occupied area, working largely through local Communists.

The United States had no such clear policy—indeed, no policy at all. During the war, Franklin D. Roosevelt was for a time persuaded to adopt a Morgenthau Plan, designed to close mines and factories and reduce Germany to agricultural status. Churchill also approved this plan; but when Secretary of State Hull and Secretary of War Stimson called attention to the unrealistic character of the proposal, it was immediately dropped. Yet nothing very definite was substituted. Nor was occupation procedure very carefully defined. In Japan, General MacArthur was given control and allowed to do just about as he chose. In Europe, the military first took charge, later giving way to a civilian administration. Occupation officials and occupation troops were inadequately trained, inadequately briefed, inadequately supervised. As a consequence, there was much confusion, and not a little corruption.

When the war ended, the emphasis was for a time on punishment. This was natural enough, considering war feeling and Axis mistreatment of Allied war prisoners. The resulting war trials did not, however, yield altogether satisfactory results. Highly questionable legal methods were used in the trials of Japanese generals Yamashita and Homma, in General MacArthur's jurisdiction. These trials, and most of those in Europe, centered around war atrocities. At the Nuremberg trials of Goering, Von Ribbentrop, and other Nazis, the Allies used the broader (and legally novel) charge of waging aggressive war. Convictions were obtained; but, since judges as well as prosecutors came from the victor nations, it could hardly be said that the principle was established in international law.

Under the actual conditions of occupation, the punishment theme gradually was deëmphasized. Instead of dismantling factories and restricting occupied populations, the American authorities used encouragement and aimed at expanded production. The reasons were various:

1. If the occupied nations were kept down, the task of occupation became expensive and difficult; the citizens of occupied countries became sullen and uncoöperative. If encouraged, they became coöperative and more nearly self-supporting, and the work of the occupying forces was made easier.

2. World economic recovery was earnestly desired for the benefit of Americans and other people. A punishment policy held down the output of occupied countries. Washington officials came gradually to feel that Germany must again become a great producer in the interest of general recovery.

3, and most important. The United States and the Soviet Union came into conflict in 1946. American occupation officials then proceeded to build up Japan and western Germany as bulwarks against an advancing Russia. Closely related was the desire to please the population of occupied areas, so as to make sure they would achieve top production and would not be tempted by communism. Often this meant coöperating with business and political groups that had been fascist in the past.

Tied into this was the desire for military bases. At the close of the war with Japan, the United States Navy took over Pacific islands formerly controlled by the Japanese. The definite desire was to have strategic bases for the future. When the Chinese Communists secured control of that country, and when the Korean Communists invaded southern Korea in 1950, American military authorities began thinking about bases in Japan. With the development of the Atlantic Pact, which linked western Europe to American military policy, control of western Germany also assumed importance.

In the main, however, American occupation policy could not be described as a success. After five years of control there was little to indicate that the United States had won the minds of the occupied populations.

International Organization

Early in World War II, President Roosevelt was doubtful as to the possibility of forming an effective league of nations at the end of the war. His hopes increased as the months went on, and he was highly optimistic by 1945. Meantime, the anti-Axis powers had had preliminary discussions at Dumbarton Oaks (political) and Bretton Woods (economic), both in 1944. A San Francisco conference, held after Roosevelt's death, perfected the United Nations organization. These three conferences that launched the new league were held in the United States, and UN headquarters would be in New York. This in itself suggested that Americans would feel a deeper interest in the UN than in the League of Nations. Also important as an indication of the new point of view was the passage of the Fulbright Resolution in the House of Representatives in 1943, favoring an organization "with power adequate to establish and maintain a just and lasting peace."

The new organization, however, had its limitations. Both Soviet Russia and the United States insisted that major states have veto power. This meant that the UN could make headway on major questions only when the great powers agreed. Hence the future of the world depended not so much on the UN as on the ability of the United States, Britain, France, and Russia to get along with each other.

For a time, things went reasonably well. The UN won some limited successes, as in Palestine. Presently, however, the UN became a sort of forum in which the United States and Soviet Russia denounced each other. Perhaps something was gained by airing such questions. Perhaps not. But the UN experiment did increase American attachment to international organizations. A basic point was the strength of the United States within the UN. Backed by Latin America, the British Empire, and the nations of western Europe, the United States could easily outvote Russia and her satellites. To escape defeat, Russia then had to resort to the veto. Americans therefore came to regard themselves as the defenders and the Russians as the opponents of international organization.

On occasion, the United States by-passed the UN, as in announcing the Truman Doctrine. Generally, however, Americans showed a definite desire to work through international organization. An interesting example of this was furnished by the government-sponsored Baruch plan for international control of atomic energy (1946). The United States offered to turn its information on atomic energy over to an international body with authority to end atomic warfare and to inspect and control civil uses of atomic energy. Russian opposition to this proposal (on the inspection issue) prevented adoption. Nonetheless, the plan represented an important American offer to yield a measure of sovereignty and work on an international plane. The close coöperation of the UN and the United States in the Korean crisis of 1950 furnished a further illustration of this point.

Military Influence

Since Russia would not accept the Baruch plan, the United States continued to handle atomic energy on a national basis. Significantly, Congress ordered this new source of energy controlled by the government, not by private industry; and by civilians, not the military. David Lilienthal, from TVA, was the first chairman of the Atomic Energy Commission.

Military influence was challenged at other points as well. Although the military supported Truman's request for universal military service, Congress would not agree. And the voters showed little interest in

Douglas MacArthur when the General was entered in the Wisconsin presidential-preference primaries for 1948.

Still, military influence was not to be disregarded. The armed forces had received much attention, leading generals and admirals much publicity in World War II. Roosevelt and Truman both held the professional military in high esteem, and sent military men as diplomats to Vichy, to Soviet Russia, to China. After World War II, Truman made General George C. Marshall Secretary of State, the first professional military man to be so named. The public seemed to approve. And, though MacArthur got nowhere politically, both Democrats and Republicans considered Eisenhower possible presidential timber in 1948. The general refused to run; but he was urged again by the Republicans for 1952.

Military appropriations remained high after World War II. For increased efficiency, Congress overhauled the military establishment in 1947, creating a Department of Defense. Under the Secretary of Defense were Secretaries for the Army, Navy, and Air. The new setup did not work very well at first, and in 1949 navy officers openly complained that their branch was mistreated. One reason for this was the new concentration on air power.

Although Congress would not vote universal military service, it did extend the draft. This meant that the armed forces had a great pool of man power on which they could draw if the need arose. As it happened, however, there was no need to use conscription in the postwar era. A higher pay scale drew enough volunteers to take care of the large American navy, the substantial air force, and the occupation units abroad. Not until actual fighting began, in Korea in the summer of 1950, did the government resume its draft calls.

Cold War with Russia

The large military appropriations of the postwar years were of course connected with the Russian question. World War II had improved Russian-American relations only temporarily. Hope for postwar coöperation faded as the Soviet Union and the United States differed over the peace treaties (those concerning Italy and four lesser states were concluded at the end of 1946; but no agreement could be reached for Germany, Austria, or Japan). Further difficulties arose as the Russians tightened their grip on eastern Europe and failed to provide the free elections which Stalin had agreed upon at Yalta. There was conflict, too, over Iran, where Anglo-American influence won out; and there was even more serious trouble further east, in China.

Secretary of State James F. Byrnes tried to work out a solution in 1946 by proposing that Soviet Russia and the United States join Britain and France in a four-power treaty to hold Germany down for a generation. When this failed to materialize, because of Russian opposition, Soviet-American relations drifted from bad to worse. The rift was all too clear by 1947, when Russia and her satellite states refused to accept Marshall Plan aid from the United States.

By then, the United States had begun to develop a program of "containing" Russia. This had several aspects. Among other things, the United States proposed to provide economic aid for the countries willing to coöperate with the American republic. To this end, the stopgap relief program of UNRRA was replaced by the Marshall Plan, proposed in 1947 and launched formally the next year. Under this program, run through an Economic Cooperation Administration, the United States supplied needed goods to Europe. This served a relief purpose and stimulated European recovery. The idea was to keep western Europe from moving into the Soviet orbit; to revive the world trade on which lasting prosperity depends; to help Latin America; and to maintain full employment and full production on farm and in factory in the United States. Besides the ECA, the United States made a special loan to Britain ($3,750,000,000); and helped finance the World Bank (International Bank for Reconstruction and Development), which also provided aid.

Along with economic help went military aid. Communist advance in the Balkans threatened Greece by 1947. Victory there would give the Soviet Union control of the Straits, which were under Turkish rule. This in turn would endanger Anglo-American control of Near East oil and of the Mediterranean. President Truman therefore asked for military aid for Greece and Turkey. In doing so, he set forth the Truman Doctrine, which announced that the United States intended to "support free peoples who are resisting attempted subjugation by armed minorities or by outside countries."

Since neither Greece nor Turkey was a democracy in the American sense, there was widespread criticism of the Truman appeal. Congress, however, coöperated, and the United States provided equipment and military advisers who helped in the move to check the Greek Communists. The program was already becoming effective when, in 1948, Marshal Tito, Communist dictator of Yugoslavia, quarreled with Moscow and became less unfriendly to the United States. Thus it could be said that Russian advance had for the time been checked in southeast Europe.

Equally serious was the question of Germany and western Europe. In June, 1948, Russia blocked the approaches to Berlin. Britain, France, and the United States all had zones in the German capital; but Berlin was surrounded by Russian-occupied territory. It was therefore easy for the Russians to establish a land blockade. Instead of yielding, Britain and America organized a Berlin airlift and sent in food and fuel by air. By the fall of 1949, when the airlift ended, over 2,000,000 tons of supplies had been shipped in on more than 250,000 flights. The operation was expensive, but successful, for Russia finally lifted the blockade.

In June, 1948, just before the announcement of the Berlin blockade, the United States Senate adopted a Vandenberg Resolution, favoring regional military alliances. A year later, an important Atlantic Pact established a ten-year military alliance or mutual defense agreement. The United States was here associated with its neighbor Canada; also with Britain, France, Italy; with Belgium, the Netherlands, and Luxembourg; with Norway, Denmark and Iceland, and Portugal. Before the end of 1949, Congress was appropriating funds for military assistance to the members of this alliance; also for Greece and Turkey, and for Asiatic friends, including Iran, Nationalist China, Korea, and the Philippine Islands. Intimately associated with this system was a military-coöperation program involving "arms for the Americas." Worked out in the Rio Pact of 1947, and in special agreements, this embraced coöperation in the face of possible danger; standardization of equipment in the Western Hemisphere; arms assistance from the

United States to Latin America; and a general anti-Communist stand.

To round out the pattern, the economic and military program was to be tied to an ideological offensive. Since Russia actively propagandized all over the world, it was only logical that the United States should endeavor to reply. This the State Department tried to do, through cultural attachés, the distribution of printed material, and short-wave radio programs (the Voice of America). Congressional suspicion of this work kept it from becoming as effective as the other parts of the check-Russia program. There were indications, however, that the program would be stepped up after 1950. More effective, perhaps, was the exchange of scholars and students, part of which was financed by the government (Fulbright grants, using money realized by the sale of surplus war equipment overseas). Also significant was the organization of unofficial bodies, such as the International Confederation of Free Trade Unions, formed in 1949 after the World Federation of Trade Unions came under Communist influence.

American efforts helped turn the tide against communism in western Europe; but the United States was not successful in eastern Asia. The Soviet Union won a crushing victory when in 1949 the Chinese Communists defeated the Chinese Nationalists and drove Chiang Kai-shek to a last stand on Formosa. In 1931, when Japan invaded Manchuria, the Chinese Nationalists controlled most of China; the Communists held only a small region. After the general Japanese invasion of 1937, the Chinese Nationalists and Communists both fought the invader. Lend-Lease aid from the United States was sent to the Nationalists. The United States hoped, however, that the Nationalists and Communists could get together, so as to strengthen the anti-Japanese cause. It was hoped, too, that both factions would serve under an American commander, General Stilwell, who could improve the fighting efficiency of the Chinese forces. Stilwell, however, quarreled with Chiang, and was recalled. The Nationalists and Communists did not join.

After World War II, General Marshall went to China on a special mission. His hope was for a coalition government, bringing the Nationalists and Communists together, but using also a middle group of American-trained Chinese liberals. This did not work either. Marshall, returning home to become Secretary of State in 1947, felt that the China situation was close to hopeless: the Chinese Communists were connected with Russia, the Chinese Nationalists were corrupt and inefficient and undemocratic. The average American citizen was little interested in the Far East, and certainly did not urge Congress to appropriate the enormous sums that would have been required to save the Chinese Nationalists. Congress did appropriate a little for Marshall Plan aid, a little later under the military-assistance program. The sums, though, were very small, and the problem was very great. And in 1949, the Chinese Nationalists went down.

When Nationalist China fell, some said that the Soviet Union could never control so vast a land, that Communist China would soon show Tito tendencies. More general, however, was a concern lest communism spread further in the Orient—into Indo-China and Tibet, which were threatened by Chinese Communists; into South Korea, which was invaded by Russian-trained North Korean Communists in June, 1950; into the Republic of the Philippines, where Communist-influenced "Huks" were campaigning against a conservative government; into other areas where the Communists were active: Siam, Malaya, newly freed Indonesia, India and Burma, and Iran.

Concerned, and denounced for having failed in China, Truman's State Department made it plain that the United States would resist further Communist advances in the Far East. When Russian-trained and Russian-equipped North Korean troops crossed the 38° parallel and invaded South Korea in June, 1950, President Truman had General Douglas MacArthur use air, naval, and ground forces against the invaders. This action was endorsed by virtually every Congressman, and by the general public. Significantly, too, Britain gave the United States support, as did the United Nations. At long last, the United States was operating on more than a national basis. And by September, 1950, the trend of battle in Korea was against the Communists.

It was recognized, too, that anticommunism was not enough; that something had to be done to aid the depressed populations of these Asiatic lands. One approach was through technological assistance—the Point Four program, which got off to a late and slow start in 1950. The UN was also pushing a Point Four program of its own. It was

PACIFIC

OCEAN

UNITED STATES

CANADA

ATLANTIC

OCEAN

SOUTH
AMERICA

A F

Flannery

In 1945, American policy makers believed that Russian-American coöperation was desirable and possible. Soon thereafter conflicts put these two powers into separate camps. Areas of friction included the Middle East, the Balkans, occupied Germany, and the Far East.

In the Cold War, both sides used economic, military, and propagandist weapons. The Russians appealed to peasants in satellite states by breaking up the large estates. Russian experts trained satellite armies, and the Soviet Union provided military equipment. Meantime, Moscow carried on

JAPAN

AUSTRALIA

U. S. S. R.

CHINA

INDIA

INDIAN OCEAN

ICA

◼ U.S.S.R. and Satellite States

◻ United States and Possessions

▨ Areas Occupied by the U.S.

⣿ Marshall and Truman Plan Areas

500   1500

Miles

a well-organized world propaganda campaign. The United States provided economic aid for its allies, notably through the Marshall Plan; also in a large loan to Britain. On the military side, the American republic gave military advice and supplies to Greece and Turkey under the Truman Doctrine; and with the signing of the North Atlantic Pact, embarked on a military-aid program for western Europe. Similar aid was to be given to coöperating states in the Middle and Far East, e.g., Iran and the Philippines. The Voice of America represented the publicity approach.

evident, however, that much more would be needed if the United States desired to figure largely in the future of the Orient.

Problems at Home

While holding the line in Europe and the Americas, the United States government also took up the question of communism at home. Early in World War II, when Stalin was working with Hitler, the Roosevelt administration took action against American Communists, sending Earl Browder to prison for passport fraud. At the time, American Communists were denouncing Roosevelt as a warmonger and World War II as an imperialist affair. After Germany invaded Russia, the Communists shifted ground, becoming interventionist and viewing the conflict as a "people's war." Browder (now out of jail) supported the war effort after Pearl Harbor, saying that Communist and capitalist nations could work together. But the party line changed again right after the war, Browder was deposed for his coöperation stand, and the American Communists (under William Z. Foster and Eugene Dennis) became violently opposed to capitalism and to American foreign policy.

As feeling against Russia increased in the United States, American Communists came to be regarded with increasing hostility by the American people. Congress and the President launched investigations. Some government officials were dropped or allowed to resign after loyalty checks. The Justice Department issued lists of "subversive organizations," groups that had been founded or used by Communists. The Taft-Hartley Act required labor leaders to swear that they were not Communists. Several cases hit the headlines. There were convictions on charges of perjury (Harry Bridges, the longshoreman labor leader, and Alger Hiss, formerly a high official in the State Department); contempt for refusing to answer questions asked by Congressional investigators (ten Hollywood writers, among others); espionage (Judith Coplon, a Justice Department employee, and Valentin Gubitchev, a Russian employed by the United Nations); violation of the Smith Act, i.e., plotting to overthrow the government (Eugene Dennis and ten other Communist party leaders). Americans were particularly disturbed to hear of spy activities, as when Harry Gold, an American scientist, confessed to helping Dr. Klaus Fuchs, a British citizen, supply Russia with information about the atomic bomb. (Russia achieved an atomic explosion in 1949.)

Anticommunist activity was not confined to government channels. Communists and procommunists who had gained influence in the labor movement were voted out of office. The C.I.O. expelled Communist-dominated unions (1949–50) and set up new unions to take over the field. There were campaigns to get Communists out of religious and veterans' organizations and out of minority-group associations. A New York Episcopal clergyman lost his post because of the activities of his son and co-worker. The Regents of the University of California required employees to swear that they were not Communists. There was a flood of books by former Communists, reciting the evils of communism. And Hollywood began turning out anticommunist movies. *The Iron Curtain* and *Conspirator*, to give two examples, were in sharp contrast with *Mission to Moscow* and *Song of Russia*, pro-Soviet pictures produced during the war years, when Russia and the United States were coöperating.

The American public whole-heartedly endorsed the efforts of the FBI to round up Russian spies. The overwhelming majority of Americans also approved of the bipartisan anti-Russian foreign policy developed after 1946; also the steps taken to prevent Communists from getting control of unions and other American organizations. At the same time, many citizens were disturbed by the tendency of some anticommunists to identify everything they disliked with Soviet Russia. Ambitious and unscrupulous politicians gained the spotlight by making wild and reckless charges. Ultraconservative newspaper columnists and radio commentators suggested that Socialists and Communists were virtually identical, and that the Socialists included all who advocated public housing or socialized medicine. David Lilienthal and other thoroughly loyal officials were harassed by investigations, so much so that many able private citizens were reluctant to enter public employment. Strong foes of communism and of Russian expansion were denounced as "Reds"—religious leaders with liberal beliefs, C.I.O. and A.F. of L. officials, liberal intellectuals. With talk of teachers' oaths, some wondered if academic freedom was in danger.

Communists eliminated civil liberties and insisted on conformity in areas under their control. Were Americans moving in the same direction?

Fortunately, the tradition of civil liberties was very strong in the United States. There were other hopeful signs. Labor had been crushed after World War I. It held its own after World War II. Minority groups had suffered after the armistice in 1918. The years after 1945 brought out some of the same difficulties; but, in addition, there was a strong and partially successful drive against discrimination. Postwar reactions had turned Americans against international cooperation by 1920. At mid-century, by contrast, citizens of the United States were generally favorable toward the UN. Associating reform with radicalism, Americans had turned away from the progressive movement after World War I; and both major parties had become very conservative. The politicians of 1950 may have lacked the crusading zeal of earlier days; but few espoused reaction. The Truman Democrats found that it paid to push the Fair Deal. And the more liberal Republicans—men like Senator Wayne Morse of Oregon and Governor James Duff of Pennsylvania—defeated conservative opponents in the 1950 primaries.

A Better World?

As they entered the second half of the twentieth century, Americans were enjoying great material prosperity. National income was enormous, well over $200,000,000,000 a year. Employment was high, around 60,000,000. Farmers were doing well, workingmen were obtaining some of the security which they had long desired. Improved educational opportunities were making it possible for an increasing number of Americans to satisfy the ambition to enter the professions. Business earnings were at peak levels. Americans had more mechanical conveniences, more cultural opportunities, more leisure than before. Women and minority groups met with less discrimination than in earlier periods. At long last, Americans were learning to conserve their natural resources. On the world front, the United States had more naval and economic power than any other nation; and America was becoming a great scientific and cultural center. If atomic energy could be put to peacetime use, still greater gains might lie ahead.

Yet, in the midst of plenty, Americans were gravely concerned about the future. The rise of Soviet Russia, the threat of communism, the horrors of atomic war bore heavily upon Americans in an age when isolation had become impossible. In the one world of 1950, domestic prosperity no longer seemed enough. It now appeared that no nation was secure while distress and want haunted other sections of the globe. And, despite American wealth and drive, it did not seem possible to build a satisfactory world in a short time, if, indeed, it could be built at all.

Even at home, all was not well. Prosperity appeared to depend in substantial part on exports for which foreign countries could not pay; and on an armament program which increased an already staggering tax burden. The individualism and the opportunity of an earlier America seemed to have faded; and some felt that the United States had suddenly grown old. Predictions of disaster were common, and despair became fashionable in intellectual circles. No longer did Americans speak of the inevitability of progress. Rather they talked of a confused and uncertain future.

In earlier generations, Americans had been overoptimistic. Now they were overpessimistic. There were problems, certainly; but there had been problems before. In facing these problems, Americans were fortunate in having a great store of natural resources; a population that was large and prosperous and relatively homogeneous; a deep attachment to democracy; an ability to meet crises and adjust to change; organizing talent and a critical spirit; and an abiding faith in the value of education. And above all else, Americans still believed in themselves. Their ancestors had conquered the wilderness and built a great republic. Looking backward, Americans were pleased with these accomplishments. Looking forward, they saw signs of trouble and sometimes felt disheartened. Deep down, however, the average citizen of the United States believed that his land would prosper in the future as in the past, and was certain that the history of the American republic was just beginning to unfold.

Bibliography

Those who use this book will want to do additional reading in the field of American history. Here are a few suggestions. By using the bibliographies in the books listed below, the interested reader will be led from these volumes to others. In addition, it is a good idea to follow the book reviews in newspapers and magazines, for example, those in the *Saturday Review of Literature*. For some reason, many persons are reluctant to use the services of reference librarians. This reluctance should be overcome; these specialists know the best guides to special fields, and can help in many other ways.

Readers who desire to explore the American past may use the references in our volume as well as those in this bibliography. As an illustration, the novels cited for each period help give one an understanding of the period and the attitude of Americans at that time. (Upton Sinclair's *Jungle* has the spirit of the muckrakers; John Steinbeck's *Grapes of Wrath* catches the mood of the depression of the 1930's.) It is worthwhile, too, to look up the writings of the leading individuals mentioned: William Jennings Bryan, Henry Ford, John Dewey, Babe Ruth, J. J. Pershing, Samuel Gompers, Frank Lloyd Wright, Booker T. Washington. Limitations of space prevent us from listing more than a handful of these. But nearly every public figure has left his written record, in an autobiography, or collection of letters, or in a volume or volumes setting forth his views and accomplishments.

All libraries have bibliographical aids. H. P. Beers, *Bibliographies in American History*, lists many of these. Special attention is called to the *Book Review Digest*; the *Readers' Guide to Periodical Literature*; G. G. Griffin's annual *Writings on American History*; the *New York Times Index*; and *Who Was Who in America, 1897–1942* (to be supplemented by *Who's Who in America*). Summaries and bibliographical references will be found in three indispensable multi-volume reference works: the *Dictionary of American Biography*; the *Encyclopaedia of the Social Sciences*; and the *Dictionary of American History*. Library card catalogues are also invaluable, especially the subject listings. Those who learn how to look things up will find that the habit sticks, and will derive pleasure from checking on historical novels, movies, and radio programs, and filling in the background as each new issue comes before the American people.

Much can be learned from the use of documents. There are now many excellent collections covering this part of American history. Among these are Merle Curti, *The Social Record* (Vol. I of Thorp, Curti, and Baker, *American Issues*); the Amherst Department of American Studies, *Problems in American Civilization;* T. G. Manning and D. M. Potter, *Government and the American Economy, 1877–present* (Vol. II of *Select Problems in Historical Interpretation*); R. A. Billington, B. J. Loewenberg, and S. H. Brockunier, *The Making of American Democracy, 1865–1950;* H. S. Commager, *Documents of American History;* L. M. Hacker and H. S. Zahler, *The Shaping of the American Tradition.* Donald Sheehan's *Democracy in an Industrial World* (Vol. II of his *Making of American History*) is a useful anthology based on works of historians.

C. O. Paullin, *Atlas of the Historical Geography of the United States,* is standard.

The most readable books in the multi-volume series are the 56 tiny volumes of the *Chronicles of America* (edited by Allen Johnson). *A History of American Life* (edited by A. M. Schlesinger and D. R. Fox) stresses social history. The nine volumes of a new *Economic History of the United States* are now appearing, as are the ten volumes of a new *History of the South* (edited by W. H. Stephenson and E. M. Coulter). *The American Nation* (edited by A. B. Hart) was long standard. A new American Nation series, conceived along somewhat broader lines, is being prepared under the direction of H. S. Commager.

Part I (1850–1896)[1]

There is no thoroughly satisfactory study of the transformation of the United States from an agrarian to an industrial nation. C. A. and M. R. Beard, *Rise of American Civilization,* remains the best introduction. There is much descriptive material in V. S. Clark, *History of Manufactures in the United States* (3 vols.). For an analytical approach, see T. C. Cochran and William Miller, *Age of Enterprise.* Gustavus Myers, *History of the Great American Fortunes,* is a pioneer work, hostile to the rising business leaders. Matthew Josephson's *Robber Barons* follows the same pattern. I. M. Tarbell, *Nationalizing of Business, 1878–98,* is worth attention, as is L. M. Hacker, *Triumph of American Capitalism.* For a popular treatment, J. B. Walker, *Epic of American Industry.* Good brief accounts are B. J. Hendrick, *Age of Big Business,* and John Moody, *Masters of Capital.* A. F. Burns, *Production Trends in the United States since 1870* is useful. For a new approach, D. W. McConnell, *Economic*

---

[1] Attention is also called to the Bibliography in our first volume, especially the General References, and the books dealing with the sectional conflict, 1850–1877. While some of the books included there are also mentioned here, we have where possible tried to add to rather than duplicate listings.

Virtues in the United States; and, for a number of suggestions, J. C. Malin, *An Interpretation of Recent American History.*

There are many histories of industrial areas, industries, and industrial companies. Bayrd Still's *Milwaukee* and Bessie L. Pierce's *Chicago* are two studies of industrial areas; and see the books by Charles Hirschfeld (Baltimore, 1870–1900), H. H. Hatcher (the Western Reserve), and C. M. Green (Holyoke, Massachusetts). For contrast, Angie Debo, *Prairie City.* Of the industry histories, mention may be made of those for carpet manufacture (A. H. Cole and H. F. Williamson), shoes (F. J. Allen), cotton textiles (M. T. Copeland), flour milling (C. B. Kuhlmann), glass (Pearce Davis), steel (H. N. Casson). The company histories include T. C. Cochran, *Pabst Brewing Company;* and G. S. Gibb, *The Whitesmiths of Taunton* (Reed and Barton, silversmiths). Here and in other particulars, H. M. Larson, *Guide to Business History,* is helpful.

Oil has received much attention from historians. Two famous older accounts are hostile to Rockefeller: W. D. Lloyd, *Wealth against Commonwealth,* I. M. Tarbell, *History of the Standard Oil Company.* The more recent studies include P. H. Giddens, *Birth of the Oil Industry;* G. W. Stocking, *Oil Industry and the Competitive System;* John Ise, *United States Oil Policy;* C. C. Rister, *Oil! Titan of the Southwest.* For contrasting interpretations, see Earl Latham (ed.), *John D. Rockefeller—Robber Baron or Industrial Statesman?*

E. R. Johnson's *History of the Domestic and Foreign Commerce of the United States,* though old, is still useful. J. G. B. Hutchins, *American Maritime Industries and Public Policy, 1789–1914,* is recommended. N. E. Whitford has written about the New York State canals. Most of the transportation story, however, is tied up in railroad history. John Moody's *Railroad Builders* is a good introduction; and see L. H. Haney, *Congressional History of Railways, 1850–87.* The regional approach has worked well in railroad history: E. C. Kirkland, *Men, Cities and Transportation* (for New England); C. R. Fish, *Restoration of the Southern Railroads;* R. E. Riegel, *Story of the Western Railroads.* For individual lines, J. B. Hedges, *Henry Villard and the Railways of the Northwest;* and books about the Union Pacific (by Nelson Trottman; by E. L. Sabin), the Central Pacific (Oscar Lewis, *The Big Four*), the Southern Pacific (Stuart Daggett); the Atlantic Coast Line (H. D. Dozier). For the special question of land, P. W. Gates, *Illinois Central Railroad and Its Colonization Work,* and R. C. Overton, *Burlington West.* J. B. Walker has written a popular survey of *Fifty Years of Rapid Transit.*

The broadening character of American business can be seen in Frank Presbrey, *History and Development of Advertising* (and see N. H. Borden's study of the economic effects of advertising); and R. M. Hower's book about N. W. Ayer & Son, an advertising agency). For another aspect of business, J. O. Stalson, *Marketing Life Insurance* (and see the histories of individual companies, by S. B. Clough, and Marquis James). R. M. Hower's history of the New York department store, Macy's, may be compared with T. D. Clark, *Pills, Petticoats and Plows*, which deals with the southern country store.

The best financial history of the United States is the one by W. J. Shultz and M. R. Caine; but see also the older study of D. R. Dewey. A. B. Hepburn's *History of the Coinage and Currency* is useful, as is Neil Carothers' *Fractional Money*. Among the excellent special studies are R. W. Hidy, *House of Baring in American Trade and Finance;* F. C. James, *Growth of Chicago Banks;* R. A. Foulke, *Sinews of American Commerce* (on Dun & Bradstreet, and business credit); J. G. Smith, *Development of Trust Companies;* C. S. Popple, *Development of Two Bank Groups in the Central Northwest;* and N. S. B. Gras, *Massachusetts First National Bank of Boston.* Sidney Ratner's *American Taxation* is an introduction to an important and neglected field. F. W. Taussig and I. M. Tarbell have both written tariff histories. On inflation, see M. S. Wildman, *Money Inflation;* D. C. Barrett, *Greenbacks and the Resumption of Specie Payments;* A. D. Noyes, *Forty Years of American Finance.* F. P. Weberg has written about the *Background of the Panic of 1893.*

In the labor field, the key book is N. J. Ware, *Labor Movement in the United States, 1860–95.* Also helpful are the short general works of M. R. Clark and S. F. Simon; F. R. Dulles; and Selig Perlman. L. L. Lorwin's *American Federation of Labor* is important for this and later periods. Samuel Yellen, *American Labor Struggles,* and Louis Adamic, *Dynamite,* deal with dramatic disputes; and see Edward Berman, *Labor Disputes and the President of the United States.* Special incidents have received attention: the Molly Maguire riots (J. W. Coleman); the Southwest railway strike of 1886 (R. A. Allen); the Haymarket affair (Henry David); the Pullman strike (Almont Lindsey); Coxey's march (D. L. McMurry). For an area approach, I. B. Cross, *History of the Labor Movement in California.*

The basic book for agricultural history in this era is F. A. Shannon, *Farmer's Last Frontier.* E. E. Edwards, *Bibliography of the History of American Agriculture* is indispensable. For general reading, N. S. B. Gras, *History of Agriculture in Europe and America.* A. C. True has written histories of agricultural research, education, and extension work. H. J. Houck's *Century of Indiana Farm Prices 1841–1941,* has general interest, as has Leo Rogin, *Introduction of Farm Machinery.* E. G. Nourse has written about *American Agriculture and the European Market;* G. G. Huebner about *Agricultural Commerce;* and see C. H. Taylor's lengthy work on the

Chicago Board of Trade. J. C. Malin gives many facts and suggests new approaches in his *Grassland of North America, Winter Wheat in the Golden Belt of Kansas,* and other works. John Ise gives a Kansas homestead case study in *Sod and Stubble.* J. G. Thompson treats the *Rise and Decline of the Wheat Growing Industry in Wisconsin,* and H. M. Larson deals with the *Wheat Market and the Farmer in Minnesota, 1858–1900.* (See also Joseph Schafer's *History of Agriculture in Wisconsin,* and E. V. Robinson, *Early Economic Conditions and the Development of Agriculture in Minnesota.*) For science and agriculture, E. J. Russell, *Plant Nutrition and Crop Production.* Edward Wiest, who has written on *Agricultural Organization in the United States,* has also made a study of the butter industry.

The special problems of the South are developed in the general histories of that area by W. B. Hesseltine, and F. B. Simkins; and E. Q. Hawk has done an economic history of the region. R. P. Brooks, *Agrarian Revolution in Georgia, 1865–1912,* is a special study of importance. B. W. Arnold has written a monograph on tobacco in Virginia in this period; and see the more general works by J. C. Robert (*Story of Tobacco*) and Meyer Jacobstein (*Tobacco Industry*). M. B. Hammond's old book on the *Cotton Industry* is still useful; and see R. B. Vance, *Human Factors in Cotton Culture;* and A. F. Raper and I. D. Reid, *Sharecroppers All;* and Shields McIlwaine, *Southern Poor-White.* W. J. Cash's *Mind of the South* is worth reading.

There is an extensive list of books on the New South. Of the older items, see Holland Thompson, *New South,* and *From the Cotton Field to the Cotton Mill;* also P. A. Bruce, *Rise of the New South.* Of the newer books, attention is directed to Broadus Mitchell, *Rise of the Cotton Mills in the South,* and his *Industrial Revolution in the South* (with G. S. Mitchell). See also B. F. Lemert, *Cotton Textile Industry of the Southern Appalachian Piedmont;* and W. K. Boyd, *Story of Durham.*

There are many general histories of the West and the westward movement: D. E. Clark, L. R. Hafen and C. C. Rister; E. D. Branch; R. A. Billington and J. B. Hedges; R. E. Riegel; F. L. Paxson. *The Early Writings of Frederick Jackson Turner* may be supplemented by the readings in G. R. Taylor's *Turner Thesis;* and for further readings, see I. F. Woestemeyer and J. M. Gambrill, *Westward Movement.* For an excellent bibliography, E. E. Edwards, *References on the Significance of the Frontier in American History.* W. P. Webb's *Great Plains* is an important interpretation. J. C. Parish, *Persistence of the Westward Movement,* E. S. Pomeroy, *Territories and the United States, 1861–90,* and F. L. Paxson, *Last American Frontier,* all cover a good deal of ground. H. E. Briggs has written about the *Frontiers of the Northwest;* G. S. Dumke, the *Boom of the Eighties in*

Southern California; E. N. Dick, the *Sod-House Frontier, 1854–90.* Much of the story of the West is told in histories of special areas, e.g., Northwest (O. O. Winther); Oklahoma (E. E. Dale and M. L. Wardell; Grant Foreman); Nevada (E. M. Mack); Montana (J. K. Howard); Colorado (P. S. Fritz); California (J. W. Caughey).

For land policy, there are general works (B. H. Hibbard, R. M. Robbins); and special studies, such as H. O. Brayer's study of the activities of the English capitalist William Blackmore; and A. N. Chandler, *Land Title Origins;* and Reuben McKitrick, *Public Land System of Texas.* P. W. Gates, *Wisconsin Pine Lands of Cornell University,* is an excellent case study. For mining, T. A. Rickard, *History of American Mining;* W. J. Trimble, *Mining Advance into the Inland Kingdom;* Oscar Lewis, *Silver Kings.* For law enforcement, Wayne Gard, *Frontier Justice;* W. P. Webb, *Texas Rangers;* and F. H. Harrington, *Hanging Judge.* L. B. Priest, *Uncle Sam's Stepchildren* deals with Indian policy, 1865–87; and see the special works on the Indians of the Southwest (E. E. Dale), the Cheyenne (G. B. Grinnell), the Apache (R. H. Ogle), the Five Civilized Tribes (M. L. Wardell; Angie Debo; Grant Foreman).

E. D. Branch, *Hunting of the Buffalo,* is most interesting. For the cattle industry, E. S. Osgood, *Day of the Cattleman,* and O. B. Peake, *Colorado Range Cattle Industry,* and the works of E. E. Dale. See also R. A. Clemen, *American Livestock and Meat Industry.*

For the overall social and intellectual pattern, see Merle Curti, *Growth of American Thought.* Also valuable are C. A. and M. R. Beard, *American Spirit;* V. L. Parrington, *Beginnings of Critical Realism* (Vol. III of his *Main Currents in American Thought*); R. H. Gabriel, *Course of American Democratic Thought;* H. S. Commager, *American Mind.* Richard Hofstadter's *Social Darwinism in American Thought* has special significance; and see P. P. Wiener, *Evolution and the Founders of Pragmatism.* There are histories of American philosophy (H. W. Schneider, I. W. Riley), political theory (R. G. Gettell), ethnological theory (R. H. Lowie). Joseph Dorfman's *Economic Mind in American Civilization* is recommended for the serious student. Much can be gained from books on the thought of individual leaders, e.g., William James (R. B. Berry), John Dewey (Sidney Hook, W. T. Feldman), Henry George (G. R. Geiger).

For social history, the best introduction is provided by Allan Nevins, *Emergence of Modern America, 1865–78,* and A. M. Schlesinger, *Rise of the City, 1878–98.* The pioneer work by A. W. Calhoun, *Social History of the American Family,* is still the best available. Among the interesting popular works are R. O. Cummings, *American and His Food, A History of Health Habits* (and see E. C. May, *Canning Clan*); Dixon Wecter, *Saga of American Society;* A. M. Schlesinger, *Learning How to Behave;* F. R.

Dulles, *America Learns to Play;* Lloyd Lewis, *Oscar Wilde Discovers America.* Bellamy Partridge and Otto Bettmann, *As We Were: Family Life in America, 1850–1900,* is one of many picture books. T. H. Greer has written about *American Social Reform Movements* (since 1865).

There are several short histories of American religion: W. W. Sweet (*Story of Religions in America; American Churches*), F. X. Curran (*Major Trends in American Church History*), W. E. Garrison (*March of Faith*), H. K. Rowe (*History of Religion in the United States*). The rise of Catholicism is described in Theodore Maynard, *Story of American Catholicism.* Three highly significant books are A. I. Abell, *Urban Impact on American Protestantism, 1865–1900;* C. H. Hopkins, *Rise of the Social Gospel in American Protestantism, 1865–1915;* and Sidney Warren, *American Freethought, 1860–1914.* Important, too, are H. F. May, *Protestant Churches and Industrial America;* Stow Persons, *Free Religion;* James Dombrowski, *Early Days of Christian Socialism in America;* D. D. Williams, *Andover Liberals;* Gustavus Myers, *History of Bigotry in the United States;* G. S. Eddy, *A Century with Youth* (Y.M.C.A.). T. H. A. LeDuc, *Piety and Intellect at Amherst College,* is a case study of great interest.

There are general histories of education (E. P. Cubberley, E. W. Knight), studies of higher education (C. F. Thwing), of education for women (Thomas Woody), of Negro education (H. M. Bond). Merle Curti's *Social Ideas of American Educators* ties education to the trend of the times. C. F. Thwing, *The American and the German University,* is worth attention; and see J. A. Walz, *German Influence in American Education and Culture.* The last few years have brought forth many excellent studies of individual universities, including studies of Wisconsin (Merle Curti and Vernon Carstensen), Pennsylvania (E. P. Cheyney), Johns Hopkins (J. C. French), Cornell (C. L. Becker; W. P. Rogers), Mt. Holyoke (A. C. Cole), Wellesley (A. P. Hackett), Catholic University (J. T. Ellis), Western Reserve School of Medicine (F. C. Waite), C.C.N.Y. (S. W. Rudy), Iowa State (E. D. Ross), College of Charleston (J. H. Easterby), Georgia Tech (M. L. Brittain), Duke (N. C. Chaffin), Vanderbilt (Edwin Mims), Dartmouth (L. B. Richardson), Chicago (T. W. Goodspeed), Wilberforce (F. A. McGinnis), Rensselaer Polytechnic Institute (P. C. Ricketts). E. D. Ross, *Democracy's College,* is important for the land-grant colleges. For literature, the new *Literary History of the United States,* edited by R. E. Spiller and others, stands out above everything else. The bibliography, which constitutes Vol. III, is excellent. Of the earlier surveys, that of F. L. Pattee deserves notice (*History of American Literature Since 1870*). Three studies merit special attention: Oscar Cargill, *Intellectual America,* W. F. Taylor, *Economic Novel,* and Van Wyck Brooks, *New England: Indian Summer, 1865–1915.* A. H. Quinn has

written *History of the American Drama from the Civil War to the Present.*
For history writing, W. S. Holt (ed.), *Historical Scholarship in the United
States, 1876–1901;* M. Kraus, *History of American History;* E. F. Goldman
(ed.), *Historiography and Urbanization;* W. T. Hutchinson (ed.), *Marcus
W. Jernegan Essays in American Historiography.* There are histories of
American journalism by F. L. Mott, by J. M. Lee, by W. G. Bleyer. See
also T. D. Clark, *Southern Country Editor;* and histories of individual pa-
pers (e.g., *The Sunpapers of Baltimore,* by G. W. Johnson and others; *The
Evening Post,* by Allan Nevins).

There is an outstanding book on the fine arts: O. W. Larkin, *Art and
Life in America.* The general reader will like Lewis Mumford, *Sticks and
Stones,* and *Brown Decades.* H. Cahill, *American Folk Art: Art of the
Common Man, 1750–1900* is instructive, as are D. Ewen, *Music Comes to
America,* and S. Spaeth, *History of Popular Music in America.* No one
should miss J. M. Fitch, *American Building.* There are many histories of
American painting (C. H. Chaffin; Samuel Isham and Royal Cortissoz;
Eugen Neuhaus), sculpture (Lorado Taft; L. H. Dodd), architecture (T.
E. Tallmadge; S. F. Kimball; T. F. Hamlin), music (J. T. Howard, L. C.
Elson). M. R. Rogers has written about *American Interior Design;* Wolf-
gang Born has specialized books on still-life and landscape painting. P. D.
Magriel's *Chronicles of the American Dance* deals with an often neglected
field. *Art in America,* edited by Holger Cahill and A. H. Barr, Jr., has much
good material.

There is no history of American science. For invention, see Roger
Burlingame, *Engines of Democracy: Inventions and Society in Mature
America;* Holland Thompson, *Age of Invention;* W. B. Kaempffert, *Popu-
lar History of American Invention;* George Iles, *Leading American Inven-
tors;* and E. W. Byrn, *Progress of Invention.* W. B. Bennett's *American
Patent System* is useful. For special fields, see H. N. Casson, *History of the
Telephone;* T. C. Martin and S. L. Coles, *Story of Electricity;* Malcolm
McLaren, *Rise of the Electrical Industry.* J. H. Collins has written the
Story of Canned Foods, and William Haynes is publishing a multi-volume
history of the chemical industry.

E. S. Dana's *Century of Science in America* has value, despite its limita-
tions. So do Bernard Jaffe's *Men of Science in America* and J. G. Crowther's
Famous American Men of Science and Paul DeKruif's *Microbe Hunters.*
J. W. Fay has written about *American Psychology before William James.*
There is more on medical history than in other fields. See R. H. Shryock,
Development of Modern Medicine; H. E. Sigerist, *American Medicine;*
H. H. Moore, *Public Health;* M. P. Ravenel, *Half-Century of Public
Health,* (1871–1921); R. D. Leigh, *Federal Health Administration.* Special
studies of importance include G. C. Whipple, *State Sanitation* (on the

Massachusetts Board of Health); K. C. Hurd-Mead, *Medical Women of America*; W. C. Posey and S. H. Brown, *Wills Hospital of Philadelphia*; Albert Deutsch, *Mentally Ill in America*. Research in other specialties is described in the histories of American chemistry (E. F. Smith), entomology (H. B. Weiss), geology (G. P. Merrill); and see C. A. Weber's *Naval Observatory*.

For immigration, see M. R. Davie, *World Immigration*; M. L. Hansen, *Immigrant in American History*; Carl Wittke, *We Who Built America*; G. M. Stephenson, *History of American Immigration*. For special groups, there are worthwhile books on the Scandinavians (K. C. Babcock), the Swedes (A. B. Benson and Naboth Hedin), Norwegians (C. C. Qualey, T. C. Blegen), Irish (E. F. Roberts), Germans (A. B. Faust), Chinese (M. R. Coolidge), Poles (W. I. Thomas and Florian Znaniecki), Russians (Jerome Davis), Jews (Samuel Joseph; B. J. Hendrick; Peter Wiernik), Hungarians (Emil Lengyel), Ukrainians (Wasyl Halich), Italians (R. F. Foerster). M. L. Hansen and J. B. Brebner have written of the *Mingling of the Canadian and American Peoples*.

The Negro has received much attention from historians in recent years. Among the general books are J. H. Franklin, *From Slavery to Freedom*; E. F. Frazier, *Negro in the United States*; C. S. Johnson, *Negro in American Civilization*; C. G. Woodson, *Negro in Our History*; and B. G. Brawley, *Social History of the American Negro*. More specialized are W. F. Nowlin, *Negro in American National Politics*; C. H. Wesley, *Negro Labor in the United States*; and V. L. Wharton, *Negro in Mississippi, 1865–90*.

Political history is described in detail in E. P. Oberholtzer, *History of the United States Since the Civil War* (5 vols.). More interesting are H. T. Peck, *Twenty Years of the Republic*; W. E. Binkley, *American Political Parties* (and see his *President and Congress*); and Matthew Josephson, *Politicos*. P. H. Buck's *Road to Reunion* treats North-South relations. F. E. Haynes, *Third Party Movements Since the Civil War*, and Nathan Fine, *Labor and Farmer Parties, 1828–1928* are survey treatments. The special studies include C. M. Destler, *American Radicalism, 1865–1901*; E. B. Usher, *Greenback Movement*; S. J. Buck, *Granger Movement* and his *Agrarian Crusade*; and J. D. Hicks, *Populist Revolt*. Populism and related movements are studied for several states: Georgia (A. M. Arnett), Alabama (J. B. Clark), Texas (R. C. Martin), Virginia (W. D. Sheldon), North Dakota (P. R. Fossum). For the regular political pattern, everyone should read James Bryce's classic *American Commonwealth*. Gustavus Myers and M. R. Werner have written histories of Tammany Hall. Edward Stanwood has covered presidential elections in his *History of the Presidency*. There are special studies for 1884 (H. C. Thomas) and 1892 (G. H. Knoles). For veteran influence, see the volumes of J. W. Oliver and W. H.

Glasson, on pensions; Dixon Wecter's general book, *When Johnny Comes Marching Home;* and F. H. Heck's monograph on the *Civil War Veteran in Minnesota.*

Constitutional history is treated in excellent surveys by A. H. Kelly and W. A. Harbison; and by C. B. Swisher. Charles Warren's standard history of the Supreme Court may be contrasted with that of Gustavus Myers; and see L. B. Boudin, *Government by Judiciary.* Other useful books are Willard Hurst, *The Growth of American Law;* E. S. Corwin, *Court over Constitution* and *Twilight of the Supreme Court;* B. F. Wright, *Growth of American Constitutional Law;* R. L. Mott, *Due Process of Law;* and C. O. Gregory, *Labor and the Law.*

The industrial leaders of the nineteenth century lend themselves to biographical treatment. Most of the biographies are either very friendly or very hostile. Thus J. K. Winkler has written somewhat critically of J. D. Rockefeller, Andrew Carnegie, James B. Duke. These figures are defended by Allan Nevins, B. J. Hendrick, J. W. Jenkins. There are biographies of many iron and steel men: Henry Clay Frick (G. B. M. Harvey), Henry W. Oliver (H. O. Evans), Abram Hewitt (Allan Nevins), Peter Cooper (E. C. Mack), the Merritts (Paul DeKruif). For other fields see lives of G. F. Swift (L. F. Swift), the Guggenheims (Harvey O'Connor), the Roeblings (D. B. Steinman), Cyrus McCormick (W. T. Hutchinson), Cornelius Vanderbilt (W. J. Lane; and, for later Vanderbilts, Wayne Andrews, *The Vanderbilt Legend*), Daniel Drew (Bouck White), Jim Fisk (R. H. Fuller).

Examples of many biographies of educators are those of D. C. Gilman (Fabian Franklin), C. W. Eliot (H. H. Saunderson). For literary figures, see lives of Mark Twain (A. B. Paine; Bernard DeVoto); William Dean Howells (O. W. Firkins); Walt Whitman (H. S. Canby); Edward Bellamy (A. E. Morgan); H. H. Bancroft (J. W. Caughey); Horatio Alger (H. R. Mayes); Helen Hunt Jackson (Ruth Odell). In the religious field, see books on Dwight Moody (Gamaliel Bradford), Mary Baker G. Eddy (L. P. Powell; E. S. Bates and J. V. Dittemore), Walter Rauschenbusch (D. R. Sharpe). In the field of ideas, there are biographies of Lester F. Ward (by Samuel Chuggerman), William Graham Sumner (H. E. Starr), Thorstein Veblen (Joseph Dorfman). F. O. Matthiessen, *James Family,* is important. In the field of science, see biographies of T. A. Edison (F. L. Dyer and T. C. Martin); George Westinghouse (H. G. Prout); Willard Gibbs the physicist (Muriel Rukeyser) and Joseph Henry (Thomas Coulson); O. C. Marsh, paleontologist (C. Schuchert and C. M. LeVene); Lewis Henry Morgan, ethnologist, (B. J. Stern); William H. Welch, medicine (Simon and J. T. Flexner).

There are many biographies in the arts. As examples, see books about

Whistler (by E. R. and Joseph Pennell), Thomas Eakins (Lloyd Goodrich), George Inness (Elizabeth McCausland), Augustus St. Gaudens (Royal Cortissoz), Albert Ryder (F. N. Price), Theodore Thomas (C. E. Russell), H. H. Richardson (H. R. Hitchcock), Winslow Homer (Kenyon Cox), F. L. Olmsted (his son and Theodora Kimble), Louis Sullivan (Hugh Morrison).

Political biographies are even more abundant. For Presidents, see biographies of Grant (W. B. Hesseltine), Hayes (H. J. Eckenrode), Garfield (R. G. Caldwell), Arthur (G. F. Howe), Cleveland (Allan Nevins), McKinley (C. S. Olcott). Lesser figures: Roscoe Conkling (D. B. Chidsey), J. G. Blaine (D. S. Muzzey), Hamilton Fish (Allan Nevins); Czar Reed (W. A. Robinson), W. E. Chandler (L. B. Richardson), J. G. Carlisle (J. A. Barnes), J. S. Morton (J. C. Olson), Philetus Sawyer (R. N. Current), B. H. Hill (H. J. Pearce), L. Q. C. Lamar (W. A. Cate), Henry M. Teller (Elmer Ellis). The biographies of Mark Hanna (Herbert Croly, Thomas Beer) are worth attention. There is no satisfactory life of Bryan, although there are biographies by Paxton Hibben, M. R. Werner, W. C. Williams, and others. For reformers, see Harry Barnard's life of J. P. Altgeld, F. E. Haynes' of James B. Weaver, C. V. Woodward's of Tom Watson, Stuart Noblin's of L. L. Polk; and see F. B. Simkins on Ben Tillman, Mary Earhart on Frances Willard, Alma Lutz on Elizabeth Cady Stanton, Caro Lloyd on Henry Demarest Lloyd. Of the journalists, there are books about E. L. Godkin (Rollo Ogden), Frank Munsey (George Britt), Henry W. Grady (R. B. Nixon). In the constitutional field, the studies include those concerning Justice Field (C. B. Swisher), Justice Miller (Charles Fairman), Chief Justice Waite (B. R. Trimble).

There are many important autobiographies. Outstanding among these is the *Education of Henry Adams*. Others who have told their own story include Andrew Carnegie, G. F. Hoar, Walter Damrosch, General Nelson A. Miles, T. V. Powderly, Boss T. C. Platt, Frances Willard, Henry Villard, Booker T. Washington.

E. H. O'Neill, *Biography by Americans* is a useful bibliography.

Part II (1896–1919)

(Books given above in Part I will not be listed again in Parts II and III.)
Several authors have written books treating the United States in the first half of the twentieth century: O. T. Barck, Jr., and N. M. Blake; F. R. Dulles; Harvey Wish; D. L. Dumond; Jeannette and R. F. Nichols; H. B. Parkes.

Roger Burlingame, *Backgrounds of Power*, deals with mass production; and see Harry Jerome, *Mechanization in Industry*. A. A. Bright, *The Electric Lamp Industry* is very useful. R. C. Epstein's *Automobile Industry* is a good survey. For recent company histories, J. W. Hammond, *Men and Volts* (General Electric); and B. Emmet and J. E. Jeuck, *Catalogues and Counters* (Sears, Roebuck).

For the rise in banker influence, G. W. Edwards, *Evolution of Finance Capitalism*; F. L. Allen, *Lords of Creation*; L. D. Brandeis, *Other People's Money*; and Lewis Corey, *House of Morgan: A Social Biography of the Masters of Money*. There are many books about the trust movement. John Moody, *Truth about the Trusts* is a good introduction. H. W. Laidler, *Concentration of Control in American Industry* is good; and see J. W. Jenks and W. E. Clark, *Trust Problem*; A. A. Berle and G. C. Means, *Modern Corporation*. There are special studies of combinations in specific fields, e.g., by Eliot Jones and by Scott Nearing for coal.

The anti-trust movement has attracted many historians. See M. W. Watkins, *Industrial Combination and Public Policy*; W. O. Knauth, *Policy of the United States towards Industrial Monopoly*; D. M. Keezer and Stacy May, *Public Control of Business*; and J. D. Clark, *Federal Trust Policy*. A. H. Walker has written a *History of the Sherman Law*.

In the labor field, Whitney Coombs has surveyed the wages of unskilled workers, 1890–1924; P. H. Douglas has studied real wages, 1890–1926; and Leo Wolman the growth of unions, 1880–1923. E. E. Witte's *Government in Labor Disputes* is good; and see M. R. Carroll, *Labor and Politics*; and L. S. Reed, *Labor Philosophy of Samuel Gompers*. *Labor and the Sherman Act*, has been handled by Edward Berman, *Labor Injunctions* by Felix Frankfurter and Nathan Greene. For the left wing, D. J. Saposs, *Left Wing Unionism*, and books on the I.W.W. by P. F. Brissenden, J. S. Gambs, and R. Chaplin. The special monographs include H. L. Hurwitz, *Theodore Roosevelt and Labor in New York State, 1880–1900*; Gladys Boone, *Women's Trade Union League*; and John Lombardi, *Labor's Voice in the Cabinet*. John Spargo's *Syndicalism, Industrial Unionism and Socialism* is also worth attention.

For the life of the people, the best survey is H. U. Faulkner, *Quest for Social Justice, 1898–1914*. Mark Sullivan's *Our Times*, a six-volume journalistic account, runs from the 1890's through the 1920's, and is well worth consulting. G. W. Johnson, *Incredible Tale*, is an effort to present the history of the average citizen since 1900. D. L. Cohn, *Good Old Days*, draws on old Sears Roebuck catalogues. Roger Butterfield, *American Past*, uses the pictorial method with some success.

The central problem of urbanization has concerned many writers: J. G. Thompson, *Urbanization*; Lewis Mumford, *Culture of Cities*, R. D. McKenzie, *Metropolitan Community*; J. A. Fairlie, *Municipal Administration*; W. G. Ogburn, *Social Characteristics of Cities*, are representative. Allan Nevins and J. A. Krout, *The Greater City*, covers New York from

1898 to 1948. For contrast, see J. M. Williams, *Our Rural Heritage*. For a study of the rich in relation to urban growth, see Wayne Andrews, *Battle for Chicago*.

M. G. White, *Social Thought in America*, is on the twentieth century. Alfred Kazin, *On Native Grounds*, and Lloyd Morris, *Postscript to Yesterday*, are interpretations based on literary materials; and see Granville Hicks, *Great Tradition*, a leftist survey.

The fight against immigration is told in R. L. Garis, *Immigration Restriction*, and in R. W. Paul, *Abrogation of the Gentlemen's Agreement*. E. N. Saveth's *American Historians and European Immigrants, 1875–1925*, suggests the need for further attitude studies.

G. B. Smith (ed.), *Religious Thought*, deals with the early twentieth century. S. G. Cole's *History of Fundamentalism* may be read in connection with F. H. Foster, *Modern Movement in American Theology*, and Maynard Shipley, *War on Modern Science*.

A *Quarter Century of Learning* covers 1904–29; and see A. E. Meyer, *Development of Education in the Twentieth Century*, and J. E. Russell, *Trend in American Education*. J. S. Noffsinger has written on correspondence schools and lyceums; W. S. Bittner and H. F. Mallory on university correspondence teaching; G. H. Wilson on education and the Y.W.C.A.; while F. P. Keppel has told the story about the early work of the foundations.

The growing interest in research is seen in R. H. Shryock's *American Medical Research*; in G. A. Weber's studies of Department of Agriculture bureaus; and in such popular works as Paul DeKruif's *Hunger Fighters* (food research) and C. M. Wilson's *Ambassadors in White* (tropical medicine). J. K. Hall and others have written *One Hundred Years of American Psychiatry*; C. E. A. Winslow, *Evolution and Significance of the Modern Public Health Campaign*. Victor Robinson, *White Caps*, deals with nursing. For an area study, see W. T. Howard's monograph on disease and public health in Baltimore, 1797–1920.

There are many books on the arts in the twentieth century. Some representative works: architecture (Sigfried Giedion), painting (M. C. Cheney), sculpture (C. L. Brummé), ballet (George Amberg), music (J. T. Howard).

There are some splendid books on the progressive movement. John Chamberlain, *Farewell to Reform*, is outstanding; so is Louis Filler, *Crusaders for American Liberalism*. Richard Hofstadter, *American Political Tradition*, is good for this period, as for others. Matthew Josephson, *President Makers, 1896–1919*, is good, as is C. C. Regier, *Era of the Muckrakers*. G. E. Mowry, *Theodore Roosevelt and the Progressive Movement*, and K. W. Hechler, *Insurgency*, both of which focus on the Taft era, are first-rate special studies. E. E. Robinson has studied the *Presidential Vote, 1896–1932.*

Lincoln Steffens' *Shame of the Cities*, introduces the municipal story. Harold Zink, *City Bosses*, and D. B. Eaton, *Government of Municipalities*, may be supplemented by C. W. Patton, *Battle for Municipal Reform.*

There should be more state studies of the progressive movement. We have some: Vermont (W. A. Flint); New Jersey (R. E. Noble, Jr.), Oregon (A. H. Eaton); Wisconsin (Charles McCarthy and A. F. Lovejoy, on the primary). Labor legislation is handled on a state basis, e.g., by E. R. Beckner (Illinois), Rhode Island (J. K. Towles), Pennsylvania (J. L. Barnard). H. F. Gosnell's realistic study of Boss Platt's New York machine helps put the progressive movement into focus.

Various issues have been dealt with in detail: woman suffrage (C. C. Catt); the initiative, referendum, and recall (W. B. Munro; and, for the referendum, E. P. Oberholtzer); food and drug regulation (Stephen Wilson); conservation (C. R. VanHise and Loomis Havemeyer; also A. E. Parkins and J. R. Whitaker; and, for state activity, C. J. Hynning; A. T. Mason's *Bureaucracy Convicts Itself* is also excellent). For those who wanted to go further, see Morris Hillquit's history of American Socialism. Wilson's approach to problems is discussed in William Diamond, *Economic Thought of Woodrow Wilson.* T. C. Blaisdell, Jr., has written about the Federal Trade Commission, E. W. Kemmerer and many others about the Federal Reserve System, A. F. Macdonald about federal aid, W. S. Holt about the farm loan system, and federal roads.

For problems of political control, see P. D. Hasbrouck, *Party Government in the House of Representatives*; G. H. Haynes, *Senate*; and several books on presidential power (E. S. Corwin; W. E. Binkley; G. F. Milton). C. E. Merriam, *American Political Ideas*, and E. R. Lewis, *History of American Political Thought*, are recommended. In constitutional history, see B. H. Meyer, *History of the Northern Securities Case*; R. G. Fuller, *Child Labor and the Constitution*; Felix Frankfurter, *Mr. Justice Holmes*; R. E. Cushman, *Independent Regulatory Commissions*; and C. G. Haines, *American Doctrine of Judicial Supremacy.*

The general histories of American diplomacy supply the background (T. A. Bailey; S. F. Bemis; R. W. VanAlstyne). For expansion, A. K. Weinberg, *Manifest Destiny*; J. W. Pratt, *Expansionists of 1898*; A. L. P. Dennis, *Adventures in American Diplomacy*; A. C. Coolidge, *United States as a World Power*; A. F. Tyler, *Foreign Policy of James G. Blaine*; Scott Nearing and Joseph Freeman, *Dollar Diplomacy.* For the Spanish war, Walter Millis, *Martial Spirit*; J. E. Wisan, *Cuban Crisis as Reflected in the New York Press*; M. M. Wilkerson, *Public Opinion and the Spanish-American War*; W. S. Holt, *Treaties Defeated by the Senate.* W. H. Haas,

American Empire, and G. L. Kirk, *Philippine Independence*, deal with the later story.

American activity in the Pacific during the expansion era is treated in A. W. Griswold, *Far Eastern Policy of the United States;* Tyler Dennett, *Roosevelt and the Russo-Japanese War;* T. A. Bailey, *Theodore Roosevelt and the Japanese-American Crises;* S. K. Stevens, *American Expansion in Hawaii;* G. H. Ryden, *Foreign Policy of the United States in Relation to Samoa;* F. H. Harrington, *God, Mammon and the Japanese* (on Korea); F. R. Dulles, *China and America;* P. J. Treat, *Diplomatic Relations between the United States and Japan;* E. H. Zabriskie, *American-Russian Rivalry in the Far East, 1895–1914.*

For Latin America, S. F. Bemis, *Latin American Policy of the United States;* Dexter Perkins, *Hands Off!;* W. H. Callcott, *Caribbean Policy of the United States;* H. C. Hill, *Roosevelt and the Caribbean;* M. W. Williams, *Anglo-American Isthmian Diplomacy;* D. C. Miner, *Fight for the Panama Route.* Sharply critical of American policy are the Vanguard books dealing with American policy in Cuba (L. H. Jenks), Puerto Rico (B. W. and J. W. Diffie), Central America (C. D. Kepner and J. H. Soothill), Bolivia (M. A. Marsh), Colombia (J. F. Rippy), Haiti (A. C. Millspaugh), the Dominican Republic (M. M. Knight).

American relations with Europe are treated in J. F. Rippy, *America and the Strife of Europe;* L. M. Gelber, *Rise of Anglo-American Friendship;* Forrest Davis, *Atlantic System;* C. E. Schieber, *Transformation of American Sentiment Toward Germany, 1870–1914;* Halvdan Koht, *American Spirit in Europe;* R. H. Heindel, *American Impact on Great Britain, 1898–1914;* Philip Rahv, *Discovery of Europe;* and M. W. Graham, *American Diplomacy in the International Community.*

H. H. and Margaret Sprout, *Rise of American Naval Power*, and W. E. Livezey, *Mahan on Sea Power*, provide the best introduction. See also D. W. Mitchell, *History of the Modern American Navy;* O. J. Clinard, *Japan's Influence on American Naval Power, 1897–1917;* and G. C. O'Gara, *Theodore Roosevelt and the Rise of the Modern Navy.* For the peace movement, Merle Curti, *Peace or War;* and his special study, *Bryan and World Peace.*

Students of Wilson's foreign policy may well begin with Harley Notter, *Origins of the Foreign Policy of Woodrow Wilson.* Charles Seymour's *American Diplomacy during the World War* covers the whole subject. Seymour's *American Neutrality*, N. D. Baker's *Why We Went to War*, and Dexter Perkins' *America and Two Wars* take a pro-Wilson view on American entry into the war. C. H. Grattan, *Why We Fought*, Walter Millis, *Road to War*, and C. C. Tansill, *America Goes to War*, take the other side. H. C. Peterson, *Propaganda for War* is important, as are the books by C. J. Child and Carl Wittke on German-Americans, and A. M. Morrissey, *American Defense of Neutral Rights, 1914–1917.*

For American participation in the war, F. L. Paxson, *American Democracy and the World War* is an overall account; its three volumes cover the years from 1913 to 1923. On the military side, T. G. Frothingham, *American Reinforcement in the World War.* J. G. Harbord has written about the army, W. S. Sims and B. J. Hendrick the navy, Johnson Hagood the Services of Supply. B. M. Baruch's *American Industry in the War* is important. See also the works of W. D. Hines (railroads), C. R. VanHise (conservation and regulation), W. C. Mullendore (food), L. P. Todd (education), A. D. Noyes (finance), W. F. Willoughby (government organization). For the C.P.I., J. R. Mock and Cedric Larson, *Words that Won the War.* Mock has also written on *Censorship, 1917;* and see Zechariah Chafee, *Free Speech in the United States.* J. M. Clark has figured the *Costs of the World War,* and J. R. Mock and Evangeline Thurber have written a Report on Demobilization. For the peace settlement, D. F. Fleming, *United States and the League of Nations,* and T. A. Bailey, *Wilson and the Peacemakers.*

Favorable biographies of business leaders include books about E. H. Harriman (George Kennan), J. J. Hill (J. G. Pyle), Elbert Gary (I. M. Tarbell), Alfred I. DuPont (Marquis James), J. P. Morgan (Carl Hovey, H. L. Satterlee). F. L. Allen and J. K. Winkler have written of Morgan in a more critical fashion. F. B. Copley's biography of Frederick Taylor, the father of scientific management, is very pro-Taylor.

There are relatively few books about labor leaders; but see Elsie Gluck on John Mitchell, R. H. Harvey on Samuel Gompers. The social settlement workers have received some attention; there are lives of Jane Addams (J. W. Linn) and Lillian Wald (R. L. Duffus). A reform lawyer, Clarence Darrow, has been written up by Irving Stone; Moorfield Storey, active in many reforms, by M. A. D. Howe.

In science and related fields, there are books about Seaman Knapp (J. C. Bailey), G. W. Goethals (J. B. and F. Bishop), George Washington Carver (Rackham Holt), the Doctors Mayo (H. B. Clapesattle), Harvey C. Cushing (J. F. Fulton), Walter Reed (L. N. Wood), William C. Gorgas (M. D. Gorgas and B. J. Hendrick), John Merle Coulter (A. D. Rodgers).

Educators are the subjects of many biographies: Booker T. Washington (B. J. Mathews), J. H. Kirkland (Edwin Mims), J. B. McMaster (E. F. Goldman), A. Lawrence Lowell (H. A. Youmans). Of the literary biographies, mention may be made of the books on Theodore Dreiser (R. H. Elias; Dorothy Dudley); Edith Wharton (Percy Lubbock); Willa Cather (René Rapin); Frank Norris (Franklin Walker); Jack London (Irving

Stone). A. S. Will has written a life of Cardinal Gibbons, P. W. Wilson a biography of Evangeline Booth.

A good many journalists have received attention from biographers. J. K. Winkler has written critically about William Randolph Hearst, as have E. S. Bates and Oliver Carlson; compare with the life by Mrs. Frémont Older. D. C. Seitz has dealt with Joseph Pulitzer, J. W. Tebbel with George Horace Lorimer, G. W. Johnson with Adolph Ochs. Elmer Ellis' book on F. P. Dunne ("Mr. Dooley") is recommended.

Of the military biographies, two are singled out for notice: W. D. Puleston's life of A. T. Mahan, E. E. Morison's of Admiral W. S. Sims.

The period is rich in political biographies. H. F. Pringle has written the best biographies of Theodore Roosevelt, and of William Howard Taft. H. C. F. Bell's *Woodrow Wilson and the People* is the best single volume; A. S. Link is bringing out a multi-volume Wilson. There are biographies of E. V. Debs (Ray Ginger), Joe Cannon (L. W. Busbey), George W. Norris (Alfred Lief), Nelson W. Aldrich (N. W. Stephenson), Elihu Root (P. C. Jessup), Henry Cabot Lodge (Karl Schriftgiesser, highly hostile), Walter Clark (A. L. Brooks), Carter Glass (Rixey Smith and Norman Beasley), Newton D. Baker (Frederick Palmer), John Sharp Williams (G. C. Osborn), Carrie Chapman Catt (M. G. Peck), E. M. House (A. D. H. Smith), Peter Norbeck (G. D. Fite), J. A. Johnson (W. G. Helmes). In the constitutional field, there are lives of Chief Justice White (M. L. Klinkhamer), Chief Justice Fuller (W. L. King), and Justices Brandeis (A. T. Mason), and Holmes (C. D. Bowen; Silas Bent).

Best of the autobiographies is that of Lincoln Steffens. Others of importance are those of Samuel Gompers, Theodore Roosevelt, Williams Jennings Bryan, Robert M. LaFollette, S. S. McClure, Cardinal Gibbons, Josephus Daniels, J. J. Pershing, Tom L. Johnson, George Creel, Edward K. Bok, Bill Haywood, Louis Sullivan.

Part III (Since 1919)

(Books given in Parts I and II will not be listed again here.)

The material on American history since World War I is enormous in every field. George Soule, *Prosperity Decade*, and Broadus Mitchell, *Depression Decade*, constitute an economic history of the period between the wars. *Recent Economic Changes* contains useful information.

For the continuing concentration movement, A. R. Burns, *Decline of Competition*; David Lynch, *Concentration of Economic Power*; Twentieth Century Fund, *Big Business*; Ferdinand Lundberg, *America's Sixty Families*; Clair Wilcox, *Competition and Monopoly*. See also Wendell Berge,

Cartels, and C. D. Edwards, *Economic and Political Aspects of International Cartels.* T. W. Arnold, *Folklore of Capitalism,* and Lewis Corey, *Decline of American Capitalism,* are worth consulting.

For the relationship of the government to business, the following are useful: Merle Fainsod and Lincoln Gordon, *Government and the American Economy;* L. S. Lyon and others, *Government and Economic Life;* A. E. Burns and D. S. Watson, *Government Spending and Economic Expansion,* J. M. Clark, *Social Control of Business;* A. H. Hansen, *Economic Policy and Full Employment;* A. H. Edgerton, *Readjustment or Revolution?;* and M. F. Gallagher, *Government Rules Industry.*

The changing structure of business is examined in O. W. Knauth, *Managerial Enterprise;* S. A. Lewisohn, *Human Leadership in Industry;* W. J. A. Donald, *Trade Associations;* C. E. Bonnet, *Employers' Associations;* C. E. Merriam, *Public and Private Government;* J. C. Bonbright and G. C. Means, *Holding Company;* Kenneth Sturges, *American Chambers of Commerce.*

R. C. Epstein has examined *Industrial Profits,* Solomon Fabricant, *Employment in Manufacturing.* For special fields, see Twentieth Century Fund, *Power Industry and Public Interest;* H. L. Smith, *Airways;* E. E. Freudenthal, *Aviation Business;* N. R. Danielian, *A. T. & T.;* Paul Schubert, *Electrical Word* and W. R. Maclaurin, *Invention and Innovation in the Radio Industry.* See also E. D. Kennedy, *Automobile Industry,* and C. L. Dearing, *American Highway Policy.*

For finance, H. G. Moulton, *Financial Organization of Society;* R. W. Goldschmidt, *Changing Structure of American Banking.* New Deal financial policies have been treated by G. G. Johnson, and A. S. Everest. C. C. Chapman, *Development of American Business and Banking Thought, 1913–36,* is worth attention, as is F. T. Pecora, *Wall Street Under Oath.*

Farmers in a Changing World, a Department of Agriculture Yearbook, is a good introduction; and see W. P. Gee, *Place of Agriculture in American Life* and Theodore Schultz, *Agriculture in an Unstable Economy.* E. G. Nourse has surveyed the first AAA, J. D. Black *Agricultural Reform* in the earlier period. For special problems, Carey McWilliams, *Factories in the Field;* C. E. Lively and Conrad Taeuber, *Rural Migration.* Sectional adjustments are treated in H. W. Odum, *Way of the South toward the Regional Balance of America;* and W. P. Webb, *Divided We Stand.*

R. R. R. Brooks, *When Labor Organizes,* and *Unions of Their Own Choosing,* Edward Levinson, *Labor on the March,* and Herbert Harris, *Labor's Civil War,* all treat the rise of unions after 1933. Benjamin Stolberg and J. R. Walsh have both written about the C.I.O. C. E. Lindblom has treated *Unions and Capitalism,* and labor leaders are discussed in C. W. Mills, *New Men of Power,* and Harold Seidman, *Labor Czars.* Special studies include V. H. Jensen, *Lumber and Labor;* Stuart Jamieson, *Labor Unionism in American Agriculture;* G. L. Palmer, *Union Tactics and Economic Change;* McAlister Coleman, *Men and Coal.* There are some good histories of individual unions, e.g., the International Ladies' Garment Workers Union (Benjamin Stolberg), the Brotherhood of Sleeping Car Porters (B. R. Brazeal).

P. W. Slosson, *Great Crusade, and After, 1914–28,* and Dixon Wecter, *Age of the Great Depression, 1929–41,* stress social history. The more popular volumes of F. L. Allen, *Only Yesterday* (1920's) and *Since Yesterday* (1930's) are valuable as well as entertaining. *The Aspirin Age, 1919–41,* edited by Isabel Leighton, is interesting, as is Charles Merz, *Dry Decade;* and G. V. Seldes' *Years of the Locust* is good for the shorter period, 1929–32.

The student of social history should not miss *Recent Social Trends,* and the splendid monographs by R. S. and H. M. Lynd, *Middletown* and *Middletown in Transition.*

H. E. Stearns (ed.), *Civilization in the United States* (1922) and his later *America Now* (1938) provide insight into the changing views of intellectuals. A Pennsylvania symposium, *Changing Patterns in American Civilization,* is one of many surveys. (For a few others, Alexander Meiklejohn, *What Does America Mean?;* Margaret Mead, *And Keep Your Powder Dry;* André Siegfried, *America Comes of Age.*)

More specialized approaches are often of greater help. C. F. Ware, *Greenwich Village, 1920–30;* Malcolm Cowley, *Exile's Return;* J. C. Ransom and others, *I'll Take My Stand* (for the Southern Agrarians); David Spitz, *Patterns of Anti-Democratic Thought,* are examples. Among the books on literature are H. E. Luccock's *American Mirror,* and Leo Gurko's *Angry Decade* (both on the depression); J. W. Beach's *American Fiction, 1920–40;* J. W. Krutch's *American Drama Since 1918.* There are books without number on education, R. F. Butts, *The College Charts its Course,* R. L. Kelly, *American Colleges and the Social Order,* and R. L. Duffus, *Democracy Enters College,* are among those worth examining. R. F. Butts, *American Tradition in Religion and Education,* J. M. O'Neill, *Religion and Education under the Constitution,* and H. K. Beale, *Are American Teachers Free?* are all works dealing with topics of current interest. R. S. Lynd, *Knowledge for What?* raises important questions.

Paul Blanshard's *American Freedom and Catholic Power* is hostile toward the Catholic hierarchy. For Catholic views see F. J. Sheen, *Peace of Soul,* J. P. Cadden, *Historiography of the American Catholic Church,* and J. A. Ryan, *Seven Troubled Years,* F. S. Loescher, *Protestant Church and the Negro,* and H. P. Douglass and E. deS. Brunner, *Protestant*

Church as a Social Institution, deal with an important problem; and see W. W. Sweet, *Methodism*, and Reinhold Niebuhr, *Faith and History*.

The National Resources Committee has prepared volumes on governmental, industrial, and business research, on technologic trends, and on energy utilization. For the work of the foundations, see E. C. Lindeman, *Wealth and Culture*; E. V. Hollis, *Philanthropic Foundations and Higher Education*. The story of scientific research during World War II is well handled by J. P. Baxter, *Scientists Against Time*; and see G. W. Gray, *Science at War*. H. D. Smyth, *Atomic Energy for Military Purposes*, tells the A-bomb story; and see Vannevar Bush, *Modern Arms and Free Men*. James Stokley, *Science Remakes Our World* is interesting.

The National Health Assembly study, *America's Health*, contains much material. L. I. Dublin, *Health and Wealth*, is valuable, as is *Length of Life*, which Dublin wrote with A. J. Lotka. Morris Fishbein has written a history of the American Medical Association. H. E. Sigerist's *Medicine and Human Welfare*, and M. M. Davis' *America Organizes Medicine*, are recommended. E. C. Andrus and others have dealt with World War II in *Advances in Military Medicine*. *Shame of the States*, by Albert Deutsch, deals with the care of the mentally ill.

There is now a large literature on the family. As an illustration, there are half a dozen studies of the family during the depression (e.g., R. S. Cavan and K. H. Ranck; and R. C. Angell). M. E. Pidgeon has written about women in the American economy, Lorine Pruette specifically on women workers in the depression. *Women in the Twentieth Century*, by S. P. Breckinridge, covers much ground.

Increasing attention has been given to minority groups. There are general studies: H. P. Fairchild, *Race and Nationality as Factors in American Life*; T. J. Woofter, *Races and Ethnic Groups in American Life*; O. C. Cox, *Caste, Class and Race*; D. R. Young, *American Minority Peoples*. M. R. Davie's *Refugees* deals with a special group. Carey McWilliams has considered the general problem (*Brothers under the Skin*), and has treated various groups: *North From Mexico*; *Mask for Privilege* (on anti-Semitism), *Prejudice* (Japanese-Americans). There are special books on the Mexican immigrants (Manuel Gamio), the Filipino immigrants (Bruno Lasker), the Japanese-Americans (Bradford Smith; Yamato Ichihashi), on anti-Semitism (L. J. Levinger), on the American Indian (Oliver LaFarge).

Among many new books on the Negro, these are representative: Arnold Rose, *Negro in America*; H. L. Moon, *Balance of Power* (Negro vote); H. R. Cayton and G. S. Mitchell, *Black Workers and the New Unions* (and see R. C. Weaver, *Negro Labor*); B. H. Nelson, *Fourteenth Amendment and the Negro since 1920*; John Dollard, *Caste and Class in a Southern Town*; C. S. Johnson, *Patterns of Negro Segregation*; R. C. Weaver,

Negro Ghetto; C. G. Woodson, *Negro Professional Man;* E. F. Frazier, *Negro Family.* No one should miss Gunnar Myrdal's *American Dilemma,* which is based upon an extensive survey.

For civil liberties, see Zechariah Chafee, *Free Speech in the United States;* J. P. Clark, *Deportation of Aliens;* Felix Frankfurter, *Case of Sacco and Vanzetti;* G. L. Joughlin and E. M. Morgan, *Legacy of Sacco and Vanzetti;* George Seldes, *Witch Hunt;* A. R. Ogden, *Dies Committee;* E. S. Corwin, *Total War and the Constitution.* For defense of the post-World War I drives, see Ole Hanson, *Americanism versus Bolshevism.* Martin Dies has written a defense of the investigational work of his committee. Subversive activity in the United States is described in the works of J. R. Carlson, Louis Budenz, Benjamin Gitlow.

Leisure-time activities have been studied by J. B. Nash, by J. F. Steiner, by G. A. Lundberg, and others. For further material on this subject, see L. R. Morris, *Not So Long Ago;* R. B. Weaver, *Amusements and Sports;* the picture book, *I Remember Distinctly;* Allison Danzing and Peter Brandwein, *Sport's Golden Age* (1920's). Among the books on radio are those by E. P. J. Shurick, and Francis Chase; and L. C. Rosten is one of many who have written about the movies. Deems Taylor's *Pictorial History of the Movies* is interesting as is Raymond Moley's book on the *Hays Office* (Hollywood self-regulation).

Recent trends are stressed in Thomas Craven, *Modern Art;* Jacques Schnier, *Sculpture in Modern America;* Aaron Copland, *Our New Music* (and see Eddie Condon, *We Called It Music,* on jazz). Grace Overmyer has dealt with an important subject in *Government and the Arts;* and, for the depression drama and art projects, Willson Whitman, *Bread and Circuses,* and George Biddle, *An American Artist's Story.* James and K. M. Ford have written about the modern house.

For politics after World War I, Mark Sullivan's *Twenties;* F. L. Paxson's *Post-War Years* (1918–23); S. H. Adams' *Incredible Era* (Harding); Karl Schriftgiesser's *This Was Normalcy* (1920–32); J. C. Malin, *United States after the World War.* Corruption is stressed in M. E. Ravage, *Story of Teapot Dome* (and see John Ise, *United States Oil Policy*); M. M. Milligan, *Story of the Pendergast Machine;* R. S. Allen (ed.), *Our Fair City.* Recent writers have given much attention to the influence of special groups: Wesley McCune, *The Farm Bloc;* S. A. Rice, *Farmers and Workers in American Politics;* H. L. Childs, *Labor and Capital in National Politics;* E. P. Herring, *Group Representation before Congress;* K. G. Crawford, *Pressure Boys;* S. Chase, *Democracy under Pressure.* P. F. Lazarsfeld, *People's Choice,* is a study of voting habits. H. A. Bone, *American Politics and the Party System,* may be supplemented by A. N. Holcombe, *Political Parties;* by J. A. Farley, *Behind the Ballots;* and by V. O. Key, *Southern*

Politics. For federal-state relations, J. P. Clark, *Rise of a New Federalism.*

For executive-legislative relations, see C. A. Patterson, *Presidential Government;* L. H. Chamberlain, *President, Congress and Legislation,* and J. M. Burns, *Congress on Trial.* For efforts to break two-party control, see the books on the Non-Partisan League (A. A. Bruce; C. E. Russell; H. E. Gaston), and on LaFollette's 1924 campaign (K. C. MacKay).

R. A. Wilbur and Arthur Hyde describe and defend the *Hoover Policies.* Basil Rauch has written the best *History of the New Deal.* The political side is seen in E. E. Robinson, *They Voted for Roosevelt,* which analyzes returns, 1932–44. See also C. W. Stein, *Third Term Tradition.* J. C. Brown, *Public Relief, 1929–39,* covers the general subject. There are special books on rural relief (C. C. Zim and N. L. Whetten), on the PWA (J. F. Isakoff), the WPA (D. S. Howard), the CCC (Kenneth Holland and F. E. Hill), the NYA (Betty and E. K. Lindley). J. K. Galbraith and G. G. Johnson, Jr. *Economic Effects of the Federal Public Works Expenditures, 1933–38,* furnishes another approach. C. F. Roos and Hugh Johnson have both dealt with the N.R.A. J. S. Davis has written *On Agricultural Policy, 1926–38,* D. C. Blaisdell, *Government and Agriculture.* H. I. Richards, *Cotton and the A.A.A.,* is one of many monographs. The history of the TVA has been told by D. E. Lilienthal, C. H. Pritchett, and others. The best book on Social Security is that of P. H. Douglas. The Twentieth Century Fund has examined the *Townsend Crusade.*

The Court fight produced many books, including E. M. Eriksson, *Supreme Court and the New Deal;* M. L. Ernst, *The Ultimate Power;* Charles Warren, *Congress, Constitution and Supreme Court;* R. H. Jackson, *Struggle for Judicial Supremacy;* J. W. Alsop and Turner Catledge, *The 168 Days;* Dean Alfange, *Supreme Court and the National Will.* For the period since 1937, C. H. Pritchett, *Roosevelt Court;* and E. S. Corwin, *Constitutional Revolution, Ltd.*

P. M. Mazur, *America Looks Abroad,* is thoughtful. For economic problems, note also Max Winkler, *Foreign Bonds, an Autopsy;* B. H. Williams, *Economic Foreign Policy of the United States;* Hiram Motherwell, *Imperial Dollar;* Ludwell Denny, *We Fight for Oil;* Cleona Lewis, *America's Stake in International Investments.* P. M. Zeis has dealt with shipping, J. M. Letiche with reciprocity. D. F. Fleming, *United States and World Organization,* is important. T. A. Bailey (*Man in the Street*) and Gilbert Almond have studied American foreign policy in its relation to public opinion; Eleanor Tupper and G. E. McReynolds, opinion with reference to Japan.

The area approach is often used in foreign policy. For Russo–American relations, see books by F. R. Dulles, *Road to Teheran,* V. M. Dean, *United States and Russia,* E. R. Stettinius, *Roosevelt and the Russians.* Mrs. Dean has also written about the United States and Europe, Dulles about American relations with China and Japan. Other volumes cover American relations with Britain (Crane Brinton), the Caribbean (Dexter Perkins), northern South America (A. P. Whitaker), China (J. K. Fairbank).

N. J. Spykman, *America's Strategy in World Politics* is a good introduction. H. H. and Margaret Sprout, *Toward a New Order of Sea Power* is significant, as are Merze Tate, *United States and Armaments*; C. L. Hoag, *Preface to Preparedness*; H. W. Baldwin, *Price of Power*. For an attack on the munitions industry, H. C. Engelbrecht and F. C. Hanighen, *Merchants of Death*. A. D. Turnbull and C. L. Lord have written a history of the beginnings of naval aviation. International air transport is considered by O. J. Lissitzyn, by H. L. Smith, and (for Latin America) by W. A. M. Burden.

For American entry into World War II, the Roosevelt position is defended by Dexter Perkins, *America and Two Wars*; Basil Rauch, *Roosevelt from Munich to Pearl Harbor*; Walter Johnson, *Battle Against Isolation*; Walter Millis, *This is Pearl*; Forrest Davis and E. K. Lindley, *How War Came*; and J. W. Alsop and Robert Kintner, *American White Paper*. For the other side, George Morgenstern, *Pearl Harbor*; C. A. Beard, *President Roosevelt and the Coming of the War*, and his *American Foreign Policy in the Making*.

There is no satisfactory history of World War II. R. W. Shugg and H. A. DeWeerd have written a survey account for the military action. General Marshall's reports are helpful. S. E. Morison is publishing a multivolume history of naval operations in the war; and there are many special monographs for naval, ground, and air operations. D. M. Nelson has written about war production in *Arsenal of Democracy*. E. R. Stettinius has treated *Lend-Lease*, while S. E. Harris has described *Price and Related Controls*. W. W. Wilcox, *Farmer in the Second World War*, is important, as is L. W. Koenig, *Presidency and the Crisis*. W. F. Ogburn has edited *American Society in Wartime*; and there are many special studies, e.g., J. A. Miller, *Men and Volts at War*, which deals with General Electric and World War II.

The biographies of business leaders include lives of Henry Ford (W. C. Richards; K. T. Sward), Andrew W. Mellon (Harvey O'Connor), Juan Trippe of Pan American Airways (Matthew Josephson), Alfred I. duPont (Marquis James), the banker A. P. Giannini (Julian Dana), Dwight Morrow (Harold Nicholson), George Eastman (C. W. Ackerman). Of the labor biographies, attention is called to J. A. Wechsler's life of John L. Lewis.

Scientists have received increasing attention from biographers. Among those who have been treated are Albert Einstein (Philipp Frank; Lincoln

Barnett); the Wright brothers (J. R. McMahon; F. C. Kelly). Representative of biographies in the arts are the lives of Grant Wood (by Darrell Garwood), Thomas Wolfe (P. H. Johnson), and John Barrymore (Gene Fowler). Virginius Dabney's life of Bishop Cannon is more of a political than a religious study.

World War II brought something of a boom in military biography. I. D. Levine has written about Billy Mitchell, the advocate of air power; W. F. Frye, Jr., about General George Marshall.

Among the judges who have been given biographical treatment are Chief Justice Stone (S. J. Konefsky), and Justices Cardozo (J. F. Pollard) and Black (J. P. Frank).

There are political biographies in abundance: Calvin Coolidge (C. M. Fuess; W. A. White); Alfred E. Smith (H. F. Pringle); Herbert Hoover (David Hinshaw); Huey Long (H. T. Kane; Carleton Beals); the Wallaces (Russell Lord); Cordell Hull (H. B. Hinton); William Allen White (Walter Johnson); James J. Walker (Gene Fowler); David Lilienthal (Willson Whitman). There is as yet no satisfactory biography of Franklin D. Roosevelt, although Alden Hatch and John Gunther, among others, have tried. Roosevelt can best be seen through R. E. Sherwood's *Roosevelt and Hopkins,* and the memoirs of those who figured in the Roosevelt administration: Frances Perkins, Mrs. Franklin D. Roosevelt, Cordell Hull, Henry L. Stimson, James A. Farley, Raymond Moley.

Other autobiographies also contribute to an understanding of recent American history. Among those of interest are the ones by Calvin Coolidge, Boss Ed Flynn, Dr. Francis E. Townsend, Huey Long, Joe Louis, Generals George S. Patton, Dwight D. Eisenhower, and Claire Chennault, Admiral W. F. Halsey, James Weldon Johnson, and Frank Lloyd Wright.

Index